Approaches to Early Childhood Education

Fourth Edition

Jaipaul L. Roopnarine
Syracuse University

James E. Johnson
The Pennsylvania State University

PEARSON

Merrill
Prentice Hall

Upper Saddle River, New Jersey
Columbus, Ohio

Library of Congress Cataloging-in-Publication Data

Approaches to early childhood education / [edited by] Jaipaul Roopnarine, James E. Johnson.—4th ed.
    p.   cm.
    Includes bibliographical references and indexes.
    ISBN 0-13-140811-9
    1. Early childhood education—United States. 2. Educational innovations—United States.
3. Early childhood educators—Training of—United States. 4. Inclusive education—United States.
5. Multicultural education—United States. I. Roopnarine, Jaipaul L. II.
Johnson, James E. (James Ewald)
LB1139.25.A66 2005
372.21—dc22   2004005446

Vice President and Executive Publisher: Jeffery W. Johnston
Acquisitions Editor: Julie Peters
Editorial Assistant: Amanda King
Production Editor: Linda Hillis Bayma
Production Coordination: *The GTS Companies*/York, PA Campus
Design Coordinator: Diane C. Lorenzo
Photo Coordinator: Valerie Schultz
Cover Designer: Ali Mohrman
Cover image: Getty One
Production Manager: Laura Messerly
Director of Marketing: Ann Castel Davis
Marketing Manager: Autumn Purdy
Marketing Coordinator: Tyra Poole

This book was set in Galliard by *The GTS Companies*/York, PA Campus. It was printed and bound by R.R. Donnelley & Sons Company. The cover was printed by Coral Graphic Services, Inc.

Photo Credits: Scott Cunningham/Merrill: 24, 282, 289; Dan Floss/Merrill: 240; James E. Johnson: 342, 346, 347, 349, 366, 390; Anthony Magnacca/Merrill: 48; Bruce Mallory: 331; National Library of Medicine: 188; Rebecca S. New: 318; Jaipaul Roopnarine: 222; Barbara Schwartz/Merrill: 142; Toos van Kuyk: 404, 406, 411; Anne Vega/Merrill: 17, 68, 91, 116, 126, 161, 167, 236, 252, 297, 301; Susan Welteroth: 45, 108; Todd Yarrington/Merrill: 85, 193, 215.

Pearson Education Ltd.
Pearson Education Singapore
Pearson Education Canada, Ltd.
Pearson Education—Japan

Pearson Education Australia Pty. Limited
Pte. Ltd. Pearson Education North Asia Ltd.
Pearson Educación de Mexico, S.A. de C.V.
Pearson Education Malaysia Pte. Ltd.

10 9 8 7 6 5 4 3
ISBN: 0-13-140811-9

To Dr. Irving E. Sigel, a child development and early education expert who has devoted himself to probing for a better understanding of how children develop and ways in which we can better enhance their learning and psychological well-being.

Foreword

The opportunity to write the foreword to the fourth edition of *Approaches to Early Childhood Education* is indeed a privilege. As a contributor to the previous editions, I am able to note the evolution of changes in the substance and reorganization of the volume. What this comprehensive text reflects is continuous growth in the breadth and depth of early childhood education (ECE) evident in the diverse programs such as Pyramid, Reggio Emilia, Portage, High Scope, and others covered herein.

The beginning chapter describes the historical background of ECE and provides insights into the various strands of knowledge from psychology, philosophy, religion, and even pediatrics among others that we know have had an influence on ECE. I believe it is immensely important for students to ground themselves in the historical literature to identify where much of current thinking about educating young children has its roots. These are the same claims on which Jaipaul Roopnarine and James Johnson base the organization of this text. What is notable for those interested in ECE as a career is that the seminal leaders in the study of the young child come from different professions and different conceptualizations regarding the nature of the developing child (see the writing of Piaget as compared to John Dewey, for example). This difference is well articulated at the beginning and throughout the text. The book should be read with an eye to the past and to the present, for it will become readily apparent that the past does reach into the present and vice versa.

The justification for a fourth edition is transparent. A change in conceptualization about the complexity of the developmental process from simplistic views of maturation and growth to the integrationist view of the whole child has changed the approach to how education should be conducted. One notable example is a shift in views of psychological development. Consider for a moment the move from behaviorist theory of learning to more experiential constructivist views of learning as a process. Roopnarine and Johnson present some perspectives (e.g., multiculturalism, special education) in the first sections of the book that enable the reader to grasp the bases for the proliferation of ECE programs that will be described in the later sections of the volume.

Although established as a text, this volume is a significant contribution to the field of early childhood education. It is a comprehensive presentation of the major educational programs in the field in one place, so anyone interested in what is available for study or emulation has the material readily available. In addition, accompanying each program, experts in that particular area provide a bibliographical reference list for further study of that program.

The readers of this text, especially students, can have an in-depth exposure to some of the major ECE curricula as well as the history of the programs' development. Such an in-depth study of these programs allows students to understand the rationale for each program's justification for being. Such knowledge would be of special value to those who are seeking enlightenment for career options in ECE. The diversity of the programs described so ably in this text creates challenges for instructors as well as for students. How does one make sense of the variations in programs when each has the same underlying objective—to enhance the quality of life for young children?

Although the editors have done an admirable job of ensuring that the style and comprehensiveness of each chapter is coherent and clearly written, they did not set out to evaluate each of these programs, and rightly so. They seem to have left the task of developing criteria for program evaluation to the faculty and students. It is to this issue that I address my subsequent comments.

If any politically oriented reader would see this array of diversity in the ECE field, chances are he or she would ask: "Why is the taxpayers' money being spent on programs when experts in childhood education cannot come to any agreement as to how children should be taught, what they expect these children to learn, or at what age the children should be taught to read?" "How do parents decide what is the optimum program for their children, especially since each program developer claims his or her program enhances the child's mental, social, and emotional development?" How to answer these questions is one of the biggest challenges facing early childhood educators. This is particularly cogent when economic times are difficult.

Let me address this criticism with an analogy to the decision making involved in preparing students for their careers. To begin with, the class "automobile" is like the class "preschool education." There are a large number of automobiles that vary in a number of characteristics but still perform the same function. The differences among them are due to the complexity of a motor transport. Yet each type has a number of common features such as wheels and a motor, it faces forward, and so on. And, of course, each is an instance of a motorized vehicle that transports people from place to place.

So too is the case with preschool programs. To compare automobiles, we would develop a rubric to categorize various characteristics to develop a taxonomy, use the population of autos as the subject, and place each in an appropriate category. So we shall use this analogy for categorizing ECE programs.

The characteristics of every ECE program can be deconstructed into a number of components to develop a taxonomy of the components expected to be present in every ECE program. Then we would apply this taxonomy to each program. This process would enable the students to articulate similarities and differences among programs. Such a procedure could be of value in just understanding a program in depth because the details of a program often help students have realistic pictures of what the program is. It has some advantages over using only observations of classrooms, which may not get at the philosophical bases of many programs that are expressed in subtle ways not evident to the observer.

As the reader of this volume will discover, founders of curricula come to the task with differing beliefs and values about the developmental trajectory. Some programs are based on psychological theories of Piaget, Vygotsky, and neo-Freudian dynamic growth. Others reflect an eclectic orientation, using elements from an ongoing program that have been shown to be effective in achieving their objectives.

In recent years, increased diversity is becoming evident, especially when the population targeted for educational intervention is the prime objective. Head Start is one of the old initial intervention programs defining its population on the basis of economic level and is a prime example of a program dedicated to helping children from economically disadvantaged homes. How the curriculum is developed will depend in part on the orientation of the agency responsible for Head Start (see Powell, chapter 3).

Another source of diversity is the interest in ECE programs of European origin. European programs in this field have a long history (e.g., Montessori). Virtually every European country has well-developed programs (see van Kuyk, chapter 17, as an example of an eclectic integrated program for immigrant children in The Netherlands).

In summary, the analysis of program similarities and differences in the service of program evaluation is analogous to comparative shopping. Which program has the most excitement and value to devote a lot of time and energy for the common good of children? Adding to this a chance to experience the program directly could be a final task before embarking on a career as an ECE educator. Roopnarine and Johnson provide the reader with a heavy diet of rich fare.

Irving E. Sigel
Educational Testing Service
Princeton, New Jersey

Preface

*E*arly childhood education (ECE) is a multisectorial and multidisciplinary field within education that embraces the challenges of complexity, diversity, and multiple perspectives. Early childhood education occurs in many different kinds of settings, is represented in many forms, and serves diverse populations. Guided by research and theory from a number of scholarly disciplines—including developmental psychology, cultural psychology, childhood studies, and psychological anthropology—as well as by history, philosophy, and teacher lore, early childhood education seeks to integrate and to utilize our best knowledge and ideas for understanding children and for finding ways of enhancing their development, learning, and well-being during the early years from birth to age 8.

This book provides current information across a number of important areas within early childhood education: child growth and development, environment, curriculum–content planning and implementation, instruction and communication, assessment, professionalism and leadership, and families, communities, and cultures. This text meets the demands of educating children in an ever-inclusive, multicultural postmodern world. In this regard, early childhood professional educators must be "inclusionists" who can work with all children who are differently "abled," and they must be culturally nonmyopic in order to serve the great diversity of children and their families in a complex, fast-changing, and pluralistic global community.

Early childhood education is a tapestry created by the energies of many different people, working with many different children and families in diverse neighborhoods, communities, and cultures. Weavers of this tapestry are all who have the thread of conviction and dedication to put into practice what they know and believe is the best for children. This book exposes the reader to a multitude of ideas and applications emanating from diverse historical, cultural, theoretical, and philosophical sources. A seminal question remains: "What concepts, realizations, insights, and ideas tied to early childhood educational practices are relevant for use in local, particular situations in today's world?" Readers are urged to judge for themselves what is meaningful to them as they strive to construct a composite, integrative view of the early childhood profession. In particular, how does one weave an understanding of current initiatives and challenges relevant to educating young children in these dynamic and turbulent times that are marked by distinct social and educational trends?

Sociodemographic changes in the United States and globally, coupled with the ever-increasing numbers of children in poverty, children who are homeless, children of immigrants and migrant children, single-parent families, children living in "trial families," lesbi-gay families, and the globalization of childhood, have all presented new challenges to early childhood education. Teachers working with young children must constantly try to find the right balance between their need to make developmental demands on children and their need to show appreciation of individual expression.

Educational trends in the early childhood area include a renewed call for effective curricula brought on by the public's growing awareness of low-quality child care in the United States and elsewhere, together with better appreciation of the importance of early social and cognitive stimulation spurred, in part, by early brain development research. There is heightened concern over curricula for English language learners, the academic performance of low-income children and children of color, and disproportionate numbers of children of color placed in remedial and special education classes in the United States. At the same time, as we achieve consensus on the importance of early education, more and more state governments are legislating, often without sufficient funding, universal pre-kindergarten programs (e.g., Connecticut, Florida, Georgia, New York). Unfortunately these trends have been accompanied by high-stakes testing, curriculum compression, and downward extension of educational demands. Needless to say, evidence-based programs place a lot of pressure on young children and their teachers. To be a good teacher means facing the many challenges caused by these interweaving educational trends that call for an emphasis on cognitive and academic learning. In the context of narrowly defined academic learning, the good early childhood teacher never loses sight of the whole child and strives to encourage social and emotional development, creativity and imagination, and play, as much as, if not more so, than intellectual development per se.

Our profession requires of us that we acknowledge the need to balance individualized emerging or established specialized interests in early childhood education (e.g., computers and young children, becoming a nanny, specializing in Montessori education, infant and toddler care) with the goal to have in our professional identity an understanding of the field taken in total. This book provides you with opportunities to develop a better grasp of early childhood education practices in order that you may form a composite, integrative view of early childhood education. Admittedly, in-depth specialization in early childhood education subfields results in professional identity, but this identity must be preserved in an inclusive meaningful context of the entire field.

✸ FEATURES OF THE FOURTH EDITION

This new edition of *Approaches to Early Childhood Education* has been reorganized to accentuate the need to examine programmatic ideas and applications through two very important thematic lenses: namely, multiculturalism and inclusion. In this vein, the revised chapters by Louise Derman-Sparks and Patricia Ramsey as well as Ellen Barnes and Robert Lehr were moved forward to Part 2. Consistent with previous editions, we have sought to give the reader an impressive array of rich and current information about important issues and trends in early childhood curricular approaches or models. We have also retained certain organizational features, specifically including in Part 1 the chapters by Patricia Monighan Nourot, Kimberlee Whaley, Douglas Powell, and David and Darlene Shearer on history, infant and toddler care, Head Start, and the Portage Model, respectively. Broad approaches, such as Eriksonian, behaviorism and mixed-age programming, are included in Part 3 and followed by specific approaches.

For this edition we have chosen to group specific approaches together: Part 4 contains four well-known "home-grown" early childhood education approaches (High/Scope, Spectrum, Bank Street or Developmental-Interaction Approach, and the Project Approach), and Part 5 contains four programs that have their origins in Europe (Reggio Emilia, Waldorf, Montessori, and Pyramid). The reader is invited to compare the approaches within and across Parts 4 and 5.

In Part 4 we have grouped them in an order that we believe goes from most focused to least focused on intellectual development, but with an increased concern for the whole child. In Part 5 the reverse is the case. A recent distinction between the experiential and functional perspectives made by David Elkind guided how we grouped these chapters. Reggio and Waldorf are considered to be more concerned with the whole child and the child's experiential perspective, and Montessori and Pyramid more enmeshed in the adult's functionalist perspective and on cognitive or learning outcomes. This arrangement permits ease of comparison between and across programs that have their roots in Europe and the United States.

This edition not only has a new author for the infant and toddler care chapter, Kimberlee Whaley (chapter 2), but also new chapter topics and authors for chapters 11, 15, 17 and an Epilogue. Spectrum, which was inspired by the theories of David Henry Feldman and Howard Gardner concerning nonuniversal development and multiple intelligences, is presented by Jie-Qi Chen; Waldorf is presented by Christy Williams and Jim Johnson, and Pyramid by Jef J. van Kuyk. All three additional approaches or models of early childhood education are growing in popularity and use, and they have solid reputations in the field. Finally, in the Epilogue, the reader is treated with Marianne Bloch's cogent and critical analysis of the field and timely suggestions as we move further into the twenty-first century.

The book overall includes much content that should add to the reader's acumen of early childhood education pedagogy, practice, and policy. Many applications are traced to philosophy and theory. Historical foundations are included in many chapters, as well as conceptual frameworks and models or images of the child. Complex particulars are introduced and discussed, as real-world issues and challenges may, and often do, collide with ideals and best-laid plans. Early childhood education is constantly on the move, and a book of this nature is meant to help all of us keep up with advancements in best practices in nurturing the minds and psyches of the most valuable resources of our world—young children.

ACKNOWLEDGMENTS

Our sincerest thanks for the support and understanding provided by our respective families during the revisions of the fourth edition of this text: Nancy Beth, Miles, and Maya, and Karen and Clayton. We are very grateful for the excellent work by Angela Packer of the Department of Curriculum and Instruction at The Pennsylvania State University who patiently organized the manuscript for us. We also appreciate the thoughtful reviews provided by our colleagues in the field of early childhood education: Berta Harris, San Diego City College; Carole Kurtines-Becker, Nova Southeastern University; and Phyllis Vokey, San Diego State University. Their comments and suggestions on both the content and organization of the book have helped to improve the quality of the material presented herein.

Jaipaul L. Roopnarine
James E. Johnson

Discover the Companion Website Accompanying This Book

THE PRENTICE HALL COMPANION WEBSITE: A VIRTUAL LEARNING ENVIRONMENT

Technology is a constantly growing and changing aspect of our field that is creating a need for content and resources. To address this emerging need, Prentice Hall has developed an online learning environment for students and professors alike—Companion Websites—to support our textbooks.

In creating a Companion Website, our goal is to build on and enhance what the textbook already offers. For this reason, the content for each user-friendly website is organized by topic and provides the professor and student with a variety of meaningful resources. Common features of a Companion Website include:

For the Professor—

Every Companion Website integrates **Syllabus Manager**™, an online syllabus creation and management utility.

- **Syllabus Manager**™ provides you, the instructor, with an easy, step-by-step process to create and revise syllabi, with direct links into Companion Website and other online content without having to learn HTML.

- Students may logon to your syllabus during any study session. All they need to know is the web address for the Companion Website and the password you've assigned to your syllabus.
- After you have created a syllabus using **Syllabus Manager**™, students may enter the syllabus for their course section from any point in the Companion Website.
- Clicking on a date, the student is shown the list of activities for the assignment. The activities for each assignment are linked directly to actual content, saving time for students.
- Adding assignments consists of clicking on the desired due date, then filling in the details of the assignment—name of the assignment, instructions, and whether it is a one-time or repeating assignment.
- In addition, links to other activities can be created easily. If the activity is online, a URL can be entered in the space provided, and it will be linked automatically in the final syllabus.
- Your completed syllabus is hosted on our servers, allowing convenient updates from any computer on the Internet. Changes you make to your syllabus are immediately available to your students at their next logon.

For the Student—

- **Introduction**—General information about the topic and how it will be covered in the website.
- **Web Links**—A variety of websites related to topic areas.
- **Timely Articles**—Links to online articles that enable you to become more aware of important issues in early childhood.
- **Learn by Doing**—Put concepts into action, participate in activities, examine strategies, and more.
- **Visit a School**—Visit a school's website to see concepts, theories, and strategies in action.
- **For Teachers/Practitioners**—Access information you will need to know as an educator, including information on materials, activities, and lessons.
- **NEW! Observation Tools**—A collection of checklists and forms to print and use when observing and assessing children's development.

- **Current Policies and Standards**—Find out the latest early childhood policies from the government and various organizations, and view state, federal, and curriculum standards.
- **Resources and Organizations**—Discover tools to help you plan your classroom or center and organizations to provide current information and standards for each topic.
- **Electronic Bluebook**—Paperless method of completing homework or essays assigned by a professor. Finished work can be sent to the professor via email.
- **Message Board**—Virtual bulletin board to post and respond to questions and comments from a national audience.

To take advantage of these and other resources, please visit the *Approaches to Early Childhood Education,* Fourth Edition, Companion Website at

www.prenhall.com/roopnarine

EDUCATOR LEARNING CENTER: AN INVALUABLE ONLINE RESOURCE

Merrill Education and the Association for Supervision and Curriculum Development (ASCD) invite you to take advantage of a new online resource, one that provides access to the top research and proven strategies associated with ASCD and Merrill—the Educator Learning Center. At **www.EducatorLearningCenter.com** you will find resources that will enhance your students' understanding of course topics and of current educational issues, in addition to being invaluable for further research.

How the Educator Learning Center Will Help Your Students Become Better Teachers

With the combined resources of Merrill Education and ASCD, you and your students will find a wealth of tools and materials to better prepare them for the classroom.

Research

- More than 600 articles from the ASCD journal *Educational Leadership* discuss everyday issues faced by practicing teachers.
- A direct link on the site to Research Navigator™ gives students access to many of the leading education journals, as well as extensive content detailing the research process.
- Excerpts from Merrill Education texts give your students insights on important topics of instructional methods, diverse populations, assessment, classroom management, technology, and refining classroom practice.

Classroom Practice

- Hundreds of lesson plans and teaching strategies are categorized by content area and age range.
- Case studies and classroom video footage provide virtual field experience for student reflection.
- Computer simulations and other electronic tools keep your students abreast of today's classrooms and current technologies.

Look into the Value of Educator Learning Center Yourself

A four-month subscription to Educator Learning Center is $25 but is **FREE** when used in conjunction with this text. To obtain free passcodes for your students, simply contact your local Merrill/Prentice Hall sales representative, and your representative will give you a special ISBN to give your bookstore when ordering your textbooks. To preview the value of this website to you and your students, please go to **www.EducatorLearningCenter.com** and click on "Demo."

Brief Contents

Contents

Note: Every effort has been made to provide accurate and current Internet information in this book. However, the Internet and information posted on it are constantly changing; it is inevitable that some of the Internet addresses listed in this textbook will change.

Part 1

Introduction

Chapter 1

Historical Perspectives on Early Childhood Education

Patricia Monighan Nourot ~ Sonoma State University

❧ INTRODUCTION

In the stories, quotations, and brief anecdotes that follow one can glimpse the essence of good practice in early childhood education during decades of history in the United States. In these examples we see common threads of ideals for the field of early childhood education that focus on particular **views of childhood** and **environments and curriculum** for teaching young children. These threads, along with varied ideas about the **role of the teacher in supporting learning** and **the relationship of schools for young children to families and the community,** are woven in a pattern of beliefs and practices that give early childhood education the rich and diverse heritage we see in contemporary theory and practice. I invite you to join me on an imaginary journey back in time to consider the people, events, and social changes that have contributed to the complexity of the fabric of early childhood education for nearly three centuries.

❧ EIGHTEENTH-CENTURY EDUCATION

A glimpse through the door of a classroom in colonial America reveals primary-age children and their younger siblings (some as young as age 3) sitting on wooden benches with rough desks. Children are copying passages from the Bible while others go to the teacher, one at a time, to recite psalms, verses, or the alphabet memorized from horn books. Some of these schools are the kitchens of older women—hence the name **Dame schools**—while others are in public buildings and are taught by men. Discipline is strict, and children are expected to work at their rote tasks alone, not speaking unless called upon to recite.

❧ VIEW OF CHILDREN

Colonial education in both the Dame schools and the few public elementary schools that existed reflected the negative view of childhood originating in Europe in the Middle Ages, when the Church dominated ideas about learning and development (Weber, 1984). Because humanity was thought to be inherently evil, learning to read scripture from the Bible was considered an avenue for salvation (Butts & Cremin, 1953). This view, reflected in the Puritan church in America, saw children as embodying the original sin of humankind; the task of the teacher was to curb this sinful nature through strict discipline.

❧ ENVIRONMENT AND CURRICULUM

In addition to the limitations posed by access to materials for copying and reading, the purpose of the colonial school environment was to force children to follow a classical curriculum and to comply with rules, not to educate them through active experiences. Teachers believed that sitting up straight focused children on their rote tasks (it probably did keep them from falling asleep). Curriculum was limited to the memorization and recitation of psalms and alphabet symbols and the meting out of discipline.

ROLE OF TEACHER

The teacher in colonial schools met with each child individually; group instruction was rare. Children recited their memorized passages to the teacher and returned to their seats. Corporal punishment was common.

From the age of 2, corporal punishment seems to have been the staple of the child's educational diet. Schoolmasters ("my system is to whip, and to have done with it") as well as parents and tutors rarely spared the rod to spoil the child (Brewer, 1979, p. 4). Other disciplinary devices included ridicule, making the child sit on the shame bench, and having the child wear a dunce cap (Gutek, 1968).

SCHOOL, PARENTS, AND COMMUNITY

Not everyone went to school during colonial times. Schooling was considered far more important for boys than for girls, and, following European traditions of the time, education was a privilege for upper-class children. Often gathered in the Dame schools, children were taught biblical passages with hornbooks, and once they were literate enough to read the Bible, further education in writing, Latin, the arts, or the trades was an extravagance only for boys of the wealthiest families (Butts & Cremin, 1953). Although efforts to teach reading to children were consistent in spirit, actual instruction depended on the proclivities of the individual teacher (Finkelstein & Vandell, 1984). Both of these early qualities of

education in America are echoed in the current debates about the language of instruction appropriate for English-language learners in schools for young children and the accessibility of high-quality education for those who are not of the dominant culture in our society (Ballenger, 1999; Chipman, 1997; Genishi, 2002; Kohn, 1998). Unlike contemporary education, however, the major component of schooling in colonial America was discipline and moral education based on the prevailing belief that to spare the rod was to spoil the child.

NINETEENTH-CENTURY EARLY EDUCATION

In sharp contrast to the practices common in eighteenth-century American and European schools, the Swiss educator Johann Heinrich Pestalozzi (1746–1827) developed a system he called elementary education, designed to integrate physical, mental, and moral development through the exercise of sense observation and reflection.

Pestalozzi's Elementary Education

Pestalozzi's work was built on the foundation of educational philosophy expounded by Plato as early as 427–347 B.C., in which early childhood was seen as a time of plasticity and expression of innate goodness, and by Comenius (1592–1670), whose ideas about education were sophisticated beyond his time. Unlike Plato, who contended that sensory experience fostered illusion about the true nature of reality, Comenius was a proponent of sensory education, believing that experiences of perception brought innate ideas to the surface of consciousness (Comenius, 1657/1953). In 1658 he published a handbook for mothers and nurses of children under age 6, arranged in short chapters of words and pictures on topics of interest to young children such as insects, plants, and animals. This handbook was the forerunner of children's texts and illustrated books (Wolfe, 2002). He also advocated for educational opportunities for children of all backgrounds (Comenius, 1967). Although popular in later centuries, Comenius's ideas found little place in the educational practice of his time (Capkova, 1970).

The philosopher John Locke also played a role in laying the foundation for Pestalozzi's ideas. Locke challenged the belief of the medieval church that children were born with a fully formed nature or soul, and he contended that children, like other natural phenomena in the universe, were subject to the effects of the environment. This notion, coupled with the work of Comenius, formed one major premise of Pestalozzi's philosophy: that children learn through sense observation and perception.

Another influence on Pestalozzi was Jean Jacques Rousseau (1712–1778) who focused on the natural environment as a vehicle for freeing the spirit of children (Gutek, 1968; Wolfe, 2002). This growing Romantic view of childhood revered children's sensibilities and innate goodness. In fact, the Romantics idealized children as the epitome of humanity as yet unsullied by greed, jealousy, and strife (Kennedy, 1988; Weber, 1984; Williams, 1987). In his school, Pestalozzi sought to protect this innate goodness in children and to mold them into a better model for the future of society. Also like Rousseau, Pestalozzi imparted his beliefs about the nature of childhood and the process of education through popular works of fiction such as *How Gertrude Teaches Her Children* (1801/1900). This, like Rousseau's *Emile* (1780/1938), broadened the influence of the ideas of the Romantics. Pestalozzi writes of the young child:

> Work and play are all one for him, his games are his work; he knows no difference. He brings to everything the cheerfulness of his interest, the charm of freedom, and he shows the bent of his own mind and the extent of his knowledge. (p. 126)

Unlike Rousseau and Locke, however, Pestalozzi did more than write about education; he founded a school, the Neuhof Institute. In 1799, after his unorthodox teaching methods led to his dismissal as an assistant teacher in a common school for working-class children, Pestalozzi found a position teaching middle-class children and was supported in his efforts to create a child-centered curriculum. Friends helped him raise funds for his own school, and in 1801 he began his Education Institute at Bergdorf, Switzerland, where he offered both childhood education and teacher preparation. One of his major contributions was the belief that all children, not just those of the upper class, might benefit from education. Students from all over Europe, and later America, carried his beliefs and practices back to their own communities.

Pestalozzi's View of Childhood   Not only did Pestalozzi believe in the innate goodness of humanity as expressed in young children, but in his work we see the seeds of contemporary ideas about developmentally appropriate practice (Green, 1969; Bredekamp & Copple, 1997). Pestalozzi subscribed to the Lockean view that humanity's existence is nested in the evolution of nature and that human development unfolded in a universal design shaped by outside forces. The functional laws of nature that call for continuous and gradual growth, as well as the proviso that each stage must come to completion before another begins, formed the basis for his developmental curriculum:

Environment and Curriculum   The following paragraph describes Pestalozzi's practice of using developmental curriculum:

> In teaching spelling Pestalozzi used simultaneous group instruction. The children began with the shortest words and then proceeded to longer ones. Movable letters were used for the first instruction in spelling and reading. In the teaching of arithmetic Pestalozzi used pebbles and beans; to teach

fractions, apples and cakes would be divided among the children. Only after acquiring complete familiarity with arithmetical processes were the children introduced to figures. (Gutek, 1968, p. 43)

For Pestalozzi, the preparation of the environment to resemble the home was of prime importance in setting the stage for children's experiential learning. He believed that a home-like environment first and foremost created a climate of *emotional security,* the first principle of education.

Based on his view of natural development, Pestalozzi designed a carefully sequenced curriculum in which materials and instruction were matched to the child's level of development:

> I saw just as soon that in making these books, the constituents of instruction must be separated according to the degree of the growing power of the child; and that in all matters of instruction, it is necessary to determine with the greatest accuracy, which of these constituents is fit for each age of the child, in order on the one hand, not to hold him back if he is ready, and on the other, not to load him and confuse him with anything for which he is not quite ready. (Pestalozzi, 1801/1900, p. 26)

Activities were organized in sequences based on Pestalozzi's concept of *Anschauung,* or ideational capacity of the brain. Sense impressions were considered the most basic form of ideas, followed by abstraction of qualities and classification of objects, which led to more generalized concepts (Gutek, 1968; Heafford, 1967; Williams, 1987). Here we see a foreshadowing of Maria Montessori's emphasis on sensory experiences and Jean Piaget's idea that logico-mathematical knowledge is built on physical experiences with concrete objects.

Another principle of his elementary education was that instruction should proceed from "the near to the far." Beginning with the learner's immediate experience, curriculum should gradually move to new objects and more remote contexts. These "ever-widening circles of mankind"

foreshadow the ideas of John Dewey and other progressive educators, as well as the contemporary emphasis on creating multiple representations of experience and learning over time prevalent in the Reggio Emilia schools in Italy and the project approach seen in the United States (Cadwell, 1997, 2002; Edwards, Gandini, & Forman, 1998; Hendricks, 1997; Katz & Chard, 2000).

Role of Teacher   For Pestalozzi and his followers, the relationship between the teacher and the student represented the foundation on which curriculum was built. Providing continuity with the mother–child love relationship as the child moved outside the home was central to the teacher's ability to match curriculum to the child's level of readiness and to create an ever-widening circle of experience.

An extension of this love principle was Pestalozzi's idea that children were to be disciplined through their desire to please the teacher rather than through fear (Wolfe, 2002). He specifically warned against connecting punishment to learning tasks, fearing that children might develop aversions to learning in this manner. He also eschewed the use of rewards, believing that they destroyed children's intrinsic motivation to learn (Gutek, 1968).

Pestalozzi originated the idea of group instruction. Before his time, children recited memorized lessons individually to the teacher and then practiced them alone. He asked children to draw, read, and recite with one another, believing that they would motivate each other's learning, and also presented lessons to the whole group at once. Of course this group instruction called for careful planning by the teacher to sequence instruction that would account for multiage groups of students and to devise ways for children to instruct one another (Downs, 1975).

School, Parents, and Community   Pestalozzi saw the home and school environments as continuous and closely linked. Although formal education was the purview of the teacher, the child's education at home and the love and support found there represented the foundation of learning. The roles of parents and teachers were closely aligned in Pestalozzi's philosophy. The nurturing attitude of the teacher and the language education, moral education, and physical education of the home were all essential to children's well-being (Heafford, 1967).

American Infant School

In America the philosophy of the Romantics and the ideas of Pestalozzi influenced the nature of the infant school movement, prominent in the 1830s and 1840s. Infant schools for children aged 3 to 5 were seen as a tool of social reform, a possible remedy to the poverty and crime brought by immigration and industrialization. An ironic twist to this view has emerged in the late 1990s, when the efforts of schools to empower children who are seen by the dominant culture as disadvantaged or at risk by immigration and poverty is met by increasingly vocal resistance from those who would prefer to use schooling to maintain the status quo of power and authority in American society (Bloch, 1991; Kessler & Swadener, 1992; Kohn, 1998, 2001).

One model for *infant* schools was based on the work of Robert Owen in Scotland. In 1816, at the height of the Industial Revolution in England, Owen founded a factory community called New Lanark in which families were housed near the workplace and health care was provided. Children attended his school until age 10 or 11, at which time they worked half days in the factory. This contrasted with child labor practices in most of England that saw children as young as 5 or 6 years working 16-hour days in the factories. Curriculum in Owen's school was based on everyday experiences of interest to children and included dance, music, and outdoor play. Play was central to the curriculum, and artificial rewards and punishments were discouraged in order for children to develop the intrinsic motivation provided by the pleasure of learning thought to be essential

for proper development of character. In fact, the school was named the Institute for the Formation of Character (Wolfe, 2002).

In the mid-1820s, Owen's school gained the attention of American reformers who saw the infant school as an avenue for providing opportunities for poor children to embark on the path of good citizenship rather than the despair and criminal behavior of the indigent poor. Before this time, children under the age of 5 were commonly enrolled in public schools with their older siblings. Primary-grade teachers were frustrated in their efforts to discipline children as young as 3 and to force them to conform to the rigid curriculum of memorization and recitation. Public schools began to exclude children under age 5 from attending.

At the same time, the new view of childhood as a period of life for freedom and play was replacing the Puritan church view in America, as it had in Europe. This led educators to express concern that small children were being harmed by harsh disciplinary practices and rigid curriculum in public schools (Strickland, 1982).

The most famous of the infant schools based on Pestalozzi's and Owen's work were programs founded in 1828 and 1834 by Bronson Alcott. Alcott's curriculum focused on conversation, singing, drawing, storytelling, and what would now be called journal writing and literature discussion groups, within a homelike atmosphere (McCuskey, 1940).

Another model of infant schooling in America presented a different picture. Samuel Wilderspin, an English educator, established infant schools based on a rigid curriculum and punitive discipline. Wilderspin's gifts were more in public relations than in early education, and his writings were widely circulated in America, so many of the infant schools did not reflect the child-centered approach of Pestalozzi, Owen, and Alcott, but instead looked much like the primary schools, except that they were for younger children (Fein, 1994; Forest, 1927; Pence, 1986; White & Buka, 1987).

Having ousted young children from public schools, those who financed public education were unwilling to fund infant schools for them, so those programs depended on the charity donations of social reformers or on parents' fees. Both models of infant schooling were doomed to decline because of this lack of support. Also, conservatives within the educational community were threatened by the association of Alcott's Temple School with utopian ideals.

The issue of support was exacerbated by Alcott himself. His fascination with transcendentalism dominated the curriculum in the Temple School he founded in Cambridge, Massachusetts, in 1834. He held conversations with children in which he idealized their notions on everything from obedience to procreation. Elizabeth Peabody, a close friend and colleague, had come to learn Alcott's model, and she faithfully recorded these daily conversations. Peabody agreed with the view of childhood and goal of self-reflection evident in Alcott's program but disagreed with the probing questions he asked children, a disagreement that eventually led to her withdrawal from the school (McCuskey, 1940; Snyder, 1972).

Against advice from both Peabody and Horace Mann, Alcott published the texts of these conversations, including children's discussions of human reproduction. In addition, he admitted a black child to the school, much to the dismay of the white parents in the community. This was the final straw in the demise of the infant school movement, and Alcott was forced to close the Temple School because of loss of support from both parents and the educational community (McCuskey, 1940).

Day Nurseries

As immigration expanded in America, another institution for the care of young children was born. In 1830 the first day nursery, modeled after the French *crèche*, was founded. This setting was viewed primarily as a service to poor working immigrants who needed help in overcoming the obstacles to success in their new country. Day nurseries were not valued for their efforts to educate children, as the infant schools had been, but as a service to adults. Because of this emphasis, day nurseries were designed as custodial care: Careful hygiene, regimented routines, and overcrowding paint the picture of their curriculum and environment. Despite a century and a half of efforts to counteract these beliefs and practices, the welfare reform efforts of the late 1990s show us that child care for young children in America is still focused on the needs of working adults, rather than on those needs of the children themselves.

By 1889 there were 175 day nurseries in the United States. The programs were often linked with settlement houses in poor communities. In the 1920s this association with settlement houses eventually led to a division between the fields of social work and early childhood education. The clinical case approach of social workers sought to change the behavior of the mother, while the day nurseries tried to provide support for victims of social and economic inequities. Because of this orientation and the social and economic pressures of the 1920s, social workers began to deny day nursery placements to all but the most "maladjusted" families in their care. Social workers emphasized the benefits of the *"mother's pension"* (an early version of Aid to Families with Dependent Children), which was instituted in many states during the early 1900s, and they encouraged mothers to stay at home with their children, even if that meant continued poverty. The stigma of day care as a program for debilitated parents rather than as a service to those who need society's support remains with us today (Goffin & Day, 1994; Stewart, 1990).

Fireside Education

The Fireside Education movement of the post–Civil War era was another influence that sealed the fate of the infant school (Strickland, 1982).

The upheaval and rapid social reform following the Civil War generated anxiety and a desire to return to conservative values including home and motherhood. Improvement in the publications industry also contributed to a parent education emphasis that remains strong in education today. Books and periodicals extolled the expertise of the mother as the child's first educator, especially in her ability and obligation to instill Christian values. Children should be sheltered from too much stimulation and from early academic pressures, a viewpoint shared by many infant school educators. Popular writing on this topic helped create popular appeal for the idea of childhood as a special time of life with special needs and privileges.

The major flaw in this movement was the exclusion of poor children from the "enlightened mother" education available in middle- and upper-class homes. Indeed, the parent education movement acquired an upper-class veneer, while programs for young children of the poor became increasingly custodial and demeaning of poor parents during the next 25 years.

Froebel's Kindergarten

In the 1880s and 1890s, as the day nurseries for poor children were flourishing, newly educated middle-class women discovered Friedrich Froebel's *kindergarten movement*. Rather than focusing on care as a service to working mothers, kindergarten programs, like their predecessor the infant school, emphasized the education of young children as a tool for social reform.

In Germany an educator named Friedrich Froebel (1782–1852) began a "garden for children" using many ideas drawn from Pestalozzi and the Romantic philosophers (Brooks, 1882). Based on Froebel's notion that women (and especially mothers) were naturally suited as children's first teachers, educated women imbued with the philosophies of the Romantics and the Transcendentalists, found the kindergarten movement a natural calling for their ideals,

skills, and place in society (DuCharme, 2000; Finkelstein, 1988; Stewart, 1990; Weber, 1969; Wiggin, 1893; Wolfe, 2002).

Froebel's View of Children　Like other Romantic educators and philosophers of his time, Froebel subscribed to the view that childhood represented a noble and malleable phase of human life. He was also influenced by the growing tide of *Transcendentalism* in Europe, a perspective that saw the divine within the human, with both humanity and nature reflecting a unity with God (DuCharme, 1996; Ross, 1976; Snyder, 1972; Weber, 1984).

This principle of unity, first realized in the home and later in the social context of the kindergarten's "extended family," was a major element of Froebel's educational philosophy. A second principle emphasized the importance of the child's self-activity. Froebel believed that children's innate goodness and creative potential would unfold naturally in the garden created for that purpose.

Froebel's kindergarten was characterized by free play, directed singing and movement games, and the use of Froebel's "gifts" and "occupations" to guide and structure play:

> When all have arrived the children form a circle, moving lightly and happily, singing a cheerful song. Then they take their seats at a long table and look around for some means of playing out the ideas which are filling their minds more or less clearly. At their request, small boxes are given them and they begin without delay to play eagerly. One child represents a breakfast table, another builds a fireplace, a third shows a shepherd followed by his flock, and such activity continues with each child following his individual interest. (Aborn, 1937, quoted in Downs, 1978, p. 43)

The boxes referred to in the preceding passage were one of the gifts, or specially designed materials that Froebel believed would help children to develop knowledge of forms of life, forms of beauty, and forms of mathematics. The first of these gifts were six 1½-inch knitted balls in red, green, yellow, violet, and orange. These were used in the many singing and movement games that Froebel described in his 1896 *Pedagogics of the Kindergarten* and built upon the "mother play" songs and fingerplays he wrote for mothers to use with children before they entered school. (See Wolfe, 2002, for a detailed description of Froebel's gifts.)

Following play with the knitted balls, children were introduced to wooden cubes, cylinders, triangles, and rectangles. The subsequent gifts were all geometric forms that could be recombined to develop children's knowledge of form and exercise their imaginations, as with the block constructions already described.

Froebel's "occupations" referred to constructive play activities including weaving, clay molding, paper folding, and embroidery that focused children's attention and exercised fine motor skills. These activities were similar in many ways to the real-life curriculum of Dewey's projects during the Progressive era.

Implicit in all Froebel's curriculum materials and guidelines were the three forms of knowledge he saw as the basis of all learning: forms of life, such as gardening, care of animals, and domestic tasks; forms of mathematics, such as geometric forms and their relationships to one another in pattern making and block play; and forms of beauty, such as design with color and shape, harmonies in music, and movement.

Role of Teacher   The teacher's role in the traditional Froebelian kindergarten was to observe and gently guide but not to interfere with children's creative processes (Snyder, 1972; Wiggin, 1893). Her role was seen as a calling and sacred in that regard. Elizabeth Peabody elucidated this view in the *Kindergarten Messenger,* a monthly journal for kindergarten teachers published from 1873 to 1875. Ross (1976) characterizes Peabody's writings:

> [She] dwelt upon such Froebelian concepts as the innocence of children and the spirit of God

in them; religious nurture rather than religious dogma; the sinfulness of breaking a child's will, respect for the child as an individual; the evaluation of children as they were in the kindergarten not as they might be when grown up; cultivating rather than drilling them. (p. 8)

This principle became severely distorted in the American kindergarten movement at the turn of the century when conservative Froebelians such as Susan Blow began to clash with the more liberal progressives led by Patty Smith Hill (Snyder, 1972; Spodek, 1986; Weber, 1969).

Rather than allowing children to explore and create with the gifts in their own way, the sequence of introduction to the gifts was carefully prescribed in the kindergarten teachers' manuals. First the child was allowed to explore the object, often sitting at a specially made table, with grids carved onto the top. Then the teacher guided the child to name properties of the objects and make comparisons with the other objects. Vocabulary related to color, shape, size, and texture would emerge from these questions. Finally the child would use the object to create original forms of art. This sequence is in opposition to current thinking about the role of play in children's learning, in which children play and create with objects before teachers ask them to reflect on their properties and name their features. Although Froebel's original intent was to promote learning through play, many of his ideas were rigidified by followers who did not fully understand his intentions (Downs, 1978; Weber, 1969; White & Buka, 1987).

As the kindergarten fell under the supervision and influence of the more rote elementary curriculum in public schools, this sequence related to the use of the gifts was codified into a structured modeling of the gifts' properties, memorization of the descriptive vocabulary, and copying of teacher-made constructions (Troen, 1975).

School, Parents, and Community   Froebel's work was designed to respect and strengthen the link between early home education and schooling.

His publications on commonly practiced mother plays represented his tribute to the family love and relationships he revered, and were an early form of parent education.

Although parents were not directly involved in Froebel's school curriculum, the continuity of domestic and school activities such as weaving, sewing, and gardening were an important element of his philosophy. Parents of Froebel's students were enthusiastic about the kindergarten, but the German government was suspicious of what it believed was an atheistic attitude in Froebel's emphasis on play and the transcendental idea of God as incarnate in humankind. In 1851 the German government banned kindergarten education. As liberal-minded Germans emigrated in Europe and to America, the stage was set for wide dissemination of Froebel's ideas.

ɷ ELIZABETH PEABODY: KINDERGARTEN IN AMERICA

After leaving her work with Bronson Alcott at the Temple School in Cambridge, Elizabeth Peabody (1804–1894) maintained her interest in early education. In 1859 she met Margarthe Schurz, a German immigrant who had founded a successful program in Watertown, Wisconsin. Peabody became intrigued with Froebel's philosophy (Snyder, 1972).

In 1860 Peabody opened the first English-speaking kindergarten in Boston. The program was very successful and was quickly filled with the children of middle-class families. But by 1867 Peabody wrote that she was disappointed in her program. Rather than creating well-balanced development, she felt her curriculum had instead created precocious learning without the spiritual aspect that Froebel felt was the essence of a kindergarten program:

> But seven years experience with my so-called kindergarten, though it has had a pecuniary success and a very considerable popularity, stimulating to other attempts, convinced me

that we were not practicing Froebel's fine art inasmuch as the quiet, certain unexcited growth of self-activity which he promised, did not come of our efforts; but there was on the contrary precocious knowledge and the consequent morbid intellectual excitement quite out of harmonious relation with moral and aesthetic growth. (Peabody, 1873, quoted in Snyder, 1972, p. 45)

As a result of her misgivings, Peabody traveled to Europe to see Froebelian kindergartens in action, bringing back with her several German teachers to train American teachers.

Susan Blow (1843–1916) worked closely with Peabody during the early years of the American kindergarten. In 1873 Blow persuaded William Harris, superintendent of the St. Louis public schools, to begin the first public kindergarten program in America. At that time most St. Louis children attended school for only 3 years, from age 7 to age 10, and educators believed that an early start in the public schools would improve the chances for children to contribute more fully to society (Snyder, 1972; Troen, 1975).

Inspired by Susan Blow, who was reported to be a gifted teacher of young children, student teachers were trained using Froebel's methods. The program was disseminated throughout the United States. One of the most enthusiastic of these early kindergarten teachers was Kate Douglas Wiggin (1856–1923), who, in 1878, started the Silver Street kindergarten in San Francisco and began the kindergarten movement on the West Coast (Association for Childhood Education International, 1940).

But the integrity of the kindergarten movement was undermined when Superintendent Harris left the St. Louis public schools. At Blow's urging he had fought moves to place kindergartens under the supervision of the more formal elementary education program, believing that such a move would destroy the spirit of play and creativity of the kindergarten. In 1884 Mary McCullough, an elementary supervisor, was assigned the kindergarten program in St. Louis, and the *trickle down phenomenon* we lament today was begun (Snyder, 1972).

In addition to the lost battle to maintain autonomy of the public kindergarten, the next three decades, 1885–1915, brought philosophical dissension in the ranks of kindergarten teachers themselves. Under the influence of G. Stanley Hall (1844–1924) of the Child Study Movement and John Dewey of the Progressive Education movement, teachers led by Patty Smith Hill (1868–1946) began to debate the appropriateness of Froebel's gifts and occupations and the rigid sequence they saw implemented in many kindergarten classrooms (Woody, 1934). These differences surfaced at the 1898 meeting of the International Kindergarten Union, where supporters on both sides "waved their white handkerchiefs and applauded" the advocates for their views (Snyder, 1972, p. 70).

In 1903 a Committee of Nineteen was formed to iron out the differences, a task that proved to be too difficult. In 1908 the committee issued three separate reports, differing primarily on perspectives regarding work versus play and the merits of free versus directed play, and the need to individualize curriculum (Fowlkes, 1991; Weber, 1969). Lucy Wheelock led the group for 6 years and edited the report published in 1913 (DuCharme, 2000).

That the inspired and truly child-centered work of Froebel became so distorted as to represent rigid and formalized instruction in the hands of less-gifted followers was unfortunate (Lilley, 1967). A similar fate befell Montessori's curriculum, which we turn to in the next section. Such is the pitfall of any curriculum, however grand its inception, and we must continue to guard against this kind of distortion by ensuring teacher preparation that includes not only methods but also the rationale for appropriate practice with young children (Almy, 1988; Bredekamp, 1987; Bredekamp & Copple, 1997; Monighan-Nourot, 1990; Wood & Attfield, 1996).

✍ TWENTIETH-CENTURY PROGRESSIVE EDUCATION

The beginning of the twentieth century brought the influence of Progressive educators, led by John Dewey (1859–1952), and the Child Study movement, begun by G. Stanley Hall (1844–1924). Both of these developments were heavily influenced by innovations in the field of science marked by the 1860 publication of Darwin's *On the Origin of Species* (Weber, 1984).

Progressives' View of Childhood

Dewey and the Progressives sympathized with many of Froebel's ideas regarding play, the importance of concrete materials, and the plasticity of early childhood. In addition, Darwin's notion that flexibility and adaptability to changing circumstances were the keys to survival appealed to the social consciences of the Progressives.

Environment and Curriculum

In 1900 Dewey published *The School and Society,* in which he called for educational institutions to step in and provide children with opportunities to learn from real objects and productive experiences formerly provided at home. School was viewed as a community of learners in which both teachers and children encountered new skills and concepts together (Dewey, 1900). Like Pestalozzi, Dewey criticized the irrelevancy of traditional schooling that relied on memorizing symbols and digesting the reports of others' opinions and experiences rather than constructing one's own ideas. He was also critical of Froebel's gifts, seeing them as contrived rather than real experiences:

> No number of object lessons got up as object
> lessons for the sake of giving information can
> afford even the shadow of a substitute for
> acquaintance with the plants and animals of the
> farm and garden acquired through active living
> among them and caring for them. No training

of sense organs in school, introduced for the sake of training, can begin to compare with the alertness and fulness of sense-life that comes through daily intimacy and interest in familiar occupations. (Dewey, 1900, p. 8)

In addition, Dewey's classroom was characterized by a hum of activity in which social negotiation and cooperation were among curriculum goals. History was the centerpiece around which child-sized versions of adult occupations such as carpentry and weaving were linked. Dewey describes how children reinvented tools to solve problems encountered by carding and weaving fibers from different sources, such as cotton and wool (Dewey, 1900). Constructive play and make-believe play were key elements of Dewey's curriculum. Coupled with the child's developing language and social skills, they formed the basis for both practical and aesthetic success (Cuffaro, 1995; Dewey & Dewey, 1915; Mayhew & Edwards, 1966).

Role of Teacher

Like his contemporary Maria Montessori, Dewey believed that a major role of the teacher was to provide a carefully prepared environment. In Dewey's environment the materials were those of a cooperative domestic society. Carpentry, weaving, cooking, and local geography were some essentials (Dewey, 1904/ 1964). Another aspect of the teacher's role was to draw on careful observation of children's play to ask questions and provide extensions that would integrate the child's understanding of experiences across several subject areas. This emphasis on questioning strategies and integrated curriculum remains a principle of appropriate early childhood education today. Discipline was seen as an evolving concept within the social spirit of the classroom, with peer pressure and the rewards of a job well done replacing external discipline by adult authority (Dewey, 1900).

School, Parents, and Community

Like Pestalozzi and Froebel, Dewey saw school as an extension of the home environment, organized to encourage specific intellectual and social goals. Likewise, the link extending from home to school to community was important as Dewey saw children's awareness of their place in a democratic society expand.

TWENTIETH-CENTURY CHILD STUDY

As Dewey's work with elementary school children was gaining momentum in the early years of the twentieth century, another movement began that was to have wide-ranging influence on the education of children too young to enter public school.

Child Study's View of Children

The many changes in the scientific community after Darwin's work was published inspired G. Stanley Hall to investigate scientifically the development of the young child. In 1893 he published the results of interviews with parents and children under the title *The Contents of Children's Minds on Entering School,* and the field of child development was born.

Arnold Gesell (1880–1961), one of Hall's students, carried child study beyond Hall's anecdotal reports to systematic observations and analyses of child behavior in his laboratory at Yale University. The norms of development established through Gesell's early work remain an important source of information for teachers and parents about age-appropriate development today (Gesell, 1948; Gesell & Ilg, 1943).

At the same time, John B. Watson (1878–1958) began to write about child study for the popular press, emphasizing the habit-training ideas of E. L. Thorndike's work in psychology. Watson's habit-training model stressed the importance of routine and consistency in children's lives. It became a feature of both the nursery schools of the early twentieth century and the kindergarten and first-grade curriculum devised by Patty Smith Hill, who attempted a unique blend of habit training and Progressivism in her *Conduct Curriculum for the Kindergarten and First Grade,* published in 1923 (Fowlkes, 1991).

Environment and Curriculum

In 1916, inspired by the writings of John Dewey and the growing Child Study movement, Lucy Sprague Mitchell (1878–1967) and Caroline Pratt (1867–1954) opened the Play School in New York City. Mitchell and Pratt adopted Dewey's emphasis on geography and the school as an extended family, as well as his ideas about play with real objects to their program for nursery school children. Play with language and storytelling that used children's own experiences as points of departure for imagined experiences were reflected in Mitchell's *Here and Now* storybooks. Block play was the forte of Pratt, whose designs for wooden blocks are used today (Antler, 1987; Hirsch, 1996). An anecdote from this period of history in early education illustrates the importance of the natural sensory world and imaginative play for young children:

> Luncheon follows, after which the children march out of doors singing a marching song. There they dig and weed and plant, water their garden beds and visit each other . . . an inviting and suitable playground is provided close to the garden. The children rush into the playground, jumping and wrestling, then unite to play games; first a game of bees, which they have just seen hovering over their flowers. Bird games follow, and a flight of pigeons over their heads suggests a pigeon game. (Aborn, 1937, cited in Downs, 1978, p. 44)

Role of Teacher

The role of the teacher in the Play School was that of guide and stage manager. Children's spontaneous play and interests brought from their lives outside school were carefully observed by the teacher, and curriculum was planned accordingly. One important legacy of the Child Study movement was the way in which Mitchell and Pratt, and later Mitchell and Harriett Johnson in their Bureau of Educational Experiments (BEE) School, saw themselves as teacher-researchers (Goffin & Wilson, 2001; Wolfe, 2002). Jotting down their insights and observations about children on a daily basis became an integral part of the teachers' craft as they guided the children's play and learning (Pratt, 1948). Another addition to the nursery teacher's traditional role as guide and architect of the environment was the role of parent-educator (National Society for the Study of Education, 1929).

School, Parents, and Community

In 1923 the Child Study movement and the field of nursery education received a significant windfall. Lawrence Frank, an economist entrusted with advising trustees on the use of the Lucy Spelman Rockefeller Memorial funds, was a colleague of Lucy Sprague Mitchell's husband. Through his friendship with Lucy Mitchell, he became convinced that early education represented the key to social reform. He convinced the trustees to fund centers for child study and parent education throughout the country. These funds reached Gesell at Yale University and other researchers in New York, Minnesota, Iowa, California, and Toronto (Antler, 1987; Weber, 1984).

University laboratory nurseries were created for three purposes: to model exemplary education practices, to provide data for research in the growing field of child study, and to educate parents about the implications of such research (National Society for the Study of Education, 1929).

In the 1920s Mitchell teamed up with Harriett Johnson to create a nursery school under the BEE in New York, where Mitchell continued the legacy of the Play School. Mitchell continued to develop imaginative language and literacy curriculum, while Johnson focused on the aesthetic elements of block play (Hewitt, 2001; H. M. Johnson, 1928; National Society for the Study of Education, 1929). This BEE school later became the Bank Street College of Education, an institution influential in the field today.

In terms of the blossoming field of parent education, the Rockefeller money also funded the efforts of teachers to communicate information about norms of child development to parents. In 1928 the National Council of Parental Education was formed in New York. *Children, the Magazine for Parents,* was founded in 1926 to disseminate information about child development through the popular press (Dittman, 1978). The 1929 yearbook of the National Society for the Study of Education (NSSE) was devoted to the link between parents and preschool education.

The parent involvement component may have served as a means of helping middle-class parents to feel good about sending their children to school, since the legacy of the Fireside Education movement was alive and well in the early decades of the twentieth century. Middle-class parents had been convinced that the proper context for early education of children was at home with their mothers (Pence, 1986). The option of coming to school with their children to learn more about child rearing from the scientific study of the child was probably a strong selling point of the nursery school.

Although the Rockefeller funding of university laboratory schools was a major source of support, other nursery schools outside university settings also became popular in the early twentieth century. One model was the parent cooperative nursery school; the first of these was founded in 1923 in Cambridge, Massachusetts, by a group of parents who had visited the Ruggles Street Nursery School in Boston. Others were simply private programs supported by parent fees. Like the open-air nurseries of Margaret McMillan and her sisters in England, these programs

emphasized raw materials for constructive play and ample opportunities for running, jumping, and climbing (Eliot, 1978). Nursery school teachers were very well educated. Those affiliated with Child Study centers had doctorates, and graduates of university programs commonly opened schools in the private sector, with parent education a major component.

Professionalization

Efforts to professionalize the field expanded during the 1920s. In 1926 Patty Smith Hill invited 25 nursery educators to a meeting at Columbia University to discuss common concerns (Finkelstein, 1988). Nursery educators at that time felt that the autonomy afforded by private sponsorship of nursery education was desirable, especially because many had been critical of the absorption of the kindergarten into the public schools and had banded together to promote autonomy (Stewart, 1990).

One result of these influences was that day nurseries remained custodial in nature and were exclusively for poor families, while middle-class children enjoyed a well-articulated curriculum grounded in child development theory and research.

Alternatives to Play-Based Nursery

In addition to the play-centered curriculum of the traditional and the psychodynamically oriented nursery schools, more structured schools were also available to the children of middle- and upper-class families.

Schlossman (1976) describes schools in the decade following World War I when the behaviorist ideas of Watson and Thorndike molded the curriculum. He attributes the popularity of these programs to the concerns of upper- and middle-class parents that their children would not learn proper manners in the Progressive elementary schools of the day, perceived by many to be permissive in their nature. The 1929 NSSE yearbook contains extensive chapters on both models of nursery education: the child-centered play approach and the habit-training model.

✎ TWENTIETH-CENTURY INNOVATIONS IN EUROPE: MONTESSORI'S CHILDREN'S HOUSE

Maria Montessori (1870–1952) was an Italian physician who gleaned many of her ideas about early childhood education from her careful observations of infants and their caregivers (Montessori, 1936). In many ways her philosophy was similar to that of her contemporaries Froebel and Dewey in other parts of the world, but she added new elements to thoughts about early childhood development and education.

Montessori's View of Children

Montessori saw education as assisting the psychological development of children rather than as teaching per se. She felt that teachers often overlooked the importance of unconscious elements in the human psyche, and that understanding children who had difficulty in adapting to society was the key to contributing to their successful development (Wolfe, 2002).

Montessori believed that the spirit of a human being developed through interactions with the environment, and she extended the notion of developmental stages seen in the philosophies of Pestalozzi and Froebel to include the ideas of sensitive periods of development. She believed that during a limited period of a child's life, particular capacities were ripe for development and must be fostered by the environment to flourish.

Like many of her contemporary Romantics, Montessori grounded her educational program on an exceptionally keen insight into the nature of childhood as well as a belief that educating the young child was the key to the salvation of society (Goffin & Wilson, 2001; Wolfe, 2002).

Environment and Curriculum

An ordered, welcoming environment was the first principle of Montessori's Casa dei Bambini, or Children's House, founded in 1907 in Rome. She believed that order in the external environment helps children to organize their often chaotic perceptions of the outside world and build a sense of predictability and security (Kramer, 1988):

> Whereas our conception that everything should be in proportion to the size of the child has been well received. The clear light rooms, with little low windows wreathed in flowers with small pieces of furniture of every shape just like the furniture of a nicely furnished home, little tables, little armchairs, pretty curtains, low cupboards within reach of the children's hands, where they can put things and from which they can take what they want, all this seemed a real, practical improvement in the child's life. (Montessori, 1936, p. 124)

Her observations of infants and toddlers led her to value purposeful activity as a highly motivating force for young children. As a result she created objects for children to allow them to experience physical activities such as stacking, opening, closing, dusting, and connecting. She saw this goal-oriented activity as children's "work" and contrasted it with play, which she saw as unfocused and frivolous. In this way she differed from Pestalozzi, Froebel, and Dewey, who saw play at the center of children's education, although her contemporaries might have classified children's self-selected activities with specially designed materials as play. Montessori defined play much more narrowly than others who wrote about the education of young children (Monighan-Nourot, 1990).

Role of Teacher

Montessori believed that children should select their own materials and claim responsibility for cleanup as well. As part of the development of this responsibility, Montessori, like Pestalozzi,

Materials such as the one pictured here are central to Montessori education today.

disapproved of rewards and punishments, believing that the child's self-dignity could best be developed by intrinsic motivation (Montessori, 1909/1912, 1936). In this way she was more flexible than teachers in the Froebelian kindergarten, who selected many of the tasks and activities for children.

She also believed that useless adult assistance to children formed the root of all future repression and that adults too frequently gave messages to children that they thought them incompetent. She noted that teachers must hold their own activities, desires, and authority in abeyance so that children could solve their own problems. In a nutshell, the good Montessori teacher operated on three principles: a carefully prepared environment, an attitude of humility, and respect for children's individuality (Montessori, 1936).

School, Parents, and Community

Montessori (1936) offers a moving account of her growing relationship with the parents in the community surrounding the Casa dei Bambini. In it she describes how parents came to her for advice on child rearing and expressed to her the ways in which school habits such as hand washing and putting objects away had influenced their home lives:

> They came instead to confide intimate family details. "These little ones of three and four," they told me, "say things to us that would offend us from anyone else. They say for instance 'You've got dirty hands, you ought to wash them. You ought to wash the spots on your dress.'" (Montessori, 1936, p. 148)

Montessori's school enjoyed financial support from the Italian government during its early years of operation. Montessori writes that the king and queen and other dignitaries visited the program. Business people hoped that the school, like educational programs for the poor in communities in America, would help to alleviate vandalism and theft in the neighborhood filled with children left unsupervised by working parents (Hunt, 1964).

In 1909 Montessori published *The Montessori Method: Scientific Pedagogy as Applied to Child Education in "The Children's Houses"* (1909/1912), and in the years 1911–1917 she received increasing attention from American educators. Her ideas were very compatible with those of educators in America who saw early education as a tool for social reform. However, her philosophy never gained the footing in America that it did in England. Educators saw Montessori's sense education curriculum as narrow in comparison with the teachings of Dewey, which were thought to be more applicable to the changing American society (Forest, 1927; Hunt, 1964).

Another reason for Montessori's limited reception in the United States was that early childhood education was just recovering from the battles waged over Froebel's curriculum, and educators were not prepared to embrace another method that was perceived as inflexible in its implementation (Lazerson, 1972; Wolfe, 2002; Wood & Attfield, 1996).

In the 1960s Montessori's work again received attention in the United States as both schools and teacher training programs were created through funds from the War on Poverty and the emphasis on early education (Pitcher, 1966).

✎ U.S. NATIONAL EMERGENCIES AND EARLY EDUCATION

The advent of the Great Depression in 1929 was the first of two national crises that had a permanent effect on the field of early childhood education.

WPA Nurseries

In 1933 the Work Projects Administration (WPA) decided that establishing nursery schools throughout the country might provide a viable avenue for increasing jobs, while at the same time offering an important service to society at large. The resulting popularization of the idea of nursery school education for all children, not just those of middle- and upper-class families, was a positive side effect of this plan (Anderson, 1947).

A negative effect was the decline in standards for teachers. Like the earlier day nurseries in the United States, the focus of the WPA nurseries was on supporting the economy through adult employment and child care rather than on educating children. Decentralized funding of these programs undermined efforts of the Children's Bureau and the National Education Association to maintain professional standards of training for teachers (Stewart, 1990). In fact, 2-week training periods were common, and the major qualification for becoming a WPA nursery teacher was liking children (Frank, 1937).

The pervasive model for the WPA nurseries was habit training, rather than the more permissive psychodynamic model that gained popularity in the 1940s and 1950s. Mary Alice Mallum recalls the WPA nursery program at the University of California, Los Angeles:

> I remember a couple of devastating things as being "appropriate and right" about how we guided children's behavior at that time, a time when there was very little focus on emotion, developmental needs and problems of children. Much emphasis was placed on social behavior and training with a big "T." (Bothman, 1976, p. 20)

Health and nutrition went hand in hand with the training of habits. Rosalie Blau recalls how children were lined up for doses of cod liver oil and a slice of orange in order to combat malnutrition in children whose families had little to eat (Bothman, 1976). Millie Almy recalls with humor the preoccupation with cleanliness she experienced:

> In previous years the emphasis had been on a particularly behavioristic model called "habit training" that was quite typical of the Nursery School in the twenties and thirties. Its emphasis was on physical hygiene. I recall calling the pediatrician attached to the school and saying,

"I just discovered we have a huge supply of surgical soap. I guess it's for the children to wash their hands. Do you think that it is necessary for us to order surgical soap?" He laughed and said, "No, but if you think children need to wash their hands with surgical soap after handling toys, maybe you should order some tongs too, then they won't have to touch the toys at all." (Stewart, 1997, p. 45)

The end of the Depression brought a group of nursery school educators looking for alternatives to the rigidity of habit training. As they looked to universities for research and theory to guide them, the more child-centered psychodynamic model became popular, but these were largely private schools for parents who could afford to pay fees for their children's education. Poor children were again without education as the WPA nurseries lost federal funds and closed.

Lanham Centers

World War II was the second national crisis to have a permanent effect on early childhood education. The war brought new funding to early education in the form of the Lanham Act nurseries. The same problems associated with inadequate teacher preparation and the lowering of standards for educational quality continued in government-funded programs. However, by this time theories and practices from the Child Study movement were more widespread, and psychoanalytic ideas about education were beginning to supplant the more rigid habit-training curriculum.

In addition, a spirit of patriotism and cooperation among nursery staff and parents replaced the stigma attached to enrollment in public nursery schools due to poverty. Docia Zavitkovsky recalls:

The enrollment cut across all economic lines and made for a very good program because one wasn't concerned whether he was at the poverty level or whether one was on Aid to Families with Dependent Children (AFDC), or if one was on Medical. You were involved

because you were freeing a person to work for the war effort and there was a great deal of feeling about doing something supportive to the national effort. (Bothman, 1976, p. 10)

Unlike the half-day programs of private nursery schools or even the 9 to 5 hours of WPA nurseries, the Lanham centers were open 10 to 12 hours a day, 6 days a week. Working mothers enjoyed the opportunity to contribute to the war effort. The support and concern for their children expressed by child-care staff alleviated some of the loneliness and anxiety of parenting alone while husbands fought the war. Hymes (1944), writing about the Lanham centers at Kaiser Steel in Oregon, discusses the need for teachers to counsel both parents and children through times of grief and stress.

But the change in attitudes toward early education did not last. With the end of the war, funding for child-care centers was suspended, and only in two states, California and New York, were early childhood educators successful in lobbying for state funding to keep programs open. Grassroots protests against closing centers were not supported by labor unions, which saw male employment as a priority, or by child welfare agencies, which had never encouraged women to work outside the home (Stewart, 1990). Widespread propaganda encouraged women to return to their places in the home, and child-care advocates had to maintain a constant battle to retain their funding from year to year (Bothman, 1976).

Psychodynamic Influences in Nursery School Education

The early years of the Child Study movement focused on children's motor and social development. By the late 1920s the influence of Sigmund Freud (1856–1939) was beginning to be seen as teachers and researchers in university laboratory schools started to address the importance of children's emotional development. Researchers studied personality development, and teachers began to incorporate such terms as complex and anxiety into their professional vocabulary (Forest, 1927).

In 1933 Susan Isaacs published *Intellectual Growth in Young Children* (1933a) and *Social Development in Young Children* (1933b), setting forth a psychodynamic perspective on early education that began to influence curriculum. Dorothy Baruch's book *Parents and Children Go to School* (1939) was widely used in the Lanham nurseries of World War II. Freud's work became a common topic in the popular press as well, and his ideas were frequently discussed (Bothman, 1976).

Psychodynamic View of Children The psychodynamic focus of attention was on the affective life of the young child. Childhood fears and behaviors such as shyness or aggressiveness took on new meanings when applied to the child's unconscious and were carefully recorded by teachers. Play as the expression of deep-seated feelings and as a catharsis for frustration was seen as the center of the child experience. Play was thought of as preventive mental health therapy or educational therapy (Hartley, Frank, & Goldenson, 1957).

Later, the work of Erik Erikson (1902–1994) added the idea of play as mastery over situations through experimentation and planning to its role in mastering unconscious impulses and conflicts (Erikson, 1963).

Environment and Curriculum Psychodynamically oriented nursery schools were characterized by a child-centered environment with a high degree of freedom and even permissiveness. Raw materials such as paint, clay, and sand were believed to offer children the most free expression of unconscious impulses, although "finished" materials such as baby dolls and puppets that might aid children in expressing their innermost conflicts were also desirable (Baruch, 1939; Biber, 1984; Fuller et al., 1947):

> The teacher provides play materials which offer children a chance to express in play the feelings that are allowed only limited expression in real life. A captain's cap gives a boy a chance to be a bold, bossy, chief-of-staff. Dolls give a submissive little girl a chance to be the dominating or deeply maternal feminine head of the household. Fear can be pantomimed without shame when a child's companion takes the part of a lion. Bold strokes of the brush, vivid massings of color may put on paper feelings which would be less acceptable if expressed in another form. (Fuller et al., 1947, pp. 139–140)

Both Isaacs (1933b) and Landreth (Fuller et al., 1947) write of a de-emphasis on eating and sleeping routines that came from psychodynamic understandings. This represented a shift from the overemphasis on such routines that characterized the habit-training model of nursery education at its peak in the 1920s and 1930s.

Role of Teacher The teacher's role became more passive under the influence of psychodynamic theory. Freudians admonished both parents and teachers not to interfere with children's expressions of feelings through play, art, and movement, and to let free expression of feelings reign. Rosalie Blau, one of the early leaders in the California Children's Centers, comments:

> Teachers were supposed to stand in the background and observe, and just step in physically if necessary if a child were going to fall—that's all. The teacher was not to interact with the children. (Bothman, 1976, p. 22)

But the psychodynamic perspective also recognized feelings of both children and adults, in contrast to the more rigid habit-training model. Mary Alice Mallum, another leader of the California Children's Center movement, recalls:

> We moved from the social-physical to the social-emotional approach. Teachers were then freer to be themselves and it was possible to recognize teachers as individuals. The children could be exposed to people who were real. A teacher who got really angry because she was

kicked could be angry because she was kicked. This is Dorothy Baruch right from the beginning. She really started when it wasn't very popular. She encouraged the expression of anger without hurting someone. (Bothman, 1976, p. 30)

School, Parents, and Community   Landreth (Fuller et al., 1947) reports that the most common reason given by parents for enrolling their children in nursery school was the social development of children. Reflecting the nursery school's concern with parent education, teachers influenced by psychodynamic theory attempted to bridge home and school for the child, explaining children's behavior to parents and encouraging children to express their feelings about experiences at home (Isaacs, 1933a, 1933b).

✌ DECLINE OF PROGRESSIVISM AND THE INFLUENCE OF *SPUTNIK*

Cremin (1961) describes the forces that began to undermine the Progressive education movement after World War II. Although Progressive ideas had been well entrenched in elementary, kindergarten, and nursery education, a conservative attitude and a decline in social reform initiatives characterized American society. The social climate was similar in many ways to that which gave rise to the Fireside Education movement after the Civil War.

In addition, Dewey's vision became fragmented in the hands of teachers who did not fully understand the implementation of Progressive curriculum. Creative self-expression often led to overpermissiveness and chaotic classrooms. This may have been partly due to psychodynamic influences but was probably more a result of poorly trained teachers who did not know how to manage a child-centered classroom effectively while integrating large quantities of new information into the curriculum (Cremin, 1961).

In 1957 the Soviet Union launched *Sputnik*, and this event exacerbated the decline of Progressive ideas in the United States. Along with concerns raised about the performance of World War II enlisted men on achievement tests, *Sputnik* symbolized an erosion of basic educational skills and concepts, and the Progressives became the scapegoat for these concerns (Goodlad, Klein, & Novotney, 1973). The pendulum of educational practice moved far to the side of skills-based instruction in the public schools until the influence of constructivism began to be evident in the latter decades of the twentieth century.

✌ CONSTRUCTIVIST THEORY IN EARLY EDUCATION

Beginning in the 1950s and accelerating in the 1960s to the present, child development research and teaching were influenced by the work of Jean Piaget (1896–1980) and his early contemporary Lev Vygotsky (1896–1934). Piaget's work became widely known before that of Vygotsky, but both theories have been influential in educational theory and practice in the 1970s and 1980s.

Both theorists emphasize the value of play in intellectual development and provide strong arguments for children's own activity with objects and in interaction with peers as the basis for early childhood curriculum.

Constructivist View of Children

The constructivist viewpoint rests on the assumption that children mentally construct knowledge through reflection on their experiences. The child is an active architect of learning (De Vries, Zan, Hildebrandt, Edmiaston, & Sales, 2002; Forman, 2000; Fosnot, 1996; Goffin & Wilson, 2001; Waite-Stupiansky, 1997). De Vries and Kohlberg (1987) express this idea succinctly: Constructivist theory means "forming the mind, not just furnishing it" (p. 17).

This view of children's development contrasts with the behaviorist view of the child as a passive receptor of knowledge, which is acquired through imitation and practice and is internalized through processes of reward and punishment (Kamii, 1985, 2000).

Piaget (1969) theorizes that children progress through universal and invariant sequences of development, with each stage marked by a characteristic way of organizing thoughts and activity. Vygotsky (1967) adds to this model the importance of the social context for children's learning. Both emphasize play as a means of developing the capacity for symbolic abstract thought (Nourot, 1997; Van Hoorn, Nourot, Scales, & Alward, 2003). Moral development, too, has its roots in the play of young children as they develop empathy and come to understand the rules and roles of society (De Vries & Zan, 1999; Piaget 1965; Vygotsky, 1967).

Environment and Curriculum

Like Montessori's, Dewey's, and Mitchell's programs, a constructivist program stresses the importance of an environment that encourages children to make choices and to pursue their play with peers. Learning centers with materials for art, block play, writing and drawing, dramatic play, and exploration with raw materials such as dirt, sand, and water are available for children to select both individual and group projects (De Vries & Kohlberg, 1987; De Vries et al., 2002; Forman, 2000; Fromberg & Bergen, 1998; Johnson, Christie, & Yawkey, 1999; Van Hoorn et al., 2003; Wasserman, 1990).

In one constructivist model, that of Kamii and De Vries (1980), group games are a central feature of the curriculum. Although these include games reminiscent of Froebel's mother play and gifts activities, a developmental sequence of the understanding of rules and the perspectives of others is implicit in these group games (De Vries, 1998; De Vries et al., 2002).

Role of Teacher

In addition to the role as environmental architect, the teacher in a constructivist program is skilled in the use of questioning strategies that encourage children to reflect on their experiences and to predict future ones (De Vries et al., 2002):

> Whichever responses teachers choose from their full repertoire, that response has power for the children. Because it comes from a person in authority, a respected teacher, the response has power to hurt or to help. It has power to be additive or subtractive, to empower or disempower, to enhance or diminish thinking. (Wasserman, 1990, pp. 199–200)

The teacher also evaluates children's progress, organizes experiences for active engagement, and collaborates with children in constructing knowledge (De Vries & Kohlberg, 1987; Jones & Reynolds, 1992; Van Hoorn et al., 2003). Recent writing regarding the role of play and interaction in constructing moral development emphasizes these collaborative dialogues (De Vries & Zan, 1999).

This use of questioning strategies to stretch children's thinking is emphasized in the High Scope Cognitively Oriented Curriculum, a model based on constructivist theory that began as one of Head Start's planned programs (Weikart, 1989), and in the Schools Are for Thinking Project in Canada (Wasserman, 1990). The British Infant School model, popular in the 1960s and 1970s, also emphasized this approach to children's learning (Entwhistle, 1970).

Another constructivist model, the developmental interaction approach, is seen at Bank Street College of Education. Biber (1984) describes how the traditional play-based model begun there by Lucy Mitchell and Harriet Johnson in the 1920s has incorporated strategies for using play to promote conflict resolution and ego strength drawn from the work of Erikson (1963) and Isaacs (1933b), as well as the cognitive goals of play gleaned from a constructivist perspective.

School, Parents, and Community

The three programs described are well-articulated examples of constructivist educational practice, but many other such programs flourish in both public and private settings for young children. Both Bank Street and High Scope were part of Head Start's programs and included parent education components, although that is not the focus of constructivist curriculum. In recent years educators have made efforts through professional books and journal articles to explain to parents major features of constructivist programs for young children, such as the value of play, children's need to learn through action with concrete objects, and the ways in which rote memorization is inconsistent with child development theory. In addition, books such as Elkind's *The Hurried Child* (1981) and *Miseducation* (1987); Winn's *Children without Childhood* (1983); Healey's *Endangered Minds* (1990); and Crain's *Reclaiming Childhood: Letting Children Be Children in Our Achievement-Oriented Society* (2003) have contributed to popular understanding of the basis for constructivist programs for young children.

New efforts at developing assessment measures based on constructivist theory have again brought an important issue to the forefront: Researchers and teachers must include parents of all cultural backgrounds in their discussions of educational reform and curriculum development (Ballenger, 1999; Delpit, 1988, 1995; Kagan, 1999; Kamii, 1990; Ramsey, 1998; Wortham, 1997).

☙ HEAD START

The increasing concern for the intellectual preparation of American school children opened a debate that began in the early 1960s and continues today. In 1961 J. McVicker Hunt published *Intelligence and Experience,* setting forth the argument that intelligence, rather than being a fixed characteristic, depended to a great extent on stimulation in early childhood. He coined the term "the match" to describe activities that optimally challenge children's development. In 1964 Benjamin Bloom published *Stability and Change in Human Characteristics.* His review of data from longitudinal research studies led him to conclude that the first 5 years of life are the optimal time for promoting intellectual development.

This work in psychology, coupled with the civil rights movement and the subsequent War on Poverty, led to the creation of Head Start, called "America's most successful educational experiment" (Zigler & Muenchow, 1992). One of the major premises of the civil rights movement was that a return of power to poverty-stricken minority communities would halt the expanding relief rolls and provide avenues to escape dependence on welfare. This idea of economic empowerment merged with the growing support for early intervention to create Project Head Start, a comprehensive program of education and health care for preschool children and their parents. In addition, teachers of Head Start preschools were to be hired from communities in which programs were located (Kagan, 1997; Kahn & Friedman, 1995; Nieto, 1996; Powell, 2000a, 2000b; Zigler & Anderson, 1979).

Information from the child development movement merged with the well-established philanthropic motives for early education. Once again, early childhood education became the rallying cry for social reform and the eradication of poverty (Lazerson, 1972).

Environment and Curriculum Models

Debates flourishing in developmental psychology for several decades found a fertile testing ground with the funding of Head Start. Lucy Spelman Rockefeller Memorial funds had been withdrawn from the Child Study movement in 1939, and Head Start was seen as a way to test theories of early education on a population quite different from the children in university laboratory schools and private nurseries (Gray & Klaus, 1965). Several models were implemented

Head Start programs were developed to provide disadvantaged young children with social and cognitive stimulation.

and systematically evaluated as part of the general evaluation of the effectiveness of Head Start (Goffin & Wilson, 2001; Miller, 1979; Powell, 2000b). The behaviorist model, a legacy from the habit-training model of earlier decades, was represented by the distar program of Bereiter and Engelmann (1966). Distar emphasized the acquisition of basic skills that poor children lacked from their home and community environments. These skills, such as standard English and recognition of symbols, were considered essential for success in elementary school. Instruction was didactic and based on a process of systematic rewards. Children's self-concepts were thought to develop as a result of experiencing success in mastering basic skills.

Another Head Start model was the traditional play-based program of nursery education based on schools founded with Lucy Spelman Rockefeller funds. These programs looked much like the Bank Street school of Mitchell and Johnson and those described in detail in the 1947 *Yearbook of the National Society for the Study of Education* (Fuller et al., 1947). Play represented

the centerpiece of the curriculum, with field trips and other activities planned around children's experiences with natural materials and real objects. The program emphasized the whole child, including social and emotional development as well as intellectual growth.

A third model, the cognitive interactionist model, was based on the constructivist theory of Piaget. On the surface, these programs resembled those of the traditional nursery school with an emphasis on play and a child-centered environment. However, in addition to observing children and setting up an environment rich in opportunities for play, teachers were trained in the use of questioning strategies and curriculum design that would challenge children's thinking with regard to specific logical-mathematical concepts.

A Montessori model was also part of Head Start's menu of programs. This model, based on Montessori's work in Italy, was similar to both the traditional and cognitive interactionist programs in taking a long-range view of child development. Positive self-esteem was seen as a basis for learning rather than an outcome of success on short-range goals of cognitive skills seen in the distar model (Monighan-Nourot, 1990).

Omwake (1979) reports that these differences regarding goals and curriculum among early childhood educators came to a boiling point when Head Start programs were evaluated by the federal government. Short-range goals of the behaviorist program were more amenable to standardized assessment measures than such goals as "social competence" that addressed the development of the whole child in the less-structured programs (White & Buka, 1987).

This lack of cohesion among early childhood educators contributed to other problems that remain with us today: a lack of well-trained teachers and paraprofessional status and pay for those who teach the youngest children in our society (Hymes, 1991). Because Head Start was conceived as a vehicle for adult employment as well as a program for children's educational needs, the adult goal took precedence in many communities.

Standards for professional competence varied widely, and budgets for in-service education of teachers were slim. Power struggles among staff drove many experienced teachers from Head Start programs, and a wide range of quality characterized Head Start programs, just as it had the WPA and Lanham centers of the past.

In the 1970s, Edward Zigler led efforts to improve child development education for Head Start staff, emphasizing the role of play and child-centered environments. Omwake (1979) reports that this staff training was not as successful as hoped, because teachers with seniority based on the early years of Head Start funding were unwilling to allow new staff to change established practices.

Another issue that surfaced during the first two decades of Head Start is the attitude of black parents toward play-based, child-centered curriculum. Joffe (1977) describes the debates among low-income black minority and white middle-class parents in the parent nursery programs in Berkeley, California, in the 1970s. Delpit (1988, 1995) and Hale-Benson (1982) write eloquently about the concerns of many black parents that their children's learning styles be respected and that they not be allowed to just play but instead learn academic skills in preschool that will allow them to succeed in public school.

Effects of Head Start

In initial evaluations, all children in Head Start programs showed significant gains in measures thought to be related to school success, compared with children not enrolled in Head Start programs. IQ gains were higher for children in the more didactic programs, while broader measures favored the less structured models (Miller, 1979). Millie Almy reflects on the evolution of thinking in the field of early education at this time:

> But these programs for the disadvantaged had another effect as well. In the early days of the renaissance many of the individuals influencing the field, as well as entering it, were primarily concerned with children's intellectual development. They were less interested in other aspects of development, or in early childhood terms, "the whole child." As time went on and as research about the programs evolved, I think that preoccupation with intellect shifted somewhat. People had to confront the reality of the complexity of children's development. (Stewart, 1997, p. 76)

However, in 1969 the Westinghouse study was released (Westinghouse Learning Corporation, Ohio University, 1969). It indicated that the early gains in intelligence scores for Head Start children washed out by third grade. Datta (1979) reports that a veil of disillusionment prevailed in early education from the time of this report until 1975 when a mood of optimism began to dawn as evaluators reanalyzed some of the Westinghouse data and designed more multifaceted studies of the effects of Head Start. Datta cites an article entitled "New Optimism About Preschool Education" appearing in a 1978 issue of the *Carnegie Corporation Quarterly,* and calls for more longitudinal research on outcome measures other than IQ.

In 1981 the promise of longitudinal data on Head Start was finally fulfilled, at least in part. Schweinhart, Weikart, and Larner (1986) published results of the Perry Preschool Project evaluation of Head Start children. At age 19, children from the Head Start program showed a significantly higher number of high school graduates, more enrollment in postsecondary education, and significantly less enrollment in special education classes than a control group who had not had preschool education. Those who had experienced the Head Start program showed lower rates of juvenile arrests, teen pregnancy, and welfare dependence, and higher rates of employment than the control group. A study of Perry Preschool Project graduates at age 27 indicated that those who attended the preschool had fewer criminal arrests, higher incomes, and more marital stability 22 years later (Schweinhart, Barnes, & Weikert, 1993). When costs were compared between programs and a control group, the high-quality preschool program yielded both long-term benefits to society and saved $7 in benefits such as remedial education for every $1 invested (Schweinhart & Weikart, 1997). By 1997 nearly 17 million children had benefited from Head Start enrollment and President Clinton's goals for 2002 included expanded enrollment of 1 million children (Powell, 2000b). Both school readiness and performance standards were encompassed in the 1998 federal reauthorization of Head Start funding, and policy makers are pushing for further focused academic outcomes in proposed legislation for 2003 (Kagan, 2003).

1970–2000: RAPID CHANGE AND SCHOOL REFORM

The two decades following the inception of Head Start brought rapid change in American society, with impact on the lives of young children and the field of early childhood education. Elkind (1986) describes the myth of competence in American society, an idea that suggests that children in these years were viewed as competent, often beyond reasonable expectations for their years, as adults sought to justify the pursuit of their own aspirations. Funding for programs for the elderly and subsidies for corporate growth overshadowed concerns for the well being of young children (Goffin, Wilson, Hill, & McAninch, 1997; Kaplan, 1991).

One of the major social changes was the huge increase in the number of working women and the concomitant need for child care. A part of this increase was due to the rising divorce rate. The number of single-parent families doubled between 1970 to 1980. Single-parent families were more often headed by women, and these families constitute over half of all families living below the poverty level in the United States (Hymes, 1991; Washington & Oyemade, 1985).

In the 1970s the birth rate declined to its lowest rate in U.S. history, and many elementary schools closed classrooms. In the early 1980s a new baby boom began as professional women born in the post–World War II years began families later in life. Unfortunately, part of the baby boom was also due to teen parents. In 1980 a half-million teenagers per year became parents, many of those younger than age 14 (Hymes, 1991).

Child care became a major political issue. Efforts to pass child-care legislation and funding were thwarted in 1970 by President Nixon's veto and in 1975 by conservative groups. In the 1970s and 1980s, private enterprise involvement in early education programs increased, as did the number of family day-care homes. In 1979 Kindercare celebrated its 10th anniversary, marking the ownership of 459 centers that operate within a corporate framework. Hymes (1991) comments, "But a day care industry is new and typical of a national hardening of the vocabulary. Increasingly we speak of caregivers rather than of teachers, of operators rather than principals or directors, of slots rather than of children" (p. 61).

However, in the noncorporate world, the income and status of teachers in child-care settings continued to decline, following the pattern started by the WPA nurseries, Lanham centers, and Head Start. Child care received much media attention in the 1980s, culminating in the topic becoming a major part of the rhetoric of both major candidates during the 1988 presidential election. In 1998 child care once again became a central issue in the debates over welfare reform and the requirements that welfare recipients join the workforce within 2 years (California Department of Education, 1998). Many of the cohesive efforts mounted by early childhood educators to raise the quality of care across the nation were undermined with the infusion of federal funding to create more slots in child care, regardless of quality in order to meet the needs of working parents.

Funding debates often centered on the effects of quality care and teacher education on the welfare of children in care outside the home. In 1989, the Child Care Employee Project released the results of a study conducted in 227 centers across the country. They documented exceptionally low wages for the teachers, who were nearly all women. Their wages were lower in relation to comparably educated women and particularly lower in relation to comparably educated men. The average turnover rate for programs was 41% per year. In addition, this study examined the effects of low-quality care on children. In low-quality programs with high turnover rates, the language and social development of children lagged behind that of children in high-quality programs with more consistent teachers (Kagan & Cohen, 1997; Kagan et al., 2002; Whitebook & Eichberg, 2002; Whitebook, Howes, & Phillips, 1990).

Environment and Curriculum: Professional Debates

In part because of these sobering statistics, efforts to professionalize the field of early childhood education and to raise standards of teacher preparation have blossomed in the last two decades. The Child Development Associate Program (CDA) began in 1973 and remained afloat even during periods of meager funding. The National Association for the Education of Young Children (NAEYC) grew to 103,500 members with over 400 affiliate groups in 1998 and continued the publication of position statements on both teacher preparation (1991b) and curriculum and assessment guidelines (1991a). The term "developmentally appropriate practice" coined by Bredekamp (1987; Bredekamp & Copple, 1997) remains a major point of discussion of early childhood educators today (Bloch, 1991; Charlesworth, 1998a, 1998b; Dickinson, 2002; Kagan, 1991; Kessler & Swadener, 1992; Lubeck, 1998; Polakow, 1992; Seefeldt, 1987; Silin, 1995).

Perhaps NAEYC's most impressive effort to date is the creation in 1984 of the National Academy for Early Childhood Accreditation, led by Sue Bredekamp. This program is based on a voluntary self-study process for early childhood education programs, from infant programs through the primary grades. By 1991 some 1,797 programs throughout the country had been accredited by the academy. Other professional organizations for early childhood educators also remain alive and well. The Association for Childhood Education International (ACEI), founded in 1892 as the International Kindergarten Union, and the Organisation Mondiale pour L'Education Prescolaire (OMEP) continue efforts both in the United States and abroad to advocate children's rights and provide professional collegiality to teachers of young children.

In the 1980s professional groups advocating the education of children began to join forces. Although many of the schisms between preschool education, kindergarten education, and elementary education remain, the importance of early intervention seems undisputed. For example, organizations formerly dedicated to elementary education have jumped on the early childhood education bandwagon. In 1985 the Association for Supervision and Curriculum Development (ASCD) and the National Association of Elementary School Principals (NAESP) issued position papers calling for public sponsorship of preschool programs (Hymes, 1991). This movement gained attention in the late 1990s in New York, Georgia, and California (Alpert, Alquist, & Strom-Martin, California Master Plan for Education, 2002; California Department of Education, Report of Universal Preschool Task Force, 1998). These reports brought forth two major issues of current debate: public school sponsorship of programs for 4-year-olds (Blank, 1985; Mitchell & Modigliani, 1989; Morgan, 1985) and the related concern for *academic pushdown* of curriculum. Academic pushdown refers to observations by educators throughout the United States that curriculum and instruction appropriate for older children have found their way into classrooms for kindergarten and preschool children. Early childhood educators express concern that public school sponsorship of preschool programs will exacerbate this trend and lead to the same fate that befell the autonomy of the kindergarten in the nineteenth century.

A 1986 survey in California revealed that nearly two thirds of kindergarten teachers surveyed listed an overemphasis on academic skills as their major concern (Smith, 1986). In the late 1980s and 1990s, position statements were issued by early childhood professional organizations to combat this trend toward "hothousing" young children to produce academic precocity at early ages (Almy 2000; Elkind, 1986; Fleege, Charlesworth, Burts, & Hart, 1992; Isenberg & Jalongo, 1997; Lewis, 1995). Among those that have published these statements are the following organizations: NAEYC (1998); the Association for Childhood Education International (1986); the International Reading Association (1986, 1998); in conjunction with ACEI, the Association for Supervision and Curriculum Development, the National Association of Elementary School Principals, and the National Council of Teachers of English; the National Association of State Boards of Education (1988); the National Black Child Development Institute (1987); and the National Association of Early Childhood Specialists in State Departments of Education (1987). Another good example of this concern is the position statement on early literacy jointly published by the International Reading Association (IRA) and the NAEYC in 1998 in response to what some call the phonics wars (Kohn, 1998) in early literacy education.

By 2002 these same organizations were still issuing alarms for the dangers of rote curriucula and high-stakes testing (Meisels, 2000; National Association of Early Childhood Specialists in State Departments of Education, 2000).

Role of Teacher

In the last decades of the twentieth century, teachers' roles with children have become increasingly demanding in terms of understanding the subtleties of age-appropriate and individual development, as well as the complexities of culturally responsive care and education (Chang, Muckelroy, & Pulido-Tobiassen, 1996; Genishi, 2002; NAEYC, 1996; Ramsey, 1998; Rust, 2001). As the early nursery school educators of the Child Study movement showed, such teaching requires far more than the mastery of subject matter. Teachers must create and support a learning environment in which children construct their own knowledge through play and social interaction and must balance direct teaching with play. The role of the teacher also is becoming more complex as it expands to include consultation and support for families in ways reminiscent of Montessori's Casa dei Bambini and the settlement houses associated with the day nurseries of the nineteenth century (Ball & Pence, 1999; Koplow, 2002). The relationships of the school, parents, and communities are perhaps the biggest challenge to early childhood educators today (Ball & Pence, 1999; Gonzalez-Mena, 2002; Isenberg & Brown, 1997; Koplow,

2002; Valdes, 1996) and include increasingly the voices of special needs children and their families (Bergen, 1994; Fuchs & Fuchs, 1998; Odom, 2002). Like the home visits associated with the early kindergarten, teachers' efforts to communicate with parents are largely informal. With so many working parents, the formalized parent education programs reminiscent of the private nursery school movement and parent cooperatives are less common than ever before. So teachers often telephone parents in the evenings or sponsor weekend picnics or workdays to draw parents into the school community. Finding ways to reach the parents of children who are new immigrants and making them feel welcome in the schools are topics on the minds of many early childhood educators today (Chang, Muckelroy, & Pulido-Tobiassen, 1996; Genishi, 2002; Okagaki & Diamond, 2000; Ramsey, 1998; Wanigarayake, 2001).

In the best of situations, schools become a centerpiece of community involvement, where preschool education and school-aged education are closely connected and summer and weekend opportunities for families are centered (California Department of Education, 1998; Hand & Nourot, 1999; Koplow, 2002). This model is reminiscent of the role of the Lanham centers of World War II, where teachers and parents worked closely together to meet the needs of the children and families in their communities. In the worst of early schooling situations, children are deemed "unready" to begin primary-grade schooling, and the frenzy to prepare children for curriculum better suited for older children continues (Cassidy, Mims, Rucker, & Boone, 2003; Graue, 1993, 2001; Graue & Diperna, 2000; Kohn, 1998; Kozol, 2000).

Professionalization Another aspect of the teacher's role increasingly debated in the literature on early education is the professionalization and training for early care and education (ECE) professionals, which increasingly considers family child care professional development as well as

those in primary-grade education, Head Start, and preschool and infant–toddler settings (Eaton, 2002). New efforts to expand subject-matter proficiency in training programs as well as to understand the developmental needs of children and to create a curriculum designed to meet those needs form the core of debates regarding the preparation of early childhood professionals to provide access to content for children from poor backgounds or who are English-language learners (Delgado-Gaitan, 1994; Genishi, 2002; Isenberg, 2000; Rust 2001).

Increasingly teachers are asked to work with disabled children in everyday early childhood programs (Bergen, 1994; Fuchs & Fuchs, 1998; Odom, 2002). PL 90-538 in 1968, PL 94-142 in 1975, and later PL 99-457 in 1986 require services to disabled young children through public schools. Head Start has steadily increased its service to disabled children, with 13% of its enrollment in 1989 consisting of preschoolers with special needs (Hymes, 1991). That percentage remained constant through 1997 (Powell, 2001). Efforts to design assessments and accommodations for children with special needs, as well as to explore the implications of inclusion expanded in the 1990s (Edmiaston, Dolezal, Doolittle, Erickson, & Merritt, 2000; Kostelnik, Onaga, Rohde, & Whiren, 2002; Mindes, 1998; Odom, 2002; Okagaki, Diamond, Kontos, & Hestenes, 1998; Sheridan, Foley, & Radlinski, 1995; Wolfberg, 1999).

School, Parents, and Community

Because of rapid social and economic changes, changes in family patterns and income, teen parents, and the growing number of young children who live in poverty or suffer from drugs and alcohol abuse in their homes, teachers often serve as the first and only sources of support for parents outside their homes (Briggs, Jalongo, & Brown, 1997; Coleman, 1991; Hart

& Risley, 1995; Koplow, 2002; Polakow, 1992; Shonkoff & Phillips, 2000). Child care, kindergarten, and primary programs struggle to find ways to offer parent education to single working parents (Driscoll, 1995; Galinsky, 1988; Greenberg, 1989; Gullo, 1990). School systems create programs for teenage parents to finish their education and learn about parenting through on-site child-care facilities.

Teachers struggle to find for themselves the meaning of developmentally appropriate practice in the lives of children whose days are touched by fear, violence, and indifference either directly or by viewing television (Carlsson-Paige & Levin, 1987; Katch, 2001; Levin, 1994, 1998; NAEYC, 1990; Polakow, 1992; Silin, 1995; Wanigarayake, 2001). They ask themselves about the appropriate use of computer and video technology for young children (Haugland & Wright, 1997; NAEYC, 1996; Wright, 2001). They struggle with the new waves of immigration to hit the United States; many different languages and cultures may be represented in a single classroom (Ball & Pence, 1999; Ballenger, 1999; Chipman, 1997; Delpit, 1995; Karweit, 1993; New & Mallory, 1994; Ramsey, 1998).

In the 1990s efforts to replace standardized tests with performance-based measures for young children met with limited success across the country (Himley & Carini, 2000; Kamii, 1990; Leavitt & Eheart, 1991; Meisels, 2000; Perrone, 1990; Wesson, 2001; Wortham, 1997). Educators are still actively seeking alternatives to paper-and-pencil testing that will recognize the learning that occurs in children's play and respect the individual intelligences and linguistic and cultural differences of young children in our schools (Gardner, Feldman, & Krechevsky, 1998; Helm, Beneke, & Steinheimer, 1998; Himley & Carini, 2000; Shepard, 2000; Van Hoorn et al., 2003).

As the twentieth century drew to a close, an atmosphere of change, healthy debate, and cau-

tious optimism prevailed among early childhood educators. In October 1990, after 20 years of lobbying for public awareness and federal support, the Act for Better Child Care (PL 101-508) was passed in Congress, providing $22 billion in funding for early education programs. By 1999 funding for child care tied to welfare reform and the expansion of Head Start were poised to come into the system. But by 2000 only half of the children eligible for Head Start were enrolled in the program (Children's Defense Fund, 2001).

CONCLUSION

As we begin the twenty-first century, debates concerning children's competence, appropriate curriculum, roles of teachers, and equity of access for children from all family and community backgrounds are sharpened. The field of early childhood education remains strong and is increasingly seen as an important key to social change and progress. Programs for young children are given a prominent role in political debates, and as such, efforts to expand these programs are beset by a double-edged sword. Because of the political nature of early care and education within the context of contemporary American society, there is a temptation to come up with simplistic and politically expedient solutions (Kagan, 1999, 2003).

The contemporary view of childhood incorporates awareness of the flexibility and resiliency of young children seen in the early decades of the field, while also recognizing the vulnerability of young children—complementary phenomena that Goffin et al. (1997) label as viewing the young child both as the savior of society and in need of saving. This dual conceptualization of children and childhood is one that has a long history in our field, and each orientation is used by policy makers to advocate for particular points of view for funding for the future. The trend of the 1970s and 1980s that children become competent at earlier and earlier ages began with the influence of *Sputnik* and appeared to be waning in the 1980s and 1990s as child development researchers and teachers united in their efforts to have curriculum honor each age and stage of development as well as individual diversity in each classroom. However, new initiatives at state and federal levels have revived the academic pushdown pressure. Some of this may be attributed to welfare reform during the Clinton administration; other trends indicate that the push for early literacy may undermine more developmentally sensitive agendas for early education (Dickinson, 2002).

With 42% of American children under the age of 6 living near or below the poverty line, equity of opportunity remains a key issue (NAEYC, 2000). As increasing research chronicles the importance of early development to brain development and future learning (Shonkoff & Phillips, 2000; Shore, 1997), high-quality early intervention in the lives of young children is critical to the health of our society.

Both program quality and level of compensation for early education caregivers and teachers have received much attention in the national debate on quality of care and education, and the difficulties are exacerbated by a roller coaster economy in the first years of the twenty-first century (Kagan, Brandon, Ripple, Maher, & Joesch, 2002; Sharpe, 2002). Some programs are of poor quality due to lack of teacher education or limited funding; other programs are of high quality with well-prepared teachers and low staff turnover. Funds that seemed promising in the 1990s have proven to be inadequate, and policy makers are calling for a cohesive infrastructure to support high-quality programs for young children (Kagan, 1999, 2003).

Environments and curricula for young children remain diverse (Goffin & Wilson, 2001).

Some programs embrace approaches based on particular theories of development or the goals of parents for their children's education (Delpit, 1988, 1995; Koplow, 2002; Polakow, 1992).

Increasingly, early childhood educators have been faced with the reality that one approach to teaching and learning does not fit all children. Developmentally responsive curricula must be seen in the context of children's families and communities as well as their individual competencies and interests (Ball & Pence, 1999; Dahlberg, Moss, & Pence, 1999; Gonzalez-Mena, 2002; Lubeck, 1996). Questions of equity and access to curriculum have become the hallmark of discussions regarding both curriculum and assessment, and a lively dialogue continues in the field (Derman-Sparks & Ramsey, 2000; Dickinson, 2002). The view of children as active learners and the importance of their social interactions drawn from child development theory have dominated recent discussions of good practice in early childhood education. But these are increasingly debated as critical, postmodern, and feminist perspectives on power and status in education, and the role of early schooling in the lives of young children and the construction of society are debated as well (Charlesworth, 1998a, 1998b; Dahlberg, Moss, & Pence, 1999; Genishi, Ryan, Ochsner, & Yarnall, 2001; Hart & Risley, 1995; Jones, Evans, & Rencken, 2001; Lubeck, 1996, 1998; Schweinhart & Weikart, 1997). These debates are healthy and should continue, lest our current notions of developmentally appropriate practice become prescriptive and suffer the fate of Froebel's, Dewey's, and Montessori's work in the hands of those who implement but do not question.

Readiness is a concept related to curriculum issues (Cassidy et al., 2003; Graue, 2001; Kagan, 1999). Although the 1990s saw a focus on the school as ready for all children, new concepts of readiness seem to be focused more on whether families and communities can prepare children to be successful in a one-size-fits-all-curriculum that is increasingly assessed only on the basis of high-stakes testing (Kohn, 2001; Meisels, 2000; Wesson, 2001). This debate is sharpened in responses to the newly authorized Elementary and Secondary Education Act (ESEA), also known as the No Child Left Behind Act (Posnick-Goodwin, 2003). Educational reforms for children of all ages are met with controversy about the relative burden of readiness on children and schools (Graue, 2001; Kohn, 1998; Maxwell, Bryant, Ridley, & Scott-Little, 2001; National Education Goals Panel, 1998; Shore, 1997).

The role of the contemporary early childhood educator continues to be complex and demanding (Almy, 1975; Kagan, 2003). It requires the visionary commitment to social change and advocacy for children that have characterized the field from the beginning. It demands comprehensive understanding of child development research and its application to practice (Biber, 1988; Frost, Worthham, & Reifel, 2001; Goffin & Wilson, 2001; Isenberg & Brown, 1997; Seefeldt, 1987). This had become even more complex at the end of the twentieth century with the proliferation of new technologies for studying early development of the brain and its relationship to education (Greenspan, 1997; Lally, 1997; Shonkoff & Phillips, 2000; Shore, 1997). It calls, more than ever before, on the consultation skills of teachers to work with parents and children of varied cultures and circumstances (Ball & Pence, 1999; Chang, Muckelroy, & Pulido-Tobiassen, 1996; Chipman, 1997; Derman-Sparks & ABC Task Force, 1989; Derman-Sparks, 1995; Gonzalez-Mena, 2002; Koplow, 2002; Ramsey, 1998; Soto, 1991; Wong-Filmore, 1991).

As part of an expanded critical professional role, Sharon Lynn Kagan, in a February 2003 keynote address to the California Association for the Education of Young Children, calls for early care and education professionals to closely examine and, in fact, redefine models for leadership that press upon our field from others. She notes that the demands of leadership and advocacy in ECE are unique to our work and that we must increasingly draw on the research and theory that stress the importance of systems and intuitive and collaborative processes. She described five types of leadership that tap different aspects of leaders who work in our field and challenged us to find ways to expand our purviews. These five leadership modes lead us to reach out with a broad vision into our communities at large to articulate and guide policy that is complex and well informed for the emerging century. She describes pedagogical leadership to bridge theory, research, and practice, administrative leadership to manage logistics and inspire innovation, advocacy leadership to invent systems for long-term initiatives that encompass legislation and policy, and conceptual leadership, which requires a vision of the field of early education and care within the forces of social, political, and economic change. She contends that each of these roles is essential in actualizing the collective vision of early education that is a legacy from our predecessors.

Millie Almy, one of the grandmothers of early childhood education in America, was interviewed in 2000, the year before her death at age 86. She discussed the guiding principles she saw as important in leading our field into the future. In her interview she emphasized the importance of play and the role of the teacher in attending carefully to each individual child. She advised,

> Well, of course each generation uses its children for its own purposes, and the purposes of the present generation seem to be to rush and to acquire. I hope that as we enter a new century, parents and teachers will protect the large blocks of time everyday, filled with simple materials and other children, that each child needs to become fully human. (Almy, 2000, p. 9)

REFERENCES

Almy, M. (1975). *The early childhood educator at work.* New York: McGraw-Hill.

Almy, M. (1988). The early childhood educator revisited. In B. Spodek, O. Saracho, & D. Peters (Eds.), *Professionalism and the early childhood practitioner* (pp. 48–59). New York: Teachers College Press.

Almy, M. (2000). What wisdom should we take with us as we enter the new century? *Young Children, 55* (1), 6–11.

Alpert, D, Alquist, E., & Strom-Martin, V. (2002). The California master plan for education May 2002 Draft. Sacramento: Joint Committee to Develop a Master Plan for Education—Kindergarten though University, California State Legislature.

Anderson, J. (1947). The theory of early childhood education. In N. B. Henry (Ed.), *The forty-sixth yearbook of the National Society for the Study of Education, Part II* (pp. 70–100). Chicago: University of Chicago Press.

Antler, J. (1987). *Lucy Sprague Mitchell: The making of a modern woman.* New Haven, CT: Yale University Press.

Association for Childhood Education International. (1940). *History of the kindergarten movement in the western states, Hawaii, and Alaska.* Bulletin presented at the 47th Annual Convention of the Association for Childhood International, Milwaukee.

Association for Childhood Education International. (1986). *When parents of kindergarteners ask "why."* Wheaton, MD: Author.

Ball, J., & Pence, A. (1999). Beyond developmentally appropriate practice: Developing community and culturally appropriate practice. *Young Children, 54* (2), 46–50.

Ballenger, C. (1999). *Teaching other people's children: Literacy and learning in a bilingual classroom.* New York: Teachers College Press.

Baruch, D. (1939). *Parents and children go to school.* Chicago: Scott Foresman.

Beardsley, L. (1990). *Good day, bad day: The child's experience of childcare.* New York: Teachers College Press.

Bereiter, C., & Engelmann, S. (1966). *Teaching disadvantaged children in the preschool.* Upper Saddle River, NJ: Prentice Hall.

Bergen, D. (1994). *Assessment methods for infants and toddlers: Transdisciplinary team approaches.* New York: Teachers College Press.

Bergen, D. (1997). Perspectives on inclusion in early childhood education. In J. Isenberg & M. R. Jalongo (Eds.), *Major trends and issues in early childhood education* (pp. 151–171). New York: Teachers College Press.

Biber, B. (1984). *Early education and psychological development.* New Haven, CT: Yale University Press.

Biber, B. (1988). The challenge of professionalism: Integrating theory and practice. In B. Spodek, O. Saracho, & D. Peters (Eds.), *Professionalism and the early childhood practitioner* (pp. 29–47). New York: Teachers College Press.

Blank, H. (1985). Early childhood and the public schools: An essential partnership. *Young Children, 40* (4), 52–55.

Bloch, M. (1991). Critical science and the history of child development's influence on education research. *Early Education and Development, 2,* 95–108.

Bloom, B. (1964). *Stability and change in human characteristics.* New York: Wiley.

Bothman, A. (1976). *Reflections of the pioneers on the early history of Santa Monica Children's Centers.* Unpublished master's thesis, California State University, Northridge.

Bredekamp, S. (1987). *Developmentally appropriate practice in early childhood programs serving children from birth through age eight.* Washington, DC: National Association for the Education of Young Children.

Bredekamp, S., & Copple, C. (Eds.). (1997). *Developmentally appropriate practice in early childhood programs* (rev. ed.). Washington, DC: National Association for the Education of Young Children.

Brewer, J. (1979). Childhood revisited: The genesis of the modern toy. In K. Hewitt & L. Roomet (Eds.), *Educational toys in America: 1800 to the present* (pp. 3–11). Burlington, VT: Robert Hull Fleming Museum.

Briggs, N., Jalongo, M. R., & Brown, L. (1997). Working with families of young children: Our history and our future goals. In J. Isenberg &

M. R. Jalongo (Eds.), *Major trends and issues in early childhood education* (pp. 56–70). New York: Teachers College Press.

Brooks, A. (1882). *The philosophy of the kindergarten.* New York: College for the Training of Teachers.

Butts, R., & Cremin, L. (1953). *A history of education in American culture.* New York: Holt, Rinehart and Winston.

Cadwell, L. B. (1997). *Bringing Reggio home.* New York: Teachers College Press.

Cadwell, L. B. (2002). Bringing learning to life: The Reggio approach to early childhood education. New York: Teachers College Press.

California Department of Education. (1998). *Ready to learn: Quality preschools for California in the 21st century. The Report of the Universal Preschool Task Force.* Sacramento: Author.

Capkova, D. (1970). The recommendations of Comenius regarding young children. In C. Dobinson (Ed.), *Comenius and contemporary education (1657/1840).* Hamburg: UNESCO Institute for Education.

Carlsson-Paige, N., & Levin, D. (1987). *The war play dilemma: Balancing needs and values in the early childhood classroom.* New York: Teachers College Press.

Cassidy, D. J., Mims, S., Rucker, L., and Boone, S. (2003). Emergent curriculum and kindergarten readiness. *Childhood Education, 79* (4), 194–199.

Chang, H. N., Muckelroy, A., Pulido-Tobiassen, D. (1996). *Looking in, looking out: Redefining child care and early education in a diverse society.* San Francisco: California Tomorrow.

Charlesworth, R. (1998a). Developmentally appropriate practice is for everyone. *Childhood Education, 74* (5), 274–282.

Charlesworth, R. (1998b). Response to Sally Lubeck's *Is developmentally appropriate practice for everyone? Childhood Education, 74* (5), 293–298.

Child Care Employee Project. (1989). *Who cares? Child care teachers and the quality of care in America: Report of the National Child Care Staffing Study.* Oakland, CA: Author.

Children's Defense Fund. (2001). *Children's Defense Fund Yearbook 2001.* Washington, DC: Author.

Chipman, M. (1997). Valuing cultural diversity in the early years: Social imperatives and pedagog-ical imperatives. In J. Isenberg & M. R. Jalongo (Eds.), *Major trends and issues in early childhood education* (pp. 43–55). New York: Teachers College Press.

Coleman, M. (1991). Planning for the changing nature of family life in schools for young children. *Young Children, 46* (4), 15–22.

Comenius, J. A. (1953). *The analytic dialogue of Comenius* (V. Jelinek, Trans.). Chicago: University of Chicago Press. (Original work published 1657)

Comenius, J. A. (1967). *The great didactic of John Amos Comenius.* (M. W. Keatinge, Trans.). New York: Russell & Russell.

Crain, W. (2003). *Reclaiming childhood: Letting children be children in our achievement-oriented society.* New York: Times.

Cremin, L. (1961). *The transformation of the school.* New York: Knopf.

Cuffaro, H. K. (1995). *Experimenting with the world: John Dewey and the early childhood class-room.* New York: Teachers College Press.

Dahlberg, G., Moss, P., & Pence, A. (1999). *Beyond quality in early childhood education and care: Postmodern perspectives.* London: Falmer.

Datta, L. (1979). Another spring and other hopes: Some findings from national evaluations of Project Head Start. In E. Zigler & J. Valentine (Eds.), *Project Head Start: A legacy of the war on poverty* (pp. 405–432). New York: Macmillan.

Delgado-Gaitan, C. (1994). Socializing young children in Mexican American families: An intergen-erational perspective. In P. Greenfield & R. Cocking (Eds.), *Cross-cultural roots of minority child development* (pp. 55–86). Hillsdale, NJ: Erlbaum Associates.

Delpit, L. (1988). The silenced dialogue: Power and pedagogy in educating other people's children. *Harvard Educational Review, 58* (3), 280–297.

Delpit, L. (1995). *Other people's children: Cultural conflict in the classroom.* New York: New Press.

Derman-Sparks, L., & the ABC Task Force. (1989). *Anti-bias curriculum: Tools for empowering young children.* Washington, DC: National Association for the Education of Young Children.

Derman-Sparks, L., & Ramsey P. (2000). A frame-work for culturally relevant, multicultural, and antibias education in the 21st century. In

J. P. Roopnarine & J. Johnson (Eds.), *Approaches to early childhood education* (3rd ed.) (pp. 379–404). Upper Saddle River, NJ: Merrill/Prentice Hall.

De Vries, R. (1998). Games with rules. In D. Fromberg & D. Bergen (Eds.), *Play from birth to twelve and beyond: Contexts, perspectives, and meanings* (pp. 409–415). New York: Garland Press.

De Vries, R., & Kohlberg, L. (1987). *Programs for early education: The constructivist view.* New York: Longman.

De Vries, R., & Zan, B. (1999). *Moral classrooms, moral children: Creating a constructivist atmosphere in early education.* New York: Teachers College Press.

De Vries, R., Zan, B., Hildebrandt, C. Edmiaston, R., & Sales, C. (2002). *Developing constructivist early childhood curriculum: Practical principles and activities.* New York: Teachers College Press.

Dewey, J. (1900). *The school and society.* Chicago: University of Chicago Press.

Dewey, J. (1964). The relation of theory to practice in education. In R. Archambault (Ed.), *John Dewey on education: Selected writings* (pp. 313–338). New York: Random House. (Original work published 1904)

Dewey, J., & Dewey, E. (1915). *Schools of tomorrow.* New York: Dutton.

Dickinson, D. (2002). Shifting images of developmentally appropriate practice as seen through different lenses. *Educational Researcher, 31* (1), 26–32.

Dittman, L. (1978). Parent education over the years. In J. Hymes (Ed.), *Living history interviews* (pp. 53–72). Carmel, CA: Hacienda.

Downs, R. B. (1975). *Heinrich Pestalozzi: Father of modern pedagogy.* Boston: Twayne.

Downs, R. B. (1978). *Friedrich Froebel.* Boston: Twayne.

Driscoll, A. (1995). *Cases in early childhood education: Stories of programs and practitioners.* Boston: Allyn & Bacon.

DuCharme, C. (1996). *Early kindergarten periodicals in the United States 1850–1930.* Long Beach: California State University. (ERIC Document Reproduction Service No. Ed 391 594)

DuCharme, C. (2000). Lucy Wheelock: her life and work. *Childhood Education, 76* (30), 164–169.

Eaton, D. (2002). Family childcare accreditaton and professional development. *Young Children, 57* (10), 23–24.

Edelman, M. W. (Speaker). (1990). *1990 NAEYC conference address* [Video]. Washington, DC: NAEYC.

Edmiaston, R., Dolezal, V., Doolittle, S., Erickson, C., & Merritt, S. (2000). Developing individualized education programs for children in inclusive settings: A developmental framework. *Young Children, 55* (4), 36–41.

Edwards, C., Gandini, L., & Forman, G. (1998). *The hundred languages of children: The Reggio approach-advanced reflections* (2nd ed.). Greenwich, CT: Ablex.

Eliot, A. (1978). America's first nursery schools. In J. Hymes (Ed.), *Living history interviews* (pp. 7–26). Carmel, CA: Hacienda.

Elkind, D. (1981). *The hurried child.* Reading, MA: Addison-Wesley.

Elkind, D. (1986, September). Formal education and early childhood education: An essential difference. *Phi Delta Kappan,* pp. 631–636.

Elkind, D. (1987). *Miseducation: Preschoolers at risk.* New York: Knopf.

Entwhistle, H. (1970). *Child-centered education.* London: Methuen.

Erikson, E. (1963). *Childhood and society.* New York: Norton.

Fein, G. (1994). Preparing tomorrow's inventors. In S. Goffin & D. Day (Eds.), *New perspectives in early childhood teacher education: Bringing practitioners into the debate* (pp. 135–145). New York: Teachers College Press.

Finkelstein, B. (1988). The revolt against selfishness: Women and the dilemmas of professionalism in early childhood education. In B. Spodek, O. Saracho, & D. Peters (Eds.), *Professionalism and the early childhood practitioner* (pp. 10–29). New York: Teachers College Press.

Finkelstein, B., & Vandell, K. (1984). The schooling of American childhood: The emergence of learning communities. In M. L. Heininger, K. Calvert, B. Finkelstein, K. Vandell, A. S. MacLeod, & H. Green (Eds.), *A century of childhood 1820–1920* (pp. 65–97). Rochester, NY: Margaret Woodbury Strong Museum.

Fleege, P. O., Charlesworth, R., Burts, D., & Hart, C. (1992). Stress begins in kindergarten: A look at behavior during standardized testing. *Journal of Research in Childhood Education 7*, 20–26.

Forest, I. (1927). *Preschool education: A historical and critical study*. New York: Macmillan.

Forman, G. (1996). The project approach in Reggio Emilia. In C. T. Fosnot (Ed.), *Constructivism: Theory, perspectives, and practice* (pp. 172–181). New York: Teachers College Press.

Forman, G. (2000). The constructivist perspective on early education: Applications to children's museums. In J. P. Roopnarine & J. Johnson (Eds.), *Approaches to early childhood education* (3rd ed.) (pp. 149–174). Upper Saddle River, NJ: Merrill/Prentice Hall.

Forman, G., & Fosnot, C. T. (1982). The use of Piaget's constructivism in early childhood education programs. In B. Spodek (Ed.), *Handbook of research in early childhood education* (pp. 185–214). New York: Macmillan.

Fosnot, C. T. (Ed.). (1996). *Constructivism: Theory, perspectives, and practice*. New York: Teachers College Press.

Fowlkes, M. A. (1991). Gifts from childhood's godmother: Patty Smith Hill. In J. Quisenberry, E. A. Eddowed, & S. Robinson (Eds.), *Readings from childhood education* (pp. 11–16). Wheaton, MD: Association for Childhood Education International.

Frank, L. K. (1937). The fundamental needs of the child. *Mental Hygiene, 22*, 353–379.

Froebel, F. (1896). *Pedagogics of the kindergarten* (J. Jarvis, Trans.). New York: Appleton.

Fromberg, D., & Bergen, D. (Eds.). (1998). *Play from birth to twelve and beyond: Contexts, perspectives, and meanings*. New York: Garland Press.

Frost, J., Wortham, S., & Reifel, S. (2001). *Play and child development*. Upper Saddle River, NJ: Merrill/Prentice Hall.

Fuchs, D., & Fuchs, L. (1998). Competing visions for educating students with disabilities: Inclusion vs. full inclusion. *Childhood Education, 74* (5), 309–316.

Fuller, E. M., Christianson, H., Headley, N., Landreth, C., Peterson, A., & Wood, S. L. (1947). Practices and resources in early childhood education. In N. B. Henry (Ed.), *The forty-sixth yearbook of the National Society for the Study of Education* (pp. 101–171). Chicago: University of Chicago Press.

Galinsky, E. (1988). Parents and teacher-caregivers: Sources of tension, sources of support. *Young Children, 43* (3), 4–12.

Gardner, H., Feldman, D. H., & Krechevsky, M. (1998). *Project Zero Frameworks for early childhood education* (Vols. 1–3). New York: Teachers College Press.

Genishi, C. (2002). Young Englsh language learners in the classroom. *Young Children, 57* (4), 66–71.

Genishi, C., Ryan, S., Ochsner, M., with Yarnall, M. (2001). Teaching in early childhood education: Understanding practices through research and theory. In V. Richardson (Ed.), *Handbook of research on teaching* (4th ed.) (pp. 1175–1210). Washington, DC: American Educational Research Association.

Gesell, A. (1948). *Studies in child development*. New York: Harper.

Gesell, A., & Ilg, F. (1943). *Infant and child in the culture of today: The guidance of development in home and nursery school*. New York: Harper.

Goffin, S. G., & Day, D. (1994). *Curriculum models and early childhood education*. New York: Merrill.

Goffin, S., & Wilson, C. (2001). *Curriculum models and early childhood education: Appraising the relationship* (2nd ed.). Upper Saddle River, NJ: Merrill/Prentice Hall.

Goffin, S., Wilson, C., Hill, J., & McAninch, S. (1997). Policies of the early childhood field and its public: Seeking to support young children and their families. In J. Isenberg & M. R. Jalongo (Eds.), *Major trends and issues in early childhood education* (pp. 13–28). New York: Teachers College Press.

Gonzalez-Mena, J. (1993). *Multicultural issues in child care*. Mountain View, CA: Mayfield.

Gonzalez-Mena, J. (2002). *The child in the family and the community* (3rd ed.). Upper Saddle River, NJ: Merrill/Prentice Hall.

Goodlad, J. I., Klein, M. F., & Novotney, J. M. (1973). *Early schooling in the United States*. New York: McGraw-Hill.

Graue, E. (1993). *Ready for what? Constructing meanings of readiness for kindergarten*. Albany: State University of New York Press.

Graue, E. (2001). Research in review: What's going on in the children's garden? Kindergarten today. *Young Children, 56* (3), 67–73.

Graue, E., & Diperna, J. (2000). Redshirting and early retention: Who gets the "gift of time" and what are its outcomes? *American Educational Research Journal, 37* (2), 509–534.

Gray, S. W., & Klaus, R. A. (1965). An experimental preschool program for culturally deprived children. *Child Development, 36,* 887–898.

Green, J. A. (1969). *The educational ideas of Pestalozzi.* New York: Greenwood Press. (Original work published 1914)

Greenberg, P. (1989). Ideas that work with young children: Parents as partners in young children's development and education: A new American fad? Why does it matter? *Young Children, 44* (4), 61–74.

Greenspan, S. I. (1997). *The growth of the mind.* New York: Addison-Wesley.

Gullo, D. F. (1990). The changing family context: Implications for the development of all day kindergartens. *Young Children, 45* (4), 35–40.

Gutek, G. E. (1968). *Pestalozzi and education.* New York: Random House.

Hale-Benson, J. (1982). *Black children: Their roots, culture, and learning styles.* Provo, UT: Brigham Young University Press.

Hall, G. S. (1893). *The contents of children's minds on entering school.* New York: Kellogg.

Hand, A., & Nourot, P. M. (1999). *First class: Guide to early primary education.* Sacramento: California Department of Education.

Hart, B., & Risley, T. R. (1995). *Meaningful differences in the everyday experiences of young American children.* Baltimore: Paul Brookes.

Hartley, R. E., Frank, L., & Goldenson, R. M. (1957). *The complete book of children's play.* New York: Crowell.

Haugland, S., & Wright, J. (1997). *Young children and technology: A world of discovery.* Needham Heights, MA: Allyn & Bacon.

Heafford, A. (1967). *Pestalozzi: His thought and its relevance today.* London: Methuen.

Healey, J. (1991). *Endangered minds: Why children don't think and what we can do about it.* New York: Simon & Schuster.

Helm, J., Beneke, S., & Steinheimer, K. (1998). *Windows on learning: Documenting young children's work.* New York: Teachers College Press.

Hendricks, J. (Ed.). (1997). *First steps toward teaching the Reggio way.* Upper Saddle River, NJ: Merrill/Prentice Hall.

Hewitt, K. (2001). Blocks as a tool for learning: An historical and contemporary perspective. *Young Children, 56* (1), 6–21.

Himley, M. & Carini, P. (Eds.). (2000). *From another angle: Children's strengths and school standards.* New York: Teachers College Press.

Hirsch, E. (1996). *The block book* (3rd ed.). Washington, DC: National Association for the Education of Young Children.

Hunt, J. McV. (1961). *Intelligence and experience.* New York: Ronald.

Hunt, J. McV. (1964). Introduction. In *M. Montessori, The Montessori method* (pp. xi–xxxix). New York: Schocken.

Hymes, J. (1944, May). The Kaiser answer: Child service centers. *Progressive Education,* pp. 222–223.

Hymes, J. (1991). *Early childhood education: Twenty years in review.* Washington, DC: National Association for the Education of Young Children.

International Reading Association. (1986). Literacy development and pre-first grade: A joint statement of concerns about present practices in pre-first grade reading instruction and recommendations for improvement in conjunction with Association for Childhood Education International, Association for Supervision and Curriculum Development, National Association for the Education of Young Children, National Association of Elementary School Principals, National Council of Teachers of English. Newark, DE: Author.

International Reading Association. (1998). Learning to read and write: Developmentally appropriate practices for young children. A joint position statement of the International Reading Association (IRA) and the National Association for the Education of Young Children (NAEYC). *Young Children, 53* (4), 30–46.

Isaacs, S. (1933a). *Intellectual growth in young children.* New York: Schocken.

Isaacs, S. (1933b). *Social development in young children.* London: Routledge & Kegan Paul.

Isenberg, J. (2000). The state of the art in early childhood professional preparation. In *New teachers for a new century: The future of early childhood professional preparation* (pp. 15–59). National Institute on Early Childhood Development and Education, Washington, DC: U.S. Department of Education.

Isenberg, J., & Brown, D. (1997). Development issues affecting children. In J. Isenberg & M. R. Jalongo (Eds.), *Major trends and issues in early childhood education* (pp. 29–42). New York: Teachers College Press.

Isenberg, J., & Jalongo, M. R. (Eds.) (1997). *Major trends and issues in early childhood education.* New York: Teachers College Press.

Jipson, J. (1991). Developmentally appropriate practice: Culture, curriculum, connections. *Early Education and Development, 2* (2), 120–136.

Joffe, C. E. (1977). *Friendly intruders: Childcare professionals and family life.* Berkeley: University of California Press.

Johnson, H. M. (1928). *Children in the nursery school.* New York: Day.

Johnson, J., Christie, J., & Yawkey, T. (1999). *Play and early childhood development* (2nd ed.). New York: Addison Wesley Longman.

Jones, E., Evans, K., & Rencken, K. S. (2001). *The lively kindergarten: Emergent curriculum in action.* Washington, DC: National Association for the Education of Young Children.

Jones, E., & Reynolds, C. (1992). *The play's the thing: Teachers' roles in children's play.* New York: Teachers College Press.

Jungck, S. (1990). Viewing computer literacy through a critical ethnographic lens. *Theory into Practice, 29* (4), 283–289.

Kagan, S. L. (1991). Children's play: The journey from theory to practice. In E. Klugman & S. Smilansky (Eds.), *Children's play and learning: Perspectives and policy implications* (pp. 173–187). New York: Teachers College Press.

Kagan, S.L. (1998). Taking our todays into tomorrow. *Young Children, 53* (6), 2–3.

Kagan, S. L. (1999a). Cracking the readiness mystique. *Young Children, 54* (5), 2–3.

Kagan, S. L. (1999b). A5: Redefining 21st century early care and education. *Young Children, 54* (6), 2–3.

Kagan, S. L. (2000). On being President: heart, head, and hands. *Young Children, 55* (5), 4–5.

Kagan, S. L. (2003). Keynote address to the California Association for the Education of Young Children. Sacramento: February 28.

Kagan, S. L., Brandon, R., Ripple, C., Maher, E., & Joesch, J. (2002). Supporting quality early childhood care and education: Addressing compensation and infrastructure. *Young Children, 57* (3), 58–65.

Kagan, S. L., & Cohen N. E. (1997). *Not by chance: Creating an early care and education system for America's children.* New Haven, CT: The Bush Center in Child Development and Social Policy.

Kahn, P. H., & Friedman, B. (1995). Environmental views and values of children in an inner-city Black community. *Child Development, 66,* 1403–1417.

Kamii, C. (1985). Leading primary education toward excellence: Beyond worksheets and drill. *Young Children, 40* (6), 3–9.

Kamii, C. (Ed.). (1990). *(No) achievement testing in the early grades: The games grown-ups play.* Washington, DC: National Association for the Education of Young Children.

Kamii, C. (with Housman, L. B.). (2000). *Young children reinvent arithmetic: Implications of Piaget's theory* (2nd ed.). New York: Teachers College Press.

Kamii, C., & De Vries, R. (1980). *Group games in early education: Implications of Piaget's theory.* Washington, DC: National Association for the Education of Young Children.

Kaplan, G. (1991, May). Suppose they gave an intergenerational conflict and nobody came? *Kappan Special Report,* pp. K-1–K-12.

Karweit, N. (1993). Effective preschool and kindergarten programs for students at risk. In B. Spodek (Ed.), *Handbook of research on the education of young children* (pp. 385–411). New York: Macmillan.

Katch, J. (2001). *Under deadman's skin: Discovering the meaning of children's violent play.* Boston, MA: Beacon Press.

Katz, L., & Chard, S. (2000). *Engaging children's minds: The project approach* (2nd ed.). Norwood, NJ: Ablex.

Kennedy, D. (1988). Images of the young child in history: Enlightenment and romance. *Early Childhood Research Quarterly, 3* (2), 121–138.

Kessler, S., & Swadener, B. B. (Eds.). (1992). *Reconceptualizing the early childhood curriculum: Beginning the dialogue*. New York: Teachers College Press.

Kohn, A. (1998, April). Only for my kid: How privileged parents undermine school reform. *Phi Delta Kappan*, pp. 568–577.

Kohn, A. (2001). Fighting the tests: Turning frustration into action. *Young Children, 56* (2), 19–24.

Koplow, L. (Ed.). (1996). *Unsmiling faces: How preschools can heal*. New York: Teachers College Press.

Koplow, L. (2002). Creating schools that heal: Real-life solutions. New York: Teachers College Press.

Kostelnik, M., Onaga, E., Rohde, B., & Whiren, A. (2002). *Children with special needs: Lessons for early childhood professionals*. New York: Teachers College Press.

Kozol, J. (2000). Foreword to *Will standards save public education?* In D. Meier (Ed.), *Will standards save public education?* (pp. vii–xv). Boston: Beacon Press.

Kramer, R. (1988). *Maria Montessori: A biography*. Menlo Park, CA: Addison-Wesley.

Lally, J. R. (1997). Brain development in infancy: A critical period. *Bridges*. The California Headstart Collaboration Project, *3* (Summer), 1.

Lazerson, M. (1972). The historical antecedents of early childhood education. In I. J. Gordon (Ed.), *Early childhood education: The seventy-first yearbook of the National Society for the Study of Education, Part II* (pp. 33–54). Chicago: University of Chicago Press.

Leavitt, R. L., & Eheart, B. K. (1991). Assessment in early childhood programs. *Young Children, 46* (5), 4–10.

Levin, D. (1994). *Teaching children in violent times: Building a peaceable classroom*. Cambridge, MA: Educators for Social Responsibility.

Levin, D. (1998). *Remote control childhood? Combatting the hazards of media culture*. Washington, DC: National Association for the Education of Young Children.

Lewis, C. (1995). *Educating hearts and minds: Reflections on Japanese preschool and elementary education*. Cambridge, England: Cambridge University Press.

Lilley, I. M. (1967). *Friedrich Froebel: A selection from his writings*. London: Cambridge University Press.

Lubeck, S. (1996). Deconstructing "child development knowledge" and "teacher preparation." *Early Childhood Research Quarterly, 11,* 147–167.

Lubeck, S. (1998). Is DAP for everyone? A response. *Childhood Education, 74* (5), 299–301.

Maxwell, K., Bryant, D. M., Ridley, S. M., & Scott-Little, C. (2001). School readiness in North Carolina: One state's attempt to do the right thing. *Young Children, 56* (6), 59–62.

Mayhew, K. C., & Edwards, A. C. (1966). *The Dewey School*. New York: Atherton Press.

McCuskey, D. (1940). *Bronson Alcott, teacher*. New York: Macmillan.

Meisels, S. (2000). On the side of the child: Personal reflections on testing, teaching and early childhood education. *Young Children, 55* (6), 16–19.

Miller, L. (1979). Development of curriculum models in Head Start. In E. Zigler & J. Valentine (Eds.), *Project Head Start: A legacy of the War on Poverty* (pp. 195–220). New York: Macmillan.

Mindes, G. (1998). Can I play too? Reflections on the issues for children with disabilities. In D. Fromberg & D. Bergen (Eds.), *Play from birth to twelve and beyond: Contexts, perspectives, and meanings* (pp. 208–214). New York: Garland.

Mitchell, A., & Modigliani, K. (1989). Young children in public schools? Only-if's reconsidered. *Young Children, 44* (6), 56–61.

Monighan-Nourot, P. (1990). The legacy of play in American early childhood education. In E. Klugman & S. Smilansky (Eds.), *Children's play and learning: Perspectives and policy implications* (pp. 59–85). New York: Teachers College Press.

Montessori, M. (1912). *The Montessori method: Scientific pedagogy as applied to child education in "The Children's Houses," with additions and revisions* (A. E. George, Trans., with introduction by H. W. Holmes). New York: Stokes. (Original work published 1909)

Montessori, M. (1936). *The secret of childhood*. Bombay, India: Orient Longman.

Morgan, G. (1985). Programs for young children in public schools? Only if. . . . *Young Children, 40* (4), 54.

National Association for the Education of Young Children. (1990). NAEYC position statement on media violence in children's lives. *Young Children, 45* (5), 18–21.

National Association for the Education of Young Children. (1991a). *Early childhood teacher education guidelines: Basic and advanced.* Washington, DC: Author.

National Association for the Education of Young Children. (1991b). NAEYC position statement: Guidelines for appropriate curriculum content and assessment in programs serving children ages 3 through 8. *Young Children, 46* (3), 21–39.

National Association for the Education of Young Children. (1996). NAEYC position statement: Technology and young children—ages 3 through 8. *Young Children, 51* (4), 11–16. Author.

National Association for the Education of Young Children. (1998). *Developmentally appropriate practices for young children—a joint position statement of the International Reading Association and the National Association for the Education of Young Children.* Washington, DC: Author.

National Association for the Education of Young Children. (2000). FYI: The faces of poverty—our young children. *Young Children, 55* (2), 66–68.

National Association of Early Childhood Specialists in State Departments of Education. (1987). *Unacceptable trends in kindergarten entry and placement: A position statement.* Lincoln, NE: Author.

National Association of Early Childhood Specialists in State Departments of Education. (2000). *Still! Unacceptable trends in early childhood entry and placement: A position statement.* Lincoln, NE: Author.

National Association of State Boards of Education. (1988). *Right from the start: A report on the NASBE task force on early childhood education.* Alexandria, VA: Author.

National Black Child Development Institute. (1987). *Safeguards: Guidelines for establishing programs for 4-year-olds in the public schools.* Washington, DC: Author.

National Education Goals Panel reports. Available online at www.negp.gov.

National Society for the Study of Education. (1929). *Twenty-eighth yearbook of the National Society for the Study of Education: Preschool and parental education.* Bloomington, IL: Public School Publishing.

New, R. S., & Mallory, B. L. (Eds.). (1994). *Diversity and developmentally appropriate practice: Challenges for early childhood education.* New York: Teachers College Press.

Nieto, S. (1996). *Affirming diversity: The sociopolitical context of multicultural education* (2nd ed.) New York: Longman.

Nourot, P. M. (1997). Playing with play in four dimensions. In J. Isenberg & M. R. Jalongo (Eds.), *Major trends and issues in early childhood education* (pp. 123–148). New York: Teachers College Press.

Odom, S. (Ed.). (2002). *Widening the circle: Including children with disabilities in preschool programs.* New York: Teachers College Press.

Okagaki, L., & Diamond, K. (2000). Research in review: Responding to cultural and linguistic differences in the beliefs and practices of families with young children. *Young Children, 55* (3), 74–92.

Okagaki, L., Diamond, K., Kontos, S., & Hestenes, L. (1998). Correlates of young children's interactions with classmates with disabilities. *Early Childhood Research Quarterly, 13* (1), 67–86.

Omwake, E. (1979). Assessment of the Head Start preschool education effort. In E. Zigler & J. Valentine (Eds.), *Project Head Start: A legacy of the War on Poverty* (pp. 221–230). New York: Macmillan.

Pence, A. R. (1986). Infant schools in North America, 1825–1840. In S. Kilmer (Ed.), *Advances in early education and day care* (Vol. 4, pp. 1–25). Greenwich, CT: JAI.

Perrone, V. (1990). How did we get here? In C. Kamii (Ed.), *(No) achievement testing in the early grades: The games grown-ups play* (pp. 1–14). Washington, DC: National Association for the Education of Young Children.

Pestalozzi, J. H. (1900). *How Gertrude teaches her children.* Syracuse, NY: Bardeen. (Original work published 1801)

Piaget, J. (1965). *The moral judgment of the child.* New York: Free Press.

Piaget, J. (1969). *The language and thought of the child.* New York: World.

Pitcher, E. (1966). An evaluation of the Montessori method. *Childhood Education, 42* (8), 189–192.

Polakow, V. (1992). Deconstructing the discourse of care: Young children in the shadows of democracy. In S. Kessler & B. B. Swadener

(Eds.), *Reconceptualizing the early childhood curriculum: Beginning the dialogue* (pp. 123–148). New York: Teachers College Press.

Posnick-Goodwin, S. (2003). Sizing up the EDEA. *California Educator, 7* (5), 6–19.

Powell, D. (2000a). Preparing early childhood professionals to work with families. In National Institute on Early Childhood Development and Education, *New teachers for a new century: The future of early childhood professional preparation* (pp. 59–88). Washington, DC: U.S. Department of Education.

Powell, D. (2000b). The Head Start program. In J. L. Roopnarine & J. Johnson (Eds.), *Aproaches to early childhood education* (3rd ed.) (pp. 55–78). Upper Saddle River, NJ: Merrill/Prentice Hall.

Powell, D. R. (1989). *Families and early childhood programs.* Washington, DC: National Association for the Education of Young Children.

Pratt, C. (1948). *I learn from children.* New York: Harper & Row.

Ramsey, P. G. (1998). *Teaching and learning in a diverse world* (2nd ed.). New York: Teachers College Press.

Ross, E. D. (1976). *The kindergarten crusade: The establishment of preschool education in the United States.* Athens: Ohio University Press.

Rousseau, J. J. (1938). *Emile.* New York: Dutton. (Original work published 1780)

Rust, F. O. (2001). The changing face of teacher education: Building bridges/forming new alliances. *Journal of Early Childhood Teacher Education, 22* (1), 3–9.

Rodger, R. (2001). *Planning an appropriate curriculum for the under fives.* London: Fulton.

Schlossman, S. L. (1976). Before Home Start: Notes toward a history of parent education in America. *Harvard Educational Review, 46* (3), 436–467.

Schweinhart, L. J., Barnes, V., & Weikart, D. P. (with Barnett, W. S. & Epstein, A. S.). (1993). Significant benefits: The High Scope/Perry Preschool study through age 27. *Monographs of the High/ Scope Educational Research Foundation,* 10.

Schweinhart, L. J., & Weikart, D. B. (1997). *Lasting differences: The High/Scope preschool*

curriculum comparison study through age 23. Ypsilanti, MI: High/Scope Press.

Schweinhart, L. J., Weikart, D. B., & Larner, M. B. (1986). Consequences of three preschool models through age 15. *Early Childhood Research Quarterly, 1,* 15–45.

Seefeldt, C. (1987). *The early childhood curriculum: A review of current research.* New York: Teachers College Press.

Sharpe, C. (2002). *Advancing careers in child development in California.* Pasadena, CA: Pacific Oaks College.

Sheridan, M., Foley, G., & Radlinski, S. (1995). *Using the supportive play model.* New York: Teachers College Press.

Shepard, L. (2000). The role of assessment in a learning culture. *Educational Researcher, 29* (7), 4–14.

Shidler, L. (2001). Teacher-sanctioned violence. *Childhood Education, 77* (3), 167–168.

Shonkoff, J., & Phillips, D. (2000). *From neurons to neighborhoods: The science of early childhood development.* Washington, DC: National Academy Press.

Shore, R. (1997). *Rethinking the brain: New insights into early development.* New York: Families and Work Institute.

Silin, J. (1995). *Sex, death and the education of children: Our passion for ignorance in the age of AIDS.* New York: Teachers College Press.

Smith, D. (1986). *California kindergarten survey.* Fresno: California State University, School of Education.

Snyder, A. (1972). *Dauntless women in childhood education 1865–1931.* Wheaton, MD: Association for Childhood Education International.

Soto, L. D. (1991). Understanding bilingual/ bicultural young children. *Young Children, 46* (2), 30–37.

Spodek, B. (1986). Introduction. In B. Spodek (Ed.), *Today's kindergarten: Exploring the knowledge base, extending its curriculum* (pp. vii–xi). New York: Teachers College Press.

Stewart, D. (1990). *Preschools and politics: A history of early childhood education in California.* Unpublished doctoral dissertation, University of California, Berkeley.

Stewart, D. (1997). *Millie Almy: Reflections on early childhood education: 1934–1994.* Berkeley: University of California Oral History Project.

Strickland, C. E. (1982). Paths not taken: Survival models of early childhood education. In B. Spodek (Ed.), *Handbook of research in early childhood education* (pp. 321–340). New York: Free Press.

Troen, S. K. (1975). *The public and the schools: Shaping the St. Louis system 1838–1920.* Columbia: University of Missouri Press.

Valdes, G. (1996). *Con Respecto: Bridging the distance between culturally diverse families and schools.* New York: Teachers College Press.

Van Hoorn, J., Nourot, P. M., Scales, B., & Alward, K. (2003). *Play at the center of the curriculum* (3rd ed.). Upper Saddle River, NJ: Merrill/Prentice Hall.

Vygotsky, L. (1967). Play and its role in the mental development of the child. *Soviet Psychology, 12,* 62–76.

Waite-Stupiansky, S. (1997). *Building understanding together: A constructivist approach to early childhood education.* Boston: Delmar.

Wanigarayake, M. (2001). From playing with guns to playing with rice: The challenges of working with refugee children: An Australian perspective. *Childhood Education, 77* (5), 289–294.

Washington, V., & Andrews, J. D. (1998). *Children of 2010.* Washington, DC: National Association for the Education of Young Children.

Washington, V., & Oyemade, U. J. (1985). Changing family trends: Head Start must respond. *Young Children, 40* (6), 12–15, 17–18.

Wasserman, S. (1990). *Serious players in the primary classroom.* New York: Teachers College Press.

Weber, E. (1969). *The kindergarten: Its encounter with educational thought in America.* New York: Teachers College Press.

Weber, E. (1979). Play materials in the curriculum of early childhood. In K. Hewitt & L. Roomet (Eds.), *Educational toys in America: 1800 to the present* (pp. 25–38). Burlington, VT: Robert Hull Fleming Museum.

Weber, E. (1984). *Ideas influencing early childhood education: A theoretical analysis.* New York: Teachers College Press.

Weikart, D. (1989). Hard choices in early childhood care and education: A view to the future. *Young Children, 44* (3), 25–30.

Wesson, K. (2001). "The Volvo effect"—questioning standardized tests. *Young Children, 56* (2) 16–18.

Westinghouse Learning Corporation, Ohio University. (1969). *The impact of Head Start in children's cognition and affective development.* Washington, DC: U.S. Office of Economic Opportunity.

White, S., & Buka, S. (1987). Early education: Programs, traditions and policies. In *Review of research in education: Vol. 14* (pp. 43–92). Washington, DC: American Educational Research Association.

Whitebook, M., & Eichberg, A. (2002). Finding a better way: Defining policies to improve child care workforce compensation. *Young Children, 57* (3), 66–72.

Whitebook, M., Howes, C., & Phillips, D. (1990). *National child care staffing study.* Oakland, CA: Child-Care Employee Project.

Wiggin, K. D. (Ed.). (1893). *The kindergarten.* New York: Harper.

Williams, L. (1987). Determining the curriculum. In C. Seefeldt (Ed.), *The early childhood curriculum: A review of current research* (pp. 1–12). New York: Teachers College Press.

Winn, M. (1983). *Children without childhood.* New York: Penguin Books.

Wolfberg, P. (1999). *Play and imagination in children with autism.* New York: Teachers College Press.

Wolfe, J. (2002). *Learning from the past: Historical voices in early childhood education* (2nd ed.). Mayerthorpe, Alberta Canada: Piney Branch Press.

Wong-Filmore, R. (1991). When learning a second language means losing the first. *Early Childhood Research Quarterly, 6,* 326–346.

Wood E., & Attfield, J. (1996). *Play, learning, and the early childhood curriculum.* London: Chapman.

Woody, T. (1934). Historical sketch of activism: Part II. In G. M. Whipple (Ed.), *The twenty-third yearbook of the National Society for the Study of Education* (pp. 9–44). Bloomington, IL: Public School Publishing.

Wortham, S. (1997). Assessing and reporting children's progress: A review of the issues. In J. Isenberg & M. R. Jalongo (Eds.), *Major trends and issues in early childhood education* (pp. 104–122). New York: Teachers College Press.

Wright, C. (2001). Children and technology: Issues, challenges, and opportunities. *Childhood Education, 78* (1), 37–41.

Zigler, E. (1998). By what goals should Head Start be assessed? *Children's Services: Social Policy, Research and Practice,* 1, 5-17.

Zigler, E., & Anderson, K. (1979). An idea whose time had come: The intellectual and political climate. In E. Zigler & J. Valentine (Eds.), *Project Head Start: A legacy of the War on Poverty* (pp. 3–21). New York: Macmillan.

Zigler, E. & Muenchow, S. (1992). *Head Start: The inside story of America's most successful educational experiment.* New York: Basic Books.

Chapter 2

Programs for Infants and Toddlers

Kimberlee L. Whaley ❧ Center of Science and Industry, Columbus, Ohio

❧ INTRODUCTION

Programs for our youngest children have become increasingly common. While child-care programs for infants and toddlers date back to 1830 when the first day nursery opened in the United States (Nourot, 2000), the use of out-of-home care for children under 3 years of age has increased dramatically, particularly in the last 20 years. In addition, recent research on early development has shifted the emphasis from programs that simply provide care at a custodial level to programs that provide high-quality educational experiences for very young children. Still, controversy rages about what is and is not appropriate for children under the age of 3. Infant stimulation programs designed to make babies smarter compete with programs focused on the more social aspects of development in the early years. This chapter presents a brief overview of the research on high-quality infant–toddler programming, stressing those factors that affect the development of infants and toddlers as they relate to programming for this unique time in life.

Most recent reports state that 61% of American mothers with children under 3 years of age were employed in 2000, compared to 34% in 1975 (Phillips & Adams, 2001). In addition, 56% of mothers with a baby under 1 year of age use some sort of care arrangement (Phillips & Adams, 2001). The location where this care occurs varies, with 27% of children under 3 cared for by one parent while the other parent works, 27% cared for by relatives, 7% with a nanny, 17% in family child-care settings, and 22% in center-based care. The fastest growing type of early education has been in center-based programming as the total number of children cared for in these settings has gone from 8% to 22% in last 20 years (Phillips & Adams, 2001). Regardless of type of setting, programs for infants and toddlers affect not only the children attending them, but also the entire family. This family systems view of early care and education considers all family members and their behaviors as being interconnected (Olson & DeFrain, 1994; Snow & McGaha, 2003). Care of infants and toddlers must take into account all members of the family and consider how the adults caring for the child relate to both the family members and the child.

Research has confirmed that experiences during the early years of life are critical to healthy growth and development. Thompson (2001) describes the first 3 years as a period of growth of body, growth of brain, growth of mind, and growth of person. High-quality programs for infants and toddlers must support learning across all of these domains. In addition, high-quality programs take a whole baby approach to programming, seeing infants and toddlers as humans whose developmental needs can't be dealt with as separate domains (Pizzo, 1990).

Growth of Body

Physical growth, perhaps the most obvious type of growth, occurs faster during the first 3 years of life than during any other time (Snow & McGaha, 2003). Changes in height, weight, and body proportion happen quickly and depend in part on the environment the child is exposed to during these early years. Environments that provide adequate nutrition, opportunities for safe exploration, and safety from exposure to environmental toxins and disease will facilitate the growth of the infant physically.

Growth of Brain

Much recent research has focused on the development of the brain during the first 3 years. The brain, already equipped for learning at birth, becomes increasingly organized during the first years of life. Massive development of synapses between neurons early in life is followed by a period of pruning that makes the brain more efficient (Huttenlocher, 1994). Experiences that stimulate the baby in appropriate ways strengthen those synapses that are most important while the others will disappear or not develop at all. Research has shown that overall quality of the child-care environment is modestly, yet consistently, related to positive cognitive and language development (NICHD Early Child Care Research Network, 2000a).

Unfortunately, this brain development research has often been misinterpreted, leading to the development of structured programs and materials for infants and toddlers designed to facilitate brain development during critical periods. These critical periods, however, are not the typical pattern of brain development, but rather are exceptions to the more typical gradual development of children's brains (Thompson, 2001). Perhaps the single most important environmental factor in brain development is a caring adult with whom the child forms a strong relationship and with whom there are ongoing interactions (NICHD Early Child Care Research Network, 2002).

A child enrolled in Early Head Start and mother enjoy the slide at the center's playground on family day.

Growth of Mind

The early years are one of the most amazing time periods in terms of growth of knowledge, with children creating new learning from everyday experiences almost constantly. Changes in thinking, memory, language, and concept understanding happen rapidly, primarily through the experiences the child does or does not have. This learning includes increased knowledge in the areas of the use of tools to accomplish goals, cause and effect, object permanence, how things move and fit in space, imitation, and organizing action and thought into patterns or schemes. Most important, knowledge comes from experiences that are live interactions between the child and other people, not from objects, videos, or television. Quality of the child-care environment has been repeatedly linked to positive language and cognitive outcomes (NICHD Early Child Care Research Network, 1999, 2000a, 2001).

Growth of Person

Much of the work associated with becoming an individual person is also begun during the first 3 years of life. This work includes development in the areas of attachment to parents and other adults, development of a strong sense of self, development of self-regulation skills, and emotional development. Consistent adults who demonstrate consistent behaviors are vital to developing all of these person skills. Strong attachment develops when there are adults who spend large amounts of time with the child and is hampered when the adults in the environment change on a regular basis. Likewise, developing a strong sense of who you are and how you fit into the world around you comes directly from your experiences with that world. Living in a world that does not value your individual needs and opinions, no matter how young you are, will not result in the development of a strong sense of self.

Self-regulation is also an important early skill. The ability to put yourself to sleep, to wait to get your needs met, and to express yourself and your needs in ways that are efficient are important skills that a good infant–toddler program supports and scaffolds.

Finally, the earliest years of life are vital in developing an understanding of and control over emotions and conflict situations. Recent research suggests that the greater the amount of time a child spends in child-care settings during the early years of life, the more problem behaviors, assertiveness, disobedience, aggression, and conflict children display in kindergarten (NICHD Early Child Care Research Network, 2003a).

Image of the Child

In order to understand what you believe about how to program for young children, it is useful to examine your view of young children—who they are, what they can do, and what your role in interacting with them really is. This image of the child has been widely discussed in writings about and by the educators in the schools of Reggio Emilia and proves useful as a starting place for all educators working with young children (Edwards, Gandini, & Forman, 1998). If infants and toddlers are seen as needy, always demanding to have their needs met by adults in their environment, programs will be implemented that are based on this deficit model and that focus on simply meeting the most basic needs of the children. On the other hand, if you view young children as competent, able to make decisions, and having feelings and preferences that are legitimate, you will program to build on these competencies. High-quality programs are those that see infants and toddlers as competent human beings and strive to provide them with the programming they are entitled to as human beings rather than programming designed to simply meet a never-ending stream of needs.

It is also important that children are viewed as individuals rather than as an age group. It can be very easy to stereotype children by expectations for a particular age group and forget that each child has his or her own individual personality. High-quality programs consider each child as an individual with his or her own personality and developmental characteristics.

✍ CHARACTERISTICS OF QUALITY INFANT–TODDLER EDUCATION

Regardless of the type of setting, research has found that there are certain characteristics of infant and toddler education that constitute high-quality programming (Fenichel, Luvie-Hurvitz, & Griffin, 1999). In addition, a significant correlation between the quality of the program and the developmental and behavioral outcomes for children in different settings has been reported (Ruopp, Travers, Glantz, & Coelen, 1979). Unfortunately, recent large-scale, multisite studies of child-care centers and homes caring for infants and toddlers found that fully half of them are providing care that rates as poor or fair, not good or excellent (Love, Raikes, Paulsell, & Kisker, 2000; Vandell & Wolfe, 2000). High-quality care is not dependent on packaged infant stimulation programs or highly structured curricula. Instead, high-quality infant and toddler programming is dependent on the quality of the environment and the quality of the relationships between the adults and the children in that environment.

Physical Environment

In a high-quality infant–toddler program, the environment serves as an organizing force for children's behavior. It is vital that environments for infants and toddlers are predictable, allow children to make choices, and provide space and freedom to explore. There are a number of factors to consider when creating a physical environment that will support the growth and development of young children. Beyond basic health and safety needs, the following environmental characteristics have been determined to be important for young children.

Settings must be designed for movement During the first 3 years of life, action plus interaction equals learning. Spaces for infants and toddlers must provide many opportunities for movement. Climbing, running, sitting, standing, and jumping are all important to development during these first 3 years. A lack of opportunity for movement can result in discipline problems as children seeking motor activity and challenge resort to pushing, biting, and hitting to satisfy their need for physical movement.

Settings should stimulate all senses, while carefully avoiding overstimulation Young chil-

dren are sensory by nature and environments should stimulate, but not overstimulate, all the senses. Calming colors, homelike scents, and a variety of sounds are all-important. Perhaps most important, and most often ignored, is touch. Babies learn not through hands-on activities, but through body-on activities, as the skin is their largest sense organ. This same sensory nature, however, means that infants and toddlers can become overstimulated. Too many primary colors, too much noise, and too many people can cause a child to become overstimulated and tense.

Rooms should have softness built in Prescott and David (1976) report that degree of softness in the environment predicts the quality of care. Softness is necessary for anyone to relax. Comfortable chairs, soft slippers, and cozy beds are all things adults associate with relaxing. Likewise, infants and toddlers need softness in their spaces to relax. Environments for these youngest children should be filled with items that respond to the child (Prescott, 1979).

Rooms should provide children with a number of minispaces Being in a group of people all day long can be hard for adults, thus it stands to reason that it can be difficult for young children as well. Still developing crucial self-regulation skills, infants and toddlers need spaces where they can separate from the group and still be safe. Greenman (1988) refers to these minispaces as places to pause and says that lack of these types of spaces leads to cocooning, where children withdraw or develop behavior issues.

Rooms should have distinct activity areas with easily recognized boundaries Spaces should be divided into clear interest areas big enough for three to four children to play. This allows children to organize their thoughts and their days. Olds (1982) refers to these areas as neighborhoods and says classrooms should include quiet, movement, wet/messy, and

Early childhood specialists provide care and learning enrichment for young children.

creative neighborhoods. Each area should have clearly defined boundaries, work/sitting surfaces, storage, and an identity that helps children know what the space is for. These boundaries are not rigid and do not mean that materials from one area can't be carried to another. Instead, the boundaries simply allow the children to make choices about their activities.

Settings for infants and toddlers should be living centers, not schools   Environments for infants and toddlers should be more like a home than like a classroom. Often, these programs are the places babies spend the majority of their time during the day. Infants and toddlers do not need classroomlike experiences, but rather, they need experiences that make them feel at home. Settings that are hard and have many people can have a deadening effect on the occupants. Creating spaces using warm, homelike colors rather than a myriad of bright, primary colors creates spaces that are warm and inviting rather than stimulating and potentially overwhelming. The area under 3 feet is the active zone for this age group, the area where they see the most and interact most often. It is important to be sure that everything at this level and below is safe, mouthable, and part of the program.

Infants and toddlers need to have items that match their scale, things that allow them to feel safe rather than overwhelmed and small. Items such as low chairs and shelves, photos at their level, and low dividers help make the infant and toddler feel secure and in control. Scale also applies to other factors in the environment, including noise level and use of time. Spaces that house groups of children have the potential to be loud and overwhelming. Environments need to be developed that keep the noise level at a scale that infants and toddlers can cope with. Reducing the number of activities that are done in large groups will help reduce the noise level as well. Finally, time has a different meaning to infants and toddlers. Although 20 minutes represents a relatively short time period to adults, it is a very long period of time for infants and toddlers.

Physical order and organization are vital An environment that is organized and orderly is more inviting than one that is chaotic and messy. The same things that appeal to us as adults appeal to young children and set the tone for the type of activity to take place in the space. Order and organization in the environment contribute greatly to a baby's ability to organize his or her thoughts and ideas. Greenman (1982) has suggested that the infant–toddler space has order that provides a clear message to babies as to how to use the space, allows for gathering and discarding modes of behavior, allows babies to focus on materials and equipment, and is easily restored. Safe, orderly storage of varied and stimulating toys, items organized into areas, and easy access to the items by the children themselves are all important factors in ordering the environment. This same concept holds true when presenting materials to infants and toddlers. Materials sorted by color and/or type of materials and presented in a way that is aesthetically appealing are more inviting and encourage more thoughtful use of them.

Environments must support the adults that live and work in them as well as the children Although we often think of children when we create a space for infants and toddlers, we rarely think about the adults in the setting. It is vital that the adults in the space are comfortable as well. Private spaces to store their personal items, chairs that comfortably seat adults, and decorations that appeal to adults as well as children are vital to a quality program.

Other suggestions for creating an appropriate environment for infants and toddlers include:

- Provide materials and settings that offer many opportunities for experimenting—opening and closing, dumping, cause and effect.

- Build low lofts to allow children to see into other classrooms or out windows.
- Create interesting ceilings with a variety of materials for babies to look at when they lie on their backs.
- Place textures along the baseboards and on the floor of the room.
- Build mirrors into the room, on the floors, on the walls, and over the changing table.
- Place ballet bars around the room low enough to allow new standers to practice and new walkers to cruise the room.
- Avoid big murals and busy walls; they add to visual confusion.
- Create built-in storage for diapers, wipes, and all the other supplies young children need.
- Consider placing windows in the bottoms of the walls as well as around the top.
- Place Plexiglas around the bottoms of the walls to slide photos, posters, and artwork in for babies and toddlers to see and touch.

Structural Factors Related to High-Quality Programming

The most important factor in high-quality programming for infants and toddlers is found in the relationships that develop between the adult and the child, relationships that are highly influenced by various structural factors. More specifically, research indicates that quality of care is highly correlated with adult:child ratios, size of group, caregiver qualifications, and level of staff turnover (NICHD Early Child Care Research Network, 2000b).

Adult-to-Child Ratios The National Association for the Education of Young Children (Bredekamp & Copple, 1997) has suggested that high-quality programs for infants and toddlers maintain adult-to-child ratios of 1:3 or 1:4 for infants (birth–18 months) and 1:5 for toddlers (18 months–3 years). In reality, each individual state determines the ratios acceptable in that state so the number of adults in classrooms for infants and toddlers varies widely. Research from 10 locations around the United States found that child outcomes were predicted by adult-to-child ratios at 24 months of age (NICHD Early Child Care Research Network, 1999, 2000b).

Group Size Infants and toddlers both enjoy and benefit from interactions with other children. Research has indicated that there are, however, an optimal number of children in any group of infants and toddlers. Whereas smaller group size has been found to be positively associated with good outcomes for children (Elicker, Fortner-Wood, & Noppe, 1999; Howes, Philips, & Whitebook, 1992), groups of infants should not consist of more than 6 precrawling babies, 9 for mobile babies through 18 months, and 12 for toddler groups of children 18 months through 3 years (Lally, Griffin, Fenichel, Segal, Szanton, & Weissbourd, 1995).

Another alternative in settings for infants and toddlers, mixed-age grouping, allows for the creation of a family-like atmosphere. Families that have multiple children rarely have them all the same age. Thus, having children in large groups of same age peers with all the same needs and all the same developmental issues creates an experience less like a family. Mixing age groups allows for more individualized care, provides older peers for modeling, reduces comparison of developmental milestones by parents and teachers, and allows adults to really know the child's individual needs (Whaley & Kantor, 1992).

Teacher Qualifications Research has shown that adults who are specifically trained in the development and care of infants and toddlers provide higher quality care (Fosberg, 1981; Honig, 1995; Honig & Hirallal, 1998; Howes, 1997; Ruopp et al., 1979). It is not enough that infant–toddler teachers be well versed in the development of preschool children, they must have knowledge about the unique developmental and behavioral needs of children under age 3. The National Child Care Staffing Study (Whitebook, Howes, & Phillips, 1990), a survey of 227 infant and preschool centers in five major cities, revealed that less than one-fifth of the teachers surveyed had attended two workshops or conferences during the previous year. In a study of child-care homes with an average of six children in their care, caregiver training predicted higher quality care and better adult–child interactions (Clarke-Stewart, Vandell, Burchinal, O'Brien, & McCartney, 2002).

Staff Turnover One of the most persistent problems in providing high-quality infant and toddler care is the high level of turnover among caregivers. Low pay, lack of training, and the high demands of caring for infants and toddlers have resulted in a turnover level estimated to be 25–40% yearly (Whitebook et al., 1990; Whitebook, Sakai, Gerber, & Howes, 2001). This turnover, although a problem at any level of education, is particularly troublesome for babies and toddlers who are learning important lessons about developing and maintaining relationships.

Even when teachers stay in settings, many centers move children from classroom to classroom based on changes in development (e.g., crawling, walking). Another way to maintain consistency of adults is to keep groups together for 3 years or to move the teacher with the children. It is important during these early years of developing trust that children have consistent people to care for them.

General Principles of Infant and Toddler Programming

Regardless of setting, there are certain principles that should be evident in any high-quality program that cares for infants and toddlers. These characteristics form the basis for everything that happens in the curriculum and are related to the image of infants and toddlers as competent members of the community with the right to developmentally appropriate experiences and spaces.

Infants and toddlers need high-quality interactions Perhaps the most important factor in early education for infants and toddlers is the quality of the interactions that occur in the environment. Infants and toddlers need interactions with adults that are intimate, stable, and individualized. In addition, research has indicated that infants and toddlers benefit from interactions with peers as well (Bleiker, 1999; Whaley & Rubenstein, 1994). Knowing how to read infants and toddlers is at the heart of quality caregiving. Care that is in tune with individual children:

- Responds to the physical and emotional needs of the child
- Shows respect for the child and her needs
- Trusts and supports the child's own cycles and routines
- Allows the child to anticipate what is about to happen to him
- Is responsive and accepting
- Relies on observation of individual children
- Does not try to force all children into a rigid schedule
- Engages children in conversations rather than talks at them.

Infants and toddlers, like any person, must be treated with respect and trust Infants and toddlers are able to tell what needs they have and when they have them. They have preferences and dislikes, know when they are hungry, cold, or wet, and prefer certain individual ways to go to sleep. Programs should respect individual children's timetables and schedules, their choices, and their decisions. In addition, adults should trust children to let them know when they need something and how they prefer things to be. A program that has a flexible schedule that can be individualized rather than a rigid group schedule will be a program that is more appropriate.

Infants and toddlers need to be exposed to a wide variety of experiences, not just easy, more practical ones Although it may be easier not to allow toddlers to paint, not to let them feed themselves, and not to allow them to dump and fill baskets of toys, these experiences are important to infants and toddlers. Avoiding experiences because they take time, are too messy, or are annoying for adults to deal with means not providing strong learning opportunities for young children. It is also important to consider the way the environment looks and to take the time to create a learning environment that is beautiful and organized rather than simply throwing things on shelves, thinking the babies will not notice. Young children are aware of beauty or chaos around them and are quite able to learn how to respect items in the environment (Edwards et al., 1998).

Infants and toddlers need to experience success at early ages Experiences need to be offered in ways that success is achieved simply by interacting with the materials. This means there are no right or wrong ways to be involved in the activities and not being involved at all is an option. Although parents may hang the ladybug their infant or toddler made on the refrigerator at home, the completion of the task of making a standard ladybug has little or no meaning to children in this age group. Expecting infants and toddlers to follow directions to create a standard product is not developmentally appropriate. As the adults in their lives, it is important that you expect enough of them that they can grow but not so much that you set them up for failure. Expecting a 2-year-old to sit quietly at a table for 20 minutes goes against who they are developmentally and sets them up to fail and you to be frustrated!

Infants and toddlers are allowed to make decisions about how to spend their days There should be very few, if any, mandatory activities, required group times, or rigid schedules. Experiences should be available throughout the day for children to choose to participate in as they

Part of Day	7:30	8:30	9:30	10:30	11:30	12:30	1:30	2:30	3:30	4:30	5:30
Creative Activities			X	X				X	X		
Sensory Activities	X	X	X	X	X		X	X	X	X	X
Play	X	X	X	X	X	X	X	X	X	X	X
Movement Activities	X	X	X	X	X		X	X	X	X	X
Snack			X	X				X	X		
Outside Play					X					X	
Other Activities	X	X					X	X			X
Diapers	X	X	X	X	X	X	X	X	X	X	X
Lunch					X	X					
Nap		X	X	X	X	X	X	X	X	X	X

FIGURE 2–1 Sample Daily Schedule of Activities

desire. A sample daily schedule can be seen in Figure 2.1. Routine activities such as eating, sleeping, and toileting are done as the individual children need and want them. This is not to say that there are no scheduled times such as lunchtime, but that children who need to nap at lunchtime have the option to nap during lunch and to eat later when they wake up.

Routines are important and reassuring to infants and toddlers Schedules should be flexible but should contain many routines that accompany each part of the day. These routines are vital for babies to develop a sense of security and trust. Routines should be in place for cleaning up toys after play, getting ready to go outside, entering and leaving the setting, eating lunch, and making transitions between parts of the day.

Maintain an unhurried pace in daily activity Infants and toddlers naturally dawdle. They should not be rushed to finish projects, eat lunch, put on shoes, and go to sleep or wake up. Infants and toddlers are not at their best when they are rushed and nobody in the setting

should be rushing through the day. In addition, times when children have to wait (to wash hands, get lunch, go outside) should be kept to a minimum. The more relaxed the adults in the environment are, the more relaxed the children will be. Babies are masters at reading adult body language and can sense tension in the environment, often responding with fussiness.

Infants and toddlers should be encouraged to be as independent as they feel comfortable with being Children often want to exercise newly developing skills. Babies who are new to walking can walk to their own space and get their lunch box or coat out. Older babies can feed themselves and toddlers can help with everything from serving lunch to cleaning up after play. Children should be encouraged to do as much as they can on their own—even when it takes more time.

Infants and toddlers need to learn the limits on their behavior and to internalize the limits In infant–toddler settings adults often sabotage themselves by creating and enforcing too many rules. Children can learn to follow the three most basic rules from early in life—do not hurt yourself, do not hurt the environment, and do not hurt others. They can be helped to learn that behaviors that violate these rules are not acceptable by actively teaching respect for self, others, and environment. Explanations should be offered frequently and children should be offered choices and encouraged to make good decisions. Even young children can and will learn to limit their own behavior if they feel they have control over their lives.

Infants and toddlers need to be engaged in conversation that is two-way   Even babies who are still nonverbal can participate in conversation. Your view of children as competent participants in relationships demands that you not spend your time giving directives to children, but that you ask them their ideas, listen to their thoughts, and engage them in conversations. Even a baby can participate by waving his or her arms or making sounds if given the time to participate. These earliest interactions are what teach a child how to engage in conversation with others. Hart and Risley (1995) report that the amount of language young children are exposed to varies widely between social classes with those children receiving less verbal stimulation being at a disadvantage during the school years.

Be explicit in what you are asking: Don't assume they know what you mean   Imagine the following scene . . . a toddler classroom, located in a church, has a large gymnasium space for large motor activity that is located down the hall from the classroom. One day the class leaves their room to head down the long hallway to the gym. Almost as soon as the door is open, these toddlers do what long hallways suggest you should do—they begin to run down the hall toward the gym. The teacher immediately yells for them to "Stop running!" The first child in the line immediately stops running . . . and begins skipping . . . as do the other 19 children in the classroom! A true story. The teacher in this case was not happy, but in point of fact, the children had done exactly what she had

told them to do . . . they had stopped running. They simply did not know she meant for them to walk instead. Be explicit.

Respect their parents and the choices they make for their lives   This is often one of the toughest parts of infant–toddler caregiving. Parents, especially first-time parents, can be demanding, inflexible, and difficult to please. It is important to remember that parents, no matter how difficult, are making their demands because they so desperately care about their child. Parents have the final say about their preferences for their child and it is vital that teachers in infant–toddler classrooms respect these choices. In addition, even for children spending the majority of their time in child care, research indicates that the quality of parent–child interactions and family characteristics are related to the developmental outcomes of their children (NICHD Early Child Care Research Network, 2003b).

Have fun . . . Laugh a lot!   This may be the single most important principle related to high-quality programming. Although the work is demanding and tiring, it is also incredibly rewarding. If you don't or can't smile and laugh, perhaps it is time to find a new career option.

INFANT AND TODDLER CURRICULUM

When we think of curriculum we often think of lesson plans and teaching in the traditional sense. In fact, every experience an infant and toddler has is a learning experience. Babies do not need direct teaching of concepts as part of their everyday experience. Daily life together becomes the curriculum, enhanced by experiences that encourage the formation of neural connections in ways that are developmentally appropriate. Anne Stonehouse (1988) has discussed five types of programming common in infant–toddler settings. In the egg carton curriculum, programming is based on unusual or novel ideas that interest the staff or will impress the parents. Lots of arts and crafts activities are planned. Activities have specific outcomes in mind rather than letting the children explore the materials, thus the activities are product oriented rather than process oriented.

An acceleration curriculum program is concerned with teaching the skills children will need in the future. For example, activities are planned to specifically teach cutting skills, children are taught to sit quietly, there are activities planned that require sharing, and formal lessons on numbers or letters are included. This model is based on a deficit view of children, seeing them as lacking in necessary skills.

The fill-in-the-blanks curriculum involves filling in the standard spaces on the lesson plan sheet. The same spaces are completed in the same time blocks weekly. Activities are chosen either because the teacher likes them or the children like them. This model frequently results in a day that is divided between learning time and free play time.

In a theme curriculum all activities, foods, and environmental additions are based around a central theme. Although themes provide structure for adults, they have little meaning to infants and toddlers. Themes also tend to lead to providing activities that are out of context for young children.

Finally, perhaps the most commonly seen curriculum in infant–toddler settings is what Stonehouse (1988) calls the noncurriculum. Many adults plan very little for infants and toddlers, saying it is inappropriate to plan for this age group. Days in these settings are frequently filled solely with free play and daily care activities.

It is true that many hours spent with infants and toddlers will be spent in daily care activities. However, these activities, far from being simply routine, form the basis for learning for young children. Routines give young children a sense of predictability and provide opportunities for adults to provide individualized care. Each baby has his or her own individual routine, own way of doing things, and own responses to various activities. Even the youngest infant knows when he needs to sleep, when she is hungry, and when he is uncomfortable. Careful observation of individual children is necessary to provide quality care to each individual child. Curriculum is developed by carefully observing the interests of the children in the setting and designing activities that will "provoke" their thinking and exploration.

Unlike more traditional educational settings, group timing for daily routines is not appropriate in infant–toddler classrooms. Days spent with infants and toddlers need to be flexible, yet planned … full of activity options that allow children to self-initiate and to participate at their own pace and on their own schedule. Infants and toddlers can certainly benefit from activities that involve the larger group, but these activities should be kept to a minimum.

Parts of the Day

The goal of programming for infants and toddlers should be to provide children with opportunities to experience many materials in their own ways and at their own pace. Parts of the day in infant–toddler settings might include play experiences, creative and sensory experiences, movement opportunities, meals, resting, literacy opportunities, routines, and unplanned spontaneous experiences. As previously stated, infants and toddlers are process oriented rather than product focused. As adults, we can anticipate the finished product while we are participating in the process of creating it. Toddlers do not do this: they get lost in the process itself. In order to allow the process to be the guiding principle, it is important to use activities that are open-ended. Open-ended experiences allow children to work at their own level, make choices about what they want to do and how they participate, and use materials in different ways. In addition, process-focused learning allows for vertical learning rather than horizontal learning. In horizontal learning, children learn a little bit about a lot of things. Vertical learning, however, allows for expansion of knowledge, for in-depth learning about fewer topics. As adults we often think that we need to provide many different activities rather than provide the same materials with different options and opportunities to experiment. Encourage divergent uses of materials. Repeat activities more than once. Build on experiences by making subtle changes in them. When planning curriculum it is important to keep the developmental characteristics of the age group in mind. Babies mouth materials. Toddlers dump and fill. Independence is growing. Table 2–1 illustrates how children at certain ages learn and the implications for programming. It is important to provide infants and toddlers with open-ended experiences with open-ended goals. Provide experiences that do not have a set product in mind.

DISCIPLINE AND GUIDANCE

One of the biggest concerns of infant–toddler teachers is discipline and guidance of children in groups. Discipline and guidance issues most often are related to environmental issues—too little to do, too much stimulation, inconsistent rules, or too many rules. An environment that provides infants and toddlers with enough

TABLE 2–1
Brief Developmental Summary Birth–3 Years

Age of Child	How They Learn	Expectations for Behavior
Birth–6 months	Learn through their senses; look, listen, and feel everything around them	Allow them to hold, touch, and taste things in the environment
	Developing attention to people in the environment	Talk with them often and give them the chance to talk back; allow them to be near other children to explore
6 months–1 year	Explore world through new ability to move around in it	Make space for them to explore; do not confine to any one area for any length of time
	Curious, may want to try everything or may be wary of trying new things	Give the opportunity to try new things but do not push them to try
1 year–18 months	Becoming more interested in peers	Provide opportunities to interact with peers and for friend to be away from the group
	Trying out new motor skills	Provide lots of opportunities to jump, run; do not expect them to sit or wait for any length of time
	Language is developing quickly; exploring the power of their words	Talk with them often, encourage them to express themselves, provide them with words when they are frustrated
	Cause–effect problem solving developing	Provide many experiences that allow children to experiment with problem solving; encourage them to find new ways to interact with materials
	May be moody and easily upset	Understand the frustrations of children, help them to calm selves and step away from situation

(*continued*)

TABLE 2–1
continued

Age of Child	How They Learn	Expectations for Behavior
18–36 months	Explore through play	Provide lots of props and opportunities for pretend
	Imitate others in the environment	Include child in everyday activities, allowing them to participate
	Desire independence	Allow them to make some decisions about what to eat, what to wear, when they are ready to rest
	Move constantly, may be noisy	Provide many opportunities to move, do not expect them to sit still for more than 15 minutes
	Tests the rules	Be consistent in rules, be sure there are not too many rules, offer choices to decrease testing behavior
	Need routine and consistency	Try to keep things as stable as possible, warn about upcoming major changes, help and comfort disoriented toddlers
	May be impulsive	Understand that many negative behaviors are simply impulses not yet controlled, replace a behavior taken away with one given back
	Process oriented	Remember that toddlers become so involved in the process that they may forget where they are heading, allow for extra time when asking them to do something, remind them gently what the goal is
	Constantly exploring, both physically and verbally	Do not expect them to sit and learn, allow them to experience things repeatedly

developmentally appropriate things to do, rules that are basic and consistent, and adults that are steady and loving will have a minimal level of behavior issues. Nonetheless, there will be some need for discipline and guidance in any setting. It is important to remember that the word *discipline* derives from the Latin word that means to teach. All discipline should teach rather than punish.

Distraction and Redirection

One of the most effective ways to redirect undesirable behavior involves directing a child to what he or she **can** do instead of what she can't do or shouldn't do. Telling a toddler to stop doing something sets up a power struggle. A general rule to remember is that for every behavior you take away ("Don't do…"), a behavior should be given back ("You can do…").

Telling a toddler to stop writing on the wall will set up a power struggle, whereas telling them they can't write on the wall but they can write on this large piece of paper will help them feel in control of the situation. Likewise, offering to remove the child from the situation can also be helpful at times ("This seems too hard for you right now. Let's go over here and play where it doesn't feel so hard.").

Choices

Providing children with choices can ease the power struggles and give the toddler a sense of control over his own life. It is important that the choices you offer are real choices and that you can live with whatever choice the child makes. Offering a young child the choice of which shoe to put on first rather than telling her to put her shoes on reduces the potential for a power struggle.

Consistent Limits

Perhaps the most important discipline and guidance technique is to create limits that are reasonable and consistently enforced. Rules that change and that are enforced one way on one day and another way on another day lead to confusion in young children and result in testing of limits. Likewise, infants and toddlers who are overwhelmed with the number of rules become frustrated and act out as a result.

Environment Structure

It is important that an adequate number of materials for the number of children are provided. Many conflicts result over toys that multiple children want to play with when there is only one item available. Research has shown that toddlers mark their friendships by playing with the same toys as well, so it is important that you have multiples of a toy in the setting (Whaley & Rubenstein, 1994).

Providing alternative activities for children in waiting situations can also reduce the need for discipline. For example, be sure there are quiet activities available for children when they get up from nap so they can stay occupied while the other children sleep.

Finally, arrange the room in ways that allow children to be as independent as possible. Place shelving and materials at their level so children can make appropriate choices on their own.

Time-Out

In the traditional view of time-out, the child is removed from the situation and placed away from the activity, often to think about the behavior he or she has been engaged in. Time-out, although perhaps effective for older children, is not appropriate for infants and toddlers. Infants and toddlers do not yet have the cognitive ability to "think about" what they have done when sitting in time-out. In addition, time-out does not replace an undesirable behavior with a desirable behavior, so it teaches nothing.

There may be times, however, when removing the child from the situation will be an effective way to help the child calm down and regain control. In this case, it is important that an adult stays nearby to reassure the child and help him or her regain control.

DIVERSITY ISSUES IN INFANT–TODDLER SETTINGS

Many might argue that there is no reason to worry about multicultural experiences in settings for infants and toddlers and that attempts to highlight cultures only reinforce differences rather than emphasizing common needs. Each child, however, is born into a culture that provides him or her with a set of expectations concerning the world. Denying children their cultures is denying children their identities.

Infants and toddlers pay close attention to the world. Studies of children less than 2 weeks old, some less that 24 hours old, reveal that they can and do pay selective attention to patterns (Snow & McGaha, 2003). By 1 month of age, infants show visual preference for patterns and by 2 months, they are able to discriminate among people and voices. At 4 months they see a variety of color shades and discriminate faces, and by 8 months infants have a mental model of the human face and are interested in variations. By 13 months infants demonstrate definite preferences for people, and around 15 months they are beginning to learn to compromise. Finally, by 3 years of age children have developed a gender identity, are starting to sympathize, and are learning fears. These milestones all suggest that multicultural programming should begin in these earliest years rather than waiting until preschool.

Multicultural programming, rather than being a curriculum, is a state of mind and should be built into the everyday experiences for infants and toddlers. The goals of multicultural programming at this level include developing self-esteem, providing exposure to multiple ways of life, creating homelike environments for all children, fostering cultural identity, and developing and encouraging empathy.

Although many might agree that providing a culturally responsive setting is important, teachers often struggle with exactly what this means in the infant–toddler classroom. The following suggestions offer a place to start.

Provide cultural consistency Know and understand the culture of every child in the setting and maintain a level of consistency between what happens at home and what happens in the infant–toddler program. This also makes the family feel welcome in the setting.

Be aware of the role of groups in the culture Whereas some societies are very group oriented, others emphasize the individual. It is important to understand how the child's home culture

views this issue as it relates to everything from how the child participates in the setting to how the parents interact with the program.

Use home languages Be sure all policies and communications are done in the native language of the family. Compile a list of volunteers in the community who are familiar with other cultures and languages and can assist in this task.

Make environments relevant Include foods, toys, equipment, music, and materials that represent the cultures of all children in the classroom. Include photos of people meeting universal needs in a variety of ways. Ask parents to contribute music, food, and materials that represent their homes. Provide each family with a small photo album to fill with photos that represent their particular definition of a family and keep these albums in baskets on the floor where infants and toddlers can access them daily.

Hire Representative Staffing

Although perhaps difficult, it is important that the staffing of a program represents diversity of age, gender, race, and cultural group. For example, although we often look for male teachers for preschool classrooms, it is just as important to attempt to find them for infant and toddler settings.

Uncover Your Own Cultural Beliefs

It is vital that teachers in infant and toddler settings are open to perspectives other than their own. A family may have a way of feeding their child or putting their child to sleep that goes against the way the teacher feels these things should be done, but it is vital that the teacher respects the values of the family. Seek out cultural and family information from the families in the setting and clarify values with parents.

ɹᴈ RECOMMENDATIONS

Although many years of research have provided us with the characteristics of high-quality educational programs for infants and toddlers, these programs are still not common. The National Child Care Staffing Study (Whitebook et al., 1990) reports that the quality of care in 227 infant and preschool programs across the United States was barely even at the adequate level in terms of performance. If we know what makes high-quality programming, why is it still so rare?

Efforts must be made to assist programs in covering the high cost of quality infant–toddler care One reason for the lack of quality programs relates to the high cost for providing quality care. This cost is significantly higher than providing the same level of quality for preschool programs due to the increased staffing, equipment, and materials necessary for infants and toddlers. Few families can afford the full cost of high-quality programming and subsidies most often do not reimburse at a high-quality rate. In many settings, the preschool classrooms are subsidizing the infant–toddler classrooms in terms of cost and revenue. Until there is assistance either to the programs to reduce their costs or to the parents to increase their ability to afford high-quality care, there will continue to be a lack of high-quality programming for this age group.

Specialized training programs for infant–toddler teachers must be made more available A second factor relates to the lack of specialized training opportunities for infant and toddler teachers. The vast majority of teachers in infant–toddler programs have been trained in preschool or elementary education rather than infant–toddler education. In addition, many teachers in infant–toddler classrooms do not have any form of specialized training in education and/or child development at all. Finally, in-service training

designed specifically for infant and toddler teachers is uncommon. We must begin to see the teaching of infants and toddlers as a specialty area for training just as we see pediatrics as a specialty in medicine, and we must develop education programs to educate those teachers interested in specializing in this age group. Likewise, pay scales for teachers in infant and toddler settings are often even lower than those found in preschool classrooms. If we truly value the development of children, we must fairly compensate those adults willing to devote their lives to carrying for and educating them.

Programming for the earliest years cannot be seen as simply basic care but as education that sets the foundation for future learning Too often, parents and the community see infants and toddlers as simply needing someone to take care of them. Education begins from the day the child is born and we must begin advocating for programs that not only meet the health and safety needs of babies but also provide them with developmentally appropriate and enhancing experiences with a wide variety of materials. We must stop settling for mediocre programs for our youngest children and expect high-quality experiences.

Changes in ratio and group size requirements are needed in some states so that all states match a nationally recognized standard Although research has shown that there are optimal numbers for adult-to-child ratios and group sizes, there continues to be a wide range of what individual states allow in infant and toddler classrooms. If we are going to have programs that are high quality, then we must begin by developing and enforcing some basic common standards for infant and toddler programming. Clarke-Stewart and her colleagues (2002) have found that infant–toddler child-care programs that are regulated by a state agency are of higher quality than unregulated programs. In addition, they report that higher quality of programs is associated with more strict state regulations.

✍ SUMMARY

This chapter has presented a very brief overview of what good programs for infants and toddlers should look like. In reality there are numerous models around the world that represent high-quality programs. These range from the infant programs of Reggio Emilia to Early Start programs in Head Start centers. The key is not the location of the program but the view the program holds of infants and toddlers and the type of programming they deserve to have.

We clearly know some of the factors that contribute to high-quality programming for our youngest citizens. It is time that we muster the will as a country to ensure that all children have access to this high-quality care and education.

REFERENCES

Bleiker, C. (1999). Toddler friendship? The case of John and Hiro. *Young Children, 54* (6), 18–23.

Bredekamp, S., & Copple, C. (Eds.). (1997). *Developmentally appropriate practice in early childhood programs.* (Rev. ed.). Washington, DC: National Association for the Education of Young Children.

Clarke-Stewart, K. A., Vandell, D. L., Burchinal, M., O'Brien, M., & McCartney, K. (2002). Do regulatable features of child-care homes affect children's development? *Early Childhood Research Quarterly, 17* (1), 52–86.

Edwards, C., Gandini, L., & Forman, G. (Eds.). (1998). *The hundred languages of children: The Reggio Emilia approach—advanced reflections.* Greenwich, CT: Ablex.

Elicker, J., Fortner-Wood, C., & Noppe, I. C. (1999). The context of infant attachment in family child care. *Journal of Applied Developmental Psychology, 20,* 319–336.

Fenichel, E., Lurie-Hurvitz, E., & Griffin, A. (1999). Seizing the moment to build momentum for quality infant/toddler child care: Highlights of the Child Bureau and Head Start Bureau's national leadership forum on quality care for infants and toddlers. *Zero to Three, 19* (6), 3–17.

Fosberg, S. (1981). *Family day care in the United States: Summary of findings (Vol. 1).* Final report of the National Day Care Home Study. Cambridge, MA: Abt Associates.

Greenman, J. (1982). Designing infant/toddler environments. In R. Lurie & R. Neugebauer (Eds.), *Toddlers: What works, what doesn't.* Redmond, WA: Child Care Information Exchange.

Greenman, J. (1988). *Caring spaces, learning places: Children's environments that work.* Redmond, WA: Exchange Press.

Hart, B., & Risley, T. R. (1995). *Meaningful differences in the everyday experience of young American children.* New York: Paul Brookes.

Honig, A. (1995). Choosing child care for young children. In M. Bornstein (Ed.), *Handbook of parenting (Vol. 4).* Mahwah, NJ: Erlbaum.

Honig, A. S., & Hirallal, A. (1998). Which counts more for excellence in childcare staff: Years in service, education level, or ECE coursework? *Early Child Development and Care, 145,* 31–46.

Howes, C. (1997). Children's experiences in center-based child care as a function of teacher background and adult-child ratio. *Merrill Palmer Quarterly, 43,* 404–425.

Howes, C., Philips, D., & Whitebook, M.(1992). Thresholds of quality: Implications for the social development of children in center-based child care. *Child Development, 63,* 449–460.

Huttenlocher, J. (1994). Synaptogenesis in human cerebral cortex. In G. Dawson & K. Fischer (Eds.), *Human behavior and the developing brain* (pp. 137–152). New York: Guilford.

Lally, J., Griffin, A., Fenichel, E., Segal, M., Szanton, E., & Weissbourd, B. (1995). *Caring for infants and toddlers in groups.* Arlington, VA: Zero to Three/National Center.

Love, J. M., Raikes, H., Paulsell, D., & Kisker, E. E. (2000). New directions for studying quality in program for infants and toddlers. In D. Cryer & T. Harms (Eds.), *Infants and toddlers in out-of-home care.* Baltimore: Paul Brookes.

NICHD Early Child Care Research Network. (1999). Child outcomes when child care center classes meet recommended standards for quality. *American Journal of Public Health, 89,* 1072–1077.

NICHD Early Child Care Research Network. (2000a). The relation of child care to cognitive and language development. *Child Development, 71,* 960–980.

NICHD Early Child Care Research Network. (2000b). Characteristics and quality of child care for toddlers and preschoolers. *Applied Developmental Science, 4,* 116–135.

NICHD Early Child Care Research Network. (2001). Before Head Start: Income, ethnicity, family characteristics, child care experiences and child development. *Early Education and Development, 12,* 545–576.

NICHD Early Child Care Research Network. (2002). Structure > Process > Outcome: Direct and indirect effects of caregiving quality on young children's development. *Psychological Science, 13,* 199–206.

NICHD Early Child Care Research Network. (2003a). Does amount of time spent in child care predict socioemotional adjustment during the transition to kindergarten? *Child Development, 74,* 976–1005.

NICHD Early Child Care Research Network. (2003b). Families matter—even for kids in child care. *Journal of Developmental and Behavioral Pediatrics, 24,* 58–62.

Nourot, P. M. (2000). Historical perspectives on early childhood education. In J. Roopnarine and J. Johnson (Eds.), *Approaches to early childhood education.* Upper Saddle River, NJ: Merrill/Prentice Hall.

Olds, A. (1982). Planning a developmentally optimal day care center. *Day Care and Early Education,* Summer.

Olson, D., & DeFrain, J. (1994). *Marriage and the family: diversity and strengths.* Mountain View, CA: Mayfield.

Phillips, D., & Adams, G. (2001). Child care and our youngest children. In *Caring for Infants and Toddlers, Spring/Summer.* Los Altos, CA: The David and Lucille Packard Foundation.

Pizzo, P. D. (1990). Whole babies, parents and pieces of funds: Creating comprehensive programs for infants and toddlers. *Zero to Three, 10,* 24–28.

Prescott, E. (1979). *The physical environment—a powerful regulator of experience.* Child Care Information Exchange.

Prescott, E., & David, T. (1976). *The effects of the physical environment on day care.* ERIC document No. 156–356.

Ruopp, R., Travers, J., Glantz, F., & Coelen, C. (1979). *Children at the center: Final report of the national day care study (Vol. 1).* Cambridge, MA: Abt Associates.

Snow, C., & McGaha, C. G. (2003). *Infant development.* Upper Saddle River, NJ: Prentice Hall.

Stonehouse, A. (Ed.) (1988). *Trusting toddlers: Programming for one-to-three year olds in child care centers.* Fyshwick, ACT: Canberra Publishing & Printing Co.

Thompson, R. A. (2001). Development in the first years of life. In *Caring for Infants and Toddlers, Spring/Summer.* Los Altos, CA: The David and Lucille Packard Foundation.

Vandell, D. L., & Wolfe, B. (2000). *Child care quality: Does it matter and does it need to be improved?* Washington, DC: U.S. Department of Health and Human Services.

Whaley, K., & Rubenstein, T. (1994). How toddlers "do" friendship: A descriptive analysis of naturally occurring friendships in a group care setting. *Journal of Social and Personal Relationships, 11,* 383–400.

Whaley, K. L., & Kantor, R. (1992). Mixed-age grouping in infant/toddler child care: Enhancing developmental processes. *Child and Youth Care Forum, 21,* 369–384.

Whitebook, M., Howes, C., & Phillips, D. (1990). *Who cares? Child care workers and the quality of care in America. National Child Care Staffing Study.* Berkeley: CA: Child Care Employee Project.

Whitebook, M., Sakai, L., Gerber, E., & Howes, C. (2001). *Then & now: Changes in child care staffing, 1994–2000.* Washington, DC: Center for the Child Care Workforce.

Chapter 3

The Head Start Program

Douglas R. Powell ∽ Purdue University

Head Start is the largest federal early childhood program in the United States. By 2003, it had served more than 21 million children since its beginnings in 1965, enrolling more than 900,000 children in 2002. The program has evolved from its original form as a summer program to a comprehensive set of services for economically disadvantaged young children and their families. Head Start has served as the nation's laboratory for experimenting in the field with quality programs for children birth through 5 years of age. The program has been a pioneer in methods of working with parents and in the development of innovative demonstration programs focused on families with very young children. It also has been at the forefront of approaches to the inclusion of children with disabilities as well as responsiveness to culturally and linguistically diverse populations. Remarkably, Head Start has gained widespread support from policy makers of contrasting political orientations. It has been called "the most important social and educational experiment of the second half of the twentieth century" (Zigler & Muenchow, 1992, p. 2).

This chapter provides an overview of the Head Start program. It is divided into four sections: the history or evolution of Head Start, including its goals and current scope; program services, staffing arrangements, and evaluation results regarding program effectiveness; innovative demonstration projects developed by Head Start; and issues regarding the future of Head Start.

∽ EVOLUTION OF HEAD START
War on Poverty Origins

Head Start was conceived in 1964 as a key part of the nation's War on Poverty during a highly optimistic time in U.S. history. Its origins are based in the social and political struggles of the civil rights era, renewed scientific interest in environmental influences on the course of human development, and the promising results of educational intervention programs for children from economically disadvantaged backgrounds (Zigler & Anderson, 1979).

The civil rights movement of the 1960s drew attention to the widespread nature of poverty and its threats to the economic and social well-being of the nation. The movement also highlighted inequitable treatment of racial and ethnic minorities as well as poor people in accessing quality education, jobs, housing, health care, and social services. The War on Poverty programs advanced by Presidents John F. Kennedy and Lyndon B. Johnson adhered to a basic belief in education as the solution to poverty. Job training and education were core features of the Economic Opportunity Act of 1964, which led to the creation of programs aimed at eradicating poverty. There also was a belief that individuals in disadvantaged circumstances should help plan and administer programs aimed at compensating for inequalities in social and economic conditions. The concept of maximum feasible participation was incorporated into the Economic Opportunity Act and subsequently into policies of War on Poverty programs such as Head Start.

During this era, social policies affecting young children were shaped by research evidence demonstrating the lasting power of environmental influences on human development. This environmental view was in marked contrast with the hereditarian perspective that prevailed in the 1950s and early 1960s. Noted scholar J. McVicker Hunt's 1961 book *Intelligence and Experience* was particularly instrumental in challenging the widespread view of intelligence and abilities as fixed by heredity. Hunt argued that intellectual development was determined largely by the quality of environmental inputs, particularly from the mother.

Benjamin Bloom, also an eminent scholar, reached a similar conclusion in an exhaustive review of a large body of research in his 1964 book *Stability and Change in Human Characteristics*. Bloom's work pointed to the first 4 or 5 years of life as the period experiencing the most rapid change in intellectual growth. He concluded that the preschool years were the best time to have long-lasting impact on cognitive functioning. This conclusion gave rise to the popularity of the "critical period" of development in the early years and to claims about half of learning taking place before the age of 5 years.

Later research clearly pointed to the extreme nature of a view of human development that disregards heredity and the significance of experiences that occur beyond 5 years of age. Eventually there was recognition of the need for elementary school experiences to be designed in a way that sustains the benefits of early childhood education. Nonetheless, the environmental perspective dominated the mid-1960s period in which Head Start was launched. The early years were seen as analogous to the importance of the foundation of a building: "If the foundation is shaky, the structure is doomed. . . . The public hailed the construction of a solid foundation for learning in preschool children as the solution to poverty and ignorance" (Zigler & Anderson, 1979, pp. 7–8).

Promising evaluation results from several early intervention programs also contributed to the decision to establish the Head Start program. Although preschool programs focused on the education of children from economically disadvantaged backgrounds were rare in the 1950s and early 1960s, a handful of innovative programs were established in this era to serve children from poor families. The Early Training Project directed by Susan Gray at Peabody College in Nashville, Tennessee, was among these prominent forerunners of Head Start. The project's focus on achievement motivation and aptitudes for learning resonated with the environmental view and had commonsense appeal among the general public. Importantly, the positive impact of this early education program on IQ and verbal abilities (Gray & Klaus, 1965) offered hope of what might be achieved on a broader scale.

Naïve Assumptions and Political Realities

Head Start was offered in the summer of 1965 to far more communities and children than recommended by many experts. One point of view was that the program should begin as a small, closely monitored pilot effort. Proponents of this view were concerned about the logistics of successfully launching a major new effort in a short period of time, and also reasoned there was insufficient information from experience and research for making informed decisions about how best to provide a preschool program for children from poor families. However, a large-scale effort initially involving 500,000 children in some 2,000 centers was envisioned by the time of President Johnson's May 18, 1965, Rose Garden speech announcing plans for Head Start. The goal was to reach as many children as possible, even if the summer program for some children entailed nothing more than modest interventions such as immunizations and badly needed health services (Richmond, Stipek, & Zigler, 1979). Importantly, there were high hopes of boosting children's IQ and intellectual competence through preschool education. Sweeping claims were made in the 1960s about the ability of a preschool program for children from disadvantaged backgrounds to eventually reduce the prevalence of poverty in the United States.

The great expectation of achieving significant improvements in children's intellectual functioning through a relatively small dose of environmental enrichment (initially a summer program) proved to be naïve and overly optimistic soon after Head Start was launched. Serious questions were raised about the prevailing view of children as clay that could be molded easily and permanently through appropriately stimulating environments. The lack of attention to biological factors in the environmentalism of the mid-1960s prompted the pendulum to swing toward a more reasonable middle ground by the late 1960s. Interactions between genetic factors and the environment were increasingly recognized as key developmental processes, a trend that continues today (Bronfenbrenner & Morris, 1998).

The early years of Head Start also were marked by simplistic assumptions about the nature of poverty and the characteristics of children and families living in economic disadvantage. A common stereotype was that low-income mothers were generally incompetent and incapable of providing appropriate guidance and affection to their children (Baratz & Baratz, 1970). Life in poor families was seen as either overstimulating (e.g., too much noise) or understimulating (e.g., too few toys). As noted by Zigler and Anderson (1979), "verbal activity in the poor household was supposed to consist of body language, monosyllables, shouts, and grunts" (p. 9). The anthropologist Oscar Lewis's studies of poverty were interpreted by many to indicate there was

a uniform "culture of poverty" and children growing up in poor families were "culturally deprived." Deviations from the norms of mainstream middle-class family life often were viewed as forms of pathology or dysfunction.

By the late 1960s there were clear challenges to stereotypical views of poor families and children. Studies heightened professionals' sensitivity to the biases of tests developed on middle-class samples of children and of testing situations that were unfamiliar to lower-income and minority children. For example, research indicated that the verbal performance of African American children was significantly better when tested by an African American tester in a nonacademic setting (Labov, 1970). Studies, program experiences, and media reports also demonstrated the diverse manifestations of poverty across regions, communities, and populations, thereby casting doubt on research and programs that assumed all poor people are alike in needs, characteristics, and aspirations. Further, the influence of community and societal contexts on individual and family functioning was emphasized in policy analyses (Keniston & the Carnegie Council on Children, 1977); families and individuals were not to be viewed as self-sufficient units to be blamed when things go wrong (Ryan, 1971). Eventually a backlash against the concept of "cultural deprivation" led to calls for educational and human service programs to celebrate cultural diversity, respect individual differences, and build on family strengths rather than weaknesses.

Over time, then, there were modifications of simplistic views of the magnitude of environmental influences, the early years as a highly malleable period of development, and poor families as uniformly incompetent. Still, the original expectation that a short-term preschool program could achieve dramatic and lasting improvements in the IQ and general competence of children from economically disadvantaged families has long persisted as a powerful albeit flawed framework for Head Start and other early childhood programs. This expectation supports a view of an early childhood program as an inoculation against future effects of poverty. As demonstrated in this chapter, the inoculation model has shaped what policy makers and the general public often expect of Head Start.

Program Goals

Head Start has long embraced a broad set of objectives focused on the developmental and learning outcomes of children in low-income families. The major domains of child development—social, emotional, cognitive, and physical—are viewed as interrelated. Accordingly, Head Start deals with the "whole child."

Currently, significant attention is being given to Head Start's role in preparing children for school success. School readiness is a strong theme in the 1998 federal legislation that reauthorizes funding for the Head Start program. School readiness also is the focus of President George W. Bush's proposed changes in the Head Start program, described in the final section of this chapter. The purpose of Head Start was revised by the 105th Congress to indicate that Head Start promotes "school readiness by enhancing the social and cognitive development of low-income children through the provision . . . of health, educational, nutritional, social, and other services that are determined to be necessary, based on family needs assessments." Performance standards also were added to ensure that children enrolled in Head Start meet the following minimum expectations: develop phonemic, print, and numeracy awareness; understand and use oral language to communicate needs, wants, and thoughts; understand and use increasingly complex and varied vocabulary; develop and demonstrate an appreciation of books; and, in the case of children for whom English is a second language, progress toward acquisition of the English language.

In 2000, the Head Start Bureau issued a Child Outcomes Framework of building blocks deemed important for school success. The framework is intended to guide programs in their ongoing assessment of progress and accomplishments of children and in program efforts to use child outcomes data for program self-assessment and continuing improvement. The framework is composed of 8 general domains, 27 domain elements, and 100 examples of more specific indicators of children's skills, abilities, knowledge, and behaviors, all aimed at 3- to 5-year-old children. The framework includes the outcomes legislatively mandated in 1998. The eight domains and their respective elements are:

- Language development: listening and understanding, speaking and communicating;
- Literacy: phonological awareness, book knowledge and appreciation, print awareness and concepts, early writing, alphabet knowledge;
- Mathematics: number and operations, geometry and spatial sense, patterns and measurement;
- Science: scientific skills and methods, scientific knowledge;
- Creative arts: music, art, movement, dramatic play;
- Social and emotional development: self-concept, self-control, cooperation, social relationships, knowledge of families and communities;
- Approaches to learning: initiative and curiosity, engagement and persistence, reasoning and problem solving;
- Physical health and development: fine motor skills, gross motor skills, health status and practices.

From the beginning, Head Start has viewed the family in general and parents and primary caregivers in particular as essential partners in achieving improved outcomes for children. It is understood that children develop in the context of their family and culture, and that "parents are respected as the primary educators and nurturers of their children" (Head Start Bureau, 1997, p. 1). The program provides numerous opportunities for parents to be involved in program decisions and activities, and to develop their own strengths and interests in a variety of adult roles, including child rearing. A premise of these provisions is the realization that no 1- or 2-year program is likely to make lasting improvements in a child's development unless the program helps parents become the "agents of change, reinforcing positive changes in the child long after the formal program's conclusions" (Zigler & Muenchow, 1992, p. 101).

Head Start's approach to working with parents has consistently been at the forefront of methods of parent participation. For example, a Head Start requirement is that parents constitute more than one-half of the local policy council for a program. This policy provision for a parent role in local program governance reflects a family empowerment perspective wherein parents are to be viewed as active, respected participants rather than passive recipients of professionally determined services. The provision stems from Head Start's War on Poverty roots and the "maximum feasible participation" language of the Economic Opportunity Act described earlier. Head Start, then, is a comprehensive program. It has "*always* been designed to be more than preschool education" (Washington & Oyemade Bailey, 1995, p. 8).

There has been confusion about Head Start's goals for many years. One area of misunderstanding has been Head Start's role in eradicating poverty. As described earlier, Head Start was established during an era of great optimism about the power of social and educational programs to successfully address numerous societal ills. President Johnson spoke to the goal of combating poverty in his May 18, 1965, speech on Head Start: "Five- and six-year-old children are inheritors of poverty's curse and not its creators. Unless we act these children will pass it on to the next generation,

like a family birthmark. This program this year means that 30 million man-years—the combined lifespan of these youngsters—will be spent productively and rewardingly, rather than wasted in tax-supported institutions and in welfare-supported lethargy" (cited in Zigler & Valentine, 1979, p. 68).

The idea that an early childhood program could reduce welfare costs and crime in adult life was given a major boost in 1984. An influential study of the Perry Preschool Project in Ypsilanti, Michigan, indicated that at age 19 years, participants in the Perry Preschool Project had better high school completion rates and less adolescent pregnancy and juvenile delinquency than youth who had not participated in the preschool program (Berrueta-Clement, Schweinhart, Barnett, Epstein, & Weikart, 1984). In 1993, results of a follow-up study of the Perry Preschool Project participants at 27 years of age showed the preschool participants had half as many criminal arrests, higher earnings and property wealth, and greater commitment to marriage than their counterparts who did not attend preschool (Schweinhart, Barnes, & Weikart, 1993). A benefit–cost analysis of the Perry Preschool Project at 27 years indicated that the preschool program produced economic benefits to participants and especially to the general public. The benefit–cost ratio was in excess of 7:1, attributable mostly to reductions in the cost of crime (Barnett, 1993).

Many policy makers and children's advocates erroneously assumed the Perry Preschool findings were applicable to Head Start and ambitiously promoted Head Start as a proven strategy for reducing welfare. Some analysts believe this inappropriate generalization of evaluation data from the Perry Preschool Project to Head Start ran into serious trouble when informed citizens realized the Perry Preschool Project is not Head Start. This realization is thought to have contributed to a period of reduced political support for the program and limited progress in allocating funds for Head Start expansion and quality improvements (Zigler, 1998).

Another point of confusion in Head Start's goals has been whether the program is primarily focused on improving children's IQ and intellectual competence. Programmatic attention to all aspects of children's development has been in place from the beginning. The original goals for Head Start set forth by the program's Planning Committee in 1965 emphasize physical health, social and emotional development, mental processes and skills, and self-confidence in future learning efforts. Children's IQ became an early focus in policy makers' and general public understanding of Head Start, however, partly because IQ is a well-known (yet poorly understood) construct in American society. Importantly, IQ tests were readily available for use by program evaluators and, in contrast, reliable, valid, and efficient tests of most other aspects of children's functioning were not available. Thus, early program evaluations held Head Start accountable for achieving gains in IQ and cognitive abilities mostly or exclusively.

Current Scope and Organization

Some key numbers offer an impressive profile of Head Start's current status. In 2002, the program served 912,345 children in all 50 states plus the District of Columbia, Puerto Rico, and the Virgin Islands. There were 18,865 Head Start centers and 49,800 classrooms. The paid staff numbered 198,000 and there were more than 1.4 million volunteers. The 2002 budget was more than $6.5 billion, and the average cost per child was $6,934 per year.

The racial/ethnic background of children enrolled in Head Start in 2002 was as follows: American Indian, 2.9%; Hispanic, 29.8%; African American, 32.6%; Caucasian, 28.4%; Asian, 2.0%; and Hawaiian/Pacific Islander, 1%. Head Start requires that 90% of enrolled families be of low-income status. In the 2000–2001 program year,

77% of Head Start families had annual incomes of less than $15,000 per year. In 2002, 13% of the Head Start enrollment consisted of children with disabilities, broadly defined to include mental retardation, health impairments, visual handicaps, hearing impairments, emotional disturbance, speech and language impairments, orthopedic handicaps, and learning disabilities. Head Start has long required that children with disabilities represent at least 10% of enrolled children in a local program.

The vast majority of Head Start children are 4 years (52%) or 3 years (36%) of age. Most Head Start programs operate a part-day program, although a growing number are seeking ways to provide full-day services. A minimum of two home visits annually is expected of all center-based Head Start programs. A relatively small number of programs provide home-based services in a significant way. In 2002, 47,000 children participated in home-based Head Start program services.

Since 1995 the program has been serving infants and toddlers through the Early Head Start program. Early Head Start programs tailor their services to meet the needs of low-income pregnant women and families with children 3 years of age or younger through home-based, center-based, or a combination of home- and center-based options. Programs are required to provide child development services, build family and community partnerships, and support staff to provide high-quality services for children and families. The program has grown steadily each year. In 2002, nearly 650 programs were given funds to provide Early Head Start child development and family support services to some 62,000 children under the age of 3 years.

Head Start is administered federally by the Head Start Bureau, located in the Administration for Children and Families office of the U.S. Department of Health and Human Services. Local programs are operated through grants to public agencies, private nonprofit organizations,

A child enrolled in Early Head Start spends some time with his mother during a field trip into the community.

faith-based organizations, and school systems. Grants are awarded by regional offices of the Department of Health and Human Services and by the Head Start Bureau's Native American and Migrant Programs Branches. In 2002, there were 1,570 local program grantees. Federal funds are limited to 80% of total program costs; there is a matching requirement of 20% from nonfederal sources. Federal law prohibits Head Start programs from charging fees of parents.

Head Start has experienced a dramatic growth in federal appropriations and number of children served annually in the last several decades. From 1992 to 2002, for example, the federal appropriation increased from $2.2 billion to $6.5 billion annually, and the number of children served annually increased from 621,078 to 912,345.

PROGRAM SERVICES AND EFFECTIVENESS

A core tenet of Head Start is that local programs need flexibility in order to meet the particular needs of their communities. The intent is to pro-

vide a range of individualized services that are responsive and appropriate to each child and family within a community context. Flexibility occurs within firm parameters set forth in Program Performance Standards by the federal Head Start Bureau (also published in the *Federal Register*). A revised set of Performance Standards was issued in November 1996, the first comprehensive revision of the standards in more than 20 years. The revised standards took effect January 1, 1998. The Program Performance Standards define the services that Head Start programs are to provide to children and families and constitute the best statement of Head Start's expectations of high quality.

The standards are organized into three major areas: Early Childhood Development and Health Services, Family and Community Partnerships, and Program Design and Management. Each area contains a set of standards, which in essence are mandated regulations for all Head Start programs, plus a rationale for the standards and guidance in the form of examples of how a standard could be implemented. There also is a detailed section on standards of working with children with disabilities and their families. To provide maximum flexibility in implementation, the Performance Standards do not prescribe *how* the services defined in the Standards are to be carried out.

Clear expectations of the scope and quality of services to infants and toddlers and pregnant women, particularly through Early Head Start, are major additions to the revised Program Performance Standards. Incorporated into the standards are requirements that address nine principles of Early Head Start. These principles include the following: a commitment to high quality; promotion of healthy child development and family functioning before conception and through the early years; positive interpersonal relationships and continuity; parent involvement; full inclusion of children with disabilities; support of the home culture and language as part of early identity formation; program services that are comprehensive, flexible, responsive, and intense; smooth transitions to and from Early Head Start; and collaborations with local community agencies and service providers that maximize resources available to families (Lally & Keith, 1997).

Head Start seeks to provide a coordinated set of services, not separate components in early childhood, health, and parent involvement. To this end, the revised standards include a number of cross-references to other standards and examples, in an attempt to support an integrated approach to service delivery.

Early Childhood Development and Health Services

A common misconception of Head Start is that a standard curriculum is implemented in all classrooms. In reality, local programs are given a good deal of flexibility to design and implement a curriculum based on developmentally and linguistically appropriate practices with young children. Program standards recognize that children have individual rates of develop-

ment as well as individual interests, temperaments, languages, cultural backgrounds, and learning styles. Head Start programs are to be inclusive of children with disabilities, as noted earlier, and to foster an environment of acceptance that respects differences in gender, culture, language, ethnicity, and family composition. The need for Head Start to support the home language, culture, and family composition is emphasized repeatedly in descriptions of program standards.

Head Start standards follow closely the developmentally appropriate practices in early childhood programs recommended by the National Association for the Education of Young Children (Bredekamp & Copple, 1997). There is to be a balance of child-initiated and adult-directed activities, including individual and small group activities, in the daily program. Social and emotional development is to be supported by building trust; fostering independence; encouraging self-control by setting clear, consistent limits and having realistic expectations; encouraging respect for the feelings and rights of others; and providing timely, predictable, and unrushed routines and transitions. Each child's learning is to be supported through experimentation, inquiry, observation, play, exploration, and related strategies. Art, music, movement, and dialogue are viewed as key opportunities for creative self-expression, and language use among children and between children and adults is promoted. Developmentally appropriate activities and materials are to be provided for support of children's emerging literacy and numeracy development. Center-based programs are to provide sufficient time, space, equipment, materials, and adult guidance for active play and movement that supports fine and gross motor development. Home-based programs are to encourage parents to appreciate the value of physical development and to provide opportunities for safe and active play.

Program standards for education and early childhood development include separate sections on infants/toddlers and preschool-age children. Services for infants and toddlers emphasize the development of secure relationships (e.g., limited number of consistent teachers over an extended period of time), emerging communication skills, fine and gross motor development, and opportunities for each child to explore a variety of sensory and motor experiences. The curriculum for preschool-age children is to foster skills that form a foundation for school readiness and later school success, including opportunities for each child to organize experiences, understand concepts, and develop age-appropriate literacy, numeracy, reasoning, problem-solving and decision-making skills. The curriculum also is to help children develop emotional security and facility in social relationships; self-awareness; and feelings of competence, self-esteem, and positive attitudes toward learning.

As noted earlier, there is growing emphasis on school readiness and especially literacy outcomes in Head Start. In 2002, the Head Start Bureau launched a Strategic Teacher Education Program (STEP) to ensure that every Head Start program and classroom teacher has a fundamental knowledge of early literacy and state-of-the-art early literacy teaching techniques. More than 3,300 local program supervisors and teachers received STEP training to serve as trainers to some 50,000 Head Start teachers in the United States. The Bureau also is sponsoring mentor-coaches to work with classroom teachers plus a Web-based resource on early literacy. Importantly, the Bureau is implementing a National Reporting System comprised of a core set of measures designed to assess all Head Start children's progress the year prior to kindergarten in developing early literacy, language, and math skills.

Parents are to be an integral part of the development of the local program's curriculum and approach to child development and education. Also, opportunities are to be provided for parents to strengthen their child observation skills and to share assessments with staff that inform

program planning for each child. Parent–staff discussion of each child's development and education is to occur in conferences and home visits. One of the purposes of home visits is to support parents in their role as their child's first teacher and to assist families in the development and attainment of family goals. Services to children with disabilities are to be consistent with each child's Individualized Family Service Plan (IFSP) or Individualized Education Program (IEP).

Head Start has had a strong commitment to improving children's health outcomes since its inception. The first director of the national Head Start program was a physician, Dr. Robert Cooke, chair of the Department of Pediatrics at Johns Hopkins University. Careful attention to children's health care needs was a central part of Head Start's original purpose.

This tradition continues today with detailed attention to child health and safety, child nutrition, and child mental health in the performance standards. Head Start functions as the leading health care system for young, low-income children in the country (Greenberg, 1990). Within 90 days of entry into a Head Start program, the staff is to collaborate with parents in determining the health status of each child. This entails an assessment of whether each child has an ongoing source of continuous, accessible health care. If ongoing health care is not accessible to a child, the program must assist parents in accessing a source of care. The child health status review also includes a determination as to whether the child is up to date on a schedule of preventive and primary health care, including medical, dental, and mental health. Again, the program is to assist parents in making arrangements to bring the child up to date if necessary. The Head Start program also is to ensure that children continue with the recommended schedule of well-child care and to track the provision of health care services. When a child has a known or suspected health or developmental problem, the Head Start program is to obtain or arrange for further diagnostic testing, examination, and treatment by a licensed or certified professional.

Within 45 days of each child's entry into Head Start, the program is to perform or obtain developmental, sensory, and behavioral screenings of motor, language, social, cognitive, perceptual, and emotional skills. The screenings must be sensitive to the child's cultural background and home language, and multiple sources of information on all aspects of each child's development and behavior are to be obtained, including input from family members, teachers, and other relevant staff. A follow-up plan is to be established and monitored with parents of children with identified health needs. Dental follow up and treatment must include fluoride supplements and topical fluoride treatments for every child with moderate to severe tooth decay and in communities where there is a lack of adequate fluoride levels. Further, Head Start programs are to develop and implement procedures that enable staff to identify any new or recurring medical, dental, or developmental concerns so as to permit prompt appropriate referrals. Parents are to be fully informed and involved in this process.

Program provisions for mental health services include collaborations with families to solicit parental information and concerns about their child's mental health and to enable staff to provide information to parents about staff observations of the child and anticipated changes in the child's behavior and development, especially separation and attachment issues. There also is to be parent–staff discussion of how to strengthen nurturing, supportive environments and relationships at home and in the program. Programs are to help parents better understand mental health issues and to support parents' participation in needed mental health interventions. Staff and/or family concerns about a child's mental health are to be addressed in a timely manner through the services of a mental health professional secured by the program. There also is to be a regular schedule of mental health con-

sultation with program staff and parents on how to address individual children's needs and ways to promote mental wellness.

Head Start performance standards also call for staff and families to work together to identify each child's nutritional needs, with consideration of a family's eating patterns, including cultural preferences and special dietary requirements. Local programs are to design and implement a nutrition program that meets the nutritional needs and feeding requirements of each child. Children in center-based programs are served a meal on a daily basis; for each child, there is a nutritious snack plus breakfast and/or lunch, depending on morning, afternoon, or full-day enrollment. A variety of foods—responsive to cultural and ethnic preferences as well as for the broadening of a child's food experience—are to be served. Food is not to be used as a reward or punishment. Each child is to be encouraged, but not forced, to eat or taste the food. At least one-third of a child's daily nutritional needs are to be met through meals and snacks in a part-day center-based program, and one-half to two-thirds of a child's daily nutritional needs are to be met in a full-day center-based program. Dental hygiene is to be promoted in conjunction with meals at programs. Parents are to be involved in planning, implementing, and evaluating a program's nutritional services, and parent education activities must include opportunities for families to learn about food preparation and strengthen nutritional skills.

Last, Head Start standards include health emergency procedures, a description of conditions for short-term exclusion from the program due to a health-related matter, and provisions for medication administration, injury prevention, hygiene, and first-aid kits.

Family and Community Partnerships

Among model early childhood programs in this country, Head Start has perhaps the most comprehensive and detailed set of provisions for working with families. Scholars have long pointed to parent involvement as a cornerstone of Head Start's success.

Head Start seeks to establish a collaborative partnership with parents that is built on mutual trust and an understanding of family goals, strengths, and necessary services and other supports. To this end, programs are to offer parents an opportunity to develop and implement an individualized Family Partnership Agreement that sets forth family goals, responsibilities, timetables, and strategies for achieving the goals plus monitoring progress. The agreement is to take into account and coordinate with preexisting family plans developed with other programs or agencies. Further, local programs are to work with parents to gain access to community services and resources that are responsive to each family's interests and goals. The services here pertain to emergency assistance with basic needs such as housing, food, clothing, and transportation; education and counseling programs focused on such mental health issues as substance abuse, child abuse and neglect, and domestic violence; and continuing education and employment training.

Head Start's concept of parent involvement is broad based and emphasizes two parental roles: parents as active contributors to program policies and practices, and parents as competent supporters of their child's healthy growth and development. Parent participation in any program activity, including home visits, is voluntary and must not be required as a condition of a child's enrollment.

Probably the best-known Head Start provision for parent participation is the shared governance requirement that 51% of the members of the local program policy group must be parents of currently enrolled children. Also, parents of formerly enrolled children may serve as community representatives on the policy group. The policy group is charged with working collaboratively with key management staff and the governing body responsible for legal and fiscal administra-

tion of the local program to determine policies and procedures in many areas, including:

- program philosophy and long- and short-term goals and objectives;
- criteria for defining recruitment, selection, and enrollment priorities;
- decisions to hire or terminate the Head Start director and any person who works primarily for the program.

The policy group also advises staff in developing and implementing local program policies, activities, and services.

There are many other provisions for parent participation. One is for parents to serve as employees or volunteers. Over 808,000 parents volunteered in their local Head Start program in 1996–1997. As noted earlier, local programs are to provide opportunities for parents to help develop the program's curriculum. Parents must be welcomed as visitors and encouraged to observe children and participate with children in group activities. Facilities must be open to parents during all program hours.

Head Start addresses numerous parenting tasks faced by adult participants in the program. Opportunities are provided for parents to enhance their parenting skills, knowledge, and understanding of the educational and developmental needs and activities of their children. Parents also are encouraged to share concerns about their children with program staff, as described in the previous section. In addition to two home visits per year, teachers in center-based programs are to hold at least two staff–parent conferences per program year. The goal of the conferences is to enhance the knowledge and understanding of both staff and parents of each child's educational and developmental progress in the program.

A wide range of content areas is addressed in the parenting education and support services. There are opportunities for parents to be involved in health, nutrition, and mental health education. Another content area is community and child advocacy. The program is to support and encourage parents to influence the nature and goals of community services in a way that makes services more responsive to their needs and interests. Programs also are to help parents become advocates for their children as they transition from home to Head Start or other early childhood program and from Head Start to elementary school. Further, support for the child advocate role focuses on parents' continued involvement in their children's education in school, including education and training for parents to exercise their rights and responsibilities regarding the education of their child in the school setting, as well as communication with teachers and other school personnel so parents can participate in decisions related to their child's education. In addition to the health and advocacy content areas, the revised program standards call for local Head Start programs to support family literacy development directly or through referrals to other local programs. An aim here is to assist parents as adult learners in recognizing their own literacy goals.

No one program can meet all of the needs of a child and family. An intent of Head Start's community partnerships is to improve the delivery of services to children and families and to ensure that a local Head Start program responds to community needs. Strong communication, cooperation, and sharing of information is to occur between Head Start and the following types of community organizations:

- Health care providers such as clinics, physicians, and dentists
- Mental health providers
- Nutritional service providers
- Individuals and agencies that provide services to children with disabilities and their families
- Family preservation and support services
- Child protective services
- Local elementary schools and other educational and cultural institutions such as libraries and museums

- Providers of child-care services
- Any other organizations or businesses that may provide support and resources to families.

Each Head Start program is to establish and maintain a Health Services Advisory Committee comprised of professionals and volunteers from the community.

The program gives considerable attention to children's transitions into Head Start and from Head Start to elementary schools or other child-care settings. Local Head Start programs are to ensure that children's relevant records are transferred to the school or the child's next setting. In addition, each Head Start program is to take an active role in encouraging communication between the program staff and their counterparts in the schools and other child-care settings, including principals, teachers, social workers, and health care staff. The aim of these communications is to facilitate continuity of programming for each child. Meetings are to be initiated for Head Start staff, parents, and kindergarten or elementary school teachers to discuss developmental progress and abilities of each child. In the Early Head Start program, transition planning is to begin for each child and family at least 6 months prior to the child's third birthday.

Program Planning and Staffing

Planning is an integral part of the management of local Head Start programs. Specifically, each program is to develop and implement a systematic, ongoing process of program planning that includes consultation with the program's governing body, policy groups, program staff, and with other community organizations that serve Head Start or other low-income families with young children. The program planning is to include an assessment of community strengths, needs, and resources; the development of both short- and long-range program goals and objectives; written plans for implementing services;

and a review of progress in meeting goals at least annually. A self-assessment of program effectiveness and progress in meeting program goals and objectives is to be conducted at least once each program year. Communication with parents, governing bodies, and policy groups, and communication among staff is to be carried out on a regular basis. Records are to be maintained on all children, families, and staff, with appropriate provisions for confidentiality.

The staffing structure for a local Head Start program entails a director, classroom teachers and home visitors, and content experts in each of the following areas: education and child development services, health services, nutrition services, family and community partnership services, parent involvement services, and disabilities services. The content experts are staff or regular consultants, depending on the size of the local program. Staffing patterns and staff organizational structures are determined by local programs.

All staff working as classroom teachers are required to obtain a Child Development Associate (CDA) or equivalent credential. The CDA credential is a competency-based certificate in early childhood education administered nationally. The federal reauthorization of Head Start in 1998 required that by September 2003, at least one-half of all Head Start teachers in center-based programs must have an associate, baccalaureate, or advanced degree in early childhood education or a related field, with preschool teaching experience. In addition, teachers of infants and toddlers must have training and experience necessary to develop consistent, stable, and supportive relationships with very young children, and must develop knowledge of infant and toddler development, safety issues in infant and toddler care (e.g., reducing the risk of Sudden Infant Death Syndrome), and methods for communicating effectively with infants and toddlers and their parents. In 1998–1999, 93% of Head Start teachers had degrees in early childhood education or had obtained the CDA

credential or a state certificate to teach in a preschool classroom.

Qualifications of staff or consultants serving as content experts are specific to the content area. For example, the content expert responsible for the education and child development services must have training and experiences in areas that include theories and principles of child growth and development, early childhood education, and family support.

Sensitivity to cultural and linguistic differences is a staff qualification. Staff and program consultants must be familiar with the ethnic background and heritage of families in the local program and, to the extent feasible, must be able to communicate effectively with children and families with no or limited English proficiency. When a majority of children speak the same language in a Head Start program, at least one classroom staff member or home visitor interacting regularly with the children must speak their language.

Although many Head Start staff have degrees in early childhood education or related fields, Head Start has consistently resisted requiring baccalaureate or graduate degrees of its staff so as to permit hiring staff from the communities served and to provide career development opportunities for parents and former parents of program children. Twenty-nine percent of Head Start staff in 2001–2002 were parents of current or former Head Start children. Parents are given preference for employment vacancies for which they are qualified. Flexibility in staff qualifications also is seen as a way to accommodate the realities of staff availability in rural areas.

There is a structured approach to staff training and development opportunities in Head Start, including regular in-service training plus an orientation for all new staff and volunteers. The Head Start Bureau developed a comprehensive set of training guides to be used with all staff in the 1990s and, as indicated earlier, launched the STEP training focused on early literacy development in 2002. The Head Start

Bureau also sponsors periodic conferences and institutes for local program administrators. In addition, training and technical assistance for Early Head Start programs is provided by regionally funded infant/toddler specialists and by the Early Head Start National Resource Center.

Program planning and staff qualifications are prescribed in the Program Design and Management section of the revised Performance Standards document.

Program Effectiveness

An extensive research literature on Head Start has accumulated since the program's inception in 1965. The amount of research conducted during the first decade of the program was especially high. Among the early studies of Head Start was an outcome evaluation conducted by the Westinghouse Learning Corporation (1969). The study indicated Head Start contributed to children's immediate modest gains on standardized tests of cognitive ability but these gains disappeared after children were in school several years. Some leading scholars criticized the study largely on methodological grounds (e.g., Campbell & Erlebacher, 1970). There also were concerns about a major focus on children's cognitive skills and limited attention to social-emotional functioning and health-related outcomes (e.g., Smith & Bissell, 1970). Nonetheless, the report had a devastating effect on the optimism that surrounded Head Start in particular and the War on Poverty programs in general. Proponents of Head Start argued that the program had immediate benefits to low-income populations by mobilizing parents to advocate for improved and expanded community services for low-income children and families (see Zigler & Freedman, 1987). An early study supported this view of Head Start as a catalyst for improved services for low-income and minority populations (Kirschner Associates, 1970). Also, an influential review of the effects of early intervention programs brought attention to the difficult contexts in which Head Start and other early education programs were attempting to achieve positive outcomes in children. Specifically, relatively brief programs such as Head Start were seen as offering experiences that ran quite contrary to children's usual and more powerful experiences in families and communities (Bronfenbrenner, 1974). This report led to increased interest in a range of support systems for families aimed at strengthening individual and family functioning. Head Start was among the developers of innovative demonstration programs focused on families, as described in the next section of this chapter.

A 1985 synthesis of 210 published and unpublished reports on Head Start research found immediate gains in children's cognitive abilities, achievement motivation, self-esteem, social behavior, and health indicators. There also were some indications of improvements in mothers' well-being and in community services, although it is not clear Head Start played a causal role in these changes (McKey, Condelli, Ganson, Barrett, McConkey, & Plantz, 1985). The synthesis review also found that cognitive test score gains achieved during Head Start did not persist over the long term (generally 2 years after participation in Head Start). Similarly, the gains in socioemotional functioning also did not persist long term (generally 3 years after participation in Head Start). Not all of the 210 research reports included in the 1985 synthesis examined each aspect of Head Start. For example, the report's findings on cognitive gains were based on 72 studies and the findings on socioemotional development were based on 17 studies.

Rigorous experimental designs have been used infrequently to assess Head Start effects. Limitations of much of the existing research on Head Start are highlighted in a 1997 U. S. Government Accounting Office (GAO) report on the impact of Head Start (GAO, 1997). From a review of some 200 reports on Head Start effects, the GAO identified 22 studies that met the following selection criteria: Head Start participation occurring in 1976 or later, comparisons of Head Start participants with children not attending any preschool or some other type of preschool or with test norms, and use of tests of statistical significance. Sixteen of the 22 studies compared Head Start participants to an unserved comparison group. Only 1 of these 16 studies used random assignment to form the Head Start and non–Head Start comparison groups. Three other studies analyzed gains on normed tests, and three compared Head Start to some other type of preschool or child-care program. Results of a reanalysis of data involving nearly 1,000 Head Start and control group children suggest that estimates of Head Start effects may be underestimated through the use of noncomparable control groups. The Head Start sample included a higher proportion of African American children, mothers with less formal education, father-absent households, larger families, and children with lower preintervention test scores of cognitive functioning than the sample in the comparison groups (Lee, Brooks-Gunn, & Schnur, 1988).

There were other limitations of the studies reviewed by the GAO. First, the studies focused mostly on academic or cognitive outcomes rather than the broad range of child functioning addressed by Head Start. Most of the studies examined the effects of Head Start on grade retention and other indicators of academic achievement such as reading and math scores. Sixteen of the 22 studies included 1 or more cognitive outcomes, while only 5 studies considered health or nutrition outcomes and only 5 examined family outcomes. Second, few studies considered program impact by subpopulations such as racial and ethnic background. These considerations are key to examining the question of whether the program has differential effects. Third, most of the studies included in the McKey et al. (1985) synthesis report noted earlier were conducted in the 1960s and 1970s. The GAO argues that Head Start programs and populations have changed significantly since this

period, thereby limiting the relevance of most prior studies. The GAO report concluded that the recent body of research on current Head Start is insufficient to draw conclusions about the impact of the program nationally (GAO, 1997).

Currently Head Start is supporting an ambitious research agenda that includes an experimental (random assignment), longitudinal study of Head Start and Early Head Start program effects, plus a range of other research projects designed to inform improvements in program effectiveness.

The Head Start Impact Study is a congressionally mandated investigation of Head Start contributions to key outcomes of development and learning and the conditions under which Head Start works best and for which children. Congressional approval of the study was based partly on the need to address the limitations of existing research information about Head Start noted in the GAO report. The Head Start Impact Study includes a nationally representative sample of approximately 5,000 Head Start–eligible children and their families with 3- and 4-year-old children who enrolled in Head Start in fall 2002. Children will be followed through the spring of their first-grade year.

The Early Head Start Research and Evaluation Project, initiated in 1995, focuses on 17 programs competitively selected by the Head Start Bureau to represent diverse program approaches, geographic locations, and participant backgrounds. Results when children were 36 months of age showed positive program impacts on children's cognitive, language, and socioemotional development, and on parents' interactions with their children during play and support of language and learning at home (e.g., more likely to read daily to their children) (Love et al., 2002). Currently the study is following children and their families as children enter kindergarten.

In addition to these two national outcome studies, the Head Start Bureau sponsors the

Head Start Family and Child Experiences Survey (FACES), a study of 3,200 children and families in some 40 Head Start programs aimed at describing characteristics, experiences, and outcomes for children and families in Head Start and after a year in kindergarten. It also supports research on program practices designed to promote school readiness.

Head Start's research agenda is guided by an Advisory Committee on Head Start Research and Evaluation established by the Secretary of Health and Human Services. The committee is comprised of individuals with expertise in program evaluation and research, education, and early childhood programs.

DEMONSTRATION PROJECTS

Head Start serves as a national field laboratory for the development of innovative approaches to working with young children and their families. Most of these demonstration programs have been developed in response to the changing circumstances of families. Two of these family focused efforts are described here. In recent years, child care and steps toward self-sufficiency have emerged as pressing needs of low-income families. Head Start's response to these needs through the development of demonstration programs also is described here.

Child Care and Family Self-Sufficiency

Child care is a pressing need in the United States as growing numbers of mothers enter school or the paid labor force when their children are young. For low-income families, welfare reform policies have escalated the need for child care due to job training and work requirements now imposed on parents who receive welfare benefits. In 1996–1997, 39% of families enrolled in Head Start needed child care for children enrolled in the program. Of those, 25% received child care through the Head Start program or its parent agency. About one half of all Head Start programs provide some form of full-day services to families who need child-care services.

In 1997, Head Start launched an initiative aimed at building partnerships with child-care providers and, in some communities, to deliver full-day, full-year Head Start services. Ways to combine Head Start and child care have been in development for some time, however, and a 1996 publication by the Children's Defense Fund offers profiles of some 23 programs across the country that are creatively combining Head Start and child-care services (Poersch & Blank, 1996).

The most common model is for child care to wrap around a part-day Head Start program. Under this arrangement, the part-day Head Start classroom maintains its identity and autonomy, with child-care services provided before and after the Head Start day and on days when Head Start is not in session. Continuity of experience for the child is potentially strengthened when a single agency offers both Head Start and the wrap-around child-care program. An alternative model is for Head Start services (e.g., health and family support services) to be provided at a child-care center. Programs that have expanded Head Start to be a full-day, full-year service typically have tapped child-care subsidies and other funding sources such as United Way subsidies in order to supplement Head Start funding (Bancroft, 1997).

Head Start also has experimented with supports for family child-care homes. Eighteen Head Start family child-care demonstration projects began in 1992 to determine whether Head Start Performance Standards could be met in family child-care homes through additional training and support services. An experimental study was undertaken to compare the impact on children and families in family child care with those participating in center-based classroom programs. Participating families had a 4-year-old child and the parent was required to be working, in job training, or in school.

Results indicated that there were no significant differences between Head Start family child-care homes and centers on quality indicators except the centers surpassed the family child-care homes in Head Start indicators of parent involvement. The children assigned to family child care performed at least as well as children in centers on measures of cognitive, socioemotional, and physical development (Faddis, Ryer, & Gabriel, 1997).

In addition to child care, welfare reform policies have major implications for Head Start's role in helping adults gain meaningful job skills. Head Start's parent involvement practices have long provided opportunities for parents to secure experiences in leadership skills (i.e., through the policy group and contributions to curriculum planning), guiding and nurturing children (i.e., through classroom volunteering), and ways to strengthen personal resourcefulness (i.e., through parenting education classes on life skills). The program also has served as the first step toward an educational or human services career for thousands of parents via volunteer or paid employment in a local Head Start program.

Recently several Head Start demonstration projects have given systematic attention to ways in which self-sufficiency can be supported through Head Start parent involvement. An example is the Step Up demonstration program in Chicago where all Head Start activities and experiences for parents are viewed as incremental steps in a "ladder" to self-sufficiency. The program is based on the lesson that leaving welfare is not an event but a "long and difficult process that involves false starts, setbacks, and incremental gains" (Herr, Halpern, & Majeske, 1995, pp. 165–166). Volunteer activities in the Head Start program are viewed as a progression of increasingly work-like demands as a step toward job readiness, for instance, and basic responsibilities of parents in the program (e.g., picking up child on time) are seen as an important foundation for building job skills (see Herr et al., 1995).

Comprehensive Approaches to Supporting Families

Head Start has built on its strong commitment to parent involvement by designing and implementing several demonstration programs aimed at testing innovative and comprehensive approaches to family support. These include the Parent-Child Centers, and the Child and Family Resource Centers, among others.

The Parent-Child Centers began in 1967 as Head Start's first experimental effort to serve children from birth to age 3 years and their families. Lessons learned in the Parent-Child Centers provided one of the bases of the Early Head Start program launched in 1995. From the outset, the Parent-Child Centers were designed to meet the needs of individual communities; as a result, each of the 36 original demonstration programs was quite different from the others in program design and methods. At the time of their initial development in the late 1960s, the Parent-Child Centers were the first national effort to focus on families with children under 3 years of age. The goals included strengthening family organization and functioning in order to maximize young children's developmental potential (Lazar, Anchel, Beckman, Gethard, Lazar, & Sale, 1970). In 1970, three Parent-Child Centers became the focus of an experimental study aimed at investigating different approaches to early intervention with parents and very young children. These centers were known as the Parent and Child Development Centers, and were based in Houston, New Orleans, and Birmingham, Alabama. Each implemented a different strategy of education and support for parenting during the early years of life. In the Houston model, for example, a year of home visits was followed by center-based activities for both mother and child. Careful evaluations found positive program effects on mothers' child-rearing skills and children's cognitive functioning (Andrews et al., 1982).

The Child and Family Resource Centers provided Head Start's "purest example of an early model family support program" (Zigler & Freedman, 1987, p. 64). Center staff developed an individualized plan for meeting the unique needs of each enrolled family through a needs assessment and goal-setting process. The age of the target child was birth to age 8 years. Home visiting was a central component as well as coordination with a range of community services to address pressing family issues such as alcohol abuse, poor health, inadequate housing and health care, and unemployment. An evaluation found improvements in family circumstances but no significant effect on child outcomes (Travers, Nauta, & Irwin, 1982). The Child and Family Resource Centers were established in the 1970s and eventually phased out.

THE FUTURE OF HEAD START

Many challenges face Head Start at the turn of the century. Two superordinate tasks are the need to strengthen attention to children's school readiness skills and to programmatically respond to changes in the needs of low-income families.

Throughout its history, questions have been raised periodically about the quality and focus of Head Start's preparation of children for school success. President George W. Bush's education reform plans emphasize the need to prepare young children to read and succeed in school through improved early childhood programs, including Head Start. The Bush administration's strategies to strengthen Head Start, outlined in its Good Start, Grow Smart initiative, include a new accountability system to ensure that every Head Start program assesses standards of learning in early literacy, language, and numeracy skills (U.S. Department of Health and Human Services, 2004). The National Reporting System described earlier in this chapter is a core part of the accountability effort. The President's plan

also includes the STEP teacher education program described earlier and improved coordination with other early childhood programs and the public schools.

The growing emphasis on early reading skills has generated concern that Head Start's comprehensive focus, including dental care, immunizations, nutrition, and family support services, will erode in favor of attention to children's literacy and school readiness experiences in classrooms. There also is concern that outcome assessments will drive curriculum emphases through "teaching to the test" practices. Head Start's challenge is to embrace literacy and school readiness goals in an approach that fully recognizes that positive growth in all developmental domains coupled with a range of appropriately focused support services contribute to early success in school.

Head Start also must grapple with the changing needs of families in poverty. Today's low-income families seeking to move off welfare generally need the following: full-day child care; services for infants and toddlers; systematic assistance with employment readiness; and sometimes with pressing family issues such as substance abuse and mental health; and more than 1 year of supportive assistance for child and family (Parker, Piotrkowski, Horn, & Greene, 1995). Clearly, Head Start has developed high-quality services in each of these areas. As described earlier, Head Start is responding to the realities of welfare reform policies by strengthening its ability to provide or arrange for full-day child care for families and by considering ways Head Start can more systematically support the development of job readiness skills among parents. These efforts are not widespread or universally available to families. The services noted above are lodged in a relatively small number of programs and/or not available with sufficient intensity due to heavy caseloads for staff. Head Start remains primarily a part-day program for 4-year-old children. It is costly yet essential to contemplate the infusion of these services into the mainstream of Head Start.

A related challenge is the availability of parents for Head Start's parent involvement opportunities. Quite simply, parents' ability to participate in Head Start programs under the current period of welfare reform appears to be reduced by the competing requirements of job training and work responsibilities. A recent study of two Head Start programs, where the majority of parents received Temporary Assistance to Needy Families (TANF) benefits, found that parents' participation in activities aimed at self-sufficiency—working, going to school, or job training—was associated with less involvement in Head Start. The study also found that parents wanted more job-related training offered through Head Start (Parker, Piotrkowski, Kessler-Sklar, Baker, Peay, & Clark, 1997).

Creative responses to these challenges will require Head Start to capitalize on its status as the "birthplace of comprehensive services in a family setting" (Zigler & Muenchow, 1992, p. 243). Head Start needs to retain and strengthen its role as a national laboratory for developing new models of innovative programs for children and their families. Strong partnerships with other institutions and resources in local communities are essential in these efforts. No matter how comprehensive or well administered, Head Start can only do so much to combat the poor prenatal care and nutrition, inadequate housing, crime-ridden neighborhoods, and racial and gender discrimination that affect the lives of many families living in poverty. Head Start is not a "panacea for poverty" (Washington & Oyemade Bailey, 1995, p. 141). It is, however, a demonstrated leader in mobilizing the energies of diverse institutions in communities on behalf of young children. Improvements in children's development and learning outcomes require not only stimulating classrooms and supportive parent–child relationships, but also communities that genuinely care about children, families, and their environments.

REFERENCES

Andrews, S. R., Blumenthal, J. B., Johnson, D. L., Kahn, A. J., Ferguson, C. J., Lasater, R. M., Malone, P. E., & Wallace, D. B. (1982). The skills of mothering: A study of Parent Child Development Centers. *Monographs of the Society for Research in Child Development, 47* (6, Serial No. 198).

Bancroft, J. (1997, June/July). Strategies for Head Start-child care partnerships. *National Head Start Bulletin, 62,* 3–4.

Baratz, S. S., & Baratz, J. C. (1970). Early childhood intervention: The social science base of institutional racism. *Harvard Educational Review, 48,* 161–170.

Barnett, W. S. (1993). Benefit–cost analysis of preschool education: Findings from a 25-year follow-up. *American Journal of Orthopsychiatry, 63,* 500–508.

Berrueta-Clement, J. R., Schweinhart, L. J., Barnett, W. S., Epstein, A. S., & Weikart, D. P. (1984). Changed lives: The effects of the Perry Preschool Program on youths through age 19. *Monographs of the High/Scope Educational Research Foundation Number 8*. Ypsilanti, MI: High/Scope Press.

Bloom, B. S. (1964). *Stability and change in human characteristics*. New York: Wiley.

Bredekamp, S., & Copple, C. (Eds.). (1997). *Developmentally appropriate practice in early childhood programs*. Rev. ed. Washington, DC: NAEYC.

Bronfenbrenner, U. (1974). *Is early intervention effect? A report on longitudinal evaluations of preschool programs*. (Vol. 2). Washington, DC: Office of Child Development, Department of Health, Education and Welfare.

Bronfenbrenner, U., & Morris, P. A. (1998). The ecology of developmental processes. In W. Damon (Ed.), R. M. Lerner (Vol. ed.), *Handbook of child psychology*, 5th ed., Vol. 1: *Theoretical models of human development* (pp. 993–1028). New York: Wiley.

Campbell, D. T., & Erlebacher, A. (1970). How regression artifacts in quasi-experimental evaluations can make compensatory education look harmful. In J. Hellmuth (Ed.), *Compensatory education: A national debate* (pp. 185–200). New York: Brunner/Mazel.

Faddis, B., Ryer, P., & Gabriel, R. (1997). *Cohort 2 report: Evaluation of Head Start family child care homes.* Portland, OR: RMC Research Corp.

Government Accounting Office (1994). *Early childhood programs: Many poor children and strained resources challenge Head Start.* Washington, DC: Author.

Government Accounting Office. (1997). *Head Start: Research provides little information on impact of current program.* Washington, DC: Author.

Gray, S. W., & Klaus, R. A. (1965). An experimental preschool program for culturally deprived children. *Child Development, 36,* 887–898.

Greenberg, P. (1990). Before the beginning: A participant's view. *Young Children, 45,* 41–52.

Head Start Bureau. (1997). *Head Start program performance standards and other regulations.* Washington, DC: Head Start Bureau, Administration on Children, Youth and Families, U.S. Department of Health and Human Services.

Herr, T., Halpern, R., & Majeske, R. (1995). Bridging the worlds of Head Start and welfare-to-work: Building a two-generation self-sufficiency program from the ground up. In S. Smith (Vol. ed.), I. E. Sigel (Series ed.), *Two generation programs for families in poverty: A new intervention strategy. Advances in Applied Developmental Psychology, Vol. 9* (pp. 161–197). Norwood, NJ: Ablex.

Hunt, J. McV. (1961). *Intelligence and experience.* New York: Ronald Press.

Keniston, K., & Carnegie Council on Children. (1977). *All our children: The American family under pressure.* New York: Harcourt Brace Jovanovich.

Kirschner Associates. (1970). *A national survey of the impacts of Head Start centers on community institutions.* Albuquerque, NM: Author.

Labov, W. (1970). The logic of nonstandard English. In F. Williams (Ed.), *Language and poverty* (pp.153–189). Chicago: Markham.

Lally, J. R., & Keith, H. (1997, October/November). Early Head Start: The first two years. *Zero to Three, 18,* 3–8.

Lazar, I., Anchel, G., Beckman, L., Gethard, E., Lazar, J., & Sale, J. (1970). *A national survey of the Parent-Child Center program.* Washington, DC: Kirschner.

Lee, V. E., Brooks-Gunn, J., & Schnur, E. (1988). Does Head Start work? A 1-year follow-up comparison of disadvantaged children attending Head Start, no preschool, and other preschool programs. *Developmental Psychology, 24,* 210–222.

Love, J. M., Kisker, E. E., Ross, C. M., Schochet, P. Z., Brooks-Gunn, J., Paulsell, D., Boller, K., Constantine, J., Vogel, C., Fuligni, A. S., & Brady-Smith, C. (2002). *Making a difference in the lives of infants and toddlers and their families: The impacts of Early Head Start.* Washington, DC: U.S. Department of Health and Human Services.

McKey, R. H., Condelli, L., Ganson, H., Barrett, B. J., McConkey, C., & Plantz, M. C. (1985, June). *The impact of Head Start on children, families, and communities. Final report of the Head Start Evaluation, Synthesis, and Utilization Project.* Washington, DC: CSR.

Parker, F. L., Piotrkowski, C. S., Horn, W. F., & Greene, S. M. (1995). The challenge for Head Start: Realizing its vision as a two-generation program. In S. Smith (Vol. ed.), I. Sigel (Series ed.), *Two generation programs for families in poverty: A new intervention strategy. Advances in Applied Developmental Psychology, Vol. 9* (pp. 135–159). Norwood, NJ: Ablex.

Parker, F. L., Piotrkowski, C. S., Kessler-Sklar, S., Baker, A. J. L., Peay, L., & Clark, B. (1997). *Parent involvement in Head Start. Final report.* New York: Center for the Child, National Council of Jewish Women.

Phillips, D. A., & Cabrera, N. J. (Eds.). (1996). *Beyond the blueprint: Directions for research on Head Start's families.* Washington, DC: National Academy Press.

Poersch, N. O., & Blank, H. (1996). *Working together for children: Head Start and child care partnerships.* Washington, DC: Children's Defense Fund.

Richmond, J. B., Stipek, D. J., & Zigler, E. (1979). A decade of Head Start. In E. Zigler & J. Valentine (Eds.), *Project Head Start: A legacy of the War on Poverty* (pp. 135–152). New York: Free Press.

Ryan, W. (1971). *Blaming the victim.* New York: Pantheon Books.

Schweinhart, L. J., Barnes, H. V., & Weikart, D. P. (1993). Significant benefits: The High/Scope Perry Preschool Study through age 27. *Monographs of the High/Scope Educational Research Foundation Number 10.* Ypsilanti, MI: High/Scope Press.

Smith, M. S., & Bissell, J. S. (1970). The impact of Head Start: The Westinghouse-Ohio Head Start Evaluation. *Harvard Educational Review, 40,* 51–104.

Travers, J., Nauta, M., & Irwin, N. (1982). *The effects of a social program: Final report of the Child and Family Resource Program's infant–toddler component.* Cambridge, MA: Abt Associates.

U.S. Department of Health and Human Services. (2004, January 16). *Good Start, Grow Smart: The Bush administration's early childhood initiative.* Retrived January 27, 2004, from http:// www.nccic.org/pubs/ literacy/ gsgs.html.

Washington, V., & Oyemade Bailey, U. J. (1995). *Project Head Start: Models and strategies for the twenty-first century.* New York: Garland.

Westinghouse Learning Corporation. (1969, June). *The impact of Head Start: An evaluation of the effects of Head Start on children's cognitive and affective development.* Athens: Ohio University, and New York: Westinghouse Learning Corp.

Zigler, E. (1998). By what goals should Head Start be assessed? *Children's Services: Social Policy, Research, and Practice, 1,* 5–17.

Zigler, E., & Anderson, K. (1979). An idea whose time had come: The intellectual and political climate for Head Start. In E. Zigler & J. Valentine (Eds.), *Project Head Start: A legacy of the War on Poverty* (pp. 3–19). New York: Free Press.

Zigler, E. F., & Freedman, J. (1987). Head Start: A pioneer of family support. In S. L. Kagan, D. R. Powell, B. Weissbourd, & E. F. Zigler (Eds.), *America's family support programs: Perspectives and prospects* (pp. 57–76). New Haven, CT: Yale University Press.

Zigler, E., & Muenchow, S. (1992). *Head Start: The inside story of America's most successful educational experiment.* New York: Basic Books.

Zigler, E., & Valentine, J. (1979). *Project Head Start: A legacy of the War on Poverty.* New York: Free Press.

Chapter 4

The Portage Model: An International Home Approach to Early Intervention of Young Children and Their Families

David E. Shearer ∾ The International Portage Association, Civitan International Research Center, University of Alabama at Birmingham
Darlene L. Shearer ∾ Lawton and Rhea Chiles Center for Healthy Mothers and Babies, University of South Florida

∾ INTRODUCTION

The past 3 decades have seen a dramatic increase in both the number of programs devoted to early intervention for young children and the amount of financial and human resources dedicated to such efforts. Early intervention services are mandated by the U.S. government for young children with developmental disabilities. State and local education systems have the option to also provide such services to young children who are at risk for developmental disabilities. These mandated services are very complex and continue to evolve into a comprehensive early intervention system. The system is currently regulated by Public Law 105-17 (the amendments to the Individuals with Disabilities Education Act, 1997). Such legislation has set the precedent that parents and families will be involved in all facets of services that are planned, implemented, and evaluated for their young children. Additionally, it mandates that services be provided in the child's least restrictive or natural learning environment. There continues to be much discussion regarding what constitutes the least-restrictive environment for older, school-age children with

disabilities. However, for very young children, the general consensus is that the most natural learning environment is the home or a child-care setting.

The target population of early intervention includes young children and their families. Providing an intervention program for young children with a disability and directly involving their parents has become a common practice (Odom & Karnes, 1988). As early as 1978, the U.S. Department of Health and Human Services (HHS), the governmental body that has provided the resources and much of the impetus for the early childhood programs in the United States, recognized the importance of parent involvement when it announced greater steps would be taken in the future to assure parental involvement in the education of children. These steps included a stronger role for parent–teacher projects, parent advisory bodies, and development of educational materials for use in the home. Today parent programs abound in the early intervention field. In the United States and internationally, the young child, the parent, and the educational program designed to meet the needs of the child are recognized as interdependent elements in the development of the society in which they exist (Weisner, 1998).

Two important principles in the study of early educational interventions for children at risk for delayed or retarded cognitive development are timing and intensity. The summative results concerning these principles are clear: high-quality, intensive educational efforts beginning early in life lead to greater cognitive gains among early intervention participants than do programs that are either less intensive or that begin later in life (Ramey & Ramey, 1992). Results from a large, nationally representative, randomized intervention trial suggest that intellectual development of young children is associated with the additive effects of intervention components (in this case, the number of home visits, days attended at child centers, and the number of meetings parents attended) and not with children's background characteristics (i.e., maternal education, birth weight) (Blair, Ramey, & Hardin, 1995). The findings suggest a dose–response relation between intervention and outcome, that the quantity of child and parent participation is of major importance for the development of cognitive skills. In these examples, there is ample evidence that an intense home-intervention program that serves children in the early years of development and emphasizes direct parent participation helps to ensure successful outcomes.

The Portage model, since its introduction in 1969, has emphasized the importance of a strong parental role and gives parents the opportunity to be their child's primary interventionist and teacher in partnership with an intervention program. The Portage model has developed, implemented, and demonstrated a highly successful intervention strategy. The model is a home-based delivery system centering on the entire family and a home teacher who helps the caregivers become more effective teachers/nurturers of their children. (The term *home teacher* will be used throughout this chapter and is intended as a generic description of a function rather than referring to a professional discipline.)

The basic premises of the model as they relate to parents and families are:

- Families care about and want their child to attain maximum potential, however great or limited that potential may be.
- With instruction, modeling, and reinforcement families will become more effective teachers/nurturers of their child.
- The socioeconomic and educational or intellectual levels of families do not necessarily determine either their willingness to teach their child or the extent of gains the child will attain as a result of parental instruction.

The precision teaching method is the preferred model because feedback is provided daily to the family and weekly to the staff, thereby reinforcing both when goals are met. Moreover, the method provides a continual data base for curriculum modification, thus maximizing the likelihood of success for families and children.

Rationale for Active Parent Participation

There were many important reasons that developers of the model chose to emphasize direct involvement of parents in the intervention model. These include:

- Parents are consumers. They pay, either directly or indirectly, for the program and the service their child receives. Most parents want a voice in what and how their child is taught and they want to participate in the teaching of their child.
- Parents, if knowledgeable about the program their child is receiving, can be the best advocates for program continuation and expansion. School boards, advisory councils, and state legislatures throughout the United States have substantially

Teaching and modeling by the home teacher help parent and child to develop an effective instructional style.

changed policy and laws as a direct result of parental advocacy.

- Family support is a dynamic system that includes those interactions and interventions that strengthen the integrity of the family unit.
- Parents of a child with a disability usually have more responsibility for their child over a significantly longer period of time than parents of a typically developing child.
- Parents serve as a vital resource to the center- or home-based staff in the area of functional program objectives for the child that will be useful in the child's home environment.
- Transferring learning from the classroom to the home has been an acknowledged problem that occurs because of insufficient or ineffective communication between the family and the program staff. Thus, planned consistency between the educational program and the educational experiences provided by the family is vitally important.

- Parent involvement can greatly accelerate the child's rate of learning. The degree of parental participation is positively related to cognitive development.

Rationale for a Home-Based Approach

As mentioned earlier, one of the key premises of an effective early intervention program is intensity (Blair et al., 1995). A home-based approach with active family participation provides the potential for daily, and sometimes hourly teaching, maintenance, and generalization of intervention opportunities. Additional rationales for using a home-based approach include:

- Learning occurs in the family's and child's natural environment, hence the need is eliminated for transfer of learned concepts from classroom or clinic to the home and daily routines.
- Home intervention allows for direct and constant access to behavior as it occurs

naturally. This is more likely to result in curriculum goals that are functional for the child within the child's own unique environment. In fact, the differences in cultures, lifestyles, and value systems held by the family are incorporated into the curriculum planning, because the family will make the final determination of what and how their child will be taught.

- Learned behaviors are more likely to generalize and be maintained if they have been learned in the child's home environment and have been taught by the child's natural reinforcing agents, the family.
- Instruction in the home offers more opportunity for full family participation in the teaching process. Father, sibling, and extended family involvement becomes realistic and obtainable goals.
- The home provides access to a fuller range of behaviors, many of which could not be targeted for modification within a classroom (e.g., having temper tantrums that only occur in the home or crawling into bed with parents each night).
- Training parents, who already are natural reinforcing agents, provides them with the skills necessary to deal with new child behaviors as they occur.
- Finally, individualization of instructional goals for the parents and child is an operational reality because the home teacher is working on a one-to-one basis with both.

✍ THE PORTAGE MODEL

The three principal ingredients that constitute the major content of the Portage model are: (a) parental involvement, (b) home-based programming, and (c) use of the precision teaching method (see Figure 4.1). The effectiveness of the components of the model have been documented over the past 30 years (Bagnato & Murphy, 1989; Bijou, 1983, 1991; Brinker & Lewis, 1982; Cameron, 1986, 1990; Jellnek, 1985; Miller,

1990; Muelen van der & Sipma, 1991; D. E. Shearer, 1991, 1995; Shearer & Shearer, 1972; Shearer & Shearer, 1976; Shearer & Snider, 1981; Thorburn, 1997; White, 1997). These components are now recognized as essential components by most successful intervention programs today and to some degree have been adapted or adopted as recommended practice (Blechman, 1984; Dunst, Trivette, & Mott, 1994; Hoyson, Jamieson, & Strain, 1984; Robinson, Rosenberg, & Beckman, 1988; Rosenberg, Robinson, & Beckman, 1984; D. E. Shearer, 1993; Shearer & Loftin, 1984; Shelton & Stepanek, 1994; Sturmey et. al., 1992; Thorburn, 1997; USGAO, 1990; Wasik, Bryant, & Lyons, 1990).

Parents as Primary Teachers

From its inception, Portage has emphasized the parent's role as the child's primary teacher. The rationale for this emphasis is that parents are the child's first teacher, a concept well supported in the literature (Bijou, 1991; Cameron, 1990; Eiserman, Weber, & McCoun, 1995; Kohli, 1991; Shearer & Loftin, 1984, 1993; Thorburn, 1992, 1997; Yamaguchi, 1988). Parents as teachers can motivate children, can reinforce newly acquired skills at home, and can provide valuable information for others working with the child (Bailey & Wolery, 1984; Cameron, 1990; White, 1997). The potential for larger and longer-lasting effects in the child increases because of the amount of time spent with the parent and the amount of reinforcement opportunity. In other words, the intensity of the intervention increases when the parent serves as the child's primary teacher. Intensity is a critical element often missing in early intervention demonstrations that fail to show positive effects on intellectual, academic, or social performance of the child (Hebbeler & Gerlach-Downie, 2002; Ramey, Ramey, Gaines, & Blair, 1995).

The question of whether all parents are capable of or want to serve as the child's primary

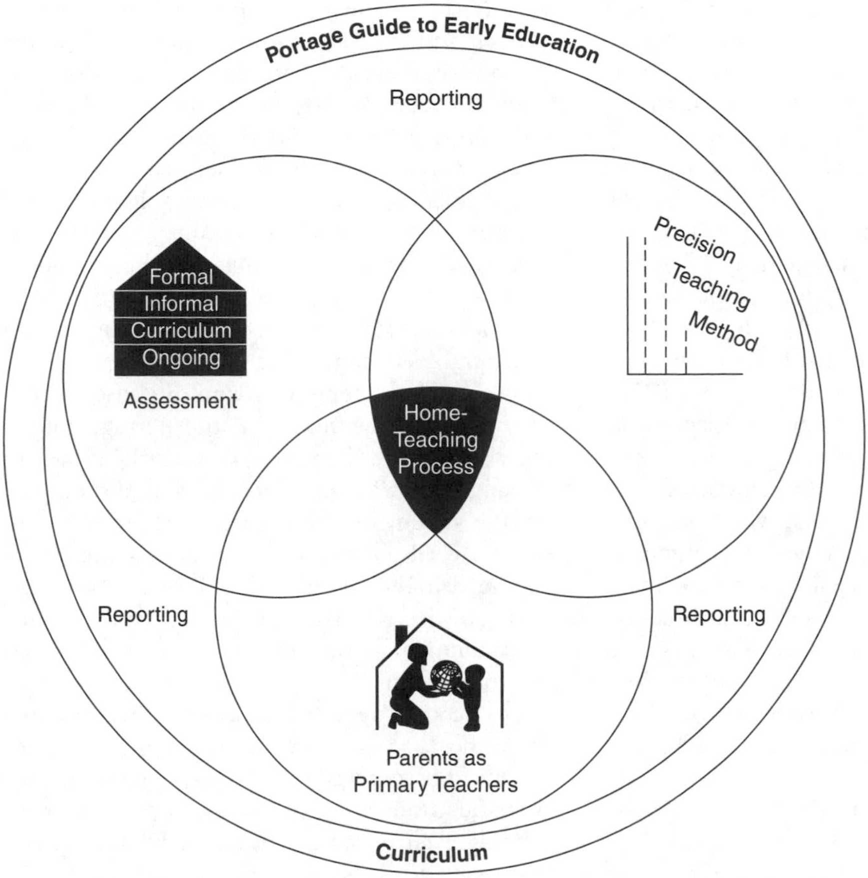

FIGURE 4–1
Components of the
Portage Model

teacher is a valid concern. However, empirical studies suggest that successful intervention gains in very young children are directly related to the level or degree of parent participation (Johnson, et al., 2000; Ramey & Ramey, 1992; Wasik et al., 1990). Involvement should be viewed as a continuum along which parents can progress based on their individual need and circumstance and with the expectation that they do not wish to remain static at any given point.

Assessment Procedures

Systematic measurement of the child's developmental status is a critical component in Portage

and occurs through four types of assessment procedures: formal (e.g., a standardized instrument such as the Alpern–Boll Developmental Profile II), informal (e.g., observation), curriculum based (e.g., The Portage Checklist), and ongoing assessment. Information from these procedures provides the means by which a curriculum can be developed to meet the child's individual needs. During formal assessment, standardized instruments are used to assess strengths and needs of the individual child. A number of formal instruments are available. Some of the most popular instruments, however, do not yield information about the child's specific developmental domains. Deficiencies of this nature make it difficult to obtain before and after measures of progress or to evaluate a program's overall effectiveness. Some practitioners have confused curriculum assessment methods (e.g., the Portage Checklist) with formal assessment and have used the checklist to document developmental status rather than to develop teaching goals for the child. Distinction between formal and curriculum assessment is critical to understanding the intent of this component.

To facilitate planning for individual children, the *Portage Guide to Early Education* (Bluma, Shearer, Frohman, & Hilliard, 1976) was devised. This curriculum guide, for use with children functioning between birth and 6 years of age, consists of a manual of instructions, a sequential checklist of behaviors, which includes five areas of development (cognitive, language, self-help, motor, and socialization), an infant stimulation section, and a set of curriculum cards to match each of the 580 behaviors stated on the checklist. The cards contain suggestions on materials and teaching procedures, along with task breakdowns to assist teachers in individualized programming.

The checklist is used to pinpoint the behaviors the child already exhibits in the developmental areas. The behaviors on the checklist that indicate emerging skills (unlearned behaviors immediately following learned behaviors) are areas that the teacher may wish to target for learning. The user can then refer to the matching cards in the deck that states the goal in behavioral terms and suggests materials and methods for teaching the skill. These materials can only serve as a guide for the teacher and parent. Fully 50% of behaviors actually prescribed for children are not found on the checklist, but they may well be a behavior leading to a long-term goal that is listed on the checklist. Thus, many behaviors listed can be thought of as long-term goals that often need to be divided into smaller behavioral segments. These can then be chained together to achieve the long-term goal. Consequently, the child not the checklist determines the curriculum.

It should be noted, however, that professionals and staff sometimes confuse the Portage home-based model with the Portage materials and curriculum. For clarification of this discussion, the Portage model is not the *Portage Guide to Early Education*. The popularity of the Portage curriculum lies within its simplicity and practicality—essential points for the many cultures and languages to which it has been adapted (see D. E. Shearer, 1991; Thorburn, 1997; Yamaguchi, 1988). The success in producing measurable change in a child's development, however, has stemmed from the use of the *Portage Guide* within the entire Portage model, specifically the benchmarks described in this chapter. The *Portage Guide* is an important part of the system but not central to the model. In other words, the Portage model is the entire home visitation model with all of the processes that are described in this chapter and not just curriculum materials that have been developed by the project.

Use and supplementation of other curricula with the *Portage Guide* has occurred because of the need to apply the model to populations with specific disabilities or needs and because of urgent need to systematically revise and update the materials. It is the authors' belief that, in the context and presence of the other components of the Portage Model, such substitutes and supplements expand the application of the model rather than hinder it.

An important change in early intervention assessment practice is the expansion of the focus of assessment beyond the individual child. The interrelatedness and impact of family support and the home environment upon the child's developmental outcome has been widely discussed (e.g., Bailey et al., 1988; Bradley & Caldwell, 1984; Bronfenbrenner, 1979; Dunst, Trivette, & Deal, 1988; Dunst et al., 1994; Ramey et al., 1992; Ramey & Shearer, in press; Turnbull et al., 1993). Consequently, comprehensive assessment includes a survey of family concerns and available resources as well as evaluation of key elements of the child's environment. The shift to a broader concept of assessment compels users of Portage to consider the additional training needs of their staff. The authors' experiences in training home teachers have shown that helping staff to develop accurate and unbiased observation skills requires significant time and effort.

Precision-Teaching Method

Precision teaching is an established paradigm based on behavioral principles and has been particularly successful with children with disabilities (Hallahan & Kauffman, 1976; Stephens, 1976). The method is based on the work of Lindsley and utilizes a set of simple but effective procedures that home teachers follow to identify, monitor, and make decisions about critical skills or behaviors a child needs to acquire (Lindsley, 1968). The procedure includes (1) precise operational definitions of the specific behaviors to teach, (2) task analysis to break down complex skills into smaller units, or subskills, (3) direct teaching methods that require practice of the new skill many times, and (4) direct daily measurement to monitor progress and evaluate the intervention.

Development proceeds rapidly during the first years of a child's life. Intervention approaches that facilitate development are heavily based on theory and methodology and support a tendency toward trial and error. Infants and young children cannot afford to wait 3 to 6 months to see if a particular intervention is successful. Hence precision teaching reduces the use of trial and error. It emphasizes watching and recording behavior to identify the unique strengths or problems of the child and recording the responses to determine results of the intervention. The likelihood of success is greatly enhanced with this method of teaching. Precision teaching is particularly advantageous when using paraprofessional or less experienced staff. It allows supervisors to specify where problems

occurred and determine why a particular approach did or did not work.

Home-Teaching Process

The centrality of the home-teaching process to other components of the Portage model (see Figure 4.1) is not by accident. It is the heart and soul of Portage, the point at which all of the components converge and where successful intervention occurs (Shearer & Shearer, 1995). The home-teaching process has four critical steps as demonstrated in Figure 4.2.

Approximately two to three behaviors or tasks are targeted for learning each week. The behaviors and criteria for success are chosen with the goal that the child (and also the family) will achieve success in one week.

1. The home visitor enters the home and takes post-baseline on the previous week's activities.
2. After discussion and planning with the family, the home teacher introduces the new tasks for the coming week. The home teacher models the teaching techniques for the parent and takes baseline data on the new tasks.
3. The parent then models the teaching activity back in the presence of the home teacher to ensure that there are no misunderstandings about the tasks or techniques to be used and to ensure that the parents feel comfortable conducting the tasks.
4. Other concerns or problems are discussed and input regarding future tasks is given by the parents.

Following both formal and informal assessment, the home teacher will suggest two or three behaviors that are emerging and could be prescribed. The parents also make suggestions of emerging behaviors they wish to see targeted. The home teacher, with the parents, writes the chosen goal(s) as a behavioral objective,

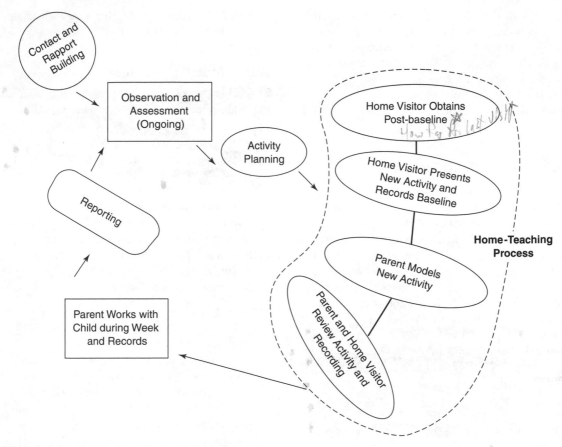

FIGURE 4–2 The Portage Home Visitation Model

together with directions, on an activity chart. Prescriptions are written with the goal that the parents and child will succeed on each prescribed task within a week. As parents experience success and gain confidence in their ability to teach their child and record the child's progress, prescriptions are gradually increased to three or four per week. These activities are often in several areas of development. For instance, the parent might be working on reducing tantrums, buttoning, and counting all within the same week.

The home teacher writes the activity chart incorporating the selection of targeted behaviors. Again, the most important point is for the

home teacher to break the tasks down and prescribe only those that can be achieved within a week. This provides the parents with rapid reinforcement because what the child learns is a direct result of parental teaching. The directions are precisely written so that the parents will have no difficulty understanding them if they need to refer to them during the week. Recording is always uncomplicated and usually involves noting frequency of success.

After the activity is pinpointed, the home teacher introduces the activity to the child and records baseline data—the frequency of correct responses prior to instruction—on the activity chart. The home teacher then follows the direc-

Mother instructs her child at home, following the Portage model.

tions written on the chart and begins the teaching process. The home teacher thus is modeling teaching techniques for the parents, showing them what to do and how to do it. After several opportunities, the parent takes over and works with the child, modeling for the home teacher. The home teacher then is able to offer suggestions and reinforcement that increases the likelihood that the parents will carry out the activities during the week.

Throughout the visit, the home teacher stresses the importance of working with the child during the week. The home teacher leaves home and office phone numbers with the parents and encourages them to call if any questions or problems arise during the week. Every attempt is made to use materials available in the home. However, at times materials are brought in and left for the parents and child to use.

When the home teacher returns the following week, post-baseline data on the previous week's activities are collected. This helps the home teacher validate the accuracy of the parent's recording and provides feedback concerning the degree of success achieved by the child and the child's readiness for the next developmentally appropriate sequential step. Based on these data, the home teacher alters the previous

prescriptions or introduces new activities, beginning with taking baseline data. And so the cycle is repeated, weekly.

This is the sequence of the home visit process. It is the direct intervention phase of the entire home visit. However, in reality, in the beginning, intermediate or additional steps are sometimes necessary in the parent-teaching process. Parents are not all alike; thus it is important to individualize the teaching process for them. Even parents with cognitive limitations can successfully participate in the teaching process. In this case, activity charts are not used; however, parents still record using a specially adapted chart. Babysitters and other caregivers can also be effective teachers with this model. Parents, and even professionals, have said that they had almost given up hope for teaching children with severe disabilities, but with the help of task analysis and precision teaching, progress and learning become more tangible in a shorter period of time.

Data Collection and Accountability

Evaluation is an ongoing process in the Portage method. Activity charts left in the home are collected weekly. The home teacher reviews these charts and completes a weekly progress report. Prescribed behaviors from the previous week, determination of whether the child has attained the criteria needed for success, and prescriptions for the coming week are all recorded on the weekly progress report (usually found on the back of the activity chart). A behavior log is kept for each child and lists all activities, the developmental domain addressed, and the date they were prescribed. This log provides an ongoing record of every behavior prescribed, whether success was achieved, and the duration of each prescription. The log also provides a percentage of success achieved by parents, child, and home teacher. The continual input of data allows supervisory personnel and each home teacher to spot problems quickly, thus providing regular feedback for program monitoring and modification.

Portage Home Visits

Each Portage home visit includes three distinct phases: (a) direct intervention, focusing on the infant or child's developmental progress, review and demonstration of activities to be left in the home, practice and return demonstration by the parent, and discussion about the purpose and expected outcome of the tasks (this is referred to as the Home-Teaching Process); (b) informal interaction and play, which provides informal play activities and assistance to the mother in helping the infant and child to generalize and maintain learned activities by incorporation into daily routines; and (c) family support efforts, in which the home teacher serves as a sounding board for the mother, provides information and assistance as it is appropriate and asked for by the family, and gains further trust and rapport with the family. (See Figure 4.3.)

✍ RESEARCH AND EVALUATION OF THE PORTAGE MODEL

In the earlier implementations of the model, several types of evaluation were conducted to examine parent's ability to teach within the model and to determine what effect the teaching had on children's growth and development. In one study, activity charts were analyzed and pre- and post-testing were done on 75 children receiving Portage intervention. The overall rate of daily recording by families was 92% and an average of 128 prescriptions were written per child. The children themselves were successful on 91% of the prescriptions. These children began the intervention with an average IQ of 75, as determined by the Cattell Infant Scale and the Stanford–Binet Intelligence Test. Their average cognitive gain was 13 months mental age in an 8-month period (Shearer & Shearer, 1972).

Another study compared Portage intervention children with randomly selected children in local Head Start programs. The Stanford–Binet Intelligence Scale, the Cattell Infant Scale, and the Alpern–Boll Developmental Profile were used as pre- and post-measures for both groups. Multivariate analysis of covariance indicated that children in the Portage service model made greater gains in IQ, language, academic, and social skills compared with the group that received classroom instruction (Peniston, 1972).

The first replication evaluation involved 44 children with language impairments who had a mean language age of 36.9 months at pretest. Changes after 8 months of Portage intervention showed gains in Peabody Picture Vocabulary ages from 35.6 to 50.7 months and Alpern–Boll Communication subscale scores from 30.3 to 47.8 months. In 8 additional Portage replications, average Alpern–Boll IQ gains were 1.2- to 1.8-month mental age per month (Ghoca, 1972). Similar findings have been documented in Portage model replications in Finland (Arvio, Hautamaki, & Tilikka, 1993); India (Kohli & Datta, 1986; Kohli, 1988, 1991); Jamaica (Thorburn, Brown, & Bell, 1979); Japan (Yamaguchi, 1987, 1996); the Netherlands (Meulen van der & Sipma, 1991; Meulen van der & Bulsink, 1992); and the United Kingdom (e.g., Barna, Bidder, Gray, Clements, & Gardner, 1980; Revill & Blendon, 1979; White, 1997).

The most recent evaluation of the Portage model was conducted with children developmentally at risk served through the Society for the Care of the Handicapped in the Gaza Strip. The 268 children between ages 3 and 30 months were divided into experimental and control groups using a stratified design. Following a 3-year Portage program, the children in the experimental group, in contrast to those in the control group, exhibited significantly higher levels of personal, social, adaptive, motor, and language development as measured by the Developmental Profile II (Alpern, Boll, & Shearer, 1980) and the Batelle Developmental Inventory

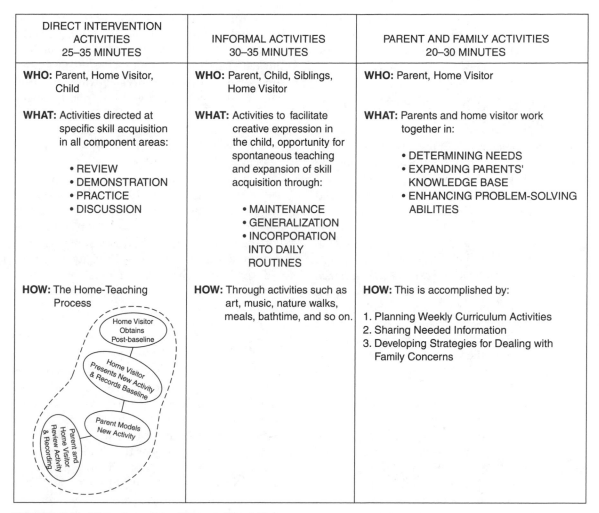

DIRECT INTERVENTION ACTIVITIES 25–35 MINUTES	INFORMAL ACTIVITIES 30–35 MINUTES	PARENT AND FAMILY ACTIVITIES 20–30 MINUTES
WHO: Parent, Home Visitor, Child	**WHO:** Parent, Child, Siblings, Home Visitor	**WHO:** Parent, Home Visitor
WHAT: Activities directed at specific skill acquisition in all component areas: • REVIEW • DEMONSTRATION • PRACTICE • DISCUSSION	**WHAT:** Activities to facilitate creative expression in the child, opportunity for spontaneous teaching and expansion of skill acquisition through: • MAINTENANCE • GENERALIZATION • INCORPORATION INTO DAILY ROUTINES	**WHAT:** Parents and home visitor work together in: • DETERMINING NEEDS • EXPANDING PARENTS' KNOWLEDGE BASE • ENHANCING PROBLEM-SOLVING ABILITIES
HOW: The Home-Teaching Process Home Visitor Obtains Post-baseline Home Visitor Presents New Activity & Records Baseline Parent Models New Activity Parent and Home Visitor Review Activity & Recording	**HOW:** Through activities such as art, music, nature walks, meals, bathtime, and so on.	**HOW:** This is accomplished by: 1. Planning Weekly Curriculum Activities 2. Sharing Needed Information 3. Developing Strategies for Dealing with Family Concerns

FIGURE 4–3   Three Parts of a Portage Home Visit

(Newborg, Stock, & Wnek, 1988). Age and gender effects generally were not significant (Ghazaleh, Ghazaleh & Oakland, 1990).

Outcome studies are essential in demonstrating the efficacy of intervention models. However, numerous practical, ethical, and methodological difficulties surround the design of research in this arena, particularly as related to young children. Most of the early studies of Portage were conducted prior to today's current emphasis on methodological soundness and rigor. It must also be noted that, contrary to many recent intervention strategies, Portage was funded solely as a demonstration model and did not have research as a contingency or mission. In addition, the use of cognitive gain as the central measure of efficacy is no longer viewed as practical given our growing understanding of other family influences on children's development (i.e., parental attitudes, expectations, and parent–child interactions). In the case of Portage and its many adaptations, the authors support the continued need for stronger and more rigorous evaluation of the model.

✍ ADAPTATIONS AND APPLICATIONS OF PORTAGE

Having discussed the Portage model and the rationale behind its development, it is also important to demonstrate the model's utility and versatility by discussing varied adaptations and applications.

The Portage Parent Program

Early in its implementation stages, Portage model staff frequently expressed concern that a systematic procedure was needed to help parents become gradually less dependent on the home teacher and eventually assume full responsibility for determining the goals and nature of the child's early education. The parents often viewed the home teacher as the educational authority who visited once a week to tell them what to do for their child. Careful consideration was given to the best way to empower these parents to gradually become their child's best advocate and interventionist. As a result, the Portage Parent Program was developed, which includes a set of readings for parents, an instructor's manual, and a parent behavior inventory (Boyd, Stauber, & Bluma, 1977). The materials provide parents with more in-depth information about skills taught in the model.

To evaluate this approach a group of children and their parents was designated to receive the systematic parent training program in addition to the basic Portage model of home teaching. The Parent Program was specifically designed to encourage acquisition and generalization of parental teaching and management skills. The evaluation compared three groups of families: those receiving the supplemental parent training program, parents receiving the basic Portage model, and a nontreatment control group of parents with preschool children without exceptional educational needs. The results of the evaluation showed that both treatment groups produced superior performance on certain child and parent measures compared with the nontreatment control group (Boyd et al., 1977). The efficacy of the evaluation findings were attributed to the Portage model's use of precision teaching and modeling. The program's emphasis on more systematic parent training and parental involvement in the planning and implementation phases of the home-teaching process yielded modest but important gains above those noted for the Portage-only group. Furthermore, parent's acquisition and generalization of child management and teaching behaviors potentially benefitted not only the child with a disability but also the child's siblings.

Urban Applications

The Portage model was originally funded as an education program for preschool children in rural areas. Its initial success prompted additional federal funding in 1974 from the U.S. Bureau for the Education of the Handicapped (BEH) for replication of the model in a large urban area in the Midwest. The program, Operation Success, opened in Milwaukee and later served as the demonstration model for the Home Start Training Center to provide training and technical assistance to Head Start programs wishing to implement a home-based option. BEH funding also provided outreach training and technical assistance to programs throughout the United States to disseminate Portage model information and materials. Through these efforts, components of the Portage model were implemented by public schools, state institutions, and private facilities; in center-based and home-based settings; in major urban communities throughout the United States; and in programs serving a wide range of disability and need.

International Applications

Through continued dissemination, the Portage model has become well-known internationally. The curriculum guide has been translated into 35 languages and the model itself has been introduced into more than 90 countries. The model's family centered orientation, clearly defined and structured curriculum, and simplistic nature have great appeal to countries and programs with limited resources or experience in serving young children. A strength of the Portage model is that it can be tailored to individual needs: it offers a focus for action, and it can provide a counseling element for families who may feel that their life has been turned upside down and feel de-skilled and inadequate as a result (Russell, 1986, p. 74).

United Kingdom   Mollie White, of the UK National Portage Association (NPA), reports that Portage was first introduced into the UK in 1976 as the subject of a research evaluation led by Albert Kushlick, director of the Wessex Health Care Evaluation Research Team (Smith, Kushlick, & Glossop, 1977). A significant research aim was the design of an effective replication model within the UK context. Following extensive dissemination during the late 1970s and early 1980s, Portage services were established in a number of areas of the country, culminating in a successful bid for central government funding in 1986. Services are now established throughout the UK, funded primarily by local education authorities and health trusts with some involvement from nongovernment organizations.

In 1983, the UK became the first country to establish a National Portage Association representing individual parents, professionals, and services working with the Portage model. The association has taken a leading role in the campaign to establish Portage services throughout the UK. The association also supports standards of local service delivery through a program of training workshops linked to a Code of Practice agreed on by the membership. There are over 150 local Portage services presently registered with the UK National Portage Association. A register of accredited trainers, with current involvement in Portage service activities, is maintained by the association. The association conducts an annual conference attended by families and professionals where new ideas and developments within the Portage movement are shared. The association has recently developed the Portage Curriculum for Further Professional Development training modules. The NPA has also taken the initiative to revise the Basic Portage Workshop. This revision responds to the raised awareness of the dynamics of the individual family as the context for the support offered by Portage services.

Portage services in the UK are playing an increasingly active role in the newly established local Early Years and Childcare Development Partnerships. The demand for quality training has put Portage trainers in great demand in programs such as the Sure Start initiatives, which promotes a family centered approach (Hassall, Weston, & Raine, 2001; Wolfendale, 2001).

Japan   The Portage model was introduced in Japan in 1977 as an experimental study funded by the Japan Ministry of Welfare. During its introduction, the Portage checklist was revised to include fewer items (562), suggested activities on the curriculum cards were modified and illustrations of material, and teaching situations were added—all to accommodate linguistic and cultural differences. In Japan, the instruction to mothers of the Portage program takes place at educational facilities because the Japanese culture and difficult conditions hinder instruction in the home. Intervention visits are conducted weekly or biweekly. Parents bring their child to consult with Portage teachers and return home with new activities to practice. Recently, families living great distances from Portage centers have been offered home-teaching services through telephone consultation and correspondence. Effectiveness of the Japanese

Portage model has been studied since 1983, particularly at seven experimental centers around Tokyo. More than 1,000 children have received services in these centers; more than 60% of them with Down Syndrome. A cohort of 200 children has been followed and results suggest significant long-term developmental gains (Yamaguchi, 1996). A Japan Portage Association was founded in 1985. Today there are 1,200 registered members, representing parents and professionals, with 40 branches throughout the country.

India   Under the direction of Dr. Tehal Kohli, a major replication and adaptation of the Portage model was implemented in India in 1980 (Kohli, 1991). After the curriculum was translated and home teachers were trained, an experimental program was offered to children with a developmental quotient (DQ) less than 75. A majority of these originally targeted children joined regular schools after early intervention, significant developmental gains were documented, as measured on the 20 Point Program of India, and the model was deemed suitable for families living in rural and slum areas as well as for families who are illiterate. With help from UNICEF, India was able to adapt the Portage materials in Hindi and to develop Portage training for professionals, paraprofessionals, and nonprofessionals. Using home advisors, Anganwadi functionaries, and parents, a low-cost affordable model was developed for the urban slums of Chandigarh. Several workshops have been conducted to promote use of the model in other major cities in India. Use of Anganwadi, or nursery teachers, is one of India's adaptations to the model, because families living in the slums have such complex child-care issues and needs. Children targeted for intervention are frequently left at home in the care of siblings—often fewer than 8 years of age themselves. The Anganwadi centers provide a variety of services besides child-care and parent instruction. In 1994 the India Portage Association was formed.

Among this organization's main areas of emphasis is the training of preschool educators, research, clearing house for dissemination of material, and night-working services through the country.

Northern Europe   Multiple applications of Portage have sprung up in several European countries. In the Netherlands, two studies have been conducted using Portage methods. The first was with children and families with parent-child interaction problems rather than developmental delays. Child development activities were used to introduce appropriate skills for behavior management to parents. Both the parents and children responded positively with the children having significant gains in social and academic domains (Meulen van der & Bulsink, 1992). A second study conducted using Portage with children who had mental disabilities also documented cognitive gains (Meulen van der & Sipma, 1991). The researchers concluded that, with some modification of the curriculum and materials, the Portage model should be introduced throughout the rest of the Netherlands.

Cyprus   Demetrios Neophytou reports that there were not many early intervention services in Cyprus prior to Portage being introduced to the country in 1996. The Christos Stelios Ioannou Foundation made this initial phase possible with the financial support of Mr. Dakis Ioannou. The initial training was conducted in 1996 by the Headquarters of the International Portage Association (IPA). A pilot Portage project was implemented to test the applicability of the Model in Cyprus. This pilot was completed in 1999 and was formally evaluated by members of the IPA Headquarters. It was deemed a successful implementation of the model and received international recognition as a certified Portage program.

The Portage program in Cyprus is a legal foundation. A board of management is the policy-making body, while the program's administration is conducted through an advisory committee that has representation from governmental and private bodies such as the Ministry of Health, the Ministry of Education and Culture, the Ministry of Labor and Social Insurance, the Christos Stelios Ioannou Foundation, the Committee for the Protection of the Rights of Persons with Mental Handicap, and the Federation of Parents of Disabled Children.

The Cyprus Portage Foundation was registered as a nongovernmental organization, which enabled the Portage program to be a successful, self-sufficient program by bringing professionals and parents into a collective and coordinated effort to empower the families and offering them guidance in meeting the needs of children with disabilities in Cyprus.

Portage in Cyprus is in a process of rapid development and expansion in other major cities in the country. The Cyprus Portage Foundation, in cooperation with and with the financial support of the European Union, is working on a large bi-communal project, which will establish three new Portage programs in the areas of Limassol, Ayia Napa, and Paphos, as well as three in the Northern part of the island.

Latvia   Ineta and Valdis J Kursietis, officers of the Latvian Portage Association, report the Latvian Portage Association was established in June 1997 and is the first and only organization to offer early intervention services to preschool-age children with special needs in Latvia. Prior to the introduction of the Portage Model to Latvia, as in other post Soviet states, the education system lacked a special education training program that could be used for preschool children with mental and physical impairments. This void has been filled by the Portage model, which is based on the classical Portage system but is modified to suit national characteristics.

Currently the Latvian Portage Association is working with over 250 children and their families. Over 110 persons have attended Portage Basic Workshops in Latvia, and approximately

50% of them work as Portage Home Visitors, with the remainder working in other special needs institutions.

The Latvian Portage Model is characterized by the following components:

- It is a home-teaching model with the aim of preparing children for the earliest possible inclusion into the society of their peers.
- It is used with children with special needs who live at home with their families and whose parents follow the model within the home
- It now has a Portage Specialist training program with a certification awarded after the specialists have completed a series of intense Portage workshops.

The Portage work in Latvia is managed by the Latvian Portage association, which operates on a statutory basis as a nongovernmental organization. The association receives financing from the local government authorities where children and families receive Portage services.

The Association is currently working on various projects to expand and develop a common Portage early intervention network in Latvia by opening new regional center's in Liepaja, Daugavpils, and Gulbene, as well as the existing centers in Riga, Valmiera, and Cesis.

Turkey   Professor Mesude Atay indicates that the Hacettepe University in Ankara became interested in the Portage Project in 1989 when advised about the model from two representatives from UNESCO. In 1999, a workshop was conducted by the headquarters of the IPA staff, which gained the attention of many professionals working in special education programs in Turkey. Currently, the Early Childhood Care Development Project is working on techniques to assess the home environment and child-care practices in Turkey. The *Portage Guide* is one tool that will be used in this process. Plans for extending the use of the Portage model throughout Turkey are in progress.

The University of Hacettepe staff conducted a study to assess the applicability of the Portage model in Turkey (Guven, Bal, & Tugrul, 1998). Over 800 normal children and children with disabilities were included in the study. It was determined that it applied to typically developing children as well as children with disabilities. A follow-up study was conducted by the university to determine the applicability of the model throughout Turkey (Guven, Bal, Metin, & Atay, 2000). Currently, the university is conducting a study to test the applicability of the model with very low-birth-weight premature infants (Karaaslan & Bal, 2002). The Portage Association of Turkey was established in July 2003 as a nongovernmental organization. One of its major goals will be the expansion of Portage throughout Turkey via a trainer's model. This training will be provided by the headquarters of the International Portage Association.

Gaza Strip   In 1984, the Sun Day Care Center, sponsored by the Society for the Care of the Handicapped in the Gaza Strip, introduced a massive adaptation of the Portage model. Today the project serves over 500 families living in the villages and camps of the Gaza Strip. Portage materials were translated from English into Arabic, with only minor cultural adaptations. Portage services have endured here despite periods of severe economic hardships and civil disruption. Curfews have frequently been imposed, during which times all persons living in the Gaza Strip were required to remain in their homes, significantly altering normal working and living conditions. During curfews, teachers did not make home visits. However, in anticipation of curfew days, teachers provided mothers with additional new activities to use should they be needed. During strike days, teachers typically maintained their teaching schedules by innocuously moving from home to home. Teachers typically live in neighborhoods in which they work and thus were better able to move about under the protection of their neighbors (Ghazaleh, Ghazaleh, & Oakland, 1990; Oakland & Ghazaleh, 1995).

Saudi Arabia   Nahla Tamin and Gerda Kuhfittig note that Portage was introduced in Saudi Arabia in the late 1990s. IPA headquarters staff have visited Jeddah three times to train staff at the help center. Since this training, early intervention services have expanded to include a Portage home visitation program for children ages birth to 9 months who have been diagnosed as having a disability. Families, especially the mothers, become very active in their child's program. This continues as the children are brought into a "home/center" program at age 9 months and eventually enrolled full time into a center-based program. The center's early intervention currently serves over 90 children. A great many more need services, because this is the only early intervention program for children with disabilities in Jeddah.

Caribbean   Portage in Jamaica has been established since 1975, beginning with the Jamaican Early Stimulation Project. The model was replicated with only relatively minor modifications. Differences include the use of Portage for all types of disabilities and for older children who are disabled, living in areas where there are few or no services. The total enrollment in 1990 was over 500 families of which 80% receive weekly home visits. The typical level of education of most community workers and home teachers is sixth to eighth grade, thus training requires intensive and ongoing effort. Dr. Marigold Thorburn has conducted numerous research activities related to the use of Portage and its application to young children with disabilities in Jamaica. She was also instrumental in introducing the model to nearly every country and island in the Caribbean (Thorburn, 1997).

Pakistan   Shagufta Shazadi of the University of Karachi reports that Pakistan has been using Portage since the early 1990s. It is felt that since the Portage model is simple to use, is economical, and is applicable for as many Pakistani children as possible, it is the most appropriate intervention that can be used in Pakistan. The model is popular with both governmental and private entities and with the Directorate General of Special Education for the Ministry of Education endorsing the translation and adaptation of the model for use in Pakistan (Shahzadi, 2002).

There is a Portage Parent Association and a National Portage Association of Pakistan, with provincial chapters. These chapters conduct the Portage training in their respective regions.

Ireland Theresa Ghalaieny reports that there have been 10 Portage workshops in Ireland, with more scheduled. The majority of home visitors are community nurses who are using the Portage materials.

✒ NEW CHALLENGES FOR PORTAGE

As a model that is now approaching its 36th year, Portage faces new challenges in both its practicality and usefulness in a world of ever-increasing sophistication in technology and knowledge. There are those service providers who see themselves as "early adopters" and who reach out to every new gadget, curriculum, or procedure that comes their way. Other providers prefer to remain in the "mainstream" and wait until sufficient research and use determines the appropriateness and staying power of new ideas. Still others become so comfortable with what is familiar to them that it takes a great deal of persuasion, or even legislation, to get them to change or try new methods. As research moves closer toward addressing what works best with families and young children, the Portage model, and indeed all intervention models, must be responsive to and incorporate research findings to remain relevant.

Applications with At-Risk Populations

Mild mental retardation accounts for approximately 70% of all developmental disabilities in the United States (Stoneman, 1990). This type of disability occurs almost exclusively in the context of psychosocial disadvantage and poverty and is transmitted intergenerationally. Early intervention is deemed essential to prevent mental retardation and poor intellectual development in children whose families do not provide adequate stimulation in the early years of life. The mounting evidence about the significance of early experience in brain development provides a stronger impetus for systematic efforts to enhance children's learning opportunities and development in the first 3 years of life (Ramey & Ramey, 1998). Whether development can be influenced directly by interventions designed specifically for the child versus indirectly by teaching parents how to provide these opportunities is an important issue and question for models such as Portage.

In this context a research prevention initiative was launched in 1995 to apply the Portage model as a primary prevention strategy for young infants deemed at risk because of being born in low-resource families and communities. Forty adolescent mothers who had not yet completed high school and who were living in a poor urban community were recruited during their last trimester of pregnancy and were randomly assigned to a weekly home visitation group or a control group. The study ran for 3 years and all children received at least 2 years of intervention, at which time families were tested on a variety of child and parenting measures. The intervention activities were primarily designed to address cognitive and language development in the children. Mothers in the home-visiting group were taught how to play and interact with their children using the Portage model and materials described in this chapter. Analysis of the study's findings has not yet been completed and problems with attrition will limit our ability to interpret the effectiveness of the intervention. However, several observations and experiences with this population are worth noting. Contrary to our previous experience working with families of children with identified disabilities or developmental delays, the children in the at-risk sample were, for all intents and purposes, "normal." The adolescent mothers were willing and eager to have weekly support and teaching during their child's first year of life when parenting experiences were relatively new and challenging. By the time their infants reached a year of age, it became more and more difficult to maintain the routine of weekly visits. Mothers returned to school or work and expressed more confidence about their roles as parents. With no outward physical or mental differences to be noted in their children, the mothers' priorities, unlike parents of children with disabilities, turned to pursuit of their own developmental needs. As the children became more independent during the second year of life, the mothers—in both the treatment and control group—demonstrated less nurturing and greater use of discipline, thus ignoring or bypassing other important learning experiences for the children. These parent attitudes were much greater than seen in the general population yet appear to reflect the understanding and values of the culture in which these adolescent mothers live. Our feeling is that once again we have demonstrated and learned that merely initiating a home-based program does not ensure that parents will be active and effective, or that the children will automatically benefit from such efforts.

We do not believe that we have yet found the answers for parenting and parent education for all types of families and children. When viewed from a global perspective, however, the implementation of Portage services or variants of them across the world is a remarkable phenomenon. Central to its success is the inherent requirement that those implementing the model have a thorough understanding of the values and norms of the population or culture to which it is applied. Our research has raised more questions than it has provided answers, yet we remain anxious to share the information. We want to put the facts on the table, to specify what we have done and what we are doing so that others may replicate, adapt, or modify our work and have the opportunity to analyze objectively and criticize what has occurred.

Although many questions concerning home-based parent training programs remain unanswered, we have learned a great deal. The Portage model has been in use since 1969. Let us look at what we know from our 36 years of experiences.

Any successful home-based parent teaching intervention must be developed in alliance with parents. They must want the alliance and see its benefit for their family.

Parents can and do teach their own child effectively when given structured sequential assistance, and if appropriately supported they can eventually plan, implement, and advocate an educational program for their child.

By using a behavioral, systematic, developmental approach, the child can achieve developmental gains in a home-based program.

Without direct and consistent parent involvement in any preschool setting, the child is not likely to maintain gains. Individualization of instruction is more likely to occur in the home rather than the classroom.

Father, sibling, and extended family member involvement in child teaching can be realistic and attainable.

Differences in cultures, lifestyles, and value systems of parents can be and should be incorporated into the curriculum because the parents share in the planning and are the final determiners of what and how their child will be taught.

Learning that occurs in the child's natural environment eliminates the problems of transferring learning from classroom to home.

The skills the child learns will more likely generalize to other areas and be maintained if they have been learned in the home environment and have been taught by the child's natural reinforcers—the parents and the family.

REFERENCES

Alpern, G., Boll, T., & Shearer, M. (1980). *Manual: Developmental profile.* Aspen, CO: Psychological Development Publications.

Arvio, M., Hautamaki, J., & Tilikka, P. (1993). Reliability and validity of the Portage assessment scale for clinical studies of mentally handicapped populations. *Child: Care, Health and Development, 19* (2), 89–98.

Bagnato, S. J., & Murphy, J. P. (1989). The validity of curriculum-based scales with young neurodevelopmentally disabled children: Implications for team assessments. *Early Education and Development, 1,* 19–29.

Bailey, D. B., Simeonsson, R. J., Winton, P. J., Huntington, G. S., Comfort, M., Isbell, P., O'Donnell, K. J., & Helm, J. M. (1988). Family-focused intervention: A functional model for planning, implementing, and evaluating individualized family services in early intervention. *Journal of the Division for Early Childhood, 10,* 156–171.

Bailey, D. B., & Wolery, M. (1984). *Teaching infants and preschoolers with handicaps.* Columbus, OH: Charles E. Merrill Publishing.

Barna, S., Bidder, R. T., Gray, O. P., Clements, J., & Gardner, S. (1980). The progress of developmentally delayed preschool children in a home-training scheme. *Child: Care, Health and Development, 6,* 157–164.

Bijou, S. W. (1983). The prevention of mild and moderate retarded development. In *Curative aspects of mental retardation: Biomedical and behavioral advances* (pp. 223–239). Baltimore: Paul Brookes.

Bijou, S. W. (1991). Overview of early childhood programs around the world. In J. Herwig & M. Stine (Eds.), *A symposium on family-focused intervention: Exploring national and international practices and perspectives* (pp. 63–71). Portage, WI: Cooperative Educational Service Agency 5.

Blair, C., Ramey, C. T., & Hardin, J. M. (1995). Early intervention for low birthweight, premature infants: Participation and intellectual development. *American Journal on Mental Retardation, 99* (5), 542–554.

Blechman, E. (1984). Competent parents, competent children: Behavioral objectives of parent training. In R. Dangel & R. Polster (Eds.), *Parent training* (pp. 15–27). New York: Guilford.

Bluma, S., Shearer, M., Frohman, A., & Hilliard, J. (1976). *Portage guide to early education* (rev. ed.). Portage, WI: Cooperative Educational Service Agency 5.

Boyd, R., Stauber, K., & Bluma, S. (1977). *Portage Parent Program.* Portage, WI: Cooperative Educational Service Agency 5.

Bradley, R., & Caldwell, B. (1984). 174 children: A study of the relationship between home environment and cognitive development during the first 5 years. In A. Gottfried (Ed.), *Home environment and early cognitive development* (pp. 5–57). Orlando, FL: Academic Press.

Brinker, R. P., & Lewis, M. (1982). Discovering the competent infant: A process approach to assessment and intervention. *Topics in Early Childhood Special Education, 2,* 1–16.

Bronfenbrenner, U. (1979). *The ecology of human development: Experiments by nature and design.* Cambridge, MA: Harvard University Press.

Cameron, R. J. (1986). Portage: Some directions for applied research. In R. J. Cameron (Ed.), *Portage: Preschoolers, parents and professionals* (pp. 101–109). Windsor, England: NFER-Nelson.

Cameron, R. J. (1989). Portage in the United Kingdom. In K. Yamaguchi, N. Shimiziu, T. Dobashi, & M. Yoshikawam (Eds.), *A challenge to potentiality: The vision of early intervention for developmentally delayed children* (pp. 58–70). Tokyo: Japan Portage Association.

Cameron, R. J. (1990). *Parents, professionals and preschoolers with special educational needs: Towards a partnership model of problem solving.* Unpublished doctoral dissertation, University of Southampton.

Dunst, C., Trivette, C., & Deal, A. (1988). *Enabling and empowering families: Principles and guidelines for practice.* Cambridge, MA: Brookline.

Dunst, C. J., Trivette, C. M., & Mott, D. W. (1994). Strengths-based family-centered intervention practices. In C. J. Dunst, C. M. Trivette, & A. G. Deal (Eds.), *Supporting and strengthening families: Vol. 1. Methods, strategies, and practices* (pp. 115–131). Cambridge, MA: Brookline Books.

Eiserman, W., Weber, C., & McCoun, M. (1995). Parent and professional roles in early intervention. *Journal of Special Education, 29,* 20–44.

Ghazaleh, H., Ghazaleh, K., & Oakland, T. (1990). Primary and secondary prevention services provided to mentally handicapped infants, children, and youth in the Gaza Strip. *International Journal of Special Education, 5,* 21–27.

Ghoca, M. L. (1972*). The development of language in preschool multiply handicapped children.* Unpublished master's thesis, University of Wisconsin–Milwaukee.

Guven, N., Bal, S., Metin, N., & Atay, M.(2000). *Usage of the Portage Project in Turkey and extending its usage throughout Turkey.* The 8th International Portage Association Conference, Birmingham, Alabama, USA.

Guven, N., Bal S., & Tugrul, B. (1998). *A contrastive study examining, on the basis of the Portage Early Education Programme checklists, cognitive development in two groups of normal children aged 37 to 72 months, attending two different kindergartens, one which had classes in the same group whereas the other had mixed-aged classes.* The 7th International Portage Association Conference, Hiroshima, Japan.

Hallahan, D. P., & Kauffman, J. M. (1976). *Introduction to learning disabilities. A psycho-behavioral approach.* Englewood Cliffs, NJ: Prentice Hall.

Hassall, L., Weston, B., & Raine, P. (2001). *Portage and Sure Start—Towards community development.* Annual Conference Proceedings, UK National Portage Association.

Hebbeler, K. M., & Gerlach-Downie, S. G. (2002). Inside the black box of home visiting: A qualitative analysis of why intended outcomes were not achieved. *Early Childhood Research Quarterly, 17,* 28–51.

Hoyson, M., Jamieson, B., & Strain, P. S. (1984). Individualized group instruction of normally developing and autistic-like children: The LEAP curriculum model. *Journal of the Division for Early Childhood, 8,* 157–172.

H. M. Inspectorate. (1990). *Education observed: Special needs issues.* London: HMSO.

Individuals with Disabilities Education Act Amendments of 1997, Part C. 105th Cong., 1st Sess. 1 (1997).

Jellnek, J. A. (1985). Documentation of child progress revisited: An analysis method for outreach or local programs. *Journal of the Division for Early Childhood, 9,* 175–182.

Johnson, Z., Molloy, B., Scallan, E., Fitzpatrick, P., Rooney, B., Keegan, T., & Byrne, P. (2000). Community mothers programme—seven years follow-up of a randomized controlled trial of non-professional intervention in parenting. *Journal of Public Health Medicine, 22,* 3, 337–342.

Karaaslan, B. T., & Bal, S. (2002). *Evaluation of the effect of home based early intervention programmes on the development of very low birth weight premature infants.* Hacettepe University, Health Sciences Institute. MD thesis in Child Development and Education, Ankara, Turkey.

Kohli, T. (1988). Effectiveness of Portage in India. In M. White & R. J. Cameron (Eds.), *Portage progress, problems and possibilities* (pp. 82–93). Windsor, England: NFER-Nelson.

Kohli, T. (1990). Impact of home centre based training programme in reducing developmental deficits of disadvantaged young children. *Indian Journal of Disability and Rehabilitation, 4* (2), 65–74.

Kohli, T. (1991). A decade of strides in Portage Programs in India. In J. Herwig & M. Stine (Eds.), *A symposium on family-focused intervention: Exploring national and international practices and perspectives* (pp. 63–71). Portage, WI: Cooperative Educational Service Agency 5.

Kohli, T., & Datta, R. (1986). Portage training: An international program for pre-school mentally retarded children with motor handicaps. *Journal of Practical Approaches to Developmental Handicaps, 9.*

Lindsley, O. R. (1968). *Training parents and teachers to precisely manage children's behavior.* Paper presented at CS Mott Foundation—Children's Health Center, New York City.

Meulen, B. F. van der, & Bulsink, R. H. H. (1992). The Portage Project Groningen. In H. Nakken, G. H. van Gemert, & Tj. Zandberg (Eds.), *Research on intervention in special education* (pp. 239–254). Lewiston, ME: Mellen Press.

Meulen, B. F. van der, & Sipma, W. G. (1991). The Portage Project Groningen: Measurement procedures and results. In J. Herwig & M. Stine (Eds.), *A symposium on family-focused intervention: Exploring national and international practices and perspectives* (pp. 125–144). Portage, WI: Cooperative Educational Service Agency 5.

Miller, D. (1990). *The importance of home-based support in providing early intervention services.* University of Wisconsin–Madison, Department of Educational Administration, Educational Administration 735.

Newborg, J., Stock, J., & Wnek, L. (1988). *Battelle Developmental Profile.* Allen, TX: DLM.

Oakland, T., & Ghazaleh, H. (1995). *Primary prevention of handicapping conditions among Palestinian children in Gaza.* Unpublished manuscript.

Odom, S., & Karnes, M. (Eds.) (1988). *Early intervention for infants and children with handicaps.* Baltimore: Paul Brookes.

Peniston, E. (1972). *An evaluation of the Portage Project.* Unpublished manuscript.

Ramey, C., Bryant, D., Wasik, B., Sparling, J., Vendt, K., & LaVange, L. (1992). Infant health and development program for low birth weight, premature infants: Program elements, family participation, and child intelligence. *Pediatrics, 89,* 454–465.

Ramey, C. T., & Ramey, S. L. (1998). Early intervention and early experience. *American Psychologist, 53* (2), 109–120.

Ramey, C. T., Ramey, S. L., Gaines, K. R., & Blair, C. (1995). Two-generation early intervention programs: A child development perspective. In S. Smith (Ed.), *Two-generation programs for families in poverty: A new intervention strategy (Vol. 9 Advances in Applied Developmental Psychology).* Norwood, NJ: Ablex.

Ramey, C. T., & Shearer, D. L. (in press). A conceptual framework for interventions with low birth weight, premature children and their families. In E. Goldson (Ed.), *Nurturing the premature infant: Developmental interventions in the neonatal intensive care nursery.* New York: Oxford University Press.

Ramey, S. L., & Ramey, C. T. (1992). Early educational intervention with disadvantaged children—To what effect? *Applied and Preventive Psychology, 1,* 131–140.

Revill, S., & Blendon, R. (1979). A home training service for pre-school developmentally handicapped children. *Behavior Research Therapy, 17,* 207–214.

Robinson, C. C., Rosenburg, S. A., & Beckman, P. J. (1988). Parent involvement in early childhood special education. In J. B. Jordan, J. J. Gallagher, P. S. Huttinger, & M. B Karnes (Eds.), *Early childhood special education: Birth to three.* Reston, VA: Council for Exceptional Children.

Rosenberg, S. A., Robinson, C. C., & Beckman, P. J. (1984). Teaching skills inventory: A measure of parent performance. *Journal of the Division of Early Childhood, 8,* 107–113.

Russell, P. (1986). Parental involvement in the 1980s. In R. J. Cameron (Ed.), *Portage: Preschoolers, parents and professionals* (pp. 72–83). Windsor, England: NFER-Nelson.

Shahzadi, S. (2002). Developing a home based programme for special needs children. *Journal of Education and Research,* Karachi Pak Organization of Workers in Educational Research, *1* (2).

Shearer, D. E. (1991). Portage makes a difference. In J. Herwig & M. Stine (Eds.), *A symposium on family-focused intervention: Exploring national and international practices and perspectives* (pp. 1–5). Portage, WI: Cooperative Educational Service Agency 5.

Shearer, D. E. (1993). The Portage Project: An international home approach to early intervention of young children and their families. In J. Roopnarine & J. Johnson (Eds.), *Approaches to early childhood education* (2nd ed.). New York: Merrill-Macmillan.

Shearer, D. E. (1995). The application of the Portage Model in developing countries [Letter to the editor]. *Actionaid Disability News, 6* (1), 33–34.

Shearer, D. E., & Loftin, C. (1984). The Portage Project: Teaching parents to teach their preschool child in the home. In R. Dangel & R. Polster (Eds.), *Parent training: Foundations of research and practice.* New York: Guilford Press.

Shearer, D. E., & Shearer, D. L. (1995, October). Has Portage experienced a paradigm shift? - *International Portage Association News, 11,* 1–6.

Shearer, D. E., & Shearer, M. (1976). The Portage Project: A model for early childhood intervention. In T. Tjossem (Ed.), *Intervention strategies for high risk infants and young children* (pp. 338–350). Baltimore: University Park Press.

Shearer, D. E., & Snider, R. A. (1981). On providing a practical approach to the early education of young children. *Child Behavior Therapy Review, 3,* 119–127.

Shearer, M., & Shearer, D. E. (1972). The Portage Project: A model for early childhood education. *Exceptional Children, 36,* 210–217.

Shelton, T. L., & Stepanek, S. S. (1994). *Family centered care for children meeting specialized health and developmental services* (3rd ed.). Bethesda, MD: Association for the Care of Children's Health.

Smith, J., Kushlick, A., & Glossop, C. (1977). *The Wessex Portage Project Research Report 125.* Southampton, United Kingdom: University of Southampton.

Stephens, T. M. (1976). *Directive teaching of children with learning and behavioral handicaps.* Columbus, OH: Charles E. Merrill Publishing.

Stoneman, Z. (1990). Conceptual relationships between family research in mental retardation. In N. W. Bray (Ed.), *International review of research in mental retardation* (Vol. 16, pp. 161–202). San Diego, CA: Academic Press.

Sturmey, P., Thorburn, M., Brown, J., Reed, J., Kaur, J., & King, G. (1992). Portage guide to early intervention: Cross-cultural aspects and intra-cultural variability. *Child: Care, Health, and Development, 18,* 377–394.

Thorburn, M. J. (1992). Parent evaluation of a community-based rehabilitation program in Jamaica. *International Journal of Rehabilitation Research, 15,* 170–176.

Thorburn, M. J. (1997). Raising children with disabilities in the Caribbean. In. J. L. Roopnarine & J. Brown (Eds.), *Caribbean families: Diversity among ethnic groups* (pp. 177–204). Greenwich, CT: Ablex.

Thorburn, M. J., Brown, J. M., & Bell, C. (1979). *Early stimulation of handicapped children using community workers.* Paper presented at the Fifth Congress of the International Association of the Scientific Study of Mental Deficiency, Jerusalem.

Turnbull, A., Patterson, J., Behr, S., Murphy, D., Marquis, J., & Blue-Banning, M. (1993). *Cognitive coping, families and disability.* Baltimore: Paul Brookes.

United States General Accounting Office (USGAO). (1990). *Home visiting: A promising early intervention strategy for at-risk families.* Report to the Chairman, Subcommittee on Labor, Health and Human Services, Education and Related Agencies, Committee on appropriations, U.S. Senate. July 1990.

Wasik, B. H., Bryant, D. M., & Lyons, C. M. (1990). *Home visiting: Procedures for helping families.* Newberry Park, CA: Sage.

Weisner, T. S. (1998). Human development, child well being and the cultural project of development. In D. Sharma & W. Fischer (Eds.), *Social emotional development across cultures: New directions for child development* (pp. 69–85). San Francisco, CA: Jossey-Bass.

White, M. (1997). A review of the influence and effects of Portage. In S. Wolfendale (Ed.), *Working with parents of special education needs children after the code of practice* (Chapter 2). London: Fulton.

White, M., & East, K. (1991). Supporting the parent role in early language development. In J. Herwig & M. Stine (Eds.), *A symposium on family-focused intervention: Exploring national and international practices and perspectives* (pp. 145–159). Portage, WI: Cooperative Educational Service Agency 5.

Wolfendale, S. (2001). Portage in contemporary contexts, in *UK National Portage Association Conference Proceedings.*

Yamaguchi, K. (1987). *The Japan adaptation of the early intervention model and some results.* Tokyo: Tokyo Gakugei University, The Research Institute for the Education of Exceptional Children.

Yamaguchi, K. (1988). The Japanese adaptation of the Portage early intervention model and some results. In M. White & R. Cameron (Eds.), *Portage: Progress, problems, and possibilities.* Windsor, England: NFER: Nelson.

Yamaguchi, K. (1996). A follow-up study of Japanese children who received early intervention through a Portage programme. In S. Cameron & M. White (Eds.), *The Portage early intervention model: Making the difference for families across the world.* Somerset, England: UK National Portage Association.

Part 2

Integral Dimensions

Chapter 5

Including Everyone:
A Model Preschool Program for
Typical and Special Needs Children

Ellen Barnes ꝏ Jowonio School, Syracuse, New York
Robert Lehr ꝏ State University of New York College at Cortland

Federal and state regulations and research support the education of children with disabilities in the least restrictive environment with their typical peers. For over 30 years Jowonio School in Syracuse, New York, has served as a program for a wide range of children, including those with physical, social, communication and cognitive needs. The curriculum developed as an integration of the knowledge from special education and early childhood developmentally appropriate practice. Special education as a field developed in public schools in the early part of the twentieth century (Sarason & Doris, 1959). In the last 40 or 50 years, as a result of both scientific knowledge about children and social changes in American society, there has been an increased interest in early education (childcare, preschool, etc.). Notably, the 1960s saw a rebirth of scientific interest in the rapid normal cognitive, language, emotional, and physical development in the early childhood (preschool) years (e.g., R. Brown, 1973; Hunt, 1961; Piaget, 1963). Women were challenging traditional roles and entering the job market in increasing numbers, government social programs were being developed, and many social issues and customs (civil rights, sexual mores, war) were being debated. Parents of disabled children, unable to get services, organized

together (e.g., Association for Retarded Children, United Cerebral Palsy) and started preschool programs. They also advocated for the development of federal and state funding for these programs. At the federal level with Head Start in 1964 (and amendments in 1972 requiring the inclusion of disabled children) and the Handicapped Children's Education Assistance Act (PL 90-538), an early intervention focus on children with disabilities was developed. The Americans with Disabilities Act (ADA, effective 1992), under its Public Accommodations Section (Title III), states that day-care centers may not discriminate on the basis of disability. Physical barriers to accessibility must be removed if readily achievable and, if not, alternative methods of providing service must be offered. Any new construction should be accessible to persons with disabilities.

The most important education act was PL 94-142, the Education for All Handicapped Children Act of 1975 (renamed in 1990 the Individuals with Disabilities Education Act), which set the standards for all of America's public schools for the education of disabled children from 3 to 21 years of age. This law included the most important ideas of what is called special education. The ideas embedded in PL 94-142 follow:

1. All children should go to school.
2. Disabled children should have an education appropriate to their individualized needs (an Individual Education Plan, IEP).
3. This education should be based on fair assessment of the child.
4. The disabled child should be educated with nondisabled children as much as possible (the "least restrictive environment").
5. Parents should have an opportunity to be actively involved in meaningful ways in their child's education, including procedural due process appeals (see Turnbull & Turnbull, 1982).

More recent legislation (PL 99-457) has resulted in these ideas being extended to children from birth to 3 years with special emphasis on the family unit as an important part of any early intervention program (see Bailey, McWilliam, Buysse, & Wesley, 1998; Gallagher, Trohanis, & Clifford, 1989). The new law is called the Individuals with Disabilities Education Act (IDEA), and it was reauthorized by Congress in 1997 and 2003. The IDEA Amendments place a strong emphasis on parent involvement in the initial evaluation process, in eligibility and placement decisions, and in the development and revision of the IEP. The IDEA has a new focus on ensuring that services be offered in natural environments. Part C encourages the provision of early intervention services for children under 3 years of age at risk for substantive developmental delay. In addition there is incentive to establish collaborative efforts with community agencies in order to identify, evaluate, and serve infants and toddlers and to create a smooth transition to preschool services.

The language describing the least restrictive environment has changed over the years. Initially, *mainstreaming* referred to the placement of students with disabilities into regular classrooms, often without supports and often on a part-time basis. *Integration* has meant that children are temporally, socially, and instructionally integrated for a meaningful amount of time, but the assumption is still made that the mainstreamed environment is designed for typical students and the special needs students must fit in. An *inclusive school* is structured to

The early intervention teacher and a child who is typically developing aid a child with cerebral palsy, providing hand-over-hand instruction to paint with a toy car. The involvement of children without special needs is one of the benefits of inclusionary practice.

serve a wide range of students; the environment is flexible and organized to meet the unique needs of all the students. In an inclusive school everyone belongs, is accepted, supports, and is supported by all members of the community while having individual educational needs met (Biklen, 1992; Sapon-Shevin, 2000/2001; Stainback & Stainback, 1990). This full inclusion is the vision of the future that is held by the people at the Jowonio School.

JOWONIO HISTORY

Created in 1969 by a group of parents in Syracuse, New York, as an alternative to the public schools, the Jowonio School reflected the humanistic free-school movement of the 1960s. It was run as a community program in which decisions were made cooperatively, and it emphasized an individualized curriculum for the whole child, including emotional and social development as well as academic achievement. Because of these values, focus, and structure, Jowonio always attracted children with special needs. In 1975, Jowonio cooperated with community agencies serving disabled people as well as the local university to develop a proposal to create a planned and well-staffed integrated program. That fall at Jowonio School, one third of the students were classified as having special needs, including students with the rather severe disability of autism, a syndrome in which language and social skills are quite delayed or different. Since that time, the school has functioned as an inclusive program in which typical students ages 2 to 5 are served with special needs peers in the same classrooms (see Knoblock, 1982; Knoblock & Lehr, 1985).

PHILOSOPHICAL BASE

A number of powerful yet simple beliefs have guided the Jowonio program since its inception, and these are described next.

All Children Can Learn

We approach the wide range of students we serve with the expectation that they can grow and change and that the impetus to do so is inherent in human nature. Children who many might call developmentally delayed have enormous potential if adults can help them find ways to express what they know and participate in their environment effectively. We are finding, for instance, that a number of nonverbal preschool children can demonstrate age-appropriate academic skills with help from adults.

Right to Participate

Just as the civil rights movement showed Americans that racial and ethnic minorities have a right to be part of American life, so it is with persons with disabilities. The segregated system of special education services arose out of a medical model as well as out of the discomfort with and prejudice against people perceived as different. In a democracy, not only should all citizens have access to the mainstream, but also diversity and heterogeneity should be valued as well. Not only those with special needs benefit from including everyone; the typical students and teachers grow from their contact and interaction as well (Odom & Diamond, 1998).

We also do not subscribe to the myth of readiness that children are included in the mainstream only when they are ready to be like their typical peers. That belief assumes that the children must change to fit the program. Our assumption is the opposite; the program should adapt to meet the needs of the children. Any child can be integrated when school personnel exhibit a willing attitude and children and adults receive appropriate supports.

Learning Through Relationships

We become open to learning when we are in trusting situations with others. We are more likely to put ourselves in new situations and respond to requests or demands of others when we feel safe and cared about (Collins, Maccoby, Steinberg, Hetherington, & Bornstein, 2000). Stanley Greenspan and Serena Wieder (1998) in their Floortime Approach describe emotions as the basis of learning. Through relationships in which significant adults interact and follow a child's interests, children are motivated to engage and learn. In a playful period of time, an adult focuses on four goals, to encourage joint attention and connection; to participate as a partner in a circle of two-way communication; to express feelings and ideas through words and play; and to link ideas together into a logical understanding of the world (e.g., classification, cause and effect).

In addition, children learn as much from other children as they do from teachers (Guralnick, Connor, Hammond, Gottman, & Kinnish, 1996; Rubin, Bukowski, & Parker, 1998). They model how their peers move through routines, how they follow directions, and how they interact with one another. Often a child who has receptive language problems and does not understand the teacher's verbal instructions imitates other children to know what to do. Developing language and appropriate social skills requires both models and practice (Guralnick, 1980; Jenkins, Odom, & Speltz, 1989). When children with special needs, particularly children with severe speech and language needs, are in segregated programs, how can they learn to talk and interact when their peers all have the same needs? Learning skills within the typical environment rather than in isolated artificial situations means that children will be more likely to demonstrate these skills in the home, school, or community. That is, they will be more likely to generalize. A good and inclusive early childhood classroom offers many opportunities for play and communication with a wide range of peers.

The emphasis must be on cooperative rather than competitive activities (Johnson & Johnson, 1999; Johnson, Johnson, & Holubec, 1990; Sapon-Shevin, 1999). Typical children need to have their questions about their peers answered and to have caring behavior modeled by adults. Teachers should explore the ways in which bias about disabilities affect their language and behavior and the classroom. Integrating nonstereotyped images of disabled and nondisabled persons in the curriculum and structuring activities for children to explore individual differences will facilitate an inclusive atmosphere (Barnes, Berrigan, & Biklen, 1978; Froschl, Colon, Rubin, & Sprung, 1984; Lieber et al., 1998).

Age-Appropriate Curriculum

Jowonio staff use the guidelines from the National Association for the Education of Young Children on Developmentally Appropriate Practice (Bredekamp & Copple, 1997). Classrooms offer many opportunities for children to manipulate a wide variety of materials; to play alone and with others in sensory, constructive, and symbolic activities; to ask questions and develop concepts about themselves and the world; to be physically active; and to express themselves in words, art, and music. A stimulating early childhood environment is designed so that any student can succeed in it. This may mean adaptations in terms of the physical environment, expectations of level of participation and amount of teacher support, size and nature of groupings during the day, schedule, and the presentation of the activities and materials used.

Communication-Based Classrooms

Just as social relationships are the basis for learning, communication is central to the establishment and maintenance of those relationships, to children's receptive understanding of the world around them, and to their ability to express that understanding to others and to have their needs and wants met. Speech and language are communicative, and our efforts with children must be geared toward enhancing their power to impact their environment through verbal or nonverbal communication. We also believe that for young children, language is learned primarily through play (Johnson, Christie, & Wardle, 2005; Musselwhite, 1986; Westby, 1980). Obviously, having typical peers as stimuli and models is very important, as is the opportunity to learn and practice language in natural contexts.

Communication occurs all day long. Even a nonverbal person is constantly communicating if another individual is present. However, what one person intends and another understands may be two different things. As teachers we must learn to read a child's behavior for its communicative intent and then learn to help a child develop appropriate ways to express those intents. The same behavior may mean different things in different contexts, and different behaviors may mean the same thing (Donnellan, Mirenda, Mesaros, & Fassbender, 1984). Children need opportunities to make real choices in their environment. We have used a number of alternative or augmentative systems for children to express themselves. These may include symbol systems, signing, and typing that occurs with adult facilitation.

Parent–Teacher Partnership

Traditionally, parents have been viewed by some teachers as irrelevant to the decision-making process of education and, at worst, as adversaries. At Jowonio we have a different definition of our role as professionals and of the role of parents. Specifically, we view parents as partners in efforts to create the best program for children. Teachers are not experts but advocates who bring a second perspective to a dialogue about children. As teachers we have access to information about available services, rights, procedures, and support networks for parents. We offer a view of a particular child from our experiences with a range of children and from seeing that child in the school setting. We are in a position to coordinate programming between home, school, and related service personnel and to communicate to other professionals about a child (e.g., when the child makes the transition to public school from preschool). Parents bring to the parent–teacher dialogue essential information about a child: historical developmental information; an understanding of a child's daily behaviors, needs, and emerging skills; and a repertoire of successful interventions. Parents will be the child's lifelong advocates, and their understanding of the child is critical in long-term effective programming (Bailey et al., 1998; Biklen, 1992).

Teachers have four major roles in relation to parents:

1. Facilitate a child's growth through parent contact.
2. Support and empower parents in their parenting role.
3. Provide resources.
4. Facilitate the transition of parents and children to their next environment.

Facilitating a child's growth through parent contact means listening to parent input and wishes and incorporating these into IEP goals that reflect the child's participation not only in school but also at home and in the community.

Teachers must establish ongoing communication with families so that expectations of the child at home and at school are known and coordinated and so that parents are aware of how their child is doing and progressing at school. At Jowonio this communication occurs through classroom observations and conferences, home visits, telephone calls, daily or intermittent exchange in a home–school notebook, and classroom social events (e.g., potluck suppers, awards ceremonies, grandparents' teas, birthdays). Teachers can help parents feel competent by listening and reinforcing them for their effective strategies, by focusing on the child's progress, and by helping them enjoy their child in the present.

Building positive and trusting relationships with parents begins with respecting their love and hopes for their child, soliciting and listening to their ideas and concerns, and sharing one's own questions. It also requires an understanding of what parents can realistically do, given all the demands on their time and energy (e.g., a single parent of several children may not be able to do a toileting program when money, meals, and laundry have top priority).

Providing resources begins with developing an understanding of family strengths and needs and natural ways to help them meet their needs (Bailey et al., 1998; Dunst, Trivette, & Deal, 1988). This may include information (e.g., literature or workshops on legal rights, autism, toilet training), problem solving to access their own networks, and, if necessary, referrals to agencies and support groups (e.g., financial-aid programs, respite care, counseling, parent or sibling support groups).

The staff members of Jowonio's community-based ENRICH program provide special education and therapy services to children with special needs ages birth to 5 years. After a comprehensive evaluation, youngsters receive itinerant services in their home or in nursery, day-care, or home child-care settings. The opportunity for intensive parent as well as child contact means that families can receive emotional and instrumental support as well as model effective teaching strategies. In these early months after diagnosis, the contact between therapists, teachers, and parents gives many opportunities to process the nature and implications of the child's developmental and unique needs and to try out strategies to support the child toward growth. The transdisciplinary team approach (including the parent) is invaluable in providing a variety of perspectives on the child's needs. Collaborating with community day-care and nursery programs not only supports individual students with special needs, but also enhances the clinical programming for all the children in these settings. The special

education staff learn to address the functional skills youngsters need to be successful in natural environments.

The transition to the next environment occurs more easily when a teacher can give parents information and a perspective on the process (e.g., school options, IEP procedures). Staff can help parents to express what they want and to work with the new school to create it, establish lines of communication between parents and the new school, and relate positive specific information about the child to the new teacher (we send a portfolio on to the new school). Preschools are often the first place where parents have trusted others to be so important in their child's life; it can be hard to move on to what seems to be a bigger, more impersonal, and less supportive setting. Teachers can help this transition by fostering positive relationships with the new school.

Teaming Skills

Quality teaching is enhanced by working within a team; we all can benefit from the ideas of others and models of different ways of doing things (Bailey, 1996; Thousand & Villa, 1990). Good teaching is never a script; it takes an experimental attitude and the openness to try things in new ways. Our program is set up with teachers working in teams of three or four full-time staff and involving additional part-time and resource staff, including language, occupational, and physical therapists. We allocate specific time each week for teachers to plan together, to have clinical conferences on children, to participate in staff development activities, and to work on their roles and relationships with one another. Most people working with young children have not been taught teaming skills; this is often the most complex part of the job in our program because of the large number of adults with whom one has contact. As we learn to problem solve about programming for children, we can also do so about one another. We have built in a system of peer and administrative supports for all our teachers.

The conscious emphasis on how we are working together pays off in the quality of the programming for children as well as in the job satisfaction of our staff. In addition, we look at adults developmentally, as we look at children, and we provide incentives for all staff to grow in their professional skill.

✍ DEALING WITH PROBLEM BEHAVIOR

Developing effective strategies for dealing with children's problem behaviors can be one of the most challenging aspects of a teacher's job. In a classroom including children with special social, behavioral, and communication needs, a wide variety of problem behaviors may require specific planned approaches. What children do is the result of an interaction with or reaction to what is going on around them. You can never look at the behavior as only coming from within the child. The adults and what they are saying and doing, the space and sensory environment, the peer group, the nature of the materials and tasks that are presented always have an important impact on the behavior. By doing a functional analysis of when the problem behavior occurs (or does not occur) and the factors that influence it, we can change the antecedent conditions as well as teach alternative behaviors that serve the same function for the child (O'Neill, Horner, Albin, Storey, & Sprague, 1990).

Behavior as Communication

What a child does must be looked at as an effort to communicate. To understand what the child is trying to tell you by a particular action (communicative intent), you must understand the context. The single behavior might mean different things in different situations; a child might scream when hurt, frustrated, or angry, or to get an adult's attention. Several different behaviors might have the same meaning; grabbing, yelling, or pinching could all be efforts to get an adult's attention (see Carr & Durand, 1985; Donnellan et al., 1984).

Using a problem-solving process, teachers and others attempt to identify the communication content of the behavior by analyzing the relationship between the environment and the occurrence of the behavior. What happens before or after the behavior? What is the setting? Who is present? When did it occur? This process attempts to discover functional relationships between the behavior and elements in the environment that we can potentially change (see Dunlap, Kern-Dunlap, Clarke, & Robbins, 1991; O'Neill et al., 1990; Touchette, MacDonald, & Langer, 1985).

The analysis may show, for example, that each time the child curses, the teacher talks to the child about using proper language in school. Maybe the child is communicating, "I want some teacher attention," and the cursing is very effective in getting it. An intervention would be to give teacher attention only for more appropriate behaviors and possibly to teach those more appropriate behaviors if the child does not use them frequently. Often prevention of the problem behavior by changing the situational variables is the best approach.

Positive Programming

Planning to teach children appropriate behaviors is the most important approach to dealing with difficult behaviors (Dunlap, Johnson, & Robbins, 1990; Evans & Meyer, 1985; Meyer & Evans, 1989). You need to teach children what you want them to do, not just tell them what not to do. This might mean teaching an alternative way to communicate (e.g., "If you want my attention, tap me on the shoulder and say my name"). Or you can teach an alternative response to a stressful situation (e.g., "If it is too noisy for you to work, put on headphones rather than flapping your hands and crying"). Many times teaching appropriate social skills or how to control emotions using role playing can effectively reduce problem behaviors (see Goldstein & McGinnis, 1990).

Reinforcing Positive Behaviors

Encouraging or rewarding someone for doing what is appropriate is always more effective than reacting to inappropriate behavior. This means that teachers need to create opportunities for children to exhibit positive behaviors and then to respond in a very reinforcing way when the positive behavior happens.

Interventions Within Relationships

Implementing interventions around difficult behaviors is always more effective within the context of a positive relationship with the child. This means teachers need to plan time each day for enjoyable positive activities, supportive attention to the child's emotions, and warm and consistent contact (physical and social) with the child. If a strong relationship exists between the adult and the child, the teacher can deal with conflict and limits in a way that is meaningful for the child.

McGee, Menolascino, Hobbs, and Menousek (1987) describe an approach to problem behavior called "gentle teaching," which generally reverses many notions about behavior problems. This point of view sees a child who throws a tantrum as a child who has not developed positive relationships ("bonded") with others. Teachers should have unconditional positive regard toward the student. Problem behaviors are prevented or ignored ("not valued"), and the child is redirected into other tasks that will develop mutual positive human relationships ("interdependence"). Because the goal is to develop human relationships, skill training or activities are used to foster these interdependent relationships. Any procedure that might interfere with the development of bonding (e.g., punishment) is excluded. If both the teacher and the learner are not having fun, then the activity is not building positive relationships.

Using Natural Consequences

As much as possible, interventions should be natural so that they will generalize to the environments in which we all function (e.g., home, school, community). If Jim dumps food on the floor, he should clean it up. In the long term, we want the normal environment to provide the control and consequences for the problem behavior. It may be necessary to be in the "real" environment to accomplish this, especially for more severely disabled children. Waiting in line at McDonald's can be simulated in the classroom, but there is no substitute for the real thing.

Aversive Treatment Is Unacceptable

We exclude the use of aversive interventions, including seclusion, physical punishment, and prolonged physical restraint, on both ethical and pragmatic grounds. For example, we often use time-out to allow students to leave a group so that they can calm down, but we never use exclusion from the group as a punishment. Teaching appropriate behaviors or positive programming is more effective and generalizable (Donnellan, LaVigna, Negri-Shoultz, & Fassbender, 1988; Dunlap et al., 1990; Evans & Meyer, 1985; LaVigna & Donnellan, 1986; McGee et al., 1987; Meyer & Evans, 1989). When using aversive methods, teachers often lose perspective, and punishment makes everyone feel bad. Focusing on positive experiences, building positive relationships, and not reinforcing (valuing) bad behaviors are more effective in the long run. (See Baumrind, Larzelere, & Cowan, 2002).

Behavioral Interventions in an Inclusive Setting

In any classroom, teachers must balance the needs of the individuals with the needs of the group. Often people opposed to inclusion talk about "the rights of the other students." The reality is that in any group setting teachers make decisions that balance the needs of the individual with the needs of the group. For a child who screams to get attention, the appropriate strategy may be to ignore the screaming. However, the screaming may be so disruptive to the rest of the children that the teacher may feel a need to address it directly. Talking with other adults will help a teacher to analyze this and similar dilemmas and develop some approaches to try.

Problem-Solving Approach

Good teachers are those who seek as much help as necessary to deal with a problem. We hold meetings that may involve speech and language pathologists, occupational and physical therapists, other teachers, aides, parents, psychologists, graduate students, and any other people who know the student and might have good ideas. The diversity of the participants is important. Working with such a diverse set of creative people requires some direction and focus, and the teacher needs to have some skills to keep the group on task.

Teachers at Jowonio use a general problem-solving approach that involves as many people and their ideas as possible. The problem to be solved may be an educational, social, emotional, or behavioral problem. The solutions are to be found in changing the environment. The child is never the problem. A single teacher never has all the right answers.

Implementing an Individualized Education Program

Because it makes sense and because it is mandated by state and federal regulations, children with special needs must have a planned description of their individual program, an IEP. This IEP must include a statement of each child's current level of functioning, annual long-term goals, a breakdown of those goals into short-term behavioral objectives, and a time line and description of the means by which these goals will be reached.

The typical curriculum and its themes and concepts are the framework within which specific goals are addressed for children with special needs. The scope and sequence of that curriculum must allow for diverse levels of achievement and diverse learning styles (see Gardner & Hatch, 1989; Goodman, 1992). Lesson plans usually incorporate multiple objectives and multiple modes of instruction. Adaptations for children with special needs may occur in a number of ways: targeted skill or skill sequence, space, groupings, level of participation expected, kinds of materials used, and nature of cues or support required (Souweine, Crimmins, & Mazel, 1981).

Technology, especially computers, allows all children to participate in highly motivating activities that encourage independence, foster positive self-esteem and sense of mastery, and increase attention span and problem-solving skills. Students prefer open-ended interactive software, and it often can be used independently after initial and intermittent adult assistance. Since children can play together at the computer, opportunities abound for turn taking, cooperation, and social interaction. Technology also offers options for students to communicate through keyboards and the increasingly sophisticated voice-output equipment. Anyone with a reliable movement can have access through a myriad of switches to computerized communication devices and enhanced learning opportunities. Nonverbal students can demonstrate their knowledge and in some cases can serve as models and teachers for their peers. As well as preparing children for the future, technology can enhance significantly the learning and social possibilities in the classroom.

✍ SCHOOL AND CLASS COMPOSITION

The wide range of children served at Jowonio includes typical students 2 to 5 years of age and peers with special needs. These include children

Inclusive classrooms will also help to sensitize children to the diverse abilities of individuals.

who have been identified by professionals as having speech or language impairments, orthopedic disabilities, autism, other health impairments, and multiple handicaps. Each class has a 1- to 2-year age range and a balance of students with skills and needs. For instance, our toddler class has 10 children, 5 with disabilities and 5 normally developing peers. Our full-day 3-, 4-, and 5-year-old rooms all have 10 typical students and 6 special needs students. It is important that the tone of the classroom group be age appropriate and that there are good models for social and language skills within the group. A cross-age student population offers a greater range of possibilities for peer interactions and friendships.

Three adults are assigned to the toddler class of 10; in the 3- to 5-year-old rooms of 16 children, 4 full-time adults are assigned. Related services of speech and language therapy, physical therapy, and occupational therapy are available as needed. In every classroom, we try to have staff trained in early childhood and special education. Background and experience with typical children lends awareness of the

usual sequence of skills and developmental tasks of each particular age. Then, for example, one can have a perspective that views issues in a 3-year-old's behavior as within normal developmental limits rather than as a symptom of a special need.

STRATEGIES FOR ACCOMPLISHING INCLUSION

To support maximum participation of a wide range of students in the classroom, we allow for flexibility in scheduling, in groupings, and in levels of support and expected participation (Stainback & Stainback, 1992). In addition, materials and activities that have multiple objectives and several modes of instruction allow for the inclusion of students with different levels of skill.

Flexibility in Scheduling

The scheduling of the day serves to provide a predictable routine within which children can gain independence while having opportunities for open-ended exploration, spontaneity, and choice making. Adults make use of teachable moments to extend play and broaden learning. We try to minimize the number of transitions and the amount of waiting between events. Time is allowed to learn skills embedded in natural situations such as cleanup and dressing. A balance must always be achieved between active gross motor activities and sitting activities, and children should have opportunities for movement throughout the building and neighborhood. A typical schedule might be as follows:

8:45–9:45	Open play/learning centers, choose and do
9:45–10:00	Meeting or circle time
10:00–10:15	Snack
10:15–10:30	Books and toileting
10:30–11:30	Special activities (movement, music, skill group, paired play, play choices, play group, acting, story stretchers, cooking)
11:30–12:00	Lunch
12:00–12:30	Rest and reading
12:30–1:00	Gym/outside
1:00–2:00	Special activities (as above) or learning centers
2:00–2:30	Goodbye preparation (music/closing circle)

The class also takes a field trip each week. The schedule is planned around a theme of the week, and efforts are made to design activities, select books, and arrange the field trip to reinforce the concepts of the theme. Therapists frequently work in the classroom and may be responsible for planning group activities designed to meet individual child goals. Classroom-based therapy maximizes the opportunities for generalization of skills, the modeling of therapeutic techniques for teachers, and the probability that therapy goals will be useful for the child in the classroom and at home.

Flexibility in Grouping

Flexibility in grouping children also facilitates inclusion. At Jowonio we use a variety of group formats to balance individualization and independence, as well as to allow for effective peer modeling and socialization. Groups vary in the level of support needed, complexity of planning, and degree of true integration. In one-to-one situations with adults, students may be working on their relationship with that adult; a one-to-one time may also be used for assessment, teaching a new skill, or rehearsing classroom content to facilitate group participation. Pairs or small groups offer opportunities for social interaction that can be teacher structured. Children also need to be able to handle large-group settings after their preschool years, so opportunities to experience larger groups are important.

Curriculum Adaptation

Typical curricula may need to be adapted so that students with special needs can participate successfully. This adaptation may involve changing the nature of the instruction in the classroom to use several modalities and to have multiple objectives. In addition, we allow for the partial participation of students, varying our expectations to meet their current capabilities (Baumgart et al., 1982). Adaptations occur in materials and cues, sequences and rules, and levels of support.

Materials and Cues   Children may need visual and object cues to comprehend language; they also benefit from manipulating objects related to the content being taught. We label everything with the written word or with symbols. Labeling the classroom is an important tool for the development of literacy (reading) in all children (Neuman & Roskos, 1993, 1994; Schickedanz, 1986). This has been a particular emphasis at Jowonio, since we realized through facilitated communication that a number of our less verbal children can read. Of course, this use of many cues to communicate the same content is good general early childhood practice. An inventory of favorite topics and materials gained through observations and child and parent interviews suggests materials that will make an activity motivating. For example, if a child is interested in cars, you can easily develop seriation, classification, and counting activities using cars.

Sequences and Rules For some students, we may change the number of steps in an activity or the rules of a game to allow all children to succeed. In addition, the number of choices may be limited, waiting time decreased, or the amount of time required to stay at an activity reduced. For example, a child who has a hard time sitting in the large-group circle may initially be expected to stay in the meeting for 5 minutes (even under protest!) and then may be allowed to get up and do something quietly in another part of the room. The goal is that by later in the year becoming comfortable in the routine will encourage the child to stay longer.

Levels of Support An important strategy for successful participation is providing support from teachers and peers that eventually can be faded so the child functions as independently as possible. The support may include physical assistance, gestures, individualized verbal cues, teacher proximity, peer partners, and peer modeling. Some students with physical disabilities may need physical assistance from adults but may become independent with technological devices such as computers.

To plan integrated activities, goals are developed around motor, social-emotional, language, behavioral, and cognitive skill areas. The general goals may be based on theme, content area, and skill level used for typical students. Then child-specific goals for the particular activity are drawn from the IEP of each child. In structuring the activity, the general sequence of events, range of materials, and group composition should be planned. Finally, necessary adaptations are made for individual children. The role of peers must be an important consideration.

The following individualized lesson plan (see Figure 5–1) is an example of how a cooking activity is adapted to include two students with special needs. Brad has severely delayed motor and cognitive skills. James, who is considered autistic, has a good deal of language, but it tends to be rote and scripted.

TRANSITIONING TO NEXT ENVIRONMENT

An important aspect of any preschool teacher's work is the preparation of children and families for their transition to their next environment, kindergarten (Donovan, 1987). A comparative study of preschool special education classrooms and regular kindergarten classrooms (Vincent et al., 1980) showed that the expectations in the two settings were very different. For example, kindergarten teachers require children to respond to directions given once to a large group, while preschool special education teachers often give their students repeated individual directions in a small group or one to one. Part of our responsibility as preschool teachers is to be conscious of the demands of the next environment and to help children acquire the task and social skills to succeed there.

A second responsibility of an early education teacher is to work with families to impact on the kindergarten placement of our students. We seek to find or create integrated programs that will meet the needs of the individual children. This often requires skills as an advocate and consultant for which teachers are not usually trained. It is important to describe the specific needs of the child in all areas to find an existing integrated program or to support the development of a new one (e.g., placement of a child in a regular kindergarten with a full-time aide and therapy services). Building positive relationships with the school district staff may begin by observing their classrooms and inviting their teachers and administrators to observe our classroom and the student in question.

Lesson Plan

DATE: _4/24   Theme: Spring Week_   TEACHER: _Rae_

ACTIVITY: _Cooking: "Grasshopper Shakes" Jowonio Cookbook p.12_

LONG-TERM GOAL: _To participate in a verbally directed sharing activity_

MATERIALS NEEDED: _blender, measuring spoons + cup, ice cream scoop, milk, ice cream, vanilla, eggs, food coloring_

Short Term Objectives	Method/Procedure	Materials	Evaluation
Group: 1. Passing materials to a peer 2. Counting, measuring concepts: whole vs. half 3. Following sequence of recipe 4. Completing a task 5. Beginning reading	small group * each child does a step in the recipe * label materials with signs		
Individualization: Brad 1. Explore ingredients - some tastes 2. Tool use - spoon for scooping pitcher for pouring blender - cause + effect 3. Follow simple commands - "put in" "give to" 4. Attend to peer	* hand over hand as needed - then fade support * encourage tasting by placing food in hand + bring to his mouth	* seat near blender * DLM pictures of milk ice cream eggs blender	
Individualization: James 1. Use vocabulary in context 2. Attend to + respond to peer requests 3. Request needed item from peer 4. Comment on activity 5. Begin reading	* review chart before activity * encourage peer to request * model comments		
Individualization: Terry, Alicia + Mary — group activity			
Individualization:			
Individualization:			

Recipe Chart
Grasshopper Shakes
Mix in ⬤ bowl:
½ cup milk
2 scoops ice cream
½ teaspoon vanilla
1 teaspoon green food coloring
1 ⬤ egg
Pour contents of bowl into the blender
Blend briefly!
Enjoy!

FIGURE 5–1 Lesson Plan

Parents and their wishes are critical in this transition process. They need to know their rights under the law, to understand the process by which their child will be evaluated and placed in a classroom, to describe program components important to them, and to develop a working relationship with school district staff to achieve the most appropriate integrated kindergarten placement for their child. As preschool teachers and administrators, we work closely with parents to give them the information and support they need to be an advocate for their child. In addition, this transition is an extremely stressful time for parents. Teachers can ease this transition by their active planning and reassurance.

Many parents are increasingly convinced of the importance of their child with special needs attending their neighborhood school rather than being bussed across town. The local school may not have served a child with these needs before. A home-school placement maximizes the development of long-term social relationships for a child, allows a child to be with siblings and neighbors, increases the communication between parents and school staff, and supports the generalization of skills to the child's natural environment (see Brown et al., 1989).

Once a child has been formally assigned a kindergarten placement, the preschool teacher communicates in person and through paperwork about the child. We develop a portfolio for the new teacher that includes samples of the child's work, evaluation reports, and descriptions of favorite activities and effective approaches in behavior management and teaching. All of our efforts are geared toward a positive transition to regular kindergarten with sufficient supports to guarantee success.

IMPLICATIONS FOR TEACHER TRAINING

Teacher preparation is an integral part of the program at Jowonio. Based on the wide variety of activities expected of teachers, new teachers need practical experience in quality inclusive settings. The effective teacher is flexible and reflective in the planning, programming, and management of the classroom, as well as in the transition to the next environment. While teachers clearly must relate well with children, they must also be able to work and interact with a variety of adults. New teachers often are overwhelmed by dealing with the various adults involved in an inclusive classroom. Teachers must be able to work well with other teachers, therapists, parents, administrators, aides, and student teachers, all of whom may have different perspectives on the classroom, different values, and different skills. Because interactions with other adults can be very difficult, teacher training must focus on working cooperatively with other adults. Developing a problem-solving approach is essential. The best way to achieve this goal is for teacher training programs to require participation in a variety of cooperative, real-life problem-solving experiences with adult peers.

ADDITIONAL INCLUSION EFFORTS

Some preschool special education programs have developed working relationships with child-care and nursery programs, by which they provide a team of special education and resource staff to work with a small group of children with special needs. Willing teachers and administrators and a commitment to teaming are central ingredients in the success of these programs. A variety of integration efforts are described in Berres and Knoblock's *Program Models for Mainstreaming* (1987) and D. Biklen's *Achieving the Complete School* (1985).

Many people are doing research on the outcomes of integrated programming at the preschool level. The major areas of focus include assessing the impact on both typical children and children with special needs, as well as on parent and teacher attitudes (e.g., Blacker & Turnbull, 1982), social interaction patterns (see Strain,

1984, 1985), developmental and behavioral outcomes (Guralnick, 1980; Jenkins et al., 1989), and methods of intervention (Strain & Odom, 1986).

Odom and McEvoy (1988), in their review of the research on integration, conclude that there is "good evidence that children with handicaps can receive an appropriate education in mainstreamed . . . preschool programs" (p. 262), but that the quality of instruction, not simply the mainstreaming, is an important factor in the success of these programs. Social interactions between disabled and nondisabled children that are available in inclusive settings do not necessarily occur spontaneously but rather require direct, planned interventions. Although the effect of integration alone is hard to separate from other variables, the empirical literature seems clear in demonstrating that "normally developing children are not adversely affected by integrated classes, and in fact benefit developmentally from the curriculum and instructional strategies" (Odom & McEvoy, 1988, p. 259).

Research findings suggest that peer interactions for children with disabilities occur more often in inclusive classrooms than in segregated classrooms (Guralnick et al., 1996); and there is less unoccupied play and less inappropriate or self-abusive behavior in inclusive classrooms (Erwin, 1993). A higher proportion of typical peers have a positive effect on peer interactions (Hauser-Cram, Bronson, & Upshur, 1993); parents and teachers report that a majority of children in inclusive classrooms have at least one friend (Buysse, 1993). Typical students in inclusive classrooms gave higher social acceptance scores in response to scenarios about children with disabilities than did their counterparts in noninclusive early childhood programs (Diamond & Hestenes, 1996); and mixed-age inclusive programs facilitated social conversations between children and led to more play mastery than same-age groupings (Blasco, Bailey, & Burchinal, 1993; Roberts, Burchinal, & Bailey, 1994).

CONCLUSION

Accepted developmentally appropriate practice in early childhood (see Bredekamp & Copple, 1997) and accepted practice in special education are consistent. Both emphasize the unique pattern of development of each child. The chosen curriculum is responsive to the child's current level of skill and interests. Effective curriculum calls on an integration of all areas of development: physical, social-emotional, language, and cognitive skills. Within a group of children, differences in ability and style are expected and valued. Each member of the community is enhanced by the diversity of the whole.

An inclusive preschool program that serves all children makes both philosophical and practical sense. In this chapter we have described one model of an early childhood setting that fully includes students with special needs and their typical peers. The Jowonio program is guided by beliefs that all children are valued; all children have a right to and can benefit from high-quality, age-appropriate early education; learning occurs through models and relationships; and problem-solving partnerships between teachers and parents and within the teaching team are central to a good program for children. The core activity in an inclusive program is the adaptation of the typical curriculum to ensure successful participation for all students. The goal is to create an inclusive community in which all children and adults can learn and feel valued.

REFERENCES

Bailey, D. (1996). An overview of interdisciplinary training. In D. Bricker & A. Widerstrom (Eds.), *Preparing personnel to work with infants and young children and their families: A team approach* (pp. 3–22). Baltimore: Paul Brookes.

Bailey, D., McWilliam, R., Buysse, V., & Wesley, P. (1998). Inclusion in the context of competing values in early childhood education. *Early Childhood Research Quarterly, 13,* 27–47.

Barnes, E., Berrigan, C., & Biklen, D. (1978). *What's the difference: Teaching positive attitudes toward people with disabilities.* Syracuse, NY: Human Policy.

Baumgart, D., Brown, L., Pumpian, I., Nisbet, J., Ford, A., Sweet, M., & Schroeder, J. (1982). Principle of partial participation and individualized adaptations in educational programs for severely handicapped students. *Journal of the Association for the Severely Handicapped, 7,* 17–24.

Baumrind, D., Larzelere, R. E., & Cowan, P. A. (2002). Ordinary physical punishment: Is it harmful? Comment on Gershoff. *Psychological Bulletin, 128,* 580–589.

Belsky, J. (1990). Parental and nonparental child care and children's socio-emotional development: A decade in review. *Journal of Marriage and the Family, 52,* 885–903.

Berres, M., & Knoblock, P. (1987). *Program models for mainstreaming.* Rockville, MD: Aspen.

Biklen, D. (1985). *Achieving the complete school: Strategies for effective mainstreaming.* New York: Teachers College Press.

Biklen, D. (1992). *Schooling without labels.* Philadelphia: Temple University Press.

Blacker, J., & Turnbull, A. P. (1982). Teacher and parent perspectives on selected social aspects of preschool mainstreaming. *Exceptional Child, 29,* 191–199.

Blasco, P., Bailey, D., & Burchinal, M. (1993). Dimensions of mastery in same-age and mixed-age integrated classrooms. *Early Childhood Research Quarterly, 8,* 193–206.

Bredekamp, S., & Copple, C. (1997). *Developmentally appropriate practice in early childhood programs* (Rev. ed.). Washington, DC: National Association for the Education of Young Children.

Brown, L., Long, E., Udvari-Solner, A., Davis, L., VanDeventer, C. A., Johnson, F., Gruenewald, L., & Jorgensen, J. (1989). The home school: Why students with severe intellectual disabilities must attend the schools of their brothers, sisters, friends, and neighbors. *Journal of the Association for the Severely Handicapped, 14,* 1–7.

Brown, R. (1973). *A first language: The early stages.* Cambridge, MA: Harvard University Press.

Buysse, V. (1993). Friendships of preschoolers with disabilities in community-based childcare setting. *Journal of Early Intervention, 17,* 380–395.

Carr, E. G., & Durand, V. M. (1985). Reducing behavior problems through functional communication training. *Journal of Applied Behavior Analysis, 18,* 111–126.

Collins, W. A., Maccoby, G. E., Steinberg, L., Hetherington, E. M., & Bornstein, M. H. (2000). Contemporary research on parenting: Nature versus nurture. *American Psychologist, 55,* 218–232.

Diamond, K., & Hestenes, L. (1996). Preschool children's conceptions of disabilities: The salience of disability in children's ideas about others. *Topics in Early Childhood Special Education, 16,* 458–475.

Donnellan, A. M., LaVigna, G. W., Negri-Shoultz, N., & Fassbender, L. L. (1988). *Progress without punishment: Effective approaches for learners with severe behavior problems.* New York: Teachers College Press.

Donnellan, A. M., Mirenda, P. L., Mesaros, R. A., & Fassbender, L. L. (1984). Analyzing the communicative functions of aberrant behavior. *Journal of the Association for Persons with Severe Handicaps, 9,* 201–212.

Donovan, E. (1987). *Preschool to public school: A teacher's guide to successful transition for children with special needs.* Syracuse, NY: Jowonio School.

Dunlap, G., Johnson, L. F., & Robbins, F. R. (1990). Preventing serious behavior problems through skill development and early intervention. In A. C. Repp & N. N. Singh (Eds.), *Perspectives on the use of nonaversive and aversive interventions for persons with developmental disabilities* (pp. 273–286). Sycamore, IL: Sycamore.

Dunlap, G., Kern-Dunlap, L., Clarke, S., & Robbins, F. R. (1991). Functional assessment, curricular revision, and severe behavior problems. *Journal of Applied Behavior Analysis, 24,* 387–397.

Dunst, C., Trivette, C., & Deal, A. (1988). *Enabling and empowering families.* Cambridge, MA: Brookline.

Erwin, E. J. (1993). Social participation of children with visual impairment in specialized and integrated environments. *Journal of Visual Impairments and Blindness, 87,* 138–142.

Evans, I. M., & Meyer, L. H. (1985). *An educative approach to behavior problems.* Baltimore: Paul Brookes.

Froschl, M., Colon, L., Rubin, E., & Sprung, B. (1984). *Including all of us: An early childhood curriculum about disabilities.* New York: Educational Equity Concepts.

Gallagher, J. J., Trohanis, P. L., & Clifford, R. M. (Eds.). (1989). *Policy implementation and PL,* 99–457. Baltimore: Paul Brookes.

Gardner, H., & Hatch, T. (1989). Multiple intelligences go to school. *Educational Researcher, 18,* 4–10.

Goldstein, A., & McGinnis, E. (1990). *Skillstreaming the preschool child.* Champaign, IL: Research Press.

Goodman, J. F. (1992). *When slow is fast enough.* New York: Guilford Press.

Greenspan, S. & Wieder, S. (1998). *The child with special needs: Encouraging intellectual and emotional growth.* Cambridge, MA: Perseus Publishing.

Guralnick, M. (1980). The social behavior of preschool children at different developmental levels: Effects of group composition. *Journal of Experimental Child Psychology, 31,* 115–130.

Guralnick, M., Connor, R. T., Hammond, M., Gottman, J., & Kinnish, K. (1996). Immediate effects of mainstreamed settings on the social interactions and integration of preschool children. *American Journal of Mental Retardation, 100,* 359–377.

Hartup, W. (1983). Peer relations. In E. M. Hetherington (Ed.), *Handbook of child psychology: Vol. 4. Socialization, personality, and social development* (pp. 103–196). New York: Wiley.

Hauser-Cram, P., Bronson, M. B., & Upshur, C. C. (1993). The effects of the classroom environment on the social and mastery behavior of preschool children with disabilities. *Early Childhood Research Quarterly, 8,* 479–498.

Hunt, J. M. (1961). *Intelligence and experience.* New York: Roland.

Jenkins, J. R., Odom, S. L., & Speltz, M. L. (1989). Effects of social integration on preschool children with handicaps. *Exceptional Children, 55,* 420–428.

Johnson, D., Johnson, R., & Holubec, E. J. (1990). *Circles of learning.* Edina, MN: Interaction.

Johnson, D. W., & Johnson, R. T. (1999). Making corporative learning work. *Theory into Practice, 38,* 67–73.

Johnson, J., Christie, J., & Wardle, F. (2005). *Play, development and early education.* Boston: Allyn & Bacon.

Knoblock, P. (Ed.). (1982). *Teaching and mainstreaming autistic children.* Denver: Love.

Knoblock, P., & Lehr, R. (1985). A model for mainstreaming autistic children: The Jowonio School. In E. Schopler & G. Mesibov (Eds.), *Social behavior in autism* (pp. 285–303). New York: Plenum.

LaVigna, G. W., & Donnellan, A. M. (1986). *Alternatives to punishment: Solving behavior problems with non-aversive strategies.* New York: Irvington.

Lieber, J., Capell, K., Sandall, S., Wolfberg, P., Horn, E., & Beckman, P. (1998). Inclusive preschool programs: Teachers' beliefs and practices. *Early Childhood Research Quarterly, 13,* 87–105.

McGee, J. J., Menolascino, F. J., Hobbs, D. C., & Menousek, P. E. (1987). *Gentle teaching.* New York: Human Science.

Meyer, L. H., & Evans, I. M. (1989). *Nonaversive intervention for behavior problems: A manual for home and community.* Baltimore: Paul Brookes.

Musselwhite, C. R. (1986). *Adaptive play for special needs children.* San Diego, CA: College Hill.

Neuman, S., & Roskos, K. (1993). Access to print for children of poverty: Differential effects of adult mediation and literacy-enriched play settings on environmental and functional print tasks. *American Educational Research Journal, 30,* 95–122.

Neuman, S., & Roskos, K. (1994). Bridging home and school with a culturally responsive approach. *Childhood Education, 70* (4), 210–214.

Odom, S., & Diamond, K. (1998). Inclusion of young children with special needs in early childhood education: The research base. *Early Childhood Research Quarterly, 13,* 3–25.

Odom, S. L., & McEvoy, M. A. (1988). Integration of young children with handicaps and normally developing children. In S. L. Odom & M. B.

Karnes (Eds.), *Early intervention for infants and children with handicaps* (pp. 241–267). Baltimore: Paul Brookes.

O'Neill, R. E., Horner, R. H., Albin, R. W., Storey, K., & Sprague, J. R. (1990). *Functional analysis of problem behavior*. Sycamore, IL: Sycamore.

Piaget, J. (1963). *The origins of intelligence in children*. New York: Norton.

Roberts, J., Burchinal, M., & Bailey, D. (1994). Communication among preschoolers with and without disabilities in same-age and mixed-age classrooms. *American Journal of Mental Retardation, 99*, 231–249.

Rubin, K. H., Bukowski, W., & Parker, J. C. (1998). Peer interactions, relationships, and groups. In N. Eisenberg (Ed.), *Handbook of child psychology: Social, emotional and personality development* (pp. 619–700). New York: Wiley.

Sapon-Shevin, M. (1980). Teaching cooperation in early childhood settings. In G. Cartledge & J. F. Milburn (Eds.), *Teaching social skills to children* (pp. 229–248). New York: Pergamon.

Sapon-Shevin, M. (1999). *Because we can change the world: A practical guide to building cooperative, inclusive classroom communities*. Needham Heights, MA: Allyn & Bacon.

Sapon-Shevin, M. (2000/2001). Schools fit for all. *Educational Leadership, 58*, 34–39.

Sarason, S. B., & Doris, J. (1959). *Educational handicap, public policy and social history*. New York: Free Press.

Schickedanz, J. (1986). *More than the ABC's: The early stages of reading and writing*. Washington, DC: National Association for the Education of Young Children.

Souweine, J., Crimmins, S., & Mazel, C. (1981). *Mainstreaming: Ideas for teaching young children*. Washington, DC: National Association for the Education of Young Children.

Stainback, S., & Stainback, W. (1992). *Curriculum considerations in inclusive classrooms*. Baltimore: Paul Brookes.

Stainback, W., & Stainback, S. (1990). *Support networks for inclusive schooling*. Baltimore: Paul Brookes.

Strain, P. S. (1984). Social behavior patterns of nonhandicapped and nonhandicapped-developmentally disabled friend pairs in mainstreamed preschoolers. *Analysis and Intervention in Development Disabilities, 4*, 15–58.

Strain, P. S. (1985). Social and nonsocial determinants of acceptability in handicapped preschool children. *Topics in Early Special Education, 4*, 47–58.

Strain, P. S., & Odom, S. L. (1986). Peer social initiations: Effective intervention for social skills development of exceptional children. *Exceptional Children, 43*, 526–530.

Thousand, J., & Villa, R. (1990). Sharing expertise and responsibilities through teaching teams. In W. Stainback & S. Stainback (Eds.), *Support networks in inclusive schooling* (pp. 201–218). Baltimore: Paul Brookes.

Touchette, P. E., MacDonald, R. F., & Langer, S. N. (1985). A scatter plot for identifying stimulus control of problem behavior. *Journal of Applied Behavior Analysis, 18*, 343–351.

Turnbull, H. R., & Turnbull, A. P. (1982). Public policy and handicapped citizens. In N. G. Haring (Ed.), *Exceptional children and youth* (3rd ed., pp. 21–44). Upper Saddle River, NJ: Merrill/Prentice Hall.

Vincent, L., Salisbury, C., Walter, G., Brown, P., Gruenewald, L., & Powers, M. (1980). Program evaluation and curriculum development in early childhood special education: Criteria for the next environment. In W. Saylor, B. Wilcox, & L. Brown (Eds.), *Instructional design for the severely handicapped* (pp. 130–182). Baltimore: Paul Brookes.

Westby, C. E. (1980). Assessment of cognitive and language abilities through play. *Language, Speech, and Hearing Services in Schools, 11*, 154–168.

Chapter 6

A Framework for Culturally Relevant, Multicultural, and Antibias Education in the Twenty-First Century

Louise Derman-Sparks ∽ Pacific Oaks College
Patricia G. Ramsey ∽ Mount Holyoke College

We are a nation of many peoples: many races, cultures, religions, classes, lifestyles, and histories. We are also a nation where access to achieving the "inalienable right" to "life, liberty and the pursuit of happiness," for which the American Revolution was fought, has not been equal for all. From their first arrival and consequent takeover of the land, European settlers encountered people whose race, cultures, religions, and history were vastly different from their own. As they consolidated their power, the Europeans established institutions and laws that embodied a fundamental contradiction between their goals to establish a democratic, free republic for themselves and their practices that enslaved or subjugated other groups. This duality has shaped our nation's history as illustrated in the current legal and extralegal efforts to exclude recent immigrants from Asia and Latin America and to roll back affirmative action and the increasing economic disparities that often follow racial lines.

As we begin the twenty-first century, these contradictions in both values and practices continue to pose an enormous challenge to all institutions, especially schools. How do educators honor their mandate to foster every child's full potential and to prepare all children to function effectively as members of a democratic society when many of these children are victims of racism and other forms of discrimination and/or live in poverty? How do educators respond to the cultural diversity of the population in this country while developing a common foundation on which to build a unified nation?

Several major responses to these questions have evolved at different points in American educational history, at the core of which are divergent philosophical and political positions, including differing demarcations of power between white European Americans and other racial/ethnic groups. Before discussing these responses, we first review what research tells us about how young children develop their identity and attitudes toward people racially, culturally, and otherwise different from themselves. This research provides an essential framework in which to consider how different approaches to diversity might apply to early childhood education.

ぷ WHAT AND HOW YOUNG CHILDREN LEARN ABOUT DIVERSITY

Young children do not arrive in early childhood programs as blank slates on the subject of diversity. Rather, they bring along a personalized

Educating children about diverse cultures will prepare them for life in the twenty-first century.

data bank that includes observations of various aspects of people's characteristics, experiences with comfortable or uncomfortable adult responses to their questions about human differences, exposure to socially prevailing biases, learned positive or negative responses to various aspects of people's identities, and self-constructed theories about what causes diversity (Derman-Sparks, 1992). Children are growing up in a world of contradictions as described in the opening paragraph of this chapter. We teach our children about equality, freedom, and fairness, but every day they are witnesses to inequities and discrimination. Often their ideas about diversity reflect these inconsistencies and confusions, as is seen in the following discussion.

Children's Responses to Race

Many studies have shown that children notice racial cues during infancy and that, by the age of 3 or 4, most children have a rudimentary concept of race (Katz, 1982; Katz & Kofkin, 1997; Van Ausdale & Feagin, 2001). Preschool children can accurately apply socially conventional labels of "black" and "white" to pictures,

dolls, and people, but they are not necessarily aware of their own ethnic affiliation (Aboud, 1977). The salience of race in children's perceptions of others and the kind and amount of information they learn about racial differences vary according to children's social milieu, their majority or minority status, and the extent and kinds of contacts they have with other racial groups (Phinney & Rotheram, 1987; Ramsey, 1991a; Ramsey & Meyers, 1990). Preschoolers have already embarked on their lifelong task of figuring out "who I am" and "who you are." They are aware of and curious about differences and similarities among people, ask questions, organize the data they gather, and construct theories about diversity congruent with their general cognitive stages of development, as well as with their life experiences (Clark, 1955; Dennis, 1981; Derman-Sparks, Higa, & Sparks, 1980; Dorris, 1978; Froschl, Colon, Rubin, & Sprung, 1984; Honig, 1983; Katz, 1982; Ocampo, Bernal, & Knight, 1993; Ramsey, 1987b; Sapon-Shevin, 1983; Sheldon, 1990; Trager & Radke-Yarrow, 1952; Van Ausdale & Feagin, 2001; Wardle, 1987, 1990).

Children's racial identity development varies across groups and across historical periods. In many early studies (e.g., Clark & Clark, 1947; Goodman, 1952; Morland, 1962; Radke & Trager, 1950), European American children never expressed a wish to be black, but African-American children frequently appeared to either wish or believe that they were white. Studies that have been done after the 1960s suggest that the positive images of blacks, now more evident in schools and in the media and more consciously promoted in families, may be reducing this dissonance.

In more recent studies, African American children usually express an own-group orientation (e.g., Cross, 1985, 1991) and in elementary school may develop a stronger own-race identity than their white peers (Aboud & Doyle, 1993; Burnett & Sisson, 1995). However, other studies suggest that racism and white dominance and affluence still negatively affect children's black self-perceptions (e.g., Gopaul-McNicol, 1988). Patterns of white identification and preference may be attempts to resolve the contradiction between feeling personally valued yet disparaged because of group membership (Corenblum & Annis, 1993; Cross, 1985, 1987, 1991). Spencer and Markstrom-Adams (1990) point out that children who are targets of discrimination have to confront conflicting values between their own group and mainstream society, prevailing negative stereotypes of their group, and lack of guidance in how to deal with discrimination.

Young children's emotional reactions to racial differences often reflect a tendency to exaggerate the intergroup differences and minimize the intragroup ones (Aboud, 1988; Katz, 1976, 1982; Ramsey, 1987b; Tajfel, 1973; Tatum, 1997). As children's awareness of different groups develops, their attitudes also evolve. Doyle and Aboud (1993) found that during the preschool and early elementary years, children became more racially biased, which coincided with an increased emphasis on

intergroup differences, difficulty differentiating individuals within different groups, and highly sociocentric views ("my view is right and yours is wrong"), all of which may contribute to their heightened prejudice. However, Aboud and Doyle (1993) found that in middle childhood (after the age of 7) prejudice declined and simultaneously children shifted from emphasizing intergroup differences to seeing similarities; they were also more able to distinguish individuals in different groups and to see others' points of view.

Some children may be more likely than others to develop and maintain stereotypes. Bigler and Liben (1993) and Bigler, Jones, and Lobliner (1997) found that young white children, who had more rigid classification systems in general, formed stronger stereotyped images of African and European Americans. Whether children become more or less own-race biased may depend in large part on their environment, the values that they are learning, and whether their assumptions and attitudes are being challenged.

Children's friendship choices in racially mixed preschool and elementary classrooms generally show that gender is a stronger determinant of friendship than race (e.g., Asher, Singleton, & Taylor, 1982; Ramsey & Meyers, 1990). However, race appears to be a factor, especially for white children who consistently over the past 3 decades have shown stronger same-race preferences than their African American classmates (Finkelstein & Haskins, 1983; Fox & Jordan, 1973; Newman, Liss, & Sherman, 1983; Ramsey & Myers, 1990; Rosenfield & Stephan, 1981; Stabler, Zeig, & Johnson, 1982; Van Ausdale & Feagin, 2001). Because white children's own-race preferences are reinforced by the society at large, they are most at risk for developing own-race bias in their friendships. During the elementary years, racial cleavage often increases as children absorb more of the prevailing social attitudes, and the awareness of "us" versus "them" becomes more established

(Katz, 1976). However, it is not inevitable. A number of research studies on racially integrated cooperative learning teams suggest that children who participate in these groups have significantly more cross-ethnic friendships (Johnson & Johnson, 2000; Rosenfield & Stephan, 1981; Slavin, 1995).

Children's Responses to Social Class Differences

Young children are not able to "see" and understand most indices of social class, such as educational level and occupational prestige. At the same time, they do notice more concrete clues including differences in clothing, homes, and possessions. Furthermore, they daily experience the effects of affluence or its absence by watching their parents interact (or not interact) with the work world and social and financial institutions. In subtle ways their images and expectations are being formed. As children learn about social class, they also absorb the prevailing attitudes that being rich is better than being poor (Leahy, 1983). Even preschoolers assume that rich people are happier and more likeable than poor people (Naimark, 1983; Ramsey, 1991b). At an early age, children's developing identities embody tacit theories about social realities that reflect their economic status at an early age. DeLone (1979) found that children with comparable IQ scores but from different social class backgrounds expressed aspirations and expectations for future jobs that fit their families' social class.

Children's understanding and attitudes related to social class change during childhood (Leahy, 1983). Between the age of 6 years and adolescence, children shift from noticing more concrete manifestations of affluence or poverty to thinking in more psychological and abstract terms. During this time, children are also developing a sense of fairness and noticing inequities (Damon, 1980), but, ironically, they are also learning to justify inequalities by claiming that poor people get what they deserve (Leahy,

1990). Taken together, these findings illustrate how children are caught in one of the underlying contradictions of our society: the ideals of fairness and equality versus the economic competitiveness and individualism that inevitably results in inequality (Chafel, 1997).

Economic differences and tensions are exaggerated and exacerbated by our consumerist culture. Even people who have adequate food, clothing and shelter often "feel poor" because their lifestyles do not match the extravagant ones portrayed in media shows and advertising. Moreover, children are learning to identify themselves as consumers and owners (Kline, 1993). In their media-induced desires for new toys and clothes, children either pressure their parents to give them money or, in some cases, get drawn into illegal activities in order to acquire highly desirable goods.

Children quickly learn to judge each other—and themselves—by the desirability and quantity of toys and clothes that they own, which can exacerbate social class differences. This passion for purchasing new items also devalues traditional values and practices and may create rifts between children and their parents and grandparents. Moreover, when children are preoccupied with having the latest and most expensive new product, they have difficulty thinking about and empathizing with the needs of other individuals or groups.

Children's Responses to Culture

A growing body of research is exploring a new and crucial perspective on how development and learning occur within sociocultural contexts (e.g., Greenfield & Cocking, 1994). Increasingly, educators and psychologists are recognizing that culture exerts a strong influence on children's development: "culture is a process which empowers people to function" (Phillips, 1990, p. 2). Through culture "children gain a sense of identity, a feeling of belonging, a notion of what is important in life, what is right and wrong, how to care for themselves and others, and what to celebrate, eat and wear" (Cortez, 1996, p. ix). They gain the power to influence their environment and to have an impact on the world (Phillips, 1988).

Despite the profound influence of culture on all aspects of learning and development, the concept of culture itself is abstract, and most children are not consciously aware of their own or others' cultures. Young children have only a vague idea about geography and cannot conceptualize the relationships between town, state, and country (Piaget, 1951). Thus, although they may notice overt cultural practices such as languages, clothing, and foods, most young children do not have a clear idea of how these differences relate to regional and national differences. Yet children's role expectations and assumptions about the world such as ideas about time, personal space, conversational conventions, and styles of teaching and learning are culturally defined. Children often react with confusion or defiance when their assumptions are violated. In their social interactions, they respond to language differences, which are more concrete expressions of culture and have practical consequences when children are playing together (Doyle, 1982; Orellana, 1994). As they get older, children are more able to identify cultural similarities and differences. However, this development occurs in a contradictory context. As children develop their capacity to see other cultural perspectives and to recognize that their own culture is only one of many, they also acquire more in-group biases against unfamiliar cultures (Carter & Patterson, 1982).

When children attend early childhood programs that are not culturally sensitive to and consistent with their home cultures, they are at risk. As Carol Brunson Phillips eloquently reminds us, "Remember what happened to E.T. when he got too far from home? He lost his power over the world. And so it is with our children when their school settings are so different from home that they represent an alien culture to them. They too lose their power" (1988, p. 47).

A nationwide study of 1,000 language-minority families (including Latin, Asian, Arab, and European immigrants and non–English-speaking Native Americans) whose children went to preschool programs conducted partly or entirely in English provides evidence that justifies this concern. The researchers found evidence of "serious disruptions of family relations occurring when young children learn English in school and lose the use of the home language" (National Association for Bilingual Education, 1990, p. 1). Lily Wong Fillmore (1990, p. 7), director of the study, concludes,

> It is important to recognize the consequences that early education programs for language minority children can have on the family's ability to perform its socializing role. Admittedly, there are positive benefits to be had from an early immersion in the ways of speaking and learning that are the most highly valued in the school. The children will find it easier to make the transition to school eventually, but such programs achieve little if they contribute to a breakdown in parent and child relations. What is at stake is nothing less than the family's continued role in the socialization of its children.

The price paid by these children includes the gradual impoverishment of communication between children, parents, and other family members; the feeling of the children that their parents must be mad at them; and the feeling of the parents that they have lost control of their children (Marquez, 1991). These dynamics lead to a serious decline in the family's ability to provide necessary socialization to their children and can lead to tragic consequences by the teenage years (Wong Fillmore, 1991).

To meet the developmental needs of an increasingly large number of children who are and will be attending early childhood part- and full-day programs, "We must examine the values and beliefs that underlie child rearing practices and ways of being in the world, and that influence children's learning styles. We need to figure out how to make our classrooms more like our [children's] homes, where children have learned to be powerful, and then we must help our children transfer their power into another cultural setting" (Phillips, 1988, p. 47).

In the well-known Kamehameha Early Education Project (KEEP), teachers adapted their teaching methods so that they were more compatible with the Native Hawaiian culture (Tharp & Gallimore, 1988). Children who had been doing poorly were much more successful in their academic work after these changes were made. Tharp (1989) argues that educators should develop practices to increase the cultural compatibility between home and school but at the same time support children as they develop new skills so that all children (including members of the dominant group) can function in a wider range of modalities.

Children's Responses to Gender Differences

From an early age, children notice, identify, and divide themselves by gender. Children appear to develop gender schemata (Bem, 1981, 1983; Martin & Halverson, 1981), theories about the characteristics of males and females that influence how children interpret social information. Gender stereotypes are self-perpetuating, because when children are presented with information that violates their expectations of gender roles, they are less likely to remember it than when they are presented with information that is congruent with their stereotypes (Mapley & Kizer, 1983). However, as with race, children may vary in the degree to which their stereotypes influence their interpretations. Children who in general make more flexible classifications less often use gender stereotypes and can remember counterstereotypic gender information better than their peers who make more rigid classifications (Bigler & Liben, 1992).

One reason that gender roles are so intransigent is the prevalent use of gender in our society to divide and differentiate people (Bem, 1981, 1983). This pattern is exacerbated by the consumerist pressures that were discussed earlier. From the time children are born, their toys and clothes are gender-typed. In toy or clothing stores there are the "pink aisles" (filled with pink and purple outfits, sneakers, and toys—even Legos come in "girl colors" now) and the "grayish-brown" aisles (filled with darker colored clothes—some imitating army camouflage—and action figures, vehicles, war toys, and guns). Many television shows target either boys or girls so that they learn and play out different gender-specific fantasies. Not only does the content of the programs differ, but the commercials for character toys encourage distinct, gender-typed fantasy play (Kline, 1993).

Children's absorption of gender stereotypes limits the development of both boys and girls. When areas of experience are closed to children simply because of their sex, neither boys nor girls are fully prepared to deal with the realities and demands of everyday life. As young as 3 and 4 years of age, children begin to self-limit their choices of learning experiences because of the gender norms they are already absorbing. One of the negative consequences of this process is a pattern of uneven development.

Despite a great deal of legal and attitudinal change, girls and boys are still not treated equally in schools (see Sadker & Sadker, 1995, for many compelling examples). Girls are often overlooked by teachers and not encouraged to excel, particularly in math and science and in physically challenging activities. They do, however, learn to be nurturing and emotionally expressive and are often more skilled at maintaining personal relationships than boys are. Boys, on the other hand, are encouraged to be aggressive, to excel, to take physical risks, and to hide their emotions. They are both the best students and the worst troublemakers (Sadker & Sadker, 1995); boys potentially grow up to take leadership positions and to earn more money than their female counterparts, but at the same time, they are at more risk than girls to fail in school or to engage in violent and dangerous activities (e.g., Garbarino, 1999; Kindlon & Thompson, 1999; Kivel, 1999; Pollack, 1998). Thus, while girls have been more materially shortchanged in schools and jobs, both sexes suffer the effects of rigid sex-role expectations.

Preschool and elementary school children clearly prefer same-sex peers—all of their hypothetical choices and actual playmate choices demonstrate this over and over (e.g., Bigler, 1999; Ramsey, 1995). Gender segregation begins before preschool and becomes increasingly entrenched during the early childhood years (Ramsey, 1995). The gap continues to widen during the elementary years and is reaffirmed by children's engagement in "borderwork" between the two groups (Thorne, 1986). As children spend more time in gender-segregated play, male and female groups form their own cultures with clearly defining characteristics (Maccoby, 1986), which further impedes cross-group play.

Sexual Orientation

Sexual orientation is related to gender roles and is the source of considerable misunderstanding and discrimination. Most people in this country are not judged by their sexual preferences and practices, but lesbians, gay men, bisexuals, and transgendered individuals are often judged *exclusively*—and harshly—by their choice of sexual partners and by others' assumptions about their sexual practices. Currently, in the United States sexual preferences are more openly acknowledged and discussed than they were 2 or 3 decades ago. Now there are a number of networks and publications for and by gay and lesbian people in many different occupations (Casper, Cuffaro, Schultz, Silin, & Wickens, 1996). Still, in most schools and centers sexual orientation is rarely mentioned and often actively avoided. Consequently, children from gay- and

lesbian-headed households do not receive the same kind of recognition and support for their families as do other children. This behavior contradicts a fundamental early childhood education tenet about the importance of partnering and supporting all families being served in a program. In one study, teachers who were recognized for their multicultural and antibias teaching and skills in discussing sensitive issues around race, class, and gender with children admitted that they often avoided the topic of sexual orientation (Alvarado, Derman-Sparks, & Ramsey, 1999).

Because so many people are vehemently opposed to any mention of sexual orientation and gay- or lesbian-headed families in schools, it is virtually impossible to interview children on this topic. Thus we have very little formal research on this topic.

Casper and Schultz (1999), however, did extensive observations of children in early childhood classrooms where there were children from gay and lesbian families. They describe several conversations that indicate that early childhood and primary-age children are interested in and aware of issues related to family composition and sexual orientation. Most of the children's questions and comments focused on whether someone needed to have had both a mother and a father to be born and what combinations of adults make a family. Casper and Schultz noted that children were most likely to bring these topics up when they had time to develop their dramatic play storylines; props that gave them the latitude to play out different family constellations (e.g., multiple adult puppets); and books and pictures that cumulatively portrayed a wide range of families including those with two mommies and two daddies.

Children's Responses to Abilities and Disabilities

Children as young as 3 years have some awareness of sensory and orthopedic disabilities (Degrella & Green, 1984; Diamond & Innes, 2001). Not surprisingly, their understanding varies across type of disability (Conant & Budoff, 1983; Diamond, 1996). Younger children notice orthopedic disabilities, largely because of the visibility of the equipment that is associated with them, such as crutches or wheelchairs, and are least aware of mental retardation or psychological disturbances (Diamond & Hestenes, 1996). When trying to explain disabilities, children often refer to immaturity (e.g., "He hasn't learned to walk yet.") or some kind of trauma (e.g., "She broke her leg and can't use it.") (Diamond, 1993; Diamond & Innes, 2001; Sigelman, 1991).

During the early childhood years, children without disabilities tend to become more biased against people with disabilities (Degrella & Green, 1984). From second to fourth grade, this trend continues (Goodman, 1989); and then children become more positive toward people with disabilities from the fourth to sixth grade (Condon, York, Heal, & Fortschneider, 1986). Acceptance or rejection of peers with disabilities is also affected by the situation and nature of disability. For example, children are more likely to reject peers with orthopedic limitations when they are thinking about or are doing physical activities (Harper, Wacker, & Cobb, 1986). Young children also frequently explain that they dislike their classmates with disabilities because they are disruptive and/or aggressive (Nabors & Keyes, 1995; Roberts & Zubrick, 1992), which suggests that children with behavioral and emotional disabilities may seem threatening to their peers and at more risk for being rejected. Children also are more accepting toward their peers who have disabilities that are no fault of their own (e.g., a specific physical disabilities such as blindness) than they are toward peers perceived as having more responsibility for their disability (e.g., obesity, poor impulse control) (Diamond & Innes, 2001).

Unfortunately, in integrated classrooms, children with disabilities are often socially isolated and rejected (Diamond, Le Furgy, & Blass, 1993; Nabors, 1995; Taylor, Asher, & Williams, 1987). In fact some findings show that children with disabilities become more isolated over the school year (Diamond et al., 1993; Guralnick & Groom, 1987), demonstrating that merely having contact does not break down the barriers between "typical" children and their peers.

When children of different abilities play together, their interactions are often strained and unequal (Siperstein, Brownley, & Scott, 1989). Even when typical and disabled children have similar interaction patterns and at the outset appear to be developing equal relationships, children with disabilities often get left behind when the play becomes more complex and requires more advanced social and cognitive skills (Guralnick, Connor, Hammond, Gottman, & Kinnish, 1996). Here again our societal contradictions may play a role. Children are learning that they should accept their peers with disabilities but are also getting caught up in judging and competing with others, which makes it hard to admire or include children who are less skilled in some way.

In spite of these challenges, isolation and inequality are not inevitable. Even children who may be quite isolated from the social mainstream often have one friend who serves as a social buffer and provides companionship (Juvonen & Bear, 1992). In one study, third and fourth graders with learning disabilities showed a considerable increase in numbers of reciprocal friends from fall to spring (Vaughn, Elbaum, & Schumm, 1996). Adults also play a crucial role in the social integration of children with disabilities (Gonsier-Gerdin, 1995; Odom, Jenkins, Speltz, & DeKlyen, 1982; Odom et al., 1996; Swadener & Johnson, 1989). First, when adults obviously enjoy interacting with children with disabilities and support interactions between them and their peers, the children with disabilities become more a part of the classroom social life. Second, adults can facilitate social interactions by closely monitoring children's social patterns, providing activities and instructions to develop social skills, and subtly supporting children as they play together by "coaching" and offering materials and ideas to maintain interest in an activity. Third, cooperative activities are more conducive to integration than competitive ones. Fourth, when teachers treat children as full members of the group, their classmates treat them that way as well. Sheridan, Foley, and Radlinski (1995) give many detailed examples of these principles in practice.

How Children Learn About Diversity

Across all dimensions of diversity, children absorb the images, stereotypes, and assumptions that are in their social milieu. They learn through direct and indirect instructions by parents, peers, and teachers and through contact with printed and electronic media. Some messages are subtle. Children may observe their parents' (possibly unconscious) reactions to different people or notice locations where their parents are uneasy. Parents' or teachers' own discomfort with issues of diversity may lead them to avoid discussing these issues. When children ask questions, parents and teachers may worry that this curiosity is a sign of incipient prejudice and dismiss children's questions and feelings about people's identities with statements such as "It's not polite to ask" or "I'll tell you later" or "It doesn't matter." This avoidance does not give children the help they need to form positive ideas about themselves or a pro-diversity disposition toward others (Derman-Sparks & ABC Task Force, 1989).

The absorption of negative and inaccurate images of different groups impairs the development of all children. Over 30 years ago, Kenneth Clark identified serious consequences of racism to both African American and European American young children. (His research was one of the decisive factors in the 1954 Supreme Court desegregation decision.) In the chapter entitled "The White Child and Race Prejudice," Clark wrote:

> The social influences responsible for the development of racial prejudices in American

children at the same time develop deep patterns of moral conflict, guilt, anxiety and distortion of reality in these children. The same institutions that teach children the democratic and religious doctrine of the brotherhood of man and the equality of all human beings—institutions such as the church and school—also teach them to violate these concepts through racial prejudice and undemocratic behavior toward others. (1955, p. 78)

The consequences of this struggle for white children include distortions of reality, lack of intellectual skills and accurate information necessary for living in today's world, a false sense of identity based on superiority simply because of skin color, tension and fears about people different from themselves, moral double standards, and conformity to undemocratic demands of silence (Clark, 1955; Dennis, 1981).

The costs to children who are targets of prejudice affect every aspect of their lives. In addition to fewer opportunities for decent health care, nutrition, education, and housing, the internalizing of societal biases against their group can "profoundly affect self-concept, behavior, aspirations and confidence. They can inhibit a child before he or she has learned to define personal talents, limits or objectives, and tend to regularly become self-fulfilling prophecies. Young people who are informed that they are going to be underachievers do underachieve with painful regularity" (Dorris, 1978, p. 2).

✍ EDUCATIONAL APPROACHES TO DIVERSITY: PAST AND PRESENT

This section discusses the five basic educational approaches to diversity and social injustice that have emerged in our society in the twentieth century (for more detailed discussions about the sociopolitical contexts of these different movements see Ramsey & Williams, 2003). For each approach, we describe the underlying assumptions about diversity and society, educational goals and methods, and current criticisms. The first three approaches focus on populations that have historically been excluded from the mainstream in the United States and ways of forcing their assimilation into the European American dominant culture. The last two approaches focus on all groups and reflect efforts to create more equitable social, cultural, economic, and political relationships among them.

Suppression of Cultural Diversity

The underlying assumption of the suppression of cultural diversity is that everyone needs to be assimilated into the European American culture to create a united nation. The justifications for this orientation rest on the racist assumptions that the European American culture is superior to others and that "it was here first." It further implies that the rights and privileges of the United States are only for those who choose to assimilate and therefore sets up a fundamentally unequal power relationship between European Americans and other racial/ethnic groups.

Early childhood curriculum that reflects this orientation does not address diversity and discourages children and parents from bringing their own languages and cultural practices into the classroom. Schools that adhere to this view reflect only European American images, beliefs, and behaviors in their curricula, physical environments, and materials. Teachers actively discourage children from retaining their own culture and language. For example, until the 1960s, schools run by the Bureau of Indian Affairs removed children from their home communities, and teachers and administrators sought to erase Native American children's culture and language and replace them with the language, values, and habits of middle-class white society. In many other schools, children were punished for speaking their native languages, and parents were urged to speak only English at home (e.g., Rodriguez, 1981). A statement made many years ago by Theodore Roosevelt exemplifies this attitude: "We have

room for but one language here and that is the English language, for we intend to see that the crucible turns our people out as Americans, of American nationality, and not as dwellers in a polyglot boarding house" (quoted in Marquez, 1991, p. 6).

In the 1960s a new form of cultural suppression emerged under the rubrics of "cultural deprivation theory" and "compensatory education." This approach argued that "the inability of culturally different families to benefit from the opportunities for social equality in this country, and thus the inability of their children to benefit from school experience is, in part (if not totally), due to their culture" (Phillips, 1988, p. 43). Therefore, the educational solution was to institute special programs for both children and parents that would teach them to assimilate into the dominant European American culture. Although appearing to be more compassionate than programs in which children were physically punished for speaking in their native tongues, these programs have shared the same ultimate goals of making all children fit a single cultural mold. Consequently, these programs embodied a deficit orientation toward the children they are designed to assist (Baratz & Baratz, 1971).

This cultural deficit orientation violates what we recognize as good early childhood education practice. It is not based on current theories or empirical research about how children learn about themselves, about becoming competent individuals, and about diversity; and it hurts all children (Tatum, 1997). Schools with this approach cannot promote feelings of safety, security, and belonging for children. These conditions undermine children's social, emotional, and cognitive development and their relationships with their families. Although these settings may be less stressful for European American children, this approach ill prepares them for their future, because increasingly, white children will grow up to live and work in diverse communities and work sites. Moreover, this perspective potentially condones or even encourages prejudice and discourages children from learning about groups other than the identified mainstream (Derman-Sparks, 1992).

Melting Pot

In the early part of the twentieth century, the national vision was one of a melting pot, an expectation that diverse groups would be fused in the crucible of the United States and emerge as common Americans. By obliterating differences, all Americans would gain equal access to the opportunities of U.S. society. Schools were expected to teach everyone the same "melted" culture. Although this ideal embodied an expectation that all cultures would contribute to the common mix, in actuality, the "common culture" comprised the ethnic worldviews of Western/Northern Europe that were fused together to become the European American dominant culture. Even as the schools touted a "melting pot" approach, they were in fact pushing toward "Anglo conformity" (Ramsey & Williams, 2003; Vold, 1989). This one-way assimilation encourages immigrants to renounce their ancestry, values, and language and become as similar to the dominant Anglo-Saxon group as possible.

Teachers who are oriented to the melting pot position often claim to be color blind. They may deny noticing whether their children are white, black, purple, or green and adhere to the position that "we are all Americans and share a common culture" and that "everyone is the same." With these pronouncements, teachers minimize differences, thereby ignoring the lifestyles and contributions of other groups as well as the effects of differential power and affluence on children's development.

This approach almost always results in teaching practices, environments, and materials that reflect European American culture and deny the realities of diversity and the absorption of societal biases. Moreover, it confuses the concept of diversity with that of Anglo conformity and thus contradicts children's daily experiences

and thwarts their efforts to understand their social worlds.

"Add-On" Multiculturalism

Criticisms of cultural suppression educational approaches began to seriously emerge as a result of the civil rights movement in the 1960s. Critics argued that recognizing cultural differences as strengths rather than problems was necessary to creating a more equitable society. A multicultural approach to education began to take shape in the 1960s with the underlying assumption that we are a society of many peoples and that we all need to learn to respect ourselves and one another. From this perspective, schools have a responsibility to support the cultures of all children, to teach children to respect themselves and others, and to get along with a wide range of people. The hope was that this approach would also result in reducing prejudice and discrimination.

Although advocates of multicultural education argue that the approach must be infused into all aspects of the education program, an insufficient version, critically termed add-on multiculturalism, has become the most frequently practiced approach. In this version of multicultural education, the existing classroom environment and curriculum continue to be based on the dominant European American culture, while other cultures (i.e., ethnic minority groups) are introduced into the curriculum from time to time through special activities. Thus, a classroom may have a special multicultural bulletin board, or may organize learning about diversity around special days or holidays, or may introduce week-long units about particular ethnic groups, and then go back to the regular curriculum.

Because add-on multiculturalism is organized around concrete and nonthreatening activities, many teachers find it easier to make these superficial gestures, or window-dressing changes, rather than to truly transform their curriculum. Many teacher education classes and inservice workshops continue to be influenced by the add-on approach. This response is abetted by the availability of (and heavily promoted) commercial curriculum materials and published curriculum guides that reflect an add-on version of multicultural education.

This form of multiculturalism has been strongly criticized as a "tourist" approach that stereotypes, trivializes, and misrepresents cultures different from the mainstream European American culture. It further perpetuates inequitable racial power relationships by keeping European American culture the center or norm and other cultures as satellites or occasional places to visit. An add-on or tourist approach to diversity does not adequately address diversity and cannot effectively support children's healthy development of identity or respectful attitudes toward others (Derman-Sparks, 1989).

Bilingualism/Biculturalism

The underlying assumption of the bilingual/bicultural approach is that children can and should learn to be effective members of both their own cultural group and of the wider, mainstream society. The prefix *bi* means *two:* two languages; two cultural ways of being. Biculturalism is based on the premise that the creation of a truly democratic society in which all groups have fair and equal access to opportunities requires that members of diverse ethnic, racial, and religious groups maintain an autonomous participation in their traditions, cultures, and special interests, while also becoming part of a shared nation (Appleton, 1983; Banks, 1988). For example, in the United States, this means people speak both English and their home, or "heritage," language (Krashen, Tse, & McQuillan, 1998). Early childhood programs that reflect this orientation foster children's ability to speak and learn in their home language and culture while learning the language and cultural rules of behavior of the dominant culture.

Bilingualism/biculturalism is not a new idea in American education. Heritage language programs have a fairly long history in North America (Krashen et al., 1998). German–English schools were established in Ohio in the mid-nineteenth century (Grosjean, 1982), and many other communities formed their own language schools in Dutch, German, Swedish, Yiddish, and Italian (Dropkin, Tobier, & City University of New York, 1976; Fishman, 1966). However, powerful attempts to destroy the language of Native Americans, the enslaved Africans, and the conquered Mexican people also have a long tradition in U.S. history. In 1923 a total of 34 states had English-only educational policies affecting European immigrant languages as well as those of Mexican and the many Native American nations (Marquez, 1991).

In the 1960s self-determination and social–political rights movements fueled a renewed demand for education to support all people's cultural rights and to reverse the tragic undermining of children's cultures, identities, and native languages that contributed to the disproportionately high school dropout rates of non–European American children. The *Lau v. Nichols* decision in 1974 led many schools to start bilingual education programs.

Early childhood education has a particularly salient and sensitive role in bilingual and bicultural education because the preschool years are key to all children's language and identity development. Knowing when to begin instruction in English for children whose home language is not English and the methods that best support continued growth in the child's home language while the child is also learning English are central to creating good programs. The National Association for the Education of Young Children recognized this in its 1997 position statement *Cultural and Linguistic Diversity,* which states that early childhood programs must focus on both educating children toward the culture of the American school while also preserving and respecting the home language and culture that each child brings with him or her.

While some educators argue that maintaining the home language interferes with the acquisition of English (e.g., Porter, 1990), most studies demonstrate that young children can learn to be bilingual (Garcia, 1980; Krashen et al., 1998; Sandoval-Martinez, 1982) and in the process benefit in other ways as well.

Maintenance of home languages fosters earlier development of academic skills and eventually more proficient English (e.g., Crawford, 1991) and supports children's overall cognitive and emotional development and their ability to communicate with their families (Cummins, 1981, 1986; Wong Fillmore, 1991). Collier and Thomas (1997) collected data on over 700,000 language minority students from 1982 to 1996 in schools that were using different kinds of well-implemented bilingual programs. They found that students in programs with the longest use of their home languages combined with strong content-based English as a second-language instruction showed most academic success. Students who received only English instruction without any home-language instruction in the early years of schooling fared the worst academically. Several researchers have also found a positive relationship between children's development of positive self-identity and the maintenance of their home language, because of the continuing connection with their cultural group. In addition, positive self and group concepts also foster the development of positive attitudes toward other ethnic and cultural groups (Tse, 1998). Nevertheless, bilingual education is "the focus of a continuing debate over language choice in the society. The arguments against bilingual education . . . carry with them underlying political and social perspectives related to people's views of American society" (Wong Fillmore, 1991, p. 2). Recently several states have virtually banned it from public schools (although families can still request that their children continue to receive bilingual education). Typically, opponents fear that bilingualism will lead to divisiveness and political unrest (Krashen et al., 1998). However, no evidence demonstrates that bilingualism or multilingualism causes political or economic problems in nations where people speak more than one language. For example, a study of the impact of 230 possible predictors of civil strife in 170 countries (Fishman, 1990) found "the correlation of linguistic heterogeneity and civil strife was a low .21, which meant that it accounted for only 4% of the variation in civil strife. When other factors were considered, it had no predictive value at all" (Krashen et al., 1998, p. 6).

Continued research is needed to determine the most effective methods to implement a bilingual/bicultural approach in varying contexts and at different developmental periods. We need to consider how bilingual education might be implemented in programs where many different languages are spoken or where only one or two children speak a language other than English. We also need to more deeply understand when and how to begin second-language English instruction and how to support early childhood teachers' progress toward becoming fluent in a language other than English. However, based on the research to date, we agree with the United Nation's *Convention on the Rights of the Child* (1989) that becoming bilingual and bicultural is a basic right of the child. Indeed, we believe that it is to the benefit of all children to become bilingual and bicultural—a necessity for effective work in our global society.

Antibias Multicultural Education

The goals of this approach are to ensure equitable individual participation in all aspects of society and to enable people to maintain their own culture while participating together to live in a common society. This approach embodies a profound acknowledgment and critique of the fundamental contradictions of our nation and a commitment to transform the inequitable power relationships in our schools and society, while also including the initial goal of multicultural education of respect for oneself and others. The antibias multicultural approach has a pragmatic as well as an idealistic intent. The realities of changing demographics mean that, as a society, we cannot afford to waste the human talent of an increasingly growing segment of the population and that "majority" (soon to be the demographic "minority") children need to learn how to live effectively and be activists in a changing and diverse society. From this perspective, schools have a responsibility not only to teach children to respect themselves and create equitable relationships with a wide range of people but also to teach children how to work toward eliminating prejudice and discrimination.

The antibias multicultural education movement has several precursors and roots. One is the intergroup education movement of the late 1940s and early 1950s (Taba, Brady, & Robinson, 1952). During this period, some of the classic studies of young children's racial awareness and attitudes toward self and others were conducted (e.g., Clark, 1955; Trager & Radke-Yarrow, 1952). Unfortunately, information about the work of the intergroup movement as well as of the pioneering research on children's development of attitudes was subsequently ignored in mainstream child development and nursery school texts. However, it has reemerged in more recent work on early attitude development, and antibias multicultural education embodies many of the goals of the intergroup education movement. Another precursor is the ethnic studies movement of the 1970s, which argued for education that truthfully taught children of color their culture and history. A third is the commitment to eliminate prejudice and discrimination that fueled the civil rights movement of the 1960s and ultimately led to the realization that white children and families must confront and unlearn their racism.

Multicultural education that began to develop during the late 1960s and 1970s initially focused on fostering respect within and across different racial and cultural groups. The antibias

approach, which first appeared in written form in 1989, argued that other aspects of identity such as gender, social class, religion, sexual orientation, and disabilities were also germane to the development of the children's positive identities and respect for others. By the 1990s, advocates of multiculturalism as well as of antibias education agreed that all educational programs should address the wider issue of underrepresentation and should incorporate all groups that have been excluded from the traditional curriculum (e.g., Derman-Sparks & ABC Task Force, 1989; Nieto, 1996; Ramsey, 1998). We choose to use the term *antibias multicultural education* to describe this perspective, although people in the field may only use one or the other of the terms.

Most recently, some antibias multicultural writers have been pointing out connections between the marginalization and subjugation of particular groups of people and the exploitation of our natural resources and the competitive consumerism in our society (Ramsey, 1998). These latter themes relate to cultural and social class differences because how one views the natural world and consumption is influenced by one's culture and level of affluence. They also embody social justice issues because environmental degradation is concentrated in poor communities and countries (Fruchter, 1999). Moreover, commercial interests often target disadvantaged groups for their most aggressive marketing (e.g., vigorous marketing of high-priced sneakers and other expensive clothing in poor urban communities [Nightingale, 1993]).

Discussion about the nature of antibias multicultural work with white children and adults is another recent development. "What if all the kids are white?" has been one of the most frequently asked questions by white early childhood teachers over the past 2 decades. It echoes the misconception that antibias multicultural education is only about people who are "different than" whites. In the early days of multicultural education, teachers in predominately white programs often assumed that education about diversity was not relevant to their children, and the question had an undertone of "Why should we bother?" After all, *their* children were not confronted by negative identity-damaging stereotypes, alienated from the images and practices in their classrooms, or subjected to racial or ethnic discrimination by school and community personnel. More recently, however, many teachers of white children have become aware of how racism affects everyone. They understand that a false sense of racial superiority is isolating and damaging and ill prepares white children to function in a diverse society. Such teachers also recognize that working for social justice is indeed also a "white thing." A society without racism will benefit *all* people, including whites, and cannot be achieved unless all groups, especially those in power, join the struggle. Thus, many teachers today believe that antibias/multicultural education IS relevant to white children. However, when such teachers serve all-white groups of children and do not perceive obvious diversity, they do not know how to engage children in learning about differences and social justice. For these teachers, the intent of the question has shifted from "why?" to "how?" The authors of this chapter are currently engaged in writing a book that explores the many issues and possible strategies to address the question of "What if all the kids are white?"

During the 1990s, antibias multicultural education more explicitly incorporated a social reconstructionist orientation that assumes that the creation of a just society requires a fundamental change in institutional structures, policies, and behaviors that inhibit the equitable participation of all racial and ethnic groups (Sleeter & Grant, 1987). As Enid Lee explains,

> It is a point of view that cuts across all subject areas, and addresses the histories and experiences of people who have been left out of the curriculum. Its purpose is to help us deal equitably with all the cultural and racial differences in the human family. It's also a

perspective that allows us to get at explanations for why things are the way they are in terms of power relationships and equality issues. (1991, p. 6)

Derman-Sparks and the ABC Task Force (1989) defined antibias education as

> An active/activist approach to challenging prejudices, stereotyping bias, and the "isms." In a society in which institutional structures create and maintain sexism, racism, handicapism, it is not sufficient to be nonbiased, nor is it sufficient to be an observer. It is necessary for each individual to actively intervene, to challenge and counter the personal and institutional behaviors that perpetuate oppression. (p. 3)

Critics who disagree with an antibias multicultural approach have raised several objections. One is the belief that learning about differences among people will make children become prejudiced. This assumption is based on a misconception, not on our knowledge about the early development of attitudes. Young children *do* absorb stereotypes about people's identities but *not* because they are learning authentic information and having an opportunity to ask their questions about differences. Rather, children's misperceptions and biases reflect those that are expressed by parents, peers, television, movies, books, and so on and become entrenched when they are left unchallenged. A second objection is that teachers are already overburdened and cannot add anything else to the curriculum. This assumption reflects a misunderstanding about the processes of antibias multicultural education. Teaching about diversity and justice is woven *into*, not added *onto*, the existing curriculum, so it is a change in perspective rather than an elaborate new curriculum.

Another criticism of antibias multicultural education rests on the belief that learning about diversity and discrimination diverts time from more important purposes of schooling. We argue that these critics are taking a myopic view of the purpose of education and not asking themselves the crucial question, "What world are we educating our children *for*?" Research and statistics about the changing demographics and the school failure and dropout rates of particular groups provide a powerful argument that multicultural education is essential to the health and success of our society. Yet another objection is that teaching the values of antibias multicultural education may conflict with the values of some of their children's families who either subscribe to biased thinking or may prefer to assimilate quietly into the society rather than challenge the system. These criticisms underscore the importance of involving families and community people in the process of designing and implementing curricula that reflect this approach. Finally, some critics have denounced multicultural antibias education for being too "political" because it presents a particular point of view. We argue that *all* education is political. Decisions about what to insert or omit in a story book or textbook, selections of topics and activities for a classroom, and strategies for working with children and parents—all reflect our priorities and values. Thus, continuing to use material that focuses only on European Americans and supports assimilation and the status quo is as political as incorporating a multicultural perspective.

Quality Education for the Twenty-First Century: Teacher Implications

In the 2000s, as the populations in our country and in many countries around the world become more racially, culturally, and linguistically diverse, educational movements advocating for multicultural, antibias, and bilingual/bicultural curriculum in early childhood care and education are active not only in the United States but also in countries such as Australia, Belgium, Canada, Denmark, Germany, The Netherlands, Sweden, South Africa, The United Kingdom, and New Zealand. In the United States, the National Association for the Education of Young Children

added diversity and antibias criteria into its accreditation standards and its national standards for basic and advanced teacher preparation (see Bredekamp & Copple, 1997).

In our conversations with teachers, we see some profound changes occurring in individual perceptions and at the systemwide and statewide level. Educators are becoming increasingly convinced that the whole curriculum and the basic structures and power relationships must be changed to create early childhood education programs in which all children and families can participate fully. Several new books provide resources to teachers wishing to use antibias multicultural approaches (Alvarado, Derman-Sparks, & Ramsey, 1999, Bisson, 1997; Kendall, 1996; Pelo & Davidson, 2000; Ramsey, 1998; Ramsey & Williams, 2003; Tatum, 1997; Whitney, 1999; Wolpert, 1999; York, 1998).

The widespread embrace of diversity and equity principles in early childhood care and education is encouraging. However, all of us who work in this area are realizing at a deeper level the psychological and social complexities and challenges of engaging in these transformations. While many early childhood educators advocate these goals, implementation in classrooms has been slower. In the name of multicultural education, many early childhood teachers are using approaches that are close to the "tourist" approach rather than reorienting their whole curriculum to incorporate a pluralistic and antibias perspective. In the name of bilingual education, many early childhood programs are using an English-as-a-second-language approach rather than implementing full bilingual/bicultural education. Antibias multicultural education is the area where programs seeking accreditation through the National Association for the Education of Young Children are still most likely to fall short. In the National Council for the Accreditation of Teacher Education (NCATE) folio reviews, the guidelines that institutions are cited most frequently for not meeting are those related to linguistic and cultural diversity (Phillips, 1998, p. 55). This remains true in 2003 as well (personal communication, NAEYC Staff).

As the antibias/multicultural and bicultural/bilingual movements have gained momentum, they have also become more controversial. In the past decade, multicultural, antibias, and bilingual/bicultural education were the targets of attacks from conservative groups and the press. For example, in several states, referenda—some successful, some not—were initiated to legislate the end of bilingual education in public schools. This backlash was in the context of wider social conservatism. At both the national and state levels, laws punishing welfare recipients, excluding immigrants, and overturning affirmative action were proposed and in some cases passed.

We argue that this backlash reflects "the tensions between those who want to press forward toward creating a more open and equitable society and those who are desperate to maintain the status quo" (Derman-Sparks & Ramsey, 1992, p. 10). People who have always been in control fear the changing demographics in this country and resist the idea of having to give up some of their economic and social power to groups that traditionally have been excluded. Many people also resent the idea that they may have to change long-held beliefs and assumptions. They want their children to go to the same schools and to learn the same things that they did.

This conservative backlash is evidence that the antibias, multicultural movement and bilingual/bicultural education now have greater visibility to people outside of the world of education, and so, in some ways, this reaction is encouraging. However, it is also an indication that the dialogue must be expanded to include people who feel threatened by educational reforms.

As we move into the first decade of the twenty-first century, we are at a crossroads. The recent criticisms of antibias multicultural education may help all educators define their mission and their goals more clearly and give them the

determination to continue and expand their work. Alternatively, the harsh voice of the conservative press may lead to retrenchment. Teachers may feel reluctant to implement activities that have been disparaged in the press, and administrators may feel more apprehensive about embarking on curriculum reforms that are potentially controversial. However, as early childhood educators, we must remain steadfast advocates for all young children and work toward the goal of a more just and open society in which young children can develop their fullest potential.

Goals for Children in the Twenty-First Century

Children of the twenty-first century cannot function effectively if they are psychologically bound by outdated and limiting assumptions about their compatriots of this country and of the world. To thrive, even to survive, in this more complicated world, children need to learn how to function in many different contexts and to recognize and respect different histories and perspectives. Moreover, as long as some groups are excluded and alienated from educational institutions and economic opportunities, the survival of our nation, as well as our world, is precarious.

Quality early childhood education and care in the twenty-first century must integrate the goals, knowledge, and methods developed by the bilingual/bicultural, multicultural, and antibias movements. These approaches mutually support each other. Antibias multicultural curriculum can enhance bilingual/bicultural education because it adds another layer of skills for effectively managing and, where appropriate, resisting the structures and strictures of the dominant society. Conversely, creating an environment and teaching styles that support the children's home culture enables children to develop the confidence that they need to become active players in the transformation of our society.

To develop creative solutions, early childhood educators, researchers, and parents need

Acknowledging someone for doing what is appropriate is often more effective than reacting to inappropriate behavior.

to talk with one another, try out ideas in practice, evaluate the results, and then modify their ideas and plans accordingly. Teachers and parents together need to make decisions about prioritizing the many goals of these two approaches. To do so they must analyze both developmental levels and cultural and economic contexts of each group of children in a given early childhood program. For example, if the children come from European American backgrounds, the currently practiced early childhood curricula are probably familiar and comfortable but may be reinforcing widespread assumptions that the European American culture is superior and desirable for everyone. In this case, the priority would be to challenge these assumptions by providing information about other groups and local and societal inequities. On the other hand, if the children's families are not culturally European American, then creating a bicultural and, if appropriate, bilingual environment would be

the first priority. Then critical perspectives can be woven in as children become more comfortable and learn about the dominant social groups. Thus, the implementation of multicultural education may vary from group to group. At the same time, the following underlying goals are consistent across groups: A few examples of activities are included with each goal to illustrate the range of potential strategies to meet them.

- Nurture each child's construction of a knowledgeable, confident self-concept and group identity by creating early childhood care and educational programs in which all children are able to like who they are without needing to feel superior to anyone else and to develop biculturally and bilingually.

Examples:
All the children in a program must be equally visible in all materials. In many cases, this will

mean searching beyond the biggest commercial companies, which tend to only or primarily sell materials reflecting dominant culture children and families, thus neglecting the range of ethnic, cultural, class, and other forms of diversity. Photographs of all the children and their families can be displayed where children can readily see them. Children can regularly talk, sing, draw, and write about themselves and their interests, fears, pleasures, competencies, and family traditions. Teachers should try to avoid the "I am special" or "all about me" or "I am what I possess" tone that some self-esteem activities convey. Rather, they can help children see how their attributes, capabilities and challenges are similar and different from those of their peers (e.g., making graphs about hair color or pet ownership; comparing family daily rituals) and as ways that they contribute to the group (e.g., cooperative activities in which everyone plays a significant role).

- Promote each child's comfortable, empathic interaction with people from diverse backgrounds by guiding children's development of the cognitive awareness, emotional disposition, and behavioral skills needed to respect differences, to negotiate and adapt to differences effectively and comfortably, and to understand the common humanity that all people share.

Examples:
In all groups of children, teachers can encourage the children to explore the ways they are both different and alike. Teachers can also use day-to-day conflicts and misunderstandings that arise in all settings to help the children learn that their ways of seeing the world are not the only or "right" ways. In diverse classrooms, teachers can encourage families to share their experiences in concrete ways such as story telling and sharing of family traditions. Daily curriculum materials will reflect all of the children in the group. Teachers expand contributions from families through regularly reading books and developing "persona doll," (Whitney, 1999)

stories to enable all children to learn about and become comfortable with a wide range of experiences. In more homogeneous classrooms, teachers can use "persona dolls," foods language, music, art materials, and classroom visitors to expose children to a wide range of ways of doing things and to work through their fearful or negative reactions to the unfamiliar.

- Foster each child's critical thinking about bias by encouraging children to identify unfair and untrue images (stereotypes), comments (teasing, name calling), and behaviors (discrimination) directed at one's own or others' identities (gender, race, ethnicity, disability, class, age, weight, etc.) *and* to develop the emotional empathy to know that bias hurts.

Examples:
Teachers can use books, persona doll stories, and puppet skits to introduce concepts about fairness, to contrast particular stereotypes with accurate images and information, and to explore how stereotypes are hurtful. As children become more aware, they can look for stereotypes and bias in books (both who is omitted as well who is misrepresented). As issues come up in the classroom, teachers can help children recognize biased language and behaviors.

- Cultivate each child's ability to act in the face of bias by helping every child learn and practice a variety of ways to act when a peer acts in a biased manner toward her or him, when a peer acts in a biased manner toward another classmate, when an adult acts in a biased manner, and when faced by injustices in the neighborhood or larger community (Pelo & Davidson, 2000). Critical thinking and empathy are necessary components of acting for oneself or others in the face of bias.

Examples:
Teachers can use the same activities described in the previous paragraph to encourage children

to talk about how they might confront bias and unfairness. They can also support children by "coaching" them to challenge a classmate or adult who is treating them in a biased way. When the children become concerned about a particular local or national issue, teachers organize group projects such as letter-writing campaigns, petitions, or letters to the editor of the local newspaper to protest biased actions in the larger community (e.g., ignoring traffic hazards near the school, reducing child-care programs in the city, inadequate maintaining or closing of a park or library).

Preparing to Teach from an Antibias Multicultural Perspective

Before planning a curriculum, teachers need to carefully scrutinize their own worldviews (Ramsey, 1998) and learn as much as they can about the current and past experiences of the children in their care (York, 1998). The following guidelines are adapted from Derman-Sparks (1992), and specific activities and discussion questions related to each of these categories have been articulated by Ramsey (1987a, 1998), Bisson (1997), Williams and De Gaetano (1985), and York (1998).

1. Teachers' history, knowledge, beliefs, values, and interests have a formative effect on the curriculum and on teaching practices. Teachers weave the curriculum together with their own thread that reflects their worldview, their beliefs about what is important for children to learn, and their underlying goals for children and our nation. What issues teachers see and hear from children, parents, and the community and what they choose to act on or ignore are strongly influenced by their own cultural beliefs and unexamined attitudes, discomforts, and prejudices. Therefore, an essential component of creating appropriate antibias multicultural curriculum is the teacher's increasing self-awareness about his or her own identity, cultural beliefs and behaviors, and attitudes toward various aspects of other people's identities (Derman-Sparks &

Phillips, 1997). Derman-Sparks and ABC Task Force (1989) suggest questions for becoming more aware of interactions between children and adults that reflect stereotypic assumptions. If a teacher is truly comfortable with diversity of race, culture, gender, sexual orientation, religion, and abilities and believes in the importance of creating an environment that promotes the goals of an antibias, multicultural approach, children will absorb these values from everything a teacher says and does.

2. Children's needs, experiences, interests, questions, feelings, and behaviors reflect their culture and social and economic status. Teachers must have a developmental perspective based on research about children's construction of identity and attitudes. In addition, teachers need a working knowledge of how children develop bilingually and biculturally. Both at the beginning and throughout the year, teachers should gather data from the specific children with whom they work. Then, throughout the year, they can monitor how children's ideas, feelings, and skills for handling diversity and injustice are changing. Information comes from observing children's interactions and their reactions to dolls, books, pictures, and other materials that portray different dimensions of diversity and inequities: It also comes from listening to and noting their questions and comments at play and in informal interactions such as at snack time. Another important source of information about the children's ideas and feelings also comes from their teachers' intentionally interviewing them on their ideas about gender, race, ethnicity, socioeconomic class, disabilities and the environment and consumerism (see Ramsey, 1998). Anecdotes from family members about their children's comments and questions are also valuable.

3. Families' beliefs, concerns, and desires for their children reflect their histories and experiences and influence the interface between children and schools. Throughout the school year, teachers should gather information from parents

about how they and their children identify themselves and whether and how their individual and group identities are changing; where family members fit on the bicultural continuum; what experiences their children have had with diversity at home and in their community; what information they want their children to learn about; what values they want their children to absorb and how they try to teach them; how they want their children to handle bias directed against them or others; and what concerns or disagreements they have about antibias/multicultural curriculum topics (see Ramsey, 1998). Teachers can gather this information in various ways, including informal conversations when family members bring or pick up their children, through written questionnaires for families who feel comfortable with this approach, and through discussions in meetings.

4. Society's events, messages, and expectations permeate children's environments. Children's ideas about themselves and others do not just come from their families—a misconception that many teachers continue to hold. One important factor is how the groups in children's communities regard one another and are regarded by the larger society. Teachers must be continually alert to the visual, verbal, and behavioral messages about human diversity, both positive and negative, that children absorb from peers, community people and events, TV, radio, movies, books, toys, greeting cards, lunch boxes, extended family members, religious and spiritual leaders, and teachers. This exploration means watching children's TV shows, visiting toy stores and book stores in children's neighborhoods, paying critical attention to the images on children's clothing and toys, and to all the materials placed in the classroom.

Planning Strategies

To be effective, all the dimensions of multicultural education must be integrated into all aspects of the daily environment and curriculum.

Teachers must create a culture within their setting that clearly communicates in everything they do, "This is a place that honors who each of you are, that recognizes diversity as a natural, key ingredient of life, and that models fairness to one another."

Several planning strategies can help teachers achieve this integration. First, teachers must weigh the multiple goals of antibias multicultural and bilingual/bicultural education in relation to the needs of their specific group of children and families. They need to decide what goals should have priority, identify what further knowledge and skills they will need to implement in their program, and set up plans for further staff development.

Second, teachers need to evaluate carefully all the materials and equipment in their classrooms or centers to determine which materials stay and go and which need modification, and to decide what additional materials need to be purchased or made. A number of useful guidelines and checklists can serve as a guide to this activity. "Ten Quick Ways to Analyze Children's Books for Racism and Sexism," written by the Council on Interracial Books for Children (in Derman-Sparks & ABC Task Force, 1989, and in Ramsey, 1998), provides criteria for evaluating children's books for stereotypes and misinformation. Derman-Sparks (1989), Kendall (1996), and Ramsey (1987a, 1998) all have guidelines for evaluating all aspects of the physical environment and examples of how classrooms can be transformed. They also provide extensive lists of resources and annotated bibliographies of children's books.

Third, antibias multicultural activities must be integrated into overall curriculum planning, not added on as an appendage or special event. Antibias multiculturalism should become a natural part of everything a teacher does (see York, 1998, for many illustrations). For example, many early childhood teachers do units about hospitals. Sometimes they are responding to children's interests in their bodies and worries about illness and injury or the hospitalization of a particular child or family member; perhaps a number of parents work at the local hospital. Activities typically include a visit to a local hospital and setting up a "hospital" in the classroom so that children can construct and enact their own understanding of hospitals. Themes of diversity and social justice can be woven into all aspects of this curriculum. Teachers might provide stories and pictures that contradict children's assumptions about male doctors and female nurses and encourage children to enact different roles. Children's ideas about hospital-related jobs can be expanded by ensuring that the visit to the hospital includes meeting custodians, nutritionists and cooks, and technicians as well as physicians and nurses (or that books about hospitals include these workers) and encouraging children to play these roles in the classroom "hospital." Honoring a wide range of workers in hospitals helps children see beyond the romanticized view of privileged doctors and to recognize and respect the contributions and dignity of all workers. To expand and challenge racial and gender stereotypes about who can do certain jobs, teachers should ensure that children meet (or at least see pictures of) members of different racial, gender, ability, and age groups doing a variety of jobs in the hospital and see pictures and books that include a diverse representation in all hospital positions. Teachers might introduce different cultural views of health and healing to help children see Western medicine in a broader perspective. They also can raise issues about the unfair distribution of health care and point out that some families cannot go to the doctor when their children are sick and engage children in activities protesting this unfairness (e.g., writing letters to federal and local officials, insurance companies, and the local newspaper).

Fourth, when planning, teachers should remember that effective antibias multicultural teaching is constructed in the context of continuous interactions between adults and children. As teachers brainstorm, plan, and initiate activities, they should constantly reflect on their children's interests and needs and talk over their ideas with parents. Careful attention to children's thinking and behavior and feedback from parents and colleagues leads to modifications and improvements to initial plans. If a teacher does not create a material and emotional environment that makes very clear that diversity is important, valued, and safe, then children will not raise issues. Conversely, if the teacher does not pay attention to their interests, ideas, and needs, then activities may not be meaningful to the children (Derman-Sparks, 1992, p. 28). Teachers need to see and take advantage of the potential for antibias multicultural work in all aspects of the curriculum: material environment, physical layout, details of routines, themes, hiring, relationships among staff, and relationships between staff and families (York, 1998).

Collaborating with Parents, Colleagues, and Community Members

To engage in teaching antibias multicultural education effectively, teachers need to be willing to give up their role as "experts" and to collaborate authentically with other adults. Because the mission and the material of antibias multicultural education are often very potent, fellow teachers, parents, and community people may be concerned about the implications of this approach. At all points, teachers need to involve them in decisions and to create networks of support.

Engaging parents in all aspects of this work is critical. Parents can participate in planning, implementing, and evaluating environmental adaptations and curricular activities. They can serve on advisory or planning committees with staff members, provide information about their families' lifestyles and beliefs, participate in classroom activities, and serve as community liaisons. Teachers need to hold frequent meetings, send home regular short newsletters to share ongoing plans and classroom activities, and elicit parent advice and resources. Parent meetings on child rearing and educational issues should incorporate culturally relevant perspectives and topics and be conducted in ways that honor and support parents' values and child-rearing styles. Meetings should also provide time and support for parents and teachers to learn from each other and to challenge their assumptions. Many schools now sponsor book groups where parents and school staff members read and discuss books related to diversity issues. Alternatively, groups could meet to watch and discuss films related to particular diversity and social justice issues.

When parents are involved in concrete ways, they can ask questions, express their concerns, and engage in discussions with teachers and one another that result in a deeper understanding of how antibias multicultural education benefits all children. Parents also gain a greater sense of their own responsibility to foster positive group identities and attitudes toward others. They feel validated and empowered by their participation in decision making about their young children's school and child-care experiences. When a family member disagrees with an aspect of the curriculum, teachers must listen carefully and sensitively to the issues underlying the disagreement. They need to find out all that they can about the cultural or other context issues that influence the concerns and problem solve with family members about ways to meet their needs while also maintaining the goals of antibias multicultural education.

The techniques for working with parents on antibias multicultural issues are generally the same as those used for other child development and education topics. The difference, however, lies in the teachers' level of comfort about addressing such topics with other adults. Working together with other staff members to explore their own feelings, beliefs, attitudes, and behaviors in relation to diversity can provide teachers with the necessary emotional foundation to use accepted methods for working with parents. Many of the same strategies used with parents apply to discussions with fellow staff members,

administrators, and community people (see Derman-Sparks, 1989, and Ramsey, 1998, for more specific suggestions).

Forming Support Groups and Networks

Antibias/multicultural and bilingual/bicultural work is emotionally demanding. Moreover, as people change their perceptions and take risks, they often have to deal with the social consequences of conflict and isolation. For these reasons, developing a support system is essential for anyone engaged in this work (Alvarado et al., 1999; Derman-Sparks, 1998).

Many teachers engaged in antibias and bicultural work have formed networks with colleagues that have provided invaluable emotional support, wider access to resources, and practical suggestions for day-to-day teaching. Networks can also provide advice and assistance for teachers who are having trouble convincing parents and colleagues of the positive aspects of these approaches. The presence of a network and the generation of ideas among its members can demonstrate the benefit of this approach to all children. Support from parents and colleagues often translates into acceptance by administrators, who frequently need reassurance that changes are being implemented thoughtfully and with participation from all interested parties. By collaborating, sharing resources, generating strategies to overcome obstacles, and providing encouragement, teachers can maintain the joy and excitement of this work and continue to build and improve their practices.

Currently many of these connections are being made electronically through organizations such as the Early Childhood Equity Alliance (www.rootsforchange.net), the National Association of Multicultural Education (www.nameorg.org). Teaching for Change (www.teachingforchange.org), and Rethinking Schools (www.rethinkingschools.org). Although these long-distance connections do not offer the intimate support of a group that physically meets and stays connected by daily contact and phone calls, they do enable people from all over the world who are struggling to create more just schools for children to share their views, resources, and support. In addition, these Web sites post information about conferences where people meet, hear about current work and research and talk together. These networks also are a wonderful tool for quickly organizing wide support for progressive national and international initiatives.

❧ CONCLUSION

It is time to act on the premise that quality education for *all* children, from the earliest years onward, requires the implementation of bilingual/bicultural and antibias multicultural education in all of their dimensions. We need to move more energetically and systematically from good intentions to good practice. As our knowledge and practices continue to develop and improve, we will all learn more about the most effective ways to meet children's developmental needs. We need to take advantage of the new models of action research in which teachers are involved directly in defining questions and conducting studies to learn in more depth about the impact of this work on both children and adults.

As early childhood and other educators work with one another and with parents and community people to create programs that meet the developmental and educational needs of *all* young children, we may no longer need to use explicit terms such as bilingual/bicultural and antibias multicultural education. Perhaps in the twenty-first century we will come to understand that the terms *care* and *education* automatically mean fostering development in linguistically and culturally consistent ways and teaching all children about diversity and how to confront and challenge stereotyping, bias, and institutional "isms." Early childhood educators will then be taking seriously Alice Walker's call to "Keep in mind always the present you are constructing. It should be the future you want" (Walker, 1989, p. 238).

REFERENCES

Aboud, F. (1988). *Children and prejudice*. New York: Basil Blackwell.

Aboud, F. E. (1977). Interest in ethnic information: A cross-cultural developmental study. *Journal of Behavioral Science, 9*, 134–146.

Aboud, F. E., & Doyle, A. B. (1993). The early development of ethnic identity and attitudes. In M. C. Bernal & G. P. Knight (Eds.), *Ethnic identity: Formation and transmission among Hispanics and other minorities* (pp. 47–59). Albany, NY: SUNY Press.

Alvarado, C., Derman-Sparks, L., & Ramsey, P. G. (1999). *In our own way: How antibias work shapes our lives*. St. Paul, MN: Readleaf Press.

Appleton, N. (1983). *Cultural pluralism in education*. New York: Longman.

Asher, S. R., Singleton, L. C., & Taylor, A. R. (1982, April). *Acceptance versus friendship: A longitudinal study of racial integration*. Paper presented at the annual meeting of the American Educational Research Association, New York.

Banks, J. (1988). *Multiethnic education: Theory and practice*. Boston: Allyn & Bacon.

Baratz, S., & Baratz, J. (1971). Early childhood intervention: The social science base of institutional racism. In R. H. Anderson & H. G. Shane (Eds.), *As the twig is bent* (pp. 34–52). New York: Houghton Mifflin.

Bem, S. (1981). Gender-schema theory: A cognitive account of sex-typing. *Psychological Review, 88*, 354–364.

Bem, S. L. (1983). Gender schema theory and its implications for child development: Raising gender-aschematic children in a gender-schematic society. *Signs: Journal of Women in Culture and Society, 8*, 597–616.

Bigler, R. (1999). Psychological intervention designed to counter sexism in children: Empirical limitations and theoretical foundations. In

B. W. Swann & J. H. Langlois (Eds.), *Sexism and stereotypes in modern society: The gender science of Janet Taylor Spence* (pp. 129–151). Washington, DC: American Psychological Association.

Bigler, R. S., Jones, L. C., & Lobliner, D. B. (1997). Social categorization and the formation of intergroup attitudes in children. *Child Development, 68* (3), 530–543.

Bigler, R. S., & Liben, L. S. (1992). Cognitive mechanisms in children's gender stereotyping: Theoretical and educational implications of a cognitive-based intervention. *Child Development, 63,* 1351–1363.

Bigler, R. S., & Liben, L. S. (1993). A cognitive-developmental approach to racial stereotyping and reconstructive memory in Euro-American children. *Child Development, 64,* 1507–1518.

Bisson, J. (1997). *Celebrate! Antibias guide to enjoying holidays in early childhood programs.* St. Paul, MN: Readleaf Press.

Bredekamp, S., & Copple, C. (Eds.). (1997). *Developmentally appropriate practice in early childhood programs* (Rev. ed.). Washington, DC: National Association for the Education of Young Children.

Burnett, M. N., & Sisson, K. (1995). Doll studies revisited: A question of validity. *Journal of Black Psychology, 21* (1), 19–29.

Carter, D. B., & Patterson, C. (1982). Sex roles as social conventions: The development of children's conceptions of sex role stereotypes. *Developmental Psychology, 18,* 812–824.

Casper, V., Cuffaro, H. K., Schultz, S., Silin, J. G., & Wickens, E. (1996). Toward a most thorough understanding of the world: Sexual orientation and early childhood education. *Harvard Educational Review, 66,* 271–293.

Casper, B., & Schultz, S. B. (1999). *Gay parents, straight schools: Building communication and trust.* New York: Teachers College Press.

Chafel, J. (1997). Children's views of poverty: A review of research and implications for teaching. *The Educational Forum, 61,* 360–371.

Clark, K. (1955). *Prejudice and your child.* Boston: Beacon.

Clark, K. B., & Clark, M. P. (1947). Racial identification and preference in Negro children. In T. M. Newcomb & E. L. Hartley (Eds.),

Readings in social psychology (pp. 169–178). New York: Holt, Rinehart and Winston.

Collier, V., & Thomas, W. (1997). *General pattern of K–12 language minority student achievement on standardized tests in English reading compared across six program models.* Washington, DC: National Clearinghouse of Bilingual Education.

Conant, S., & Budoff, M. (1983). Patterns of awareness in children's understanding of disabilities. *Mental Retardation, 21* (3), 119–125.

Condon, M. E., York, R., Heal, L. W., & Fortschneider, J. (1986). Acceptance of severely handicapped students by nonhandicapped peers. *Journal of the Association for Persons with Severe Handicaps, 11* (3), 216–219.

Corenblum, B., & Annis, R. C. (1993). Development of racial identity in minority and majority children: An affect discrepancy model. *Canadian Journal of Behavioral Science, 25* (4), 499–521.

Cortez, J. (1996). Introduction. In J. Cortez & C. Young-Holt (Eds.), *Infant/toddler caregiving: A guide to culturally sensitive care* (pp. x–xii). San Francisco: Far West Laboratory for Educational Research and Development.

Crawford, J. (1991). *Bilingual education: History, politics, theory, and practice.* Trenton, NJ: Crane.

Cross, W. E. (1985). Black identity: Rediscovering the distinction between personal identity and reference group orientation. In M. B. Spencer, G. K. Brookins, & W. R. Allen (Eds.), *Beginnings: The social and affective development of black children* (pp. 155–171). Hillsdale, NJ: Erlbaum.

Cross, W. E. (1987). A two-factor theory of black identity: Implications for the study of identity development in minority children. In J. Phinney & M. J. Rotheram (Eds.), *Children's ethnic socialization* (pp. 117–133). Beverly Hills, CA: Sage.

Cross, W. E. (1991). *Shades of black.* Philadelphia: Temple University Press.

Cummins, J. (1981). The role of primary language development in promoting educational success for language minority students. In California State Department of Education, *Schooling and language minority students: A theoretical framework* (pp. 3–49). Los Angeles: Evaluation Dissemination and Assessment Center, California State University.

Cummins, J. (1986). Empowering minority students: A framework for intervention. *Harvard Educational Review, 56* (1), 18–36.

Damon, W. (1980). Patterns of change in children's social reasoning: A two-year longitudinal study. *Child Development, 51*, 1010–1017.

Degrella, L. H., & Green, V. P. (1984). Young children's attitudes toward orthopedic and sensory disabilities. *Education of the Visually Handicapped, 16* (1), 3–11.

DeLone, R. H. (1979). *Small futures.* New York: Harcourt Brace Jovanovich.

Dennis, R. (1981). Socialization and racism: The white experience. In B. Bowser & R. Hunt (Eds.), *Impacts of racism on white Americans* (pp. 71–85). Beverly Hills, CA: Sage.

Derman–Sparks, L. (1989). How well are we nurturing racial and ethnic diversity? *Connections, 18* (1), 3–5.

Derman-Sparks, L. (1992). Anti-bias, multicultural curriculum: What is developmentally appropriate? In S. Bredekamp & T. Rosegrant (Eds.), *Reaching potentials: Appropriate curriculum and assessment for young children.* (pp. 114–127). Washington, DC: National Association for the Education of Young Children.

Derman-Sparks, L. (1998). *Future vision, present work: Learning from the culturally relevant antibias leadership project.* St. Paul, MN: Redleaf Press.

Derman-Sparks, L., & ABC Task Force. (1989). *Anti-bias curriculum: Tools for empowering young children.* Washington, DC: National Association for the Education of Young Children.

Derman-Sparks, L., Higa, C., & Sparks, B. (1980). Children, race and racism: How race awareness develops. *Bulletin, 11* (3 & 4), 3–9.

Derman-Sparks, L., & Phillips, C. B. (1997). *Teaching/learning anti-racism: A developmental approach.* New York: Teachers College Press.

Derman-Sparks, L., & Ramsey, P. (1992). Multicultural education reaffirmed. *Young Children, 47* (2), 10–11.

Diamond, K. E. (1993). Preschool children's concepts of disability in their peers. *Early Education and Development, 4* (2), 123–129.

Diamond, K. E. (1996). Evaluating preschool children's sensitivity to developmental differences in their peers. *Topics in Early Childhood Special Education, 14*, 49–63.

Diamond, K. E., & Hestenes, L. L. (1996). Preschool children's conceptions of disabilities: The salience of disability in children's ideas about others. *Topics in Early Childhood Special Education, 16*, 458–475.

Diamond, K. E., & Innes, F. K. (2001). The origins of young children's attitudes toward peers with disabilities. In M. J. Guralnick (Ed.), *Early childhood inclusion: Focus on change.* Baltimore: Paul Brookes.

Diamond, K., Le Furgy, W., & Blass, S. (1993). Attitudes of preschool children toward their peers with disabilities: A year-long investigation in integrated classrooms. *Journal of Genetic Psychology, 154*, 215–221.

Dorris, M. (1978). Why I'm not thankful for Thanksgiving. *Bulletin, 9* (7), 2–9.

Doyle, A. (1982). Friends, acquaintances, and strangers. In K. H. Rubin & H. S. Ross, *Peer relationships and social skills in childhood* (pp. 229–252). New York: Springer-Verlag.

Doyle, A., & Aboud, F. E. (1993). Social and cognitive determinants of prejudice in children. In K. A. McLeod (Ed.), *Multicultural education: The state of the art* (pp. 28–33). Toronto: University of Toronto Press.

Dropkin, R., Tobier, A., & City University of New York, City College Workshop Center for Open Education. (1976). *Roots of open education in America: Reminiscences and reflections.* New York: City College Workshop Center.

Finkelstein, N. W., & Haskins, R. (1983). Kindergarten children prefer same-color peers. *Child Development, 54*, 502–508.

Fishman, J. (1966). *Language loyalty in the United States.* The Hague, The Netherlands: Mouton.

Fishman, J. (1990). Empirical explorations of two popular assumptions: Inter-policy perspective on the relationships between linguistic heterogeneity, civil strife, and per capita gross national product. In G. Imhoff (Ed.), *Learning in two languages* (pp. 209–225). New Brunswick, NJ: Transaction Publishers.

Fox, D. J., & Jordan, V. B. (1973). Racial preference and identification of black, American

Chinese, and white children. *Genetic Psychology Monographs, 88,* 229–286.

Froschl, M., Colon, L., Rubin, E., & Sprung, B. (1984). *Including all of us: An early childhood curriculum about disability.* New York: Educational Equity Concepts.

Fruchter, J. (1999). Linking social justice concerns with environmental issues. *ZPG Recorder* (Special Issue on Kid-Friendly Cities), *31* (4), 10–11.

Garbarino, J. (1999). *Lost boys: Why our sons turn violent and how we can save them.* New York: Free Press.

Garcia, E. (1980). Bilingualism in early childhood. *Young Children, 35* (4), 52–66.

Gonsier-Gerdin, J. (1995, March–April). *An ethnographic case study of children's social relationships in a full inclusion elementary school.* Poster presented at the biennial meeting of the Society for Research in Child Development, Indianapolis.

Goodman, H., Gottlieb, J., & Harrison, R. H. (1972). Social acceptance of EMR's integrated into a non-graded elementary school. *American Journal of Mental Deficiency, 76,* 412–417.

Goodman, J. E. (1989). Does retardation mean dumb? Children's perceptions of the nature, cause, and course of mental retardation. *The Journal of Special Education, 23,* 313–329.

Goodman, M. E. (1952). *Race awareness in young children.* New York: Collier.

Gopaul-McNicol, S. (1988). Racial identification and racial preference of black preschool children in New York and Trinidad. *The Journal of Black Psychology, 14* (2), 65–68.

Greenberg, S. (1980). Eliminating sex bias in early childhood. *Equal Play, 1* (4), 5.

Greenfield, P. M., & Cocking, R. R. (Eds.). (1994). *Cross-cultural roots of minority child development.* Hillsdale, NJ: Erlbaum.

Grosjean, F. (1982). *Life with two languages: An introduction to bilingualism.* Cambridge, MA: Harvard University Press.

Guralnick, M. J. (1980). Social interactions among preschool children. *Exceptional Children, 46,* 248–253.

Guralnick, M. J., Connor, R. T., Hammond, M. A., Gottman, J. M., & Kinnish, K. (1996). The peer relations of preschool children with communication disorders. *Child Development, 67,* 471–489.

Guralnick, M. J., & Groom, J. M. (1987). The peer relations of mildly delayed and nonhandicapped preschool children in mainstreamed playgroups. *Child Development, 58,* 1556–1572.

Hanes, M. L., Flores, M. I., Rosario, J., Weikart, D. P., & Sanchez, J. (1979). *Un marco abierto.* Ypsilanti, MI: High/Scope Educational Research Foundation.

Harper, D. C., Wacker, D. P., & Cobb, L. S. (1986). Children's social preferences toward peers with visible physical differences. *Journal of Pediatric Psychology, 11* (3), 323–342.

Honig, A. (1983). Sex role socialization in early childhood. *Young Children, 38* (6), 37–70.

Iano, R. P., Ayers, D., Heller, H. B., McGettigan, J. F., & Walker, V. S. (1974). Sociometric status of retarded children in an integrative program. *Exceptional Children, 40* (4), 267–271.

Johnson, D. W., & Johnson, R. T. (2000). The three Cs of reducing prejudice and discrimination. In S. Okamp (Ed.), *Reducing prejudice and discrimination* (pp. 239–268). Mahwah, NJ: Erlbaum.

Juvonen, J. & Bear, G. (1992). Social adjustment of children with and without learning disabilities in integrated classrooms. *Journal of Educational Psychology, 84,* 322–330.

Katz, P. A. (1976). The acquisition of racial attitudes in children. In P. A. Katz (Ed.), *Towards the elimination of racism* (pp. 125–154). New York: Pergamon Press.

Katz, P. (1982). Development of children's racial awareness and intergroup attitudes. In L. G. Katz (Ed.), *Current topics in early childhood education* (pp. 17–54). Norwood, NJ: Ablex.

Katz, P. A., & Kofkin, J. A. (1997). Race, gender, and the young child. In S. Luthar, J. Burack, D. Cicchetti, & J. Weisz (Eds.), *Developmental perspectives on risk and pathology* (pp. 51–74). New York: Cambridge University Press.

Kendall, F. (1996). *Diversity in the classroom: A multicultural approach to the education of young children* (Rev. ed.). New York: Teachers College Press.

Kindlon, D., & Thompson, M. (1999). *Raising Cain: Protecting the emotional lives of boys.* New York: Ballantine Books.

Kivel, P. (1999). *Boys will be men: Raising our sons for courage, caring, and community.* Gabriola Island, BC, Canada: New Society Publishers.

Kline, S. (1993). *Out of the garden: Toys and children's culture in the age of TV marketing.* London: Verso.

Krashen, S. L., Tse, L., & McQuillan, J. (Eds.). (1998). *Heritage language development.* Culver City, CA: Language Education Associates.

Leahy, R. (1990). The development of concepts of economic and social inequality. *New Directions for Child Development, 46,* 107–120.

Leahy, R. L. (1983). The development of the conception of social class. In R. L. Leahy (Ed.), *The child's construction of inequality* (pp. 79–107). New York: Academic Press.

Lee, E. (1991). Taking multicultural, anti-racist education seriously. *Rethinking Schools, 6* (1), 6–7.

Maccoby, E. E. (1986). Social groupings in childhood: Their relationship to prosocial and antisocial behavior in boys and girls. In D. Olewus, J. Block, & M. Radke-Yarrow (Eds.), *Development of antisocial and prosocial behavior* (pp. 263–284). New York: Academic.

Mapley, C. E., & Kizer, J. B. (1983). *Children's process of sex-role incongruent information: "The nurse's name was Dr. Brown."* Paper presented at the biennial meeting of the Society for Research in Child Development, Detroit.

Marquez, N. (1991). *The language of learning: A framework for developing two languages in preschool education.* Unpublished manuscript, Administration for Children, Youth and Families, Washington, DC.

Martin, C., & Halverson, C. F. (1981). A schematic processing model of sex typing and stereotyping in children. *Child Development, 52,* 1119–1134.

Morland, J. K. (1962). Racial acceptance and preference of nursery school children in a southern city. *Merrill-Palmer Quarterly, 8,* 271–280.

Nabors, L. (1995, March). *Attitudes, friendship ratings, and behaviors for typically developing preschoolers interacting with peers with disabilities.* Paper presented at the biennial meeting of the Society for Research in Child Development, Indianapolis.

Nabors, L., & Keyes, L. (1995). Preschoolers' reasons for accepting peers with and without disabilities. *Journal of Developmental and Physical Disabilities, 7* (4), 235–255.

Naimark, H. (1983). *Children's understanding of social class differences.* Paper presented at the biennial meeting of The Society for Research in Child Development, Detroit.

National Association for Bilingual Education. (1990, January). *The NABE No-Cost Study on Families* [press release].

National Association for the Education of Young Children. (1997). *Cultural and linguistic diversity* [brochure]. Washington, DC: National Association for the Education of Young Children.

Newman, M. A., Liss, M. B., & Sherman, F. (1983). Ethnic awareness in children: Not a unitary concept. *The Journal of Genetic Psychology, 143,* 103–112.

Nieto, S. (1996). *Affirming diversity: The sociopolitical context of multicultural education* (2nd ed.). White Plains, NY: Longman.

Nightingale, C. H. (1993). *On the edge: A history of poor Black children and their American Dreams.* New York: Basic Books.

Ocampo, K. A., Bernal, M. E., & Knight, G. P. (1993). Gender, race, and ethnicity: The sequencing of social constancies. In M. E. Bernal & G. P. Knight (Eds.), *Ethnic identity: Formation and transmission among Hispanics and other minorities* (pp. 11–30). Albany, NY: SUNY Press.

Odom, S. L., Jenkins, J. R., Speltz, M. L., & DeKlyen, M. (1982). Promoting social interaction of young children at risk for learning disabilities. *Learning Disability Quarterly, 5,* 379–387.

Odom, S. L., Peck, C. A., Hanson, M., Beckman, P. J., Kaiser, A. P., Lieber, J., Brown, W. H., Horn, E. M., Schwartz, I. S. (1996). Inclusion at the preschool level: An ecological systems analysis. *Social Policy Report of the Society for Research in Child Development, 10* (2 & 3), 18–30.

Orellana, M. F. (1994). Appropriating the voice of the superheroes: Three preschoolers' bilingual language uses in play. *Early Childhood Research Quarterly, 9,* 171-193.

Pelo A., & Davidson, F. (2000). *That's not fair! A teacher's guide to activism with young children.* St. Paul, MN: Redleaf.

Phillips, C. B. (1988). Nurturing diversity for to-day's children and tomorrow's leaders. *Young Children, 43* (2), 42–47.

Phillips, C. B. (1990). Culture: A process that empowers. In J. Cortez & C. Young-Holt (Eds.), *Infant/toddler caregiving: A guide to culturally sensitive care* (pp. 2–9). San Francisco: Far West Laboratory for Educational Research and Development.

Phillips, C. B. (1998). Preparing teachers to use their voices for change. *Young Children, 52,* 55–60.

Phinney, J., & Rotheram, M. J. (1987). *Children's ethnic socialization: Pluralism and development.* Beverly Hills, CA: Sage.

Piaget, J. (1951). *The child's conception of the world.* New York: Humanities Press.

Pollack, W. (1998). *Real boys: Rescuing our sons from the myths of boyhood.* New York: Random House.

Porter, R. P. (1990). *Forked tongue: The politics of bilingual education.* New York: Basic.

Radke, M., & Trager, H. G. (1950). Children's perceptions of the social roles of Negroes and whites. *Journal of Psychology, 29,* 3–33.

Ramsey, P. G. (1987a). *Teaching and learning in a diverse world.* New York: Teachers College Press.

Ramsey, P. G. (1987b). Young children's thinking about ethnic differences. In J. S. Phinney & M. J. Rotheram (Eds.), *Children's ethnic socialization: Pluralism and development* (pp. 56–72). Beverly Hills, CA: Sage.

Ramsey, P. G. (1991a). The salience of race in young children growing up in all-white community. *Journal of Educational Psychology, 83,* 28–34.

Ramsey, P. G. (1991b). Young children's awareness and understanding of social class differences. *Journal of Genetic Psychology, 152,* 71–82.

Ramsey, P. G. (1995). Changing social dynamics of early childhood classrooms. *Child Development, 66,* 764–773.

Ramsey, P. G. (1998). *Teaching and learning in a diverse world: Multicultural education for young children* (2nd ed.). New York: Teachers College Press.

Ramsey, P. G., & Myers, L. C. (1990). Salience of race in young children's cognitive, affective and behavioral responses to social environments. *Journal of Applied Developmental Psychology, 11,* 49–67.

Ramsey, P.G. & Williams, L.R. with Vold, E.B. (2003). *Multicultural education: A source book* (2nd edition). New York: Routledge Falmer.

Roberts, C., & Zubrick, S. (1992). Factors influencing the social status of children with mild academic disabilities in regular classrooms. *Exceptional Children, 59* (3), 192–202.

Rodriguez, R. (1981). *Hunger of memory: The education of Richard Rodriguez.* Boston: Godine.

Rosenfield, D., & Stephan, W. G. (1981). Intergroup relations among children. In S. S. Brehm, S. M. Kassin, & F. X. Gibbons (Eds.), *Developmental social psychology* (pp. 271–297). New York: Oxford University Press.

Sadker, M., & Sadker, D. (1995). *Failing at fairness: How our schools cheat girls.* New York: Simon & Schuster.

Sandoval-Martinez, S. (1982). Findings from the Head Start bilingual curriculum development and evaluation effort. *NABE Journal, 7,* 1–12.

Sapon-Shevin, M. (1983). Teaching young children about differences. *Young Children, 38* (2), 24–32.

Serbin, L. (1980). Play activities and the development of visual-spatial skills. *Equal Play, 1* (4), 5.

Serbin, L. A., Tonick, I. J., & Sternglanz, S. H. (1977). Shaping cooperative cross-sex play. *Child Development, 48,* 924–929.

Sheldon, A. (1990). Kings are royaler than queens: Language and socialization. *Young Children, 45* (2), 4–9.

Sheridan, M. K., Foley, G. M., & Radlinski, S. H. (1995). *Using the supportive play model: Individualized intervention in early childhood practice.* New York: Teachers College Press.

Sigelman, C. K. (1991). The effect of causal information on peer perceptions of children with physical problems. *Journal of Applied Developmental Psychology, 12,* 237–253.

Siperstein, G. N., Brownley, M. V., & Scott, C. K. (1989, April). *Social interchanges between mentally retarded and nonretarded friends.* Paper presented at the biennial meeting of the Society for Research in Child Development, Kansas City, MO.

Slavin, R. E. (1995). Cooperative learning and intergroup relations. In J. A. Banks & C. A. M. Banks (Eds.), *Handbook of research on multicultural education* (pp. 628–634). New York: Macmillan.

Sleeter, C., & Grant, C. (1987). An analysis of multicultural education in the United States. *Harvard Educational Review, 57*, 421–444.

Spencer, M. B., & Markstrom-Adams, C. (1990). Identity processes among racial and ethnic minority children in America. *Child Development, 61*, 290–310.

Stabler, J. R., Zeig, J. A., & Johnson, E. E. (1982). Perceptions of racially related stimuli by young children. *Perceptual and Motor Skills, 54* (1), 71–77.

Swadener, E. B., & Johnson, J. E. (1989). Play in diverse social contexts: Parent and teacher roles. In M. N. Bloch & A. D. Pellegrini (Eds.), *The ecological context of children's play* (pp. 214–244). Norwood, NJ: Ablex.

Taba, H., Brady, E. H., & Robinson, J. T. (1952). *Intergroup education in public schools.* Washington, DC: American Council on Education.

Tajfel, H. (1973). The roots of prejudice: Cognitive aspects. In P. Watson (Ed.), *Psychology and race.* Chicago: Aldine.

Tatum, B. D. (1997). *"Why are all the black kids sitting together in the cafeteria?" and other conversations about race.* New York: Basic Books.

Taylor, A. R., Asher, S. R., & Williams G. A. (1987). The social adaptation of mainstreamed mildly retarded children. *Child Development, 58*, 1321–1334.

Tharp, R. G. (1989). Psychological variables and constants: Effects of teaching and learning in schools. *American Psychologist, 44*, 349–359.

Tharp, R. G., & Gallimore, R. (1988). *Rousing minds to life: Teaching, learning, and schooling in social context.* Cambridge, England: Cambridge University Press.

Thorne, B. (1986). Girls and boys together . . . but mostly apart: Gender arrangements in elementary schools. In W. W. Hartup & Z. Rubin (Eds.), *Relationships and development* (pp. 167–184). Hillsdale, NJ: Erlbaum.

Trager, H., & Radke-Yarrow, M. (1952). *They learn what they live.* New York: Harper & Brothers.

Tse, L. (1998). Affecting affect: The impact of heritage language programs on student attitudes. In Krashen, S. L., Tse, L., & McQuillan, J. (Eds.), *Heritage language development.* Culver City, CA: Language Education.

United Nations. (1989). *Convention on the rights of the child, proceedings.* New York: Author.

Vaughn, S., Elbaum, B. E., & Schumm, J. S. (1996). The effects of inclusion on the social functioning of students with learning disabilities. *Journal of Learning Disabilities, 29* (6), 598–608.

Van Ausdale, D. & Feagin, J.R. (2001). *The first R: How children learn race and racism.* Lanham, MD: Rowman & Littlefield.

Vold, E. B. (1989). The evolution of multicultural education: A socio-political perspective. In P. G. Ramsey, E. B. Vold, & L. R. Williams (Eds.), *Multicultural education: A source book* (pp. 3–42). New York: Garland.

Walker, A. (1989). *The temple of my familiar.* New York: Pocket Books.

Wardle, F. (1987). Are you sensitive to interracial children's special identity needs? *Young Children, 42* (2), 53–59.

Wardle, F. (1990). Endorsing children's differences: Meeting the needs of adopted minority children. *Young Children, 45* (5), 44–46.

Whitney, T. (1999). *Kids like us: Using persona dolls in the classroom.* St. Paul, MN: Redleaf.

Williams, L. R., & De Gaetano, Y. (1985). *ALERTA: A multicultural, bilingual approach to teaching young children.* Menlo Park, CA: Addison-Wesley.

Wolpert, E. (1999). *Start seeing diversity: The basic guide to anti-bias curriculum.* St. Paul, MN: Readleaf Press.

Wong-Fillmore, L. (1990). Latino families and the schools. In J. Cabello (Ed.), *California perspectives Vol. I: An anthology from the immigrant students project* (pp. 1–8). San Francisco: California Tomorrow.

Wong-Fillmore, L. (1991). Language and cultural issues in early education. In S. L. Kagan (Ed.), *The care and education of America's young children: Obstacles and opportunities. The Ninetieth Yearbook of the National Society for the Study of Education* (pp. 30–49). Chicago: University of Chicago Press.

York, S. (1998). *The big as life: The everyday inclusion curriculum.* Vols. 1 & 2. St. Paul, MN: Readleaf Press.

Part 3

Broad Approaches

Chapter 7

The Eriksonian Approach

Alice Sterling Honig ✣ Syracuse University

During the past half-century in the United States, major innovative educational programs were launched to break intergenerational cycles of social distress and lack of academic achievement that disproportionately affect young children living in poverty. Some model projects were narrow in focus and dealt with specific aspects of child functioning, such as language or sensorimotor skills. Other programs were global in their approach to enrichment. Duration, program site, ages of children served, educational model, and outcome measures varied with the model (Consortium for Longitudinal Studies, 1983; Honig, 1983a, 1996b). Some programs were center based, some home based; some served children for a season, some for several years. Most provided cognitive enrichment for preschoolers, but some programs worked primarily to enhance parent–infant interactions as the foundation for later competence and resiliency in child functioning (Bromwich, 1997; Brophy-Herb & Honig, 1999; Honig, 1974b, 1982b, 1984, 1990, 1995a, 1997b). Unlike programs in other countries, such as France, these model programs did not reflect a national consensus toward provision of child care as a societal responsibility for all young children (McGovern, 1998).

Projects sometimes chose curricula eclectically and with a specific applied goal. Some demonstrated that they could enhance intellective functioning in infants from low-education, poor homes (Heber, Garber, Harrington, Hoffman, & Fallender, 1972; Honig, 1982a, 1994b; Keister, 1977). Early programs had the important goal of demonstrating that group care for infants would not attenuate infant attachment with mother (Caldwell, Wright, Honig, & Tannenbaum, 1970). Another applied goal has been to discover educationally facilitative methods to provide group care for poor children to support parents, so that school-dropout mothers could return to classes or enter job training (Brophy & Honig, 1995). Other projects have tried carefully to implement *theoretical* principles in constructing curricula and staff goals and in training caregivers to create learning environments for young children (Honig, 1992, 1994a).

The Children's Center in Syracuse, New York, founded by Drs. Caldwell and Richmond in the early 1960s (Caldwell et al., 1968) served children from 6 to 60 months of age. Dr. Lally and Honig (1977a, 1977b) continued the Children's Center with programmatic changes in group-care delivery via an open-education model and with an expanded parent involvement component. Eriksonian and Piagetian principles were coordinated in choosing curriculum activities and materials and in specifying interaction processes for creation of an "optimal learning environment" in the Children's Center (Caldwell, 1967; Honig, 1977, 1991; Honig & Lally, 1982).

Integration of these two theoretical perspectives was seen as particularly critical in programming for infants and toddlers. Later research has borne out Erikson's theoretical prediction, based on extensive clinical experience, that the *emotional climate* of infant learning affects the infant's ability to become an active, curious, focused, and self-motivated learner and to persist at difficult problem-solving tasks during the preschool years (Clarke-Stewart, 1973; Matas, Arend, & Sroufe, 1978).

Zigler (1970) has claimed that even the test–retest gain scores attributed to intervention program efforts with disadvantaged youngsters may accrue partly because of the positive emotional climate of the classroom and testing situations rather than cognitive curricula per se. He pointed out that many parents have had experiences that have alienated them from society, and therefore parents and children need experiences that will help them to actualize themselves within the social framework. "We must be just as concerned with the development of positive attitudes and motives as with the development of the intellect" (p. 408).

Zigler and Trickett (1978) urged that socioemotional nourishing of disadvantaged young children should be a cardinal objective of enrichment programs and that social competence rather than IQ ought to be employed as a major measure of program success. Enhancing self-esteem and positive motivation for learning would, in turn, increase the probability that children would become better able to focus on, and maintain interest in, intellectual tasks. It is interesting to note that these prescient recommendations were made before publication of the extensive longitudinal research outcomes of the effects of early attachment patterns, based on the work of Bowlby, Ainsworth, Bretherton, Sagi, Main, and others. We are now far more knowledgeable about long-term consequences of insecure attachment patterns in the earliest years for less optimal interactions with peers and caregivers. Sroufe and Fleeson (1986) provided powerful research illustrations of these effects. Having measured attachment classifications (with the Ainsworth Strange Situation) years earlier in infancy, they set up a preschool with

highly trained teachers, blind to the children's infancy attachment classifications, and then observed classroom interactions. Pairs of peers (carefully chosen according to the children's infant attachment ratings) were also observed in a special playroom. Preschoolers who had been rated as avoidantly attached infants were significantly more likely to bully a peer who had been rated as ambivalent/insecure in infancy. When both children in a pair had been earlier rated as ambivalent/insecure, they showed immaturity and social ineptitude in peer play together. Adults gave these youngsters more nurturance and leeway for misbehaviors. The teachers sometimes got angry, but only with children formerly rated as avoidantly attached. Highest teacher expectations were for the securely attached preschoolers. Thus, it is a tribute to Erikson's clinical skills that decades earlier he had accurately described children's clinical difficulties in socioemotional interactions based on early parental interaction patterns in childrearing.

The twenty-first century has seen a sharp rise in out-of-home care for infants and toddlers. Thus, both *teacher training* to ensure positive early socioemotional relationships in child care and the importance of helping parents make informed *choices* for care in order to optimize the development of their little ones have become critical societal issues (Honig, 2002a, 2002b). Already, beginning in 1969, the Family Development research program was deeply committed to these goals.

✒ DESCRIPTION OF FAMILY DEVELOPMENT RESEARCH PROGRAM

The Family Development Research Program (FDRP) was an omnibus model (Honig & Lally, 1982; Lally & Honig, 1977a, 1977b) that served 108 low-income, low-education families and their first- or second-born children from the last trimester of pregnancy until the child entered elementary school. None of the mothers (mean age = 18 years) had either a high school diploma or skilled-work history at time of entry into the project. Family income for the predominantly single, black mothers was less than $5,000 per year. A variety of program components were devised to meet family needs.

Home Visit Component

Parents were empowered to take initiatives as teachers of their own children through the outreach work and support of a cadre of highly trained paraprofessional home visitors. The home visitors, known as CDTs (child development trainers), served as teachers, friends, family advocates, and partners of parents in promoting the learning career of each child. During the years that the family was in the project, CDTs visited the home weekly. Their goals expanded to meet the changing needs of families as the children grew through new developmental stages and as special family circumstances (such as fatal fire in household) arose. The role of the CDT included:

1. Building a trusting relationship with mothers. CDTs offered positive support and encouragement to mothers as they carried out a given activity with their own children. The mothers rather than the children were the focus of the home visitors' attentions and teaching. They were seen as autonomous, actively involved change agents in their children's lives. CDTs gave generously of their time and assistance. They escorted parents to weekly toy-making sessions and monthly group meetings at the centers.
2. Modeling for parents positive discipline techniques (Honig, 1996a) and responsive processes of interaction with children that could enhance the growth of basic trust, autonomy, initiative, and task persistence.
3. Providing prenatal and child nutrition information and explanations to families.

4. Developing maternal skills in providing Piagetian sensorimotor games, language interactions, and learning tasks (Gordon & Lally, 1967) appropriate to each child's developmental level. The CDTs placed particular emphasis on carrying out such learning games with parents in the context of warm and loving interactions with children in daily routines and care situations (Honig & Brophy, 1996). A library of toys and books was created and shared with the family.
5. Helping mothers to learn ways to modify games and activities so that children were more apt to maintain interest in an activity and to learn to work industriously and cheerfully at tasks. Matching parental learning goals for a child with the child's current developmental capabilities required sensitive attention to the unique individual characteristics of each child and to interaction models that we characterized as "dancing the developmental ladder" (Honig, 1983b).
6. Serving as liaisons between available community support services (e.g., pediatric clinics, food stamp programs, legal counseling services) and the families. The community liaison function expanded and varied as the needs of the families were clarified.
7. Encouraging family members to take an active role as facilitators of children's development. This involved helping families learn to find and use neighborhood resources and learning environments such as libraries, supermarkets, and parks.
8. Helping mothers to observe their children's development and to devise their own appropriate learning games and activities as their children continued to grow.
9. Aiding parents to fulfill their aspirations for themselves. The project director hypothesized that parental feelings of self-confidence and self-competence generated

by mothers undertaking a job or job training or further schooling would be reflected in more secure and positive relations between parents and children. Home visitors offered personal attention and friendship to the mothers. Different families need different personal support strategies.

10. Encouraging mothers to take an active role when the children were ready to enter public school. Mothers were given specific practice in learning how to make and maintain contacts with school personnel so that the parents could continue to be positive educational change agents and advocates for their children in the public school system (Honig, 1982a).

Children's Center Component

The Children's Center served as an integral part of the omnibus FDRP project, although conceptualized as an *adjunct* to the parent program. The main goal of the FDRP was to help parents initiate and maintain loving, learning interactions with their children. This was to be done through trusting relationship CDTs built with families and through the modeling that teachers provided in classrooms when parents visited, which was highly encouraged.

The Children's Center was organized to serve younger infants (6–18 months) in half-day care, with full-day care for 15- to 18-month-old toddlers in a transition group and full-day care for 18- to 60-month-old preschoolers in open education mixed-age classrooms.

Infant-Fold   Younger infants were cared for in the "infant-fold." Four infants were assigned to one caregiver for special tender attention, cognitive and social games, Piagetian sensorimotor activities, and language stimulation. Play materials were devised, emphasizing the use of homemade toys, to help children develop means–ends relationships, object permanence, spatial concepts, causality understandings, and receptive and expressive language skills in a climate of basic trust and respect for the personhood of babies (Honig, 1974a, 1981, 1991; John Tracy Clinic, 1968).

Two key concepts infused program provision. One, in paraphrasing Piagetian *equilibration,* I call *Matchmaking:* offering new tasks and challenges just slightly new or more difficult or discrepant from the child's present capabilities and understandings. Another I labeled *Dancing the developmental ladder,* signifying that the adult constantly adjusts to the child's pace, understandings, and knowledge base in making lessons easier or more difficult in each developmental area (Honig, 1978, 1982c). Tasks and learning opportunities were based on each individual infant's developmental capability. Infants were *lured* forward in responsive, loving interactions to solve slightly more novel or difficult tasks.

The third key to successful implementation of curriculum was the conscious use of "homey" routines, such as diapering, shepherding, and dressing situations to promote secure emotional learning, turn taking, language interactions, and sensorimotor experiences. Regular monitoring of classroom transactions revealed that program provision was carried out as planned (Honig & Lally, 1975b, 1990).

Family Style Setting   Preschoolers (18 to 60 months) attended a full-day multiage group experience in four distinct activity rooms, which they could freely choose to enter and leave.

In the four available areas were offered:

- Small-muscle games (pegboards, puzzles, poker chips in cans, bead-stringing, etc.).
- Sensory experiences (touching, smelling, tasting, listening, viewing film strips, stroking pets, and reading books).
- Creative expression (clay, Play-Doh, fingerpainting, water play, housekeeping, rice or sand play, easel painting, and snacks).
- Large-muscle activities (tumbling, climbing, balancing, sliding, scooting, riding tricycles).

Sensory experiences such as touching are the building blocks of early exploration and peer play.

The family style settings were spatially structured rather than time bound. Two teachers supervised each setting for a week and rotated to a new setting the next week. Setting structure and accompanying limits were defined mainly by the area materials and concepts. Because concepts to be learned transcended areas, teachers applied *concept links* to each area. For example, no running was allowed in the sensory perception area, yet the concepts of faster or slower could be used appropriately in relation to materials and activities in that area as well as in the large-muscle play room and other areas. The first rule for use of space was that materials were to stay in their appropriate area. Older preschoolers had a great influence on younger children in helping them to remember these rules. Choices were given to children if an activity they wanted to do was not appropriate for the area in which they were playing. A child who wanted to run, for example, would be given the choice of going to the large-muscle room or staying in the creative expression room and participating in an activity there.

The second and third rules had to do with caring for and respecting other children's rights to play and with respecting materials. Books could not be walked on or put into a water play tub. Dolls could not be banged with a hammer. We emphasized that the children were to use language rather than hitting as a medium for establishing social justice. In the creative activity area one day, Johnny was pulling the big chunk of Play-Doh more and more toward his side of the table. Jenny, seated on the other side of the small worktable, grew angrier and more frustrated as she could not reach the Play-Doh to create animal shapes with her cookie cutters. She clenched her fist. Then, instead of leaning over and hitting Johnny, she half stood in her chair and yelled out, "Teacher, Johnny ain't sharing!" The teacher moved quickly to the table and restated sharing rules in a firm, caring fashion. Staff persistently promoted the use of verbal methods to redress conflict situations and increase prosocial resolutions.

Rich language experiences were an integral part of daily activities in each area and were embedded in care-giving routines, such as feeding and shepherding down hallways. Helping caregivers increase their use of *turn-taking-talk* with infants and their use of *Socratic questions* to lure youngsters into sharing more elaborate language descriptions and explanations is a challenge for trainers of child-care personnel (Honig, 2001).

Piagetian games suitable for sensorimotor and early preoperational functioning were carefully specified for teachers through weekly in-service training. Implementation was monitored daily by caregivers themselves using Piaget Task Checklists as well as by staff observations using the ABC Scales (Honig & Lally, 1981). Although Piagetian activities were an integral part of daily activities, the primary theoretical model that informed staff interactions with the children and with their parents was Eriksonian. Caregivers were to

create a sense of trust in their children by that kind of administration which in its quality combines sensitive care of the baby's individual needs and a firm sense of personal trustworthiness within the trusted framework of their community's life style. This forms the basis in the child for a sense of identity which will later combine a sense of being "all right," of being oneself, and of becoming what other people trust one will become ... [Caregivers] must also be able to represent to the child a deep, an almost somatic conviction that there is a meaning to what they are doing. (Erikson, 1950, p. 65)

✍ ERIKSONIAN THEORY: TENETS AND PRINCIPLES

Erik Erikson's theory is primarily a conceptualization of the stages in development of an emotionally healthy personality. Building on Freud's work, Erikson accepted his ideas of unconscious motivation, defenses of the ego, and psychosexual stages, but broadened these to include *psychosocial* development. Erikson gives a more important role to ego functioning, the influence of the cultural milieu, the entire life span rather than the early years exclusively, and the possibility that positive social experiences can redirect children's stressed or conflicted emotional growth toward healthier functioning:

> I shall present human growth from the point of view of the conflicts, inner and outer, which the healthy personality weathers, emerging and re-emerging with an increased sense of inner unity, with an increase of good judgment, and an increase in the capacity to do well according to the standards of those who are significant to him. (Erikson, 1980, p. 52)

It follows that caregivers in a loving, responsive relationship that provides "focused attention" (Briggs, 1975) to the needs of young children are most likely to rear well-motivated learners and prosocial youngsters with high self-esteem. An Eriksonian approach in no way can accept the premise, inherent in some enrichment models, that teachers are replaceable cogs in a highly structured program, or that cognitive curriculum lesson plans are the single critical ingredient in learning success for the very young, regardless

of the teaching style of the persons delivering such a curriculum.

Erikson postulates eight nuclear conflicts that must be struggled with in turn throughout the life span and resolved with a predominantly positive outcome if humans are to develop a healthy personality. His epigenetic principle states that "anything that grows has a ground plan, and that out of this ground plan the parts arise, each part having its time of special ascendancy until all parts have arisen to form a functioning whole" (1980, p. 53). Careful attention to rate and sequencing of tasks proposed for children as well as to their readiness for handling new challenges can thus be seen as a corollary precept. This precept for caregiving also is corollary to the Piagetian principle of equilibration. Epigenetic development creates a "succession of potentialities for significant interaction with those who tend" children (1980, p. 54).

Teacher training based on Eriksonian theory, therefore, has to focus adult attention not just on particular skills, toys, room arrangements, and curriculum activities. Teacher training has to include sensitivity and *attunement to the individual infant's or preschooler's readiness for planned experiences and interactions, and on ways to enhance such readiness and cooperation with the learning experiences.*

According to Erikson's theory, each component of a healthy personality comes to its ascendance, meets its crisis, and finds a lasting solution (which will influence the adequacy of later conflict resolutions) toward the end of a particular stage. All conflicts exist in some form before their special critical periods. All stages are dependent one on the other. However, caregivers need to be aware of the *particular* crisis of the nuclear conflict at each stage to help children deal with that crisis more effectively. Erikson observed that a baby's growth consists of a series of challenges to caregivers to serve the infant's newly developing potentialities for social interactions. During the rapid physical growth of the early years, radical adjustments of developmental perspective from supine to sitting to vertical toddling to running easily are additional sources of potential crises at each stage. Caregiver *mutuality* in relating to each child's unique developmental situation is the key to more optimal conflict resolution.

Components of a Healthy Personality

Only the first three nuclear conflicts will be discussed, because they pertain to the preschool period during which the Children's Center cared

for children. Table 7–1 diagrams this system of stages and nuclear conflicts during the early years. Descriptions of appropriate child tasks and caregiver tasks that can facilitate optimal conflict resolution have been noted for each of the three stages.

Oral-Sensory Stage   A basic sense of trust rather than mistrust as an attitude toward the world (parents and caregivers initially) and toward the self is the positive outcome of the first nuclear conflict.

TABLE 7–1
Eriksonian Nuclear Conflicts of the Preschool Years: An Epigenetic Diagram

Approximate Child Age	Psychological Stage	Nuclear Conflict	Dominant Organ Modes and Zones	Developmental Tasks and Goals	What the Eriksonian Approach Suggests for Caregivers	Basic Virtues or Strengths as Outcomes of each Nuclear Conflict
Birth to 1 year	Oral-sensory	Trust vs. mistrust	Incorporative mode Oral Zone	Infant develops a sense of inner goodness rather than badness. Infant must learn mutual balance between getting what is given and getting to become a giver. Infant learns to trust own neediness and give clear signals, as well as trusting that needs will be met by reliable caregiver(s).	Sensitive interpretation of distress plus responsive tuned-in care coupled with tender body holding and turn-taking games increase infant chances for favorable ratio of basic trust to mistrust.	Faith and hope Optimism/joy
1 year to 3 years	Anal-urethral-muscular	Autonomy vs. shame or doubt or rage	Retentive vs. eliminative modes	Toddler must learn to harmonize the duality of rigidity and relaxation, between holding on and letting go, appropriating and then	"Matchmake" so that adult socialization pressures (for neatness, toilet learning, obedience to social rules) are adapted to skill levels of	Self-control and willpower Pride and self-esteem.

(continues)

TABLE 7–1
continued

Approximate Child Age	Psychological Stage	Nuclear Conflict	Dominant Organ Modes and Zones	Developmental Tasks and Goals	What the Eriksonian Approach Suggests for Caregivers	Basic Virtues or Strengths as Outcomes of each Nuclear Conflict
				throwing away. Toddler expresses self willfully with sense of pride rather than shame about self. Learns to be self-sufficient in some care/play domains such as self-feeding, walking, toileting, using words to communicate and express wishes.	the toddler. Firm controls (but without shaming) and calm handling or negativisms increase toddler autonomy without burden of shame at temporary failures, while child struggles with develop-mental tasks.	
3–6 years	Locomotor-genital	Initiative vs. guilt	Intrusive and Inceptive modes Genital zone	Preschooler com-bines pleasurable mastery in toy manipulation with zest for construc-tive play with toys. Learns to cooper-ate and play with peers. Struggles to resolve oedipal rivalry with same-sex parent. Conscience develops. Curiosity and intrusive talk are strong.	Arrange environments so that rich variety of toys, activities, and peers are available for construction play senarios and cooperative social games. Help child make choices, select goals, and persist at tasks. Promote self-control. Encourage moral and prosocial reasoning.	Direction and purposefulness Responsibility for choices and play

Anal-Urethral-Muscular Stage A lasting sense of good will and pride is the outcome of the second nuclear conflict (autonomy vs. shame or doubt) for toddlers in the second and third year of life. Caregivers need to nurture a sense of self-control without loss of self-esteem. Otherwise, a lasting sense of doubt or shame can be the legacy of either overcontrol by caregivers or a sense of loss of control by the child. Keen appreciation of the sense of rightful dignity of a toddler is needed. This may be difficult unless adults are well trained to respect the personhood of a small child who may still be in diapers, not very articulate, and often not too skillful in motor acts, whether with hands or sphincters.

If not protected against meaningless and arbitrary experiences of shame the toddler may try to gain power by stubborn and minute control, become secretly determined to get away with things that adults disapprove of, or act defiant toward those who force the child to consider self or body products evil (Erikson, 1950, p. 252).

Locomotor-Genital Stage Exuberant enjoyment of new locomotor and mental skills and an eager ability to make things cooperatively and to play well socially is the positive outcome of the third nuclear conflict (initiative vs. guilt) in the later preschool years. Prechoolers' humor develops a playful quality and they begin to learn how to create compromises to settle social conflicts (Shure, 1993).

> An inner powerhouse of rage must be suppressed at this stage, as some of the fondest hopes and the wildest fantasies are repressed and inhibited. The resulting self-righteousness—often the principal reward for goodness—can later be most intolerantly turned against others in the form of persistent moralistic surveillance so that the prohibition rather than the guidance of initiative becomes the dominant endeavor. (Erikson, 1950, p. 257)

Young children who are encouraged in a well-paced manner to interact responsibly with playmates, materials, and tools can gradually during this stage develop a sense of moral responsibility as well as retain some of the exuberance from the earliest years.

Zones, Modes, and Modalities

Along with the nuclear crises, Erikson postulated that certain organ modes, zones, and modalities characterize each stage, and some will dominate certain stages (see Table 7–1). For example, in the oral-sensory stage, the *incorporative mode* is dominant. Babies suck and take in fluids with the mouth; they also stare and take in whatever tableaux enter the visual field. After the middle of the first year, their hands reach for, swat at, and grasp whatever can be taken in manually. Yet other modes coexist, though they are less important. The *retentive mode* is seen when the baby resists feeding and holds food in cheek pouches, perhaps unnoticed by the caregiver shoveling in food. The *eliminative mode* is seen when infants spit out unwanted foods or spit up if fed too rapidly with a nipple with too large a hole.

Awareness of the importance of the *incorporative mode* for the oral-sensory period can alert the adult to provide sufficient nonnutritive sucking as well as feeding opportunities, to provide interesting visual spectacles for the eyes, language and song variety for the ears, and stroking and cuddling for the skin.

According to Erikson, possible deviations and fixations are associated with distortion in satisfaction of the predominant mode for a given stage. A new stage does not mean that a new zone or a new mode is initiated. But the young child *is* then ready to experience a given mode or organ zone (such as the mouth or the anus) more exclusively during each stage, to master zones and modes more coordinately, and "to learn their social meaning with a certain finality" (Erikson, 1950, p. 78). *Eliminative and retentive modes* predominate during the second stage. Caregivers must avoid forced feeding or coercive toilet training.

The *intrusive mode* characterizes the Erikson stage three child. Preschoolers shout, yell, endlessly ask why, and generally intrude into the auditory and physical space of their peers and caregivers. They sometimes act flirtatious, interact playfully, and begin to accommodate to a companion's wishes in peer play.

Delivery to the child's senses during each of these stages, says Erikson, "must have the proper intensity or else the child's openness changes abruptly into diffuse defense" (1950, p. 72).

Caregiver fine-tuning to the individual emotional sensibility of each child becomes a cornerstone requirement of an Eriksonian approach to childcare (See Table 7–1).

Social Modalities   Social modalities also characterize the stages. The first social modality learned by infants is a readiness to get what is given by the caregiver.

> In a mutually well-regulated relationship, the caregiver permits the child to develop and coordinate his means of getting as she develops and coordinates her means of giving. . . . The mouth and the nipple seem to be the mere centers of a general aura of warmth and mutuality which are enjoyed and responded to with relaxation. . . . The mutuality of relaxation thus developed is of prime importance for the first experience of friendly otherness. One may say (somewhat mystically, to be sure) that in thus getting what is given and in learning to get somebody to do for him what he wishes to have done, the baby also develops the necessary ego groundwork to get to be a giver. (Erikson, 1950, p. 76)

Where custodial or indifferent caregiving is provided, a child may try to get by random activity, constant thumbsucking, compulsive self-rocking, or fantasy day-dreaming that which could not be obtained by reciprocity. Erikson observes that if an infant has a lack of mutuality in the feeding relationship with the mothering one, a sensitive caregiver can make up for what is missed orally by satiating other than oral receptors. The baby takes "pleasure in being held, warmed, smiled at, talked to, rocked, etc. We cannot afford to relax our remedial inventiveness" (1950, p. 76).

The simultaneous social modalities that must be experimented with and brought into harmony in stage two are *holding on* and *letting go*. As with all modalities (if adults do not provide firm reassuring controls), their basic conflict can lead to imbalance toward hostile rather than harmonious expectations and attitudes.

Thus, to hold can become a destructive and cruel retaining or restraining, and it can become a pattern of care: to have and to hold. To let go, too, can turn into an inimical letting loose of destructive forces, or it can become a relaxed "to let pass" and "to let be." . . . The infant must come to feel that the basic faith in existence, which is the lasting treasure saved from the rages of the oral stage, will not be jeopardized by this about-face of his, this sudden violent wish to have a choice, to appropriate demandingly, and to eliminate stubbornly. Firmness [of caregivers] must protect him against the potential anarchy of his as yet untrained sense of discrimination, his inability to hold on and let go with discretion. (Erikson, 1950, pp. 251–252)

The basic modalities of the third stage, during the later preschool years, Erikson calls "making" or "being on the make." This involves the use of *phallic-intrusive modes* and "suggests pleasure in attack and conquest" (1950, p. 255). In girls, Erikson says that the emphasis may be on catching or snatching, as in catching attention by making oneself endearing and attractive.

Eriksonian conflicts are indeed just that—conflicts. The theory in a sense postulates that children will always face trauma. The baby encounters trauma as teeth erupt painfully. Failures in early walking lead to sprawling tumbles and hard falls. There are "tantrums of muscular and anal impotence" (Erikson, 1950, p. 79). For this reason, *mutual regulation,* and judicious and gentle introduction of socialization practices, such as weaning and toilet training, are counseled. In the first year of life, if caregivers are abrupt or insensitive or there is a drastic loss of accustomed mother love that could occur when infants are in outside care situations for long hours, children may be subject "to acute infantile depression or to a mild but chronic state of mourning which may give a depressive undertone to the whole remainder of life" (1950, p. 80).

Eriksonian theory implies, then, that the *quality* of caregiver interactions is critical for positive resolution of the nuclear conflicts of the early years.

✍ CAREGIVER INTERACTIONS: AN ERIKSONIAN APPROACH

In their interactions, caregivers in the Children's Center nurtured the child's development of basic trust and pleased sense of self. They supported, in a secure environment with clear rules, toddlers' growing sense of will, ability to make responsible choices, and capacity to take initiatives freely. The arrangements of environments, coupled with responsive personalized care, embodied Eriksonian prescriptions for ensuring positive emotional, social, and intellectual development of the children (Honig, 1978; Honig & Lally, 1981).

Responsive Attunement of Caregivers

In the "infant-fold," babies were held in arms frequently. Each infant was assigned a special caregiver. That is, each caregiver had charge of four infants and each of those infants had one specific nurturing person who "belonged" to that infant. Building basic trust was not easy for some of the infants. One infant, with a veiled, impassive face, spent several weeks at the center entirely unresponsive to the caregiver's ministrations. Despite Delores's best efforts to implement our cognitive-language curriculum through an Eriksonian process, the baby remained solemn and unresponsive. Delores felt discouraged in her caregiving. We urged her to keep faith with the process of responsive, caregiving interactions and mutually pleasureful body cuddling and games. After another few weeks, suddenly the baby burst into tears when Delores went on coffee break. When she returned to the room, the infant brightened and greeted her with extended hands. Almost immediately thereafter, cognitive gains became noticeable. The infant would play peek-a-boo and pat-a-cake. Sounds of "ba-ba" and other babbling began. Development of a basic Eriksonian trusting relationship had been necessary before more intellective or sensorimotor learning could be ventured.

Holding baby on the caregiver's lap, hugging, and stroking the baby help in the development of a trusting parent–child relationship.

Feeding   What kinds of transactions build basic trust? Leisurely bottle feeding with baby in arms was the daily experience of each infant. When infants graduated to solid foods, caregivers would talk with them during the meal and give a baby spoon to any baby who wanted to try to get food also. *Mutuality* means that we allow an infant to try self-feeding even when we must still do the majority of the spoon-feeding.

Holding   Babies were often rocked in arms or while draped on a caregiver's lap. Their backs were rubbed; hugs and holding were freely available. Little walks about the room were taken with an infant in arms, even for simple activities such as enjoying a view out of the window.

Diapering   Diapering was an important routine for enhancing bodily comfort, language learning, and trust building. Babies were crooned to and talked with as they were diapered. Admiring glances and smiles reflected the goodness of their bodies. Hands caressed them. Language lessons and skin pleasuring were intertwined. The salience of Erikson's incorporative mode in the first year made diapering table time an ideal opportunity for skin sharing and vocal exchanges. Year-old infants who are wooed with shiny eyes, loving conversation, and deft care that leaves their bottoms clean and comfortable will wriggle their rounded tummies with delight and often kick rhythmically in deep pleasure. Babies who either submit passively or angrily resist diapering are not learning mutual positive attunements with caregivers. The diapering table is a language lesson locale par excellence! The caregiver is so close to the baby's body. It is easy to croon loving words and enjoy baby babbles directed to the caregiver.

Why are such Eriksonian mutual attunements so crucial for quality care? Research on securely and insecurely attached infants whose low-income mothers returned to work early (before the child was 1 year old) shows the potential disorganizing effects of out-of-home care on the emotional security of the children at 24 months (Vaughn, Deane, & Waters, 1985). Toddlers whose mothers had returned to full-time employment during the first year of infancy and who had been previously securely attached as infants showed more opposition and less persistence when presented with difficult tool-using tasks than did the toddlers who had initially been insecure as infants. The vulnerability of the securely attached infants to disruption of maternal care because of mothers' early return to full-time employment emphasizes for us the critical nature of the *quality* of out-of-home care that infants receive. Eriksonian principles are more likely to engender secure trusting relationships with substitute caregivers and possibly lessen the jeopardy of disruption in the primary trusting relationship with parents. This disruption in infancy can have long-lasting effects. Caregivers (blind to the children's infancy care conditions) have rated preschool children as behaviorally

more aggressive when full-time care had begun in the first year of life (Park & Honig, 1991).

Washing   Personal respect for each infant also extended to routine cleansing. At cleanup time after lunch, for example, face washing was carried out as courteously as possible with verbal notice. "Now I am going to wash up your face. Let's get your face all cleaned off; now you will feel nice and clean and comfortable." Sing-song tones and explanations ease routine clean-up times (Honig, 1995b). Such gentle handling and forewarning contrasts sharply to scenes I have observed in group care centers where large adults swoop down without warning from behind tiny children to wipe their faces as infants struggle to escape the "help." Where cleansing or filling up with food are done as mechanical, efficient actions such as one would carry out with inanimate objects, then the prime Eriksonian goal of establishing reciprocal trust and mutuality in relationships cannot easily be met. As the philosopher Martin Buber has so beautifully taught us, an "I-Thou" (rather than an I-It) relationship is fundamental to sensitive cherishing and respect. In an Eriksonian framework:

> trust is built on a four way signal system. Adults who trust themselves to be loving and facilitative and are sensitive to the infant's signals and responsive to his expressed needs, nurture that infant's trust in adults as well as in his own ability to express his needs and to get someone to meet those needs. (Honig, 1974a, p. 637)

Reading   Loving touches were also part of the learning experience during reading times. Babies were read to in innumerable ways and spaces. One frequent technique was for a caregiver to sit on a low couch with infants leaning against each knee and two more snuggled under the arms. A teacher could then read to four babies while touching them all. Caregivers attuned to the different learning levels of some babies can change a story, shorten it, vary voice tones to increase child interest as they share picture books with babies.

Some toddlers can sit for a 50-page story. Some are highly active and not used to story sharing with an adult. Adult skills for picture book sharing are in short supply in some care settings. Honig and Shin (2001) observed in middle-class child care centers that caregivers rarely read to babies younger than 1 year. Across the infant/toddler period, the length of a reading episode in that study was barely more than 1 minute!

Comforting All babies were picked up promptly if they cried or were distressed. Infants who showed difficulty in adjusting to group care were carried about on a hip for weeks. Longitudinal studies of infant temperament styles has revealed that babies differ markedly in their ability to adjust to new social situations, such as child care (Honig, 1997a). Although our staff training did not include the nine specific aspects of temperament we now recognize so easily, because of the Eriksonian framework of our care, teachers were indeed sensitive to differing temperament styles. They were able to reassure the slow-to-warm-up infant or provide more nurturance for a more *triggery* baby. Always, caregivers have to be sensitive and not ignore the more outgoing, easy-to-soothe baby. Evaluation of caregiver trans-actions with the ABC (Adult Behaviors in Caregiving) Checklists (Honig & Lally, 1975a) showed that adults ignored infant bids for attention during only .1% of 840 two-minute observations of five "infant-fold" teachers.

ERIKSONIAN IDEAS BLENDED WITH PIAGETIAN GAMES

Many of the sensorimotor activities that teach-ers carried out were not presented as formal les-son plans but embedded in loving interactions. Even when special activities (e.g., presentation of a dangling toy to enhance eye-hand coordi-nation) were initiated, the infant would be snug-gled on the caregiver's lap for the "lesson."

Caregivers provided bodily reassurance. They used the human body for Piagetian games even though toys and furnishings also fre-quently served as lesson props. For example, in promoting spatial understandings, caregivers not only used detour and barrier games with objects, but also used the body as a Piagetian "screen" (Honig, 1991). After slowly moving a toy car to a position in back of the caregiver's own or the baby's body, a caregiver would encourage the infant to lean, turn, and reach to find the hidden object. Thus, bodies as well as conventional cloths, pillows, and cups were used for Piagetian object permanence and spa-tial games.

An infant would be lifted onto a seated care-giver's hip and then onto the chest. Baby's face reflected wonder and amazement as the vantage point changed and the spatial view of the world enlarged.

For other spatial games, homemade origami birds or animals were attached by thin strings and hung from the ceiling with sticky tape. Coordinations of vision and prehension in reaching upward required the sturdy security of a caregiver's arms, from which baby could trust-ingly stretch upward in space to reach for the paper bird.

Tying sensorimotor activities to body close-ness and comfort adds a dimension of somatic surety to early learning that may make it easier for infants to absorb the "lessons" planned for them.

Toddlers: The Need to Keep Building Trust

Trust building continued by adults in the tod-dler period takes on more subtle dimensions. Caregiver patience and good humor becomes particularly important. Tempers fray as toddlers find that their wills are stronger than their skills. Toddlers have seesawing needs between fiercely independent "no-no" saying and op-posite needs for laps and cuddling. They need unobtrusive help that does not diminish their pride in early efforts at more mature behaviors.

Teachers support early autonomy strivings while continuing to secure toddler confidence in adult kindness despite the provocations of toddler negativism. These adult skills require special sensitivity (Wittmer & Honig, 1990). As a caregiver sang with and helped toddlers act out ring-around-the-rosy, endless times little hands came apart. Endless times adults would gently re-form the circle and rejoin their hands. Game rules or social interaction rules were calmly restated. Tolerance and good-humored patience with toddler ungainliness prevailed. Seeing banana in the hair of a dining toddler as a "vitamin hair treatment" rather than a grim reminder of extra work to be done helps caregivers keep their sense of humor. One older toddler could not figure out how to press pasted strips of paper together to make loops for a long daisy chain as the others were busily doing. The teacher smoothly helped the child press the paper strips together, giving help that did not intrusively take over the job or shame the child as clumsy compared to others. Innumerable tiny acts of kindness increased toddler assurance that adults were their helpers in learning struggles. Adults respected slow eating tempos or endless tries to do something "myself." *Timing* and *pacing of activities* became critical. Fortunately, the open-education settings permitted the self-directed choices and independent initiatives that children needed to feel in control of their own pacing for length of activity.

Firm rules had to be sustained concerning aggressive acts. No child was allowed to hurt another. Biting or hitting children were promptly and firmly led to cooling-off spaces. Thus, even during the second Eriksonian struggle, trust building went on. Teachers could be trusted to prevent anarchy within and without. Teachers provided firm classroom control balanced with the freedom to make choices in eating, in voiding, and in play bouts with peers.

Teachers were low-keyed in listening to and handling toddler "Nos." Positive luring techniques often brought a toddler into an activity or routine. The *"magic triangle"* technique (Honig, 1982c) whereby adult and child are focused on the apex of the triangle, the activity, rather than on a potential interpersonal struggle, often eased toddlers into an activity and so avoided direct confrontations.

Toilet training was carried out persistently, but at a pace comfortable for each toddler. Neither criticism nor shame was given for toileting accidents (Honig, 1993). In this, Children's Center caregivers often differed dramatically from some parents. One 2-year-old girl, painting at an easel, stood frozen with fear as she had a urinary accident. Her teacher noticed and called out reassuringly that she would come right over and help clean up the urine and find fresh panties. But the little girl's mother habitually switched the child on the legs with a stick to punish her for urinary accidents. Expecting to be whipped, petrified with fear at the unexpected difference in handling techniques, the little girl burst into almost uncontrollable crying. Building trust, so that it can sustain a child against the surges of shame some parents actively evoke in toddlers through coercive socialization practices, can be difficult work in group programs. In-service training for caregivers needs to help adults see how corrosive shame can be. Guilt (beginning in Erikson's stage 3) is important for caregivers to be aware of when they need to use "victim-centered discipline" to help a toddler or preschooler understand how another has been hurt and how healing gestures can be offered (Honig, 1996a).

EVALUATION

Assessment of the parent outreach program, testing of the children, and observation of caregiver transactions were part of an ongoing evaluation program integral to the FDRP effort to monitor and ensure the implementation of the program. We have already spoken of the ABC Scales used to monitor caregivers in the center. In addition, the parents were interviewed in depth when the children were 3 and 5 years of age.

The Parent Evaluation of Program (PEP) interview at 36 months revealed the quality of relationship that the home visitors had developed with the families. To the question "What are the qualities that make your CDT effective in working with you?" parents replied:

"I feel I'm equal to her. She never puts me down. And you know that she has the same problems—just normal everyday people who don't try to run your life. She knows that everyone is different."

"She has always been friendly and helpful in any way she could. Always there to contact for any problem."

"She's very understanding. She's gone through a lot with me. I don't answer the door or phone. It takes a person with a lot of nerve to try to see me. If she weren't so patient and understanding, my child wouldn't be in the center. I don't think most people would put up with someone like me. I know I wouldn't!"

"She's patient. I'm awfully moody at times."

"She's never down or mean though she has problems, too."

"She's given help on personal problems and taken us to her home."

"She's helped me out of certain personal jams."

"She's frank with you. She tells you what she thinks about things. You can believe her. She doesn't twist things."

"She's not afraid to come into my house and eat my cooking."

"She worked her schedule around mine."

"The way she puts things gives me choices; though she tells me when she's upset by something I've done."

"She's always there to contact for every problem."

"She likes her job more than just for the money."

"She's one of the best friends I've got." (Honig, 1979, pp. 53–54)

Optimal Testing: An Eriksonian Approach to Evaluation with Children

A variety of measures were chosen to assess aspects of children's functioning and progress. Up to the age of 3 years, FDRP infant progress was compared to that of low socioeconomic status infants who had participated in other community programs (e.g., a nursery for infants of unwed teenagers) and of high socioeconomic status infants (children of college-educated parent volunteers) matched by sex and age to program infants. Note in Table 7–2 that cognitive differences between program infants and low or high educational control group were not found at 12 or 18 months with the Cattell Infant Intelligence Scale.

From 36 months of age onward, a matched group of control children was recruited. They were carefully chosen to meet the same initial demographic requirements as families enrolled in the FDRP. When the children were 36 months old, a contrast group of children, also carefully matched for age and sex, was chosen from

TABLE 7–2

Cattell Mean IQ Scores for Center, Low-Education Control, and High-Education Contrast Children

	12 Months			18 Months		
	Center	Low Ed	High Ed	Center	Low Ed	High Ed
n	100	60	39	100	60	39
IQ score	107.18	105.89	107.49	114.68	112.22	115.46

middle-class, two-parent, college-educated families. The control families were followed throughout the duration of the project and in the longitudinal follow up 10 years after the project ended (Lally, Mangione, & Honig, 1988). Child measures across age groups included:

Language

ELAS (Early Language Assessment Scale)
CLOC (Classroom Language Observation Checklist)
ITPA (Illinois Test of Psycholinguistic Ability)
Peabody Picture Vocabulary Test

Cognition

Piagetian Infancy Scales
Cattell Infant Intelligence Scale
Stanford-Binet Intelligence Scale
Caldwell Preschool Inventory
Boehm Test of Basic Concepts
Bayley Infant Behavior Record
Cornell Descriptive Scanning Record of Infant

Activity and Infant Environment

AAS (Beller Autonomous Achievement Striving Scales)

Socioemotional Functioning

Schaefer Classroom Behavior Checklist
Schaefer Behavioral Rating Form
Emmerich Ratings of Personal-Social Behaviors
CAT (Children's Apperception Test)—selected pictures
Coopersmith Behavioral Rating Form
Maternal Comparisons of Project Children with Peers

Nutritional and Medical Status

Weekly and monthly baby diet forms (collected from mothers)
Pediatric examination
Visual, dental, and hearing examination
Lead poisoning and iron deficiency examinations

In accordance with Eriksonian philosophy, testing staff was trained first in positive ways to build trust with children while ensuring that test items were presented so that item-pass requirements were rigorously met (Honig & Lally, 1989). "Optimal testing" was the technical name for this positive testing procedure. When a child was tired or hungry, that child would be fed, or taken to a play space with other toys for a rest, or even taken for a walk around the block. Sometimes a child was brought back for a second session another day to finish the testing procedures. Our implicit operating procedure was to trust the child's signals and value the child's needs for rest or refreshment while luring the child into participation with the test materials and tasks.

Evaluation staff was trained to recognize infant signals that let adults know that rapport is not yet well established. They realized when more wooing and interesting the child would have to be done before valid scores could be obtained. Infant testers had to watch for arched backs, furrows between brows, hands under the table rather than up and ready to grasp proffered toys. Testers were taught how to lure children into feeling comfortable by offering them blocks or bells or toy cars to interest them in the test materials. If one Cattell item proved difficult, a tester was advised to offer an easier item or one that involved more toy manipulation the next turn. Thus, motivation could be kept high throughout the testing procedures from basal through ceiling items with each child.

Optimal testing was carried out with control-group children as well. An example from the early history of the Children's Center illustrates this: A control mother brought her 4-year-old son in for a Stanford–Binet test. Mother did not want to stay in the test room. She brought her youngster to the door and said to me, "Here, you take him. Good luck with him. He never sits still for anyone or anything." With that definitive pronouncement, she then left. As I seated the youngster at the test table, I explained to him that we were going to play games and I would ask him some questions. Then I would need time to write down everything he said and how he did some of the games such as building a tall tower of blocks. So would he please help me out by running back and forth to the end of the room after each activity while I was writing down his special words and activities? The child was a model of cooperativeness. After each Stanford–Binet item, he ran to the end of the room, then came back and slid into his seat for the next item. Thus, when children had very short attention spans, deliberate efforts to create a climate of mutuality in testing interactions helped to ensure that optimal testing was carried out.

Longitudinal Follow-Up

Preschool Scores In general, intellectual attainments of the program children at 36 and 48 months were quite satisfactory (Stanford–Binet IQs of 110.3 and 109) in comparison with low education controls (96.6 and 100.7) (Honig & Lally, 1982). Possibly as a result of optimal testing, control low education children's scores in the FDRP project were much higher than those reported in other enrichment projects (Honig & Lally, 1989). High education contrast children had significantly higher IQ scores, in the 120–129 range. IQ differences did not persist between the experimental and control low education groups by 72 months (see Table 7–3).

Social-emotional functioning of the children was assessed with the Emmerich Observation Scales. Children's Center participants at 36 months scored significantly higher than controls on the following unipolar scales:

1. Exhibits interest in or concern for others in distress.
2. Friendly toward adult.
3. Friendly toward child.
4. Gets intrinsic satisfaction from activity or task.
5. Attempts to communicate verbally to child.

6. Seeks physical affection from other child.
7. Seeks help or guidance from adult.
8. Engages in complementary behavior.
9. Praises or expresses approval toward other child.
10. Nurturant toward other child.
11. Engages in gross motor activity.
12. Engages in fantasy activity.
13. Takes initiative in carrying out own activity.
14. Threatens to act aggressively toward other child.
15. Imitates behavior of adult.

Control children scored significantly higher on the following behaviors:

1. Restlessness.
2. Does not concentrate on activity (Honig, Lally, & Mathieson, 1982).

Kindergarten and First-Grade Scores

The Emmerich Scales were again used in kindergarten and first grade in 15 elementary schools within the city classrooms to assess the socioemotional functioning of center graduates. In each classroom, the center child was matched to a noncenter child by race, sex, and socioeconomic status. Teachers were interviewed to ensure the appropriateness of the classroom matches, and permission for observation of these control children was obtained from their parents. The Emmerich Scales were used to assess specific categories of social and emotional behavior, such as social motives, coping mechanisms, and activities and interests. Bipolar items (e.g., sensitive to others vs. self-centered, dependent vs. independent, aggressive vs. affectionate to others, socially secure vs. socially insecure) were based on ratings from specific unipolar item behaviors. Each child was observed (by observers blind to child status) for four 20-minute class time periods. In the kindergarten study, Children's Center

TABLE 7–3
One-Way Analysis of Variance Comparing the Stanford–Binet IQ Means of Center, Control, and Contrast Children

Group	36 Months				48 Months			
	n	M	SD	F Ratio	n	M	SD	F Ratio
Children's center	81	110.33	13.78	Center and low ed. 41.54*	75	109.97	10.67	Center and Low ed. 21.73*
Low ed. controls	68	96.59	11.89	High ed. and center 32.69*	71	100.77	13.11	High ed. and center 108.24*
High ed. contrast	47	125.87	16.45	High ed. and low ed. 122.78*	43	136.05	16.54	High ed. and low ed. 158.64*

Group	60 Months				72 Months			
	n	M	SD	F Ratio	n	M	SD	F Ratio
Children's center	64	106.59	12.39	Center and low ed. 2.55	38	109.05	12.84	Center and low ed. 1.10
Low ed. controls	52	102.63	14.34	High ed. and center 121.93*	15	105.07	11.40	
High ed. contrast	30	138.26	14.26	High ed. and low ed. 117.97*				

graduates continued to show a profile of significantly more positive, friendly, task-persistent behaviors than controls.

The bipolar items indicated that the 37 center children in kindergarten were more involved, relaxed, dominant, energetic, independent, social, purposeful, affectionate to others, and flexible than their school matches. They were more sensitive to adults and other children, less submissive to adults and other children, less dependent on adults and other children, more affectionate

toward peers and adults, and more socially secure around adults and other children. The classroom controls were significantly more restrained, self-centered, passive, unstable, timid, destructive, socially insecure, and unhappy than the center graduates.

In the first-grade follow up, for which only 20 center graduates were able to be observed with matched controls, the outcome picture became far more troubling. Although center graduates still significantly more than controls sought attention from teachers through positive bids, they now also sought attention from teachers through negative bids. They still made more positive bids to peers than did controls, but they were more verbally loud, aggressive, and defiant as well, compared to classroom controls. Controls showed increased threats to act aggressively toward peers and significantly more criticism of adults and children. These results were puzzling and disturbing, although they were based on a very small sample. First-grade classrooms were far more teacher dominated than kindergartens. Freedom to choose activities, opportunity to get intellectual needs met promptly by having adults in fairly plentiful supply—these center benefits were no longer available. We ask with concern, "How can we alter these settings to maintain positive personal-social behaviors engendered in preschool and family-centered programs?" (Honig, Lally, & Mathieson, 1982, p. 145).

Data from the Adolescent Years   The premise of the Eriksonian program was that a strong emphasis on building positive parenting skills and family closeness, plus home-visitor support for parental self-esteem and achievement goals, would enhance the effectiveness of the program for the target children. In the center, teachers had promoted prosocial techniques for children to resolve social conflicts as well as admired and cheered on the youngsters' learning efforts. Thus we hypothesized that, in the socioemotional domain, as the children grew up, program children and their kin would feel closer as families and that parents would be more supportive of their children's learning and career goals and more admiring of their children's accomplishments.

Ten years after the children graduated from the program, the project attempted to locate graduates and their matched controls. All interviewers were blind to initial status of the youngsters and did not know the families. Of the 108 children who started the program, 82 had completed the full 5-year intervention, and 79% of these families were located and signed consent forms. Of the 74 matched controls who had remained in the sample through 60 months of age, 73% were found and signed the consent form. No differential attrition was found, although control families required far more creative and persistent efforts to locate (Lally et al., 1988). Single-parent families with the mother working at a low wage were characteristic of both groups at follow-up.

Both cognitive and socioemotional data were gathered, from interviews with the teenagers and their families, from school records, and from teacher descriptions. The impact of program was favorable for the school functioning of girls only, both in terms of grade reports and frequency of school absence or truancy. Facet theory analysis was applied to teacher ratings. No significant group differences were found for the males. Compared with control girls, program girls, however, were rated as having more positive attitudes toward themselves and others.

The family interviews consisted of open-ended questions about use of leisure time, values, concerns, aspirations, accomplishments, and support systems. A content analysis of the major trends revealed that the major group differences pertained to the parents' comments about what made them feel proud about themselves as parents and what advice they would give to youngsters (Lally et al., 1988). Only 10% of control parents talked about their child having a prosocial orientation, while 28% of program parents did so, saying things like, "He cares about other people." Also, a significantly higher percentage of program parents (18% vs. 5% of controls) mentioned that unity of the family (e.g., "We're all close with each other") made them feel proud of their parenting efforts. Some 29% of program parents said they would advise young people to learn something about themselves and to do everything they could to reach their full potential. But only 14% of control parents said they would offer such advice; they were more likely to advise youngsters to concentrate on getting by.

Program teens significantly more often asserted that they liked one or more of their physical attributes (e.g., physique or appearance), and there was a trend toward their also liking more of their personality attributes, such as their sense of humor, compared with the controls. Twice as many control students as program students felt that "the worst thing about school was getting into trouble." Thus, program students felt more positive about themselves.

Rates of Juvenile Delinquency The most marked finding of the positive social effects of FDRP's Eriksonian program was in the differential juvenile delinquency rates of program and control children. Data available on 65 program youngsters and 54 control youngsters from 13 to 16 years of age revealed that court costs, probation supervision, placement in foster care, and detention costs to the community differed significantly for the two groups.

Compared with 6% of program children convicted of juvenile delinquency (four cases, of which three were PINS, or "persons in need of supervision," a courtroom term for children who are considered unmanageable but not a threat to society), 22% of control adolescents had been processed by the County Probation Department (12 youths, of whom five were repeat offenders) (Lally et al., 1988). The control youth had committed much more serious acts, including robbery, physical assault, burglary, and sexual assault. Costs to the community for program youths were $12,000 vs. $107,192 for control youths. Thus, more antisocial acts and more aggravated ones characterized the group of young people who had been in the control group.

Further attempts to follow up the FDRP graduates and the controls when they were adults proved frustrating. Very few of the control young adults could be found, despite extensive efforts to enlist community supports for locating families.

LESSONS FROM FDRP AND SUGGESTIONS FOR FUTURE PROGRAMS

The Children's Center and FDRP data have made clear the ways in which an Eriksonian approach to the education of infants, toddlers, and preschoolers can be implemented in a program that serves children and their parents. During the time that children were in program, extensive observational data confirmed that their socioemotional development and their scores on psychometric tests were essentially predictive of normal functioning in a group of children from high-risk families. Yet difficulties in the lives of very low socioeconomic status families continued to impact on the children who had graduated from the program.

What do the follow-up findings suggest must be emphasized or added to an Eriksonian plus Piagetian curriculum in an omnibus early intervention program for disadvantaged preschoolers and their families?

- Poverty is long lasting. Educational programs need to network and collaborate with community agencies to serve clients after program participation ends for the preschoolers. Note that FDRP parents were still living in poverty when the FDRP graduates were teenagers. Programs may choose to collaborate with other community agencies to enhance job training and placement opportunities for parents of the children served. Collaboration with school boards could strengthen efforts to keep in contact with dropout parents and persist in helping them eventually achieve high school equivalency diplomas. Collaboration with helping agencies is now required of Head Start programs nationwide.
- Educational programs for teen parents are more effective if begun prior to a child's birth. The FDRP program enrolled families prior to the birth of the infant. More

programs need to promote this option. In a recent 2-year home-based intervention program, some high-risk teens were randomly enrolled several months *prior* to the baby's birth and others only post-birth. Several years later, home visitation begun *prior* to birth was associated with significantly lower rates of confirmed child abuse or neglect cases, even for program drop-outs when compared with drop-outs enrolled *after* baby's birth with a mean of seven home visits (Honig & Morin, 2001).

- Schools need to implement prevention programs with teens to prevent high-risk behaviors, such as teen drug use that can lead to fetal harm and child developmental difficulties. Interventions early in pregnancy can support teens in avoidance of alcohol, smoking, and drugs that often have devastating effects, such as prematurity, drug addiction in the newborn, and learning problems, that are particularly severe for FAS (Fetal Alcohol Syndrome) children.

- Intensive, in-depth, ongoing training is crucial for home visitors and care providers who serve families with more severe risk factors. What kinds of therapeutic techniques must be added to the repertoire of the home visitor? In the FDRP program, home visitors were paraprofessionals dedicated to serving high-risk families. Both training and supervision were provided on an ongoing basis. However, clinical research has revealed the power of attachment status in parental family of origin as it impacts on the mother's and father's ability to support a baby's development of secure attachment (Fonagy, Steele, & Steele, 1991).

Ainsworth's (1982) attachment research has borne out Erikson's proposed relationship between early care-giving practices and latter patterns of attachment (Bretherton & Waters, 1986; Sameroff & Emde, 1990).

Such data add more urgency to the question of *how much training* workers need to be effective with young parents who may have experienced harsh childhoods and themselves had insecure attachments. Fraiberg's kitchen therapy model (Fraiberg, Adelson, & Shapiro, 1987) was an intensive psychoanalytically based model successful with mothers at severe risk for neglect. This model requires intensive personnel training in clinical therapeutic skills.

Increased *reflectivity* by teen parents about how they were parented and their wishes for their own children proved a significant predictor of more empathic and prompt response to infant distress in a home visitation program for low-income teen mothers (Brophy-Herb & Honig, 1999). Developmentally nurturing interactions with young children depend on caregiver attunement to the child's feelings, rather than one's own, plus the ability to respond supportively. Such awareness when it includes the realization that one can *choose* to parent the same or differently from one's own parents are abilities Piaget would characterize as "decentering." Erikson specified that the main nuclear conflict for teenagers is an identity crisis. But adolescents struggling with figuring out who they really are and want to become may not be prepared for the role of parent. Outreach workers and child-care staff interacting with young parents need to boost parental noticing skills and competencies. Workers need to enlarge the repertoire of parental skills in managing difficult or inappropriate child behaviors. Then young parents can more accurately interpret a young child's emotional distress and respond to that child's needs adaptively and generously. Eriksonian theory would predict that such help for the teen parent allows her to struggle through the socioemotional crisis of identity versus a confused sense of her new role as a parent with responsibilities. The young parent with increased ability to *reflect* on her or his own past relationship with parents is better able to choose and implement appropriate rearing strategies with a baby.

• More outreach programs for at-risk new parents need to be funded. Study of the effects of family learning environment and poverty on cognitive test scores of infants born premature and at low birth weight reveal "the power of the learning environment inside the home" (Klebanov, Brooks-Gunn, McCarton, & McCormick, 1998, p. 1431). Their data confirmed that provision of learning experiences for the babies was clearly a "central parental behavior" that impacted the young children's cognitive test scores. Home visitors are often skilled at helping parents use ordinary household utensils to promote language and learning experiences. FDRP data revealed that home visitors have talents for helping families use homey materials, even when parents cannot afford store-bought toys.

• Explanations of *temperament issues* must be integrated into any model for training infancy caregivers. Teachers and home visitors need more knowledge about infant temperament. Teaching parents about inborn *temperament* characteristics of young children helps them gain increased insight into ages, stages, and response styles of a young child. Half of a group of low-income mothers with highly irritable infants in Holland were randomly assigned to receive supports for becoming more attuned to and responding more sensitively to their irritable infants. These babies had far higher rates of secure attachment to mother at 1 year than the group who had not received help with soothing skills (Van den Boom, 1993).

Group-care staff also can benefit from more awareness of temperament characteristics and from more training in appropriate interactions regardless of child temperament. This must include family child-care providers, whom parents are often more apt to choose for services when they have young infants (Honig, 2002a).

• Male children from at-risk families may require more specific focus and efforts to ensure positive development. The FDRP program, along with many other experimental studies of model programs, reveals far larger achievement score effects for females than for males (David and Lucile Packard Foundation, 1995). In center group care, low-income male toddlers are markedly more needy than females (Wittmer & Honig, 1987). The special vulnerability of *male children* from high-risk single-parent families in terms of lower school achievement, repeated grades, and social difficulties presents a challenge to early childhood programs to target more nurturant supports for these youngsters. In the NICHD study across many sites in the United States, male infants, regardless of social class, have shown higher vulnerability than females to early maternal full-time employment. Infant boys whose mothers worked 30 hours or more per week scored nearly 9 points lower on the Bracken School Readiness test at 36 months when compared with boys whose mothers did not work by 9 months (Brooks-Gunn, Han, & Waldfogel, 2002). Thus, child-care personnel and policy makers need to become aware of male infant vulnerability both to maternal insensitivity and to increased hours in nonmaternal care and find creative ways to program more tender responsive care for male babies.

• Program goals that are *exclusively cognitive* are too narrow. Research with FDRP graduates increases our understanding that intervention programs must provide for the building of Eriksonian positive outcomes as well as for cognitive attainments. Many enrichment programs report that an exclusively cognitive curriculum is insufficient to ensure successful outcomes for youth. IQ scores tend to decline as high-risk children leave the program and enter public education institutions with other youngsters from disadvantaged families. Truancy and delinquency rates may increase during adolescence even for children who have been in such programs during the entire preschool period (Garber, 1988). Haskins (1985) reported significantly more aggression in kindergarten children who had attended a high-quality infant–toddler program with emphasis on cognitive enrichment. Not until a prosocial program was introduced for subsequent waves of enrolled program children did later kindergarten aggression rates equalize for program graduates and control children. As reported, the long-term delinquency findings of the FDRP program underscore the importance of including Eriksonian goals and techniques to build trust, autonomy, and initiative as well as intellective skills.

- Nutrition is crucial for young children's optimal development. Breast-feeding of infants needs to be promoted. FDRP teenagers felt negatively about breast-feeding. More efforts need to be made to help prospective parents understand the positive nutritional and emotional benefits of breast-feeding. Often, new mothers need help, such as the La Leche League provides, in order to breast-feed successfully. In some at-risk families, fast food diets are the norm. Obesity and juvenile diabetes are increasing in society. Our task is even more urgent then for children in out-of-home care that we nourish the growing brain. The brain needs good nutrition and restful sleep times. Daily routine care must provision for optimal nutrition and sleep.
- Brain research findings should be added to every caregiver-training program. Caregivers who become aware of the new findings will become empowered with a realization of how important their interactions and roles are (Honig, 2003). One of the most exciting findings of the past decade has been how awesomely prepared the toddler mind is for learning. What does the new brain research have to teach us that can increase our motivation to support high-quality infant/toddler caregiving?

At birth, a baby's brain contains 100 billion neurons and a trillion glial cells that protect and nourish the neurons. But these neurons need to become wired together so that chemical and electrical messages can flow easily across the synapses, the connections between one neuron and another. During the early years, the baby's brain grows trillions of these connections. Toddlers' brains contain twice as many synapses and consume twice as much energy as the brains of normal adults (Nash, 1997). To ensure that these connections are wired in, caregivers need to provide infants and toddlers with repeated enriched-learning opportunities and engage in language-rich interpersonal interactions. Unused neuronal connections are pruned, beginning before 10 years of age. Our frontal lobes give us an advantage in decision making because they allow humans to be proactive rather than only reactive. They allow for conscious anticipations and preparations for responding to challenges in time and space. A safe, secure human web of relationships helps to wire neurons together. *Parents and caregivers are teachers of the baby's brain!*

Touch is important. "Children who don't play much or are rarely touched develop brains 20% to 30% smaller than normal for their age" (Nash, 1997, p. 51). Cuddling is not only an Eriksonian imperative! Stroking and cuddling increase brain development. Excellent videos exist to help caregivers learn to provide infant massage for young babies.

Although we attribute only motor control to the cerebellum, some neurologists are now asserting that motor and cognitive development may be fundamentally interrelated and "intertwined" (Diamond, 2000, p. 44). Adults need to provide more opportunities for infants to stretch, crawl, reach, twist, bend, toddle, and safely clamber to enhance cerebellar functioning. Given lots of opportunities to practice motor skills safely, young children can learn more coordinated responses, more optimal timing of actions, and correct errors of estimating distance or body functioning in space. Toddlers learning impulse control are learning to resist temptations to respond too early or to inhibit an action a caregiver has labeled as dangerous. Cognitive functions are importantly allied with skilled motor performances. And motor practice is very important during the Piagetian sensorimotor stage. Concerns have been raised that in some cultures, prolonged carrying of infants without allowing them opportunities for physical mastery of objects in space "may have detrimental effects on the development of the visual integration pathways" (Pretorius, Naude, & Van Vuuren, 2002, p. 173). Babies need to negotiate a variety of spaces and materials with graduated challenges. When a care facility provides a cramped space as a result of adding babies into the program they have for preschoolers, then they may be shortchanging development of motor skills and visual integration.

Some children live with abuse and violence in the home. Perry (1993) has described in painful detail how the amygdala and the limbic area of the brain respond when young children frequently observe and experience violence. The neural connections that are wired in when children experience violence result in habitual responses of flight or freeze or fight. Teachers cannot expect that a few weeks of nurturing and reassuring care will change these sadly inappropriate brain connections. Dr. Perry has explained how long and arduous the brain retraining process needs to be. Caregivers faced with young children in care who require the patient rewiring of limbic area circuits in order to promote more positive social and emotional responses deserve special community support and rewards.

The effects of maternal depression on infant cerebral functioning have been clarified by research. About 40% of babies with depressed mothers show reduced brain activity. If the maternal depression can be lifted by 6 months of age, babies will not show cognitive deficits (Shore, 1997). Such findings can be used in training staff to increase caregiver motivation to provide more animated and cheerful engagements with infants.

- Mix and match theoretical curricular models to serve families optimally. The challenge for staff training lies in creative implementation of a judicious *mixture* of theories, including ideas from Piaget, Vygotsky, language and attachment theorists, Eriksonian dialectics, and family systems theory (Honig, 1997b).
- Programs need more emphasis on transitions to elementary school. Children's transitions to elementary school may be very difficult even when Eriksonian principles have been generously used in the preschool environment. FDRP graduates at 6 years of age were immersed in first-grade classrooms that were teacher

dominated with no adult assistants. This elementary school model was not congruent with the responsive model to which the children had been accustomed in the open-education, free-choice, high adult-to-child-ratio classrooms and settings of the FDRP program. Just as positive interactions with teachers and therapists can re-create more favorable outcomes in the ratio of positive to negative poles in Erikson's nuclear conflicts, so too can more frustrating later experiences change the ratio toward more negative outcomes. Within families, Vaughn, Egeland, Sroufe, and Waters (1979) reported an association between stressful events in the second year of life and change to nonoptimal child–mother attachment patterns as measured by Ainsworth's Strange Situation procedure. Life stress and lack of support for positive emotional interactions in learning situations in schools increase children's vulnerability to social and academic difficulties (Honig, 1986b).

- Long-term commitment to high-risk families may be a *necessity*. Stability of positively nurturing environments to ensure the continued positive socioemotional functioning of young children with adult caregivers and teachers requires more of a commitment to families and projects than is currently provided when projects serving vulnerable families are limited to the preschool years. For some children, supportive involvement means keeping children with the same caregiver for the first 3 years of the program. Nurturing at-risk families through the child's *transition to school years* will increase some children's chances for positive outcomes. Elementary schools, too, need to find ways to bolster child autonomy, provide choices, foster industriousness, and continue to ensure that young children trust the goodwill of the teachers who guide their learning careers.

- Finding families for research longitudinal follow-up demands imaginative solutions. For successful longitudinal evaluations, program personnel may well need to devise inexpensive techniques such as frequent phone call follow ups and sending out birthday cards and holiday greetings to family members in order to keep contact over many years. Close relationship with high school personnel are another way to ensure that long-term outcomes will be able to be gathered from early intervention projects (Levenstein, Levenstein, Shiminiski, & Stolzberg, 1998).

✿ CONCLUSION

Follow-up findings for FDRP program youngsters support the significance of emphasizing the fostering of: (1) tender nurturing relationships with very young children in an enrichment program designed also to enhance cognitive functioning, (2) *prosocial* interactions even with very young children in the program (Honig & Wittmer, 1996), and (3) outreach support for parents to sustain and integrate positive socioemotional development that is fostered by program personnel who work directly with the children.

Programs for children at risk will ensure more long-lasting gains if they include among their goals for young children's education the building of: basic trust, a strong sense of self-esteem and creative initiatives, industriousness, judicious balance between striving for autonomy and empathic sensitivity for the needs and rights of others, as well as prosocial skills in relating with adults and peers. Erikson's insistence on the importance of *mutuality* and his clarification of the *dialectic* dance necessary for optimal child rearing provide guiding beacons for future work in optimally rearing and educating young children.

REFERENCES

Ainsworth, M. D. (1982). Early caregiving and later patterns of attachment. In M. H. Klaus & M. O. Robertson (Eds.), *Birth, interaction and attachment* (pp. 35–43). Skilman, NJ: Johnson & Johnson Baby Products.

Bretherton, I., & Waters, E. (Eds.). (1986). Growing points of attachment theory and research. *Monographs of the Society for Research in Child Development, 50* (1–2, Serial No. 209).

Briggs, D. (1975). *Your child's self esteem.* Garden City, NY: Doubleday.

Bromwich, R. (1997). *Working with families and their infants at risk: A perspective after twenty years of experience.* Austin, TX: Pro-Ed.

Brooks-Gunn, J., Han, W., & Waldfogel, J. (2002). Maternal employment and child cognitive outcomes in the first three years of life: The NICHD study of early child care. *Child Development, 73,* 1052–1072.

Brophy, H., & Honig, A. S. (1995). Working with teenage mothers: The prevention pathway. *International Journal of Adolescence and Youth, 5,* 1–20.

Brophy-Herb, H. E., & Honig, A. S. (1999). Reflectivity: Key ingredient in positive adolescent parenting. *The Journal of Primary Prevention, 19* (3), 241–250.

Caldwell, B. M. (1967). What is the optimal learning environment for the child? *American Journal of Orthopsychiatry, 37,* 8–12.

Caldwell, B. M., Richmond, J. B., Honig, A. S., Moldovan, S. E., Mozell, C., & Kawash, M. B. (1968). A day care program for disadvantaged infants and young children—observations after one year. In G. A. Jervis (Ed.), *Expanding concepts in mental retardation* (pp. 103–115). Springfield, IL: Thomas.

Caldwell, B. M., Wright, C., Honig, A. S., & Tannenbaum, J. (1970). Infant day care and attachment. *American Journal of Orthopsychiatry, 40,* 397–412.

Clarke-Stewart, A. (1973). Interactions between mothers and their young children: Characteristics and consequences. *Monographs of the Society for Research in Child Development, 38* (6–71, Serial No. 153).

Consortium for Longitudinal Studies. (1983). *As the twig is bent: Lasting effects of preschool studies.* Hillsdale, NJ: Erlbaum.

David and Lucile Packard Foundation. (1995, Winter). *The future of children.* Long-term outcomes of early childhood programs. *5* (3).

Diamond, A. (2000). Close interrelation of motor development and cognitive development and of the cerebellum and prefrontal cortex. *Child Development, 71* (1), 44–56.

Erikson, E. H. (1950). *Childhood and society.* New York: Norton.

Erikson, E. H. (1980). *Identity and the life cycle.* New York: Norton.

Fonagy, P., Steele, H., & Steele, M. (1991). Maternal representations of attachment during pregnancy predict the organization of infant-mother attachment at one year of age. *Child Development, 62,* 891–905.

Fraiberg, S., Adelson, E., & Shapiro, V. (1987). Ghosts in the nursery: A psychoanalytic approach to the problems of impaired infant-mother relationships. In L. Fraiberg (Ed.), *Selected readings of Selma Fraiberg* (pp. 100–136). Columbus: Ohio State University Press.

Garber, H. L. (1988). *The Milwaukee Project: Preventing mental retardation in children at risk.* Washington, DC: American Association on Mental Retardation.

Gordon, I. J., & Lally, J. R. (1967). *Intellectual stimulation for infants and toddlers.* Gainesville: Institute for Development of Human Resources, University of Florida.

Haskins, R. (1985). Public school aggression among children with varying day care experience. *Child Development, 56,* 689–703.

Heber, R., Garber, H., Harrington, S., Hoffman, C., & Fallender, C. (1972). *Rehabilitation of families at risk for mental retardation: A progress report.* Madison: University of Wisconsin Rehabilitation Research and Training Center in Mental Retardation.

Honig, A. S. (1974a). Curriculum for infants in day care. *Child Welfare, 53* (10), 633–643.

Honig, A. S. (1974b). The developmental needs of infants: How they can be met in a day care setting. *Dimensions, 2* (2), 30–33, 60–61.

Honig, A. S. (1977). The Children's Center and the Family Development Research Program. In B. Caldwell & D. Stedman (Eds.), *Infant education: A guide for helping handicapped children in the first three years* (pp. 81–99). New York: Walker.

Honig, A. S. (1978). Training of infant care providers to provide loving, learning experiences for babies. *Dimensions, 6* (2), 33–43.

Honig, A. S. (1979). *Parent involvement in early childhood education* (2nd ed.). Washington, DC: National Association for the Education of Young Children.

Honig, A. S. (1981). What are the needs of infants? *Young Children, 37* (1), 3–10.

Honig, A. S. (1982a). Intervention strategies to optimize infant development. In E. Aronowitz (Ed.), *Prevention strategies for mental health* (pp. 25–55). New York: Watson.

Honig, A. S. (1982b). Parent involvement in early childhood education. In B. Spodek (Ed.), *Handbook of research in early childhood education* (pp. 426–455). New York: Free Press.

Honig, A. S. (1982c). *Playtime learning games for young children*. Syracuse, NY: Syracuse University Press.

Honig, A. S. (1983a). Evaluation of infant/toddler intervention programs. In B. Spodek (Ed.), *Studies in education evaluation* (Vol. 8, pp. 305–316). London: Pergamon.

Honig, A. S. (1983b). Meeting the needs of infants. *Dimensions, 11* (2), 4–7.

Honig, A. S. (1984). Reflections on infant intervention programs: What have we learned. *Journal of Children in Contemporary Society, 17* (1), 81–92.

Honig, A. S. (1986a). Research in review: Stress and coping in children, Part 1. *Young Children, 41* (4), 50–63.

Honig, A. S. (1986b). Research in review: Stress and coping in children, Part 2. *Young Children, 41* (5), 47–59.

Honig, A. S. (1990). Infant–toddler education: Principles, practices, and promises. In C. Seelfedt (Ed.), *Continuing issues in early childhood education* (pp. 61–105). Columbus, OH: Merrill/Macmillan.

Honig, A. S. (1991). Piagetian and psychometric development of 12-month-old disadvantaged infants in an enrichment program. In A. S.

Honig (Ed.), Varieties of early child care research [Special issue], *Early Child Development and Care, 68*, 71–88.

Honig, A. S. (1992). Infant intervention and enrichment programs. In L. R. Williams & D. Fromberg (Eds.). *Encyclopedia of Early Childhood Education* (pp. 131–132). New York: Garland Press.

Honig, A. S. (1993). Toilet learning. *Day Care and Early Education, 21* (1), 6–9.

Honig, A. S. (1994a). Assessing the preparation of infant/toddler caregivers. In S. Reifel (Ed.), *Advances in Early Education and Day Care, 6* (pp. 107–151). Greenwich, CT: JAI Press.

Honig, A. S. (1994b). Intervention, infant and preschool: Effects on intelligence. In R. Sternberg (Ed.), *Encyclopedia of Intelligence.* Vol. 1 (pp. 599–607). New York: Macmillan.

Honig, A. S. (1995a). Choosing child care for young children. In M. Bornstein (Ed.), *Handbook of Parenting* (Vol. 4, pp. 411–435). Hillsdale, NJ: Erlbaum.

Honig, A. S. (1995b). Singing with infants and toddlers. *Young Children, 50* (5), 72–78.

Honig, A. S. (1996a). *Behavior guidance for infants and toddlers from birth to three years.* Little Rock, AR: Southern Early Childhood Education Association.

Honig, A. S. (1996b). Evaluation of early childhood enrichment programs. *Early Child Development and Care, 120*, 29–37.

Honig, A. S. (1997a). Infant temperament and personality. What do we need to know? *Montessori Life, 9* (3), 18–21.

Honig, A. S. (1997b). Training early childhood educators for the future. *International Journal of Early Childhood Education, 2*, 37–54.

Honig, A. S. (2001, Fall). Language flowering; language empowering: 20 ways parents and teachers can assist young children. *Montessori Life*, 31–35.

Honig, A. S. (2002a). Choosing child care for young children. In M. Bornstein (Ed.), *Handbook of parenting* (2nd ed.), (Vol. 5, pp. 375–405). Mahwah, NJ: Erlbaum.

Honig, A. S. (2002b). *Secure relationships: Nurturing infant/toddler attachment in early care settings.* Washington, DC: National Association for the Education of Young Children.

Honig, A. S. (2003, April/May). Twenty brain-boosting tips for your baby. *Scholastic Parent and Child*.

Honig, A. S., & Brophy, H. E. (1996). *Talking with your baby: Family as the first school*. Syracuse, NY: Syracuse University Press.

Honig, A. S., & Lally, J. R. (1975a). Assessing teacher behaviors with infants in day care. In B. Friedlander, G. Kirk, & G. Sterritt (Eds.), *Infant assessment and intervention* (pp. 528–544). New York: Brunner/Mazel.

Honig, A. S., & Lally, J. R. (1975b). How good is your infant program: Use an observational method to find out. *Child Care Quarterly, 1*, 194–207.

Honig, A. S., & Lally, J. R. (1981). Infant caregiving: A design for training. Syracuse, NY: Syracuse University Press.

Honig, A. S., & Lally, J. R. (1982). The family development research program: Retrospective review. *Early Child Development and Care, 10*, 41–62.

Honig, A. S., & Lally, J. R. (1989). Effects of testing style on language scores of four-year-old, low-income "control" children in an intervention project. *Early Child Development and Care, 41*, 195–211.

Honig, A. S., & Lally, J. R. (1990). Behavior profiles of experienced teachers of infants. In A. S. Honig (Ed.), *Optimizing early child care and education* (pp. 181–199). London: Gordon & Breach.

Honig, A. S., Lally, J. R., & Mathieson, D. H. (1982). Personal and social adjustment of school children after five years in the Family Development Research Program. *Child Care Quarterly, 11* (2), 138–146.

Honig, A. S., & Morin, C. (2001). When should programs for teen parents and babies begin? Longitudinal evaluation of a teen parents and babies program. *Journal of Primary Prevention, 21* (4), 447–454.

Honig, A. S., & Shin, M. (2001). Reading aloud to infants and toddlers in childcare settings: An observational study. *Early Childhood Education Journal, 28* (3), 193–197.

Honig, A. S., & Wittmer, D. S. (1996). Helping children become more prosocial: Part 11. Ideas for classrooms, families, schools, and communities. *Young Children, 51* (2), 61–70.

John Tracy Clinic. (1968). *Getting your baby ready to talk: A home study plan for infant language development*. Los Angeles: Author.

Keister, M. E. (1977). *"The good life" for infants and toddlers: Group care of infants* (2nd ed.). Washington, DC: National Association for the Education of Young Children.

Klebanov, P. K., Brooks-Gunn, J., McCarton, C., & McCormick, M. C. (1998). The contribution of neighborhood and family income to developmental test scores over the first three years of life. *Child Development, 69*, 1420–1436.

Lally, J. R., & Honig, A. S. (1977a). The family development research program: A program for prenatal, infant and early childhood enrichment. In M. C. Day & R. D. Parker (Eds.), *The preschool in action: Exploring early childhood programs* (pp. 149–194). Boston: Allyn & Bacon.

Lally, J. R., & Honig, A. S. (1977b). *Family Development Research Program*. Final Report to the Office of Child Development. Syracuse, NY: Syracuse University.

Lally, J. R., Mangione, P., & Honig, A. S. (1988). The Syracuse University Family Development Research Program: Long-range impact of an early intervention with low income children and their families. In D. Powell (Ed.), *Parent education as early childhood intervention: Emerging directions in theory, research, and practice* (pp. 79–104). Norwood, NJ: Ablex.

Levenstein, P., Levenstein, S., Shiminiski, J.A., & Stolzberg, J. E. (1998). Long-term impact of a verbal interaction program for at-risk toddlers: An exploratory study of high school outcomes in a replication of the Mother-Child Home Program. *Journal of Applied Developmental Psychology, 19* (2), 267–285.

Matas, L., Arend, R. A., & Sroufe, A. L. (1978). Continuity of adaptation in the second year: The relationship between quality of attachment and later competence. *Child Development, 49*, 547–556.

McGovern, M. P. (1998). Early child care and education: Lessons from the French. *Child & Youth Care Forum, 27* (1), 21–37.

Nash, M. (1997, February 3). Fertile minds. *Time*, 48–56.

Park, K., & Honig, A. S. (1991). Infant child care patterns and later teacher ratings of preschool behaviors. *Early Child Development and Care, 68*, 89–96.

Perry, B. D. (1993, Spring). Neurodevelopment and the neurophysiology of trauma. 1. Conceptual considerations for clinical work with maltreated children. *The Advisor, 6* (1), 1–20.

Pretorius, E., Naude, H., & Van Vuuren, C. J. (2002). Can cultural behavior have a negative impact on the development of visual integration pathways? *Early Child Development and Care, 172* (2), 173–181.

Sameroff, A. J., & Emde, R. N. (Eds.). (1990). *Relationship disturbances in early childhood: A developmental approach.* New York: Basic.

Shore, R. (1997). *Rethinking the brain.* New York: Families and Work Institute.

Shure, M. B. (1993). I can problem solve (ICPS): Interpersonal cognitive problem solving for young children. *Early Child Development and Care, 96*, 49–64.

Sroufe, L. A., & Fleeson, D. (1986). Attachment and the construction of relationships. In W. W. Hartup & Z. Rubin (Eds.), *Relationships and development* (pp. 51–71). Hillsdale, NJ: Erlbaum.

Van Den Boom, D. C. (1993). Do first-year intervention effects endure? Follow-up during toddlerhood of a sample of Dutch irritable infants. *Child Development, 66*, 1798–1816.

Vaughn, B. E., Deane, K. E., & Waters, E. (1985). The impact of out-of-home care on child-mother attachment quality: Another look at some enduring questions. In I. Bretherton & E. Waters (Eds.), Growing points of attachment theory and research. *Monographs of the Society for Research in Child Development, 50* (1–2, Serial No. 209).

Vaughn, B., Egeland, B., Sroufe, L. A., & Waters, E. (1979). Individual differences in infant-mother attachment at twelve and eighteen months: Stability and change in families under stress. *Child Development, 50*, 971–975.

Wittmer, D. S., & Honig, A. S. (1987). Do boy toddlers bug teachers more? *Canadian Children, 12* (1), 21–27.

Wittmer, D. S., & Honig, A. S. (1990). Teacher re-creation of negative interactions with toddlers. In A. S. Honig (Ed.), *Optimizing early child care and education* (pp. 77–88). London: Gordon & Breach.

Zigler, E. (1970). The environmental mystique: Training the intellect versus development of the child. *Childhood Education, 46* (8), 402–412.

Zigler, E., & Trickett, P. K. (1978). IQ, social competence, and evaluation of early childhood intervention programs. *American Psychologist, 33*, 789–798.

Chapter 8

Behavior Analysis and Principles in Early Childhood Education

John T. Neisworth ❧ The Pennsylvania State University
Thomas J. Buggey ❧ The University of Memphis

*I*s good teaching an art or a science? We propose that the really effective preschool teacher artfully applies science, so that children benefit from evidenced-based practices in a humanistic program. "Behaviorism versus humanism" is a false distinction. In fact, we contend that the use of behavior principles in a planned program can be the most humanistic way to help children become increasingly competent. We ask the reader to try to study this chapter with an "open mind" (if you will pardon a behaviorist's use of the expression!) and to seriously consider the behavioral approach as a positive and effective way to build competence and self-esteem as a real contribution to humanism.

In this chapter, we (1) summarize the foundations underlying the behavior analytic approach, (2) describe several major principles that help us to explain behavior and deliver educational and therapeutic interventions, and (3) provide illustrations of applications.

❧ FOUNDATIONS OF THE BEHAVIORAL MODEL

Several fundamental assumptions underlie *behaviorism, behavior principles, behavior analysis,* and *behavior modification*. A differentiation among these several terms will set the stage for the subsequent discussion of applications of a behavior analysis approach (cf. Peters, Neisworth, & Yawkey, 1985; Watkins & Durant, 1992; Wolery, Strain, & Bailey, 1992). Within this chapter, we provide brief descriptions of the philosophy underlying the approach.

Behaviorism

Behaviorism is a philosophy, a worldview, and belief system concerning the nature and causes governing behavior and development. It refers to the point of view that human behavior is natural (not supernatural) and that behavior is lawful. Translated to early childhood education, the behaviorist, as natural scientist, believes that child behavior is lawful, that cause–effect (functional) relationships can be discovered and employed to help manage and direct child progress (see Bijou & Baer, 1978). It is an optimistic view that a child's development is shaped by the qualities of that child's experience. Teachers and parents can do much to plan and orchestrate the child's experiences. Studying the behavioral approach offers caregivers knowledge of specific factors that can be arranged to promote the best experiences for the children they serve. Behaviorism is the belief that child behavior and development are subject to scientific analysis and can be improved through environmental engineering.

Behavior Principles

Statements of behavior principles provide explanations of behavior. *Behavior principles* are statements of the fundamental functional relationships among variables (i.e., laws) that govern (and explain) behavior. A major principle, for example, is that behaviors that are successful (i.e., result in some reward or escape from aversive circumstances) become stronger and more reliable. Later, we describe several principles that teachers can use to solve behavior problems and enhance development.

Behavior Analysis

Behavior analysis refers to the identification of the critical circumstances surrounding a behavior, especially what comes before and after a behavior. Such analyses allow us to infer what behavior principles may be operating and to suggest ways to build (develop) or change behavior.

Applied Behavior Analysis (ABA)

Behavior modification is an older term that is roughly synonymous with ABA and refers to methods for building and altering behavior. After we analyze a behavior, we can then use the analysis to select behavior change techniques. Behavior techniques are available to educators and have proven to be powerful ways to build, reduce, and redirect child behavior. Recent publications and videos are available that are extremely helpful in illustrating use of behavior change techniques with young children (e.g., Beck, 1997/ 2004; Rule, Utley, Qian, & Eastmond, 1999; YAI NIPD, 2001).

Operants

Behaviors that operate on the environment and are modified by it are termed *operants* (Skinner, 1938, 1963). An operant is dynamic and interactive. The child is not seen as passive, like a puppet being controlled by the strings of the environment. Both the child and the situation have characteristics, and both are important to the interaction and changed by it.

Accessible Variables versus Explanatory Fictions

Scientific explanations must be based on accessible variables that refer to real (not theoretical) factors that can be accessed in order to make change possible. In the field of biology, little progress was possible when disease was explained by the use of concepts such as sin, the revenge of the Gods, demonic possession, or imbalance of the four humors. These explanations offered no variables that could be accessed, no leverage for intervention; these explanatory fictions (Skinner, 1977) do not offer real factors that can be managed to produce change. When people adopted a natural science model to study disease and disorder, the modern science of biology was born along with modern medical practice: the view that disease is related to the presence of bacteria, viruses, or dysfunctions of bodily organs allows us to study and alter these real circumstances.

Various explanatory fictions are used in child psychology and development such as cognitive structure, schemata, ego, language acquisition device, and drive state, but behavior analysis focuses on detailing the (accessible) variables of which behavior is a result. When explanations are based on real (not theoretical) variables that are reliably related, prediction and manipulation are made feasible.

A major strength, then, of the behavioral approach is its solid foundation of scientific evidence. The pioneering efforts of Pavlov, Watson, Thorndike, and Skinner, as well of current research of behavior analysts, are accumulating to give us an increasingly better explanation of behavior that provides clear methods for improving child education and parenting (Kazdin, 2001). While other theoretical viewpoints have come and gone, behavior analysis continues to build on itself. Behavior principles discovered 50 years ago remain the same today, although applications of principles change with shifting cultural perspectives and practices.

Some early behaviorist preschool programs were characterized by teacher-directed, fast-paced, task-oriented approaches that emphasized drill, repeated trial sessions, and food rewards similar to animal training. Many of these programs were well intentioned and were a reaction to the prevailing approaches of simply hoping that a child might accidentally learn something in a "nursery" custodial program. The point here is that the effective teaching methods and materials developed by behavior analysts can be misused and abused as well as appropriately used. Almost any resource that is truly effective can become a danger simply because it is effective. Electricity, nuclear power, and drugs are obvious examples of resources that can be friend or foe. Within education, the use of television, computers, whole language, ability segregation, standardized achievement testing, direct instruction, inclusion, and other practices can be praised or criticized—depending on how they are used.

Developmentally Appropriate Practice (DAP)

DAP guidelines (Bredekamp & Copple, 1997) developed by the National Association for the Education of Young Children (NAEYC) were initially seen as quite opposed to practices advocated by behaviorists. Indeed, much controversy has been generated by these guidelines. However, DAP guidelines are not etched in granite nor are they the only criteria for quality early childhood programs (Johnson & Johnson, 1992). Today, DAP and behavioral methods should no longer be seen as antagonistic (Sandall, McLean, & Smith, 2000). A number of professionals recognize the value of blending behavioral practices into a program based on developmentally appropriate practices (cf. Davis,

B. F. Skinner was instrumental in introducing operant psychology education pursuits.

Kilgo, & Gamel-McCormick, 1998; Sandall et al., 2000).

The principles, procedures, and materials described in this chapter can, and should, be employed within a program that is neither teacher centered nor child centered, but teacher–child dyad centered. The teacher and child are partners, or dynamic duos, wherein the teacher has the big picture of developmental goals and the skills to guide the way, and the child has the present skills and interests that guide the teacher and drive learning experiences.

As you read this chapter, try to view the methods and materials described as effective tools to be judiciously used. The behaviorally oriented teacher arranges learning environments and events to help children to learn and grow and does not depend on accidental or an unplanned program. The behavior principles and methods summarized in this chapter provide a glimpse of an increasingly effective approach to early childhood education, an approach that celebrates the possibilities for human achievement through a natural science approach to development and learning.

Role of the Body and Behavior

Physical development and behavior have two sources or basic causes: biology and experience. *Nature* and *nurture* are terms that have been used to identify these two sets of determinants. A child's physical characteristics (e.g., eye color, general body type, facial features, skin color) are determined genetically. Early childhood education, of course, has little or no effect on such basic features. Likewise, many basic behaviors are somewhat automatic and come with the child's human heritage. All children (in the absence of genetic or other damage) are born with general behavioral features, just as they are born with general physical features. Just as children are typically born with two arms, legs, eyes, and ears, a digestive tract, and a brain, they also possess general behavioral capabilities such as bending, blinking, reaching, reacting to pain, crying, and making vocal sounds. As children mature, other general behaviors are typically evidenced (e.g., crawling, babbling, and other behaviors that become possible when biological mechanisms are available).

Maturation   Maturation refers to the development and availability of a biological (natural) characteristic. Maturation makes possible certain behaviors. As an illustration, children cannot be expected to chew foods until their teeth have erupted or to walk until their bones are sufficiently hardened, and numerous perceptual-motor activities cannot be manifested until there is maturation of the nervous system (e.g., myelinization of nerves). We see, then, that the child's fundamental physical features and early general behavioral capabilities are biologically driven.

Phylogenetic Behaviors   Phylogenetic behaviors (e.g., blinking, crying, reaching, crawling, walking, babbling) are behaviors common to all members of the species. All children come with a "package" of these general biological and behavioral features. Any approach to early childhood education must recognize the fundamental role of biology in providing the enabling mechanisms for behavioral development. After very early development, however, almost all behavioral development comes under the increasing influence of the environment and is no longer the automatic product of biological maturation. Put simply, most behavior is learned as a result of individual experience.

Ontogenetic Behavior   This behavior refers to the skills acquired by the child through individual experience. Phylogenetic behavior is molded and shaped through experience into complex, ontogenetic (individual) skills. The random general behavior of infants is the raw material for learning through experience. We cannot expect behavioral advancement unless the child interacts with the environment, and the circumstances of the environment are the critical determinants of the child's development and behavior.

Learning   Learning can be defined as relatively permanent changes in behavior as a result of experience. Note that this definition does not rely on explanatory fictions (e.g., changes in cognitive structure, lattices). The definition focuses on measurable behavior changes and accessible environmental variables. Obviously, the experiences encountered by the child can vary greatly. The qualities of environments can have much to do with how well a child will benefit from experience. To provide an extreme illustration, great restrictions on experience (e.g., being kept in a dark attic) can certainly retard and distort development when compared with a more typical or standard environment. Once the critical role of experience is acknowledged, the next questions are: What qualities of the environment are important for development? How can behavioral development be encouraged? The behavioral approach to early childhood education focuses on exactly this issue of environmental circumstances and provides the principles and analyses for describing and changing environmental circumstances for behavioral development. When you adopt a behavioral approach to early childhood education, you recognize the paramount importance of the circumstances for learning, and you employ basic behavior principles to construct favorable environments. The behavioral early childhood educator becomes a kind of engineer who manipulates environmental circumstances to build and elaborate child behavior. Measurement of child progress then permits further environmental adjustments as well as documentation of progress.

✍ TWO FUNDAMENTAL PRINCIPLES OF BEHAVIOR

First, it must be understood that the fundamental principles of behavior are not speculations or hypothetical. The principles of behavior are facts of life; they operate as surely as do the law of gravity or other forces of nature. One's belief in behavior principles—whether they are likeable or not—has nothing to do with their operation. The principles of behavior operate in nature and can be used to explain and direct many aspects of children's development and activities: That is what a behaviorally based preschool is all about.

Principle 1: Behavior Is Controlled by Its Consequences

Learning depends on its outcome. Some things a child does are followed by positive, rewarding events. Whenever a behavior is followed by immediate positive consequences (positive reinforcement), that behavior becomes stronger. On the other hand, if a behavior is followed by no reinforcement (extinction) or aversive events (punishment), that behavior is weakened.

From a behavioral perspective, children come to a situation with a particular repertoire of behaviors. Some behaviors work; they are useful or instrumental to the child. Other behaviors have little or no utility, and some behaviors may result in negative or aversive outcomes. As previously described, the child is viewed as active or, better, interactive. The child interacts with a specific environment with whatever behaviors are available at the time. As the child engages the environment, some behaviors result in rewarding outcomes. Technically speaking, some behaviors are reinforced by their consequences. Behaviors that are reinforced are repeated, receive even more reinforcement, and become established within the child's repertoire; they are successful behaviors, and they survive. Other behaviors, not followed by favorable results, will not become established but will drop out of the child's repertoire. Thus, a weak, fledgling behavior becomes strong and established when it produces favorable (reinforcing) outcomes. As an illustration, if a child discovers a favorite toy hidden under a cloth or in a box, the behaviors of reaching out and uncovering are reinforced. We can say that those behaviors are learned through reinforcement, and those behaviors are more likely to be used in other similar situations and be strengthened and elaborated through further success.

Consider how rapidly a child learns to yammer when such behavior "produces" a cookie! As another illustration, Emma accidentally drops the rattle from the highchair; Mommy picks up the toy and returns it to the little darling, who drops it again—such fun! We can see that Emma is learning about cause—effect and social behavior as well as having fun. This is an example of countless experiences that build a child's control of his/her physical and social worlds. When parents and teachers also unintentionally reward unwanted behaviors, they unwittingly build the very behavior they don't want to encourage. Unfortunately, parents and teachers get trapped into rewarding unwanted child behavior when it produces some immediate relief. When the adult gives the child a cookie for yammering (i.e., contingent on yammering), the yammering will probably be used by the child more often, and, because the cookie stopped the noise (at least temporarily), the adult behavior of providing the cookie will probably be used more often. Thus, we see that a vicious cycle can be generated until the undesirable child behavior reaches intolerable levels that can produce adult frustration, aggravation, and even abusive behavior. Clearly, the child cannot be blamed for learning the aggravating behavior; the behavior was built through misguided reinforcement. Of course, just as unwanted behaviors are accidentally reinforced, desirable developmentally constructive behaviors can be reinforced, and that is the focus of a constructive behavior program.

Although much more could be said about positive reinforcement and punishment, the crucial point here is that the preschool teacher can attempt to provide strengthening or weakening consequences after a given child behavior. When the teacher is systematic about providing consequences, child behaviors can be changed rapidly, and that teacher is acting as an applied behavior analyst.

Teachers probably can name many events that can act as positive reinforcers. Getting a gold star (that may or may not be reinforcing for a given child) is a familiar example of an old-fashioned technique for encouraging behavior. Many other events reinforce children's behavior. Here are some things or events that typically act to strengthen child behavior:

- food or drink
- prizes
- tokens exchangeable for desirable items or events
- praise

- preferred activities
- positive feedback
- task-imbedded reinforcement (e.g., pieces of puzzle fitting together or task completion)

Principle 2: Circumstances That Exist When a Behavior Is Reinforced Become Cues, or Signals, for the Behavior

This principle is known as *stimulus control*. Many everyday behaviors are cued, or set off, by specific stimuli. A good illustration is the signaling of eating by a television set. If one frequently eats while watching television, then television viewing also becomes *discriminative* for eating. People may not be hungry at all, but because eating has been reinforced while watching TV, they will find themselves wanting to eat when the set is on. If this is the case, it can be said that the TV not only is discriminative for viewing but that it also has come to set the occasion, or be discriminative, for snacking.

Of course, there are many appropriate discriminative stimuli for behavior. A green light is discriminative for proceeding; a picture or printed word is discriminative for saying the corresponding word; a teacher's finger against the teacher's lips is a signal for being quiet; a bell is a signal for starting or stopping an activity.

The basic technique for establishing a discriminative stimulus for a behavior is simple: The behavior must be reinforced when the intended stimulus is present and not reinforced when it is absent. Teachers can devise special signals deliberately to occasion specific behaviors. Teachers can increase the chances that children will display an appropriate behavior when a *prompt* is added when the natural stimulus does not yet occasion the wanted behavior. Children can learn to pay attention, begin work, put away their toys, and talk or not talk to one another, when these behaviors come under the control of special prompts, which can then be faded (eliminated gradually) in favor of the natural stimuli. Blinking the room lights can be established as a prompt for being quiet, when the teacher's presence is not discriminative for quieting down.

Teachers may not always want to use the same signal for a behavior. Often, they will want to shift signals or fade them. New stimuli can become signals for specific behaviors when they are paired with one that already is a prompt for a behavior. Gradually, the new stimulus gains prominence and can share or replace the control of the original one. Fading is accomplished by gradually reducing the presence of a prompt. These strategies, discussed in this chapter, are powerful techniques for the modern educator. You can see from this discussion that teachers and parents can have a tremendous impact on children's learning by "engineering" environmental circumstances and events.

✍ SIX IMPORTANT STRATEGIES[1]

Teachers will want to try many strategies for teaching children new skills and for encouraging the growth of present ones.

Strategy 1: Shaping

Educators often are faced with teaching new, difficult behaviors to children. Ms. Shari cannot simply ask 2-year-old Sammi to throw a ball across the room and expect she will then do it. Sammi will at first experience difficulty in aiming the ball in the correct direction and in throwing the ball such a great distance. Nor can the teacher simply wait for Sammi to accomplish such a difficult task, so that a perfect performance can be reinforced. The teacher must use

shaping (i.e., reinforce small approximations toward the terminal performance of the task). Sammi first could be rewarded for simply throwing the ball. After she becomes proficient at the first approximation of the task, reinforcement is withheld until the performance moves a step closer to the desired behavior. Thus, Sammi might be told, "Good, but now throw it to me"; then, only throws that are toward the teacher would be reinforced. The teacher cannot always predetermine the steps in the shaping process but must watch the child closely and reinforce even slight improvements.

Strategy 2: Sequencing (Chaining) Behaviors

Much of what educators wish to teach children involves sequences or chains of behavior, rather than single behaviors. *Chaining* refers to the putting together of behaviors to produce more complex acts. A given sequence of behavior may be built in a forward or backward fashion.

Washing one's hands is, for example, a complex act consisting of several steps. After the steps are identified, the child may be taught the initial step, and subsequent ones may be added until the whole sequence is learned. On the other hand, sometimes it is preferable to teach the final step first, and then to work backward to the initial step (backward chaining).

In backward chaining, the teacher initially does every step of a sequence except the last one and then lets the child perform that final step. Because this last bit of behavior is closest to the end and success, it may be learned most easily. When a child can perform that step well, the teacher does everything but the last step and next to the last step, leaving those for the child to complete. This procedure continues until the child can carry out the whole sequence.

Forward chaining also involves determining the sequence of steps in a task and having the teacher initially do every step except one. However, in forward chaining, the teacher begins by

---

[1]Material for this section is adapted from *Individualized Education for Preschool Exceptional Children* by J. T. Neisworth, S. J. Willoughby-Herb, S. J. Bagnato, C. A. Cartwright, & K. W. Laub, 1982, Germantown, MD: Aspen.

Modelling for others is one way through which children learn.

letting the child complete the first step. The teacher then completes the task. When able to do the first step well, the child is required to do the second step, and so on. Because people do have the ability to use language and remember starting from the beginning (forward chaining), this should be attempted first. If forward chaining seems difficult for the child, then backward chaining is preferred.

Strategy 3: Modeling

"Monkey see, monkey do" is an adage that aptly describes a characteristic of many children. They will often imitate behaviors that they see. *Modeling* refers to presenting an example to be imitiated. Good modeling can become a powerful technique for encouraging the development of a variety of new behaviors with children.

Children do not imitate all models, however. What influences whether a child will imitate a particular person's behavior? First of all, the prestige or importance of the person to the child can be a big influence in the power of the model. If the child looks up to or respects the person, the child will imitate that person's behavior much more readily. Most teachers, then, who are important in the lives of children, will be readily imitated. A second variable of importance is similarity of the model to the child. Children will tend to imitate those persons who are more like themselves. As an example, advertisers use children to demonstrate eating certain cereals ("Mikey likes it!") or playing with certain toys. Children will then copy the behavior of these children.

You can employ the technique of model similarity with your group of children. For example, you can decide to teach an important behavior to a child who seems to be well liked and imitated by the other children. Once the new behavior is acquired, the child will act as a model for the others, and the behavior may spread without any deliberate instruction on your part. Many parents report with amazement how their toddler instantly learned to use the potty after seeing another child do so. (In many cases the problem is not one of capability but motivation provided by peer modeling!) The trick is to decide who will learn the behavior most rapidly, teach them the new behavior, and then let them be the exemplars for others. Finally, a very powerful variable in the effect of a model is whether or not the model receives reinforcement for the behavior. Children who act as models and are rewarded for their behaviors are much more likely to be imitated. Make sure, then, that your "demonstrator children" are seen by other children to receive reinforcement for their model behaviors. The technique of modeling, especially when you attend to the variables mentioned, can really make instruction much more effective and fun in your classroom.

Strategy 4: Prompting

A *prompt* is a signal or cue that the teacher can use to get a specific behavior. Specifically arranged prompts are used to help children do things that they otherwise would not or could not do. However, the eventual goal is for children to do things without the use of contrived prompts.

In most cases, prompts should be faded as the child learns the new behaviors. Because of this, there are two important considerations when using prompts: (1) choose a prompt that can be faded easily, and (2) choose a prompt that helps the child focus on some significant feature of the task. For example, in teaching children to discriminate between circles and triangles, placing colored dots at the apex of a triangle focuses the children's attention on the three points of the triangle; these dots should then be faded, allowing the characteristics of the shapes themselves to be discriminative for correct identification.

There are several ways to fade prompts. The *intensity* of the prompt can be faded. In teaching Peter to recognize his left shoe, the teacher could put a red dot on that shoe and this would be his cue. To fade its intensity, the red dot could be made lighter and lighter over trials until it is pink and then lighter and lighter again

until it finally disappears. To fade *magnitude* of this same prompt, the red dot could be large at first and then made smaller and smaller over trials until it no longer is used. To fade the *frequency* of this cue, the teacher could begin by presenting the task occasionally without the cue. As Peter begins to recognize his left shoe without the cue, that cue should be faded. Typically, it is good practice to begin with the least prompt needed to occasion the correct behavior; fading will then be easier.

Strategy 5: Behavior Rehearsal

The technique of *behavior rehearsal* consists of having children practice a new skill. In teaching children to count to 10, the teacher might assemble many sets of objects to be counted and then have the children count aloud in various voices (roaring like lions, squeaking like mice). At times the technique resembles the good old-fashioned method of "practice makes perfect" and, yes, drill—like it or not—can be extremely effective and even fun!

At other times the teacher is interested not merely in the repeated practice of the skill but in the situations in which the skill is practiced. Children often must be taught skills that are not typically practiced at school, such as taking a bus ride. It is usually not possible to take children on a bus ride daily until they learn to step up, pay the driver, and take a seat. These skills, therefore, are rehearsed in a dramatic play situation until learned. When the children do take a bus ride, they will likely use the behaviors they have rehearsed. Of course, it would be good teaching to take the children out to a real bus stop in the final phase of training.

On other occasions the teacher may want children to rehearse difficult behaviors in comfortable, behavior-conducive settings. In teaching children to play with wooden blocks, the teacher might have the children rehearse block construction during a small-group lesson so that later they will build with them during a free-play period.

Two points must be kept in mind while doing behavioral rehearsal: (1) shape behaviors as the children rehearse, and (2) use task-embedded (built-in) reinforcers liberally so that the repetition of tasks does not become tedious.

Strategy 6: Discrimination Training

In using *discrimination training,* the teacher attempts to establish specific signals for specific behaviors. Sometimes the concern lies in teaching children to discriminate between two or more signals (e.g., to choose the appropriate restroom from the Men and Women door signs). This might be called a double or multiple discrimination problem because the teacher wants the child to behave appropriately in the presence of two or more similar signals: a girl should enter the door marked Girls or Women and look elsewhere when she sees the door marked Boys or Men. Teaching recognition of the right restroom is a good opportunity to use the prompt/fade technique. Easily recognized photos or icons of men and women (the prompts) can be paired with their respective words; these can then be faded until children reliably recognize the appropriate words and don't need to depend on the prompts.

At other times the educator is not concerned directly with teaching children to discriminate between words or objects. In some instances, the teacher wants children to discriminate by choosing appropriate behavior in a certain situation, such as to say "please" at the lunch table, to be quiet in the library, or to sit on chairs during circle time.

✎ THE BEHAVIORAL PRESCHOOL

The main purpose of a behaviorally based preschool is to build the child's constructive repertoire and, thus, to facilitate growth and development in a planned and sequential manner. Preschools and day-care centers that emphasize "freedom" and "open curricula" are often putting the child's development into the hands of chance. Moreover, they may be unknowingly placing some children at risk. While some children's developmental skills will progress in unplanned activities, many children do not benefit from an "ad lib" program. Although learning occurs spontaneously and in ways unintended and unplanned, the behavioral teacher takes time to assess each child's developmental skills, plan activities, and advance these skills through careful engineering of the environment to structure and maximize learning opportunities. This "engineering" of the environment can somewhat guarantee skill development. Other skills will be developed or practiced during unstructured time.

In a behavioral preschool, the teacher plans, and is accountable for, developmental progress of the children. Careful planning allows the teacher to target skills that are just beyond the children's present developmental levels. Rather than waiting for the teachable moment, the behavioral teacher prepares for the reinforceable moment. Following a child's lead is not unheard of; in fact, behavioral teachers use the child's current interests as opportunities to teach. The behavioral preschool is not a setting in which children participate in robotic repetitions of teacher-dictated behaviors. Rather, it is a dynamic, positive place that maximizes children's learning. Recognize the central behavior principle is that people learn and repeat behaviors that are reinforced. In the preschool environment, this translates to exciting, motivating, and fun activities (Figure 8–1).

Preschool Design

Many behavioral techniques have been adopted and used effectively by the advertising industry. Attention-getting and -motivating prompts are used in commercials and store displays to attract attention to products. Although many of the stimuli in modern advertising are unsuitable for use in preschool settings, the principles used have direct

Student _____ Age _____   Date _____

General Education Activities	Opening	Center Time	Circle Time	Music	Art	Lunch	Motor Skills	Closing					Other Activities						Home
Length of Time																			
Adaptations needed																			
Goal Areas																			
Point to body parts	X						X												
Identify shapes			X		X														
"Where is Lane?"	X					X		X											
"How old are you?"						X													
2 step commands		X	X	X		X	X												
Mouse control & "L"																			
Communicate: Potty						X		X											
5 min attending	X		X	X	X		X	X											
Play w/ turn taking		X																	
Follow peers to activity		X	X	X	X	X	X	X											
Respond to "stop"		X		X	X														
Stair walking							X												
Walk backwards							X												
Stand on 1 foot							X												
Jump small object							X												
Throw ball overhead							X												

X = Activities where student objectives will be addressed

FIGURE 8–1   Activity-Based Instruction Matrix—Planning
Source: Bigge, J. (1991). *Teaching individuals with physical and multiple disabilities* (3rd ed., p. 137). Upper Saddle River, NJ: Merrill/Prentice Hall. Copyright 1991 by Merrill/Prentice Hall. Reprinted with permission.

relevance to instruction. A good preschool design will motivate (reinforce) children to pay attention to tasks and materials. Both the overall layout and specific learning materials should serve to engage the child with the learning environment. The design of the preschool classroom (stimulus control) should be considered an instructional tool (form follows function), with all design elements arranged to facilitate learning.

Design for Stimulus Control   An important behavioral principle related to the arrangement of

the environment is stimulus control. As described earlier, the principle of stimulus control refers to the fact that a behavior is more apt to occur in the presence of circumstances that are reliably present when that behavior has been reinforced and not to occur (not reinforced) when the circumstances are absent. Circumstances in the learning environment can become discriminative for behaviors. For example, a study area for a college student should include items that are discriminative for study behavior, such as a computer, desk, and books. Such an area should not contain items such as a bed or pool that are cues for other behaviors antagonistic to studying.

A clear example of confused stimulus control is provided by an anecdotal study of preschoolers playing with smearing and otherwise being messy with their food at the lunch table (Neisworth, 1995). Several strategies were considered: use high-strength, contrived reinforcers for nonmessy behavior—for example, tokens, stickers, high rates of praise; time-out was also considered. In this case, however, it was the stimulus control of the table setting that was the culprit. The same table and chairs were frequently used for finger painting—where smearing and "creative messiness" were encouraged. No wonder the peanut butter and jelly were smeared at lunch time! Technically, the situation was a discrimination problem. The whole problem was dispelled by using a distinctively different table in another part of the room.

A common use of stimulus control in preschools is the use of learning areas to divide the classroom (Bailey & Wolery, 1992; McEvoy, Fox, & Rosenberg, 1991). Examples of these areas might include gross motor, math, science, reading, bathroom, dramatic play, and individual learning stations. The reading area might be decorated with letters, posters of children reading (models), and attractive book covers that serve as reminders for looking at picture books and other reading materials. Stimulus control can be further facilitated by color coding the areas. Brightly colored free-play and gross motor areas can cue the children that louder noise levels are permissible. Softer, pastel hues in the reading and math areas can serve to prompt quiet behavior. To limit distractions and interference, quiet areas should not be in close proximity to noisier areas. As matters of safety and efficiency, learning areas can be partitioned by using shelving or dividers that are approximately 3 feet in height. This will allow the teacher to have a clear field of vision across the preschool classroom, it provides a sense of privacy to the areas, and it creates places for storage of materials

adjacent to the site where they will most likely be used.

Stimulus control is also relevant to generalization or transfer of learned behaviors across settings and individuals. Research since the 1980s has emphasized the need to use naturalistic or milieu teaching strategies (Halle, Alpert, & Anderson, 1984; Warren & Kaiser, 1988). Behaviors taught in isolation (or in settings not reflecting the expected milieu for the behavior) do not automatically transfer to new situations. For example, language behaviors taught in traditional "pull-out" language therapy sessions are often found to be mastered within the clinic, but the same behaviors do not occur outside the therapy setting (Fey, 1986). Research in language intervention (e.g., Hart & Risely, 1980; Warren & Gazdag, 1990; Yoder, Kaiser, & Alpert, 1991) indicates that the transfer of learned language to normal conversational use, such as in lunch and free play, is enhanced by teaching language with children in the milieu where the behaviors will naturally occur. Vocational schools often make good use of stimulus control to prepare their students for the world of work. For example, food preparation courses are taught in situations resembling that expected in the work environment (i.e., a kitchen). A traditional lecture approach probably would not produce graduates who could easily transition to restaurant milieus.

Similarly, stimulus control can be used in preparing children for transition from preschool to kindergarten (Buggey, DeHaas-Warner, & Bagnato, 1991; McEvoy et al., 1991). The preschool environment can be altered to approximate the kindergarten environment as transition time draws near. Social and academic skills acquired in this transition area will tend to generalize more easily to the kindergarten environment. Kitchen areas provide an excellent opportunity for applying stimulus-control techniques. Generalization of learned skills in etiquette, nutrition, and cooking will more likely occur when taught in an environment that includes or resembles the discriminative circumstances present in the other environments in which the behaviors will be expected. A general practice that can be applied across the preschool curriculum is to analyze behavioral objectives in terms of where, when, and with whom the desired skills could or should occur. Instruction can then take place in natural or stimulated environments that approximate these settings.

Design for Reinforcement The preschool environment can also serve as a reinforcer for children's behavior. Learning areas can be manipulated so that children receive immediate feedback and reinforcement. For example, a child working in the math area who has successfully completed a problem may be rewarded with time to work on the class computer (or another reinforcer that has high value to the child). Learning centers can also be arranged so that they permit flexible sequencing of child activities. The Premack principle (Premack, 1959) can be used in scheduling activities so that children move from less desirable activities to more desirable activities. "Premacking" involves sequencing activities so that less probable (desirable) activities are followed by more probable (motivating) activities. College students often apply this principle when they interrupt periods of tedious studying and insert an activity that allows them to relax or unwind. If a child is uninterested in the reading area and highly motivated by the gross motor area, time in the gross motor area can serve as a reinforcement following participation at the reading area. A similar effect can be obtained by using contracting. If Andrea enjoys the dress-up center, she can attend this area contingent on completion of prescribed activities in a less desirable setting (Figure 8–2).

The possibilities for arranging the classroom, learning centers, and schedules to best facilitate child interaction, and thus learning, are virtually endless. Classroom dynamics provide the behavioral preschool teacher with the challenge to create new and exciting environ-

ments for the child. Certain aspects of the preschool environment should become routine to provide the child with a sense of security. Behind the scenes, however, the teacher provides an ever-changing, ever-expanding learning environment.

Design for Accessibility The term *accessibility* is often used in the context of providing equal opportunity for children with disabilities to enter into an environment; however, for educational purposes the term has a broader implication. Accessibility in preschool contexts includes adaptations necessary to ensure successful goal attainment by children with disabilities; this may require changes in the communication methods as well as the physical arrangements. More and more children with disabilities are being included with their age-appropriate peers in regular preschool programs. These children will have educational objectives outlined in Individualized Education Programs (IEPs) or Individualized Family Service Plans (IFSPs), which are required as part of the Individuals with Disabilities Education Act (IDEA). Staff of programs who work with special needs will find it relatively easy to adapt circumstances for children with sensory or physical disabilities. In these programs, modifications to meet the needs of students are part of the presentation of daily activities. Programs that are more free-form, relying on child-directed activities, will need more adaptation to accommodate children with special needs (Buggey, 1999).

As a rule, adaptations to an environment to accommodate a child should be kept to a minimum. Adaptations should be as unobtrusive as possible to minimize pointing out the differences in the child with the disability. The adaptations needed will depend on the type and severity of the disability. Preschoolers with severe physical disabilities may need additional room for maneuvering and may require a range of adaptive equipment to facilitate therapy and to aid in accessing aspects of the preschool

Student _____   Age _____   Date _____

General Education Activities	Opening	Center Time	Circle Time	Music	Art	Lunch	Motor Skills	Closing					Other Activities						Home
Length of Time																			
Adaptations needed																			
Goal Areas																			
Point to body parts	0						0												
Identify shapes			+		+														
"Where is Lane?"	+						+	+											
"How old are you?"							0												
2 step commands		−	0	0		+	0												
Mouse control & "L"																			
Communicate: Potty						−		0											
5 min attending	−		0	+	0		0	0											
Play w/ turn taking		0																	
Follow peers to activity		−	0	0	0	+	+	+											
Respond to "stop"		−	0		0														
Stair walking							0												
Walk backwards							0												
Stand on 1 foot							−												
Jump small object							0												
Throw ball overhead							0												

− = behavior not demonstrated   0 = behavior demonstrated with prompting   + = behavior demonstrated without prompting

FIGURE 8–2 Activity-Based Instruction Matrix—Evaluation
Source: Bigge, J. (1991). Teaching individuals with physical and multiple disabilities (3rd ed., p. 137). Upper Saddle River, NJ: Merrill/Prentice Hall. Copyright 1991 by Merrill/Prentice Hall. Reprinted with permission.

program. Equipment often used in this context includes wedges, wheelchairs, sidelyers, posture chairs, prone standers, and support bars.

Collaboration with physical and occupational therapists and parents will be necessary to ensure that individual needs for successful participation are met. For example, the purpose of a wedge is to give the lower trunk and torso support so that head, arms, and hands are free to manipulate objects. A child using a wedge may freely participate in activities such as block play, art, and role playing with human figures and dolls. Sidelyers and prone standers serve the same purpose for youngsters with a variety of physical disabilities.

Adaptations to the communication environment may require the adoption of augmentative or alternative communication material. This may include methods such as signing, communication boards, flip-picture cards, as well as high-tech devices such as scanning computer keyboards that can be operated with switches adapted for a particular disability. It may be necessary to modify bulletin boards and other classroom materials to accommodate these alternative forms of communication. The use of signs or symbols with the printed word on materials may facilitate learning of these techniques by all class members, thus improving accessibility of children who are nonverbal by providing a universal method of classroom communication. Preschool teachers must develop the skills and knowledge to teach children with diverse cognitive, emotional, and physical abilities for the inclusive preschool.

Some Design Recommendations   Researchers have found five elements of preschool design that are positively related to cognitive growth (Bailey & Wolery, 1992; Buggey, 1999; Wachs, 1979): (1) a physically responsive environment; (2) adequate space/limiting overcrowding; (3) provisions for private, individual areas; (4) predictable scheduling; and (5) opportunities for exploration.

Responsiveness of the environment is a factor that relates consistently to cognitive growth (Wachs, 1979). A setting that provides immediate and consistent reinforcement of behaviors permits children to acquire a sense of power in controlling their environments. This sense of empowerment can be an important motivator for children to encourage them to explore the next nook or cranny within the preschool. Self-correcting materials are good examples of instructional technologies that can provide immediate feedback. Because self-correcting materials can be completed without the teacher, the child can also develop independence skills. Montessori preschools have long used self-correcting materials. Currently, many software programs developed for preschool-age children use a self-correcting format. In some materials, an animated creature appears on the screen and says "good work" or provides a soft form of correction and urges the child to try again.

Providing consistent feedback adds to children's sense of security by allowing them to participate in a predictable environment. The rules applied yesterday will be the same today. Variation of displays and materials within this predictable environment then allows children to extend their exploration from the secure base of operation into the "frontiers" defined by the preschool environment.

The ratio of classroom size (area) and the child population is an important factor in the preschool design. Some time ago, research findings indicated that within given classrooms, aggressive behaviors among children increased as the classroom population increased (Hutt & Viazey, 1966). However, positive social interactions are more likely to occur when learning areas are small and proximity is maximized (Brown, Fox, & Brady, 1987). Although the findings of these two studies may seem contradictory, this may not be the case. Other research has indicated that, as the amount of play material available in a given space is increased, the number of disruptions in the setting decrease (McWilliams, Trivette, & Dunst, 1985). Possibly an optimal space/population ratio for specific classrooms depends on the interactions of many variables including the quality of environmental arrangement, type of activity, and student characteristics.

We must recognize the influence of space and materials on social behavior. We cannot expect children to be happy, sharing, and cooperative in a crowded room with few toys and materials. Such a setting might encourage a "survival of the fittest" set of competitive behaviors.

Research also has shown that prosocial and cooperative behaviors can be promoted through environmental arrangements (Titus, 1975). A seesaw, large toys, and telephones are materials that either require or favor cooperative play. Much can be done in the preschool and community to provide environmental circumstances favorable to prosocial behavior (see Odom & Brown, 1993).

Here are five suggestions for improving the responsiveness of the environment and the attractiveness of materials (Bailey & Wolery, 1992):

- *Provide appealing materials.* Colorful materials are better than drab ones. Three-dimensional objects are more appealing than pictures. Toys that provide immediate feedback (sounds, visual displays, movement) are also motivating.
- *Make participation a privilege rather than a duty.* Have some high-interest activities be a reward for helping or appropriate behaviors.
- *Give children immediate roles in activities.* Children could use puppets, stuffed animals, or their imaginations to take on roles of characters during story time. Each child could have a specific role designed for his or her skill level for an "assembly line" art project.
- *Use instructions to initiate or prompt interactions.* Children who sit idly in an activity may need a model or prompt to begin.
- *Identify children's preference for materials.* The most motivating materials are those the child plays with most, and these materials vary among children. Know who likes what.

Early childhood educators know that children frequently want time and space to be alone. A sense of independence and the need for privacy can be addressed by providing individual cubbies for storage of personal items (much like lockers in high school) and attractive and comfortable areas designed specifically for individual quiet time. Children should view these places as positive areas. Preschools often have time-out areas where children are sent for brief periods of social isolation when they are disruptive. The sites for time-out and personal quiet areas should be clearly delineated so that no aversive qualities are paired with the privacy areas. Picture books, listening materials, and items of personal value should be available in the privacy areas.

An important outcome for any objective being taught to a child is that the acquired behavior generalizes to other situations beyond the environment in which it was taught. Environmental manipulation can be a powerful tool in ensuring that generalization occurs and can cue desired behaviors within areas of the classroom.

The Behavioral Teacher

Besides being the environmental engineer as mentioned in the previous sections, the behavioral teacher takes on other roles: observer, scheduler, instructor, evaluator, behavior model, and parent consultant. Although these numerous roles may seem overwhelming, careful organization of time and environment can make behavioral teaching very manageable. Unlike the traditional teacher model in which the teacher dominates in front of the class and dispenses knowledge, the teacher in the behavioral preschool model stands aside and orchestrates the carefully arranged learning environment. The onus is then on the teacher to be an astute observer of children's behavior (environmental interaction) so that instruction, reinforcement, prompting, and modeling can be applied to maximize effectiveness. Above all else, the behavioral teacher must be organized. A central concept to all organizational skills is task analysis, and this technique can be applied to many aspects of teaching. For example, given a goal of teaching etiquette at lunchtime, the task can be analyzed into its component behaviors: using a spoon, filling glasses from a pitcher, using a napkin, and passing food. Each of these elements can be broken down further into their constituent parts. For example, the use of the napkin involves unfolding, placement, and wiping or dabbing and the use of task analysis with instructional goals aids in determining teaching sequences and in establishing starting points for instruction. Daily activities can also be task analyzed to facilitate instructional planning. Storytelling time can be broken down into the sequence of events that the teacher anticipates taking place during the activity: sitting in the circle, role assignment, silent listening, questioning, and closure.

The teacher also serves as a behavior model for children. The teacher is probably the only adult the child sees in a daily work role. The saying "Do as I say, not as I do" does not work in an educational setting, especially with impressionable preschoolers. An absentminded, disorganized teacher cannot expect children to be any better. Children will know something is wrong or unfair if a teacher with a cluttered desk expects children to be neat and tidy. Children can learn other important behaviors through modeling such as patience, persistence, acceptance of cultural differences, child care, and politeness. Make sure to demonstrate behaviors such as first-aid care, sympathy for others, and the comforting of distraught children within the purview of the children.

The following list summarizes some basic procedures:

- Analyze tasks to make them simpler to learn.
- Reward constructive behavior; ignore behavior that is undesirable.
- Teach skills in simulated approximations or in the actual circumstances where the skills are expected.
- Practice what you teach; teacher behavior will be imitated by children.
- Behavioral teaching is by definition individualized.
- Plan developmentally appropriate sequences for each child.
- Choose rewards that are appropriate and motivating to the child.
- Learning occurs when the child is interacting with the environment; maximize interaction.
- Plan for generalization; use shaping and/or stimulus control; evaluate acquired skills across settings, time, and persons.

- Periodically reinforce and evaluate previously acquired behaviors; do not permit learned behaviors to become extinct.

Two Program Models

Teaching technologies derived from behavioral principles have proven to be powerful and effective methods of facilitating learning. In the past 25 years, behaviorally based methods such as Milieu or Incidental Teaching (Hart & Risley, 1980; Warren & Kaiser, 1988), Activity-Based Instruction (Bricker & Cripe, 1992), Nurturant-Naturalistic Intervention (Duchan & Weitzner-Lin, 1987), and Teacher-Mediated Facilitation (Malmskog & McDonnell, 1999) have been developed that are powerful new tools for teachers. Many of the newer approaches are developmentally appropriate and address group instruction that facilitate inclusion of children with a wide range of abilities. Furthermore, because these methods are practiced in natural environments, the likelihood of "generalization" increases (i.e., the skills will be evidenced in the child's real circumstances—not just in the preschool). We now briefly discuss two models that blend behavior principles and developmentally appropriate practice.

Milieu Teaching   One of the most common differences cited as separating behaviorist and constructivist preschools is that the behaviorist preschool is teacher directed and the constructivist preschool is child directed. Following the child's lead and careful arrangement of the environment are two of the major components of Milieu Teaching, a teaching model based on behavior principles. This approach is typically used in language instruction and has evolved over the years, beginning with the Incidental Teaching work of Hart and Risley (1968, 1980).

Activity-Based Instruction   Activity-based intervention (ABI) grew from the need to merge developmentally appropriate practice and best practices in early childhood special education (Bricker, 2001; Bricker & Cripe, 1992; Garrett, 1997). The primary feature of ABI is that teachers plan how to accomplish individual goals by embedding them into daily routines. For example, lunch time provides opportunities for working on eating (self-help and fine motor goals), requesting food items (socialization and communication goals), and sharing (socialization goal). Teachers can weave instructional objectives into the routines of the program (e.g., snack time, circle time, playground time).

Activity-based instruction requires careful planning and environmental manipulations. When designing a daily ABI plan, teachers should carry out the following steps:

- describe child by age and abilities (both strengths and weaknesses)
- identify and prioritize goals
- describe the setting, including adaptations that may be needed for individuals
- develop an antecedent/behavior consequence (ABC) schedule (identify antecedents, consequences, and reinforcers associated with the target goal) (Bricker, 2001)
- establish a systematic monitoring system with the matrix as part of the record

Activity-based intervention has several inherent positive features. By providing instruction within ongoing natural routines, generalization is facilitated. Additionally, ABI provides a format for addressing individual goals within a group teaching situation, especially important for planning inclusionary programs. Finally, activity-based instruction goes beyond milieu methods by addressing the needs of the child across the curriculum rather than just focusing on language. Once again, the concept of the teacher as environmental engineer comes into play, as the teacher is responsible for orchestrating environmental events, antecedents, and consequences to promote development. Excellent inservice materials (printed and video) are available to help teachers learn how to use effective behavior principles and activity-based methods in developmentally appropriate ways (Rule et al., 1999).

The Preschool Curriculum

Although behavioral technologies provide a sound basis of "how to teach," they are not designed to prescribe "what to teach"; this role falls to the preschool curriculum. Several excellent new curriculum systems are now available that are consistent with behavior principles. These curricula have three major features: (1) authentic content, (2) a system for planning and evaluating child progress in the program, and (3) teaching strategies that are behaviorally based and done *in context* (Neisworth & Bagnato, in press).

Authentic content means that the curricular objectives are skills that are useful to the child in typical circumstances. For example, children are not taught how to stack blocks, string beads, stand on one foot. Rather, children learn useful skills (e.g., to dress themselves, tie their own shoes—not model shoes—share toys, walk up steps). Systems for evaluating progress are based on objective observation checklists to track child mastery to set criteria. Often, progress evaluation is possible on a daily basis and can be shared with parents. The suggested teaching activities emphasize structured procedures such as those described in this chapter (reinforcement, modeling). Finally, teaching is not decontextualized, but, as much as possible, is done in the actual circumstances where the child will need the skill. Examples of curricula that are exemplars for the effective preschool are AEPS: Assessment, Evaluation, and Programming System (Bricker, Cripe, & Slentz, 2003) and HELP: Hawaii Early Learning Program (1995). (See Wolery, 2000, for recommended practices in delivering child programs.)

Several factors should be considered when choosing a curriculum to meet the needs of your situation. A curriculum should be age appropriate. Some curricula are designed for specific age groups such as newborns, infants, toddlers, or preschoolers, while others cover a broad developmental span. The chosen curriculum provides accommodations for developmental variations. Providing for the needs of children with physical problems or who have delayed or advanced development is becoming increasingly important with the national trend toward inclusive preschool programs. Therefore, a curriculum with a broad developmental span or adaptations to a narrower range curriculum may be required to meet the instructional needs of all children. A good curriculum can form the nucleus of the preschool program, and many excellent preschool curricula are available (see Bagnato, Neisworth, & Munson, 1997, for a description and discussion of numerous high-quality curricula).

A good curriculum includes objectives that address maintenance and generalization. The purpose of maintenance objectives is to facilitate the development of behavior that is reliable over time. High school students who learn a foreign language in class often lose their language skills because they do not have an opportunity to practice the language in daily life. Skills taught in preschool can be developed and practiced beyond preschool. To accommodate this need, many curricula use a spiral design that repeats objectives with increasing complexity over time. Likewise, the curriculum should address the need to generalize learned skills to other situations. A child may be able to use the potty with a verbal prompt by the teacher, but if the child cannot perform the behavior in different situations and without the verbal prompt, things may become messy.

The curriculum should be well-balanced across developmental domains. As stated previously, most curricula present objectives in the domains of communication, self-help, motor, cognitive, and social skills. The curriculum should also present the objectives in a sequential, developmental format. The behavioral approach to education offers some suggestions for ways to sequence objectives:

- *Teach prerequisite skills first.* A behavioral view suggests that complex behaviors can be arranged and taught according to a hierarchy of difficulty. Rather than waiting for a child to reach a developmental stage, the teacher can proceed directly through this hierarchy.
- *Maximize chances for success.* Each new learning experience should lead to positive results. Curricula should be developed so that units begin with review and that tasks proceed from concrete to abstract experiences, from simple to complex learning, from rote to problem-solving techniques, and from the familiar to the unfamiliar. Within these hierarchies, children should begin instruction at a level that ensures success and gradually move toward the more complex.
- *Incorporate intermittent reviews.* Reinforcement of previously learned skills is essential. Behaviors that are not being reinforced may well be forgotten. Spiral curricula that periodically reinforce and expand on previously learned skills are helpful and provide a format for continuous evaluation. A good curriculum can form the nucleus of the preschool program, but this must be coupled with innovative and flexible teaching practices and will be greatly enhanced by the use of behavioral technologies.

ILLUSTRATIONS OF BEHAVIORAL PROCEDURES IN EARLY CHILDHOOD EDUCATION

To demonstrate the use of behavioral strategies in the preschool classroom, we illustrate some applications of these techniques to common behavior management and instructional problems. We begin with one small but common childcare/preschool problem. Next, because most preschool curricula cover the domains of language, self-help, cognitive, and social skills, we provide one example from each of these domains.

A Minor Behavior Problem

It's nap time at the Happy Valley Daycare Center. The fifteen 3- to 4-year-old cherubs lie on their nap mats on the floor, the lights are dimmed, and quiet music is played. The staff, too, deserve a break and find relief in this quiet time. A few children, however, squirm and yammer instead of napping quietly. Clara, a day-care aide, sees Rachel fussing and goes to quiet her. Clara can quickly get Rachel to stop squirming and yammering by rubbing her back as she explains why it's important for her to be quiet and to cooperate. This works for that nap time—but the staff has noted that Rachel persists at her fussing at the next nap time. In fact, it seems that she is now doing it even more at every nap time. Why would Rachel not cooperate, even though Clara has repeatedly explained why she should be quiet?

The teacher, Ms. Shari, has just returned from a professional development course in applied behavior analysis. Here is what Ms. Shari did to solve the problem of Rachel's continued fussing at nap time.

- First, Ms. Shari asked Clara (the aide) to keep a record of the times Rachel yammered and did not nap.
- Second, she saw that children who did cooperate and nap quietly were ignored—but Rachel (and a few other children) got attention, back rubs, and "counseling" when they did NOT cooperate.
- Third, Ms. Shari met with the aides and asked them to (1) ignore the children who fuss and yammer, and (2) visit with the children who are lying quietly on their mats.

We can see that the wrong behaviors were inadvertently being reinforced, while desired behavior was taken for granted. The simple redirection of attention was enough to remedy the nap-time problem.

Self-Help

A preschool teacher, Ms. Young, notices that Jennifer, a 4-year-old, has difficulty buttoning her sweaters and jackets. Ms. Young decides, along with the parents, that buttoning would be a worthwhile instructional objective. Jennifer has demonstrated no difficulty in unbuttoning or in putting on her sweaters and jackets and has normally developed fine motor skills; her prerequisite skills seem appropriate for the task. Ms. Young analyzes and records the steps necessary for Jennifer to button her clothing (task analysis):

- locate and grasp top button with left hand (if button is on left side)
- locate and insert right index fingertip through top button hole
- move button so that the edge touches right index finger
- push the button through hole using the right index finger as a guide
- use pincer grasp with right hand to pull button through hole
- locate and grasp button next to top

Each of these steps can be further broken down into smaller elements if the teacher finds that Jennifer has difficulty comprehending directions or carrying out the task. Children often need to have a task broken down into simple steps, just the way adults might for complex tasks. It is helpful, for example, when specific printed instructions are provided for assembling kits that might otherwise be perplexing.

Ms. Young also decides to teach the skill to Jennifer near the coatroom so that Jennifer will get to practice the skill in an area that will eventually be the circumstance for the desired behavior (stimulus control). The teacher or a paraprofessional and Jennifer begin to work at a table near the coatroom, and the teacher explains the purpose of the activity. Because Ms. Young is the consummate planner, she had previously contacted Jennifer's parents and had them send in their daughter's sweater with the largest buttons to minimize fine motor coordination problems. The teacher has also predetermined that with every button successfully buttoned, Jennifer will receive a reward specifically designed to have high motivation value for her, a hug and a comment on "what a big girl she is" (positive reinforcement, contingent on skill improvement).

Ms. Young has Jennifer put on her sweater, then buttons all the buttons for her, except the one closest to the neck. Of course, the always-prepared Ms. Young is also wearing a sweater, prebuttoned to the same location. She now demonstrates the successive steps to Jennifer by buttoning the last button of her own sweater (modeling). Now it is Jennifer's turn, and Ms. Young takes both of Jennifer's hands and guides her through the steps (physical prompts). When completed, Jennifer gets her warm, fuzzy reward and wants to try again. As the instruction proceeds, the physical prompts are gradually withdrawn (fading), and the positive reinforcement is reduced. Because Ms. Young began instruction with the last step of the buttoning task, she now proceeds to have Jennifer work on the last two buttons, then the last three, until Jennifer has mastered the entire row of buttons (backward chaining). Voila! Jennifer is a happy buttoner, having experienced success and feeling a little bit more grown-up. However, questions remain unanswered about Jennifer's proficiency with the task: (1) Will she be able to successfully complete the task with buttons of different sizes and shapes, and (2) will she be able to produce the behavior in different settings, such as her home?

Realizing the importance of Jennifer being able to transfer what she has learned to other settings and material (generalization), Ms. Young has made arrangements to address these issues in the instruction. Once Jennifer has acquired the skill in the first setting, instruction will proceed across different forms of outerwear, and across different times and settings. Because blouse buttoning may be inappropriate in the preschool setting, Ms. Young made arrangements with Jennifer's parents to continue instruction at home using the same procedures implemented in the classroom.

Social

Andrea is a 4-year-old student in Mr. Mike's Head Start class who has difficulty in sharing toys with the other children. Mr. Mike has talked to Andrea's mother, and they both concluded that this was a behavior that deserved attention. Mr. Mike has a system in place in the classroom where positive behaviors (e.g., completing tasks, following rules, showing consideration) are rewarded with play money, which, in turn, can be turned in at the end of the day for stickers or free-play passes (token economy). Mr. Mike takes Andrea aside one day and proceeds to make a deal with her. He explains to Andrea that for every time she offers a toy that she is playing with to another child, she will receive a play dollar (contracting). It is made clear to Andrea that she must be playing with a toy before she shares it, otherwise she may begin distributing all the toys in the classroom to all the children, all of the time. The teacher asks his assistant to observe Andrea's behavior during free play and lunch to ensure that she catches any demonstration of the contracted behavior and so that she can immediately deliver positive reinforcement. This contrived reward system seemed reasonable because Andrea apparently got more pleasure out of hoarding toys than sharing them. Once Andrea reached a certain level of sharing, Mr. Mike began reducing the token reinforcement. Again, the teacher must look to the child for clues about how rapidly the tokens can be withdrawn. Mr. Mike was pleased to see that the children who benefited from Andrea's sharing reacted positively to her; their social reinforcement of Andrea's sharing easily replaced the tokens. At that point, Andrea's sharing was influenced by the natural social consequences that should operate—mutual give and take, share and share alike.

Cognitive

Mr. Manhart is initiating a lesson to a group of 3-year-old students concerning the concept of "one more." He demonstrates the concept to the children by acting out the instructions for a follow-the-leader game (modeling): "I clap my hands one time." "I clap my hands one more time." Mr. Manhart proceeds to give other examples using motor movements, and then begins the game with the children. He is careful to monitor the responses of students, noting those who quickly master the game and those who need assistance. A student who is exhibiting mastery of the game is selected to be the new game leader (peer modeling) so that the teacher is free to help others. Mr. Manhart stays in close proximity to those having difficulty and intervenes as unobtrusively as possible by using modeling and physical manipulation (modeling and partial physical prompts used in a system of least prompts). Positive verbal reinforcement is used contingent on skill improvement; thus, Mr. Manhart must be aware of each child's baseline performance in order to apply an individualized set of criteria for reinforcement.

Following the game, the children and Mr. Manhart move to a table with a supply of raisins. He again demonstrates the desired behavior by eating one raisin and then eating one more. He then instructs students to do the same behavior only after being told to do so (verbal prompts). The children are eager to eat the raisins (task-imbedded reinforcer). This second activity in the lesson serves to reinforce the concept of "one more" (overlearning) and provides a different scenario for practicing the skill (generalization across settings and objects).

Language

Jonathan has just turned 5 years old and still has not mastered the use of "I" in the subject position. He consistently substitutes the pronoun me for I in his normal conversation. Mrs. Rogers, the speech pathologist, Ms. Burns, the preschool teacher, and Jonathan's parents meet to discuss the problem and to discuss an intervention program. It is decided that Mrs. Rogers will provide direct instruction within the preschool setting and that instruction will be supplemented at home, by the parents, and in school, by Ms. Burns. Mrs. Rogers arranges her schedule so that instruction will take place in the free-play area of the classroom when it is not being used; this is the circumstance that is or should be discriminative for Jonathan to use normal conversation (stimulus control). The therapy consisted of modeling the correct behavior and evoking imitation using verbal and visual cues. Mrs. Rogers reinforced correct responses with verbal praise. Ms. Burns's role in the intervention plan was to catch Jonathan when he used me or I in the subject position during the daily activities of the classroom. If he used me, Ms. Burns asked Jonathan to repeat the utterance after she provided the correct model (corrective feedback). If Ms. Burns caught Jonathan using I correctly, she verbally praised him by using phrases that had implications of how mature his language sounded. Ms. Burns also paired Jonathan in activities with children who had mastered the target behavior (peer modeling). At home, Jonathan's parents were to watch for correct occurrences of I in the subject position and to reward the behavior (generalization across settings). Ms. Burns and Mrs. Rogers kept careful records of Jonathan's progress. Once he reached a pre-established criterion of performance (in this case, 80% correct usage), Ms. Burns began to reduce the reinforcement, and Mrs. Rogers began to fade her instruction on I and me and moved on to another language objective. Attention was given to ensuring that the desired behavior was maintained and applied in different settings. Within 3 weeks, Jonathan had discontinued his incorrect pronoun use and was successfully using his new language behavior in all settings.

✍ CONCLUSION

The behavioral approach to education has been practiced since the early 1940s and has continued to be a mainstay in language therapy, preschool education, special education, and regular education. A new generation of teachers and therapists are studying behavioral principles and procedures and becoming Certified Behavior Analysts (see www.bacb.com). The field of education has seen its share of fads. New-wave ideas have come and gone within the last 50 years, but the solid documentation for the effectiveness of a behavioral approach allows it to stand apart from fads in education. The early childhood educator who employs a behavioral approach in developmentally appropriate ways can be a model for effective, efficient, humanistic instruction.

REFERENCES

Bagnato, S. J., Neisworth, J. T., & Munson, S. M. (1997). *LINKing assessment and early intervention: An authentic curriculum-based approach.* Baltimore: Paul Brookes.

Bailey, D. B., & Wolery, M. (1992). *Teaching infants and preschoolers with disabilities* (2nd ed.). Upper Saddle River, NJ: Merrill/Prentice Hall.

Beck, R. (1997/2004). Project RIDE. Longmont, CO: Sopris West.

Bijou, S. W., & Baer, D. M. (1978). *Behavior analysis of child development.* Upper Saddle River, NJ: Prentice Hall.

Bredekamp, S., & Copple, C. (Eds.). (1997). *Developmentally appropriate practice in early childhood programs* (Rev. ed.). Washington, DC: National Association for the Education of Young Children.

Bricker, D. (2001). The natural environment: A useful construct? *Infants and Young Children, 13* (4), 21–31.

Bricker, D., & Cripe, J. (1992). *An activity-based approach to early intervention.* Baltimore: Paul Brookes.

Bricker, D., Cripe, J., & Slentz, K. (2003). *Assessment, evaluation, and programming systems.* Baltimore: Paul Brookes.

Brown, W. H., Fox, J. J., & Brady, M. P. (1987). The effects of spatial density on the socially directed behavior of three- and four-year-old children during free play: An investigation of a setting factor. *Education and Treatment of Children, 10,* 247–258.

Buggey, T. (1999). Designing learning environments for young children with special needs. In R. M. Gargiulo & J. L. Kilgo (Eds.), *Young children with special needs: An introduction to early childhood special education* (pp. 209–238). Albany, NY: Delmar.

Buggey, T., DeHaas-Warner, S., & Bagnato, S. (1991). Can professionals forecast and plan for kindergarten success? In S. Bagnato & J. Neisworth (Eds.), *Assessment for early intervention: Best practices for professionals* (pp. 142–163). New York: Guilford.

Davis, M. D., Kilgo, J. L., & Gamel-McCormick, M. (1998). *Young children with special needs.* Needham Heights, MA: Allyn & Bacon.

Duchan, J., & Weitzner-Lin, B. (1987). Nurturant-naturalistic intervention for language-impaired children. *ASHA, 29,* 45–49.

Fey, M. E. (1986). *Language interventions with young children.* Boston: College-Hill Press.

Garrett, J. (1997). Activity-based intervention: A strategy for supporting inclusive practices. *Focus on Early Childhood, 9* (3), 1–3.

Great Falls Public Schools. (1997). *Project RIDE: Responding to individual differences in education (program manual).* Longmont, CO: Sopris West.

Halle, J. W., Alpert, C. L., & Anderson, S. R. (1984). Natural environment language assessment and intervention with severely impaired preschoolers. *Topics in Early Childhood Special Education, 4* (2), 36–56.

Hart, B. M., & Risley, T. R. (1968). Establishing the use of descriptive adjectives in the spontaneous speech of disadvantaged children. *Journal of Applied Behavior Analysis, 1,* 109–120.

Hart, B., & Risely, T. R. (1980). In vivo language intervention: Unanticipated general effects. *Journal of Applied Behavior Analysis, 13,* 407–432.

HELP: Hawaii Early Learning Program. (1995). Palo Alto, CA: Vort Corp.

Hutt, C., & Viazey, M. J. (1966). Differential effects of group density on social behavior. *Nature, 209,* 1371–1372.

Johnson, J., & Johnson, K. (1992). Clarifying the developmental perspective in response to Carta, Schwartz, Atwater, and McConnell. *Topics in Early Childhood Special Education, 12* (4), 439–457.

Kazdin, A. E. (2001). *Behavior modification in applied settings.* Belmont, CA: Wadsworth.

Malmskog, S., & McDonnell, A. P. (1999). Teacher-mediated facilitation of engagement by children with developmental delays in inclusive preschools. *Topics in Early Childhood Special Education, 19,* 203–216.

McEvoy, M. A., Fox, J. J., & Rosenberg, M. S. (1991). Organizing preschool environments: Suggestions for enhancing the development/learning of preschool children with handicaps. *Topics in Early Childhood Special Education, 11,* 18–28.

McWilliams, R. A., Trivette, C. M., & Dunst, S. J. (1985). Behavior engagement as a measure of the efficacy of early intervention. *Analysis and Intervention in Developmental Disabilities, 5,* 59–71.

Neisworth, J. T. (1995). *Mixed stimulus control at the preschool lunchtable.* Unpublished manuscript. The Pennsylvania State University, University Park.

Neisworth, J. T., & Bagnato, S. J. (in press). The mis-measure of young children. *Infants & Young Children.*

Neisworth, J. T., Willoughby-Herg, S. J., Bagnato, S. J., Cartwright, C. A., & Laub, K. W. (1982). *Individualized education for preschool exceptional children.* Germantown, MD: Aspen.

Odom, S. L., & Brown, W. H. (1993). Social interaction skills interventions for young children with disabilities in integrated settings. In C. Peck, S. Odom, & D. Bricker (Eds.), *Integrating young children with disabilities into community programs* (pp. 39–64). Baltimore: Paul Brookes.

Peters, D. L., Neisworth, J. T., & Yawkey, T. D. (1985). *Early childhood education: From theory to practice* (pp. 83–214). Monterey, CA: Brooks/Cole.

Premack, D. (1959). Toward empirical behavior laws: I. Positive reinforcement. *Psychological Review, 66,* 219–233.

Rule, S., Utley, G., Qian, A., & Eastmond, N. (1999). *Strategies for preschool intervention in everyday settings (SPIES) video series.* Logan: Utah State University.

Sandall, S., McLean, M., & Smith, B. (2000). *DEC recommended practices in early intervention/ early childhood special education: Birth to age 5.* Longmont, CO: Sopris West.

Skinner, B. F. (1938). *The behavior of organisms: An experimental analysis.* New York: Appleton-Century-Crofts.

Skinner, B. F. (1963). Operant behavior. *American Psychologist, 18,* 503–515.

Skinner, B. F. (1977). Why I am not a cognitive psychologist. *Behaviorism, 5,* 1–10.

Titus, R. M. (1975). Environmental behavior modification: Responses of "isolate" preschool children to a cooperation–contingent treatment environment and associated changes in free play behavior. Ann Arbor, MI. *Dissertation Abstracts.* Publication No. AAT7617234.

Wachs, T. (1979). Proximal experience and early cognitive-intellectual development: The physical environment. *Merrill Palmer Quarterly, 25,* 3–41.

Warren, S. F., & Gazdag, G. (1990). Facilitating early language development with milieu intervention procedures. *Journal of Early Intervention, 14,* 62–86.

Warren, S. F., & Kaiser, A. P. (1988). Research in early language intervention. In S. L. Odom & M. B. Karnes (Eds.), *Early intervention for infants and children with handicaps: An empirical base* (pp. 89–108). Baltimore: Paul Brookes.

Watkins, K. P., & Durant, L. (1992). *Complete early childhood behavior management guide.* West Nyack, NY: Center for Applied Research in Education.

Wolery, M. (2000). Recommended practices in child focused interventions. In S. Sandall, M. McClean, & B. Smith (Eds.), *DEC recommended practices in early intervention/early childhood special education* (pp. 29–38). Longmont, CO: Sopris West.

Wolery, M., Strain, P., & Bailey, D. (1992). Reaching potential of children with special needs. In S. Bredekamp & T. Rosegrant (Eds.), *Reaching potentials: Appropriate curriculum and assessment for young children* (Vol. 1, pp. 92–111). Washington, DC: National Association for the Education of Young Children.

YAI/National Institute for People with Disabilities Network (NIPD). (2001). *Everything you need to know about behavior modification* (manual and video). Brooklyn, NY: Author.

Yoder, P., Kaiser, A., & Alpert, C. (1991). An exploratory study of the interaction between language teaching methods and child characteristics. *Journal of Speech and Hearing Research, 34,* 155–167.

Chapter 9

Mixed-Age Educational Programs for Young Children

Jaipaul L. Roopnarine, Aysegul Metindogan, and Hyun Jung Yang ❦ Syracuse University

Within the United States, interest in mixed-age classrooms, variously termed *ungraded, multiage, multigrade, combination classes, open education,* and *multilevel,* has waxed and waned throughout the twentieth century. After a steady decline into the 1950s and a limited resurgence of interest in the 1960s, it was not until the last 2 decades of the twentieth century that systematic implementation of mixed-age classrooms garnered greater attention again (see Kannapel, Aagaard, Coe, & Reeves, 2000; Kentucky Education Association & Appalachia Educational Laboratory, 1991; McIntyre & Kyle, 1997). Noting the educational benefits of mixed-age groupings, some states (e.g., Florida, Kentucky, Louisiana, and Mississippi) have called for the implementation of mixed-age primary programs (in Kentucky, K–3) (Mason & Stimson, 1996), and they are not uncommon in elementary schools in other states (e.g., Wisconsin). At the same time, a sizable number of day-care and preschool programs provide care and intellectual and social experiences for typically developing infants, toddlers, and preschoolers in mixed-age groups (Katz, 1995, 1998; Pratt, 1999; Whaley & Kantor, 1992; Winsler et al., 2002). The merits of mixed-age groupings have also caught the attention of those providing inclusive educational training for children with disabilities (see Darwish, 2000; McWilliam & Bailey, 1995; Roberts, Burchinal, & Bailey, 1994).

Undoubtedly, the increased attention to classroom age-group composition in the United States is a result of a sizable body of work that has examined the potential benefits and drawbacks of educating grade school (see Burns & Mason, 2002; Caverly, Lemerise, & Harper, 2002; Hoffman, 2002; Kelly-Vance, Caster, & Ruane, 2000; Mason & Burns, 1996; Lloyd, 1999; Veenman, 1995, 1996) and preschool-aged children in mixed-age classrooms (see Derscheid, 1997; Winsler et al., 2002); the need to provide culturally and developmentally appropriate instruction and experiences for young children (Bredekamp & Copple, 1997; Roopnarine & Metindogan, in press; Roopnarine, Bynoe, & Singh, in press); and a strong educational reform movement that focuses on flexibility in the curriculum and school day (Cesarone, 1995; Fu et al., 1999), teacher training and empowerment, cost–benefit of extra-year programs to students and educational institutions (Nason, 1991; Shaeffer & Hook, 1993; Tanner & Decotis, 1995), a greater emphasis on emergent literacy and peer collaboration (Christie & Stone, 1999), and technological skills (Espinosa & Chen, 2001). Relatedly, some have questioned the wisdom of a mass educational system that emphasizes traditional modes of intelligence testing, tracking, and ability grouping (see Feldman, 1994, 1998; Gardner, 1987; Katz, Evangelou, & Hartman, 1990).

As we will see, mixed-age groupings appear ideal for providing a curriculum that is not rigid and has few age-graded expectations (Katz et al., 1990; Whaley & Kantor, 1992). Mixed-age milieus provide children with opportunities to develop leadership skills and to display nurturance, and they are rich contexts for the development of prosocial behaviors in general. They allow for uneven development in diverse ethnic and cultural groups—a goal that is espoused by the National Association for the Education of Young Children (see Bredekamp & Copple, 1997) and may be an appropriate alternative for "gifted" children (Lloyd, 1999). The cognitive conflicts that the mixed-age classroom may engender, because of differences in developmental levels, allow children to operate within wider cognitive domains (see Katz et al., 1990).

This chapter explores the benefits and drawbacks of mixed-age classrooms, their implementation in the United States, and issues pertaining to teacher training and educational practice. Although we focus on younger children, an attempt is made to include some of the curricular issues and findings that pertain to grade-school children as well.

✒ CONCEPTUAL FRAMEWORK

Children's everyday environments are characterized by mixed-age social milieus: In their neighborhoods, children often play with peers who are at least a year younger or older than themselves (see Barker & Wright, 1955; Ellis, Rogoff, & Cromer, 1981), and mixed-age play participation is present in school playgrounds (Boulton, 1992). Observations in older civilizations such as the! Kung San of the Kalahari Desert suggest that mixed-age play groups are quite prevalent. These multiage groups consist of siblings and cousins who range from infants to adolescents (Konner, 1975). Postindustrialized societies may have evolved from mixed-age social milieus, with same-age grouping in formal settings a more recent phenomenon,

possibly a product of mass education and industrialization (see Eisenstadt, 1956).

With the renewed interest in mixed-age classrooms, educators and policy makers are taking a closer look at the adaptive benefits of mixed-age arrangements for children's social and intellectual growth. Taken as a whole, the research findings and meta-analyses on mixed-age classrooms are confusing (see Anderson & Pavan, 1993; Matthews, Monsaas, & Penick, 1997; Slavin, 1987; Veenman, 1995). The data on mixed-age groupings are examined within the context of five broad categories: (1) reinforcement and social learning, (2) imitation, (3) cognitive functioning, (4) tutoring and therapeutic benefits, and (5) other social behaviors.

Reinforcement and Social Learning

Behavioral observations of children in mixed-age and same-age groupings suggest that positive reinforcements and social interchanges are more common between mixed-age than same-age peers. Goldman (1981) found that 3-year-olds in mixed-age classrooms, compared with 3-year-olds in same-age classrooms, engaged in more positive interactions, less parallel play, and fewer teacher-directed activities. Similarly, 4-year-olds in mixed-age classrooms engaged in more positive interactions, less parallel play, fewer teacher-directed activities, and more solitary play than 4-year-olds in same-age classrooms. Mounts and Roopnarine (1987) also found higher levels of participation in more mature modes of play among children in mixed-age than in same-age settings. Three-year-olds in mixed-age settings were more likely to engage in solitary-constructive, interactive-constructive, and parallel-constructive play than 3-year-olds in same-age classrooms, while 3-year-olds in same-age classrooms were more likely to engage in parallel-manipulative play than 3-year-olds in mixed-age classrooms. Other studies (Brownell, 1990; Rothstein-Fisch & Howes, 1988; Urberg & Kaplan, 1986; Winsler et al., 2002) also report more mature play and social participation by younger children in mixed-age than in same-age settings and on the ability of young children to adjust their interaction patterns as a function of the partner's age. But mixed-age and same-age preschool classrooms may offer different opportunities for social participation; cooperative and constructive play were observed more often in mixed-age classrooms, while dramatic play was observed more often in same-age classrooms (Roopnarine et al., 1992). Three-year-olds in mixed-age classrooms spent more time in goal-directed on-task activities than 3-year-olds in same-age classrooms, whereas 4-year-olds in mixed-age classrooms behaved more like their 3-year-old classmates than comparable age children in same-age classrooms (Winsler et al., 2002).

Laboratory studies tend to confirm the asymmetrical social interaction patterns of children grouped in mixed-age and same-age dyads. Lougee, Grueneich, and Hartup (1977) found that reinforcements were least frequent between dyads of 3-year-olds, most frequent between dyads of 5-year-olds, and intermediate between dyads of 3- and 5-year-olds. These results point to the ability of young children to make accommodative shifts in accordance with their play partner's developmental levels (see Shatz & Gelman, 1973).

Imitation

The importance of imitation and observational learning for social and personality development has been addressed extensively (Bandura, 1992, 2002). Likewise, the effect of the model's age on imitation and observational learning (Davidson & Smith, 1982; Graziano, Musser, & Moore, 1984; Lougee, 1979a; Peifer, 1972; Robert & Charbonneau, 1977; Thelen & Kirkland, 1976; Williams, 2001) and the impact of rehearsal of different skills on processes of understanding have been articulated (O'Donnell, 1999). For example, Peifer (1972) found that 6-year-olds were more likely to imitate older models than

younger ones. Other investigations (Lougee, 1979b) have also reported that older models were imitated more than younger ones across different tasks, that children find it more rewarding if they are imitated by older peers rather than younger ones (Thelen & Kirkland, 1976), and that more leader-style social role behaviors were enacted when children were perceived as younger compared to older (Blume, 1987). Children are capable of switching roles by imitating model/teacher (Williams, 2001). Although the efficacy of a model might depend on such other factors as social competence and power (Mischel & Grusec, 1966), these findings generally indicate that the greater social competence of older children might increase the likelihood of imitation by younger peers. The cognitive or social mechanisms underlying imitation in mixed-age settings are not clearly understood, however.

Cognitive Functioning

Some would argue that children derive unique adaptational advantages through interacting with peers who are similar in age (Piaget, 1932). Such interactions might lead to conflicts during play that in turn might result in the acceptance of others' perspectives, thereby allowing children to decenter, or become less egocentric. Given that children make accommodative shifts according to the developmental levels of their peers (see Hartup, 1983), decentration might be facilitated in mixed-age milieus (Derscheid, 1997).

This latter point merits more attention in the treatment of mixed-age socialization. In a sense, if children are capable of making the developmental shifts necessary to interact with younger or older peers, they may be operating within overlapping cognitive domains. That is, older children may be providing the scaffolding that is necessary for younger children to move beyond their own level of cognitive functioning (Tudge, 1986; Tudge & Hogan, 1999). In Vygotsky's framework, children in mixed-age settings would tap into one another's "zone of proximal development," especially during collaborative activity (see Katz et al., 1990; Sapon-Shevin, 1999; Wertsch, 1985).

Although little evidence exists with respect to cognitive decentration and children's age relationships per se, three studies provide related information on this issue. Shatz and Gelman (1973) found that the speech of 4-year-olds to 2-year-olds was shorter and simpler than their speech to other 4-year-olds. Sachs and Devin (1976) found that children adapt and modify their speech according to the developmental status of the listener, and Derscheid (1997) found associations between moral (helping) behaviors and vocal turns to a younger partner, to perspective-taking ability, and to length of attendance in a mixed-age program. Working with grade-school children, McCloskey (1996) found that in mixed-age dyads girls were more instructive in their speech to younger partners, and tutorial speech was more common in mixed-age than in same-age dyads.

Turning to cognitive gains and mixed-age classrooms, a bulk of the research has focused on older grade-school children. As noted above, reviews of the research literature (Anderson & Pavan, 1993; Mason & Burns, 1996; Veenman, 1996) and individual studies (Matthews et al., 1997; Ong, Allison, & Haladyna, 2000; Tanner & Decotis, 1995) have provided equivocal results on the impact of nongraded classrooms on children's achievement. In studies (Richard, Miller, & Heffer, 1995; Tanner & Decotis, 1995) of developmental trends and adjustment in kindergartners, first-, and second-grade children enrolled in mixed-age classrooms, there were no age-related differences in achievement in children, but in two separate samples, first- and third-grade children in nongraded classrooms performed better academically (e.g., grades, reading, writing, mathematics) than those in graded classrooms (Grant & Richardson, 1999; Tanner & Decotis, 1995). Another study (Winsler & Diaz, 1995) found no differences in the private speech

of kindergartners enrolled in same-age and mixed-age classrooms.

By contrast, some researchers (Bailey, Burchinal, & McWilliam, 1993) have reported a quadratic developmental trajectory for children in mixed-age classrooms and a linear developmental trajectory for young children in same-age classrooms. Children in mixed-age classrooms showed higher cognitive growth rates than children in same-age classrooms between 2 and 4 years. Greater gains in reading scores for older at-risk students have also been noted in multiage classrooms (Mackey, Johnson, & Wood, 1995), and interactions with same-age and younger peers were associated with less cognitive and social play and lower receptive language scores (Dunn, Kontos, & Potter, 1996). Collaborative literacy activities—functional reading and writing, reading aloud, and recreational reading and writing—were more prevalent during sociodramatic play among children in multiage than in same-age classrooms. Furthermore, collaborative strategies (e.g., assisting, tutoring, directing) were more varied in the multiage than in the same-age setting (Christie & Stone, 1999).

Tutoring and Therapeutic Benefits

The mixed-age classroom appears to be an ideal arrangement for peer tutoring (see Christie & Stone, 1999; Tudge, 1992). Research findings suggest that children tutored by peers who are very discrepant in age performed significantly better than when they were taught by peers who are less discrepant in age (Linton, 1973; Thomas, 1972). Thus, the most gains in learning were produced if the age difference between the tutor and learner was great.

A second issue that has received increased attention is using peers as behavioral change agents (Strain, Shores, & Timm, 1977). The role of age-mates and non–age-mates in social rehabilitation has been demonstrated in experiments conducted on rhesus monkeys. Suomi and Harlow (1972) showed that monkeys who

Children are afforded many opportunities to teach one another in mixed-age classrooms.

were socially deprived can be "rehabilitated" if they are exposed to younger playmates. Although the social interactions of the younger monkeys were initially rebuffed by the socially deprived ones, the persistent attempts of the younger monkeys led to significant improvements in the social behaviors of the maladjusted monkeys. Similar findings on mixed-age rehabilitation have been noted by others (Novak, 1979).

The potential of mixed-age peer socialization in rehabilitating human children has also been demonstrated. Furman, Rahe, and Hartup (1979) systematically exposed socially withdrawn children to same-age and younger socially competent partners. The younger play partners were more effective in eliciting social interactions from the withdrawn children than were their age-mates. Basically, similar conclusions can be reached from a study of rejected aggressive children (Kim, 1990). Young children experiencing social behavioral problems benefited from extensive exposure to cross-age peers in play groups. Perhaps the younger partners appeared nonthreatening, thereby allowing their older counterparts to gain

control over the bouts of social interactions. This may have been the crucial factor in the success of the intervention program.

While not directly related to social rehabilitation, it is noteworthy that peer popularity and social reputation were stable during the transition from same-age kindergarten to ungraded primary classrooms (Lemerise, Harper, & Howes, 1998) with younger children in mixed-age settings less likely to have friends than their older classmates (Caverly et al., 2002), aggression was far less in mixed-age than same-age classrooms (McClellan & Kinsey, 1999), and rates of conflicts were not significantly different in mainstreamed same-age and mixed-age classrooms (Lund, 1989) or were reduced after behavioral intervention (Finley, Pettinger, Rutherford, & Timmes, 2000). Children who were older and intermediate in age were seen as more popular compared with their younger classmates (Lemerise, 1997). Mixed-age settings may have a moderating effect on school adjustment (Diehl, Lemerise, Caverly, Ramsay, & Roberts, 1998) and on negative social overtures because children are aware of the benefits and nature of peer collaboration (Williams, 2001).

Other Social Behaviors

Finally, studies of leadership, nurturing, and cooperative behavior in children's groups have received considerable attention. Early studies suggest that a good relationship exists between leadership and age (Goodenough, 1930; Parten, 1933).

Later work (French, 1984; Straight & French, 1988) has also reported a link between age and leadership. Younger children seem to ascribe leadership and instructive, helpful, and sympathizing roles to older children, whereas older children perceive their younger peers in a more needy light as requiring help and instruction. Further, older children were assessed to have better leadership skills than younger children (Blume, 1987; French, Waas, Straight, & Baker, 1986), and older girls seem to assume a more managerial role during social conversations than older boys in mixed-age dyads (McCloskey, 1996).

Children were more nurturing to infants than to age-mates (40% vs. 11%) (Whiting & Whiting, 1975), and young girls offered a good deal of nurturing to infants (Liederman & Liederman, 1974). Sibling care is ubiquitous in several societies around the world (see Flinn, 1992; Weisner & Gallimore, 1977). The degree to which mixed-age classrooms facilitate nurturing behaviors in older children is largely undetermined, but qualitative descriptions suggest their existence among very young children in mixed-age settings (Whaley & Kantor, 1992).

Last, research on the cooperative behavior of children in mixed-age groups has mainly focused on grade-school children in laboratory situations. In a series of experiments, Graziano and his colleagues (Brody, Graziano, & Musser, 1983; Graziano, French, Brownell, & Hartup, 1976) reported that the division of labor in task completion was more pronounced in mixed-age triads than in same-age triads, with older

children increasing their performance when their partners were younger. Apparently, the age of the partner is an important factor in task completion. Let us now turn our attention to collaboration within the framework of the cooperative learning movement.

Cooperative Education

Arguably, the cooperative education movement in the United States has fueled greater attention to heterogeneous age and racial/ethnic and inclusive classroom communities (Sapon-Shevin, 1999). Essentially, the cooperative educative process centers on the basic principles of noncompetitive, active learning using small heterogeneous age groups of children with diverse abilities and from diverse cultural backgrounds. It taps into the motivational power of the learners and peer group assistance (see Johnson & Johnson, 1990, 1999; Sapon-Shevin, 1999; Slavin, 1990).

Although cooperative learning has as its major premise the notion of positive interdependence and individual accountability, approaches to cooperative learning vary. Some approaches are more structured, while others offer greater flexibility in curriculum method and materials (see Hurley, Chamberlain, Slavin, & Madden, 2001; Johnson & Johnson, 1999, 2001; Sapon-Shevin, 1999, 2000/2001; Slavin & Madden, 2001) and assessments (Johnson & Johnson, 1999). Nevertheless, cooperative learning approaches have broad applications and provide teachers with new methods to augment "one-sided" traditional approaches to educating young children.

The research data on cooperative learning are wide ranging. Greater gains in language and mathematics skills have been noted for children in cooperative education classrooms versus control children (see Slavin, 1990). But equally important are the findings that cooperative learning approaches lead to a more prosocial orientation among students, better race relations, improved self-concept, and greater acceptance of mainstreamed academically disabled students (Kagan, 1990; Odom & Diamond, 1998b; Slavin, 1990). It can lead to reduced conflicts (Johnson & Johnson, 2001) and to more promotive interactions during chat room dialogues on the computer (Jensen, Johnson, & Johnson, 2002).

Summary of Empirical Bases

Across a range of social–cognitive constructs and in different settings, children appear quite sensitive to their peers' level of development. The mixed-age grouping seems to elicit a number of social behaviors and cognitive input from children of varying developmental statuses. The debates regarding the cognitive and social merits of mixed-age classrooms notwithstanding, the mixed-age philosophy has gained broader appeal across the United States and in other countries around the world (e.g., Australia), and more systematic assessments of the cognitive and social gains young children might accrue from them are being further discerned.

✍ OVERALL GOALS AND OBJECTIVES

Mixed-Age Programs

In earlier editions of this book, discussion focused mainly on the mixed-age program at the Laboratory School at the University of Wisconsin. Because mixed-age programs have recruited wider attention today (e.g., there are multiage Web sites and chat rooms—Mulitage-Education.com, resource guides and handbooks—Northwest Regional Education Laboratory Guide to Multigrade Education, professional organizations such as Multiage Association of Queensland, Australia), in this chapter we expand our treatment of mixed-age programs to include a discussion of some aspects of Kentucky's initiatives toward ungraded primary programs during the last decade of the previous century, a brief look

at mixed-age inclusive programs, and mixed-age programs internationally.

As stated already, several states have mandated the implementation of mixed-age classrooms as a part of educational reform efforts. Whether mandated by states or embraced by individual schools and teachers, mixed-age programs vary tremendously and have been implemented broadly with diverse groups of learners. We refer you to a few of them that have been implemented or are currently operating: A. Sophie Rogers Laboratory School at the Ohio State University (see Whaley & Kantor, 1992); Project Friends at the University of Florida (Adams et al., 1997); Hillcrest Professional Development School at Baylor University (Baker, 1996); Rainerd School in Houston, Texas (Bouchard, 1991); Slatonhall Elementary School in Salem, Massachusetts (Fowler & Corley, 1996); The San Carlos Charter Learning Center (Darwish, 2000); and M.A.G.I.C. (Multi-age Groupings Interweaving the Curriculum) program in southwest Texas (Mackey et al., 1995) (see Wisconsin's multiage Web site for a list of elementary schools around the state that employ the mixed-age approach and looping). Other reports have indicated that children with disabilities are enrolled in mixed-age inclusive classrooms (see Roberts et al., 1994). A.I.M. (Avondale Integrative Model) in the Avondale School District in Auburn Hills, Michigan, is one such program (Avondale Public Schools, 1992). Efforts have also been made to integrate senior citizens, 5-year-olds, and at-risk grade school children in educational activities (Freeman & King, 2001).

General Goals of Mixed-Age Programs

Fundamentally, mixed-age programs strive to attain the same general goals of all early childhood programs: Provide a cognitively and socially stimulating environment in which children can flourish; provide teachers and parents with the challenge of developing curricula and working with children who vary widely in terms of competence, socioeconomic, and cultural backgrounds; and build partnerships between the school and natal culture. Nevertheless, there are some important differences between most early childhood programs and mixed-age classrooms. The asymmetry in the developmental levels of children provides greater opportunities for dispensing with traditional boundaries in the curriculum and focusing on integrated thematic units that attend to the individual needs of children. In the spirit of cooperative education, this process capitalizes on peer teaching and enriches the continuous learning process.

Preschool Mixed-Age Classrooms

A sizable number of early childhood programs are built on the idea that play is central to children's cognitive and social development (Johnson, Christie, & Wardle, 2005). Through fantasy play and engagement in games with rules, children's cognitive competence is bolstered. Such assumptions are based on the growing literature on the importance of early peer relationships and play for later social and cognitive development. Authoritative reviews (e.g., Coie & Dodge, 1998; Parker & Asher, 1987; Rubin, Bukowski, & Parker, 1998) outline the link between inadequate early peer relationships (unpopularity, behavioral problems such as aggressiveness, withdrawal, and shyness) and later criminality, academic problems, and psychopathology. Conversely, ample evidence shows that peers contribute to sex role development (see Hartup, 1992; Maccoby, 1998); that an understanding of personal relationships is advanced and friendships are solidified through repeated peer contacts (see Rubin et al., 1998); and that peer play contributes to intellectual development, the acquisition of various social skills, and the regulation of affect (Johnson et al., 2005).

Furthermore, links between play and creativity, language development, perspective-taking ability, and problem solving are well acknowledged (see Hughes, 1998; Johnson et al., 2005 for overviews). Beyond these general links, play researchers have argued that constructive play may be related to problem-solving abilities, that solitary play involves goal-directed and independent activity, and that pretend modes of behaviors may help divergent thinking, language refinement and vocabulary, and representational skills (see Johnson et al., 2005; Roopnarine, Suppal, Shin, & Donovan, 1999; Rubin et al., 1998), and may possibly be connected to the child's theory of mind (see Lilliard, 2001).

At a theoretical level, a mixed-age program that is rooted in peer interactions provides children with ample opportunities for observational learning, imitation, and tutoring, and it is an environment for engaging in simple to complex modes of cognitive and social play. Older children have opportunities to sharpen skills already learned, while younger children are exposed to the behaviors of more competent older peers.

At this point we describe globally the efforts at implementing a mixed-age program at the University of Wisconsin Preschool Laboratory. This exercise is geared toward providing the reader with a more concrete view of the internal dynamics of one mixed-age program that was designed for 3- to 8-year-olds. This experimental program is atypical, since most mixed preschool programs enroll children who are less discrepant in age. As you peruse the mixed-age preschool literature, you will find that mixed-age groupings vary widely in terms of age-group admixture and social and educational philosophies.

Implementation

The basic goal of the Wisconsin program was to provide an environment that was safe and functional in terms of children's physical size and developmental levels. The University of Wisconsin Mixed-Age Laboratory School was an experimental program that contained two classrooms equipped with standard preschool- and school-related materials. The classrooms were divided into activity areas. Each area contained objects and materials that were conducive to the various forms of cognitive and social play. In addition, each area was designed to promote curriculum objectives and to encourage individual and small group activities.

Curriculum

The program had an educational as well as a recreational focus and involved both indoor and outdoor activities. The program had an open classroom orientation that emphasized language and communication, science and nature, dance and movement, arts and crafts, and dramatic themes. Also included were field trips, drawing groups, visits from guests, carnivals, and circuses.

- *Language and communication* involved reading and prereading activities; pictures that tell a story; songs, verses, and poems; photographic essays; reading books; telephoning; writing letters; verbal and nonverbal communication; charades; topic discussions; drawing stories; and board games.
- *Science and nature* included premathematics and number activities; logical reasoning tasks; plants and animals; solids, liquids, and gases; mixtures and combinations; colors, sizes, and shapes; magnets and electricity; sounds and vibrations; fire and heat; weather and air; gravity; machines; planting seeds; and lights.
- *Dance and movement* consisted of exercise and body movements; climbing; folk dances; spontaneous and rhythmic motion; finger play; and musical chairs and other quick reaction games.
- *Dramatics* focused on puppet play; playing people and animals; play skits; sociodramatic play (barbershop, ice cream shop, camping, bakery, superheroes, housekeeping, hospital); treasure hunts; and building sand castles.
- *Arts and crafts* involved doing construction work with soft modeling clay, puzzles, blocks, and cubes; building cranberry necklaces; making crayon rubbings and finger paintings with pudding; creating sand, yarn, and nature pictures; making collages; doing easel and stencil painting; working with macramé; and making sculptures.

The curriculum emphasized the role of the child as an active learner and experimenter. The socially and cognitively oriented curriculum allowed children to participate actively in various elements of the physical and sociocultural environment. It also permitted children to enter the world of make-believe through simple-to-more complex sociodramatic themes. In sum, knowledge of the social and the intellectual world came through personal interaction with peers and objects.

Role of Teachers

The teacher/child ratio in this program was 1:3. The teachers were informed about the specific goals of the program and assumed a supervisory role without engaging in didactic instruction. This met with the overall goals of the program because we wanted the children to engage in discovery-based learning, and we wanted to provide them with the opportunity to tutor or instruct their peers during social encounters. However, teachers did introduce new materials and props to facilitate social interaction in each of the activity areas and provided encouragement to children who had difficulty joining the activities of others. Additionally, they met with the preschool director and core of research faculty members to discuss problem behaviors, the curriculum, the process of social integration, and general program objectives. Teachers were undergraduate and graduate students majoring in early childhood education and child development.

Role of Parents

Parental participation and cooperation is key to any successful early childhood program. Quite a bit has been written about the links between parental participation in school-related activities and children's school functioning (see Lopez, 2001). Initially, parents had to be convinced that 3- and 8-year-olds do benefit cognitively and socially if grouped together. Parents of older children were concerned about the benefits of the program for their children. Thus, the information flow between parents and staff members was critical to solidifying the philosophy behind mixed-age socialization. Moreover, parental feedback on curricular issues, provision of materials, and their direct participation in field trips reflected the bidirectional emphasis that is so essential to the success of early childhood programs.

Observation and Assessments

With the rise in mixed-age classrooms, the cognitive benefits of age-group admixtures have come under greater scrutiny (see Kelly-Vance et al., 2000; Lloyd, 1999; Veenman, 1996). Nevertheless, the long-term benefits of mixed-age preschool education remain untapped. As is clear from the overview provided in an earlier section, most of the research on mixed-age programs in the preschool years has sought to assess patterns of interactions between children. Building on this database, research and childhood evaluations were central to the Wisconsin program and to our subsequent attempts to assess the benefits of mixed-age classrooms in the Syracuse area. Some of the research focused on the phenomenon of social segregation on the basis of age, social participation in different behaviors such as peer tutoring and imitation, children's play, cooperation during group art projects, and children's knowledge of age relationships. Our findings have been presented in several published reports and will be presented in summary form here (see Johnson, Koester, & Wanska,

1984; Mounts & Roopnarine, 1987; Roopnarine, 1984; Roopnarine et al., 1992; Roopnarine, Church, & Levy, 1990; Roopnarine & Johnson, 1983, 1984).

1. *We found significant differences in kindergartners' behaviors toward younger and older peers.* In general, kindergartners exhibited primarily sociodramatic play (55%) followed by parallel-constructive (13%) and interactive-constructive (12%). They spent about 33% of their time playing with preschoolers, 40% of their time playing with other kindergartners, and 27% of their time playing with school-agers. Kindergartners were more likely to engage in parallel-functional, interactive-functional, and interactive-dramatic play with other kindergartners than with school-agers. They were also more likely to engage in interactive-dramatic play with other kindergartners than with preschoolers but showed more of a tendency to engage in parallel-constructive play with preschoolers than with other kindergartners. Thus, considerable cross-age play occurred.

2. *Mixed-age classrooms were more conducive to cooperative and constructive play, while same-age classrooms were more conducive to dramatic play.* Preference for same-gender playmates was far greater in same-age than in mixed-age classrooms (see Winsler et al., 2002, as well).

3. *During art projects, younger children tended to prefer age-mates, while older children displayed equal interest for age-mates and younger peers.* Older children seemed to facilitate the task-oriented behaviors of younger children, but their effects depended on group composition.

4. *Interviews of children suggest that kindergartners and school-agers project an understanding of preschoolers' social and cognitive competence.* Preschoolers were generally viewed as being less mature cognitively and

socially. While younger children may have been perceived as deficient in cognitive and social competence, our observational data do not indicate that younger children were excluded from the play of their older counterparts in the classroom setting. A few researchers have illustrated the difficulty younger children in mixed-age classrooms encounter in forming and maintaining friendships (see Diehl et al., 1998)

5. *We found no significant relationships between performance on The Preschool Interpersonal Problem Solving Task, Peabody Picture Vocabulary Test, and a referential communication task and children's social interactions with peers.* The lack of significant relationships between the measures might be attributed to problems associated with the reliability, validity, and task equivalency of the instruments used and to the small number of children in our sample.

6. *Modes of parenting and marital relations were associated with children's level of play in the peer group.*

The Kentucky Experiment: Primary Ungraded Programs

The Kentucky Education Reform Act of 1990 mandated the implementation of ungraded primary programs in all elementary schools across the state by 1992–1993 (Kentucky Education Association & Appalachia Educational Laboratory, 1991). Initially, the Kentucky Education Association (KEA) and the Appalachia Educational Laboratory (AEL) conducted case studies of 10 successful ungraded programs that were already in existence in the State of Kentucky (e.g., Jefferstown Elementary School in Louisville, Kentucky) and three other states (e.g., Townsend Continuous Progress School in Milwaukee, Wisconsin). Subsequently, both qualitative and quantitative assessments were conducted of student achievement, and the attitudes of parents, teachers, and administrators were

solicited regarding mixed-age education (Kannapel et al., 2000; McIntyre & Kyle, 1997). The programs assessed varied in terms of their emphasis (e.g., independent lifelong learners, building self-esteem, experiential learning, promoting high levels of achievement, development of whole child), age ranges of children served (combinations ranged from K–5, 1–3, K–3, Pre-K–2, 1–5), teacher/child ratio, the teacher's role in the classroom, and commitment to implementing mixed-age education, and outcomes. KEA-AEL identified concepts, procedures, and materials used in ungraded schools; highlighted commonalties among the programs; and provided links to ungraded schools for educators and teachers. However, a 1994 law relaxed the emphasis on mixed-age groupings.

As you may have gathered by now, there is no "one right way" to implement ungraded primary programs (see Kasten & Lolli, 1998; Katz, Allison, Clark, Bergman, & Gainer, 1998). Consequently, the KEA-AEL case studies revealed that grouping children appeared flexible: one on one; small groups; independent activities; subgroups based on skill mastery levels; and groups based on a consideration of socioeconomic and ethnic backgrounds, gender, and achievement levels. Curriculum methods involved cooperative learning approaches; learning centers; learner capacity-paced lessons; instruction-/individually paced lessons; computer-assisted instruction; peer tutoring; team teaching; skill sequence levels; integrated thematic units; whole-language instruction; Montessori methods; positive-assertive discipline techniques; student-initiated assignments; basal texts in reading, spelling, and mathematics; and hands-on materials (e.g., Box It, Bag It Math, LOGO, SUM, TOPS).

As the methods of instruction varied, so did the teacher's role in the classroom and his or her commitment to the mixed-age approach. Although teaming was not required in some of the schools and teachers learned from expert teachers or collaborated with the principal to develop individual student schedules and class schedules,

A display of cross-age caring—a commonly seen occurrence and an important advantage of mixed-age classrooms.

most teachers worked in teams drawing on each person's strength. Teams often developed plans for sharing information, worked on curricular issues, and obtained additional training. Thus, shared decision making and ongoing inservice training were hallmarks of most of the programs featured by KEA-AEL (see Kentucky Department of Education Web sites for a description of Instruction Resource Documents).

Outcomes Across Programs

In early program assessments, the KEA-AEL case studies pinpointed several benefits of ungraded primary classrooms: increased student achieve-ment, cooperative attitudes and increased sensitivity among children, fewer discipline referrals, parent satisfaction, improved standardized test scores, reduced student retention, improved student attitudes, enhanced self-esteem, decreased teacher isolation, increased teacher empowerment, reduced teacher preparations, and improved teacher–student bonding (Kentucky Education Association & Appalachia Educational Laboratory, 1991). Later assessments and reviews of a corpus of studies (Gnadinger, McIntyre, Chitwood-Smith, & Kyle, 2000; Kannapel et al., 2000) suggested largely similar findings in student achievement or, at the very least, that mixed-age programs did not have a negative effect on student outcomes. Across Kentucky, fourth-graders demonstrated improvements in all subject areas with the largest increments occurring in reading (Kannapel et al., 2000).

The overall picture was not totally positive, however. There were disagreements between parents and teachers about program concept, lack of time for teachers to plan instruction, weak administrative support, problems in management, and the feeling that developmental education is for weak students. No doubt, these problems could have been attenuated by permitting more time for teachers to plan and share information about instruction, by encouraging teachers to make appropriate adjustments in their approach, and by emphasizing continuous progress (Kentucky Education Association & Appalachia Education Laboratory, 1991). The 1994 Kentucky legislation that permitted more flexibility in educational reforms did not help matters much. Some teachers began to abandon the mixed-age concept altogether in favor of the long-standing, fully entrenched age-graded classrooms and "traditional" education (Kannapel et al., 2000). To complicate matters further, the links between the primary reforms and those of the entire educational system were never clearly laid out (Kannapel et al., 2000).

It is worth mentioning that the mixed-age approach was never fully implemented in schools across the state of Kentucky. In several instances, parents and teachers did not sway far from the aged-graded concept of education. Like their counterparts whose children were enrolled in the Wisconsin Preschool Laboratory, parents questioned the wisdom of grouping kindergartners with older children and emphasized the preparatory role of early schooling. They became increasingly uncomfortable with assessment procedures that were not grounded in the assignment of grades for each subject (Kannapel et al., 2000).

Mixed-Age Inclusive Classrooms

With the push toward inclusive educational practices in North America (see Friend & Bursuck, 1999; Sapon-Shevin, 1999; Walther-Thomas, Korinek, McLaughlin, & Williams, 2000), educators and researchers have begun to examine the benefits of mixed-age classrooms for children with disabilities (see entire issue of *Early Childhood Research Quarterly*, Odom & Diamond, 1998a). Again, the educational philosophies of the programs vary a good deal; some have used the High/Scope Model (A.I.M. in the Avondale School District in Auburn Hills, Michigan), whereas others have employed gentle teaching strategies (e.g., Jowonio Program in Syracuse, New York, see Chapter Four), multidisciplinary units (Darwish, 2000), collaborative partnership (Appal, Troha, & Rowell, 2001), or a play-based curriculum.

The findings on mixed-age inclusive programs are generally positive. Preschool-aged children in mixed-age classrooms engaged in more turn-taking conversations with peers with disabilities, and, in turn, children with disabilities were more likely to reciprocate compared with children in same-age classrooms (Roberts et al., 1994). Researchers noted developmental trajectories for children with disabilities, with the most cognitive growth occurring between 2 and 4 years of age (Bailey et al., 1993). Children with disabilities in mixed-age classrooms demonstrated more complex play mastery than their counterparts do in same-age classrooms (Blasco, Bailey, & Burchinal, 1993).

Mixed-Age Programs Internationally

We are unable to gauge the extensiveness of mixed-age early childhood programs internationally. Scattered reports indicate that mixed-age programs are popular in Sweden (43% of preschoolers were enrolled in 1991) (Aberg-Bengtsson, 1996; Sundell, 1993), there is a growing movement toward mixed-age education in some parts of Australia, implemented at the Child Development Research Institute at Yonsei University in Seoul, Korea (Tieszen & Lee, 1993), and their impact has been assessed in Slovenia (Plastenjak, 1993; Umbek & Musek, 1997), New Zealand (Meade & Dalli, 1992), and Holland among other societies (see Veenman, 1996). The available data indicate that in Slovenia symbolic play was more complex in mixed-age than in same-age classrooms (Umbek & Musek, 1997); that the performance of Swedish students in small rural schools, which are more likely to be mixed-age than urban schools, was equal to that of students in urban same-age schools (Aberg-Bengtsson, 1996); and that teacher effectiveness in mixed-age classrooms in Holland increased after systematic intervention (Roelofs, Raemaekers, & Veenman, 1989).

Implications for Teachers

The obvious challenge for teachers in mixed-age classrooms is designing lessons and activities for children who are discrepant in developmental levels. The age discrepancy could undermine children's attempts to make accommodative shifts or adjust their language and social skills according to their playmates' developmental level (Richard et al., 1995). Other factors such as group size, time together, and context-specific activities may also affect the functioning of mixed-age classrooms (Stegelin, 1997). To avoid social and cognitive segregation, teachers may have to direct a lot of energy in developing thematic units that appeal to diverse ability levels.

Because of the diverse nature of mixed-age programs, there are no set curricular guides in implementing them. Consequently, the teaching strategies are diverse. Cooperative learning, peer play, and peer tutoring are common strategies used in promoting children's intellectual and social development in mixed-age settings. Teachers, though, may have to be proactive in encouraging children to engage in joint ventures. For example, in specific situations, younger children may be encouraged to seek assistance from older classmates, or older children may have to be reminded of the skills of younger classmates (Katz et al., 1990). In some cases, older children may be directed to assist and assume responsibility for younger children; however, teachers must guard against inadvertently limiting challenges for older children by providing enriching experiences across groups (Lodish, 1992).

Teachers can also help older children appreciate their own advances while simultaneously discouraging the stereotyping of younger children's abilities (Katz et al., 1990). Moreover, due to the gap or decalage that exists in developmental levels in mixed-age classrooms, children may become frustrated over differences in their performances. Teachers can assume a central role in designing activities that tap into different skill levels (e.g., when making books, older children do the writing and younger children do the illustrations, the same for joint activities involving computers). Children should be encouraged to articulate their feelings, needs, and desires to their peers and to accept comfort from them (Katz et al., 1990; Lodish, 1992).

In meeting the instructional needs of mixed-age classrooms, teachers may need extra time and support to redesign lessons and topical units. In this regard, teaming may free up time for reflection, shore up thematic units, permit teachers to instruct to their strengths, eliminate teacher isolation and frustration, and increase feelings of empowerment. Assistance in other areas of curriculum and staff development may be sought from parent volunteers and teacher mentors (Jeanroy, 1996; Kentucky Education Association & Appalachia Educational Laboratory, 1991). Support in these domains may encourage greater acceptance of approaches to schooling that stand in contrast to age-graded practices that are so widespread and firmly rooted in the educational system in the United States.

Teachers need a solid understanding of childhood development (including the acquisition of mathematics and language skills, cultural competence), family development, sociocultural practices and beliefs about education among the parents of diverse groups of learners, and the effects of one's own beliefs and ethnic identity on curriculum planning and assessments of children's progress (Ladson-Billings, 2000; Roopnarine et al., in press; Roopnarine & Metindogan, in press). Further, strong and respectful relationships between the school and natal cultures can only facilitate working with an increasingly diverse U.S. population.

CONCLUSION

American educators have segregated children on the basis of age, perhaps because of the belief that same-age classrooms are best suited to the needs of young children in a postindustrialized world, and because it is often difficult to change institutional patterns that form the foundation of a school system (Tyack & Tobin, 1994). Considering the developmental significance attributed to peer socialization and the unique adaptational advantages children might derive from mixed-age versus same-age educational experiences, mixed-age programs offer tremendous hope for early childhood education worldwide.

Observations and assessments of preschoolers and grade school children suggest that, overall, mixed-age programs that emphasize cooperative ventures may be very adaptive in facilitating the educational and social growth of young children (Kannapel et al., 2000; Lloyd, 1999). With the large number of American children in preschools and day care and in attempts at reforming the educational system in the United States for diverse learners (see U.S. Department of Education, 2002), educators and policy makers may want to take a serious look at heterogeneous classroom groupings. Although age-graded and non–age-graded classrooms may each have unique adaptational advantages vis-á-vis the technological needs of industrialized nations, exposure to peers of varying developmental levels offers any curriculum breadth and scope that are antithetical to differentiation by ability levels in children's groups. In the long run, interdependence and the motivational power evident in heterogeneous cooperative groups can only foster interpersonal respect and intellectual and sociocultural understanding and can enable the mastery of basic academic subjects.

REFERENCES

Aberg-Bengtsson, L. A. (1996, September). *Education in small rural Swedish schools: An initial overview of the field*. Paper presented at the European Conference on Educational Research, Seville, Spain. (ERIC Document Reproduction Service No. ED 413 118).

Adams, D., Harmon, C., Reneke, S., Adams, T. L., Hartle, L., & Lamme, L. (1997). Project friends: A multi-age learning community. *Early Childhood Education Journal, 24,* 217–221.

Anderson, R. H., & Pavan, B. N. 1993. Nongradedness: Helping it to happen. Lancaster, PA: Technomic Publishing Company. (ERIC Document Reproduction Service No. Ed 355–005).

Appal, D., Troha, C., & Rowell, J. (2001). Reflections of a first-year team. *Teaching Exceptional Children, 33,* 4–8.

Avondale Public Schools. (1992, December 2–6). *Avondale integrated model*. Paper presented at the Annual International Conference of the Council for Exceptional Children, Washington, DC.

Bailey, D. B., Burchinal, M. R., & McWilliam, R. A. (1993). Age of peers and early childhood development. *Child Development, 64,* 848–862.

Baker, B. R. (1996). *The role of the professional development school to prepare teachers of young children*. Unpublished manuscript, Baylor University, Waco, TX.

Bandura, A. (1977). *Social learning theory*. Upper Saddle River, NJ: Prentice Hall.

Bandura, A. (1992). Social cognitive theory. In R. Vasta (Ed.), *Six theories of child development* (pp. 1–60). London: Jessica Kingsley Publication.

Bandura, A. (2002). Social cognitive theory: An agentic perspective. *Annual Review of Psychology, 52,* 1–26.

Barker, R. G., & Wright, H. G. (1955). *Midwest and its children*. New York: Harper & Row.

Blasco, P. M., Bailey, D. B., & Burchinal, M. R. (1993). Dimensions of mastery in same-age and mixed-age integrated classrooms. *Early Childhood Research Quarterly, 8,* 193–206.

Blume, L. B. (1987). *Perceived-age ascriptions as a factor in the social-role perception and social-role behavior of preschool children in a mixed-age setting*. Unpublished doctoral dissertation. Texas Tech University, Lubbock.

Bouchard, L. L. (1991). Mixed age grouping for gifted students. *Gifted Child Today, 14,* 30–35.

Boulton, M. J. (1992). Participation in playground activities at middle school. *Educational Research, 34,* 167–182.

Bredekamp, S., & Copple, C. (Ed.). (1997). *Developmentally appropriate practice in early childhood programs* (rev. ed.). Washington, DC: National Association for the Education of Young Children.

Brody, G. H., Graziano, W. G., & Musser, L. M. (1983). Familiarity and children's behavior in same-age and mixed-age peer groups. *Developmental Psychology, 19,* 568–576.

Brownell, C. (1990). Peer social skills in toddlers: Competencies and constraints illustrated by same-age and mixed-age interaction. *Child Development, 61,* 838–848.

Bruner, J. S. (1972). The nature and uses of immaturity. *American Psychologist, 27,* 687–708.

Burns, R. B., & Mason, D. A. (2002). Class composition and student achievement in elementary schools. *American Educational Research Journal, 39* (1), 207–233.

Burns, S. M., & Brainerd, C. J. (1979). Effects of constructive and dramatic play on perspective taking in very young children. *Developmental Psychology, 15,* 512–521.

Caverly, S. L., Lemerise, E. A., & Harper, B. D. (2002). Patterns of friendship in ungraded primary classes. *Early Education & Development, 13* (1), 5–21.

Cazden, C. B. (1976). Play with language and meta–linguistic awareness: One dimension of language experience. In J. S. Bruner, A. Jolly, & K. Sylva (Eds.), *Play: Its role in development and evolution* (pp. 603–608). New York: Basic.

Cesarone, B. (1995). Mixed-age grouping. *Childhood Education, 71,* 182–184.

Christie, J. F., & Stone, S. J. (1999). Collaborative literacy activity in print-enriched play centers: Exploring the "zone" in same-age and multi-age groupings. *Journal of Literacy Research, 31* (2), 109–131.

Coie, J. D., & Dodge, K. A. (1998). Aggression and antisocial behavior. In N. Eisenberg (Ed.), *Handbook of Child Psychology: Social, emotional, and personality development* (pp. 779–862). New York: Wiley.

Darwish, E. (2000). An intentional laboratory: The San Carlos Charter Learning Center. *Teaching and Change, 7,* 258–264.

Davidson, E. S., & Smith, W. P. (1982). Imitation, social comparison, and self-reward. *Child Development, 53,* 928–932.

Derscheid, L. E. (1997). Mixed-age grouped preschoolers' moral behavior and understanding. *Journal of Research in Childhood Education, 11,* 147–151.

Diehl, D. S., Lemerise, E. A., Caverly, S. L., Ramsay, S., & Roberts, J. (1998). Peer relations and school adjustment in ungraded primary children. *Journal of Educational Psychology, 90* (3), 506–515.

Dunn, L., Kontos, S., & Potter, L. (1996). Mixed-age interactions in family child care. *Early Education and Development, 7,* 347–366.

Eisenstadt, S. N. (1956). *From generation to generation: Age groups and social structure.* New York: Free Press.

Ellis, S., Rogoff, B., & Cromer, C. (1981). Age segregation in children's social interactions. *Developmental Psychology, 17,* 399–407.

Espinosa, L. M., & Chen, W. J. (2001). The role of technology in supporting multi-age practices. *Information Technology in Childhood Education Annual,* 5–31.

Feldman, D. H. (1994). *Beyond universals in cognitive development* (2nd ed.) Norwood, NJ: Ablex.

Feldman, D. H. (1998). How spectrum began. In J. Q. Chen, M. Krechevsky, & J. Veins (Eds.), *Building on children's strengths: The experience of project spectrum* (pp. 1–17). New York: Teachers College Press.

Finley, D., Pettinger, A., Rutherford, T., & Timmes, V. (2000). *Developing emotional intelligence in a multiage classroom.* Dissertation, Saint Xavier University & Skylight Professional Development, Chicago, Illinois

Flinn, M. U. (1992). Parental care in a Caribbean village. In B. Hewlett (Ed.), *Father-child relations: Cultural and biosocial contexts* (pp. 57–84). New York: Aldine DeGruyter.

Fowler, R. C., & Corley, K. K. (1996). Linking families, building community. *Educational Leadership, 53,* 24–26.

Freeman, N. K., & King, S. (2001). Service learning in preschool: An intergenerational project involving five-year-olds, fifth-graders, and senior citizens. *Early Childhood Education Journal, 28,* 211–217.

French, D. C. (1984). Children's knowledge of the social functions of younger, older, and same age peers. *Child Development, 55,* 1429–1433.

French, D. C., Waas, G. A., Straight, A. L., & Baker, J. A. (1986). Leadership asymmetries in mixed-age children's groups. *Child Development, 57,* 1277–1283.

Friend, M., & Bursuck, W. D. (1999). *Including students with special needs: A practical guide for classroom teachers* (2nd ed.). Boston: Allyn & Bacon.

Fu, D., Hartle, L., Lamme, L. L., Copenhaver, J., Adams, D., Harmon, C., & Reneke, S. (1999). A comfortable start for everyone: The first week of school in three multi-age (K-2) classrooms. *Early Childhood Education Journal, 27* (2), 73–80.

Furman, W., Rahe, D. F., & Hartup, W. W. (1979). Rehabilitation of socially withdrawn preschool children through mixed-age and same-age socialization. *Child Development, 50*, 915–922.

Gardner, H. (1987). Beyond the IQ: Education and human development. *Harvard Educational Review, 57*, 187–193.

Gaustad, J. (1996). Implementing multiage education. *Research Roundup, 13,* 1–4.

Gnadinger, C., McIntyre, E., Chitwood-Smith, T., & Kyle, D. (2000). *2000 review of research on the Kentucky Education Reform Act: Primary Program.* Frankfort: Kentucky Institute for Education Research.

Goldman, J. (1981). The social participation of preschool children in same-age versus mixed-age groupings. *Child Development, 52*, 644–650.

Goodenough, F. L. (1930). Interrelationships in the behavior of young children. *Child Development, 1,* 29–47.

Grant, J., & Richardson, I. (1999). When your students need one more year. *High School Magazine, 7* (4), 8–13.

Graziano, W., French, D., Brownell, C. A., & Hartup, W. W. (1976). Peer interactions in same-age versus mixed-age groupings in relation to chronological age and incentive condition. *Child Development, 47*, 707–714.

Graziano, W. G., Musser, L. M., & Moore, J. S. (1984). *Developmental and situational influences on the processes of peer imitation.* Unpublished manuscript, University of Georgia, Athens.

Hartup, W. W. (1983). Peer relations. In P. H. Mussen (Ed.), *Handbook of child psychology* (4th ed., Vol. 4, pp. 103–196). New York: Wiley.

Hartup, W. W. (1992). Social relationships and their developmental significance. *American Psychologist, 44*, 120–126.

Hoffman, J. (2002). Flexible grouping strategies in the multiage classroom. *Theory into Practice, 41*, 47–52.

Hughes, F. P. (1998). *Children, play, & development.* Needham Heights, MA: Allyn & Bacon.

Hurley, E. A., Chamberlain, A., Slavin, R. E., & Madden, N. A. (2001). Effects of Success for All on TAAS reading scores: A Texas statewide evaluation. *Phi Delta Kappan, 82* (10), 750–756.

Jeanroy, D. (1996). The results of multiage grouping: An elementary principal documents the outcomes of meeting students' developmental needs. *The School Administrator, 53*, 18–19.

Jensen, M. S., Johnson, D. W., & Johnson, R. T. (2002). Impact of positive interdependence during electronic quizzes on discourse and achievement. *Journal of Educational Research, 95*, 161–166.

Johnson, D. W., & Johnson, R. T. (1990). Social skills for successful group work. *Educational Leadership, 47*, 29–33.

Johnson, D. W., & Johnson, R. T. (1999). Making cooperative learning work. *Theory into Practice, 38*, 67–73.

Johnson, D. W., & Johnson, R. T. (2001). Peer mediation in an inner-city elementary school. *Urban Education, 36*, 165–178.

Johnson, J., Christie, J., & Wardle, F. (2005). *Play, development and early education.* New York, Longman.

Johnson, J., Christie, J., & Yawkey, T. (1999). *Play and early childhood development.* New York: Longman.

Johnson, J., Koester, L., & Wanska, S. (1984). Preschoolers' social and task-oriented behaviors in multi-age small groups. *Child Study Journal, 14* (3), 237–249.

Kagan, S. (1990). The structural approach to cooperative learning. *Educational Leadership, 47*, 12–15.

Kannapel, P. J., Aagaard, L., Coe, P., & Reeves, C. A. (2000). Implementation of the Kentucky Nongraded Primary Program. *Education Policy Analysis Archives, 8*, 1–34.

Kasten, W. C., & Lolli, E. M. (1998). *Implementing multiage education: A practical guide.* Norwood, MA: Christopher-Gordon Publishers. (ERIC Document Reproduction Service No. ED 416956).

Katz, L. (1995). *The benefits of mixed-age grouping.* Urbana: IL: ERIC Clearinghouse on Elementary and Early Childhood Education. (ERIC Document Reproduction Service No. ED382411).

Katz, L. (1998). *The benefits of the mix* (Report No. PS026946). Illinois: National Center for Research on Teacher Learning. (ERIC Document Reproduction Service No. ED423993).

Katz, L. G., Allison, J., Clark, M., Bergman, R., & Gainer, S. (1998). Multi-age caregiving. Beginnings workshop. *Child Care Information Exchange, 124,* 45–60.

Katz, L. G., Evangelou, D., & Hartman, J. A. (1990). *The case for mixed-age groupings in early education.* Washington, DC: National Association for the Education of Young Children.

Kelly-Vance, L., Caster, A., & Ruane, A. (2000). Nongraded versus graded elementary schools: An analysis of achievement and social skills. *The Alberta Journal of Educational Research, XLVI,* 372–390.

Kentucky Education Association & Appalachia Educational Laboratory. (1991). *Ungraded primary programs: Steps toward developmentally appropriate instruction.* Frankfort, KY and Charleston, WV: Author.

Kim, S. H. (1990). *The effect of cross-age interaction on socially at risk children.* Unpublished doctoral dissertation, University of Illinois, Urbana.

Konner, M. (1975). Relations among infants and juveniles in comparative perspective. In M. Lewis & L. Rosenblum (Eds.), *Friendship and peer relations* (pp. 99–129). New York: Wiley.

Ladson-Billings, C. (2000). Fighting for our lives: Preparing teachers to teach African-American children. *Journal of Teacher Education, 51,* 206–214.

Lamb, M. E., Easterbrooks, A., & Holden, G. (1980). Reinforcements and punishments among preschoolers: Characteristics, effects, and correlates. *Child Development, 51,* 1230–1236.

Lamb, M. E., & Roopnarine, J. L. (1979). Peer influences on sex-role development in preschoolers. *Child Development, 50,* 1219–1222.

Langlois, J. H., & Downs, A. C. (1980). Peer relations as a function of physical attractiveness: The eye of the beholder or behavioral reality? *Child Development, 50,* 409–418.

Lemerise, E. A. (1997). Patterns of peer acceptance, social status, and social reputation in mixed-age preschool and primary classrooms. *Merrill-Palmer Quarterly, 43,* 199–218.

Lemerise, E. A., Harper, B. D., & Howes, H. M. (1998). The transition from kindergarten to ungraded primary: Longitudinal predictions of popularity and social reputation. *Early Education and Development, 9,* 187–201.

Liederman, S. H., & Liederman, G. F. (1974). Affective and cognitive consequences of polymatric infant care in the East African Highlands. In A. D. Pick (Ed.), *Minnesota symposia on child psychology,* (Vol. 8, pp. 81–110). Minneapolis: University of Minnesota Press.

Lilliard, A. (2001). Explaining the connection: Pretend play and theory of mind. In S. Reifel (Ed.), *Theory in context and out: Play and Culture Studies* (Vol. 3., pp. 173–177). Westport, CT: Ablex.

Linton, T. Jr. (1973). The effects of grade displacement between student tutors and students tutored (Doctoral dissertation, University of Cincinnati, 1973). *Dissertation Abstracts International, 33,* 4091A. (University Microfilms No. 72–32034).

Lloyd, L. (1999). Multi-age classes and high ability students. *Review of Educational Research, 69,* 187–212.

Lodish, R. (1992). The pros and cons of mixed-age grouping. *Principal, 71,* 20–22.

Lopez, G. R. (2001). The value of hard work: Lessons of involvement from an (im)migrant household. *Harvard Educational Review, 70,* 417–437.

Lougee, M. G. (1979a). Age relations and young children's social interactions. *Journal of Research and Development in Education, 13,* 32–41.

Lougee, M. G. (1979b). Peer imitation and the influence of age and gender of the model (Doctoral dissertation, University of Minnesota, 1979). *Dissertation Abstracts International, 40,* 897B. (University Microfilms No. 79–18362).

Lougee, M. G., Grueneich, R., & Hartup, W. W. (1977). Social interaction in same- and mixed-age dyads of preschool children. *Child Development, 48,* 1353–1361.

Lund, I. A. (1989). *Features of conflict: Evidence of a developmental trend among same-age and mixed-age mainstreamed preschool playgroups.* Unpublished doctoral dissertation, University of North Carolina, Chapel Hill.

Maccoby, E. E. (1998). *The two sexes: Growing up apart, coming together.* Cambridge, MA: Belknap.

Mackey, B., Johnson, R. J., & Wood, T. (1995). Cognitive and affective outcomes in a multi-age language arts program. *Journal of Research in Childhood Education, 10,* 49–61.

Mason, D. A., & Burns, R. B. (1996). "Simply no worse, and simply no better" may simply be wrong: A critique of Veenman's conclusion about multigrade classes. *Review of Educational Research, 66,* 307–322.

Mason, D. A., & Stimson, J. (1996) Combination and nongraded classes: Definitions and frequency in twelve states. *Elementary School Journal, 96* (4), 439–452.

Matthews, M. W., Monsaas, J. A., & Penick, J. M. (1997). A comparative study of the literacy development of at-risk children in graded versus nongraded classrooms. *Reading Research and Instruction, 36,* 225–239.

McClellan, D. E. (1991). *Children's social behavior as related to participation in mixed-age or same-age groups.* Unpublished doctoral dissertation, University of Illinois, Urbana-Champaign.

McClellan, D. E., & Kinsey, S. J. (1999). Children's social behavior in relation to participation in mixed-age or same-age classrooms. *Early Childhood Research and Practice, 1,* 1–19.

McCloskey, L. A. (1996). Gender and the expression of status in children's mixed-age conversations. *Journal of Applied Developmental Psychology, 17,* 117–133.

McIntyre, E., & Kyle, D. (1997). Primary program. In J. C. Lindle, J. M. Petrosko, & R. S. Pankratz (Eds.), *1996 review of research on the Kentucky Education Reform Act* (pp. 119–142). Frankfort: Kentucky Institute for Education Research.

McWilliam, R. A., & Bailey, D. B. (1995). Effects of class structure and disability on engagement. *Topics in Early Childhood Special Education, 15,* 123–147.

Meade, A., & Dalli, C. (1992). Review of the early childhood sector. *New Zealand Annual Review of Education, 1,* 113–132.

Mischel, W., & Grusec, J. (1966). Determinants of the rehearsal and transmission of neutral and aversive behaviors. *Journal of Personality and Social Psychology, 3,* 197–205.

Mounts, N. S., & Roopnarine, J. L. (1987). Social cognitive play patterns in same-age and mixed-age preschool classrooms. *American Educational Research Journal, 24,* 463–476.

Nason, R. B. (1991). Retaining children: Is it the right decision? *Childhood Education, 67* (5), 300–304.

Novak, M. A. (1979). Social recovery of monkeys isolated from the first years of life: II. Long term assessment. *Developmental Psychology, 15,* 50–61.

Odom, S. L., & Diamond, K. E. (1998a). Inclusion in early childhood settings [Special issue]. *Early Childhood Research Quarterly, 13,* 1–209.

Odom, S. L., & Diamond, K. E. (1998b). Inclusion of young children with special needs in early childhood education: The research base. *Early Childhood Research Quarterly, 13,* 3–26.

O'Donnell, A. M. (1999). Structuring dyadic interaction through scripted cooperation. In A. M. O'Donnell & A. King (Eds.), *Cognitive perspectives on peer learning* (pp. 179–196). Mahwah, NJ: Erlbaum.

Ong, W., Allison, J., & Haladyna, T. M. (2000). Student achievement of 3rd-graders in comparable single-age and multiage classrooms. *Journal of Research in Childhood Education, 14,* 205–215.

Parker, J. G., & Asher, S. R. (1987). Peer relations and later personal adjustment: Are low-accepted children at risk? *Psychological Bulletin, 102,* 357–389.

Parten, M. B. (1933). Social participation among children. *Journal of Abnormal and Social Psychology, 27,* 243–269.

Peifer, M. R. (1972). The effects of varying age–grade status of models on the imitative behavior of six-year-old boys (Doctoral dissertation, University of Delaware, 1972). *Dissertation Abstracts International, 32,* 6216A–6217A. (University Microfilms No. 72-14516).

Piaget, J. (1932). *The origins of intelligence in children.* New York: International Universities Press.

Plastenjak, M. (1993). *Flexible organisation of educational work in kindergarten.* Urbana: IL: ERIC Clearinghouse on Elementary and Early Childhood Education. (ERIC Document Reproduction Service No. ED 368 476).

Pratt, M. W. (1999). The importance of infant/toddler interactions. *Young Children, 54* (4), 26–29.

Richard, R. J., Miller, G. A., & Heffer, R. W. (1995). Developmental trends in the relation between adjustment and academic achievement for elementary school children in mixed-age classrooms. *School Psychology Review, 24,* 258–270.

Robert, M., & Charbonneau, C. (1977). Extinction of liquid conservation by observation: Effects of model's age and presence. *Child Development, 48,* 648–652.

Roberts, J. E., Burchinal, M. R., & Bailey, D. B. (1994). Communication among preschoolers with and without disabilities in same-age and mixed-age classes. *American Journal on Mental Retardation, 99,* 231–249.

Roelofs, E., Raemaekers, J., & Veenman, S. (1989, September 4–7). *Training teachers in complex classroom organizations (mixed-age classes) to improve instruction and classroom management behavior: Effect of a staff development programme.* Paper presented at a meeting of the European Association for Research on Learning and Instruction, Madrid, Spain.

Roopnarine, J. L. (1984). Sex-typed socialization in mixed-age preschool classrooms. *Child Development, 55,* 1078–1084.

Roopnarine, J. L., Ahmeduzzaman, M., Donnely, S., Gill, P., Mennis, A., Arky, L., McLaughlin, M., Dingler, K., & Talukder, E. (1992). Social and cognitive play behaviors and playmate preferences in same-age and mixed-age classrooms. *American Educational Research Journal, 28,* 757–776.

Roopnarine, J. L., Bynoe, P. B., & Singh, R. (in press). Factors tied to the schooling of English-speaking immigrants in the United States. In U. Gielen, & J. L. Roopnarine (Eds.), *Childhood and adolescence across cultures.* (2 Vols.). Westport, CT: Praeger.

Roopnarine, J. L., Church, C. C., & Levy, G. D. (1990). Day care children's play behaviors: Relationship to their mothers' and fathers' assessments of their parenting behaviors, marital stress, and marital companionship. *Early Childhood Research Quarterly, 5,* 335–346.

Roopnarine, J. L., & Johnson, J. E. (1983). Kindergarteners' play with preschool and school-age children within mixed-age classroom. *Elementary School Journal, 83,* 578–586.

Roopnarine, J. L., & Johnson, J. E. (1984). Socialization in mixed-age experimental program. *Developmental Psychology, 20,* 828–832.

Roopnarine, J. L., & Metindogan, A. (in press). Cultural beliefs about childrearing and schooling in immigrant families and "developmentally appropriate practices": Yawning gaps! In O. N. Saracho and B Spodek (Eds.) *Contemporary Perspectives in Early Childhood Education.* Greenwich, CT: Information Age Publishers.

Roopnarine, J. L., Suppal, P., Shin, M., & Donovan, B. (1999). Sociocultural contexts of dramatic play: Implications for early education. In J. Christie & K. Roskos (Eds.), *Literacy and play in the early years: Cognitive, ecological, and sociocultural perspectives.* Mahwah, NJ: Erlbaum.

Rothstein-Fisch, C. R., & Howes, C. (1988). Toddler peer interaction in mixed-age groups. *Journal of Applied Developmental Psychology, 9,* 211–218.

Rubin, K. (1980). Fantasy play: Its role in the development of social skills and social cognition. In K. Rubin (Ed.), *Children's play* (pp. 69–85). San Francisco: Jossey-Bass.

Rubin, K. H., Bukowski, W., & Parker, J. C. (1998). Peer interactions, relationships, and groups. In N. Eisenberg (Ed.), *Handbook of child psychology: Social, emotional, and personality development* (pp. 619–700). New York: Wiley.

Rubin, K. H., Maioni, T. L., & Hornung, M. (1976). Free play behaviors in middle- and lower-class preschoolers: Parten and Piaget revisited. *Child Development, 47,* 414–419.

Sachs, J., & Devin, J. (1976). Young children's use of age-appropriate speech styles in social interaction and role-playing. *Journal of Child Language, 3,* 81–98.

Sapon-Shevin, M. (1999). *Because we can change the world: A practical guide to building cooperative, inclusive classroom communities.* Needham Heights, MA: Allyn & Bacon.

Sapon-Shevin, M. (2000/2001). Schools fit for all. *Educational Leadership, 58,* 34–39.

Shaeffer, M. B., & Hook, J. (1993). Are extra-year classes worth it?: Research and cost analysis say no. *The American School Board Journal, 180,* 31–32.

Shatz, M., & Gelman, R. (1973). The development of communication skills: Modifications in the speech of young children as a function of listener. *Monographs of the Society for Research in Child Development, 38* (5, Serial No. 152).

Slavin, R. E. (1987). Developmental and motivational perspectives on cooperative learning; A reconcilation. *Child Development, 58,* 1161–1167.

Slavin, R. E. (1990). Research on cooperative learning: Consensus and controversy. *Educational Leadership, 47,* 52–55.

Slavin, R. E., & Madden, N. A. (2001). *Success for all and comprehensive school reform: Evidence-based policies for urban education.* Baltimore: Disseminated by the success for All Foundation. (ERIC Document Reproduction Service No. ED 459 301).

Stegelin, D. A. (1997). Outcomes of mixed-age groupings: Research highlights. *Dimensions of Early Childhood, 25,* 22–28.

Straight, A. L., & French, D. C. (1988). Leadership in mixed-age children's groups. *International Journal of Behavioral Development, 11,* 507–515.

Strain, P., Shores, R., & Timm, M. (1977). Effects of peer imitations on the social behavior of withdrawn preschoolers. *Journal of Applied Behavior Analysis, 10,* 289–298.

Sundell, K. (1993). *Mixed age groups in Swedish nursery school and compulsory school.* Paper presented at the European Conference on the Quality of Early Childhood Education, Kriopigi, Greece.

Suomi, S. J., & Harlow, H. F. (1972). Social rehabilitation of isolate-reared monkeys. *Developmental Psychology, 6,* 487–496.

Tanner, C. K., & Decotis, J. D. (1995). The effects of continuous-process nongraded primary school programs on student performance and attitudes toward learning. *Journal of Research and Development in Education, 28,* 135–143.

Theilheimer, R. (1993). Something for everyone: Benefits of mixed-age grouping for children, parents, and teachers. *Young Children, 48,* 5, 82–87.

Thelen, M. H., & Kirkland, K. S. (1976). On status and being imitated: Effects on reciprocal imitation and attraction. *Journal of Personality and Social Psychology, 33,* 691–697.

Thomas, J. L. (1972). Tutoring strategies and effectiveness: A comparison of elementary age tutors and college age tutors (Doctoral dissertation, University of Texas, 1972). *Dissertation Abstracts International, 32,* 3580A. (University Microfilms No. 72–2425).

Tieszen, H. R., & Lee, Y. (1993). The Yonsei preschool open education program. *Early Child Development and Care, 85,* 47–54.

Tudge, J. (1986). *Beyond conflict: The role of reasoning in collaborative problem solving.* Paper presented at the Piaget conference, Philadelphia. (ERIC Document Reproduction Service No. ED 275 395).

Tudge, J. (1992). Processes and consequences of peer collaboration: A Vygotskian analysis. *Child Development, 63,* 1364–1379.

Tudge J., & Hogan D. (1999). *Collaboration from a Vygotskian perspective.* Greensboro, NC.

Tyack, D., & Tobin, W. (1994). The "grammar" of schooling: Why has it been so hard to change? *American Educational Research Journal, 31* (3), 453–479.

Umbek, L. M., & Musek, P. L. (1997). Symbolic play in mixed-age and same-age groups. *European Early Childhood Education Research Journal, 5,* 47–59.

Urberg, K., & Kaplan, M. (1986). Effects of classroom age composition on the play and social behavior of preschool children. *Journal of Applied Developmental Psychology, 7,* 403–415.

U.S. Department of Education. (2002). *No child left behind.* Washington, DC.: U.S. Government Printing Office.

Veenman, S. (1995). Cognitive and noncognitive effects of multigrade and multi-age classes: A best-evidence synthesis. *Review of Educational Research, 65,* 319–381.

Veenman, S. (1996). Effects of multigrade and multi-age classes reconsidered. *Review of Educational Research, 66,* 323–340.

Walther-Thomas, C., Korineck, L., McLaughlin, V. L., & Williams, B. T. (2000). *Collaboration for inclusive education: Developing successful programs.* Boston, MA: Allyn & Bacon.

Weisner, T. S., & Gallimore, R. (1977). My brother's keeper: Child and sibling caretaking. *Current Anthropology, 18,* 169–190.

Wertsch, J. V. (1985). *Culture, communication, and cognition: Vygotskian perspectives.* Cambridge, England: Cambridge University Press.

Whaley, K. L., & Kantor, R. (1992). Mixed-age grouping in infant/toddler child care: Enhancing developmental processes. *Child and Youth Care Forum, 21,* 369–384.

Whiting, B. B., & Whiting, J. M. W. (1975). *Children of six cultures.* Cambridge, MA: Harvard University Press.

Williams, P. (2001). Children's ways of experiencing peer interactions. *Early Child Development and Care, 168,* 17–38.

Winsler, A., & Diaz, R. D. (1995). Private speech in the classroom: The effects of activity type, presence of others, classroom context, and mixed-age grouping. *International Journal of Behavioral Development, 18,* 463–487.

Winsler, A., Caverly, S., Willson-Quayle, A., Carlton, M. P., Howell, C., & Long, G. N. (2002). The social and behavioral ecology of mixed-age and same-age preschool classrooms: A natural experiment. *Journal of Applied Developmental Psychology, 23,* 305–330.

Part 4

Specific Approaches/USA

Chapter 10

The High/Scope Curriculum for Early Childhood Care and Education

David P. Weikart (deceased) and Lawrence J. Schweinhart ⌁ High/Scope Educational Research Foundation, Ypsilanti, Michigan

The High/Scope curriculum provides teachers with an open framework of educational ideas and practices based on the natural development of young children. The approach was created by David P. Weikart and his colleagues in the 1960s for use in the High/Scope Perry Preschool program (Weikart, Rogers, Adcock, & McClelland, 1971). The High/Scope Educational Research Foundation continues to develop the High/Scope curriculum, including within it art, music, movement, and computer usage, and to help people apply the curriculum to new circumstances and new populations of children around the world (Hohmann, 1997, 2002; Hohmann, Banet, & Weikart, 1979; Hohmann & Weikart, 1995, 2002). Thousands of early childhood programs throughout the United States and in other countries now use the High/Scope curriculum (Epstein, 1993).

Based on the child development theories of Jean Piaget (Piaget & Inhelder, 1969), the High/Scope curriculum views children as *active learners,* who learn best from activities that they themselves plan, carry out, and reflect on. Adults use complex language as they observe, support, and extend the work of the child as appropriate. Adults arrange interest areas in the learning environment; maintain a daily routine that permits children to plan, carry out, and reflect on their own activities; and join in children's activi-

ties, engaging in conversations that extend children's plans and help them think things through. The adults encourage children to engage in key experiences and help them learn to make choices, solve problems, and otherwise engage in activities that contribute to their intellectual, social, and physical development.

Unlike many other curriculum models, such as the materials required for a Montessori classroom or teacher and student workbooks for academic instructional classroom, the High/Scope curriculum does not require the purchase and use of special materials; the only cost involved is that of equipping the learning environment as would be typical of most good nursery school programs. In less-developed countries or other settings with limited resources, material from nature, household discards, and other found materials are employed. Although often challenging for adults to learn initially, the methods implementing the curriculum, once mastered, free staff for comfortable work with children, other classroom adults, parents, and supervisors. Rooted firmly in developmental theory and historical early childhood practice, the High/Scope curriculum is an organized and transferable expression of what has worked well with children in many programs over the years. The curriculum is an example of developmentally appropriate practice as commonly defined today by the early childhood field, and it has been validated through longitudinal studies over 30 years (Berrueta-Clement, Schweinhart, Barnett, Epstein, & Weikart, 1984; Oden, Schweinhart, & Weikart, 2000; Schweinhart, Barnes, & Weikart, 1993; Schweinhart & Weikart, 1997). Perhaps more important, it lends itself to training, supervision, and implementation assessment so that parents and administrators can rest assured that their children are receiving a high-quality, validated program. Delivery of high-quality programs is the most important task the early childhood field faces, as program ideas move from research laboratories and demonstration schools into large-scale service to children, their families, and society at large.

✍ HISTORY

The High/Scope curriculum's development began in 1962 under the leadership of David P. Weikart with the High/Scope Perry Preschool program, a program for 3- and 4-year-olds operated at the Perry Elementary School in Ypsilanti, Michigan. This program was one of the first in the 1960s designed to help children resist the negative effects of poverty on schooling, an idea later embodied in Head Start programs. It was also one of the first to achieve an exacting experimental design—children were randomly assigned to attend or not—permitting researchers to trace the program's effects throughout the subsequent lives of participants. This study showed that the preschool program had a striking variety of short- and long-term benefits for participants, such as better preparation for school, less failure throughout schooling, lower arrest rate as young adults, a higher employment rate, and a lower welfare rate. The program was found to pay for itself many times over in economic returns to taxpayers with $7.16 returned for every $1 spent (Barnett, 1996).

In the late 1950s, Ypsilanti Public Schools Special Education Director David Weikart was concerned that easily identifiable children were failing in school—repeating grade levels, being placed in special education, and dropping out of school. Seeking changes in the schools to address these problems, he was frustrated that school administrators had few realistic alternatives. He developed one idea that seemed useful. He turned to the preschool years as a way of reaching children before they fell into the traditional school patterns that spawned their failure.

Staffed by both research psychologists and teachers, the preschool program established a creative tension between the psychologist's demand for explicit rationale and the trained preschool teacher's more intuitive approach to dealing with children. The High/Scope curriculum evolved from give and take among a team of people who had definite ideas about how to do things, but were open to new ideas and could integrate them into their thinking and practice.

As the High/Scope Perry Preschool program entered its second year, the staff encountered and embraced the child development ideas of Jean Piaget (Piaget & Inhelder, 1969). Piaget offered a conceptual structure around which a preschool curriculum model could be built, an explicit rationale for the preschool activities. Piaget offers the idea of the child as an active learner, an idea not only with intuitive appeal but also with strong roots in early childhood tradition dating back at

Both children and teachers are active learners.

least to Friedrich Froebel (1887) in the first half of the nineteenth century.

As the High/Scope curriculum developed, the national enthusiasm for early childhood curriculum models also emerged. The federal government nurtured this enthusiasm by taking an active interest in early childhood education as a means of helping poor children avoid school failure and its tragic consequences. President Lyndon Johnson's War on Poverty and the Economic Opportunity Act of 1964 initiated the federal role in early childhood education through the National Head Start project. Subsequently, even as Head Start grew steadily as a service program, it consistently invested a small fraction of dollars in curriculum experimentation and scientific study.

Several projects permitted the High/Scope Foundation to develop the High/Scope curriculum further and extend it into the elementary school years. In 1968 the federal government initiated the Follow Through project to provide enrichment to children in the primary grades who had attended Head Start (Weikart, Hohmann, & Rhine, 1981). The Follow Through project was perhaps the largest funded effort ever offered for the development of early childhood curriculum models. The Planned Variation Head Start project also used the multiple curriculum model approach from 1969 to 1973 (Smith, 1973).

In the late 1970s, federal assistance permitted the High/Scope Foundation to develop and adapt its curriculum model to children with special needs and children from Spanish-speaking families (Hanes, Flores, Rosario, Weikart, & Sanchez, 1979). High/Scope also actively applies the curriculum model in other countries throughout the world. As of 2003, licensed national High/Scope training centers were in operation in Canada, Great Britain, Indonesia, Ireland (a cross-borders institute), Mexico, Singapore, and The Netherlands. Centers are under development in Chile, South Africa, Taiwan, and Turkey. The basic textbooks and/or assessment instruments are translated into Arabic, Chinese,

Dutch, Finnish, French, Korean, Norwegian, Portuguese, Spanish, and Turkish. The institutes are coordinated by the High/Scope International Council, made up of all the directors of official centers. This diverse work helps mold a curriculum model that is essentially democratic in operation, adaptable to local culture and language, and open to use by thoughtful adults everywhere.

ACTIVE LEARNING BY THE CHILD

Adults who use the High/Scope curriculum must be fully committed to providing settings in which children learn actively and construct their own knowledge. The child's knowledge comes from personal interaction with ideas, direct experience with physical objects and events, and application of logical thinking to these experiences. The adult's role is to supply the context for these experiences, to help the child think about them logically, and, through observation, to understand the progress the child is making. From an adult view, children are expected to learn by the scientific method of hypothesis generation, experimentation, and inference at a level of sophistication consonant with their development.

ROLE OF THE TEACHER

Even as children are active learners in the High/Scope curriculum, so, too, are the teachers. By daily evaluation and planning using the High/Scope key experiences as a framework, teachers study their experience with children and classroom activities and strive to achieve new insights into each child's unique tapestry of skills and interests. Teaching teams challenge themselves by observing one another's performance and interacting with one another in mutually supportive ways.

An important aspect of the High/Scope curriculum is the role of the teacher in interacting with the child. Although broad developmental milestones are employed to monitor the youngster's progress, the teacher does not have a precise script for teaching the child. Instead, the adult listens closely to what children plan and then actively works with them to extend their activities to more challenging levels as appropriate. Adult questioning style is important. The adult emphasizes questions that seek information from the youngster that will help the adult participate. Test questions such as those about color, number, or size are rarely used. Instead, the adult asks, "What happened?" "How did you make that?" "Can you show me?" "Can you help (another child)?" and so on. Conversation is stressed. The teacher is a participant rather than an imparter of knowledge. "Did you see that butterfly?" "May I touch the pizza, or is it too hot?" This questioning and conversation style permits free interaction between adult and child and models language for child-to-child interaction. This approach permits the teacher and the child to interact as thinkers and doers rather than in the traditional school roles of active teacher and passive pupil. All are sharing and learning as they work.

✍ DAILY ROUTINE TO SUPPORT ACTIVE LEARNING

To create a setting in which children learn actively, a consistent daily classroom routine is maintained that varies only when children have fair warning that things will be different the next day. Field trips are not surprises, and special visits or events are not introduced to the classroom on the spur of the moment. This adherence to routine gives children the security and control necessary to develop a sense of responsibility and to enjoy the opportunity to be independent.

The High/Scope curriculum's daily routine is made up of a *plan-do-review* sequence and several additional elements. The plan-do-review sequence is the central device in the curriculum that permits children opportunities to express intentions about their activities while keeping the teacher intimately involved in the whole process. The following paragraphs describe the elements in the daily routine.

Planning Time: Stating an Intention

Children make choices and decisions all the time, but most programs seldom have them think about these decisions in a systematic way or help them realize the possibilities and consequences of their choices. Planning time gives children a consistent, predictable opportunity to express their ideas and intentions to adults and to see themselves as individuals who act on decisions. They experience the power of independence and the joy of working with an attentive adult as well as with peers. They can carry out their intentions.

The teacher talks over the plans with the children before they carry them out. This helps children form mental pictures of their ideas and get a notion of how to proceed. For adults, developing a plan with the children provides an opportunity to encourage and respond to the children's ideas, to suggest practical ways to strengthen the plans so they will be successful, and to understand and gauge the children's levels of development and thinking styles. But the teacher accepts the plans and their limits as determined by the children. Both children and adults receive benefits: children feel reinforced and ready to start their plans, while adults have ideas as to what to look for, what difficulties children might have, where help may be needed, and what levels of development children have achieved. In such a classroom, all are playing appropriate roles of equal importance.

Work Time: Executing the Intention

The "do" part of the plan-do-review cycle is work time, the period after children have finished planning. Generally the longest time period in the daily routine, it is an active period of play for both children and adults. Adults new to the High/Scope curriculum sometimes find work time confusing because they are not sure of their role. Adults do not lead work-time activities—children execute their own plans of work—but neither do adults just sit back and passively watch. The adult's role during work time is to first observe children to see how they gather information, interact with peers, and solve problems, and then to enter into the children's activities to encourage, extend, set up problem-solving situations, and engage in conversation. Because the children are working in many different areas, the adult is limited in the amount of time it is possible to engage with any specific child or group.

Cleanup Time

Cleanup time is naturally integrated into the plan-do-review cycle in the obvious place, after the doing. During this time, children return materials and equipment to their labeled place and store the incomplete projects. This process restores order to the classroom and provides opportunities for the children to learn and use many basic cognitive skills. Of special importance is how the learning environment is organized to facilitate children's use of materials. All materials in the classroom available for children's use are on open shelves within reach. Clear labeling is essential, usually with a direct representation of the objects on the shelves. With this organizational plan, children can realistically return all work materials to their appropriate places. It also gives them a sense of confidence in their initiative by knowing where everything they need is located.

Recall Time: Reflecting on Accomplishments

Recall time is the final phase of the plan-do-review sequence. It is the time when the children reflect on what they have accomplished or experienced. The children represent their work-time experience in a variety of developmentally appropriate ways. They might recall the names of the children they involved in their plan, dictate a story of their activity, or recount the problems they encountered. Recall strategies include drawing pictures of what they did, making models, reviewing their plans, or verbally recalling the past events. Recall time brings closure to their planning and work-time activities; it provides them opportunities to express insights on what they have experienced and thought about. It provides opportunity to use language and illustrations to inform others. The teacher supports the linkage of the actual work to the original plan. The use of complex language to discuss, describe, and predict outcomes are key in this support process by the teacher.

Small-Group Time

The formal setting of small-group time is familiar to all preschool teachers: The teacher creates an activity in which children participate for a set period. These activities are drawn from the children's cultural backgrounds, from field trips the group has taken, from new materials available in the classroom, from the seasons of the year, and from age-appropriate group activities such as cooking and group art projects. Although teachers offer structure for the activities, children are encouraged to contribute ideas and solve problems presented by the activities in their own ways. Activities follow no prescribed sequence but respond to the children's needs, abilities, interests, and cognitive levels. Once each child has had the opportunity for individual choice and problem solving, the teacher extends the child's ideas and actions by engaging in conversation, asking open-ended questions, and supporting additional problem-solving situations. In planning and implementing small-group time, active involvement by all children is important. Children move physically, use objects and materials,

During small-group activities, children explore materials and objects, make choices, and solve problems.

make choices, and solve problems. An active small-group time gives children the chance to explore materials and objects, use their bodies and their senses, and work with adults and other children.

Large-Group Time

At large-group time, the whole group meets together with an adult to play games, sing songs, do finger plays, perform basic movement activities, play musical instruments, or reenact a special event. This time provides an opportunity for each child to participate in a large group, share and demonstrate ideas, and imitate the ideas of others. Although the adult may initiate the activity, children provide some leadership and make as many individual choices as possible. Large-group time is especially important as an opportunity to support the development of a steady beat through patting the floor or their bodies, marching, rocking, and moving to high-quality instrumental music. (See *Rhythmically*

Moving Series, Recordings 1–9, P. S. Weikart, 2nd ed., 2003.)

 KEY EXPERIENCES IN CHILD DEVELOPMENT

Child progress in the High/Scope curriculum is organized around a set of key experiences developed from research findings and development theory. Although the plan-do-review sequence conducted within a consistent daily routine is the hallmark of the High/Scope curriculum for the child, these key experiences are the central feature for the teacher. Key experiences are a way of helping the teacher understand, support, and extend the child's self-designed activity so that developmentally appropriate experiences and growth are constantly available to the child. These experiences guide the teacher in planning small- and large-group activities. They provide a way of thinking about curriculum that frees the teacher from the workbook of activities that characterize some early childhood programs or the scope-and-sequence charts that dominate the behavioral approaches. They form the basis of the framework an adult uses to plan for and observe each child.

The key experiences are important to the growth of rational thought in children the world over, regardless of nation or culture. They are also very simple and pragmatic. Preschool key experiences have been identified in the following:

- Creative representation
- Language and literacy
- Initiative and social relations
- Movement
- Music
- Classification
- Seriation
- Number
- Space
- Time

Each of these categories is divided into specific types of experiences. For example, the key experiences in creative representation are:

- Recognize objects by sight, sound, touch, taste, and smell
- Imitate actions and sounds
- Relate models, pictures, and photographs to real places and things
- Pretend and role play
- Make models out of clay, blocks, and other materials
- Draw and paint

And the key experiences in movement are:

- Act on movement directions
- Describe movement
- Move the body in nonlocomotor ways
- Move the body in locomotor ways
- Move with objects
- Express creativity in movement
- Feel and express steady beat
- Move in sequences to a common beat

Classroom learning experiences are not mutually exclusive, and any given activity will involve several types of key experiences. This approach gives the adult a clear tool to think about the program and observe the youngsters. In addition, the key-experience approach provides a way to give the curriculum a structure while maintaining its openness to child-generated experiences. Thus, as High/Scope staff develop the new curriculum areas such as art, movement, music, computer usage, and drama, we have a vehicle for outlining the research findings into additional experiences to be included. The key experiences provide a device that enables the High/Scope curriculum to continue to evolve as a forceful tool in promoting children's healthy growth and development.

✍ HIGH/SCOPE CHILD OBSERVATION RECORD

The High/Scope Child Observation Record (COR, 2nd ed. High/Scope Educational Research Foundation, 2003) measures the developmental status of young children 3 to 5 years old as affected by early childhood education. Originally developed to assess the outcomes of the High/Scope curriculum, the COR was later expanded for use in all early childhood programs that engage in developmentally appropriate practice, whether they use the High/Scope curriculum or not. For example, in 1998 the British Government Ministry of Education and Employment accepted the High/Scope COR, with several additions, for use in British schools to assess student progress under their new national standards.

To use the High/Scope COR, the teacher writes brief notes over several months describing episodes of young children's behavior in six domains of development: (1) initiative, (2) social relations, (3) creative representation, (4) music and movement, (5) language and literacy, and (6) logic and mathematics. The teacher then uses these notes to classify the child's behavior on 30 five-level COR items in these domains. For example, the item on Expressing Choices has the following five levels, from lowest to highest:

1. Child does not yet express to others.
2. Child indicates a desired activity or place of activity by pointing or saying a word.
3. Child indicates a desired activity, place of activity, materials, or playmates with a short sentence.
4. Child indicates with a short sentence how plans will be carried out ("I want to drive the truck on the road").
5. Child presents detailed descriptions of intended actions ("I want to make a road out of blocks with Sara and drive the truck on it").

The High/Scope COR demonstrated its feasibility, reliability, and validity in a study involving 64 teams of Head Start teachers and assistant teachers in southeastern Michigan (Schweinhart, McNair, Barnes, & Larner, 1993). The COR's feasibility was demonstrated in a project that offered 3 days of training and involved a high level of quality control. Teacher-scored COR subscales demonstrated acceptable levels of internal consistency and correlation with subscales on the same children scored by assistant teachers. The concurrent validity of teacher-scored COR subscales was demonstrated by modest correlations with children's ages; zero-order correlations with mothers' years of schooling; and moderate correlations with similar subscales on the McCarthy Scales of Children's Abilities (McCarthy, 1972).

✍ ROLE OF PARENTS AND COMMUNITY

From the outset of development of the High/Scope curriculum, parent participation has been one of its hallmarks. In the initial period during the 1960s, teachers made home visits each week to each participating family, with the focus usually on the mother and participating child. Reflecting the movement of women into the work-force, parent participation now is more focused on group meetings and other means of contact.

The key to effective parent involvement is the dual nature of information flow. Although the school and its staff have knowledge and training to provide to the family, the staff must also be trained by the parents concerning the child, the family's culture, and their language and goals. The belief that parents and staff are both experts in their own domains is essential to the success of the program and its use in various settings.

✍ HIGH/SCOPE CURRICULUM TRAINING

Effective training in the High/Scope curriculum has several key elements. Training has to be on site and curriculum focused. It must be adapted to the actual work setting of the teacher, physically and socially, adapted to the group for children involved (e.g., children with disabilities or who are bilingual), related to the culture of the children, and enable parent involvement in some systematic way. Training sessions should be scheduled about once a month because teachers need time to study training materials, think about the training experience, put new ideas into practice, see the gaps in their own thinking and in the program being presented, and make adaptations to their own setting. Consistent delivery to the individual teacher must be maintained by observations and feedback.

Nearly 2,000 early childhood leaders in the United States and other countries have successfully completed High/Scope's 7-week Training of Trainers program and are training teachers in the High/Scope curriculum. In 1993 an estimated 29% of all Head Start staff, for example, had received some High/Scope curriculum training from these trainers (Epstein, 1993; Larner & Schweinhart, 1991).

Throughout this presentation of the High/Scope curriculum, we have indicated its flexibility in various ways. It is open to all who understand its developmental principles. Perhaps the High/

Scope approach is not so much a curriculum as a methodological framework for education. The teachers and parents employing the framework arrange the context of the program; the child actually provides the content. Thus, the program grows from the users rather than from the developers. This fact gives it extraordinary flexibility and usefulness as an effective framework for adults.

✒ RESEARCH SUPPORT FOR THE HIGH/SCOPE CURRICULUM

Weikart and his staff of the High/Scope Perry Preschool program in the Ypsilanti Public Schools first developed and used the High/Scope curriculum to assist disadvantaged children. By virtue of its experimental design (random assignment) and long-term duration (since 1962), the evaluation of the High/Scope Perry Preschool program is one of the most thorough examinations

of program effects ever undertaken. The basic evaluation question is whether the High/Scope Perry Preschool program using the High/Scope curriculum affected the lives of participating children. The study focused on 123 African American children born in poverty and at high risk of failing in school. In the early 1960s, at ages 3 and 4, these children were randomly divided into a program group who received a high-quality preschool program and a no-program group who received no preschool program. The two groups have been carefully studied over the years. At age 27, 95% of the original study participants were interviewed, with additional data gathered from their school, social services, and arrest records (Schweinhart, Barnes, & Weikart, 1993). Postpreschool program differences between the groups represent preschool program effects (see Figure 10–1). Findings were statistically significant (with a two-tailed probability of less than .05). The U.S. Department of Health and Human

FIGURE 10–1 High/Scope Perry Study Findings at Age 27

Source: From *Significant Benefits: The High/Scope Perry Preschool Study through Age 27* (p. 190), by L. J. Schweinhart, H. V. Barnes, & D. P. Weikart, with W. S. Barnett & A. S. Epstein, 1993, Ypsilanti, MI: High/Scope Press. Copyright 1993 by High/Scope Educational Research Foundation. Adapted with permission.

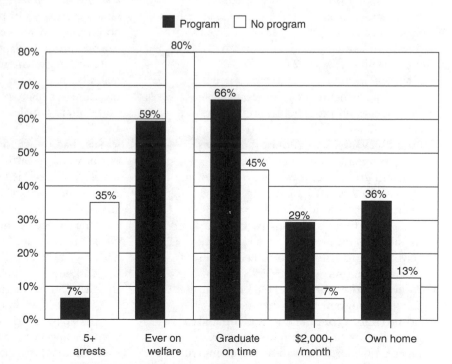

FIGURE 10–2
High/Scope Perry Study
Return on Investment
Source: From *Significant Benefits: The High/Scope Perry Preschool Study through Age 27* (p. 168), by L. J. Schweinhart, H. V. Barnes, & D. P. Weikart, with W. S. Barnett & A. S. Epstein, 1993, Ypsilanti, MI: High/Scope Press. Copyright 1993 by High/Scope Educational Research Foundation. Adapted with permission.

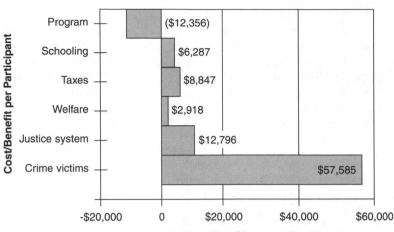

Services and the Ford Foundation funded the age-27 phase of the study. The basic outcomes included findings in the following areas:

- *Social responsibility:* By age 27, only one fifth as many program group members as no-program group members were arrested 5 or more times (7% vs. 35%), and only one third as many were ever arrested for drug dealing (7% vs. 25%).
- *Earnings and economic status:* At age 27, four times as many program group members as no-program group members earned $2,000 (1992 dollars) or more per month (29% vs. 7%). Almost three times as many program group members as no-program group members owned their own homes (36% vs. 13%); and over twice as many owned second cars (30% vs. 13%). Only three fourths as many program group members as no-program group members received welfare assistance or other social services at some time as adults (59% vs. 80%).
- *Educational performance:* One third again as many program group members as no-program group members graduated from regular or adult high school or received General Education Development

certification (71% vs. 54%). Earlier in the study, the program group had significantly higher average achievement scores at age 14 years and literacy scores at age 19 years than had the no-program group.
- *Commitment to marriage:* Although the same percentages of program males and no-program males were married (26%), the married program males were married nearly twice as long as the married no-program males (averages of 6.2 years vs. 3.3 years). Five times as many program females as no-program females were married at the age-27 interview (40% vs. 8%). Program females had only about two thirds as many out-of-wedlock births as did no-program females (57% of births vs. 83% of births).
- *Return on investment:* A benefit–cost analysis was conducted by estimating the monetary value of the program and its effects, in constant 1992 dollars discounted annually at 3% (see Figure 10–2). Dividing the $88,433 in benefits per participant by the $12,356 in cost per participant results in a benefit–cost ratio of $7.16 returned to the public for every dollar invested in the High/Scope Perry program, substantially exceeding earlier estimates. The program

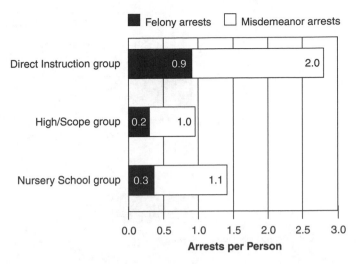

FIGURE 10–3 Curriculum Study Adult Arrests by age 23
Source: From *Lasting Differences* (p. 53), by L. J. Schweinhart & D. P. Weikart, 1997, Ypsilanti, MI: High/Scope Press. Copyright 1997 by High/Scope Educational Research Foundation. Adapted with permission.

was an extremely good economic investment, better than most other public and private uses of society's resources (Barnett, 1996). By increasing the number of children per adult from five to eight, the program's cost per child per year could be reduced to $5,500 with virtually no loss in quality or benefits. This increase in numbers per teachers was implemented in the next High/Scope study.

In 1967, a second longitudinal study, the High/Scope Preschool Curriculum Comparison Study (Schweinhart & Weikart, 1997), was undertaken to explore possible effects of early education programs based on several major theoretical approaches. The question was whether the High/Scope curriculum success was unique, or would any early education program be equally effective when applied with high standards?

Conducted by the High/Scope Educational Research Foundation since 1967, the High/Scope Preschool Curriculum Comparison Study has followed the lives of 68 young people born in poverty who were randomly assigned at ages 3 and 4 to one of three groups, each experiencing a different curriculum model:

• In the Direct Instruction model, teachers initiated drill and practice activities,

following a script with academic objectives, and rewarded children for responding correctly and following the teacher direction.

• In the High/Scope model, teachers and children both initiated actions. Teachers arranged the classroom and the daily routine so children could plan, do, and review their own activities and engage in key learning experiences as described in this chapter.

• In the traditional Nursery School model, teachers responded to children's self-initiated play and introduced projects in a loosely structured, socially supportive setting. Program staff implemented the curriculum models independently and to high standards, in $2\frac{1}{2}$-hour classes held 5 days a week and $1\frac{1}{2}$-hour home visits every 2 weeks, when children were 3 and 4 years old.

Except for the curriculum model, all aspects of the programs were essentially identical. The three groups did not differ significantly on most background characteristics. The findings presented here are corrected for differences in the gender makeup of the groups (see Figure 10–3 and 10–4).

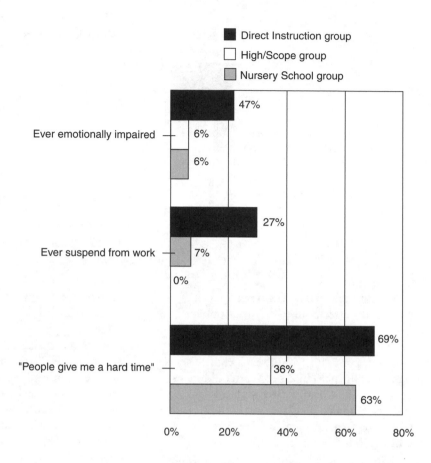

FIGURE 10–4   Other Curriculum Effects through age 23

Source: From *Lasting Differences* (pp. 40, 48, and 51), by L. J. Schweinhart & D. P. Weikart, 1997, Ypsilanti, MI: High/Scope Press. Copyright 1997 by High/Scope Educational Research Foundation. Adapted with permission.

By age 23 years, the High/Scope group had eight significant advantages over the Direct Instruction group:

- Fewer felony arrests
- Fewer arrests for property crimes
- Fewer years in needed treatment for emotional impairment or disturbance
- Fewer reporting that other people give them a hard time
- Less teen misconduct
- A higher percentage living with a spouse
- More who ever did volunteer work
- More who plan to graduate from college

By age 23 years, the Nursery School group had four significant advantages over the Direct Instruction group:

- Fewer felony arrests at age 22 and over
- Fewer years in needed treatment for emotional impairment or disturbance
- More who did volunteer work
- The only one not in common with the High/Scope curriculum group, fewer suspensions from work

By age 23, the Direct Instruction group had no significant advantage on any outcome variable.

By age 23, the High/Scope group and the Nursery School group did not differ significantly on any outcome variable.

Through age 10, the main finding of this study was that the overall average IQ of the three groups rose 27 points from a borderline impairment level of 78 to a normal level of 105 after 1 year of their preschool program and subsequently settled in at an average of 95, still at the normal level. By age 15 in spite of 2 years of academic training for the Direct Instruction group, throughout their school years, curriculum groups did not differ significantly in school achievement. The conclusion at that time was that well-implemented preschool curriculum models, regardless of their theoretical orientation, had similar effects on children's intellectual and academic performance. Time has proved otherwise.

The research supports the conclusion that, by age 23, scripted, teacher-directed instruction, touted by some as the surest path to school success, seems to purchase a modest improvement in academic performance at the cost of a missed opportunity for long-term improvement in social behavior. Child-initiated learning activities, on the other hand, seem to help children develop their social responsibility and skills so that they less often need treatment for emotional impairment or disturbance and are less often arrested for felonies as young adults.

While the High/Scope curriculum and Nursery School curriculum groups did not differ significantly on any outcome variable at age 23, the High/Scope approach is easier to replicate than the Nursery School approach because of its extensive documentation of actual practice, validated teacher training program, and well-developed program and child assessment systems. The Nursery School approach used in this study was the unique product of two teachers trained in a general child development approach. For this reason, it is unclear whether the results of this study apply to children who experience other versions of the Nursery School approach developed by their own teachers.

These findings constitute evidence that early childhood education works better to prevent problems when it focuses not on scripted, teacher-directed academic instruction but, rather, on child-initiated learning activities. Because bi-weekly home visits were part of each program, it seems that home visits by themselves do not account for these differences. These findings suggest that the goals of early childhood education should not be limited to academic preparation for school but should also include helping children learn to make decisions, solve problems, and get along with others—*the precise goals of the High/Scope curriculum.*

Implications

The High/Scope Perry Preschool Study (Schweinhart et al., 1993) and the High/Scope Curriculum Comparison Study (Schweinhart & Weikart, 1997) suggest that the High/Scope early childhood curriculum has significant, lasting benefits because it:

- Empowers children by enabling them to initiate and carry out their own learning activities and make independent decisions
- Empowers parents by involving them in ongoing relationships as full partners with teachers in supporting their children's development
- Empowers teachers by providing them with an effective curriculum, systematic inservice curriculum training with supportive curriculum supervision, and observational tools to assess children's development

Combined with similar findings from other studies (Marcon, 1992; Nabuco & Sylva, 1997), these High/Scope data have wide-ranging implications. They indicate that high-quality preschool programs for children living in poverty can have a positive long-term effect on their lives. Their early educational success leads to later school success, higher employment rates, and fewer social problems such as crime and welfare dependence. Early childhood education can help individuals realize their potential. But the findings show more than good outcomes for individuals. They also indicate that citizens can expect substantial improvement in the quality of community life. An effective program can help reduce street crime and bring welfare dependency down to a more manageable level.

Further, an important improvement can be made in the available workforce because of better educational attainment and improved job-holding ability. However, such outcomes are not the results of all programs. Especially suspect are the outcomes for teacher-scripted programs.

RELATIONSHIP OF RESEARCH TO THE HIGH/SCOPE CURRICULUM

The High/Scope curriculum defined the essential program elements in the day-to-day experience of children and teacher that were largely responsible for the program effects, that is, plan-do-review and key experiences as a basis of planning and observation. Also among the key program elements were staffing, staff planning and development, class sessions, and a high level of parent involvement. The staff/child ratio was 1:5, with 4 teachers for 20 to 25 children in the High/Scope Perry Preschool program; and 1:8, with 2 teachers and 16 children in the High/ Scope Curriculum Comparison study. The teaching staff worked together in teams that planned, implemented, and evaluated each day's activities. Indeed, working in tandem with researchers and consultants, they developed and refined the High/Scope Preschool Curriculum. The preschool program had two components—daily 2½-hour classroom sessions and weekly 1½-hour home visits by the teacher to each mother and child. These program elements can be applied with some flexibility. Staffing could safely go as high as 20 children in a class with 2 trained adults. Teachers need to develop intellectual ownership of the curriculum, preferably through daily planning, evaluation, and teamwork, and with the active support of the administration, the provision of inservice curriculum training opportunities. Contrary to general opinion, home visits are not a prerequisite for program effectiveness, as witnessed by the data from the Direct Instruction group (Schweinhart & Weikart, 1997). Parents and teachers do need to work together as real partners in the education of children, which means regular, substantive communication concerning the developmental status of the child. In short, the High/Scope Perry Preschool program group (Schweinhart et al., 1993) and the High/Scope group of the Curriculum Comparison Study (Schweinhart & Weikart, 1997) were successful because they implemented the essential elements of the High/Scope curriculum and because they maintained consistent program policies that permitted the curriculum to operate effectively.

To recapitulate, these program policies are followed in a high-quality preschool program:

- Teachers use and "own" a validated curriculum model through regular inservice training in the curriculum model.
- The teaching staff work as teams in planning, implementing, and evaluating each day's activities.
- The staffing ratio is no more than 10 children per staff member, and group sizes are no greater than 20.
- Parents join with teachers as partners in the education of the child and engage in substantive discussion on the topic.
- The administration provides curriculum leadership, supervision, and assistance.

Many existing programs of early childhood care and education are not of adequate operational quality. Improving them is a major task of caregivers and educators. As with elementary and secondary school programs, early childhood programs must meet basic standards. These elements are neither easy to put into practice nor cheap to maintain. Yet the advantages of high-quality programs far outweigh the effort and cost of providing them.

What is it about young children's development that presents the opportunity for such effective programs? The preschool years are a watershed for several dimensions of child development. Physically, by age 3, young children have matured to the point that they have achieved both fine- and gross-motor coordination and are able to move about easily and freely. Mentally, they have developed basic language capabilities and can use objects for self-chosen purposes. In the terms of Jean Piaget, they have shifted from sensorimotor functioning to preoperational thinking. Socially, they are able to move away from familiar adults and social contexts to unfamiliar ones. The fear of strangers so common earlier is much reduced, and youngsters welcome relations with new peers and adults. What stands out among the basic accomplishments of early education is that children develop additional social, physical, and intellectual abilities. Armed with these acquired competencies, children learn to relate to new adults who respond to their performance very differently from their families. In short, children learn to demonstrate abilities in novel settings and to trust new adults and peers enough to display these skills willingly. Children's willingness to try things and develop competencies is the seed that is transformed into later school and life success. Early success grows grade by grade, year by year, into young adult success; each stage leads to a better performance at the next. These steps are documented by the research. The thrust is captured in the old folk adage, "As the twig is bent, so grows the tree."

CONCLUSION

The High/Scope curriculum is an open framework of developmental theories and educational practices based on the natural development of young children. It is currently used in thousands of early childhood programs throughout the United States and in other countries. Based on Piaget's (Piaget & Inhelder, 1969) child development ideas, the High/Scope curriculum views children as active learners who learn best from activities that they themselves plan, carry out, and reflect on. Adults arrange interest areas in the learning environment; maintain a daily routine that permits children to plan and pursue their own activities; join in children's activities and help them think; and provide language through conversations and observations. The adults encourage children to engage in key experiences and help them learn to make choices, solve problems, and generally engage in activities that promote intellectual, social, and physical development. Decades of careful research indicate that the High/Scope curriculum works to significantly improve the life chances of participating children.

High/Scope Educational Research Foundation
600 North River Street
Ypsilanti, Michigan 48198-2898
phone: (734) 485-2000
fax: (734) 485-0704
email: www.highscope.org

REFERENCES

Barnett, W. S. (1996). Lives in the balance: Age-27 benefit–cost analysis of the High/Scope Perry Preschool program. *Monographs of the High/Scope Educational Research Foundation, 11.*

Berrueta-Clement, J. R., Schweinhart, L. J., Barnett, W. S., Epstein, A. S., & Weikart, D. P. (1984). Changed lives: The effects of the Perry Preschool program on youths through age 19. *Monographs of the High/Scope Educational Research Foundation, 8.*

Epstein, A. S. (1993). *Training for quality: Improving early childhood programs through systematic inservice training.* Ypsilanti, MI: High/Scope Press.

Froebel, F. (1887). *The education of man.* W. N. Hailman, Trans. New York: D. Appleton.

Hanes, M., Flores, L., Rosario, J., Weikart, D. P., & Sanchez, J. (1979). *Un marco abierto: A guide for teachers.* Ypsilanti, MI: High/Scope Press.

High/Scope Educational Research Foundation. (2003). *The child observation record* (2nd ed.). Ypsilanti, MI: High/Scope Press.

Hohmann, M. (1997). *A study guide to educating young children: Exercises for adult learners.* Ypsilanti, MI: High/Scope Press.

Hohmann, M. (2002). *A study guide to educating young children: Exercises for adult learners* (2nd ed.). Ypsilanti, MI: High/Scope Press.

Hohmann, M., Banet, B., & Weikart, D. P. (1979). *Young children in action: A manual for preschool educators.* Ypsilanti, MI: High/Scope Press.

Hohmann, M., & Weikart, D. P. (1995). *Educating young children: Active learning practices for preschool and child care programs.* Ypsilanti, MI: High/Scope Press.

Hohmann, M., & Weikart, D. P. (2002). *Educating young children* (2nd ed.). Ypsilanti , MI:.High/Scope Press.

Larner, M. B., & Schweinhart, L. J. (1991, Winter). Focusing in on the teacher trainer: The High/Scope registry survey. *High/Scope ReSource,* pp. 1, 10–16.

Marcon, R. A. (1992). Differential effects of three preschool models on inner city four-year olds. *Early Childhood Research Quarterly, 7,* 517–530.

McCarthy, D. A. (1972). *Manual for the McCarthy scales of children's abilities.* San Antonio, TX: Psychological Corporation.

Nabuco, M., & Sylva, K. (1997, September). *A study on the quality of three early childhood curricula in Portugal.* Paper presented at 7th European Conference on the Quality of Early Childhood Education, Munich.

Oden, S., Schweinhart, L. J., & Weikart, D. P. with Marcus, S., & Xie, Y. (2000). *Into adulhood: A study of the effects of Head Start.* Ypsilanti, MI: High/Scope Press.

Piaget, J., & Inhelder, B. (1969). *The psychology of the child.* New York: Basic Books.

Schweinhart, L. J., Barnes, V., & Weikart, D. P., with Barnett, W. S., & Epstein, A. S. (1993). Significant benefits: The High/Scope Perry Preschool study through age 27. *Monographs of the High/Scope Educational Research Foundation, 10.*

Schweinhart, L. J., McNair, S., Barnes, H., & Larner, M. (1993, Summer). Observing young children in action to assess their development: The High/Scope Child Observation Record study. *Educational and Psychological Measurement, 53,* 445–455.

Schweinhart, L. J., Barnes, H. V., & Weikart, D. P., with Barnett, W. S., & Epstein, A. S. (1993). *Significant benefits: The High/Scope Perry Preschool Study through age 27.* Ypsilanti, MI: High/Scope Press.

Schweinhart, L. J., & Weikart, D. P. (1997). Lasting differences: The High/Scope preschool curriculum comparison study through age 23. *Monographs of the High/Scope Educational Research Foundation, 12.*

Smith, M. S. (1973). *Some short-term effects of project Head Start: A preliminary report on the second year of planned variation, 1970–71.* Cambridge, MA: Huron Institute.

Weikart, D. P., Hohmann, C. F., & Rhine, W. R. (1981). High/Scope cognitively oriented curriculum model. In W. R. Rhine (Ed.), *Making schools more effective: New directions from Follow Through* (pp. 201–247). New York: Academic Press.

Weikart, D. P., Rogers, L., Adcock, C., & McClelland, D. (1971). *The cognitively oriented curriculum: A framework for preschool teachers.* Urbana: University of Illinois Press.

Weikart, P. S. (Producer). (2003). *Rhythmically moving series, recordings 1–9* [CD; 2nd ed.]. Ypsilanti, MI: High/Scope Press.

Chapter 11

The Project Spectrum Approach to Early Education

Jie-Qi Chen ∽ Erikson Institute, Chicago

❧ INTRODUCTION

Project Spectrum is a 10-year research project dedicated to the development of an innovative approach to assessment and curriculum for the preschool and early primary school years. Spectrum's work is based on the belief that each child exhibits a distinctive profile of cognitive abilities or a spectrum of intelligences. These intelligences are not fixed; rather, they can be enhanced by educational opportunities, such as an environment rich with stimulating materials that support learning and self-expression. The Spectrum approach to early education emphasizes the identification of young children's areas of cognitive strengths and the use of this information as the focus for reflecting and evaluating the needs of individual children in the teaching and learning processes.

Project Spectrum began its work in the early 1980s in the midst of growing national concern about the education and well-being of children. In 1983, the publication of *A Nation at Risk* led to a close examination of the educational system in the United States (National Commission on Excellence in Education [NCEE], 1983). While attempting to analyze the problems of our schools and propose solutions, the authors unfortunately did not take into consideration the rapidly growing body of knowledge about the development of children (Association for Supervision and Curriculum Development [ASCD],

1988; Early Childhood Education Commission [ECEC], 1986; Elkind, 1987; Katz, 1987). Instead, they lumped together all levels of education in their discussions and recommendations, without regard to the specific needs and abilities of children at different ages. Moreover, out of concern for the nation's future economic strength, the authors advocated a "competitive" approach to education, including an increased use of standardized tests to assess and rank children with the focus on students' deficits rather than their strengths. Early childhood educators feared that such an approach would lead to children being labeled as failures at younger and younger ages (National Association of State Board of Education [NASBE], 1988).

In an effort to inform and redirect the school reform movement, the National Association for the Education of Young Children (NAEYC) published a position statement on developmentally appropriate practices for children from birth through age 8 (Bredekamp, 1987). The statement outlined a set of principles for early childhood programs based on the most current knowledge about how young children develop and learn; in particular, it recommended the use of more active learning approaches based on young children's diverse educational needs and abilities. While NAEYC's position statement was not without problems, it stimulated greater discussion of so called "best practices" for young

Early childhood teachers foster learning across an array of developmental dimensions.

children. The work of Project Spectrum contributed to this effort in a significant way by focusing on the emergence and nurturing of diverse cognitive strengths in young learners (Adams & Feldman, 1993; Feldman, 1998; Krechevsky & Gardner, 1990; Malkus, Feldman, & Gardner, 1988; Project Spectrum, 1984).

Of significant importance to the work of Project Spectrum is its theoretical foundation, which includes David Feldman's theory of nonuniversal development (1980, 1994) and Howard Gardner's theory of multiple intelligences (1983, 1993a). Different but complementary, both theories strive for a better understanding of varied human cognitive abilities in diverse knowledge systems and cultural contexts. Based on these theoretical perspectives, the initial goal of Spectrum's work was to develop a new means of assessing the diverse cognitive abilities of preschool children (Krechevsky, 1998; Project Spectrum, 1984). We soon discovered this was no easy task—we were challenged by an array of issues, including: (1) devising an assessment instrument reflective of the project's theoretical underpinnings;

(2) determining how to focus on the unique proclivities of individual children in a laboratory situation while providing teachers with a useful tool for classroom-based assessment; (3) assessing developmental trajectories and changes in children's cognitive abilities across varied domains; and (4) extending the assessment of cognitive abilities to include young children's experience and interaction with different materials. It took us a full 4 years to develop Project Spectrum's assessment activities and an additional 5 years to revise and refine these activities.

Spectrum's initial work also drew our attention to the inextricable connection between assessment and curriculum. This led to the second phase of the project: developing curriculum activities based on the wider range of abilities that Spectrum materials assessed. Specifically, curriculum activities were developed for children in public elementary schools who were struggling with academics at the beginning of formal schooling. The product of this phase of the project, *Spectrum Early Learning Activities*, provides teachers with a tool to observe children's key cognitive abilities while engaging them in a range of curricular activities in diverse areas (Chen, Isberg, & Krechevsky, 1998; Project Spectrum, 1988).

During the third phase of Spectrum's work, we expanded its scope beyond the school walls. More specifically, we collaborated with a children's museum and a preschool to develop sets of classroom-based instructional units and interactive museum exhibits that would reinforce each other by drawing on the unique features of each learning environment. We also established a mentorship program to give children opportunities to work with adults who shared an area of intellectual strength or interest. Mentors, including park rangers, urban planners, a musician, and a poet, visited the classroom once a week throughout the academic year, conducting hands-on activities that they developed with the support of Spectrum researchers.

In its 10-year history, Project Spectrum's work has been used for a variety of purposes in a wide range of settings. Thus, we believe that Spectrum is best thought of not as a discrete program or specific set of activities, but as a theory-based approach that emphasizes the importance of recognizing and nurturing children's diverse cognitive abilities. This approach can be used to help bring about important changes in educational assessment, curriculum development, and instruction (Chen, Krechevsky, & Viens, 1998).

Because Spectrum's work is theory based, this chapter begins with a brief overview of Feldman's and Gardner's theories. It proceeds with a description of the first and second phases of the Spectrum work—the development of the assessment instruments and the early learning activities. Related research studies and their implications for teaching and learning in early childhood classrooms are also discussed. In addition, a critical review of the Spectrum work is offered in light of its developmental and historical context. The chapter concludes with a discussion of Spectrum's approach in the context of current national debate about the federal No Child Left Behind Act.

❧ THEORETICAL FRAMEWORK

For much of the twentieth century, two models have dominated our understanding of human cognition: the psychometric model of intelligence (IQ) and Piaget's model of universal intellectual development (Flavell & Markman, 1983; Sternberg, 1985). According to the psychometric model, the most accurate way to measure people's intelligence is to use standardized intelligence tests, such as the Kaufman or Wechsler Intelligence Test. Based on the results of such tests, we can calculate an IQ score and array individuals from superior to below average based on their IQ. This model considers intelligence to be a single entity that is general and representative of the entire range of cognitive behaviors. Moreover, intelligence is relatively constant. Children tend to maintain their rank order over time in comparison with their peers (Neisser et al., 1996; Plomin & Petrill, 1997; Sameroff, Seifer, Baldwin, & Baldwin, 1993).

In a significant departure from the psychometric view of intelligence as IQ, Piaget emphasized that the nature of intelligence is developmental, rather than static; the mind of the child is qualitatively, rather than quantitatively, different from that of an adult (Ginsburg & Opper, 1987; Piaget, 1977). However, similar to the psychometric view is Piaget's notion of general abilities. In Piaget's theory, mental structures are general rather than specific, universal rather than cultural. In common with the psychometric view, Piaget's theory also assumes that cognitive development is essentially the result of the child's spontaneous tendencies to learn about the world, with the environment playing a minor role in the process. Piaget was primarily interested in the universal development of children as a group and he paid little attention to the individual differences among children. Finally, while IQ tests concentrate on people's linguistic and logical-mathematical abilities, Piaget defined intelligence in terms of logical-mathematical thought about the physical

FIGURE 11–1   **Developmental Continuum from Universal to Unique**
(Feldman, 1994; Feldman & Fowler, 1997a)

aspects of the world, including the understanding of causality, time, and space. As such, both Piaget's measures and psychometric tests sample from a subset of human intelligences; they do not, and cannot, measure the operations of other forms of intelligence or cognitive abilities (Ceci, 1996; Feldman, 1994; Gardner, 1993a; Sternberg, 1985).

Trained as developmental psychologists, both Feldman and Gardner concentrated their scholarly works on the development of human cognition. Arguing that Piaget's theory of universal development cannot account for development that is not experienced by all children, Feldman (1980, 1994) further differentiated cognitive changes to include nonuniversal development—that is, development that is neither spontaneous nor fully achieved by all individuals. In a radical departure from the notion of intelligence as a unitary construct of human cognition, a view held by Piaget and many psychometricians, Gardner (1983, 1993a) proposed the theory of multiple intelligences. Gardner's theory recognizes and values the existence of several distinct and relatively independent forms of human competence that are geared to specific contents in the world. While Feldman's theory focuses primarily on cognitive development in knowledge systems and Gardner's framework focuses on understanding the human mind, both theorists emphasize a more differentiated view of cognitive development and learning. It is this shared concern that sets the cornerstone for Project Spectrum.

Feldman's Nonuniversal Theory

Nonuniversal theory proposes that there are many *domains* of activity that are not universally developed by all individuals and groups; rather, their attainment requires individual effort and external support such as education and technology (Feldman, 1994, 1998). By domain Feldman refers primarily to a body of knowledge or a knowledge system. Feldman maintains that, in order to account for a wider range of cognitive changes, we must embrace a continuum of domains ranging from universal to unique (see Figure 11–1).

Embedded in the continuum are several distinctive features essential to the understanding of Feldman's theory. First, the continuum delineates different types of knowledge domains. The structure of knowledge in these different types of domains varies (Feldman, 1994). Universal domains are basic developmental competences that all normal humans in normal human environments acquire. An example of a universal domain is Piaget's work on logical cognitive structure. Pancultural domains refer to certain domains such as language that are acquired in all cultures by all intact individuals but may take different forms in different cultures and are not acquired by human beings in the absence of a human community. Cultural domains are bodies of knowledge and skills that all individuals within a given culture are expected to become proficient in through informal and formal instruction. Reading and writing are examples of cultural domains in American society. Discipline-based domains involve the development of expertise in a particular discipline, such as law and chemistry. Idiosyncratic domains represent one's specialty in sub-areas of a discipline. Patent law and organic chemistry are examples of such specialties. Finally, unique developmental achievements occur when the existing limits of a domain are transcended. The discovery of DNA is

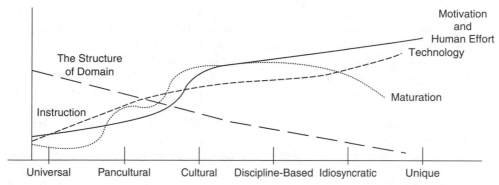

FIGURE 11–2 Sample of Contributing Factors to the Developmental Changes on Feldman's Continuum from Universal to Unique
(Adapted from Feldman & Fowler, 1997a.)

a case of unique transformation in biological knowledge.

In addition to examining the continuum from left to right, Feldman also calls attention to an analysis based on vertical development within each domain (Feldman, 1994). According to Feldman, development in each domain on the universal-to-unique continuum can be fruitfully and plausibly organized into a set of qualitatively distinct stages or levels. However, there are no general structures that are applied to every domain. Rather, what exists in the mind of the child at a given moment in time is a variety of skills in different domains, with each skill functioning at a certain level of mastery with respect to that domain (Feldman, 1974, 1986, 1987). To support this notion, Feldman refers to his study of child prodigies and argues that radical decalage can occur at an early age. Child prodigies, for example, generally advance at an extraordinary rate in specific fields while developing in others at a more typical pace (Feldman & Goldsmith, 1991). In contrast to many developmental theories (Case, 1992; Karmiloff-Smith, 1992; Piaget, 1977; Siegler, 1996), Feldman's theory holds that developmental levels are tied to specific bodies of knowledge and are not based on the operation of a general cognitive structure across domains (Feldman, 1994; Feldman & Fowler, 1997a, 1997b).

Finally, Feldman considers factors that contribute to the development of an individual's knowledge structures within and across domains (see Figure 11–2). These factors include maturation, motivation and human effort, the structure of domains, instruction, and technology (Feldman & Fowler, 1997a, 1997b). Some factors are internal to the child whereas others are external in the culture; some are more biologically based whereas others are more psychological; and still some are more readily observable and measurable than others. The diverse sources of influential factors and their interactions add to the complexity of accounting for developmental change. In Figure 11–2, notice that the five illustrated factors are involved in all domains of the universal-to-unique continuum, but to differing degrees. For example, instruction is highly influential for developmental changes in cultural, discipline-based, and idiosyncratic domains; it is much less influential for development in universal and unique domains, the two ends of the continuum. When focusing on unique domains, maturation plays a rather trivial role, as it is achieved long before an individual reaches the unique domain in his or her development. In contrast, human creativity in the unique domains demands almost obsessively strong motivation, tremendous efforts, and often the support of advanced technology. For this reason, the number of individuals who master the higher levels of development decreases as one moves from left to right on the universal-to-unique continuum. The sources of individual differences lie in the varying potential for mastery of different domains and the availability and degree of access to various domains (Feldman, 1989, 1994). As such, Feldman describes individual differences in cognition in terms of how advanced individuals are in different domains (Feldman, 1985, 1989; Feldman & Adams, 1989).

Gardner's Theory of Multiple Intelligences

For most readers of this book, the theory of multiple intelligences (MI) by Howard Gardner requires little introduction. Briefly stated, MI theory contends that human intelligence is neither a single complex entity nor a unified set of processes. Rather, as a species, human beings have evolved over the millennia to use several distinct, relatively autonomous intelligences. An individual's intellectual profile reflects a unique configuration of these intelligences (Gardner, 1993a, 1999). Gardner proposes eight different intelligences: linguistic, logical-mathematical, musical, spatial, bodily kinesthetic, naturalist, interpersonal, and intrapersonal. Though the linguistic and logical-mathematical intelligences have been emphasized in traditional psychological testing and school settings, the eight intelligences in the MI framework have equal claims to priority and are seen as equally valid and important (Gardner 1987a, 1987b, 1993a). Apart from specific numbers is the emphasis of MI on the "concepts of plurality, possibility, richness, expansion, and dialogue" (Rinaldi, 2001, p. 30).

Since the publication of *Frames of Mind* in 1983, MI theory has become one of the most influential theoretical forces in the fields of developmental psychology and education. Its inspiration and impact are evident in a wide range of areas, including cognition and learning, curriculum design, instructional strategies, programs for gifted and special needs children, assessment, career counseling, college teaching, and the development of toys and educational software programs. Gardner's books have been translated into more than 20 languages and the impact of MI shows no signs of diminishing. MI theory draws such wide attention for a number of reasons: Ideologically, it fits the contemporary cultural views of American society that stress diversity and egalitarianism. It is humane in nature by attending to human potential and valuing individual differences. It confirms the beliefs that many educators hold and practice, and provides them with language for clarification and communication. Last, but not least, is the beauty in the simplicity of its expression. Embedded in complex concepts, the theory is not hard to grasp—its basic ideas can be understood by people from grandmothers to elementary school students.

For the purposes of this chapter, we emphasize only the MI features most relevant to Spectrum's work: Gardner's methodology, his definition of intelligence, the relationship between intelligence and domain, and intelligences in context. First is the methodology, as it is influenced by and contributes to the development of a theory (Kuhn, 1962). In a radical departure from the traditional means of studying intelligence, Gardner began developing his theory by considering the range of adult end-states that are valued in diverse cultures around the world. To uncover the abilities that support these end-states, he examined a wide variety of empirical sources from different disciplines, many of which had not been used for the purpose of defining human intelligence. Gardner's focus on end-states led him to develop a theory of intelligence that accounts for how people function in diverse real-life situations (Gardner, 1993a).

In his most recent formulation of MI theory, *Intelligence Reframed* (1999), Gardner defines intelligence as "a biopsychological potential to process information that can be activated in a cultural setting to solve problems or create products that are of value in a culture" (p. 33). By considering intelligence a potential, Gardner asserts its emergent and responsive nature, thereby differentiating his theory from traditional approaches that claim human intelligence is fixed and innate. Whether a potential will be activated depends on the values of the culture in which an individual grows up and the opportunities available in that culture. Finally, in this definition Gardner regards the creation of products, such as writing a book or composing a symphony, to be as important an expression of intelligence as abstract problem solving is. Traditional theories of intelligence do not recognize human artifacts as manifestations of intelligence and therefore are limited in how they conceptualize and measure it.

In Gardner's work, intelligence and domain are related but different concepts. *Intelligence* refers to biological and psychological potential whereas *domain* speaks of a body of knowledge valued and exercised within a culture. Any one intelligence may be deployed in a number of domains. For example, naturalist intelligence involves the abilities to distinguish among, classify, and make sense of features of the environment. It can be used in the domains of archaeology, botany, and chemistry. In fact, human activity normally reflects the integrated functioning of several intelligences. An effective teacher, for example, relies on linguistic and personal intelligences and possesses knowledge of particular subject areas as well (Gardner, 1993b). Understanding the relationship between the concepts of intelligence and domain avoids confusion and the misuse of MI theory in educational practice. Given that intelligences do not function in isolation, for example, any assessment designed to measure pure intelligence would be fruitless.

Finally, considering intelligence in context is vital for understanding the relation of MI theory to Spectrum's work. From an MI perspective, the notion of intelligence in context has a number of meanings. One is that an intelligence is not an abstract entity: It must have its own identifiable core operations or set of operations and must be susceptible to encoding in a symbol system such as language, numbers, graphics, or musical notations (Gardner, 1993a). Also, intelligence is distributed: Human intelligence is so inextricably involved with people and objects that it is impossible to understand intellectual activities without also considering the use of tools and reliance on other human efforts (Gardner, 1993b). Third, intelligence is domain specific: Mental faculties do not operate according to general laws; rather, they are sensitive to content and each content area has its own principles of perception, memory, and problem solving (Gardner, 1987a, 1993a, 2000). In sum, human beings are biological, social, and cultural creatures. Intelligence is always an interaction between biological proclivities and the opportunities for learning that exist in a culture (Gardner, 1991, 1994; Kornhaber, Krechevsky, & Gardner, 1990).

Highlights of Spectrum's Conceptual Framework

Although distinctive in significant ways, Feldman's and Gardner's theories share certain features in the conceptualization of human cognition, and it is these commonalities that provide the theoretical foundation for Project Spectrum. First, both theorists argue that cognitive ability is pluralistic. Feldman and Gardner recognize many different and discrete facets of knowing and doing, acknowledging that people have varied cognitive strengths, interests, and weaknesses. It is in recognition of such a diversity of intellectual profiles that their joint project selected the name "Spectrum." More specifically, Project Spectrum's work, whether in assessment or in curriculum development, involves a range of domains including language, mathematics, movement, science, music, visual arts, and social understanding. Such a wide selection of domains is deliberate: Only by exposing children to a range of learning experiences in these various domains can we begin to identify and support the full complement of their diverse cognitive abilities.

Closely related to the notion of a pluralistic human intellect is Feldman and Gardner's belief in domain-specific cognitive abilities. Their works suggest that cognitive abilities are more accurately described as specifically attuned to particular domains rather than seen as reflecting one general capacity. This assertion entails a prediction that individuals often exhibit uneven profiles of ability when a wide range of domains is assessed. In Spectrum's work, domain-specific competence is defined in terms of key abilities that are essential to performance in a specific area of learning. In the domain of music, for example, key abilities for music perception include sensitivity to rhythmic patterns, pitch discrimination, and identification of different musical instruments (Dempsey, 1998).

Finally, both nonuniversal theory and MI theory maintain the need to recognize cognitive abilities as they are influenced by educational experiences and expressed in diverse cultures. Human culture actively constructs and significantly influences both the content of individual cognitive abilities and the course of their development. When we assess a child's cognitive abilities, we are assessing the child's intellectual proclivities, past experience in the area, familiarity with the assessment material, opportunity to practice using the material, and the scaffolding offered by the assessor. Variability in intellectual proclivities reflects not only the individual child, but also educational practices, environmental factors, and cultural values.

THEORY INTO PRACTICE: PROJECT SPECTRUM

A more differentiated view of cognition, articulated in both Feldman's and Gardner's theories, requires field tests of its construct validity and its potential benefit to educational practice. This call for empirical evidence led to the inception of Project Spectrum. Spectrum began its research at the preschool level and continued with primary grades throughout its course. This emphasis on early childhood was deliberate (Adams & Feldman, 1993; Malkus, Feldman, & Gardner, 1988). Theoretically, we wanted to know how early in life the specific expression of different cognitive abilities could be reliably discerned. Educationally, we believed that young children would benefit the most from a pedagogical approach attending to their diverse proclivities. Practically, curriculum and classroom environment during the early childhood years tend to be more open to innovation. Ideologically, we were eager to participate in the national discourse on DAP in early childhood education with arguments based on sound theories and empirical data.

Because the theoretical framework of Project Spectrum was original, its research and development had to be inventive. For this reason, many of the research questions that guided Spectrum's work were exploratory in nature: Could we develop an appropriate means to assess a wide range of cognitive abilities in young children? What would such an assessment instrument look like and in which ways would it differ from traditional tests of intelligence or cognitive ability? Could teachers use such assessment techniques to document the behavior and performance of children with diverse backgrounds on an ongoing basis during regular school days? How could we integrate assessment, curriculum, and instruction so that children's diverse cognitive profiles could be the basis for personalized teaching and learning? To pursue these questions, the Project Spectrum staff engaged in a decade-long field experiment and we can now confidently address some of our research questions. In the 10 years of Spectrum work, we also developed two major products: the *Preschool Assessment Handbook* and a book of *Early Learning Activities*. The following section is devoted to the discussion of these two products and their educational implications. Some of Spectrum's research questions are also addressed.

The Spectrum Assessment System

The Spectrum assessment system includes three components: *Preschool Assessment Activities, Observational Guidelines,* and the *Spectrum Profile* (hereafter referred to as *Activities, Guidelines,* and *Profiles*). The *Activities* include 15 activities in the seven domains of knowledge described earlier: language, math, music, art, social understanding, sciences, and movement. Some activities are structured tasks that can be administered in a one-on-one situation; others are more spontaneous and can take place in a group setting. Each activity measures specific abilities, often requires particular materials, and is accompanied by written instructions for task administration. These instructions include a score sheet that describes different levels of the key abilities exercised in the activity so that the child's performance on many activities is quantifiable. Finally, upon completion of each assessment activity, the child's working style during the task is recorded. Working style refers to the way in which a child interacts with the materials of a content area, such as degree of engagement, confidence, or attention to details (for a detailed description of Spectrum preschool assessment activities, see Krechevsky, 1998).

The *Guidelines* are observational checklists in eight different domains. In the *Guidelines,* the domain of science is divided into natural science and mechanical construction to capture the different uses of different key abilities and materials. Each guideline describes a set of key abilities and core components similar to those measured in the preschool assessment activities. Designed for preschool and primary grades, teachers can use the *Guidelines* for ongoing classroom observation that focuses on domain-specific cognitive abilities.

The *Activities* and *Guidelines* can be used independently. However, when used together,

they provide a more complete and accurate picture of a child's abilities. Because both instruments use similar sets of domain-specific key abilities to gauge a child's performance, comparing and contrasting results from the two assessments is straightforward and meaningful. The *Activities* help describe the child's place in a developmental process at a particular point in time, whereas the *Guidelines* direct ongoing observation so that the child's progress can be tracked over time. The *Activities* focus on degrees or levels of a child's strengths or weaknesses while the *Guidelines* look at the consistency of these identified abilities across settings. Finally, the *Activities* allow close examination of one child at a time, making it possible to document the child's performance in detail, including her working style. In contrast, the *Guidelines* help teachers obtain a rough approximation of the ways in which children differ from one another in a natural learning environment.

The third component of the Spectrum assessment system, the *Profile,* is a narrative report based on the information obtained from the two assessment processes described above (Krechevsky, 1998; Ramos-Ford & Gardner, 1991). Using nontechnical language, the report focuses on a range of cognitive abilities examined by the Spectrum assessment instruments. It describes each child's relative strengths and weaknesses in terms of that child's own capacities, and only occasionally in relation to peers. The strengths and weaknesses are described in terms of the child's performance and working styles in different content areas. For example, a child's unusual sensitivity to different kinds of music might be described by reference to her body language, facial expressions, movement, and attentiveness during and after listening to various music pieces. It is important to note that the child's profile is described not only in terms of capacities, but also in terms of preferences and inclinations. In so doing, the report stresses the importance of developmental assessment—the child's profile is not a static image but a dynamic composition of her interests, capability, and experience at a particular point in time. Changes in the profile are inevitable as the child's life experience changes. The conclusion of the *Profile* typically includes specific recommendations to parents and teachers in terms of possible ways to support the identified strengths and improve weak areas (Adams & Feldman, 1993; Krechevsky, 1998).

Embedded in the three components of Spectrum's assessment system are several premises that we deem important for the accurate assessment of cognitive abilities in young children. These premises, described in detail later, pertain to four issues in child assessment: measures, instruments, materials, and context.

Measures: Valuing Intellectual Capacities in a Wide Range of Domains

It has been widely acknowledged in the field of child assessment that, in order to accurately portray a child's cognitive ability, multiple measures must be taken. As all forms of assessment contain errors, no one measure can adequately represent the complex nature of human cognition (Greenspan & Meisels, 1996; Horton & Bowman, 2002; Sattler, 2001). The Spectrum approach to assessment adds another dimension to the meaning of multiple measures; namely, the need to sample from a range of areas in order to capture different facets of human intellectual capacities. In practice, the meaning of multiple measures for Spectrum is triplefold: multiple methods of assessment (e.g., testing, observation, and portfolios), multiple administrations (e.g., three times per school year or an ongoing process), and multiple domains that include mechanical construction, visual arts, language and literacy, and math.

To use the results of multiple measures in a range of intellectual domains, Spectrum emphasizes supporting children's learning and development on the basis of their complete cognitive profile, including strengths, interests, and weaknesses. At the same time, Spectrum focuses on the value of building on children's strengths. This approach does not ignore weak areas but sees strengths as promising stepping stones for effective intervention (Chen, 1993; Chen, Krechevsky, & Viens, 1998). In focusing on the child's strengths in the assessment process, we acknowledge that perceived deficits may shift during the rapid changes in the early childhood period (Bowman, Donovan, & Burns, 2001; Sameroff & Haith, 1990). We also assert that every child has strengths; the challenge is to sample widely enough to accurately identify them. Last but not least, we believe in the efficacy of building the teaching and learning process based on what the child is capable of. To build the process based on what the child is incapable of is to further limit their opportunities for learning (Chen, 1993; Chen, Krechevsky, & Viens, 1998).

The identification of strengths in the Spectrum approach is based on key abilities. A child's art portfolio, for example, can be examined on the basis of three key abilities: representation, exploration, and artistry (Chen & Feinburg, 1998). The range of scores for each of these key abilities is 1 to 9. With a total possible score of 27, scores on the art portfolio can be used to delineate high performers from low performers in the area of drawing. However, the same quantitative score for two children does not necessarily reflect the same levels of ability. One child may earn a score of 19, based on a score of 9 for representation, 4 for exploration, and 6 for artistry. A second child may also earn a score of 19 for her portfolio, but this 19 may be the sum of 3, 9, and 7 points for representation, exploration, and artistry respectively. Thus, to interpret a score, one must look not only at the total number of points, but also at the level of performance for each key ability (Adams, 1993). The use of key abilities, defined in terms of different performance levels, makes it possible to identify both cognitive strengths and the composition of these strengths. For designing learning experiences, this level of detail is much more informative than a single global score.

Instruments: Using Media Appropriate to the Domain Supported and constrained by one or more symbol systems, key abilities are integrated mental processes that ensure performance in specific domains. For this reason, domain-specific cognitive abilities can be accurately assessed only by employing media that are appropriate for a particular domain, or to put it briefly, by using "intelligence-fair instruments" (Gardner, 1993b). Attention to appropriate means in the Spectrum assessments sharply contrasts with traditional intelligence tests, which funnel information largely through linguistic and logical means.

To illustrate the point, consider several examples from Spectrum's preschool assessment activities. To measure mechanical abilities, a child is asked to disassemble and assemble a meat grinder, an oil pump, or some other common household gadgets. In the process of dismantling and constructing these objects, the child's key abilities in the area of mechanical construction are observed and documented. These key abilities are visual-spatial abilities, understanding of causal and functional relationships among parts, using a problem-solving approach with mechanical objects, and fine motor skills. In the domain of music, a child's music perception key abilities are assessed through a game with Montessori Bells that look the same but produce distinctive sounds. To differentiate one pitch from another, the child cannot use her eyes; she must rely exclusively on her sense of hearing. In these Spectrum assessment activities, domain-specific cognitive abilities are measured through the use of domain-specific media to solve domain-specific problems.

Using "intelligence-fair" instruments to assess key abilities is not only theoretically sound; it also has a number of educational implications. For gifted education, the identification of unique talent can go beyond IQ tests to include instruments employing media to assess a wide range of exceptional abilities, including exceptional social abilities and leadership (Kornhaber, 1997; Maker, 1997; Wu, 2003). For learners of English as a second language, educators can support their students by using other media or symbol systems, in addition to language, to elicit their understanding and competence (Haley, 2003; Stefanakis, 2003). For all children, learning can be stimulated through multiple entry points and documented through "hundred languages" (Edwards, Gandini, & Forman, 1998; Gardner, 2000).

Materials: Engaging Children in Meaningful Activities and Learning Of critical importance to the assessment of young children is active engagement with materials. Young minds often rely on concrete objects for mental operations (Piaget, 1954, 1977; Piaget & Inhelder, 1969) and cognitive ability is manifested through a wide variety of artifacts and other human efforts (Feldman and Fowler, 1997a; Gardner, 1993b). Although materials in and of themselves cannot automatically lead to meaningful learning, *intelligent materials,* a term educators from the Municipal Preschool and Infant–Toddler Centers in Reggio Emilia, Italy, often use to refer to their conscious selection of objects and tools for learning, are more likely to invite questions, stimulate curiosity, facilitate discoveries, promote communication, and encourage the use of imagination and multiple symbol systems (Krechevsky, 2001; Rinaldi, 2001).

In the development of the Spectrum assessment activities, choosing appropriate materials was a careful and deliberate process. Veteran teachers and domain experts were among the consultants asked to recommend and evaluate materials to ensure that materials would be engaging and meaningful to children. To assess children's understanding of number concepts, for example, Spectrum responds to preschoolers' fascination with dinosaurs. While a board game motivates participation, the child's manipulation of dinosaur game pieces reveals her counting skills, ability to adhere to rules, and use of strategy. Similarly, children's social understanding is assessed in Spectrum through a classroom model with small wooden figures. The figures have the photos of the teacher and each child in the classroom. In the process of using the figures to act out, and react to, scenarios in their own classroom environment with their peers, children's abilities to observe, reflect on, and analyze familiar social events and experiences are examined. Because they are attractive and actively engage children in the assessment process, the Spectrum assessment materials are more likely to reveal children's cognitive strengths and to motivate their learning (Bransford, Brown, & Cocking, 1999).

Because cognitive abilities are contextualized, children's prior experience with assessment materials directly affects their performance on tasks. In recognition of the role that experience plays, the Spectrum approach to assessment emphasizes using materials that are familiar to children. It follows that children who have little experience with blocks are less likely to do well in a block design task. Similarly, it would be unfair to assess a child's musical ability by asking the child to play a xylophone if she has never seen such a musical instrument. In Spectrum's assessment, if a child were not familiar with a material, she would be given ample opportunities to explore the material prior to the assessment.

Context: Focusing on Ecological Validity and Relevance for Instruction

To assess young children's cognitive abilities, the first and foremost criterion for context is ecological validity (Gardner, 1993b); that is, the assessment environment must be natural, familiar, and continuing. Learning is not a one-shot experience, nor should assessment be. When a child's ability is measured through a one-shot experience in a strange or stressed situation, the child's profile is often incomplete and distorted. In contrast, when assessment is naturally embedded in the learning environment, it allows teachers to observe children's performance in various situations over time. By collecting multiple samples of a child's abilities, it is possible to document the dynamics and variation of the child's performances both within and across domains and therefore more accurately assess the child's intellectual profile. Ongoing assessment is especially important to young children, as their response to a given assessment can be largely affected by their emotional status, physical well-being, or willingness to participate (Cohen & Stern, 1997; Sattler, 2001). It is precisely for this reason that Spectrum advocates the use of both assessment activities and ongoing guided observations to capture young children's cognitive abilities.

Focus on a problem-solving process in a meaningful situation is another criterion for a sound assessment context. In the Spectrum assessments, for example, instead of asking children to exhibit isolated behaviors such as hopping on one foot, the child's athletic ability is assessed through the use of an obstacle course. To gather information about a child's ability to draw logical inferences and generate hypotheses, Spectrum engages the child in a treasure hunt game. This is in strong contrast to tests that assess logical inference by asking children to sequence a series of pictures that often bear little connection to their life experience. Rather than presenting young children with abstract moral dilemmas to assess their social ability, Spectrum invites children to play with a classroom model and reconcile peer conflicts that happen in their own classroom. Spectrum maintains that when the assessment context is meaningful to children and they work on tasks that genuinely engage them in problem-solving processes, children are motivated to do well and the assessment is more likely to elicit their best performance.

A primary reason for child assessment is to improve instruction. Yet too many standardized assessments used in our classrooms bear little, and often distant, relation to curricular plans and instructional practice. For assessment to be instructive for teachers, it must connect to classroom learning and performance (Meisels, Bickel, Nicholson, Xue, & Atkins-Burnett, 2001; Wiggins, 1998). The *Spectrum Observational Guidelines* are designed to direct teachers' attention to domain-specific key abilities that naturally occur in various classroom situations. As children work, teachers can use the *Guidelines* to observe and document children's interests and abilities in different domains. The more regularly teachers receive feedback from an assessment, the more the assessment would become part of daily classroom life, and the more likely teachers would use it to help plan curriculum and instruction (Chen & Gardner, 1997). In this process, assessment and instruction inform and enhance each other, becoming an integrated, enriched, and spiraling whole.

Spectrum Early Learning Activities

The *Spectrum Early Learning Activities* are curricular activities in eight areas identical to the domains of the *Observational Guidelines* described earlier. Each area begins with a description of the *Observational Guideline* for that area; this serves to reinforce the notion that ongoing assessment is part of the *Spectrum Early Learning Activities*. To help teachers track the development of specific student abilities, we organized the activities for each area in terms of the key abilities stimulated by the activity (Science area is an exception as it is organized based on short experiments and long-term projects). This enables teachers to focus their observations of children's interests and cognitive abilities and record their observations in greater detail. Finally, for each activity, we also describe the objectives, materials, and step-by-step procedures to assist teachers with the implementation (Chen, Isberg, & Krechevsky, 1998).

Each area includes 15 to 20 classroom activities and several take-home activities appropriate for children in kindergarten and first grade. In terms of the activity format, some

occur in free play whereas others are structured. With regard to the content, some activities help exercise domain-specific skills while others focus on the understanding of topics or concepts drawn from different domains of knowledge. As for the source of the activities, some were developed by Spectrum staff and others are based on existing curriculum activities familiar to most early childhood teachers. For activities to be selected, they generally had to: (1) highlight and exercise key abilities in a designated domain; (2) involve hands-on problem solving in a meaningful context; and (3) provide information that will help teachers adapt their curriculum to better meet the needs of individual children (Chen, Isberg, & Krechevsky, 1998).

It is important to note that the *Spectrum Early Learning Activities* are not designed to be a full-fledged curriculum. They do not present "an organized framework" with particular learning goals, knowledge systems, and teaching strategies (Bowman, Donovan, & Burns, 2001). They are in no way intended to substitute for a systematic approach to skills acquisition or the development of major concepts in typical school subject areas. Instead, the *Learning Activities* are for teachers to use to supplement their regular curricula, to expand into territories they do not usually teach, or to support classroom observations in accordance with key abilities. The *Learning Activities* also can serve as catalysts, providing ideas to help teachers develop their own projects or find ways to teach children who are not responding to more traditional approaches. We encourage teachers to adapt these activities to fit their own situation, teaching styles, and classroom composition.

The *Spectrum Early Learning Activities* were field tested in four first-grade public school classrooms in Somerville, Massachusetts, in the early 1990s. The primary focus of the work was to examine the effects of these activities on students at risk for school failure (Chen, 1993). The teachers' experiences indicate that these activities should not be used in isolation, but in the context of Spectrum's theoretical framework. This framework encompasses four interrelated intervention steps: (1) introducing children to a wide range of learning experiences; (2) identifying children's areas of strength; (3) nurturing the identified strengths; and (4) extending children's strengths to other subject areas and academic performance.

Introducing Children to a Wide Range of Learning Experiences

Spectrum's theoretical framework holds that rich educational experiences are essential for the development of an individual's particular configuration of interests and abilities. To do justice to our respect for the minds, bodies, and spirits of young children, we need to provide them with joyful, rich, and stimulating learning experiences through a variety of learning modes, such as touch, smell, conversation, drawing, acting, manipulation, observation, investigation, and exploration. Only by exposing children to a range of learning areas and encouraging them to use varied modes of learning do we set an optimal environment for the development of their intelligences.

In our schools, particularly those in poor communities, too many children fall through the cracks. However, children who have trouble with some academic subjects, such as reading or math, are not necessarily inadequate in all areas. They may shine when asked to portray their understanding of a story in "spontaneous theater" through story acting (Paley, 2003) or to solve a math problem using graphics (The New City School, 1994). The *Spectrum Early Learning Activities* provide these students with the same opportunities to demonstrate their competence that students who excel in linguistic and logical pursuits already find in the daily school routine.

It is noteworthy that not only individual children, but also society as a whole, would benefit from an educational approach that recognizes and cultivates diverse intellectual potential. For any functional society, there is a clear need for diverse

professionals, including teachers, writers, lawyers, artists, mathematicians, psychologists, and many others. Each of these professionals requires a combination of different intelligences. When school curriculum focuses on only a narrow band of subject areas and evaluates student achievement through primarily paper and pencil tests, we poorly serve our future by not supporting the wide range of talent society needs.

The notion of exposing children to a range of learning experiences is not a new concept in the field of early education (Edwards, Gandini, & Forman, 1998; Froebel, 1897; Montessori, 1964). Indeed, many of our nation's early childhood classrooms are organized based on this belief (Bowman, Donovan, & Burns, 2001). In this regard, classrooms based on the Spectrum approach share many features with other quality early education programs, including hands-on materials, learning centers, and student choice.

What distinguishes the Spectrum classroom, however, is the attempt to engage students in real-world tasks while introducing them to a rich educational experience. Gardner's concept of "end state" was used to focus on skills and abilities needed for successful performance in adult roles or in the world of work. To develop understanding of causal and functional relationships and visual-spatial abilities, for example, children use tools and materials to create mobiles, bridge structures, or a model of their classroom. Similarly, to develop oral language skills, children might conduct an interview in the style of a television journalist. These activities help children relate the skills they are learning in school to what they wish to perform in everyday life. Also distinctive in the Spectrum classroom is the variety of domains available, particularly their systematic use for identifying and supporting children's areas of strength and interest. Guided by the Spectrum framework, teachers are continually expanding the curriculum to reach an ever wider and more diverse range of learners.

TABLE 11–1
Identified Areas of Strength in At-Risk Children across Domains

Spectrum Domain	Areas of Strength Related to		
	Class	Self	Total
Math		1	1
Social		1	1
Science	1	1	2
Language	2		2
Mechanical	2	1	3
Movement		3	3
Visual Arts	2	4	6

Identifying Children's Areas of Strength

The next step in the Spectrum educational process is to identify children's (and particularly at-risk children's) areas of strength through observation and analysis of their participation in a variety of rich educational experiences. In this approach, intervention begins with the identification of a child's strengths from a wide range of areas, rather than the remediation of deficits in a very limited number of traditional academic disciplines such as reading and math. We do not disregard the value of and need for remedial services in specific areas. Rather, we contend that while some at-risk students might benefit from this strategy, others might be more responsive to building on strengths. By using only one strategy, intervention programs may restrict their effectiveness.

In the Somerville study, the classroom teachers and Spectrum researchers identified children's strengths on the basis of their demonstrated interest and competence. Interest was assessed in terms of the frequency with which a child chose a particular domain-specific activity and the length of their involvement in that activity. Competence was evaluated using the *Observational Guideline* that specifies key abilities and describes core components of activities.

Many teachers gather information through classroom-based observation, but they are not always clear about what they see or what they are looking for. Consequently, their observations may be of limited use for planning learning experiences. Spectrum maintains that observations are more informative when they are domain specific. The specificity of the key abilities enables teachers to observe students' work and assess their level of competence in particular domains. Using these guidelines, teacher observations in our Somerville study became more specific and more useful for learning about each child's unique cognitive profiles (Chen, 1993; Chen, Krechevsky, & Viens, 1998).

Using the criteria described above, we identified areas of strength for 13 of the 15 (87%) at-risk students in four Somerville classrooms. As seen in Table 11–1, these children's strengths spanned almost all of the *Spectrum Early Learning Activities* areas. Also noteworthy, these children demonstrated more strengths in nonacademic areas than in academic ones—6, 3, and 3 in the areas of art, mechanics, and movement, respectively, versus 2 and 1 in the language and math areas. This result clearly indicates that at-risk students, although they often perform poorly in traditional academic areas, are not in-

TABLE 11–2
Mean Scores of At-Risk Students' Behavior When Working in Strength Versus Nonstrength Areas

	Areas of Strength	Other Areas
Self-Direction	3.98**	2.25
Self-Confidence	3.96**	2.33
Positive Classroom Behavior	3.67**	2.40
Positive Affect	3.96**	2.58
Self-Monitoring	3.19**	1.87
Active Engagement	4.26**	3.17

**$p < .01$

competent in all areas of learning. When a wide range of learning areas is made available for them to explore and pursue, at-risk children demonstrate competence and skills in a variety of areas. Drawing attention to at-risk childrens' areas of strength offers a promising alternative to the typical characterization of this population only as deficient.

Nurturing the Identified Strengths Equally important to the identification of children's areas of strength is continuing educational support. Only through a sustained effort can children's areas of strength be nurtured and developed. In the Somerville study, the classroom teachers and Spectrum researchers worked together to provide this support. Among the many strategies they used were making available a range of materials based on children's identified strengths and building time into the daily schedule for children to choose an area of work. These strategies invite the child to act as a leader in areas of strength, thereby increasing her sense of competence and confidence. These practices also create opportunities to extend children's interests through project-based learning. As children choose activities and develop their skills, teachers have successful experiences to share with parents.

Teacher, child, and parents begin to see a child's strengths, often for the first time since the child was identified as at risk (Chen, Isberg, & Krechevsky, 1998).

The effect of working in areas of strength was tested in our Somerville study using the Child Behavioral Observation Scale (Chen, 1992). Table 11–2 presents the results of analyzing at-risk children's behavior when working in areas of strength versus nonstrength. The MANOVA analysis indicates a significant effect on all six measures in favor of children working in strength areas, namely, self-direction ($F = 3.98$, $p < .01$), self-confidence ($F = 3.96$, $p < .01$), positive classroom behavior ($F = 3.67$, $p < .01$), positive affect ($F = 3.96$, $p < .01$), self-monitoring ($F = 3.19$, $p < .01$), and active engagement ($F = 4.26$, $p < .01$). Also, an analysis of individual subjects indicates that all 15 at-risk students showed a statistically significant difference on at least 1, and in some cases as many as 5, of the aforementioned behaviors. These findings indicate that all at-risk children had positive experiences when working in their areas of strength (Chen, 1992).

The results of this empirical study support Spectrum's position: When children recognize that they are good at something, and when that skill is also recognized by the teacher and peers, children experience success and feel valued. When children work in an area of strength, they not only have the chance to be effective and productive, but also to be of help to others who are less skilled in the area. When their competence is acknowledged in the classroom, the children start to see themselves as capable in the school environment. As children develop further competence in their areas of strength, they are more likely to experience feelings of satisfaction and self-worth. These feelings, in turn, help children develop greater self-confidence, enhanced self-esteem, and improved classroom behavior (Project Spectrum, 1989).

It is important to note that nurturing children's strengths does not mean "labeling" them or limiting their experience in other areas. For example, a child known as a willing helper should not be expected to help all the time. A child with strong verbal skills could be encouraged to take risks and experiment in areas where she has less experience and may feel less comfortable. The early childhood years are not the time to narrow children's learning experience, nor are they the time to focus on only children's interests. On the contrary, young children need years of exposure to the possibilities of development in all domains. Rich educational experiences enable children to develop fully their potentials and interests and help them succeed in school (Barnett, 1998; Dunn, 1993).

Extending Children's Strengths to Other Subject Areas and Academic Performance

The development of children's basic skills and knowledge is one of the fundamental tasks of schooling. In America, skills acquisition is now pushed to such an extent that academic success in the early elementary years, which is often equated with the ability to read, write, and count, has almost become a critical prerequisite for success in later schooling (The Department of Health and Human Services [DHHS], 2003).

Spectrum's work does not ignore the value of the three Rs for later learning, but proposes an alternative instructional approach to reach the same destination. This approach is based on extending children's strengths to other subject areas and academic performance, a process referred to as "bridging" by Spectrum staff.

The process of bridging entails two fundamental concepts critical to Project Spectrum's work. First, it acknowledges the relative independence of skills and abilities in different domains (Adams, 1993; Bransford et al., 1999; Gardner, 1993a). For example, strengths in constructing mechanical objects or creating artwork do not automatically transfer to skill in language arts or math. To help a child transfer skills, a teacher must construct activities that provide a unique blend of elements from one domain with those of another. Second, the concept of bridging is consistent with Spectrum's aim to support the achievement of educational goals. The Spectrum learning activities were developed as a means to help teachers uncover a more complex and comprehensive profile of a child's learning potential to inform educational planning. They were not intended to stand alone to provide a catalog of intellectual strengths as an end in itself.

Spectrum staff have identified and described a number of strategies that can be used to initiate the process of bridging. These strategies include: (1) social/emotional readiness—the child discovers an area of strength, enjoys exploring it, and feels more confident. The experience of being successful gives the child the confidence needed to enter more challenging domains; (2) learning style resemblance—a musical child may find reading and writing appealing when the text is poetry; the aural mode of processing or style of learning is used as a vehicle for engaging the child in an area of challenge; (3) content connection—a child with a mechanical aptitude can be asked to read and write about machines. As such, the content of a child's area of strength is used to engage the child in other areas, particularly those central to success in school; and (4) structural comparison—a child sensitive to the rhythmic aspect of music might respond to rhythmic aspects of language, math, or movement because of the comparable structural component involved in these disciplines.

The process of bridging is not accomplished by simply linking one area to another. It calls for a deep understanding of the domains of knowledge involved (Gardner, 1998, 2000). For successful bridging to take place, the teacher must know the knowledge base he or she wants the child to develop. The teacher also needs to consider possible instructional strategies that will engage the child and motivate skill acquisition through the identified strengths. Each Spectrum domain can and should be used as an entry point for skill acquisition and knowledge development. Young children, at risk or not, learn best when multiple sensory faculties are activated and their natural proclivities are utilized (Marcon, 1992; Montessori, 1964; Smith, 1999).

Due to a limited intervention period, our Somerville study was unable to document measurable effects of the bridging process on classroom achievement. However, the field of education is not short of evidence that bridging is a viable instructional strategy to improve academic performance and that it is particularly effective in reaching students with learning difficulties (Bolanos, 2003; Campbell, Campbell, & Dickinson, 1996; Hoerr, 2003; Kornhaber, 1999; Kornhaber & Krechevsky, 1997; Kornhaber, Veenema, & Fierros, 2003). We believe that for the Spectrum approach to fully reach its promise, the bridging process must be further developed. Successful bridging is a time-consuming process, requiring great effort to plan and implement. However, when we ponder the enormous human potential currently wasted in our society and realize that an alarmingly large number of children are labeled for school failure at a very early age, such an investment seems not only worthwhile, but necessary.

☙ PUTTING PROJECT SPECTRUM'S WORK IN PERSPECTIVE

Because of its strong theoretical framework and unique approach to assessment and curriculum development, Project Spectrum has attracted much attention in the field of early childhood education. The three published volumes documenting Spectrum's work have been translated into Spanish, Chinese, Italian, and Portuguese, and there are now more than three dozen assessment instruments in the field inspired by the Spectrum work (Hsueh, 2003). Many early childhood teachers and schools endorse the Spectrum approach to early education and use it to guide the teaching and learning process in daily classroom practices (Campbell, 1992; Chen, Krechevsky, & Viens, 1998; Kornhaber, 1999). For a research project with only 10 years of history, these achievements are truly remarkable.

The work of Project Spectrum is not without constraints, however. Some of them are due to the nature of the grants that shaped the direction of the project, others relate to our own developmental process in understanding the issues involved, and still others are simply a matter of time—the time needed to see the long-term effects and to engage in reflective research practice. Among the issues raised by Spectrum researchers and practitioners in the field, four warrant special attention: the concept of domain in Spectrum's work, the development of domain-specific abilities, the study of group process in learning, and the connection between assessment and teaching. To be sure, these issues concern what Project Spectrum didn't or wasn't able to do; they also help people see how to build on Spectrum's work and extend its applications.

The Concept of Domain in Spectrum's Work

Domain is a concept key to Spectrum's work, yet it is also vague and perplexing. This is due partially to the lack of a clear definition for domain in the field of cognitive development (Hirschfeld & Gelman, 1994; Keil, 1994; Leslie, 1994; Wellman & Gelman, 1992). In the field, the word *domain* has been used quite loosely and often implies different meanings, including subject matter (e.g., math, sciences), developmental area (e.g., physical, social/emotional, cognitive), aspect of cognition (e.g., memory, perception), type of activity (e.g., chess, soccer, cooking), and body of knowledge (e.g., dinosaurs, cars). As Hirschfeld and Gelman (1994) claim, "we lack an explicit and well articulated account of what a domain is. It is easier to think of examples of a domain than to give a definition of one" (p. 21). The different meanings attached to domain reflect the richness of the term and diverse interests in the field. At the same time, however, they contribute to confusion and possible misunderstanding. Project Spectrum joined the club and added an additional meaning.

Influenced by Feldman's theory, Project Spectrum deliberately set out to examine nonuniversal, rather than universal, domains. Guided by Gardner's theory, Spectrum's selection of domains intends to help foster the development of diverse intellects in young children. Spectrum's domains do not directly correspond to the multiple intelligences identified by Gardner, nor are they a direct application of Feldman's theory of nonuniversal domains. The two theories guided, but did not dictate, selection of the domains Spectrum used. The concept of domain in Spectrum's work reflects the integration of both Feldman's and Gardner's theories as well as the application of this theoretical framework in the context of education (see Figure 11–3).

The confusion about Spectrum's domains often comes from looking at the theories individually, instead of looking at the framework that emerged through integration and application. For example, when people compare domains in Feldman's theory with the domains examined in Spectrum's work and do not see a

direct match, they may underestimate the contributions of nonuniveral theory. On the other hand, many people equate Spectrum's domains with the intelligences of MI theory because of their seeming resemblance. This leads to the mistaken beliefs that the Spectrum assessments are designed to assess multiple intelligences in young children and the Spectrum early learning activities are intended to exercise multiple intelligences in early childhood classrooms. Despite strenuous efforts from Spectrum's staff to challenge the misguided attempts to devise intelligence tests based on MI theory and to expose the possible dangers of such practices, misuses of MI theory still occur. The development of multiple intelligences-based tests or assessments is lucrative and people frequently use Spectrum's work as an example to support their endeavors (Shearer, 1999; Teele, 2000; Wu, 2003). In response, we contend that understanding Spectrum's domains as an integration of Feldman's and Gardner's theories is a prerequisite for adapting the Spectrum work to other settings.

The Development of Domain-Specific Abilities

Recall that one of the central research questions in Spectrum's initial work concerns how early one can reasonably identify diverse cognitive abilities in different domains. Spectrum research indicates that children as young as 4 years old often display varying levels of competence when abilities from distinctive areas are evaluated (Adams, 1993; Malkus, Feldman, & Gardner, 1988). This finding suggests that cognitive abilities are domain specific at an early age. When individuals are described in terms of either a single numerical score (e.g., IQ) or a global category (e.g., a Piagetian stage), meaningful variations within a child's repertoire of abilities are concealed (Adams, 1993).

In view of Spectrum's research findings on domain-specific abilities, naturally researchers and teachers ask questions about the development

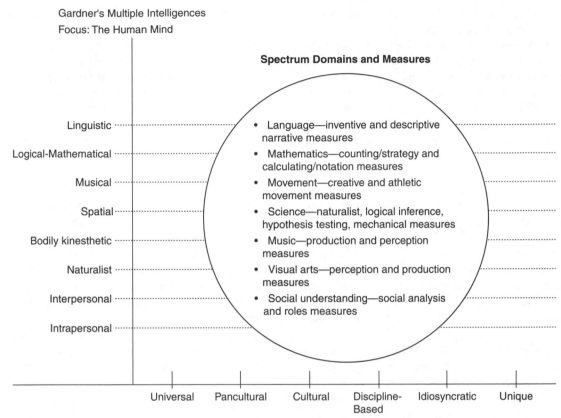

Gardner's Multiple Intelligences
Focus: The Human Mind

Spectrum Domains and Measures

- Linguistic
- Logical-Mathematical
- Musical
- Spatial
- Bodily kinesthetic
- Naturalist
- Interpersonal
- Intrapersonal

- Language—inventive and descriptive narrative measures
- Mathematics—counting/strategy and calculating/notation measures
- Movement—creative and athletic movement measures
- Science—naturalist, logical inference, hypothesis testing, mechanical measures
- Music—production and perception measures
- Visual arts—perception and production measures
- Social understanding—social analysis and roles measures

Universal   Pancultural   Cultural   Discipline-Based   Idiosyncratic   Unique

Feldman's Developmental Continuum from Universal to Unique
Focus: The Change of Knowledge Systems

FIGURE 11–3 Domains Examined in Spectrum's Work

of such abilities in young children. For example, what are the developmental trajectories that characterize young children's progress through Spectrum's domains? Do some domain-specific abilities display patterns of discontinuity with new skills emerging from the reorganization of earlier ones, whereas others change in a more continuous and quantitative fashion? Do some domain-specific abilities develop at very early ages whereas others are slower to emerge, and if so, what factors account for these variations? Are children's strengths and weaknesses in various domains constant over time? How does nonuniversal development in the domains ex-

amined in Spectrum's work relate to the universal competence defined by Piaget? These are some of the basic questions identified during the 10-year history of Project Spectrum. Further study of these developmental issues would be of great value, both theoretically and practically.

The Study of Group Process in Learning

Attention to group effects and teacher guidance is a constant underlying dimension in Spectrum's work. Some Spectrum assessment activities, such as creative movement and the peer interaction checklist, are conducted in a group setting. Also, small group work is the primary context for all Spectrum early learning activities. In addition, Spectrum profiles are based on performance relative to the particular group of children being assessed rather than norm-referenced benchmarks. Last but not least, teacher scaffolding in the Spectrum assessment is permitted and accounted for in scoring, and teacher guidance is essential to the implementation of all Spectrum learning activities. However, the primary focus of Spectrum's work is on individuals. Indeed, one of the most distinctive strengths of Spectrum's work is its genuine attention and deep commitment to individual differences. Because the unit of analysis in Spectrum's work is the individual, examining and documenting the development of the individual in groups has yet to be explored in detail.

In today's field of cognitive development, more and more people have accepted the theoretical proposition that cognition is a collaborative process (Rogoff, 1998). When studying collaborative, collective, or distributed cognition, the unit of analysis switches from the individual to the group, social interaction, cultural practice, or sociocultural activity (Leont'ev, 1981; Rogoff, 1998; Vygotsky, 1978; Wertsch, 1981). In the Spectrum context, research on group process might include investigations of how a child learns from and with others in developing strengths, how a child's strengths become part of one's identity in a group, and how children help each other by using their strengths. In addition, it would be of great interest to examine the effects of group process on individual learning as a covariance of the strengths of individual children and how the composition of team members including their cognitive compatibility affects individual learning.

In collaboration with Reggio educators, Mara Krechevsky, the director of Project Spectrum, and her colleagues at Harvard's Project Zero have taken a significant leap in pursuing this line of work. Their most recent publication, *Making Learning Visible: Children as Individual and Group Learners* (Project Zero & Reggio Children, 2001), provides numerous vivid examples of how individual children benefit from, as well as contribute to, the group learning process. Their description of the nature of learning groups and the features of learning in groups focuses on interconnection and holistic structure, arguing that the whole is larger than the sum of parts (Project Zero & Reggio Children, 2001; Turner & Krechevsky, 2003). However, challenges remain when studying individuals in relation to the group. The primary one is methodology—such study requires lengthy observation and documentation of relatively small numbers of children in natural settings. This methodology yields data that are rich and authentic, as it draws on research skills from psychology and anthropology as well as education. It nonetheless can be subject to interpretation, difficult to replicate, hard to establish reliability, and time consuming. The full implications of such research methodology are yet to be realized as psychologists and educators pursue studies about group process in learning (Cole, 1996; McNamee, 1990, 2000; Paley, 2003; Rogoff, 1998).

The Connection Between Assessment and Teaching

Educational application is a primary focus of Project Spectrum. For the Spectrum assessment activities to be more teacher friendly, two aspects of the work require further attention: procedures for implementation and interpretation of results. In contrast to standardized tests, the Spectrum assessment activities use varied procedures and evaluation systems to fit the nature of specific activities. Some Spectrum assessment activities are structured and yield a numerical score. Other activities are open ended, with the child's performance evaluated using checklists. Some checklists are based on a "yes" or "no" system, others require checking "correct" or "incorrect," and still others are simple checks. While these varied procedures and evaluation systems are necessary to make the assessment diverse and flexible, the variability also makes the instrument less easy to comprehend, more difficult to learn, and harder to implement.

The issue of interpreting results concerns the meaning of Spectrum assessment results for each child's education. As described earlier, Spectrum's assessment system is designed to assess the cognitive abilities of individual children by focusing on key abilities within different domains. Domains examined in Project Spectrum, however, are not synonymous with school subject areas, nor are key abilities equivalent to key concepts, such as phonemic awareness and word knowledge in the area of emergent literacy (Burns, Griffin, & Snow, 1999). The differences between what Spectrum emphasizes and what schools teach enrich the classroom environment. They may also make it difficult for teachers to translate the results of Spectrum's assessments into curriculum planning. For example, the key abilities identified by Spectrum in the language domain include invented narrative, descriptive language, and poetic use of language, apparently all relating to oral language. If a child displays a language strength based on the Spectrum assessment, what does it mean to a teacher for instructional practice in the following days and months? How would this strength relate to benchmarks in speaking and communicating for preschoolers? How might this strength lead to the development of emergent literacy skills—a fundamental task for early educators and a key for children learning to read? Clearly, making the connection between assessment results and instructional practice transparent is not an easy task for assessment designers. Given that the primary purpose of assessment is improving instruction and providing appropriate intervention (Greenspan & Meisels, 1996; Horton & Bowman, 2002), we

have no choice but to work on this task wholeheartedly.

CONCLUSION

This is a time of educational conformity and rigidity. Influenced by the "No Child Left Behind" Act of 2001, an enormously important federal law intended to improve America's public schools, the Bush administration has proposed a new early childhood initiative—*Good Start, Grow Smart*—to help states and local communities strengthen early learning for young children (DHHS, 2003). The intention is undoubtedly laudable, as it is based on the belief that all children must begin school with an equal chance at achievement and no child can be left behind.

A closer examination of the initiative reveals that the only areas focused on are early literacy, language, and numerical skills. The primary method of assessing these learning goals is standardized testing, largely of isolated skills. What is more, all Head Start programs will soon be scrutinized with such high-stakes tests; data on whether a Head Start program is successfully reaching these standards will be used in the Human Health Services' evaluation of local Head Start agency contacts (DHHS, 2003). This narrowed focus on early learning and ways of evaluating early learning has caused great concern among early childhood educators (Anyon, 2003; Ryan, 2003; Silin & Schwartz, 2003).

The concern that educators express today about the use of standardized tests to assess narrowly defined cognition and learning is a concern that educators have voiced before. Recall, both Feldman's nonuniversal theory and Gardner's theory of multiple intelligences represented significant departures from this view and practice. Also, a similar concern was voiced 20 years ago in response to the rhetoric of the report entitled *A Nation at Risk*. And indeed, the birth of Project Spectrum was in part a response to the national debate about developmentally appropriate education for young children. A primary difference between the current debate and the debate 20 years ago is that we now know much more about young children's learning and development.

From the work of Project Spectrum, we know that diversity, individuality, and flexibility are keys to developmentally appropriate education and young children's learning. Learning standards are important. To foster meaningful learning and development, standards should recognize diverse human cognitive abilities, encourage the use of multiple symbol systems to express and facilitate understanding, and allow for the varied developmental rates of young children. By focusing on only one or two areas of learning, we significantly reduce the possibility of developing all human potential and limit the opportunities for children's success in school and in life.

Stressing the value of diverse learning areas does not disregard the importance of early literacy and numerical skills. They are critical to functioning in an industrial society. They are also cornerstones for learning. However, as revealed in the work of Project Spectrum, a rich and deep understanding of key concepts and ideas is as important as the mastery of discrete skills in the areas of early literacy and math. Further, there are numerous ways of exposing young children to these concepts, ideas, and skills. Direct instruction has its place; so do hands-on manipulation and all kinds of play activities. Some children might benefit from an educational approach focused on overcoming deficits whereas others might be more responsive to an approach building on strengths.

Project Spectrum advocates and models the use of performance-based assessment in early childhood classrooms for instructional purposes. We believe in accountability but do not support the use of standardized tests because they do not provide accurate information about what children learn and what teachers teach in early childhood classrooms (Horton & Bowman, 2002). Our work indicates that young children's learning is highly integrated, episodic, and nonlinear. The breadth and depth of their skills and knowledge cannot be assessed accurately through a point-in-time, content-driven test with a standard format. Also shown in our work is the complexity of young children's learning processes. The learning process involves both internal factors such as the child's motivation and interests and external factors such as materials and social structure. While these factors are extremely important for instructional practice, they are often controlled for or disregarded as noise in standardized tests.

When we overemphasize uniformity, conformity, and rigidity, we lose diversity, individuality, and flexibility. Education is the science and art of balancing extremes and finding ways to reach every child. Consider what dangerously large numbers of our youngsters are neither understood nor nurtured in the schools they are required to attend. Consider how many children have already been left behind. Narrowing the criteria for success further restricts opportunities for children to discover and build on their strengths. Let us hold ourselves, as educators, administrators, and policy makers, accountable too. To help ensure that no child is left behind, let's find more doors for children to open and more ways for them to succeed in school.

REFERENCES

Adams, M. (1993). *An empirical investigation of domain-specific theories of preschool children's cognitive abilities.* Unpublished doctoral dissertation, Tufts University, Medford, MA.

Adams, M., & Feldman, D. H. (1993). Project Spectrum: A theory-based approach to early education. In R. Pasnak & M. L. Howe (Eds.), *Emerging themes in cognitive development: Vol. II:*

Competencies (pp. 53–76). New York: Springer-Verlag.

Anyon, J. (2003, April). *Rethinking the process of reform.* Paper presented at the annual meeting of the American Educational Research Association, Chicago, IL.

Association for Supervision and Curriculum Development (ASCD). (1988). *A resource guide to public school early childhood programs.* Alexandria, VA: Author.

Barnett, W. S. (1998). Long-term effects of early childhood programs on cognitive and school outcomes. In W. S. Barnett & S. S. Boocock (Eds.), *Early care and education for children in poverty: Promises, programs, and long-term outcomes* (pp. 11–14). Buffalo: State University of New York Press.

Bolanos, P. (2003, April). *Implementing MI in the Key Learning Community.* Paper presented at the annual meeting of the American Educational Research Association, Chicago, IL.

Bowman, B. T., Donovan, M. S., & Burns, M. S. (Eds.). (2001). *Eager to learn: Educating our preschoolers.* Washington, DC: National Academy Press.

Bransford, J., Brown, A. L., & Cocking, R. R. (Eds.). (1999). *How people learn: Brain, mind, experience, and school.* Washington, DC: National Academy Press.

Bredekamp, S. (Ed.). (1987). *Developmentally appropriate practice in early childhood programs serving children from birth through age 8* (Exp. ed.). Washington, DC: National Association for the Education of Young Children.

Burns, M. S., Griffin, P., & Snow, C. E. (Eds.). (1999). *Starting out right: A guide to promoting children's reading success.* Washington, DC: National Academy Press.

Campbell, B. (1992, Summer). Multiple intelligences in action. *Childhood Education, 197–202.*

Campbell, L., Campbell, B., & Dickinson, D. (1996). *Teaching and learning through multiple intelligences.* Needham Heights, MA: Allyn & Bacon.

Case, R. (1992). *The mind's staircase: Exploring the conceptual underpinnings of children's thought and knowledge.* Hillsdale, NJ: Erlbaum.

Ceci, S. J. (1996). *On intelligence: A bio-ecological treatise on intellectual development* (2nd ed.). Cambridge, MA: Harvard University Press.

Chen, J. Q. (1992). *Building on children's strengths: Examination of a Project Spectrum intervention program for students at risk for school failure.* Unpublished doctoral dissertation, Tufts University, Medford, MA.

Chen, J. Q. (1993, April). *Working with at-risk children through the identification and nurturance of their strengths.* Paper presented at the biennial conference of the Society for Research of Child Development, New Orleans, LA.

Chen, J. Q., & Feinburg, S. (1998). Visual arts scoring criteria. In M. Krechevsky (Ed.), *Project Spectrum preschool assessment handbook* (pp. 159–162). New York: Teachers College Press.

Chen, J. Q., & Gardner, H. (1997). Alternative assessment from a multiple intelligences theoretical perspective. In D. P. Flanagan, J. L. Genshaft, & P. L. Harrison (Eds.), *Contemporary intellectual assessment: Theories, tests, and issues* (pp. 105–121). New York: Guilford Press.

Chen, J. Q., Isberg, E., & Krechevsky, M. (Eds.). (1998). *Project Spectrum: Early learning activities.* New York: Teachers College Press.

Chen, J. Q., Krechevsky, M., & Viens, J. (1998). *Building on children's strengths: The experience of Project Spectrum.* New York: Teachers College Press.

Cohen, D. H., & Stern, V. (1997). *Observing and recording the behavior of young children* (4th ed.). New York: Teachers College Press.

Cole, M. (1996). *Cultural psychology: A once and future discipline.* Cambridge, MA: Harvard University Press.

Dempsey, R. (1998). Music activities. In J. Q. Chen, E. Isberg, & M. Krechevsky (Eds.), *Project Spectrum: Early learning activities* (pp. 81–106). New York: Teachers College Press.

Department of Health and Human Services (DHHS). (2003). *Good Start, Grow Smart.* www.whitehouse.gov/infocus/earlychildhood.

Dunn, L. (1993). Proximal and distal features of day care quality and children's development. *Early Childhood Research Quarterly, 8* (2), 167–192.

Early Childhood Education Commission (ECEC). (1986). *Take a giant step.* New York, NY: Author.

Edwards, C., Gandini, L., & Forman, G. (Eds.). (1998). *The hundred languages of children: The*

Reggio Emilia approach–advanced reflections (2nd ed.). Greenwich, CT: Ablex.

Elkind, D. (1987). *Miseducation: Preschoolers at risk.* New York: Knopf.

Feldman, D. H. (1974). Universal to unique: A developmental view of creativity and education. In S. Rosner & L. Abt (Eds.), *Essays in creativity* (pp. 45–85). Croton-on-Hudson: North River Press.

Feldman, D. H. (1980). *Beyond universals in cognitive development.* Norwood, NJ: Ablex.

Feldman, D. H. (1985). The concept of nonuniversal developmental domains: Implications for artistic development. *Visual Arts Research, 11,* 82–89.

Feldman, D. H. (1986). How development works. In I. Levin (Ed.), *Stage and structure: Reopening the debate* (pp. 284–306). Norwood, NJ: Ablex.

Feldman, D. H. (1987). Developmental psychology and art education: Two fields at the crossroads. *Journal of Aesthetic Education, 21,* 243–259.

Feldman, D. H. (1989). Universal to unique: Toward a cultural genetic epistemology. *Archives de Psychologie, 56,* 271–279.

Feldman, D. H. (1994). *Beyond universals in cognitive development* (2nd ed.). Norwood, NJ: Ablex.

Feldman, D. H. (1998). How Spectrum began. In J. Q. Chen, M. Krechevsky, & J. Veins. *Building on children's strengths: The experience of Project Spectrum* (pp. 1–17). New York: Teachers College Press.

Feldman, D. H., & Adams, M. L. (1989). Intelligence, stability, and continuity: Changing conceptions. In M. Bornstein & N. Krasnegor (Eds.), *Stability and continuity in mental development: Behavioral and biological perspectives* (pp. 293–309). Hillsdale, NJ: Erlbaum.

Feldman, D. H., & Fowler, R. C. (1997a). The nature(s) of developmental change: Piaget, Vygotsky, and the transition process. *New Ideas in Psychology 15* (3), 195–210.

Feldman, D. H., & Fowler, R. C. (1997b). Second thoughts: A response to the commentaries. *New Ideas in Psychology 15* (3), 235–245.

Feldman, D. H., & Goldsmith, L. (1991). *Nature's gambit* (2nd ed.). New York: Teachers College Press.

Flavell, J. H., & Markman, E. M. (1983). Preface. In J. H. Flavell & E. M. Markman (Eds.), *Handbook of child psychology: Vol. 3. Cognitive development* (4th ed., pp. viii–x). New York: Wiley.

Froebel, F. (1897). *The education of man* (W. N. Hailmann, Trans.). London: Chapman.

Gardner, H. (1983). *Frames of mind: The theory of multiple intelligences.* New York: Basic Books.

Gardner, H. (1987a). Beyond the IQ: Education and human development. *Harvard Educational Review, 57* (2), 187–193.

Gardner, H. (1987b). The theory of multiple intelligences. *Annals of Dyslexia, 37,* 19–35.

Gardner, H. (1991). *The unschooled mind: How children think and how schools should teach.* New York: Basic Books.

Gardner, H. (1993a). *Frames of mind: The theory of multiple intelligences* (10th-anniversary ed.). New York: Basic Books.

Gardner, H. (1993b). *Multiple intelligences: The theory in practice.* New York: Basic Books.

Gardner, H. (1994). Multiple intelligences theory. In R. J. Sternberg (Ed.), *Encyclopedia of human intelligence* (pp. 740–742). New York: Macmillan.

Gardner, H. (1998). The bridges of Spectrum. In J. Q. Chen, M. Krechevsky, & J. Veins (Eds.), *Building on children's strengths: The experience of Project Spectrum* (pp. 138–146). New York: Teachers College Press.

Gardner, H. (1999). *Intelligence reframed: Multiple intelligences for the 21st century.* New York: Basic Books.

Gardner, H. (2000). *The disciplined mind: Beyond facts and standardized tests, the k-12 education that every child deserves.* New York: Penguin Books.

Ginsburg, H., & Opper, S. (1987). *Piaget's theory of intellectual development* (3rd ed.). Upper Saddle River, NJ: Prentice Hall

Greenspan, S. I., & Meisels, S. J. (1996). Toward a new vision for the developmental assessment of infants and young children. In S. J. Meisels & E. Fenichel (Eds.), *New visions for developmental assessment of infants and young children* (pp. 11–26). Washington, DC: ZERO TO THREE/National Center for Infants, Toddlers, and Families.

Haley, M. (2003, April). *Learner-centered instruction and the theory of multiple intelligences with second language learners.* Paper presented at the annual meeting of the American Educational Research Association, Chicago, IL.

Hirschfeld, A. L., & Gelman, R. (1994). Toward a topography of mind: An introduction to domain specificity. In A. L. Hirschfeld & R. Gelman (Eds.), *Mapping the mind: Domain specificity in cognition and culture* (pp. 3–37). Cambridge: Cambridge University Press.

Hoerr, T. (2003, April). *How MI informs teaching at the New City School.* Paper presented at the annual meeting of the American Educational Research Association, Chicago, IL.

Horton, C., & Bowman, B.T. (2002). *Child assessment at the preprimary level: Expert opinion and state trends.* Occasional Paper of Herr Research Center. Chicago, IL: Erikson Institute. Available on the Internet at http://www.erikson.edu/Research/horton-bowman.pdf.

Hsueh, W. C. (2003, April). *The development of a MI assessment for young children in Taiwan.* Paper presented at the annual meeting of the American Educational Research Association, Chicago, IL.

Karmiloff-Smith, A. (1992). *Beyond modularity: A developmental perspective on cognitive science.* Cambridge, MA: MIT Press.

Katz, L. (1987). Early education: What should young children be doing. In S. L. Kagan & E. F. Zigler (Eds.), *Early schooling: The national debate* (pp. 151–167). New Haven, CT: Yale University Press.

Keil, F. (1994). The birth and nurturance of concepts by domains: The origins of concepts of living things. In A. L. Hirschfeld & R. Gelman (Eds.), *Mapping the mind: Domain specificity in cognition and culture* (pp. 234–255). Cambridge: Cambridge University Press.

Kornhaber, M. (1997). *Equitable identification for gifted education and the theory of multiple intelligences.* Unpublished doctoral dissertation. Harvard University, Cambridge, MA.

Kornhaber, M. (1999). Multiple intelligences theory in practice. In J. Block, S. T. Everson, & T. R. Guskey (Eds.), *Comprehensive school reform: A program perspective.* Dubuque, IA: Kendall/Hunt Publishers.

Kornhaber, M., & Krechevsky, M. (1997). Expanding definitions of learning and teaching: Notes from the MI underground. In P. W. Cookson (Ed.), *Creating school policy: Trends, dilemma, and prospects.* New York: Garland Press.

Kornhaber, M., Krechevsky, M., & Gardner, H. (1990). Engaging intelligence *Educational Psychology, 25* (3–4), 177–199.

Kornhaber, M., Veenema, S., & Fierros, E. (2003). *Multiple intelligences: Best ideas from research and practice.* Boston: Allyn & Bacon.

Krechevsky, M. (1998). *Project Spectrum preschool assessment handbook.* New York: Teachers College Press.

Krechevsky, M. (2001). Form, function, and understanding in learning groups: Propositions from the Reggio classrooms. In Project Zero & Reggio Children, *Making learning visible: Children as individual and group learners* (pp. 246–271). The Municipality of Reggio Emilia, Italy: Reggio Children.

Krechevsky, M., & Gardner, H. (1990). The emergence and nurturance of multiple intelligences: The Project Spectrum approach. In M. J. A. Howe (Ed.), *Encouraging the development of exceptional skills and talents.* Leicester, England: British Psychological Society.

Kuhn, S. (1962). *The structure of scientific revolution.* Chicago: University of Chicago Press.

Leont'ev, A. N. (1981). The problem of activity in psychology. In J. W. Wertsch (Ed.), *The concept of activity in Soviet psychology* (pp. 37–71). Armonk, NY: Sharpe.

Leslie, M. A. (1994). ToMM, ToBY, and agency: Core architecture and domain specificity. In A. L. Hirschfeld & R. Gelman (Eds.), *Mapping the mind: Domain specificity in cognition and culture* (pp. 119–149). Cambridge: Cambridge University Press.

Maker, C. J. (1997). Authentic assessment of problem solving and giftedness in secondary school students. In B. Torff (Ed.), *Multiple intelligences and assessment* (pp. 133–152). Arlington Heights, IL: Skylight.

Malkus, U., Feldman, D. H., & Gardner, H. (1988). Dimensions of mind in early childhood. In A. D. Pellegrini (Ed.), *The psychological bases for early education* (pp. 25–38). Chichester, England: Wiley.

Marcon, R. A. (1992). Differential effects of three preschool models on inner-city 4-year-olds. *Early Childhood Research Quarterly, 7* (4), 517–530.

McNamee, G. D. (1990). Learning to read and write in an inner-city setting: A longitudinal study of community change. In L. Moll (Ed.), *Vygotsky and education* (pp. 287–303). New York: Cambridge University Press.

McNamee, G. D. (2000). Child development research in early childhood classrooms. *Human Development, 43* (4–5), 246–251.

Meisels, S. J., Bickel, D. D., Nicholson, J., Xue, Y. G., & Atkins-Burnett, S. (2001). Trusting teachers' judgments: A validity study of a curriculum-embedded performance assessment in kindergarten to grade 3. *American Educational Research Journal, 38* (1), 73–95.

Montessori, M. (1964). *The Montessori method.* New York: Schocken Books.

National Association of State Board of Education (NASBE). (1988). *Right from the start: The report of the NASBE task force on early childhood education.* Alexandria, VA: Author.

National Commission on Excellence in Education (NCEE). (1983). *A nation at risk: The imperative for educational reform.* Washington, DC: U.S. Government Printing Office.

Neisser, U., Boodoo, G., Bouchard, T. J., Boykin, A. W., Brody, N., Ceci, S. J., Halpern, D. F., Loehlin, J. C., Perloff, F., Sternberg, R. J., & Urbina, S. (1996). Intelligence: Knowns and unknowns. *American Psychologist, 51,* 71–101.

The New City School. (1994). *Multiple intelligences: Teaching for success.* St. Louis, MI: Author.

Paley, V. G. (2003, June). *The disappearance of play from the early childhood classroom.* Paper presented at the annual meeting of the Jean Piaget Society, Chicago, IL.

Piaget, J. (1954). *The construction of reality in the child.* New York: Basic Books.

Piaget, J. (1977). The origins of intelligence in children. In H. Gruber & J. J. Vonche (Eds.), *The essential Piaget* (pp. 215–249).

Piaget, J., & Inhelder, B. (1969). *The psychology of the child.* New York: Basic Books.

Plomin, R., & Petrill, S. A. (1997). Genetics and intelligences: What's new? *Intelligence, 24,* 53–77.

Project Spectrum. (1984). *The monitoring of intellectual propensities in early childhood.* Harvard Project Zero, Cambridge, MA: Author.

Project Spectrum. (1988). *The early detection of children "at risk" for school problems.* Harvard Project Zero, Cambridge, MA: Author.

Project Spectrum. (1989) *Building on children's strengths: A Project Spectrum intervention for children at risk for school failure.* Cambridge, MA: Author at the Harvard Graduate School of Education.

Project Zero & Reggio Children. (2001). *Making learning visible: Children as individual and group learners.* The Municipality of Reggio Emilia, Italy: Reggio Children.

Ramos-Ford, V., & Gardner, H. (1991). Giftedness from a multiple intelligences perspective. In N. Colangelo & G. A. Davis (Eds.), *Handbook of gifted education* (pp. 55–64). Boston, Allyn & Bacon.

Rinaldi, C. (2001). Introduction. In Project Zero & Reggio Children, *Making learning visible: Children as individual and group learners* (pp. 28–31). The Municipality of Reggio Emilia, Italy: Reggio Children.

Rogoff, B. (1998). Cognition as a collaborative process. In D. William, D. Kuhn, & R. S. Siegler (Eds.), *Handbook of child psychology: Vol. 2. Cognition, perception, and language.* (5th ed., pp. 679–744). New York: Wiley.

Ryan, S. (2003, April). *Message in a model: Teachers' responses to a court-ordered mandate for curriculum reform.* Paper presented at the annual meeting of the American Educational Research Association, Chicago, IL.

Sameroff, A. J., & Haith, M. M. (1990). *The five to seven year shift.* Chicago: Chicago University Press.

Sameroff, A. J., Seifer, R., Baldwin, A., & Baldwin, C. (1993). Stability of intelligence from preschool to adolescence: The influence of social risk factors. *Child Development, 64,* 80–97.

Sattler, J. (2001). *Assessment of children: Cognitive applications* (4th ed.). San Diego, CA: Sattler.

Shearer, B. (1999). *Multiple intelligences developmental assessment scale.* Kent, OH: Multiple Intelligences Research and Consulting, Inc.

Siegler, R. S. (1996). *Emerging minds: The process of change in children's thinking.* New York: Oxford University Press.

Silin, J., & Schwartz, F. (2003, April). *Progressive pedagogy as school reform.* Paper presented at the annual meeting of the American Educational Research Association, Chicago, IL.

Smith, A. B. (1999). Quality child care and joint attention. *International Journal of Early Years Education, 7*(1), 85–98.

Stefanakis, E. (2003, April). *Multiple intelligences and portfolios: A window into the learner's mind.* Paper presented at the annual meeting of the American Educational Research Association, Chicago, IL.

Sternberg, R. J. (1985). *Beyond IQ: A triarchic theory of human intelligence.* New York: Cambridge University Press.

Teele, S. (2000). *Rainbows of intelligence: Exploring how students learn.* Thousand Oaks, CA: Corwin Press.

Teele, S., & Yemenici, A. (2003, April). *Multiple intelligences and emergent literacy with second language learners.* Paper presented at the annual meeting of the American Educational Research Association, Chicago, IL.

Turner, T., & Krechevsky, M. (2003). Who are the teachers? Who are the learners? *Educational Leadership, 4,* 40–43.

Vygotsky, L. S. (1978). *Mind in society: The development of higher psychological processes* (M. Cole, V. John-Steiner, S. Scribner, & E. Souberman, Trans.). Cambridge, MA: Harvard University Press.

Wellman, M. H., & Gelman, R. (1992). Cognitive development: Foundational theories and core domains. *Annual Review of Psychology, 43,* 337–375.

Wertsch, J. W. (1981). (Ed.). *The concept of activity in Soviet psychology.* Armonk, NY: Sharpe.

Wiggins, G. (1998). *Educative assessment: Designing assessment to inform and improve student performance.* San Francisco, CA: Jossey-Bass.

Wu, W. T. (2003, April). *Multiple intelligences, educational reform, and successful careers.* Paper presented at the annual meeting of the American Educational Research Association, Chicago, IL.

Yoong, S. (2001, November). *Multiple intelligences: A construct validation of the MIDAS Scale in Malaysia.* Paper presented at the International Conference on Measurement and Evaluation in Education, Penang, Malaysia.

SELECTED PUBLICATIONS OF PROJECT SPECTRUM'S WORK

Adams, M. (1993). *An empirical investigation of domain-specific theories of preschool children's cognitive abilities.* Unpublished doctoral dissertation, Tufts University, Medford, MA.

Adams, M., & Feldman, D. H. (1993). Project Spectrum: A theory-based approach to early education. In R. Pasnak & M. L. Howe (Eds.), *Emerging themes in cognitive development: Vol. II: Competencies* (pp. 53–76). New York: Springer-Verlag.

Chen, J. Q. (1992). *Building on children's strengths: Examination of a Project Spectrum intervention program for students at risk for school failure.* Unpublished doctoral dissertation, Tufts University, Medford, MA.

Chen, J. Q., & Gardner, H. (1997). Alternative assessment from a multiple intelligences theoretical perspective. In D. P. Flanagan, J. L. Genshaft, & P. L. Harrison (Eds.), *Contemporary intellectual assessment: Theories, tests, and issues* (pp. 105–121). New York: Guilford Press.

Chen, J. Q., & Gardner, H. (in press). Assessment based on multiple intelligences theory. In D. P. Flanagan, J. L. Genshaft, & P. L. Harrison (Eds.), *Contemporary intellectual assessment: Theories, tests, and issues* (2nd ed.). New York: Guilford Press.

Chen, J. Q., Isberg, E., & Krechevsky, M. (Eds.). (1998). *Project Spectrum: Early learning activities.* New York: Teachers College Press. (General editors: H. Gardner, D. H. Feldman, & M. Krechevsky.) (Translated into Spanish, Portuguese, Chinese, and Italian.)

Chen, J. Q., Krechevsky, M., & Viens, J. (1998). *Building on children's strengths: The experience of Project Spectrum.* New York: Teachers College Press. (General editors: H. Gardner, D. H.

Feldman, & M. Krechevsky.) (Translated into Spanish, Portuguese, Chinese, and Italian.)

Feldman, D. H., & Adams, M. L. (1989). Intelligence, stability, and continuity: Changing conceptions. In M. Bornstein & N. Krasnegor (Eds.), *Stability and continuity in mental development: Behavioral and biological perspectives* (pp. 293–309). Hillsdale, NJ: Lawrence Erlbaum.

Gardner, H., & Viens, J. (1990). Multiple intelligences and styles: Partners in effective education. *The Clearinghouse Bulletin: Learning/ Teaching Styles and Brain Behavior, 4* (2), 4–5. Seattle, WA: Association for Supervision and Curriculum Development.

Gray, J., & Viens, J. (1994). Multiple intelligences and multicultural education: Adding intelligences to our understanding of diversity. *Phi Kappa Phi,* Winter.

Kornhaber, M., & Gardner, H. (1993). *Varieties of excellence: Identifying and assessing children's talents.* New York: Teachers College Press.

Kornhaber, M., & Krechevsky, M. (1997). Expanding definitions of learning and teaching: Notes from the MI underground. In P. W. Cookson (Ed.), *Creating school policy: Trends, dilemma, and prospects.* New York: Garland Press.

Krechevsky, M. (1991). Project Spectrum: An innovative assessment alternative. *Educational Leadership, 48* (5), 43–48.

Krechevsky, M. (1998). *Project Spectrum preschool assessment handbook.* New York: Teachers College Press. (General editors: H. Gardner, D. H. Feldman, & M. Krechevsky.) (Translated into Spanish, Portuguese, Chinese, and Italian.)

Krechevsky, M., & Gardner, H. (1990). The emergence and nurturance of multiple intelligences: The Project Spectrum approach. In M. J. A. Howe (Ed.), *Encouraging the development of exceptional skills and talents.* Leicester, England: British Psychological Society.

Krechevsky, M., & Gardner, H. (1994). Multiple intelligences in multiple contexts. In D. Detterman (Ed.), *Current topics in human intelligence* (Vol. 4). Norwood, NJ: Ablex.

Krechevsky, M., Hoerr, T., & Gardner, H. (1995). Complementary energies: Implementing MI theory from the laboratory and from the field. In J. Oakes & K. H. Quartz (Eds.), *Creating new educational communities: Schools and classrooms where all children can be smart. 94th yearbook of the National Society for the Study of Education-Part I* (pp. 166–186). Chicago: University of Chicago Press.

Krechevsky, M., & Malkus, U. (1997). Telling their stories, singing their songs. In J. Flood, S. Brice-Heath, and D. Lapp (Eds.), *Handbook of research on teaching literacy through the communicative and visual arts.* New York: Macmillan.

Krechevsky, M., & Seidel, S. (1998). Minds at work: Applying multiple intelligences in the classroom. In R. J. Sternberg & W. Williams (Eds.), *Intelligence, instruction, and assessment.* Hillsdale, NJ: Lawrence Erlbaum.

Malkus, U., Feldman, D. H., & Gardner, H. (1988). Dimensions of mind in early childhood. In A. D. Pellegrinin (Ed.), *The psychological bases for early education* (pp. 25–38). Chichester, England: Wiley.

Ramos-Ford, V., Feldman, D. H., & Gardner, H. (1988). A new look at intelligence through Project Spectrum. *On the Beam, 6,* 15.

Ramos-Ford, V., & Gardner, H. (1991). Giftedness from a multiple intelligences perspective. In N. Colangelo & G. A. Davis (Eds.), *Handbook of gifted education* (pp. 55–64). Boston: Allyn & Bacon.

Sherman, C., Feldman, D. H., & Gardner, H. (1988). A pluralistic view of early assessment: The Spectrum approach. *Theory into Practice, 27,* 77–83.

Viens, J. (1999a). Project Spectrum: A pluralistic approach to intelligence and assessment in early education, part I. *Teaching Thinking and Problem Solving, 12* (2), 1–4.

Viens, J. (1999b). Project Spectrum: A pluralistic approach to intelligence and assessment in early education, part II. *Teaching Thinking and Problem Solving, 12* (3), 1–4.

Chapter 12

The Developmental-Interaction Approach at Bank Street College of Education

Harriet K. Cuffaro, Nancy Nager, and Edna K. Shapiro ∽ Bank Street College of Education, New York

Although some use the term the *Bank Street approach* to early childhood education, and that is the title used in earlier editions of this volume, many practitioners and proponents prefer the term the *developmental-interaction approach*. Although admittedly more cumbersome, developmental-interaction specifies key features of the approach and also removes it from its geographically specific site of origin. Many schools for children, as well as individual classroom teachers, consider themselves exemplars of this approach to teaching, although Bank Street College of Education claims the longest consistent association with this way of thinking about and practicing education.

The term *developmental-interaction* calls immediate attention to the centrality of the concept of development, the ways in which children's (and adults') modes of apprehending, understanding, and responding to the world change and grow as a consequence of their continuing experience of living. The term *interaction* refers to the tenet that thinking and emotion are interconnected, interacting spheres of development; and it highlights the focus on the importance of engagement with the environment of people and the material world.

The term has been in use since 1971 (see, e.g., Biber, Shapiro, & Wickens, 1971; Goffin, 1994; Nager & Shapiro, 2000; Shapiro & Biber, 1972; Shapiro & Weber, 1981), but the basic ideas have a much longer history. We begin with the origins of these principles and practices both to indicate the forerunners of several of the key educational ideas and also to demonstrate that programs for young children have a more extensive history than is often recognized.

🖎 HISTORY AND EVOLUTION

One notable aspect of the early days of the twentieth century, a period now known as the Progressive era, was that many women were rebelling against conventional restrictions on women's lives. Social reformers were exposing social inequities and working to show ways toward a more democratic, egalitarian society. For example, Jane Addams and Lillian Wald were pioneering social workers; Susan B. Anthony, Lucretia Mott, and Elizabeth Cady Stanton fought for women's suffrage. In New York City alone, there were innovative educators such as Caroline Pratt, who founded the Play School, later known as the City and Country School; Elisabeth Irwin, who founded the Little Red School House; and Margaret Naumberg, who began the Walden School.

Among the small, independent educational enterprises designed to model new ways of teaching and new social arrangements was the Bureau of Educational Experiments. Founded in 1916 by Lucy Sprague Mitchell, it later became Bank Street College of Education. Mitchell was strongly influenced by the work of John Dewey.

A philosopher, psychologist, educator, and prolific writer, his ideas still inform thinking about education. Dewey's belief in the importance of education for the development of a democratic society was crucial. Central too was the proposition that school learning should be connected to children's lives in meaningful ways. The school that Dewey founded at the University of Chicago in 1896 was a laboratory, synthesizing the study of human development and the creation of curriculum. The school was an experiment in guiding children's development toward greater collaboration and living out democratic ideals (see, e.g., Cahan, 1992; Dewey, 1991a/1937, 1991b/1936, Tanner, 1997).

Mrs. Mitchell founded the Bureau as a research organization; Harriet Johnson, who had been working for the Public Education Association, became the founding director of the Bureau's nursery school in 1919. The school was designed to be an arena for studying children and for devising teaching practices that fostered growth and development. When Bureau staff—teachers and researchers—spoke of development or of schooling, they did not refer only to cognitive gains. They saw children's growth as encompassing physical, social, emotional, and aesthetic as well as intellectual domains. The concept of the whole child captures a salient aspect of this approach to education (see Biber, 1972). The Bureau was part of an informal network of experimental schools that shared a commitment to progressive pedagogy and a spirit of inquiry (see Winsor, 1973, for a compilation of bulletins from these schools).

Mitchell combined a full-scale career with an active family life; she was a pioneer of what her biographer, Joyce Antler (1981, 1987), calls "feminism as life process." Like Dewey, she was a strong believer in the then remarkable idea that schools that would enhance and support children's growth should be based on knowing more about how children learn, how to build on their interests, and how to introduce concepts and knowledge in ways that made sense to chil-

dren. In *Two Lives,* a book that combines her autobiography and a biography of her husband, the economist Wesley Clair Mitchell, she wrote: "It seemed to me that knowledge gained through all the kinds of work I had seen . . . was relevant to a study of children, and surely one had to understand children in order to plan a school that was right for their development" (Mitchell, 1953, p. 273).

Over time there was a growing interest in making this kind of education available to more children of preschool age and extending it into the elementary years. In 1930 the Cooperative School for Teachers was initiated to prepare teachers to work in these new kinds of ways and to help teachers learn as the children did, by active experimentation. This approach is compatible with what is now known as constructivism.

Subsequently, Mrs. Mitchell and the Bureau (later, College) staff worked in public school classrooms where teachers volunteered to have staff members bring curriculum ideas and materials to their classrooms and model teaching techniques. The Public School Workshops, as they were called, continued for many years in New York City and neighboring communities. The staff introduced progressive educational ideas to many schools that followed basically traditional teaching methods. In turn, staff had the opportunity to work with a more diverse student and teacher population. In this sense, the workshops laid the groundwork for Bank Street's leadership and participation in national educational programs such as Head Start and Follow Through (Shapiro, 2003). More recently, Bank Street has been engaged in a notably successful collaboration with the Newark, New Jersey Public Schools in a multiyear restructuring of early childhood education (Silin & Lippman, 2003).

Mrs. Mitchell was joined by dedicated colleagues who made important contributions to clarifying and expanding the fundamental philosophy of the developmental-interaction approach. Many deserve mention, but Barbara Biber stands out. A volume of her collected papers represents

50 years of thoughtful attention to the blending of psychological and educational insights (Biber, 1984; see also, Zimiles, 1997). Her work demonstrated psychological depth, a keen understanding of children's development, and a pervasive faith in the potential power of schooling to provide a context for living democratic ideals.

Two concepts of broad scope were central to the evolving developmental-interaction approach: progressivism and mental health. Although the term *mental health* is no longer in common use, its meaning has been incorporated into generally accepted views of the potential of schooling for fostering healthy development. The school was seen as a vehicle for promoting mental health by providing opportunities for creative and satisfying work; by cultivating cooperation rather than competitiveness; by offering children meaningful and stimulating rather than rote and fragmented learning; by nurturing individuality; and by furthering values of social democracy. The school was, and is, seen as much more than simply a place to learn basic cognitive skills. Certainly, the developmental-interaction approach does not fit what Freire (1970) described as a "banking model" of education, one in which the expert teacher deposits knowledge into the passive child recipient.

BASIC PRINCIPLES

As noted, the roots of the developmental-interaction approach are found in two major areas: educational theorists and practitioners, primarily John Dewey and early progressive pioneers such as Lucy Sprague Mitchell, Harriet Johnson, Caroline Pratt, and Susan Isaacs; and developmental theorists, especially those who saw development in dynamic terms and in social context, such as Anna Freud (1974), Erik Erikson (1963), Heinz Werner (1961), Jean Piaget (1952), and Kurt Lewin (1935).

Several general principles about development and children's interactions with the social and physical environment are basic to understanding the developmental-interaction approach. A fun-

The utility of the Bank Street approach has been demonstrated in the public school system as well.

damental tenet has already been mentioned in the definition but bears repeating because it is a distinctive feature of the approach: "that the growth of cognitive function . . . cannot be separated from the growth of interpersonal processes" (Shapiro & Biber, 1972, p. 61). This guiding principle governs the theory and practice of the developmental-interaction approach. The concept of development is dynamic. It is not a simple maturational unfolding but, rather, involves shifts in the way individuals organize and respond to experiences. True to the constructivist paradigm, the child is viewed as an active maker of meaning; the school must provide opportunities for authentic problem solving.

Another basic principle is that engaging actively with the environment is intrinsic to human motivation. Further, as children grow, they construct more and more complex ways of making sense of the world. In general, the direction of growth involves movement from simpler to more complex and integrated modes.

When thinking about developmental sequences, one must remember that individuals are never at a fixed point on a straight line but operate within a range of possibilities. Earlier ways of organizing experience are not eradicated but become integrated into more advanced systems. While the concept of stages was invoked in the past to describe sequential patterns of developmental organization, recent research has raised serious questions about the invariance and universality of stage concepts.

A central idea shared with numerous other educational approaches is the importance of the development of a sense of self as a unique and independent being. The idea of self described in developmental-interaction is informed by the thinking of George Herbert Mead:

> the self is both image and instrument. It emerges as the result of a maturing process in which differentiation of objects and other people becomes progressively more refined and self-knowledge is built up from repeated awareness and assessment of the powers of the

self in the course of mastering the environment. The shape and quality of the self reflect the images of important people in the growing child's life (Biber & Franklin, 1967, pp. 13–14; Mead, 1934).

Growth and maturing involve conflict. Conflict is necessary for development—sometimes within the self, sometimes with others. The nature of interaction with significant figures in the child's life and the demands of the culture will determine the way conflicts are resolved.

In recent years, the work of the Russian psychologist and educator Lev Vygotsky has had a major impact on our conceptualization of interaction. We cannot claim that his work influenced earlier formulations, because the relevant writings were not translated into English until 1978. However, his work and that of his followers is now providing an important perspective that highlights the social context for children's learning and development and emphasizes the interactive nature of learning (see, e.g., Moll, 1990; Rogoff, 1990; Vygotsky, 1978; Wertsch, 1985).

From these general principles of development and interaction, a picture emerges of the learner and future citizen. School becomes a place to promote the development of competence in all areas of children's lives and helps them attain a sense of autonomy and personal and group identity. The development of social relatedness is equally stressed.[1] The school empowers children to deal effectively with their environments. It is an active community, connected to the social world of which it is a part,

---

[1]In an analysis of the evolution of the Bank Street approach, Nager and Shapiro (2000) point out that in earlier formulations the development of an autonomous and independent sense of self was seen as a goal. Until relatively recently, the concept of individuality was so deeply embedded in developmental theory that its assumptions were seldom noticed or questioned. Today, however, we have become more aware that different cultural groups place quite different values on independence as opposed to community or collectivity. We are more sensitized to the depth and scope of the formative impact of culture on growth and development.

rather than an isolated place for learning lessons. This means that the school shares responsibility with children's families and neighborhood institutions. Sharing responsibility means sharing power and actively seeking engagement. In a time of increased immigration and greater diversity in school populations, these points take on new meanings.

CURRICULUM

Explicitly or implicitly, any theory or philosophy of education holds within it a view of the learner, consideration of the relationship between learning and teaching, as well as a statement of what knowledge is deemed most worthy of knowing. As evident throughout this volume, approaches to early childhood education differ in the degree of exactness and specificity required in the relationship between theory or philosophy and practice. Some educational programs translate theory into explicit goals and strategies and the teacher is seen as a skilled implementor of a delivered curriculum. In contrast, in educational programs like developmental-interaction, the underlying philosophy generates principles that guide, rather than determine, practice. In such programs, teachers are expected to develop curriculum content and practices within a stated framework of valued aims and beliefs (Schoonmaker & Ryan, 1996). From the history, philosophy, and developmental theory of Bank Street how are ideas and expectations realized in and through practice? How does this approach to education respond to the fundamental *how, what, when, where,* and *why* questions of curriculum? What choices are made concerning knowledge? How are the teacher and learner portrayed?

The Learner

From birth, children are seen as curious beings who are actively engaged in interaction with their social and physical environment and who, through sensorial exploration and experimentation, work eagerly to make sense of the world in which they live. Each child has a history of experiences in a world shaped and influenced by the social forces of family, community, and culture. In their encounters with the social and physical environment, children respond with a wholeness of self. As Lucy Sprague Mitchell (1951) noted,

> . . . a child is not to be regarded as a sum of special faculties to be trained or developed separately; (the child) is to be regarded as a person, an organism, reacting to experiences as a whole . . . for purposes of discussion a child may be divided into a physical body; an intelligence with certain capacities and limitations; a social being reacting to others—either adults or his peers; a creature capable of definite social responses. But no one has ever met such split-off division of a child all by itself. (p. 189)

The concept of a democratic society guides the development and education of the learner in the developmental-interaction approach, influencing curricular decisions about content, practices, and the quality of the social and physical environment. This all-permeating concept reflects Bank Street's historical roots in the Progressive movement and the influence of Dewey's educational philosophy in which school and society, democracy and education, are intrinsically connected. The communication, participation, and associated living essential to a democratic society become a way of life to be experienced in the community of the classroom (Cuffaro, 1995; Dewey, 1991b/1936). "If we really want to know what democracy is like, we have to have firsthand contacts with it—that is, we have to live democratically. This holds true for teachers and children alike" (Mitchell, 1942, p. 1). What might democracy look like in a classroom of 3- or 5- or 8-year-olds?

Knowledge and Experience

In the Bank Street approach social studies is the core or center of the curriculum. Social studies is about the relationships between and among people and their environment, the world in which we live and our place in it. It concerns the near and far and past and present. Fundamental to this approach is that the school provides consistent opportunities for children to experience democratic living.

> . . . the responsibility of the social studies program is to give children a sense of man's use of his environment and the role which technology plays in the development of that environment, and understanding of the meaning and structure of society and appreciation of man's striving toward the beautiful, the attainment of his goals. (Winsor, 1957, p. 397)

It is essential that the *what* and *how* of learning are interconnected. *What* one learns about the world is not separated from *how* that knowledge is gained and used. From its inception, fundamental to this approach to education is the concept of learning from experience.

> To learn from experience is to make a backward and forward connection between what we do to things and what we enjoy and suffer from things in consequence. Under such conditions, doing becomes a trying; an experiment with the world to find out what it is like; the undergoing becomes an instruction—the discovery of the connection of things. (Dewey, 1966/1916, p. 140)

To learn from experience, children must engage directly and actively with the environment, motivated by their interests and curiosities, and the questions raised in classroom discussions and conversations. For experience to be educative there must also be continuity—where "every experience both takes up something from those which have gone before and modifies in some way the quality of those which come after" (Dewey, 1963/1938, p. 35). *Experience, community, connections, relationships, experiment, continuity,* and *problem solving* are key words in the developmental-interaction approach.

Teacher

The classroom is a learning situation in which the teacher becomes the link between the child's personal world of interests and experiences and the objective, ordered world of the fields of study (Dewey, 1959a/1902). Teaching is complex and demanding, requiring a specialized set of knowledge, skills, and dispositions. Firmly grounded in knowledge of development, coupled with understanding each child's individuality, and with deep knowledge of the curriculum content, the teacher's task is to consider, analyze, and integrate meaningfully the *what, how, when,* and *where* of daily classroom life. Teachers must be knowledgeable in the content of the social study not for giving children information but as a guide to asking meaningful questions; for planning opportunities for their experiencing (trips, books, activities); to know available resources; and to assess the development of the study. Academic and practical skills are embedded throughout the curriculum. Guiding the teacher's consideration of these many factors is the *why* of education, the principles of a democratic community. Consequently, attention is given to creating a social atmosphere in the classroom that will invite discussion and the presence of varied perspectives while also encouraging and supporting a common purpose in working together.

Mediating the intricate connections between teaching and learning is a difficult and multilayered undertaking that we believe requires careful preparation (see Nager & Shapiro, 2003, for a fuller discussion). The contemporary policy debate pits those who view teaching as a complex profession against those who want to deregulate the preparation of teachers and provide simpler and faster routes to teaching along with ready-made curriculum for teachers to follow by rote (see, for example, Cochran-Smith & Fries, 2001; Darling-Hammond & Sykes, 1999; U.S. Department of Education, 2002).

The developmental-interaction approach places considerable emphasis on the complexity of enacting the kinds of classroom situations we are describing. The ability to skillfully interweave knowledge of children, families and communities, subject matter content, and pedagogy within a coherent value system represents a demanding conceptualization of teaching that requires both careful preparation and considerable practice.

Learning Environment

What does a developmental-interaction classroom look like? It is a dynamic environment that welcomes active participation, cooperation and independence, and variety in expression and communication. There are unit and hollow blocks, clay, paint, water, sand, paper, crayons, and wood, materials whose lack of structure invites activity, experimentation, imagination, and transformation. There are also more structured materials such as puzzles, manipulatives, Cuisenaire rods, Dienes blocks, teacher-made materials, paper and pencils for writing, and a wide range of books. Activities such as cooking, planting, weaving, and computer use are offered. The inclusion of materials and activities is determined on the basis of the richness of the opportunities they provide for exploration, discovery, and further learning. The allocation of space provides ample room for dramatic play, block building, and group meetings as well as space to work alone or in a small group. Flexibility in the schedule provides extended periods of time for children to actively explore the potential of materials, to take trips, to become involved in expanding ideas and interests, and to work together. Flexibility also exists within the familiar context of the expected routines of time for snack or lunch, story, rest, and outdoor periods.

A consistent part of daily classroom life is creating an environment that stimulates literacy with many and varied opportunities for conversation, discussion, listening to and writing stories, reading, singing, and rhyming. Recent developments in the fields of anthropology, social theory, and linguistics have influenced our understanding of literacy. Guiding the teaching of reading and writing is that all children have ideas they want to communicate. To respond to the individuality of children, a range of strategies is necessary, including features from whole language and the earlier language experience approach, as well as phonetic understanding. Children also communicate their thoughts and feelings through art materials—paint, clay, wood, paper, crayons—which provide essential nonverbal opportunities for expression (Gwathmey & Mott, 2000; Levinger & Mott, 1992).

Experiencing and Integrating Knowledge

In social studies, the history and story of people's lives—their struggles, aspirations, accomplishments, hopes—are viewed from the perspective of different fields of knowledge. The centrality of the *social* in social studies brings questions and ideas back to people. As Dewey noted in a discussion of geography, one of the disciplines within social studies, "the ultimate significance of lake, river, mountain, and plain is not physical but social; it is the part it plays in modifying and directing human relationships" (Dewey, 1975/1909, pp. 34–35). Lucy Sprague Mitchell (1934) adds further detail to this perspective in her discussion of "human geography":

> For human geography deals with the interrelations between the needs of human beings and the outside environment in which they must satisfy their needs. One half of human geography is what people do to modify the earth's surface; the other half is what the phenomena of the earth's surface do to condition men's activities, most of which are concerned with their work. (p. 100)

In social studies multiple opportunities are offered for questioning, problem solving, and making sense of the social and physical environment of our interactions. In such studies there is an ever-widening spiral of learning and understanding of self and the world, for example,

3-year-olds' interest and exploration of themselves and their families; 5-year-olds' study of community services and jobs; 8-year-olds' research on the history of the original settlers of the area in which they live.

The Family

It is essential that the teacher is aware of the multiple meanings that family can have for the children in the class and makes no assumptions about the composition of the family or the values it holds. It seems safe to assume that all families want the best for their children, but it does not necessarily follow that we know what a particular family considers best. In many instances family values and the values of the school and the larger culture may conflict (see, for example, Wasow, 2000).

Self and family are topics of abiding interest for children and a familiar place from which to branch out into the larger world. In a classroom of 3-year-olds, the study of family might be evident in photographs of children's families posted at the children's eye level. Conversations are stimulated between and among children as they make comparisons and find similarities and differences. Diversity among family structures is discussed at group meetings and ideas and conversations are extended through books and stories that include the many ways in which families are constituted—traditional and extended families, gay- and lesbian-headed families, or single parents (see, for example, Casper, Cuffaro, Schultz, Silin, & Wickens 1996). From each family in the group there are songs and stories to hear, favorite foods to be tasted, and holidays and traditions to learn about. Trips within the school and in the immediate neighborhood begin to expand the children's worlds. And in their dramatic play children reconstruct their experiences and experiment with their increasing understanding of their immediate world. Within such multiple sharing of interests and stories, of self and family, a sense of community begins to grow.

The Community

Gradually, children's interest in the world outside the family broadens. Making sense of the world now includes unraveling the mysteries of a highly technological and complex world where origins are often hidden. "How does that work?" "Who's the boss?" "Why?" are the questions of 5-year-olds. When the teacher adds a simple question, "What is a neighborhood?" a foundation can be laid for focusing, organizing, and directing children's curiosities and interests and beginning a study of community life. In the discussions that follow, children have the opportunity to think about and express their ideas, their information, and their misinformation. Extending the scope of the initial question, a new question can be posed: "What do families need?" This may lead to investigating different types of housing; the services provided in the community; the variety of neighborhood stores; available means of transportation; and people's work. In researching and exploring these varied questions, children come to know the detail of people's work through observing and interviewing workers.

One question leads to another, increasing both the scope and depth of children's learning. Children seek not only facts and information but also an understanding of relationships. As knowledge is constructed through many neighborhood trips, it is recorded through trip sheets, graphs, charts, children's written stories and drawings, and murals. Trips and discussions are essential to developing a dynamic social studies program at all ages. Connections are extended and strengthened in daily group meetings and in the children's imaginative dramatic play with blocks as they symbolically create the social and physical world of a neighborhood. In the interactions of their dramatic play, children test hypotheses using the data they have collected and in the process experience and reconstruct their knowledge. The perspectives of both scientist and artist are encouraged in the work of the classroom. And, in the reality of the world the children have constructed in play, new questions surface, interrelationships are discovered, and the need for further information becomes evident.

On Monday morning during the 5-year-olds' group meeting, the children choose what they will build. Painted on the floor are two blue lines for the river that will wind through the block scheme. The structures the children have chosen to build are a hospital, a pizza store, a school, a fire station, a house, a zoo, a bus company, and a doctor's office. During the morning discussion, the "bus drivers" state that they will build a bridge so that they can go back and forth between both parts of the town. This leads to children asking where the bus stops will be. An animated discussion follows with questions such as: Will you stop at every building? Should there be a bus stop in front of the fire station? What will happen if the fire engines have to rush out and there's a bus there? Should the fire station be next to the hospital (because sick people have to sleep and rest)? If there's a fire in the hospital how will the sick people get out?

By midweek there is much activity. The "teacher" at the school is gathering the wooden block figures to go on a trip to the zoo and asks, "Did everyone go to the bathroom?" Using the information they learned on a recent trip to a fire station, the "fire fighters" are inspecting the hospital to check that it is safe. A sign is posted at the pizza store. "GD PIZA $5 NO SMCNG." Beside the house, a child is holding a block figure and waiting impatiently for the bus. Then, with obvious irritation, goes to the teacher. "They don't come! I just wait and wait. We need a meeting! It's not fair." And an argument is breaking out at the doctor's office. "No, they don't." "Yes, they do." "I'm going to ask." The building partners go to the teacher and ask, "Do doctors give shots or give lollipops?" Nearby, a child comments, "My doctor gives me a shot *and* a lollipop." Interactions continue and multiply. Observing individual children and the group dynamics, the teacher notes possible trips to take and questions to ask at the next group meeting.

While the type of trip taken depends on the age of children, going out into the world often may include unexpected encounters with societal problems and issues. For example, on a trip to a local railroad station by a group of 6-year-olds studying transportation, besides gaining information about train tracks and workers, schedules and waiting rooms, the children also see several people who are homeless sitting on benches. Does the unexpected, homelessness, become part of the curriculum? In the partnership between children and teachers in the development of curriculum, how is this question answered? Does the teacher wait to see if the children include homelessness in their discussion, wait to see what appears as the children include the train station in their block scheme? If homelessness does not appear in the children's conversations or buildings, does the teacher introduce the topic?

These questions are fundamental to curriculum planning and are connected intrinsically to the *why* of what is worth knowing. Such questions go beyond the happenings of a specific trip because the world with all its complexities and problems always *is* in the classroom. Children are in and part of the world. They hear adults talk; they watch television. They feel adult tensions and anxieties. They hear words they do not understand; they have questions. Children encounter and are affected by societal issues and attitudes, whether directly or indirectly.

For children to truly make sense of the world, the social atmosphere of the classroom should create opportunities for children to express their thoughts and feelings. A democratic community invites rather than silences questioning and discussion. The questions teachers ask, or choose not to ask, extend or narrow children's view of the world. At times, adults may believe that they must protect children from disturbing aspects of the world. In our protective caring, "what we neglect to present to children may shape their vision of the world and their place in it." As Dewey noted,

Learning is extended beyond the classroom setting to other sources of knowledge.

"the crucial question is the extent to which the material of the social studies . . . is taught simply as information about present society or is taught in connection with things that are done, that need to be done, and how to do them" (1991a/1937, 14:185). Raising questions offers children varied opportunities to reflect on their experiences and to extend their thinking. As children reveal their thoughts, feelings, and questions in their play, drawings and paintings, stories, and conversations, adults have the opportunity to clarify, to support, and to share concerns and feelings. And, it is in associated living, in the daily interactions and work of classroom life, that children experience what is valued and the community we strive to achieve.

Communities of the Past

In the primary grades, children's curiosities gradually turn from interest in the present "here and now" to the lives of people in the past. To be relevant and meaningful to children, and mindful of the still emerging development of children's understanding of historical time, the teacher might select for study immigration or the early settlers of their community.

"What do people need?" remains a primary question but it is now viewed from a different perspective as children must imagine and research change in the physical environment over time. Human geography comes explicitly to the forefront as children take local trips noting physical changes as well as the geographic features that have influenced the possibilities and direction of an area's growth. As Mitchell (1934/1991) noted, "Everywhere people have been conditioned by the earth forces around them; and everywhere they have to a greater or lesser extent changed the earth they live in" (p. 24). Questions such as "How have people worked together to solve ever present human problems?" come to the forefront, as do the concepts of change and interdependence. Trips in the area are supplemented with research in libraries and with museum trips where children may study artifacts from the past. There are also regularly scheduled times for learning and practicing the skills necessary to read, write, and compute at increasingly complex levels.

To integrate and communicate their growing knowledge and research, children become deeply involved in refining their mathematical and mapping skills. They learn to work in scale. They create relief maps and dioramas as ways of expressing and consolidating knowledge. Writing becomes an increasingly important tool as children write reports about researched information such as family stories of immigration, or create imaginative reconstructions of what it might have been like to be a child in their community in the past. Science experiments help children to understand how food was kept and preserved in the past, how herbs and plants were used to create simple remedies. Play appears again but in a more organized, planned manner as the children bring together what they have learned over months of study and create a play. They work on story development and dialogue, simple scenery, and props. The social studies may culminate in an extensive exhibit created by the children in which they display their work—murals, science experiments, books, maps, dioramas, charts. In whatever form the culminating activities may appear, they are shared with other groups and parents.

Curriculum becomes integrated and whole as various skills and subjects are used as means or tools to organize and understand social studies content. At the same time, art, science, math, music, movement, language—each represents a way of knowing the world. These ways of knowing and expressing are explored in their own time within the days and weeks of classroom life. Further, independent of the social studies, there are animals to observe and care for, processes and changes in cooking to be investigated, seeds to be planted, simple machines to construct that illustrate basic laws of physics. Together, these activities encourage the development of a scientific attitude that requires observation, investigation, hypothesizing, and experimentation.

The educator's aim is to create a dynamic learning environment offering multiple opportunities for the expansion and realization of children's potential and capacity. Guided by the philosophical principles of the developmental-interaction approach, the teacher's choice of content will expand and deepen the children's view of the world and their place in it, while encouraging questioning, reflection, responsibility, shared work and community. These attitudes and activities are necessary to experiencing democratic living.

Assessment

Assessment, a valued and integral aspect of the developmental-interaction approach, gives the teacher a means to know how children are learning and growing and therefore provides a guide for curricular decisions. This is consistent with what is referred to as authentic assessment or a learner-centered approach (Cenedella, 1992; McCombs & Whisler, 1997; Meier, 2000; Perrone, 1991). Current school reform movements have placed assessment at the forefront of educational change to achieve higher standards of academic achievement. Desirable outcomes for students are defined primarily in terms of test scores, leading many schools to emphasize teaching to the test at the expense of complex curriculum. In our view this indicates an oversimplified cause-and-effect view of teaching and learning. In addition, the use of test scores as a high-stakes barrier to passing a grade or completing a program of study reflects a narrow and fundamentally undemocratic approach to the education of children (Cuffaro, 2000).

Bank Street has long advocated a broader approach to assessment, based on understanding how the learner makes sense of his or her world and providing a range of opportunities for the student to represent that understanding. Competence in basic skills, the development of an analytic capacity, and a wide range of knowledge in subject areas are fundamental. Of equal importance are attitudes and characteristics of the learner in interaction with the environment, such as the ability to work both independently and collaboratively, to exercise initiative, and to be a socially responsible member of the community. There are many measures of basic skills. In contrast, no readily administered assessments adequately measure the attributes of the learner that are desired outcomes of this approach (see also Zimiles, 1987).

When classroom teachers who use a developmental-interaction approach must comply with mandated educational testing, teachers are urged to advocate for children in two important ways: first by examining the quality of the assessment tools and raising appropriate questions about implementation; and second, by preparing children for test taking without sacrificing a rich curriculum. Assessment requires rigorous, systematic, reflective observing and recording of children's work and behavior over time (see Cohen, Stern, & Balaban, 1997; Haberman, 2000, for valuable guides). Meaningful data include teacher's observations of the ways in which children demonstrate their understanding (e.g., reading, mathematics, working with materials, interacting with others); portfolios of children's work (e.g., artwork, writing, computations, constructions); and, for older children, teacher-designed techniques for checking the quality of student learning (e.g., reading and writing logs, lab reports, inventories, tasks at the end of a unit of study). Analyzing and summarizing these data illustrate Dewey's (1938/1963) scientific method. This process enables the teacher to understand each child's characteristic strengths and needs, what a child knows and can do, as well as what he or she needs to know. In this way, assessment and instruction can mutually inform each other in a constructivist, dynamic manner (see Shepard, 2000, for discussion of paradigms of assessment). Assessment gives the teacher a basis for parent–teacher conferences as well as ongoing planning. In this way, assessment, learning, and the curriculum are integrated, a basic premise of the experimental attitude of progressive education.

IMPLICATIONS FOR TEACHER EDUCATION

Bank Street's central tenets apply equally to the education of children and their teachers. Lucy Sprague Mitchell was convinced that learning processes for adults and children were fundamentally similar, and so "we tried in all fields to give firsthand experiences (in studio, laboratory, and field work) to supplement 'book learning'" (Mitchell, 1953, p. 471).

The conviction that teachers need experiences as learners that parallel the ways they will teach children remains central to teacher education at Bank Street. The developmental assumption is that becoming a competent teacher is tied not only to information but also to the ways in which teachers experience, internalize, and construct their growing knowledge and sense of self as a maker of meaning. It is a process of epistemological development in which teachers come to value

their own voice, self, and mind, enabling them to create opportunities for children to achieve similar processes of discovery and invention (Nager, 1987). Active participation in real problems is the kind of experience that is the basis for both child and adult learning. Therefore, the interrelated set of opportunities that comprise supervised field work is at the heart of the teacher's education.

A system of advisement encompasses the graduate student's entire academic program at Bank Street (Nager, 1987) and thereby serves an integrative function. Advisement incorporates fieldwork, conference group, and course work. In preservice fieldwork, the student works with a cooperating teacher and comes to assume increasing teaching responsibility. When the student is already a classroom teacher, the work setting becomes the inservice fieldwork site. Guiding the student's work is the advisor, a member of the Graduate School faculty. The term *advisor* rather than *supervisor* is noteworthy and indicates a process of guiding learning and thinking and modeling communication and interpersonal relations. The student has a biweekly individual conference with the advisor. One of these meetings follows an observation of the student's teaching and entails shared reflection on that work. Each student also participates in a weekly conference group with the advisor and five to six other students. This group provides an opportunity for peer learning and support as well as an opportunity to participate in the broader and deeper project of democratic culture building (Pignatelli, 2000).

The content of group discussion is open ended. Students bring issues of personal and professional importance to the group, learning and gaining support from the advisor and the peer interaction. Considerable personal growth is required for teachers to assimilate and practice this approach to education (Shapiro, 1991). In attending to individual learning needs, advisement affords the kind of nurturing and stimulating environment that teachers are encouraged to provide for children. Again, the parallel to attending to the complex interrelationships between children's cognitive and affective development is made explicit.

"The image in advisement is of senior and junior colleagues setting individual goals, solving specific problems, attaining mutual insights, evaluating approaches and outcomes, defining and refining values. It combines approaches of the artist, the philosopher, and the scientist" (Bloomfield, 1991, p. 86). Pignatelli (2000) notes that this model challenges "an understanding of professional development defined largely as a matter of enlarging skill level and technical knowledge base" (p. 23). Knowledge is valued as a process of inquiry, reflection, and construction. Teachers are helped to achieve a sense of competence that is both cognitive and affective.

Not surprisingly, knowledge of development constitutes a core foundation of the teacher education curriculum. Teachers learn to think about education in terms of children's developmental needs and characteristics and the values their families and cultures have emphasized. Academic study of child development is combined with learning to observe and record children's behavior as a critical tool for understanding children and planning curriculum.

In all areas of curriculum, students are offered principles and theory and the opportunity to experience them in practice. In curriculum courses, students explore questions about content—what is worth knowing—and consider the implications of their choices for room arrangement and scheduling. They take trips connected to social studies and participate in block workshops. In addition, they have opportunities to paint, sculpt, and create; they visit schools to consider what different philosophies of education look like in practice and work with math manipulatives to reconstruct their understanding of number and mathematical problem solving. Writing logs and research essays as well as creating portfolios provide opportunities to reflect on self, children, and content.

CONCLUSION

In this chapter, we briefly summarized the developmental-interaction approach, long associated with the Bank Street College of Education. Its roots are in the Progressive era and the educational philosophy of John Dewey and Bank Street's founder, Lucy Sprague Mitchell. Concepts found in the dynamic psychologies of Erik Erikson, Anna Freud, and, more recently, Lev Vygotsky contribute a developmental understanding of teaching and learning.

Principles of the approach serve as a context for the teacher's decision making concerning choice of content, methodology, and the physical and psychological environment of the classroom. The developmental-interaction approach is not a codified set of procedures. Rather, the teacher has the complex task of using these values and principles to guide planning, implementation, and assessment of curriculum and children's growth.

These same principles apply to the education of teachers. Through direct experience, children and adults engage actively with the environment, expand their knowledge base, and strengthen their sense of competence and mastery. Teachers educated at Bank Street are expected to have a broad understanding of children's developmental needs and the ability to create caring, intellectually challenging, and democratic classrooms.

ACKNOWLEDGMENTS

We thank the editors and Herbert Zimiles for permission to use material from his chapter "The Bank Street Approach," which appeared in earlier editions of this volume. The utility of the Bank Street approach has been demonstrated in the public school system as well.

REFERENCES

Antler, J. (1981). Feminism as life process: The life and career of Lucy Sprague Mitchell. *Feminist Studies, 7*, 134–157.

Antler, J. (1987). *Lucy Sprague Mitchell: The making of a modern woman.* New Haven, CT: Yale University Press.

Biber, B. (1972). The "whole child," individuality and values in education. In J. R. Squire (Ed.), *A new look at progressive education.* ASCD yearbook (pp. 44–87). Washington, DC: Association for Supervision and Curriculum Development.

Biber, B. (1984). *Early education and psychological development.* New Haven, CT: Yale University Press.

Biber, B., & Franklin, M. (1967). The relevance of developmental and psychodynamic concepts to the education of the preschool child. *Journal of the American Academy of Child Psychiatry, 6,* 5–24.

Biber, B., Shapiro, E., & Wickens, D. (1971). *Promoting cognitive growth: A developmental-interaction point of view.* Washington, DC: National Association for the Education of Young Children.

Bloomfield, D. (1991). A theoretical framework for advisement. *Thought and Practice, 3,* 85–93.

Cahan, E. D. (1992). John Dewey and human development. *Developmental Psychology, 28,* 205–214.

Casper, V., Cuffaro, H. K., Schultz, S., Silin, J. G., & Wickens, E. (1996). Toward a most thorough understanding of the world: Sexual orientation and early childhood education. *Harvard Educational Review, 66,* 271–293.

Cenedella, J. (1992). Assessment through the curriculum. In A. Mitchell & J. David (Eds.), *Explorations with young children: A curriculum guide from The Bank Street College of Education* (pp. 273–282). Mt. Rainier, MD: Gryphon House.

Cochran-Smith, M., & Fries, M. K. (2001). Sticks, stones, and ideology: The discourse of reform in teacher education. *Educational Researcher, 30,* 3–15.

Cohen, D., Stern, V., & Balaban, N. (1997). *Observing and recording the behavior of young children* (4th ed.). New York: Teachers College Press.

Cuffaro, H. K. (1995). *Experimenting with the world: John Dewey and the early childhood classroom.* New York: Teachers College Press.

Cuffaro, H. K. (2000). *Educational standards in a democracy: Questioning process and consequences.* Occasional Paper #4. Bronxville, NY: Child Development Institute, Sarah Lawrence College.

Darling-Hammond, L., & Sykes, G. (1999). (Eds.). *Teaching as the learning profession: Handbook of policy and practice.* San Francisco: Jossey-Bass.

Dewey, J. (1959). The child and the curriculum. In M. S. Dworkin (Ed.), *Dewey on education* (pp. 91–111). New York: Teachers College Press. (Original work published 1902).

Dewey, J. (1963). *Experience and education.* New York: Collier Books. (Original work published 1938).

Dewey, J. (1966). *Democracy and education.* New York: Free Press. (Original work published 1916).

Dewey, J. (1975). *Moral principles in education.* Carbondale: Southern Illinois University Press. (Original work published 1909).

Dewey, J. (1991a). The challenge of democracy to education. In J. A. Boydston (Ed.), *The later works of John Dewey,* 1935–1937 (Vol. 11, pp. 181–190). Carbondale: Southern Illinois University Press. (Original work published 1937).

Dewey, J. (1991b). The Dewey School: The theory of the Chicago experiment. In J. A. Boydston (Ed.), *The later works of John Dewey,* 1925–1953 (Vol. 11, pp. 202–216). Carbondale: Southern Illinois University Press. (Original work published 1936).

Erikson, E. (1963). *Childhood and Society.* New York: Norton.

Franklin, M. (2000). The meanings of play in developmental-interaction. In N. Nager & E. Shapiro (Eds.), *Revisiting progressive pedagogy: The developmental interaction approach.* Albany, NY: SUNY Press.

Freire, P. (1970). *Pedagogy of the oppressed.* New York: Seabury.

Freud, A. (1974). *The writings of Anna Freud* (5 Vol.). New York: International Universities Press.

Goffin, S. G. (1994). *Curriculum models and early childhood education: Appraising the relationship.* Upper Saddle River, NJ: Merrill/Prentice Hall.

Gwathmey, E., & Mott, A. M. (2000). Visualizing experience. In N. Nager & E. Shapiro (Eds.), *Revisiting progressive pedagogy: The developmental interaction approach.* Albany, NY: SUNY Press.

Haberman, E. (2000). Learning to look closely at children: A necessary tool for teachers. In N. Nager & E. Shapiro (Eds.), *Revisiting progressive pedagogy: The developmental interaction approach.* Albany, NY: SUNY Press.

Levinger, L., & Mott, A. M. (1992). Art in early childhood. In A. Mitchell & J. David (Eds.), *Explorations with young children: A curriculum guide from the Bank Street College of Education* (pp. 199–214). Mt. Rainier, MD: Gryphon.

Lewin, K. (1935). *A dynamic theory of personality.* New York: McGraw-Hill.

McCombs, B., & Whisler, J. (1997). *The learner-centered classroom and school.* San Francisco: Jossey-Bass.

Mead, G. H. (1934). *Mind, self, and society: From the standpoint of a social behaviorist.* Chicago: University of Chicago Press.

Meier, D. (2000). Educating a democracy. In J. Cohe and J. Rogers (Eds.), *Will standards save public education?* Boston: Beacon Press.

Mitchell, L. S. (1934). Social studies and geography. *Progressive Education, 11,* 97–105.

Mitchell, L. S. (1942). *The people of the U.S.A.: Their place in the school curriculum* (with Johanna Boetz and others). New York: Progressive Education Association.

Mitchell, L. S. (1951). *Our children and our schools.* New York: Simon & Schuster.

Mitchell, L. S. (1953). *Two lives: The story of Wesley Clair Mitchell and myself.* New York: Simon & Schuster.

Mitchell, L. S. (1991). *Young geographers: How they explore the world and how they map the world.* New York: Bank Street College of Education. (Original work published 1934).

Moll, L. C. (Ed.). (1990). *Vygotsky and education: Instructional implications and applications of socio-historical psychology.* New York: Cambridge University Press.

Nager, N. (1987). Becoming a teacher: The development of thinking about knowledge, learning, and the self. *Thought and Practice, 1,* 27–32.

Nager, N., & Shapiro, E. (2000). (Eds.). *Revisiting progressive pedagogy: The developmental interaction approach.* Albany, NY: SUNY Press.

Nager, N., & Shapiro, E. (2003). *Some principles for teacher education.* New York: Bank Street College of Education.

Perrone, V. (1989). *Working papers: Reflections on teachers, schools, and communities.* New York: Teachers College Press.

Perrone, V. (1991). *A letter to teachers: Reflections on schooling and the art of teaching.* San Francisco: Jossey-Bass.

Piaget, J. (1952). *The origins of intelligence in children.* New York: International Universities Press.

Pignatelli, F. (2000). Furthering a progressive educational agenda: Advisement and the development of educators. In N. Nager & E. Shapiro (Eds.), *Revisiting progressive pedagogy: The developmental interaction approach.* Albany, NY: SUNY Press.

Rogoff, B. (1990). *Apprenticeship in thinking: Cognitive development in social context.* New York: Oxford University Press.

Schoonmaker, F., & Ryan, S. (1996). Does theory lead to practice? Teachers' constructs about teaching: Top-down perspectives. In S. Reifel & J. A. Chafel (Eds.), *Advances in early education and day care* (Vol. 8, pp. 117–152). Greenwich, CT: JAI Press.

Shapiro, E. (1991). Teacher: Being and becoming. *Thought and Practice, 3,* 5–24.

Shapiro, E., & Biber, B. (1972). The education of young children: A developmental-interaction point of view. *Teachers College Record, 74,* 55–79.

Shapiro, E., & Weber, E. (Eds.). (1981). *Cognitive and affective growth: Developmental-interaction.* Hillsdale, NJ: Erlbaum.

Shapiro, E. K. (2003). Precedents and precautions. In J. Silin & C. Lippman (Eds.), *Putting the children first: The changing face of Newark's public schools.* New York: Teachers College Press.

Shepard, L. (2000). The role of assessment in a learning culture. *Educational Researcher, 29,* 4–14.

Silin, J., & C. Lippman (Eds.). (2003). *Putting the children first: The changing face of Newark's public schools.* New York: Teachers College Press.

Tanner, L. N. (1997). *Dewey's laboratory school: Lessons for today.* New York: Teachers College Press.

U.S. Department of Education. (2002). *Meeting the highly qualified teachers challenge: The Secretary's Annual Report on Teacher Quality.* Washington, D.C.: U.S. Department of Education, Office of Postsecondary Education, Office of Policy, Planning, and Innovation.

Vygotsky, L. (1978). *Mind in society: The development of higher psychological processes* (M. Cole, V. John-Steiner, S. Scribner, E. Souberman, Eds.). Cambridge, MA: Harvard University Press. (Original work published 1922–1935).

Wasow, E. (2000). Families and schools: New lenses, new landscapes. In N. Nager & E. Shapiro (Eds.), *Revisiting a progressive pedagogy: The developmental-interaction approach.* Albany, NY: SUNY.

Werner, H. (1961). *Comparative psychology of mental development.* New York: Science Editions.

Wertsch, J. V. (1985). *Vygotsky and the social formation of mind.* Cambridge, MA: Harvard University Press.

Winsor, C. B. (1957). *What are we doing in social studies? Forty-fifth annual School Men's Week proceedings.* Philadelphia: University of Pennsylvania Press. Reprinted by Bank Street College.

Winsor, C. B. (Ed.). (1973). *Experimental schools revisited: Bulletins of the Bureau of Educational Experiments.* New York: Agathon Press.

Zimiles, H. (1987). Progressive education: On the limits of evaluation and the development of empowerment. *Teachers College Record, 89,* 201–217.

Zimiles, H. (1997). Viewing education through a psychological lens: The contributions of Barbara Biber. *Child Psychiatry and Human Development, 28,* 23–31.

Chapter 13

The Project Approach: An Overview

Lilian G. Katz ∽ *University of Illinois*
Sylvia C. Chard ∽ *University of Alberta, Canada*

The inclusion of in-depth investigations in the early childhood and primary school curriculum has a long history. First inspired by the ideas of John Dewey, during the Progressive era, it was advocated by William H. Kilpatrick, who referred to its use as the "project method." The project method was also used in Dewey's Laboratory School at the University of Chicago at the turn of the century (Tanner, 1997).

In more recent times, project work was a central part of preschool and primary education in Britain during the so-called Plowden Years in the 1960s and 1970s, which inspired many U.S. educators to adopt the project method under the name "open education" (cf. Smith, 1997). A highly creative variation of the project method can now be seen as part of the curriculum in preprimary schools in the small northern Italian city of Reggio Emilia (Edwards, Gandini, & Forman, 1993). A contemporary extension and elaboration of these earlier practices, now referred to as the Project Approach, has been adopted in preschool and primary classes in many parts of North America and is being widely adopted in many other countries (see Katz & Chard, 2000).

We use the term *project approach*, rather than *method* or *model*, to suggest that children's investigations constitute one of many important elements of an early childhood or primary curriculum. As a *part* of the curriculum for children from the ages of about 3 to 8 years, project work functions in a *complementary* relationship to

other aspects of the curriculum, rather than as a total pedagogical method or curriculum model, and thus does not require the abandonment of a wide variety of other curriculum elements that support children's development and learning.

We begin this overview with a definition of a project, followed by a summary of the theoretical rationale for its inclusion in the curriculum (discussed in greater detail in Helm & Katz, 2001; Katz, 1991; Katz & Chard, 2000). A brief description of how the project approach can be implemented is also presented.

∽ WHAT IS A PROJECT?

A project is an extended in-depth investigation of a topic, ideally one worthy of the children's attention and time. Projects are usually undertaken by a whole class, sometimes by small groups within a class, and occasionally by an individual child. Even when a project is undertaken by the whole class, children typically work in small groups and often individually on specific subtopics related to the larger one under investigation. In discussions with their teacher, children generate questions about specific aspects of the topic that will constitute the main thrust of the investigation.

The investigation undertaken in a project involves the application of a variety of intellectual dispositions, as well as social and academic skills. Depending on the range of skills already available to the participating children, the work

These children work on an art project they planned.

ideally includes sharing and discussing previous experiences and knowledge related to the topic, gathering and recording new data, looking things up in a library and on the Internet, reading, writing, taking measurement, sketching and drawing, painting, model making, creating stories, having dramatic play and fine arts, interviewing experts on the topic, and so forth. A project ideally also involves the acquisition of worthwhile knowledge and concepts in a variety of disciplines such as the sciences, social studies, literature, and all the arts. In addition, the activities usually employed in project work at all ages ideally include collecting information through direct observations, conducting surveys and distributing questionnaires, conducting experiments related to subtopics of interest, making collections of related artifacts, and preparing visual and verbal reports of the findings.

Furthermore, in project work, the children are encouraged to identify subtopics of special interest to them and to accept responsibility for particular types of tasks that will contribute to the overall investigation. In addition to the value of the new knowledge acquired, and the skills ap-

plied, the feelings of mastery of a topic resulting from such sustained effort can lay the foundation for a lifelong disposition to persevere and to reach for in-depth understanding of worthwhile topics.

Main features of project work that distinguish it from the traditional didactic way of introducing children to new knowledge are (1) the direct involvement of the children in identifying the topic to be studied, (2) the children's role in formulating the questions to be answered by their investigation, (3) openness to possible shifts in the direction of the inquiry as it proceeds, and (4) the children's acceptance of responsibility for the work accomplished and for the kinds of representations of findings that are prepared and reported.

PROJECT WORK AND OTHER PARTS OF THE CURRICULUM

The project approach is advocated on the assumption that during the primary years project work is the informal part of the curriculum that complements and supports its more formal components such as systematic instruction in basic literacy and numeracy skills. *Systematic instruction* refers to formal instruction of an individual or of small groups of children—and in the case of older children, the whole class—who require adult assistance with learning the specific skills and subskills involved in becoming literate and numerate. By comparison, in the case of preschool children—for whom spontaneous play, informal activities, music, story reading, and so on are more typical and appropriate than formal instruction—project work constitutes the more formal part of the curriculum.

In the early primary years, project work and formal instruction can be seen as complementary in several ways:

1. Formal instruction aids children with the acquisition of basic skills, while project work gives them opportunity to apply skills in meaningful contexts.

2. In formal instruction the teacher addresses children's deficiencies, while project work gives children opportunities to apply and strengthen their proficiencies.

3. In formal instruction, the teacher directs the instructional sequences and organizes the work on the basis of expert knowledge of how the skills are best learned by individual children with particular learning characteristics. In project work, children choose the tasks and the level of task difficulty most appropriate for them.

4. During systematic instruction, learners are in a passive and receptive posture as the teachers provide them with the information and instructions. In project work, they are actively engaged in planning and conducting the investigation and applying knowledge and skills, making decisions and choices on all aspects of the work.

5. While children are intrinsically motivated to remain engaged in their project work, in systematic instruction, the teacher takes advantage of children's motivation to please him or her and to meet his or her expectations. Furthermore, in project work the usefulness, relevance, and purposes of basic literacy and numeracy skills typically become self-evident. The experience of relevance tends to strengthen children's motivation to improve such skills and increases their receptivity to the teacher's help in mastering them through systematic instruction.

In project work, the teacher's role is more consultative than instructional. The teacher facilitates the progress of the work by supervising and monitoring the children's progress. The teacher uses observation of the children at work during the project to identify cues concerning the kinds of instructional activities that might be needed by individual children and notes the readiness of individuals or groups of children for the introduction of new knowledge and skills.

In the case of preschool children, the teacher's role includes both consultation and leadership in helping to organize the progress of the investigation, encouraging in-depth and extended attention to the work of answering the questions raised in discussion with the children. The teacher arranges the time schedule so that the project can proceed. The teacher also makes suggestions for how children can represent their findings. At both the preschool and primary levels, the teacher plays an important role in documenting the experiences of the children as the work proceeds (Katz & Chard, 1996).

In summary, we suggest that young children's development and learning are best served when they have frequent opportunity to be involved in investigations about worthwhile topics *and,* especially during the primary years, when the teacher's formal instruction in basic skills is also available for those who cannot achieve mastery without such assistance. Teachers are encouraged to balance the two important provisions for learning in the early years.

In addition, throughout the preschool and primary years, children can learn to make increasingly sophisticated use of computers in the course of project work. In the preschool years, many children begin to use computers for writing, preparing signs, and other elementary graphics. With increasing age and experience, children can use computers for writing, preparing graphs, compiling posters, producing visual essays, designing simple games, and other forms of representation. They can also have access to a wide variety of types of information via selected Internet sites as they seek answers to the questions that represent the main thrust of their investigation.

THEORETICAL RATIONALE FOR THE PROJECT APPROACH

The recommendation for including project work in the early childhood curriculum is based partly on our conception of the goals of education and partly on our view of a developmental approach to implementing those goals. We begin by defining the goals and follow with the principles of practice based on combining the goals and our understanding of how young children develop and learn. A fuller discussion of these points can be found in Katz and Chard (2001).

Four Types of Learning Goals

We suggest that at every level of education four types of learning goals must be addressed: knowledge, skills, dispositions, and feelings. At the early childhood level, they can be broadly defined as follows:

1. *Knowledge* during the preschool and early primary school period can consist of ideas, concepts, schemas, facts, information, stories, myths, legends, songs, and other such contents of the mind.
2. *Skills* are defined as small, discrete, and relatively brief actions that are fairly easily observed or inferred from behavior (e.g., cutting, drawing, counting a group of objects, coordinating activities with peers, fine and gross motor skills).
3. *Dispositions* are relatively enduring habits of mind, or characteristic ways of responding to experience across types of situations (e.g., persistence at tasks, curiosity, generosity or avarice, the disposition to read or to solve problems). Unlike an item of knowledge or a skill, a disposition is not an end-state to be mastered once and for all. It is a trend or consistent pattern of behavior, and its possession is established only by its repeated manifestation.
4. *Feelings* are subjective emotional or affective states, such as feelings of belonging, self-esteem, confidence, adequacy and inadequacy, competence and incompetence, anxiety, and so forth. Feelings about significant phenomena may vary from being transitory to enduring, intense to weak, or ambivalent.

The inclusion of project work in the curriculum helps to ensure that the construction and acquisition of worthwhile knowledge and the mastery of basic skills can occur in such a way that the *dispositions* to use them are also strengthened (Katz, 1994). Our hypothesis is that if knowledge and skills are acquired in meaningful contexts with ample opportunity to apply them, then the dispositions to seek and deepen knowledge and to use the skills acquired will be strengthened; conversely, without such meaningful application, the dispositions to use knowledge and skills may not be developed or may even be weakened. In addition, our experience is that children's involvement in project work is typically accompanied by *feelings* of self-confidence, engagement, enthusiasm, and often of pleasure and satisfaction with what is accomplished. In principle, then, the incorporation of project work in the curriculum helps to ensure that all four categories of learning goals are addressed concurrently.

Implications for Practice

Learning in all four goal categories—knowledge, skills, dispositions, and feelings—is facilitated in different ways. In the case of knowledge and skills, learning can be aided by active research, observation, appropriate instruction, and many other processes. However, dispositions and feelings cannot be learned from study or from direct or systematic instruction. Furthermore, for dispositions to be strengthened, they must be enacted, and their enactment must be associated with satisfaction.

Some of the most important dispositions included in the goals of education are inborn. All children are born with the disposition to learn, to observe, to investigate, to make sense of experience, to play, and to develop attachments to others—granted, stronger in some children than in others. Thus, experience should be provided to young children that support and strengthen these inborn dispositions. Other dispositions, however—desirable and undesirable ones—are likely to be learned from being around and interacting with adults who have them and in whose behavior they are visible.

Feelings related to schooling are likely to be learned as by-products of experience, rather than from instruction or exhortation. Both dispositions and feelings can be thought of as incidental learnings in that they are incidental to the processes by which knowledge is constructed and acquired and by which skills are learned. However, to label feelings as incidental is not to belittle them or to devalue the role of the teacher or the curriculum in their development; rather, it is to emphasize that feelings cannot be taught didactically. Children cannot be instructed in what feelings to have or not to have!

Principles Related to the Acquisition of Knowledge

Recent insights into children's development suggest that, in principle, the younger the child, the more readily knowledge is constructed and acquired through active and interactive processes rather than passive, receptive, and reactive ones. With increasing age, children become more able to profit from passive reception of instruction. This developmental principle suggests that, in practice, young children in the preschool and early primary years best construct and master knowledge from their own firsthand, direct experiences and from interaction with primary sources of knowledge.

The interactive experiences from which knowledge can be constructed and acquired must have meaningful content. We suggest that, in principle, the content of interaction should be related to matters of actual or potential interest to the children involved. However, because not all of children's interests are equally deserving of attention, and because adults can and should help children acquire new interests, some selection by the teacher of what content is most worthy of attention is required. We suggest that the

interests most worthy of strengthening in young children are those likely to extend, deepen, and improve understandings of their own environments and experiences.

We suggest furthermore that, in principle, the younger the learner, the more integrated the curriculum should be; conversely, as children increase in age and experience, their capacity to profit from subject- or discipline-based study increases. Young children do not differentiate their ideas, thoughts, and interests into categories like science, language, and mathematics. They are more likely to gain knowledge and understanding by pursuing a topic to which scientific, linguistic, mathematical, and other discipline-related concepts can be applied.

Principles Related to the Acquisition of Skills

Skills can be acquired and strengthened through a variety of processes (e.g., observation, imitation, trial and error, coaching, and instruction) and can be improved with optimum drill and practice. In principle, the younger the child, the more likely skills can be acquired and strengthened by their purposeful application in meaningful contexts (Bransford, Brown, & Cocking, 1999; Brown, Collins, & Duguid, 1989). With increasing age, children grasp more fully the relationship between skillfulness and drill and more easily accept the need for practice and exercise of disembedded or decontextualized skills—even if they do so reluctantly.

Principles Related to Both Knowledge and Skills

We suggest that, in principle, the younger the children, the more important it is that what they learn about (knowledge) and what they learn to do (skills) have more horizontal than vertical relevance. *Vertical relevance* refers to learning in preparation for the next rather than the current school experience. In other words, the knowl-

Collaboration on connnected curricular activities is commonplace.

edge and skills are expected to be relevant at a future point in time. It is a type of education for the next life; the content of the curriculum is justified on the basis of what will be required of the children in the future rather than what is meaningful in the present. *Horizontal relevance* means that the children's learning is applicable and meaningful on the same day, on the way home, and in their contemporary lives within and outside of the educational setting. With increasing age and experience, children become more able to acquire knowledge and skills with little immediate significance or applicability.

The Development of Social Competence

Contemporary developmental research suggests that the first 6 or 7 years of development are a critical period of the achievement of social competence and that failure to do so can have long-term negative consequences (Katz & McClellan, 1997; Parker & Asher, 1987). In principle, a

curriculum for young children must provide frequent activities in which cooperation, collaboration, and coordination of effort and resolution of conflicts among the children is functional, consequential, and satisfying to them.

Strengthening Desirable Dispositions Parents, teachers, and school officials invariably include many dispositions in their lists of desirable outcomes of education. Among them are the desire to learn, to be cooperative and creative, and to be eager to approach and solve problems. The underlying assumption is that mastery of knowledge and skills must be accompanied by robust dispositions to employ them.

As suggested earlier, dispositions cannot be taught directly. We suggest that, in principle, if dispositions are to be strengthened, ample opportunity for their enactment must be available. For example, the disposition to be problem solvers can be strengthened only if children have real and meaningful problems to solve in the course of their daily activities. Similarly, the disposition to be responsible can be strengthened only when children have appropriate responsibilities. The findings of the research in this area suggest that, in principle, a curriculum that emphasizes child-initiated meaningful learning tasks is more likely to strengthen such dispositions as to seek mastery, to exert real effort, and to persist at challenging tasks, and many others usually alluded to in lists of goals and desirable educational outcomes.

Feelings Related to School Experiences Like dispositions, feelings cannot be taught directly; they are experienced and strengthened or weakened in the context of the interactions and activities that give rise to them. However, when a curriculum is focused on a narrow range of academic tasks (e.g., drill and practice in workbooks, lessons in phonics), it is likely that a substantial proportion of the learners will be unable to work effectively and thus will be prevented from developing feelings of competence. Indeed, when a single instructional approach is employed with any group of children who are diverse in background, ability, and development, some feel left out and are prone to develop feelings of incompetence or inadequacy (Slavin, Madden, Dolan, & Wasik, 1996). The inclusion of project work increases the variety of types of tasks and levels of difficulty available, such that all members of the class are likely to find meaningful work that can enhance feelings of competence, of belonging, and of being a contributor to the group effort.

In summary, the incorporation of project work into the curriculum of early childhood and primary education addresses all four categories of learning goals and makes possible the application of the principles of practice derived from current knowledge of young children's development and learning.

✍ IMPLEMENTING PROJECT WORK

As defined earlier, a project is an extended investigation of a topic typically undertaken by a whole class working in small groups or individually. It is a good idea for the teacher to propose possible project topics until children become experienced in project work. Based on knowledge of the children, the teacher can nominate topics of potential interest and can make a selection based on the discussion that follows. In addition, it is a good idea to propose topics based on local or state curriculum guides and to engage the children in discussions of aspects of the topic they are interested in investigating in depth. For detailed descriptions of project implementation, see Chard (1998a, 1998b).

Selecting Topics for Projects

To a very large extent, the benefits of project work are related to the topic being investigated. The sheer number of possible topics is so large that some kind of selection process is advisable. Teachers have the ultimate responsibility for judging whether the topic is worthy of children's time and energy and of the school's resources. Furthermore, to support good project work, teachers must often undertake extensive preparation, study, and exploration. Thus, topic selection warrants serious consideration by the teacher and by those who define the curriculum.

Many factors contribute to the appropriateness of a topic. Much depends on characteristics of the particular group of children, the teacher's knowledge and experience related to the topic and his or her own interest in it, the local resources available, the larger context of the school and community, and various mixes of all these. Furthermore, it is important to keep in mind that many topics of importance are not suitable for projects. It is also difficult to predict which topics will work well with a given group of children.

Responding to Children's Interests   Teachers sometimes select project topics on the basis of the children's expressed or assumed interest in them. However, the interest of an individual, a group, or a whole class presents a number of potential pitfalls in topic selection. On a practical level, in a class of 25 children, the number of possible interests is potentially too large to be able to address in a single year. Thus, teachers need some criteria to determine which of the interests is worthy of being addressed. Furthermore, it is not clear what children mean when they say that they are interested in a topic. Interests can be of relatively low value to the child's total learning (e.g., interest in pirates or in the Titanic stimulated by exposure to a movie). Some interests might be passing thoughts or fancies, fleeting concerns, phobias, fetishes, or topics nominated by a child who wants to please the teacher.

In addition, the fact that an individual or group expresses interest in a given topic (e.g., dinosaurs) does not necessarily mean that the teacher should support and strengthen interest in it. Children's enthusiastic response to a Disney movie about pirates, for example, does not mean that the topic is worthy of a project. The children can be given opportunity for spontaneous dramatic play involving pirates; they can be encouraged to discuss their reactions to the film, and so forth. But such interest does not imply that an in-depth study of the topic of pirates is in their best developmental, educational, or even moral interests. We suggest that it is useful to distinguish between providing opportunity for child-initiated spontaneous play around a topic and a teacher investing time and energy in organizing a long-range effort to investigate the topic around their play and thereby according the topic greater value than it warrants. The topic of a project should be part of the general commitment of the teacher and the school to taking children and their intellectual powers seriously, and to treating them as young investigators of worthwhile phenomena.

We suggest that adults have substantial responsibility to educate children's interests. This does not mean that the teacher indicates disrespect or disdain for the children's own expressed interests. However, children's awareness of the teacher's real and deep interest in a topic (e.g., the changes in the natural environment over a 6-week period) is likely to engender some level of interest in the topic among the children who respect and look up to the teacher. In this way, adults take responsibility for educating children's interests.

Exciting Children's Interest Sometimes teachers select exotic and glamorous topics in the hope of capturing the attention of children who are sometimes reluctant or uninvolved members of the group. For example, projects revolving around the rain forest in U.S. midwest schools may entice young children into participation and certainly do no harm. However, our experience of working with many teachers all over the world indicates that young children can be no less fascinated and intrigued by the experience of close observation and study of their own immediate natural environments, whether corn fields, apple orchards, or a nearby

bicycle shop. Furthermore, if the topic is an exotic and therefore remote one, it is difficult for the children to contribute to the direction and design of the project. The less firsthand experience the children have in relation to the topic, the more dependent they are on the teacher for the ideas, information, questions, hypotheses, and so forth that constitute the essence of good project work. Young children are indeed dependent on adults for many important aspects of their lives. However, project work is that part of the curriculum in which children are encouraged to take the initiative in setting the questions to be answered and the direction of the study, as well as in accepting responsibility for the work accomplished.

Along similar lines, topics are sometimes chosen because they are expected to amuse or even entertain the children. Such topics are thought by teachers to stimulate children's imaginations (e.g., the Little Mermaid, teddy bears). However, these topics are more fanciful than imaginative. In good project work, children have ample opportunity to use and strengthen their imaginations when they make predictions about what they will find before taking a field trip, when they predict the answers to their questions that a visiting expert might give, or when they argue with each other about possible causes and effects related to the phenomenon under investigation. Project work stimulates and strengthens young children's imaginations in many other ways as well; for example, during the early phases of a project, they are encouraged to report their actual experiences and memories related to the topic but also to make up their own stories related to it (e.g., stories of actual experiences of riding a tricycle and imaginary and fictional stories of bike rides).

Diversity Concerns

Diversity of Experiences In some classes, the diversity of the incoming pupils' experiences might be so great that it would be beneficial to *begin* the year with a topic that the teacher is reasonably certain is familiar to all children. At the beginning of the life of the classroom group, it is probably best to ensure that all the children have sufficient experience related to the topic to be able to recognize and share their own experience and participate in discussion with some confidence. As the school year progresses and children become adept at project work, they can more readily appreciate that classmates have different interests and prefer to work on different subtopics. In this way, children's appreciation of differences in experiences, interests, and abilities among their peers can be deepened.

Diversity of Culture and Background The project approach is highly responsive to diversity of cultures and backgrounds within the group of children being served. One consideration to be made when selecting topics for diverse groups is that some topics may be considered delicate in some cultures and not others. Furthermore, some topics might embarrass children of some backgrounds. However, we find it useful to make a distinction between a child's culture and a child's heritage. *Culture* refers to the current day-to-day experiences and environment of the children; *heritage* refers to historic and ancestral characteristics and past experiences associated with their origins. From a developmental perspective, young children can deepen their understanding of their culture through good project work; deepening their knowledge of their heritage is more appropriately accomplished through other parts of the curriculum, especially as children get older.

Preparation for Participation in a Democratic Society

An important consideration in the selection of the topics of projects is a commitment to building children's abilities to participate competently in a democratic society. In the service of this goal, good topics are those that deepen children's understanding, knowledge, and appreciation of the contribution of others to the well-being of all. In addition, one of the many potential benefits of good project work is that it provides a wide range of experiences within the classroom itself that constitute participation in democratic processes: collaboration, listening and responding to each others' ideas, coordinating their efforts, diverse contributions of members of the whole and of subgroups, negotiating disagreements, reaching consensus on how to solve problems and accomplish tasks, and so forth. All of these processes help to lay the foundation for competence in democratic living.

Furthermore, in the interests of the goal of preparing for participation in democracy, we ask, "Will the study of this topic strengthen and/or deepen the disposition to examine closely the real world and its complexities?" Thus, we suggest avoiding topics that are frivolous, banal, or of trivial consequence. Choose topics that involve children in unpacking the familiar, deepening their understanding of what goes on behind the scenes, and of how various people's efforts contribute to daily community life; these topics can contribute to children's growing capacity to appreciate the diverse ways that others contribute to their well-being, which is basic to a democratic community.

Criteria for Selecting Topics

Based on the preceding discussion, we offer the following list of criteria for selecting topics: *A topic is likely to be a good one if*

1. Relevant phenomena are directly observable in the children's own environments.
2. It is within children's experiences (most of them? some of them?).
3. Firsthand direct investigation is feasible (and involves no potential dangers).
4. Local resources are favorable and readily accessible.

5. It has good potential for a variety of representational media (role play, construction, graphic, multidimensional, graphic organizers, etc.).
6. Parental participation and contributions are likely; parents can become involved in the investigation with little difficulty.
7. It is sensitive to local culture as well as culturally appropriate in general.
8. It is potentially interesting to many of the children or is an interest that adults consider worthy of developing in children.
9. It is related to curriculum goals of the school and district.
10. It provides ample opportunity to apply basic skills (appropriate to the ages of the children).
11. The topic is *optimally* specific—not too narrow and not too broad (e.g., a study of the teacher's own dog at one end, and the topic of "music" at the other).

PHASES OF PROJECT WORK

Once the topic of a project is selected, a central feature of project work is the children's involvement in identifying which aspects of it to explore, in planning the work, and in defining the kinds of representations of findings and reports to be prepared.

Planning by the teacher produces some preliminary ideas about the work that might be done and of the resources needed; then projects can be planned and conducted in three approximate phases (see Chard, 1998a, 1998b). These phases are discussed next.

Phase 1: Getting Started

In the first phase of a project, the teacher encourages the children to share their own personal experiences and recollections related to the topic and to review their knowledge of it, using representational and expressive competencies such as dramatic play, drawing, reporting their experiences, and writing about them. During these initial activities, the teacher can learn of the special interests of individual children and their parents; this sharing also helps establish a baseline of understanding for the whole group involved in the project. Parents may be able to contribute to the project in a variety of ways such as arranging places to visit, lending items for display, being interviewed by the children, and providing access to information.

In the process of reviewing their current understanding of the topic during the first phase of a project, children raise questions about the topic. Often the questions reveal gaps in knowledge or even misunderstandings, which can form the basis for planning the second phase of the project. In the role of consultant, the teacher is not too quick to correct misconceptions that emerge during phase 1; these can be excellent resources for learning as the children investigate and test their theories against reality.

Phase 2: A Project in Progress

The main thrust of the second phase is gaining new information, especially by means of firsthand, direct, real-world experience. The sources of information used can be primary or secondary. Primary sources include field trips to real settings and events, such as an actual construction site to be observed, the working of a machine, or the goods-delivery section of a supermarket. Talking with people who have direct experience of the topic also provides firsthand information. Secondary sources of information such as books, relevant educational films, videotapes, brochures, and pamphlets can be examined at this time as well.

Fieldwork During phase 2, a field visit can be planned by the children and teacher together. Field visits do not have to be elaborate, involving expensive transportation to distant places. They can involve going to places close to the schools, shops, stores, parks, construction sites, or walks. With teacher aides, the children can go to these sites in small groups, enjoying the opportunity of having an adult to talk with about what they are observing.

The preparatory work completed *before* conducting fieldwork includes identifying questions to be answered, people to talk to about their work, equipment, objects, and materials to observe closely. Children can carry simple clipboards (if necessary, made with cardboard and paper clips) and sketch or write things of special interest to be used upon return to the classroom. During the visit, children can also be encouraged to count, note the shapes and colors of things, learn any special words for things, figure out how things work, and use all their senses to deepen their knowledge of the phenomena studied.

Back in the Classroom   On return to the classroom, the children can recall many details and represent them in increasingly elaborate ways as the children learn more about the topic. At this time, the children apply skills already learned: talking, drawing, dramatic play writing, making simple mathematical notation, taking measurement, and diagramming. If a field site is close by, such as a construction site in the vicinity of the school, it can be visited on several occasions and comparisons can be made between what was observed on one visit and on subsequent ones.

The children's work can be accumulated in individual project folders, in wall displays, and in group record books in which work is shared with others. Children can be fully involved in discussing and planning what will be displayed and how. The information collected from interviews can be represented in various similar ways. The work can also be stimulated and enriched by a variety of secondary source materials, books, charts, leaflets, maps, pamphlets, and pictures.

As the work progresses in phase 2, the children often develop a strong concern for realism

and logic about the topic, and drawing real objects becomes an increasingly absorbing activity. In their observational drawing, young children can look closely at the plants and animals, see how the parts of a bicycle interconnect within the whole, or note how the pattern inside a carrot dissected different ways indicates the way water and other nutrients contribute to its growth. Interest is stimulated by frequent recognition and review of the progress in the development of the project.

Phase 3: Concluding a Project

The main thrust of the last phase of a project is the completion of the individual and group work and summary and review of what has been learned. For 3- and 4-year-olds, this last phase is largely taken up with dramatic play in their project constructions. Thus, if they have built a store or a hospital, they will be enacting roles associated with those settings.

With older children, a discussion to develop plans for sharing their project experience and learning with others should be initiated before their interest in the topic wanes. It is possible that a project could go on too long; almost any topic can be run into the ground. The third phase of the project can include inviting visitors to see the work at an open house, or the class next door could be invited to see some of the displays of the children's work. It is also satisfying for the children to share their ideas with the principal and other interested teachers; this offers a good debriefing experience for the class following the investment of considerable effort. Preparation for such an occasion provides real purpose for a review of the work achieved. At this time, the children can also be encouraged to evaluate their own work, to compare what has been found out with the questions they generated during phase 1.

We next present a brief outline of how a whole-class project on the topic of shoes might proceed.

✒ A KINDERGARTEN PROJECT ON SHOES

The following account of a project on shoes was undertaken by a kindergarten class. The topic arose in discussion among the children, provoked by the fact that several of them had new shoes at the beginning of the school year. The shoes had many interesting features: some lit up, some made noises, some had laces with different patterns and colors. The teacher and her assistant thought of many possible directions in which the children's interests might develop through a study of shoes. They brainstormed ideas and represented them in a topic web.

Phase 1: Getting Started

The children in the class talked about their shoes and their experiences of buying shoes. The children began to wonder about shoes and raised questions. The teacher began compiling a list of their questions and added to it throughout the first week of the project. The children painted and drew pictures of shoes and of their experiences of buying shoes. The children were encouraged to ask their parents, friends, and neighbors for any kinds of shoes they might have to contribute to the class shoe collection for the study. The teacher brought in some shoes from her 16-year-old daughter's closet and added these to the dramatic play corner. They set up a simple shoe store in the dramatic play area and tried on the different shoes there. The parents were informed of the topic of study and were invited to discuss shoes with their children. They were also invited to share with the class any special knowledge they might have about shoes. At the end of the first week, the teacher arranged for a child in the class to bring in his baby brother to show the class his first pair of walking shoes.

Phase 2: Developing the Project

The teacher and the children talked about what they could do to get answers to their questions

about shoes. The questions included, "What are shoes made of? Where are shoes made? How much do they cost? How do you know what size you wear?"

As the children began to discuss money, they talked about what the storekeepers did with the money people paid when they bought shoes. Some thought the salespersons gave it to poor people, others thought they took it home for their pay, and some thought the boss kept it all. The variety of predicted answers to questions heightened the children's curiosity and desire to find out more details about what goes on in the shoe store. The teacher arranged a trip to a family shoe store in their city. The children worked for a whole week to prepare for the trip. They decided what parts of the store needed to be investigated, who would take responsibility for drawing what parts of the store, for asking which questions of the boss and of the salespersons. The fieldwork was planned to get the information needed to make a more elaborate shoe store in the classroom on their return.

Five groups formed around the children's special interests. They were interested in the following:

1. The cash register, how many shoes are sold in a day, and the amount of money collected each day
2. How the shoes are displayed in the shop windows and presented for customers' viewing in the store
3. The storeroom, how the shoe boxes are arranged (e.g., men/women/children, sizes, dress/sport, etc.)
4. The shoe salesperson's responsibilities, activities
5. Different kinds of shoes available
6. Sizes, colors, and number of shoes in stock
7. Where the shoes came from, where delivered, and the frequencies of deliveries
8. Studying the shoe collection brought by children to the class in terms of their materials, their special functions and style, model, and manufacturers' names

The teacher and her assistant worked in turn with each group to talk about the questions they wanted to ask and what they wanted to find out from the questions. The teachers helped the children develop ways to record the information to be gathered at the store.

The teacher contacted the personnel in the shoe store in advance to prepare them for the visit by explaining the expectations she had for the field experience. She outlined the questions the children wanted them to answer and described the drawings planned, the observations the children wanted to make of them at work, and the items the children wanted to examine closely.

When the big day arrived, the 3 people at the shoe store spent about 20 minutes with each group of children. The students returned to school with a great deal to think about. The teacher and her assistant led discussions in large and small groups to debrief the children about the visit.

Each group told the whole-class group about the information they had acquired. Then they set out to build a shoe store in their classroom. Groups and individual children found out what they needed to know to make what they wanted to add to the shoe store. Throughout the next 3 weeks, the teacher talked to each group about their progress, and the children listened to each other's ideas and made suggestions to each other.

The children worked on making cars to get to the store. They made a bird in a cage like the one they had seen in the store. They made a television set to resemble the one they had seen in the store. They made catalogs for the shoes in their store. They marked the shoe boxes so they would know which kinds of shoes were in the boxes. Some children made money for the little cash register the teacher provided. They made a shoe chart so shoppers in their store could see their shoe size. They worked on a book to tell new shop workers how to sell shoes. They made a wooden bench for children to sit on while waiting to be served. In some cases, several versions of these things were made because children personally wanted to be involved in particular contributions to the store. For example, they especially made many shoe catalogs. A Turkish guest worker also helped two children from her country to use their own language in the context of the project by producing a Turkish version of a shoe catalog and by posting advertising and directional signs in Turkish.

During this period of investigating and representing the items they wanted to put in their shoe store, the children invited several visitors to their classroom. Another teacher in the school was a dancer and showed her tap shoes and her special jazz dancing shoes. One father was a member of the police force. He helped the children understand the importance of the evidence of shoe prints at the site of a crime in finding criminals. Another parent visitor showed her special shoes for bicycle racing. A grandfather of one of the children had repaired shoes in his work and was able to tell the children about how shoes are made and what they are made of. With this knowledgeable man's help, the children were able to examine the parts of a shoe: the leather, thread, tacks, and glue used in shoe construction. Various other kinds of sports shoes were shown to the children by older siblings and their special features discussed: ice skates, roller blades, Doc Martins, ski boots, fishing waders, golf shoes with cleats, wooden shoes from the Netherlands, ballet slippers, cowboy boots from Texas, and soccer shoes.

During the field visit, the children had been able to watch the process of selling a pair of shoes to a customer. They had followed the sale/purchase, noting the steps in the process from the salesman's and the customer's points of view. They were able to use these steps in the dramatization of the sale and purchase of shoes in their own shoe store. They took pride in showing several pairs of shoes to prospective buyers, measuring their feet, and interviewing them as to the kind of shoe they wanted, the color, and the price they wanted to pay. Then they concluded the sale and put the unsold shoes back in their boxes and back on the storage shelves after the sale had been concluded.

The children who made the dollar bills set up a bank so their money could be used in the purchase of shoes in the store. A number line was provided to help those children who wished to use it to count out the money they wanted to spend. Prices were added to the information on the shoe boxes.

Phase 3: Concluding the Project

After several weeks, the children became interested in new kinds of play. They wanted to explore the bus travel that had begun during the shoe project, as some customers came to town to buy shoes using the local transit system. The teacher arranged an opportunity for the parents to come to the school to visit the children's shoe store and see what had been learned in the process of developing the children's interests in shoe store construction and play. The parents had the opportunity of buying shoes in the store and being served by their children.

The parents were able to look at the children's drawings and paintings. They were able to read the documentation of the project, reading the word labels and captions written by children and teachers on the representational work and the photographs taken throughout the project to record the high points and various aspects of the children's learning. Among the skills applied by the children were counting, measuring, using technical vocabulary, developing color, shape, and size recognition, and interviewing and other social skills. The knowledge they had gained concerned the processes of designing, manufacturing, and selling shoes and much information about the variety of materials used in making the various kinds of shoes and for different parts of the shoes. They also appreciated the working of a store and the interdependence of the number of different people involved in enabling people

to wear something as basic as shoes. The parents who had participated in the final sharing of the children's work were left in no doubt that valuable in-depth learning had taken place over the 8 weeks of the project.

Commentary This project is described as fairly typical for a class of kindergarten children. However, it is difficult to describe projects as typical, because much of the work of any project with any teacher or group of children is related to the availability of local resources for firsthand investigation and to the interests expressed by the particular participants.

The availability of parent experts willing to help the children made a crucial contribution to the quality of what was accomplished. The parents of any class group might include a number of people involved in house construction, vehicle driving and maintenance, food services, farming, the health services, and so on. Teachers who make themselves aware of the particular expertise among the parents of any class group can often plan project work to take account of the opportunities afforded for this kind of parent support. Bilingual parents can help to sensitize the children to words that are used in different cultures to describe the same objects and processes. This can ensure that all children are involved in the study and that an awareness of different languages can begin early in children's lives.

The age of the children affects the extent to which project work can involve a class of children for an extended period of time. Younger children would probably not have benefited from quite such elaborate dramatic play, and the project probably would not have continued to develop over so many weeks. Older children, on the other hand, might have seen a video of a shoe factory, built an assembly line on one side of the classroom, focused on their understanding of the process of shoe design and production, studied the workings of a shoe store, and included a variety of mathematical studies involving average sizes, costs, and surveys of classmates' shoes and preferences.

✎ CONCLUSION

The inclusion of project work in the curriculum for young children addresses the four major learning goals of all education: the construction and acquisition of worthwhile knowledge, the development of a wide variety of basic intellectual, motor, and social skills, strengthening desirable dispositions, and engendering positive feelings about themselves as learners and participants in group endeavors. Because project work is complementary to formal instruction, children have the opportunity to apply their basic skills in the course of studying meaningful topics. In this way, school experience becomes interesting not only to the children but to the teacher as well.

REFERENCES

Bransford, J. D., Brown, A. L., & Cocking, R. R. (Eds.). (1999). *How people learn. Brain, mind, experience, and school.* Washington, DC: National Academy Press.

Brown, J. S., Collins, A., & Duguid, P. (1989). Situated cognition and the culture of learning. *Educational Researcher, 18*, 32–42.

Chard, S. C. (1998a). *The project approach. Practical guide 1. Developing the basic framework.* New York: Scholastic.

Chard, S. C. (1998b). *The project approach. Practical guide 2. Developing curriculum with children.* New York: Scholastic.

Edwards, C., Gandini, L., & Forman, G. (Eds.). (1993). *The hundred languages of children. The Reggio Emilia approach to early childhood education.* Norwood, NJ: Ablex.

Helm, J. H. (Ed.). (1996). *The project catalogue.* Champaign, IL: ERIC Clearinghouse on Elementary and Early Childhood Education.

Helm, J. H., & Katz, L. G. (2001). *Young investigators. The Project Approach in the early years.* New York: Teachers College Press.

Katz, L. G. (1991). Pedagogical issues in early childhood education. In S. L. Kagan (Ed.), *The care and education of America's young children: Obstacles and opportunities. Ninetieth Yearbook of the National Society for the Study of Education.* Chicago: University of Chicago Press.

Katz, L. G. (1994). *The project approach. ERIC Digest.* Champaign, IL: ERIC Clearinghouse on Elementary and Early Childhood Education.

Katz, L. G., & Chard, S. C. (1996). *The contribution of documentation to the quality of early childhood education.* Champaign, IL: ERIC Clearinghouse on Elementary and Early Childhood Education.

Katz, L. G., & Chard, S. C. (2000). *Engaging children's minds: The project approach* (2nd ed.). Stamford, CT: Ablex.

Katz, L. G., & McClellan, D. (1997). *Fostering social competence: The teacher's role.* Washington, DC: National Association for the Education of Young Children.

Parker, J. G., & Asher, S. R. (1987). Peer relations and later personal adjustment: Are low-accepted children at risk? *Psychological Bulletin, 102,* 367–389.

Slavin, R. E., Madden, N. A., Dolan, L. J., & Wasik, B. A. (1996). *Every child, every school: Success for all.* Thousand Oaks, CA: Corwin.

Smith, L. S. (1997). Open education revisited. *Teachers College Record, 99* (2), 371–415.

Tanner, L. N. (1997). *Dewey's laboratory school. Lessons for today.* New York: Teachers College Press.

Part 5

Specific Approaches/European

Chapter 14

The Reggio Emilia Approach
Provocations and Partnerships with U.S. Early Childhood Educators

Rebecca S. New ~ Tufts University

In 1988, at the annual conference of the National Association for the Education of Young Children (NAEYC), approximately 25 people attended a small session dedicated to Italian perspectives on early care and education. At that session, Lella Gandini and Baji Rankin shared slides and stories about a small northern Italian city that had developed its own particular approach to providing early care and educational services to its youngest citizens, beginning in the first year of life and continuing through the kindergarten year. At about the same time, a traveling exhibition from this same Italian city was making its way through New England, having already made several stops in New York and Massachusetts. Two years later, the city of Reggio Emilia was featured on the cover of *Young Children* (New, 1990). A few months after, at the 1990 NAEYC conference in Washington, DC, crowds spilled out into the halls trying to see and hear more from the Italian educators (e.g., Filippini, 1990) who were sharing some provocative new ways of thinking about and teaching young children. Today, Reggio Emilia's municipal early care and educational program is a major reference point for early childhood educators in the U.S. and around the world.[1]

This chapter describes this city's interpretation of early care and education with particular attention to its Italian origins and, more recently, its entrance into the field of early childhood education in the United States. Against this backdrop, the discussion highlights key features of Reggio Emilia's municipal program for young children that have become synonymous with the city's name—that is, those elements that are now part of the constellation of what is referred to as "the Reggio Emilia approach" or REA.[2] Following this description of Reggio Emilia's municipal program for children, including its interpretations of the physical environment, curriculum as extended projects or *progettazione,* teachers as researchers, documentation as a tool for collaborative inquiry, and parents as essential partners in children's early education, the chapter illustrates some of the ways in which U.S. educators have applied these principles to their own work in American early childhood settings. The chapter concludes by considering the challenges of using

---

[1]The Reggio Children network of international relations now includes Canada, Greenland, Mexico, Costa Rica, Guatemala, Cuba, Puerto Rico, Trinidad, Brazil, Bolivia, Paraguay, Chile, Norway, Sweden, Denmark, Finland, Iceland, Spain, United Kingdom, The Netherlands, Germany, Belgium, Israel, Switzerland, France, Portugal, Tanzania, Senegal, India, Nepal, China, Korea, Japan, Taiwan, Hong Kong, Thailand, Malaysia, Phillipines, Singapore, Australia, New Zealand, and the United States.

[2]REA is a frequently used anachronym to refer to the Reggio Emilia approach.

what is now understood about Reggio Emilia's municipal early childhood program within the changing context of U.S. early childhood education. But first—what and where is Reggio Emilia, and why is it so special?

✍ UNDERSTANDING REGGIO EMILIA'S HISTORY: A KEY TO UNDERSTANDING ITS ROLE IN U.S. EARLY CHILDHOOD EDUCATION

Few would deny the role of history in making sense of contemporary cultural phenomena, and the case of Reggio Emilia aptly illustrates this premise. Examining Reggio Emilia's place in two distinct cultural settings—its Italian home and the United States, where it has become a frequent and familiar visitor—helps to explain Reggio Emilia's cultural bases as well as its current status in the United States and worldwide. The most essential key to understanding how Reggio Emilia has come to have such influence on early childhood education is, of course, its own particular story within the Italian culture.

Reggio Emilia, Italy: A Particular Response to Cultural Values and Traditions

Reggio Emilia is a small city of 150,000 inhabitants in northern Italy. Many early admirers assumed that the city is either like all Italian cities, or like none other, in its interpretation of high-quality early care and educational services. In fact, Reggio Emilia is both. As a contemporary of other Italian cities, large and small, Reggio Emilia citizens share many of the same cultural values that characterize the Italian culture writ large, including a centrality of the family in community life, an image of children as a shared social responsibility, and a keen appreciation of local dialects and interpretations of quality—whether of wine, cheese, or early childhood services (New, 1993b).

Beyond this shared membership with the Italian culture, Reggio Emilia has an identity that is linked to its regional address.[3] One of several small, wealthy, and progressively minded cities in the region of Emilia Romagna, Reggio Emilia has much in common with its neighbors Parma and Modena, including a jointly produced and world-famous cheese (*Parmigiano-Reggiano*) as well as the local wine, *Lambrusco*. Reggio Emilia also shares a cultural and political history with the region, including a commitment to the arts and industrial innovation, a tradition of collaboration and civic engagement, and a leading role in the resistance movement of World War II. Equally important to note is the common history, not only within the region of Emilia Romagna but much of north and central Italy, of well-financed public early childhood services for young children and their families.

As is now the case in most Italian communities,[4] Reggio Emilia has three forms of early childhood services for young children: private (*scuola materna*) services typically provided by the Catholic church; state[5]-funded preschools; and a municipal program (which is the focus of this chapter). Much of what is regarded as particular to Reggio Emilia's early childhood services (for example, the continuity of children's class membership and teachers from one year to the next) is also common to other high-quality Italian early childhood programs. Where Reggio Emilia has distinguished itself is in its persistent efforts to reconceptualize early care and educational services—and to share its discoveries with the world.

---

[3]Indeed, the city's official name, *Reggio nel Emilia*, distinguishes it from another Reggio city in Italy, that of *Reggio nel Calabria*.

[4]Readers who are interested in contemporary Italian child care and early educational services and the history of their development are urged to see other more extensive descriptions (e.g., Corsaro & Emiliani, 1992; Mantovani & Musatti, 1996; New, 1993b) as well as the recent OECD review, *Starting Strong* [2001].

[5]The term *state* when used in this context refers to the national Italian government.

While some Italians will argue that Reggio Emilia cannot be considered "the best" in a culture where local innovations and standards must prevail, few would disagree with Reggio Emilia's leading role in exploring the potentials of (1) children's multiple symbolic languages in their learning; (2) teachers as active classroom researchers; and (3) parents as willing and able partners in designing and evaluating early care and educational services. These features have roots that extend deep into the city's political history, including its reputation for resisting the status quo, particularly when those norms limit the possibilities for active engagement of all citizens in the life of the community.

Several historic events are routinely highlighted in depictions of Reggio Emilia's early history of services for *infanzia* [early childhood],[6] including the fact that the current citywide program was begun by a small group of parents following World War II, who were soon joined by a philosopher-journalist by the name of Loris Malaguzzi (Malaguzzi, 1998). The Reggio Emilia parents wanted a different sort of child care for their children—not the custodial model as developed by the Catholic Church, but, rather, one that would allow parents to play an active role in a preschool setting where children could learn how to live in and contribute to a free and democratic society. Under Malaguzzi's leadership, these new goals for an early education expanded to include the promotion of children's multiple symbolic languages, not just those associated with traditional language and literacy development. Thus Vea Vecchi was hired—the city's first *atelierista*—with expertise in the arts, not in child development. Early accounts also point to Reggio Emilia's leadership with respect to the professional development of teachers. Responding to Italy's

lack of provisions for preservice teacher education,[7] Reggio Emilia's early childhood programs were conceptualized from the very beginning as learning environments for teachers as well as for young children. These early initiatives soon became hallmarks of the "Reggio Emilia approach." This attitude of resistance to more traditional Italian interpretations of children early learning potentials and the roles of adults in those processes continued to characterize Reggio Emilia's work locally and nationally over the next several decades.

Throughout the 1960s and 1970s, as the city of Reggio Emilia continued to develop its own services for children, leaders of the municipal program participated in a series of national campaigns drawing attention to the benefits of early childhood services for children, families, and the larger society. Reggio Emilia's own municipally funded early childhood services preceeded by several years the 1968 national law proclaiming the rights of all Italian children to pre-primary schools. As state-run services were soon added to the hundreds of municipal ones already in place, Reggio Emilia's solidarity with leaders of other cities' services helped to ensure a continued role for local innovation and experimentation (New, 2001). More modest laws for increased provision of infant/toddler care were eventually passed in 1971. By the late 1970s, city leaders demonstrated another feature of Reggio Emilia—one that distinguishes it from other cities both within and outside of Italy— and that is its eagerness to share, on a global scale, its compelling interpretation of "a new culture of childhood." Again under the charismatic leadership of Loris Malaguzzi, city leaders collected, organized, and displayed their observations

---

[6]C.f., both editions of *The Hundred Languages of Children* (Edwards, Gandini, & Forman, 1993; 1998) and a new video dedicated to the story of Reggio Emilia's infant–toddler centers and pre-primary schools (*Not Just Anywhere* [Washington, DC: Reggio Children, USA, 2002]).

[7]In 1998 a law was passed making university training mandatory for newly hired preschool and elementary teachers in Italy. Prior to that time, a vocational high school degree with course work in child development were the only prerequisities to applying for a teaching position in early and elementary education.

and new understandings of children's learning in a traveling exhibition that soon attracted attention from educators in countries as diverse as Sweden and Germany, Portugal and Denmark. It was a full decade later, in 1987, that an English-language version arrived in the United States.

What Americans saw in the exhibit were beautifully arranged graphic displays and photographs of children accompanied by their drawings and constructions, translated texts of their conversations, hypotheses, and explorations about the natural world (rain clouds, shadows, reflections) and their sense of self in relation to others (emotions as expressed through hands and voices, gender roles), as well as fantastical constructions—a dinosaur, a horse, clouds. The exhibition was overwhelming in its size, its complexity, its beauty, and its message—that children have social and intellectual and creative potentials not fully realized in traditional early care and education programs, even those that espouse a play-based and child-initiated curriculum; and that they could, and adults should, do much better.

Reggio Emilia's Early History Within the United States

Reggio Emilia's arrival in the United States by way of the exhibit was timely, coinciding with a growing debate between early childhood and elementary educators regarding the "developmental appropriateness" of direct instruction in early academics versus child-initiated and play-based approaches to learning. The first widely distributed document outlining these differences—NAEYC's *Guidelines to Developmentally Appropriate Practice* (Bredekamp, 1987)—was seen as a watershed moment for early childhood educators who were eager to use the document's child development research base to defend their preferred early educational practices. Within this same time period, the early childhood community began to actively debate the merits of Reggio Emilia's examples of children's long-term projects as they contrasted to stage-based inter-

pretations of children's developmental limitations in determining curriculum possibilities. By 1991, one of Reggio Emilia's preschools had been proclaimed by *Newsweek* magazine as "the best in the world." As news of this Italian city spread, parents, policy makers, and the larger educational community began to take note. As Reggio Emilia was being hailed as an "inspiration to U.S. educators" (Cohen, 1992),[8] new concerns were raised regarding NAEYC's DAP (developmentally appropriate practice) guidelines.

Challenges to DAP guidelines and especially the identification of practices labeled as "inappropriate" continued to come from elementary educators as well as some parents who wanted young children to enter school already acquainted with basic numeracy and literacy skills and understandings. Other criticisms came from those engaged in the reconceptualist movement (e.g., Kessler, 1991). Still other critiques were from advocates for children with special needs (Mallory, 1992) and those from cultural and linguistically diverse families (New, 1993a). These and other criticisms converged in their focus on the outdated theoretical premises, highly individualistic orientation, and American middle-class values embedded in the guidelines (Mallory & New, 1994). Eventually, Reggio Emilia became an illustrative example in support of many of these critiques, including the false dichotomy of teacher-directed versus child-initiated learning as well as the positioning of the teacher as recipient of someone else's "knowledge base" (New, 1994).

Throughout the 1990s, U.S. early childhood educators continued to study and visit Reggio Emilia, and a growing number of national leaders were explicit about their admiration for the city's efforts and understandings regarding children's early learning potentials (c.f., Bredekamp, 1993; Katz & Cesarone, 1994). Accompanying these

---

[8]Two versions of the exhibition (including an updated version of the original) continue to travel from city to city in the United States, while other versions of the exhibition have recently toured Asia and South America.

and other pronouncements of support was a voluminous and growing body of literature (including two lengthy edited volumes with contributions from Italian educators [Edwards, Gandini, & Forman, 1993; Edwards, Gandini, & Forman, 1998]) that had a powerful effect on U.S. early childhood educators locally and nationally, including those in national positions of authority (e.g., Child Development Associates, NAEYC). It came as no surprise, therefore, when references to Reggio Emilia—once used as a counter example— were used to illustrate NAEYC's revised interpretations of developmentally appropriate practices (Bredekamp & Copple, 1997). By the end of the century, the "Reggio Emilia approach" was a dominant theme in discussions among U.S. classroom teachers, program directors, early childhood teacher educators, local and state policy makers, and members of national organizations concerned with early care and education. But what was it about Reggio Emilia that attracted so much attention?

PRINCIPLES AND PRACTICES OF THE REA: A COMBINATION OF THE OLD AND THE NEW

The philosophy of education behind Reggio Emilia's municipal program has been described in various ways by Italian educators (c.f., chapters by Malaguzzi in both the 1993 and 1998 edited volumes by Edwards, Gandini, & Forman), each time with reference to several key principles:

- Schools are systems of relations, such that the well-being of children is dependent on the well-being of teachers and families.
- Children have numerous creative, intellectual, and communicative potentials, each of which deserve to be respected and nurtured.
- Teachers must learn about children as they try to teach them, and the incentive of uncertainty is central to processes of collaborative inquiry.

- Educational spaces must serve the needs of all who utilize them, such that early childhood centers are conceptualized as centers of exchange and relationship building among and between children, teachers, and families.

Although these principles do not strike U.S. early childhood educators as particularly new or problematic, as "students" of Reggio Emilia got closer and more deeply engaged in exploring the principles and practices found in the Italian classrooms, they discovered elements that are distinctively *Reggiano* and clearly challenging to U.S. beliefs and practices in many early childhood settings. This discussion describes Reggio Emilia's translation of their philosophical foundation as they appear in practices and features common to the town's municipal *asili nido* and *scuola del'infanzia*, including:

- the use of the environment to promote learning and relationships;
- curriculum projects based on inquiry and the "hundred languages" of children;
- documentation as a means of observation, research, and advocacy;
- partnerships with parents that exceed current notions of parent education.

1. An Environment that Welcomes, Nurtures, and Inspires

The feature most visible to those who come to observe Reggio Emilia's municipal program is also regarded as central to those who work inside of the city's infant–toddler centers (*asili nido*) and pre-primary schools (*scuole dell'infanzia*). Functioning as what anthropologists would call a "developmental niche" (Super & Harkness, 1986), the Reggio Emilia schools are characterized by a number of environmental features purposefully designed to create a school culture that reflects and promotes the values and goals of the larger community. For example, the communal ethos maintained by the central piazza found in every

Even the bathroom becomes a space for play and contemplation. Parents and teachers designed this tube arrangement through which colored water flows when children turn on the faucets.

Italian city and town is echoed in the large central space through which children, parents, and teachers must traverse as they move about the school. The environments designed for young children are also, in a word, *beautiful*. The strong and colorful Italian aesthetic as observed in the arrangement of red and yellow peppers at the market, rainbows of *gelato* cones, or dignified rows of cypress trees on the hillside is made explicit in Reggio Emilia classrooms through purposeful arrays of toy irons on shelves, bottles of colored water lining bathroom windows, and the careful and colorful way in which art supplies have been arranged. Mobiles with light-catching materials, simple arrangements of fragile shells, puddle-shaped mirrors on the floor, expansive leaf-laden

lattice-work serving as room dividers, and large colorful cushions—these features and others contribute to a space that conveys not only a concern with appearance, but also a welcoming message of respect and possibilities for children and their families. The Reggio Emilia early childhood environments are also highly *personal and purposeful*. Few, if any, mass-produced images or furniture are found in the classrooms; rather, images are of the children and their parents, together and separately, who make up the school's population; number charts and other forms of instructional aids, if they exist at all, have been created by the children; messages to parents are displayed on carefully arranged panels that include samples of children's work. The artifacts that are displayed come from the children's experiences at home, at school, or in the community. None have been ordered from a catalog. Each infant–toddler center, each pre-primary school is, as Lella Gandini (1984) has described, "not just anywhere." Rather, teachers and parents have worked hard to make their early childhood centers into "particular" places that are both caring and supportive of children's early learning (Gandini, 1998).

The early childhood environments in Reggio Emilia's municipal schools are not just visually pleasing and personally relevant reminders of the larger community culture. They are also explicitly designed to foster social activity, elicit curiosity and exploration, and promote an awareness of the history of the school community. These goals are in evidence as soon as one enters a Reggio Emilian *nido* or *scuola del'infanzia,* where there are messages to read, displays to contemplate, invitations to linger. The entranceway is filled with photographic images of children working on their projects, of parents engaged in discussions at council meetings, of teachers and staff in humorous poses. Throughout are carefully tended plants, cozy arrangements of adult-sized furniture, and more displays of children's work, some of which is from previous years. The centrally located *piazza* includes natural light whenever possible, and there is usually some form of enticing play apparatus that parents designed and built for the children and that has now become a part of the center's physical history. The qualities of the materials displayed, sometimes fragile and delicate, acknowledge children's capacities to notice and take care of their environment.

The potentials of school spaces to serve as another "teacher" of young children is especially apparent upon entering the classrooms, each of which is filled with what Reggio Emilian educators describe as "messages and possibilities" (Filippini, 1990). As might be expected, classrooms are divided into spaces for group gatherings, dramatic play, and large and small construction activities. Spaces for small-group and teacher-led activities are available at child-size

tables dispersed throughout the classroom. Other features are more particular to Reggio Emilia, including a *mini-atelier* or small work space adjacent to the classroom, where teachers and children can pursue long-term projects without distraction. Reflecting Italian beliefs regarding the importance of one's sense of self in relation to others, there are mirrors and other reflective surfaces throughout the classroom space as well as in the bathrooms and hallways. A keen appreciation for the pleasure and possibilities of light is also apparent in the frequent use of light boxes and illuminated light tables to display collections of leaves or other found objects, or an array of tissue paper just waiting to be composed. In most classrooms large windows open up to the outside, allowing shadows and sunshine as well as the sounds of the neighborhood to enter into the classroom.

The environment also serves as an essential source for the development of relationships among and between adults and children, such that the physical space is arranged and furnished in a manner that brings children and adults together. Children are invited to connect with each other within and outside of their classrooms, by way of "talking tubes" and transparent openings that allow them to call, speak, and gesture to one another from opposite sides of the classroom wall. Even the dress-up clothes are arranged in ways that invite the development of new relationships, stored as they often are in a central location outside the classroom. Children often visit each others' classrooms, and their project work often spills out into the large open spaces beyond their classroom doors. Everywhere one looks, there is evidence of the thought given to the potential interface between children, spaces, and relations (Ceppi & Zini, 1998). Adult relations—with each other, with teachers, and with the children—are also promoted through the careful arrangement of adult-sized furniture in the central space as well as in classrooms, including the occasional rocking chair that invites the visiting parent or grandparent to linger.

Within this adult-friendly environment, teachers create occasions that purposefully foster the development of relationships among parents. As is the case in most Italian early childhood programs, parents are invited to stay at the center during the child's initial transition period.[9] In Reggio Emilia, the goal is not only to support the child's transition to the new environment, but also to support the development of adult friendships among parents. Thus mothers and fathers are encouraged to share coffee together in a small room adjacent to the classroom, where they may also make some materials for use in the classroom. The environment continues to support adult relationships throughout the school year, and not only between parents and teachers. The kitchen, typically surrounded by glass divides or open windows, is often frequented by children and their parents upon arrival, when the cooks share tastes of the menu for the noontime *pranzo*. Evening gatherings of parents sometimes take place in the kitchen, where recipes are shared and the cooks again provide samples of food that they are serving to their children. The relationships with teaching and nonteaching staff are also supported during the daily meals, when teachers take turns enjoying a leisurely lunch with the cooks who have prepared it for them. Teacher work spaces are also designed so that teachers will enjoy their time working together while children nap or after they have gone home for the day. Such relationships are not only valued; they are essential, given the lack of a principal or head teacher in charge of the school and thus the need for group decision making.

Combined, these features of the environment support the philosophical premise of schools as systems of relations and create a sense of *place* for children and their families (Bruner, 1998) that is not captured by the use of terms such as *programs* or *services*. This sense of place, in turn, makes possible some of the other features that make Reggio Emilia's municipal program so compelling, including its conception of an early childhood curriculum.

2. Curriculum as Collaborative Explorations through Symbolic Representations

Reggio Emilia's early childhood environments are fascinating to visitors who are accustomed to settings filled with manufactured cartoons, look-a-like furniture, and primary colors, and yet the implications are straightforward and compelling—classrooms can, with purposeful and creative planning, become inviting, stimulating, and highly personalized places for adults as well as children. It is not so easy, however, for U.S. educators to understand and make use of the Reggio Emilia interpretation of a developmentally appropriate early childhood curriculum. For most observers of and visitors to Reggio Emilia, the most essential and perplexing aspect of the Reggio Emilia curriculum is their long-term projects known as *progettazione,* many of which are represented in the traveling exhibitions.[10]

The complexities of children's projects, sometimes spanning periods of weeks if not months; the quality of their drawings and other forms of representation of their ideas,

---

[9]The initial period of home-school transition is treated with a great deal of attention and respect in Italy. Many communities have devised distinct ways of ensuring that children, families, and teachers have ample opportunity to get to know one another. See Bove (1999) and New (1999) for further discussion of Italian approaches to the period of *inserimento* or *transizione*.

[10]Reggio Emilian educators, under the guidance of Loris Malaguzzi, created two elaborate traveling exhibitions on their work. *L'Occhio se Salta il Muro* (When the Eye Jumps over the Wall) was the first to open in Europe in 1981 and continues to travel to nations outside of Italy, most recently to Latin America. Another exhibition was created for Japan and yet a third exhibition has recently traveled across Australia. These exhibitions are *in addition to* the English-language version (The Hundred Languages of Children) that has been traveling through the United States since 1987. For information about the exhibition schedule, contact exhibit curator Pam Houk at the Dayton Art Institute in Ohio.

designs, and understandings; and the extensive and collaborative nature of what appears to be constructive play all suggest that the children in Reggio Emilia schools are either gifted or specially trained. And yet these examples of what *Reggiani* children are challenged and invited to do are also part of the normal course of a day's events in a Reggio Emilia classroom—they represent the results of purposeful and carefully designed early learning opportunities—in other words, an early childhood curriculum.

But educators in Reggio Emilia rarely talk about curriculum issues in terms familiar to American educators. That is, there are no specified goals and objectives as they might pertain to specific developmental or learning potentials such as developing fine motor skills or learning how to tell a story in sequence. Rather, goals are discussed in broad culturally valued aims such as (1) developing relationships, (2) learning how to collaborate, and (3) appreciating diversity in ideas and their expression. These aims are then pursued through the exploration of concepts that have already captured the attention of the children and/or the adults— for example, Where do shadows come from? Can an enemy become a friend? What makes it rain? As such, the curriculum in Reggio Emilia emerges from the shared experiences of children, teachers, and families (Rinaldi, 1993).

Reggio Emilia teachers use children's questions and curiosities to promote their exploration of materials, to experiment with various ways of communicating and then testing out hypotheses, to debate and negotiate their multiple points of view. In such explorations, embedded within a pedagogical process described as *progettazione,* Reggio Emilia teachers create conditions by which children are supported in their efforts to participate in the world that is around them, making sense of and adding their own interpretations to the events of the day. A trip to the market can become the first step in a long exploration of the city boundaries, leading to map making and the development of new relationships as children discover side streets,

buildings, and merchants previously unknown. Teachers do not necessarily wait on children to convey a curiosity or interest; rather, they carefully observe and document children at play, paying close attention to their conversations, and then talk with colleagues in other classes and with parents as part of the decision making about how best to prepare for the next day's learning encounters, which may involve one of the two classroom teachers with a small group of children (four or five)—or perhaps the entire class. It is not by accident that numerous such *progettazione* involve the use of developing numeracy and mathematical skills, but those are generally regarded as the means rather than the aims of the children's collaborative efforts.[11]

Although it is difficult to identify the starting point of such a problem-based curriculum, the aims are always to understand, first, the directions that children wish to take in pursuing their own questions; and then to support children's ongoing inquiry and problem-solving efforts as responses to initial hypotheses lead to the articulation of new ideas and possibilities. Such curriculum practices reflect a fundamental Reggio Emilia principle of curriculum as something that should "enable children to utilize their own skills and competence" (Rinaldi, 2003, p. 1).

Progettazione, the Project Approach, and an Emergent Curriculum Some U.S. educators have noted the similarity between Reggio Emilia's *progettazione* and other popular curriculum models, particularly the "Project Approach" as described by Katz and Chard (1989). The two interpretations of curriculum share in common (1) the selection of a topic that is of interest to children, (2) the use of

[11]See, for example, a project involving children's exploration of mathematics as they attempt to re-create a much beloved table in their classroom that was carefully documented and eventually published as "*Scarpe e metro*" (the shoe and the meter) by Reggio Children. This small publication and those of other projects are available for purchase through Reggio Children, USA, Washington, DC 20005-3105.

collaborative working groups, and (3) the creation of a learning "problem" with multiple avenues for exploration. Advocates of the Project Approach also recommend the use of highly detailed webs that identify learning goals—a strategy that sometimes supports teachers' curriculum planning processes in Reggio Emilia as well. Still others have noted the commonalities between Reggio Emilia's *progettazione* and U.S. interpretations of an emergent curriculum (Jones & Nimmo, 1994), which expand upon principles associated with the Project Approach through greater emphasis on the processes by which adults identify curriculum themes. Central tasks for teachers attempting to implement an emergent curriculum are to discern the interface between teachers' interests and those of the children; and to connect children's school experiences with their family and community lives. Clearly, these two approaches have much in common with Reggio Emilia's project-based curricula, and yet there are several features of *progettazione* that distinguish it from these curriculum interpretations.

- *An emphasis on creativity and symbolic representation.* One of the most obvious distinguishing characteristics of Reggio Emilia's *progettazione* is the level of creative exploration and symbolic representation associated with children's collaborative work. Beyond an emphasis on group learning to promote children's social relations, Reggio Emilia educators are purposeful in creating conditions by which children will find it necessary to share their understandings. Thus teachers ask children to explain their ideas through drawings, to create visual hypotheses through the creation of models or designs to help others envision the essential steps of a problem-solving agenda. As children share their understandings with one another, they are often challenged to revisit and revise their own ideas. This sequence of representation and

exploration, regarded as central to children's processes of knowledge construction, has been described by others in both text form (c.f., Forman & Fyfe, 1998) and on videotape.[12]

No way. The hundred *is* there.

The child
is made of one hundred.
The child has
a hundred languages
a hundred hands
a hundred thoughts
a hundred ways of thinking
of playing, of speaking.
A hundred always a hundred
ways of listening
of maraveling of loving
a hundred joys
for singing and understanding
a hundred worlds
to discover
a hundred worlds
to invent
a hundred worlds
to dream.
The child has
a hundred languages
(and a hundred hundred hundre
more)
but they steal ninety-nine.
The school and the culture
separate the head from the body.
They tell the child:
to think without hands
to do without head
to listen and not to speak
to understand without joy
to love and to marvel
only at Easter and Christmas.
They tell the child:

---

[12]A listing of available videos of Reggio Emilia *progettazione* can be obtained by writing to Reggio Children, USA, Washington, DC 20005-3105.

to discover the world already there
and of the hundred
they steal ninety-nine.
They tell the child:
that work and play
reality and fantasy
science and imagination
sky and earth
reason and dream
are things
that do not belong together.
And thus they tell the child
that the hundred is not there.
The child says:
No way. The hundred *is* there.

Loris Malaguzzi*

Teachers frequently reference Malaguzzi's hypothetical "hundred languages of children" (see the poem above) as the rationale for providing multiple means by which children can explore and share and reflect on their understandings. Thus, pairs of children may be invited to represent their understandings of trees blowing in the wind, one with clay and another with a fine-tipped felt pen. As they compare the details afforded by their diverse materials, they can also compare their experiences and their understandings, eventually co-constructing new understandings as supported by their diverse representations that reveal the best of what each has learned. While some observers consider this element of children's project work to be an art activity, Malaguzzi was explicit about his belief that creativity is not a separate mental faculty but rather a characteristic

"way of thinking, knowing, and making choices." As such, he regarded the development of children's creative potentials as inseparable from other curriculum goals and activities. The practical consequences of his theory of the relationship between creativity and intelligence include the hiring of an *atelierista* (art educator) who works closely with teachers to discover and promote children's developing symbolic languages, and daily opportunities for children to explore multiple types of media and symbolic representation through the use of clay, fine-tipped graphic drawings, painting, shadow play, as well as large and small constructive activities that far exceed the typical and brief periods of block play as found in U.S. early childhood settings. These activities are further supported through the use of a separate *atelier* or studio space, where children can work together in small groups on projects over longer periods of time with support from the *atelierista*.

- *Taking risks with a reality-based curriculum.* Another distinguishing feature of Reggio Emilia's *progettazione* is likely linked to cultural differences in the roles of adults in protecting children from certain realities of the world in which they live. In the Italian culture at large, for example, in contrast to middle-class U.S. norms, young children are more often included in adult activities and conversations, have fewer restrictions placed on nudity, have relatively easy access to sexually explicit language and information, and are more likely to understand that before one eats chicken for dinner, someone must kill and pluck the chicken. Thus, while many of the *progettazione* found in Reggio Emilia's municipal schools are based on the sorts of children's curiosities about the physical and social worlds (What is the nature of a

---

*Note. From "No Way. The Hundred Is There" by L. Malaguzzi, translated by L. Gandini, in the *The Reggio Emilia Approach—Advanced Reflections* (p. 3) edited by C. Edwards, L. Gandini, and G. Forman, 1998, Greenwich, CT: Ablex. Copyright 1998 by Ablex. Reprinted with permission.

shadow? Why are there so many crowds?), or practical propositions (Why don't we build an amusement park for the birds? Let's have an athletic event!) that might also be pursued in U.S. early childhood settings, other topics of potential exploration are much less likely to be pursued by U.S. early childhood educators. Such topics as found in Reggio Emilia classrooms include children's philosophical dilemmas (Can an enemy become a friend? What is love? Who is God?) as well as their anxieties or insights about the world around them, including their views of sexuality, their conceptions of children's rights, and their fears for themselves and the soldiers during the ongoing conflicts in the Middle East. Not only are such projects as common in Italy[13] as they are rare in the United States, they are also highly engaging and unlikely to bore the children and teachers who participate in their collaborative explorations.

This description of *progettazione* is not meant to imply that the children in Reggio Emilia classrooms spend most of their time engaged in long-term collaborative explorations of physics or philosophy. In fact, much of the child's day at the center is spent doing the sorts of things that children do elsewhere, including engaging in sociodramatic and constructive play as well as fine and gross motor activities. Classrooms are filled with blocks of various sizes, puzzles, clay, and other manipulative materials, as well as dolls, housekeeping supplies, and other play materials frequently found in high-quality early childhood settings. What is different about the use of these materials is not how

the children are engaged; rather, it is how teachers use this time to observe, listen to, and record children's conversations and activities, and subsequently link these insights to their planning for long-term projects. This role of the teacher is linked to a third distinguishing feature of Reggio Emilia's work with young children—which is, that it is not only focused on the children.

3. Documentation as a Tool for Research, Reflection, and Relationships

Under the guidance of Loris Malaguzzi, Reggio Emilian teachers have consciously adopted a Deweyian approach to scientific inquiry, posing hypotheses about children's social and intellectual capacities, creating experimental conditions to test those hypotheses, and then systematically collecting artifacts of children's activities as well as transcripts of children's and adults' conversations. Together, sometimes with parents and teachers from other schools, often with the *atelierista*, teachers analyze their data and frame new hypotheses. They move through the *progettazione* in a process remarkably similar to the one that characterizes the children's learning. Where the children's contemplative and communicative efforts associated with their projects are captured under the rubric of symbolic languages, for the teachers, this process is facilitated through documentation.

Documentation as a Support for Teacher Research   The administrators, teachers, and parents in Reggio Emilia have engaged in a form of collaborative action research for the past 35 years—research as they have defined it within their own classrooms and community. The primary aim of this research has been to better understand children in order to design learning experiences and environments that foster the development of multiple forms of communication and cognition. Within this

---

[13]Reggio Emilia is not alone in this use of the surrounding sociocultural context for curriculum content. A wine-making project was observed in a Naples preschool, where parents and grandparents worked together with the teacher to ensure that children were well acquainted with the traditions indigenous to the community (New, 1999).

context, teachers in Reggio Emilia have fine-tuned the art and science of careful observations and documentation of children's behaviors and understandings in both the social and physical realms. As children are learning through their active engagement with each other and through long- and short-term projects, the teachers are learning about the children as individuals and as members of groups. Teachers routinely debate the significance of these observations and develop their own questions and hypotheses about children's existing understandings as well as the processes associated with their meaning making. As explained previously, many of the questions or proposals associated with *progettazione* come from the children's own activities; teachers may also initiate an exploration based on a proposition that they present to the children. This role of teacher as *provocateur* builds upon teacher observations and documentation of what is (or is not) happening in the classroom or the community (New, 1990). This use of documentation also helps teachers to address questions that the teachers or parents themselves may have about children's development and learning. Each of the previously mentioned types of Reggio Emilian curriculum projects (practical ideas, questions about the world, or philosophical inquiries) are also based, in some way, on *adult* hypotheses regarding children's developing theories about the world around them. Thus documentation serves as an essential tool for a "projecting curriculum" for teachers to learn from (Rinaldi, 1998).

Documentation as a Form of Reflection for Children

Teachers are not the only ones to benefit from their ongoing documentation efforts. Reggio Emilia classroom walls are filled with evidence of the processes and high-quality products associated with children's school experiences, and especially their participation in long-term projects. The frequent use of photographic images of children at work, coupled with samples of their finished products and their conversations, has been described previously. Such displays provide children with the opportunity to reflect upon their prior abilities and understandings even as they develop more elaborate and sophisticated skills and knowledge. Such displays are not only of ongoing and recently completed activities but also from previous years, often eliciting questions from the children about a particular event or child. In this way documentation serves both to represent and promote an interest in the history of the school itself, with images of families, teachers, children, and their work from previous years making explicit the community that new classes of children will join. Also implicit in the documentation products displayed throughout the early childhood environment is an advocacy for the work being done by the children and their teachers, and the rights of parents to be informed about and involved in these experiences.

Documentation as a Means of Connecting with Families and Communities

Early childhood educators in Reggio Emilia as well as those in Pistoia and San Miniato have spent several decades exploring the possibilities of documentation as a means of promoting parent relationships as well as fostering a better understanding and greater interest among the community at large in children's early childhood education. Everywhere, it seems, there is testimony to children's work and the respect it garners from their teachers. Photographs, transcriptions of conversations, and teacher descriptions of the aims and outcomes of various short- and long-term projects supplement elegant displays of the products of children's collaborative activities. Combined, these features of the environment convey messages of welcome as well as an invitation to learn more about the activities that characterize this learning environment. They also direct attention to the qualities of children's competencies and the context that supports and inspires their development. By reading teacher explanations regarding children's processes of knowledge construction and viewing the numerous visual images of their activities, parents and community leaders alike can learn about children's development as it is supported within the school environment. In this sense these documentation displays serve as a form of advocacy for children as well as for the program. The recent project *Reggio Tutta* that entailed children's exploration throughout the city exemplifies the role of documentation in helping children to connect with their city and ensuring that the city stays mindful of the children in its midst (Bruner, 2002).

Documentation efforts also support parental understanding of their individual child's learning and developmental progress. Rather than provide assessment results typical of many U.S. early childhood programs, parents in Reggio Emilia and other like-minded communities "receive extensive descriptive information about their children's daily life and progress. . . and share in culminating productions or performances" (Edwards, personal communication April, 2002). Documentation strategies provide the materials to use in creating these descriptions as well as more elaborate "portfolios or other products of children's individual and group work, some of which are displayed and others sent home at key intervals and transitions" (Edwards, 2002). As do teachers in a number of other municipal programs in Italy (Gandini & Edwards, 2001), teachers prepare *diarios* (memory books) with samples and stories from children's experiences in the *nido* and *scuola del'infanzia*. This use of documentation to promote shared understandings between parents and teachers is one element in a larger component that is likely the key to the success of Reggio Emilia's municipal program—the notion of *partecipazione* as essential to the design and maintenance of the city's early childhood services.

4. Parent Engagement, Not Parent Education

Of all of the elements associated with Reggio Emilia's work with children and their families, the concept of parental engagement is probably the least visible to outsiders and yet most central to their philosophy, their practices, and their 30-year success story. Grounded in cultural values regarding the importance of adult collaboration and fine-tuned in a region distinguished by high levels of civic engagement (*partecipazione*) (Putnam, 1993), Reggio Emilia played a leading role in establishing national guidelines and implementing practices that support community involvement and parent engagement in early childhood settings.

The concept of *gestione sociale* (social management), originally developed for the labor market, is premised on the essential right of parents to be directly involved in the running of local child-care centers. In most Italian cities with municipal early childhood programs, the concept of *gestione sociale* is represented in various forms of parent–teacher–citizen advisory councils. Reggio Emilia has further elaborated upon the general principle of an advisory council to create specific practices that promote the collaborative engagement of families in the early childhood services (New, Mallory, & Mantovani, 2000).

This importance of family participation is directly linked to the philosophical premise of schools as "systems of relations," but Reggio Emilia's interpretation goes beyond ensuring that parents feel welcome and included in the school environment. As interpreted in Reggio Emilia, the concept of *partecipazione* requires that parents and citizens become intimately involved with the processes and aims of the educational enterprise. The intent is to offer "the possibility of the citizens (most of all the parents) to contribute actively to the conducting of educational services, refusing to delegate their potentials and their responsibility" (Spaggiari, 1991, p. 112 [translated from Italian]).

The concept of participation is more than a set of ideals; it also has multiple practical interpretations aimed at developing trusting and reciprocal relations with parents (New & Mallory, in press). In addition to the formal advisory councils (which include both citizen and parent representation), numerous other strategies have been designed to ensure that parents and citizens have opportunities to play what the Italians refer to as "co-protagonist" roles (Spaggiari, 1998). For example, each class has regular individual and full-class meetings regarding events particular to their group; there are also small-group meetings of parents and teachers for discussion of particular topics of interest. Groups of parents and sometimes grandparents are invited to come together in the evenings to have cooking lessons with the cook, or to get together on weekends to make something for the school. Schoolwide meetings may focus on educational issues (such as the role of technology) or a topic on child development (i.e., the changing role of grandparents), or issues associated with budgetary matters. While many such meetings involve the sharing of teacher documentation to inform the discussion, other meetings may include a guest speaker. *All* meetings with parents and the larger community are documented to validate their importance and to ensure that those who were not present can share in the learning that took place.

In addition to meetings where parents, teachers, and other citizens talk about their own understandings of and responsibilities for children's learning, other occasions serve as culminating events to children's long-term project work. Although not the case with every project, every Reggio Emilia school finds occasions during the year to share and celebrate children's work to which families and members of the larger community are invited. These and many other strategies have been designed to promote the development of reciprocal home-school relationships and community involvement. The success of these strategies is apparent in the high levels of participation that characterize these events. It is also apparent in the quality and sustainability of their highly successful and municipally funded program of early educational services over the past 40 years.

Reggio Emilia's creation of a school environment that nurtures adult as well as child relations, their interpretation of curriculum as a catalyst for children's and teacher's collaborative investigations, and their commitment to ensuring ongoing communication and exchanges with families and community members represent much more than an approach to early childhood education. Rather, this collection of principles and their related practices reflect an attitude that draws upon political, philosophical, and cultural views of what it means to live and contribute to a democratic community (New, 1998). The particulars of Reggio Emilia's history, culture, and politics make it risky to blithely assume that U.S. early childhood educators might incorporate various features of Reggio Emilia's municipal program for use in their own work with young children. And yet, thousands of teachers and teacher–educators across the U.S. have done just that. The following discussion suggests that the REA in the United States has taken on a life of its own, in a context of its own.

✍ REGGIO EMILIA'S INFLUENCE IN THE UNITED STATES

It is difficult to adequately describe the current and potential influences of REA-inspired conversations and collaboration that are taking place in the United States. Once considered an exotic point of reference for those fortunate enough to have traveled to Italy, Reggio Emilia is now regarded as a major curriculum approach in the professional literature, as evidenced by its inclusion in this volume and its many references as found in contemporary early childhood texts in the United States and abroad.[14] Reggio Emilia has its own track of sessions at NAEYC's national conference, multiple list serves and study groups, a newsletter, annual U.S. delegations, and dozens of Internet reference sites. As a result of this widespread exposure, tens of thousands of teachers and teacher educators are now striving to understand and apply "the Reggio Emilia approach" to U.S. education, including, in a few instances, elementary (New, 2003) and middle school (Hill, 2002) settings. Thirty-seven of the 50 states have contacts who help teachers connect with others who are interested in exploring premises of Reggio Emilia's work with young children. Teachers in early childhood programs in Chicago, St. Paul, Boulder, St. Louis, Columbus, Santa Monica, Miami, Atlanta, and San Francisco are currently collaborating directly with Reggio Emilia educators, as is the World Bank Children's Center in Washington, DC (New, 2002). Besides generating this large-scale interest and enthusiasm, what influence has Reggio Emilia had in U.S. early childhood education? The following discussion outlines Reggio Emilia's role in challenging and expanding upon U.S. theory and practice in early childhood settings.

New Understandings of How Children Learn

As outlined in the introduction, Reggio Emilia played a central role in expanding U.S. conceptions of developmentally appropriate practices. This influence was in great part due to the exhibition's success in illustrating changing understanding of contemporary theories of children's learning and development. Already under criticism for a too-heavy reliance on Piagetian theories and associated interpretations of an activity-based and child-centered early childhood

curriculum, early childhood teacher educators and many among the NAEYC leadership welcomed Reggio Emilia's ability to demonstrate more advanced conceptual understandings of children's learning. Many of Reggio Emilia's principles about how children learn are embedded within the theoretical construct of the zone of proximal development, a Vygotskian construct central to the theoretical framework of sociocultural theory and one that has major implications for how we conceptualize and experience educational change (New, 1998). Reggio Emilia's *progettazione,* for example, provided numerous and compelling illustrations of the interplay between social and intellectual processes. It was not just academics who experienced paradigm shifts in their theoretical interpretations of children's learning. Classroom teachers also became fascinated with the question of how children learn as a result of seeing and learning about Reggio Emilian teaching strategies.

The practical examples of Reggio Emilia were seen by many as "a helpful way for the field to understand that Piagetian theories did not explain everything."[15] In particular, the intensity of engagement over periods of weeks and months by Italian children as young as 3 and 4 years, in projects that they co-constructed with their teachers, served as a powerful provocation for early childhood educators to rethink their dichotomous distinctions between teacher-directed and child-initiated learning. Because they were illustrated with fascinating photographs and vignettes rather than in strictly academic terms, these theoretical insights led many classroom teachers and teacher educators to more carefully explore contemporary Vygotskian and neo-Vygotskian literature (e.g., Rogoff, 1990) as it could inform and improve educational practice. Seeing and reading about teachers who carefully attend to children's questions as they up the ante in presenting new

---

[14]C.f., Abbott & Nutbrown, 2001, for a discussion of Reggio Emilia's growing influence in the United Kingdom.

[15]John Nimmo, 2002, personal communication.

problems to ponder helped U.S. educators to re-think the instructional implications of readiness in the new terms of "zoped" or zones of prox-imal development, a state which is characterized by a dynamic tension between what is known and what is being sought (Brown & Ferrera, 1985). Numerous publications have since utilized Reggio Emilia as an example of theory into prac-tice, linking Reggio Emilia to theories of con-structivism and social constructivism (New, 1998) for typically developing children as well as those with special needs (Mallory & New, 1994).

Reggio Emilia's influence on theoretical un-derstandings has not been limited to views on cognitive development. Reggio Emilia's work also "draws attention to children's need for comfort and security" as essential to their suc-cessful engagement in Reggio Emilia projects (Edwards, personal communication). This rela-tionship between children's emotional well-being and cognitive development "resonates with what we are learning about attachment as well as the new brain research" (Carolyn Ed-wards, personal communication, April 2002). And beyond the theoretical abstractions of the processes of children's learning, Reggio Emilia has also challenged our understandings and ex-pectations of the content and consequences of children's learning. As revealed through the documentation of children's conversations and constructions, Reggio Emilia educators have demonstrated beyond doubt that the limits in our theoretical understandings have been ac-companied by vast underestimations of the po-tentials that children bring with them to early childhood settings (Katz, 1998).

From Traditional Scripts to Purposeful and Collaborative Teaching

It is one thing to have a foreign experience pro-vide a new way of understanding, of theorizing, and of planning for children's learning processes and potentials. It is altogether different to begin to change the day-to-day practices that might be linked with these abstractions. For some class-room teachers the changes to practice came first. Beginning with increased attention to the phys-ical environment (such that bottles of colored water began appearing in bathrooms across the country), teachers became emboldened to think more critically about their classroom work with young children. Taking advantage of supports provided by the growing number of study groups and Reggio Emilia dedicated list serves, teachers began to more actively explore ways to use what they were learning about young chil-dren as they planned more purposeful but also open-ended learning encounters. Some of these teacher explorations took place in isolated set-tings; others, in places that dedicated their entire program to exploring ways to re-create relevant principles and practices from Reggio Emilia in new contexts. Two examples are worth men-tioning here—the St. Louis schools (three pri-vate preschool settings) and the Chicago Com-mons project (a consortium of federal, state, and locally funded early childhood and parent–child centers for low-income families). As described by program directors of these two communities, each of whom has been exploring implications from Reggio Emilia for the past decade, the chal-lenge has been to figure out what and how to "bring Reggio Emilia home" (Cadwell, 1997). Over the slow and deliberate process, teachers in each setting—as distinct from each other as they are from Reggio Emilia—embarked on a study of and debate about the principles of Reggio Emilia as they might pertain to and improve their services for young children. Thus, for example, in St. Louis, teachers have focused on pedagog-ical documentation as a link to the creation of an investigative framework that guides teachers' work with children (Cadwell, 2002). In Chicago, African American parents who have recently as-sumed roles as Head Start teachers have visited Reggio Emilia, returning to initiate schoolwide discussions on what it really means to involve parents in children's learning. And these are only two of the hundreds of early childhood settings where teachers, individually and together, continue to use their experiences and understandings from Reggio Emilia to promote their ongoing reflection about their own work with young children and families (see, for example, the 2002 issue of *Innovations* for discussions with directors of three different American schools). Reggio Emilia educators have worked closely with many of these teachers and program directors, illustrating through their international partnerships the benefits of "collaboration in all its meanings" (Bredekamp, 2002).

New Forms and Functions of Parent–Teacher Relationships

The REA has also influenced teachers' thinking with respect to how they relate to and work with parents, although the translation of these ideas into actual practices has been somewhat less widespread. Traditional interpretations of professional responsibilities have often placed parents in a consumer rather than in a partner role with educators. The demands of contemporary family life make the idea of 3-hour classroom meetings a rarity rather than a reality in most U.S. settings. And the diversity of perspectives likely found among a group of parents in a pluralistic society such as the United States makes some teachers hesitant to even inquire as to what parents actually want for their children. Nonetheless, some U.S. teachers have creatively found ways to minimize the assumed hierarchy of teachers over parents and to seek more active and reciprocal relationships. Thus two kindergarten teachers invited a group of parents to help them with a problem—a real problem, not one that they had manufactured for the occasion—having to do with the need for a "birthday policy" that would acknowledge and respect the diverse cultural and religious perspectives represented in their classroom. Subsequent to that decision, the teachers described a slow but significant change in parents' relationships to each other as they came to understand that their hopes and preferences for their own children did not always coincide with the goals for other people's children. In a similar vein, after several years of exploring principles from Reggio Emilian and other Italian early childhood programs, one Early Head Start teacher invited teenage parents to take on the role of documenting children's learning, trusting them with the videocameras and, eventually, with selecting, arranging, and writing about the images on bulletin board displays. These parents came to increasingly value their roles in helping the teacher to identify and promote children's learning and development. Each of these examples illustrates a Reggio Emilia principle that has been appropriated for a particularly American controversy or context.

Documentation as a Tool for Professional Development

One of the most visible consequences of Reggio Emilia's influence on U.S. early childhood practices is the growing use of documentation—not only as a means of observing and assessing young children, but also as a vehicle for teacher development. Described in terms of its potentials for sharing and reflecting, classroom teachers (e.g., Oken-Wright, 2001) describe with detail the importance of more carefully listening to and observing the children with whom they work so that these insights can guide their ongoing curriculum decisions. U.S. educators are also increasingly utilizing documentation strategies as a means for systematically following and studying the ways that individuals as well as groups of children develop ideas, theories, and understandings (Project Zero & Reggio Children, 2001; Turner & Krechevsky, 2003). More recent advocates of documentation highlight its usefulness in illuminating the processes of *teaching* (Project Zero, 2003) as well as learning. These potentials of documentation have not been lost on early

As an example of the nature and focus of *partecipazione* in Reggio Emilia, parents, teachers, grandparents, and citizens engage in series of meetings addressed to questions of education today.

childhood teacher educators who advocate for the potentials of documentation to help preservice teachers learn how to observe, record, and understand child development (Goldhaber, Smith, & Sortino, 1997). Increasingly, Reggio Emilia–inspired teacher education programs now incorporate the practices of teacher research (Rinaldi, 2003) through collaborative documentation into their university-based teacher professional development programs (Gandini & Goldhaber, 2001). Together with other Reggio Emilia principles, documentation has helped to provoke and sustain a paradigm shift among an increasing number of university laboratory schools (Stremmel, Hill, & Fu, in press) and early childhood teacher education programs (Fu, Stremmel, & Hill, 2002).

CONCLUSION

The story of Reggio Emilia is only one of many such stories in contemporary Italy (Gandini & Edwards, 2001; Mantovani & Musatti, 1996), each characterized by a respect for cultural traditions as well as innovation (Mantovani, 2001). One of the aims of this discussion has been to distinguish between what happens in the classrooms of one particular Italian city and what has come to be known, in the United States, as the Reggio Emilia approach. The point here is that any educational innovation becomes transformed as others attempt to understand and make use of it. Some transformation is unintentional or unavoidable. There are a number of practical and policy-related challenges of interpreting Reggio

Emilia in the United States beyond the challenges of implementation, including the trivializing of Reggio Emilia principles and practices, the American tendency to seek out "quick fixes" for complex educational challenges, the lack of infrastructures at the local and state levels to support teacher collaboration, the difficulties of retaining poorly paid teachers over time, not to mention the lack of a nationwide commitment to the provision of early childhood services. This is not to say that Reggio Emilia has nothing to offer to U.S. early childhood education. The previous discussion has highlighted some of the ways in which Reggio Emilia has already changed at least some U.S. educators' ways of thinking about and working with young children and their families.

A second aim of this discussion has been to reveal the wealth of possibilities that exist when teachers and others involved in education don't try to imitate, but rather try to learn from such international examples. Such possibilities are conveyed in the sincerity of Sergio Spaggiari's message: "If you want to be like us, don't copy us. We have never copied anyone. If you want to be like us, be original" (cited in Cadwell, 2002, p. 163). Thus a growing number of U.S. educators are attempting to "reinvent" the promise of Reggio Emilia as it might be realized elsewhere (Fu, 2002), keeping in mind the particular facts and circumstances of that Italian city itself—what Peter Moss (2001) refers to as the "otherness" of Reggio Emilia—as a means of keeping in the forefront the inextricable relationship between culture and education (Bruner, 1996).

What Reggio Emilia has been most successful at doing is setting an example—of a commitment to hard work and collaborative inquiry on behalf of young children. What is really exotic about Reggio Emilia is not the beautiful images on the walls, or the carefully rendered drawings by children of their ideas and understandings. What has inspired American educators to rethink, collaboratively and over time, about their images of children, parents, and their own professional identities is the *fact* of Reggio Emilia (New, 2002). It is difficult to imagine a city in the United States that dedicates 10% of its annual budget to the care and education of its young children, that continues to do so for 30+ years no matter what is happening in other parts of the nation, and that does so in a way that involves families, engages teachers, and promotes children's skills and understandings beyond imaginable levels. Indeed, the United States remains far behind most other industrialized nations in developing any sort of system, national or otherwise, for the early care and education of its children (OECD, 2001). That Reggio Emilia has done these things, and successfully, in the face of its own challenges (Piccini, as quoted in Gambetti, 2002) gives educators around the world the message that, in their settings as well, things could change. If nothing else from Reggio Emilia makes a lasting impression, the city and her citizens have demonstrated what might happen when parents, teachers, and other citizens refuse to accept the status quo and come to collectively imagine that there might be another way to care for and educate young children.

REFERENCES

Abbott, L., & Nutbrown, C. (Eds.). (2001). *Experiencing Reggio Emilia: Implications for pre-school provision*. Buckingham, UK: Open University Press.

Bove, C. (1999). *L'inserimento del bambino al nido* [Welcoming the child into child care]: Perspectives from Italy. *Young Children, 54* (2), 32–34.

Bredekamp, S. (1987). *Developmentally appropriate practice in early childhood programs serving children from birth through age eight*. Washington, DC: National Association for the Education of Young Children.

Bredekamp, S. (1993). Reflections on Reggio Emilia. *Young Children, 49* (1), 13–17.

Bredekamp, S. (2002). Developmentally appropriate practice meets Reggio Emilia: A story of collaboration in all its meanings. *Innovations, 9* (1, Winter Issue), 11–15.

Bredekamp, S., & Copple, C. (Eds.) (1997). *Developmentally appropriate practice for early childhood programs serving children from birth through age eight* (Rev. ed.). Washington, DC: NAEYC.

Brown, A., & Ferrara, R. (1985). Diagnosing zones of proximal development. In J. V. Wertsch (Ed.), *Culture, communication, and cognition: Vygotskian perspectives* (pp. 273–305). New York: Cambridge University Press.

Bruner, J. (1996). *The culture of education.* Cambridge, MA: Harvard University Press.

Bruner, J. (1998). Some specifications for a space to house a Reggio pre-school. In G. Ceppi and M. Zini (Eds.), *Children, space, and relations—A metaproject for an environment for young children.* Reggio Emilia: Reggio Children; and Modena: Domus Academy Research Center.

Bruner, J. (2002). Commentary. In *Reggio Tutta: A guide to the city by the children.* Reggio Emilia: Reggio Children.

Cadwell, L. B. (1997). *Bringing Reggio Emilia home.* New York: Teachers College Press.

Cadwell, L. (2002). *Bringing learning to life: The Reggio approach to early childhood education.* New York: Teachers College Press.

Ceppi, G., & Zini, M. (Eds.). (1998). *Children, spaces, relations: Metaproject for an environment for young children.* Modena: Reggio Children and Domus Academy Research Center.

Cohen, D. L. (1992). Preschools in Italian town inspiration to U.S. educators. *Education Week, 12,* Nov 20.

Corsaro, W., & Emiliani, F. (1992). Child care, early education, and children's peer culture in Italy. In M. E. Lamb, K. J. Sternberg, C. P. Hwang, & A. G. Broberg (Eds.), *Child care in context* (pp. 81–115). Hillsdale, NJ: Erlbaum.

Edwards, C. (2002). Three approaches from Europe: Waldorf, Montessori, and Reggio Emilia. *Early Childhood Research and Practice, 4* (1), Available online: http://ecrp.uiuc.edu/V4n1/edwards.html [accessed 2003, March].

Edwards, C., Gandini, L., & Forman, G. (Eds.) (1993). *The hundred languages of children: The Reggio Emilia approach.* Norwood, NJ: Ablex.

Edwards, C., Gandini, L., & Forman, G. (Eds.) (1998). *The hundred languages of children: The Reggio Emilia approach—Advanced reflections* (2nd ed.). Greenwich, CT: Ablex.

Filippini, T. (Novermber, 1990). *Introduction to the Reggio approach.* Paper presented at the annual conference of the National Association for the Education of Young Children, Washington, DC.

Forman, G., & Fyfe, B. (1998). Negotiated learning through design, documentation, and discourse. In C. Edwards, L. Gandini, & G. Forman (Eds.), *The hundred languages of children: The Reggio Emilia approach—Advanced reflections* (2nd ed.; pp. 239–260). Greenwich, CT: Ablex.

Fu, V. R. (2002). The challenge to reinvent the Reggio Emilia approach: A pedagogy of hope and possibilities. In V. Fu, A. Stremmel, & L. Hill (Eds.), *Teaching and learning: Collaborative exploration of the Reggio Emilia approach* (pp. 23–35). Upper Saddle River, NJ: Merrill/Prentice Hall.

Fu, V. R., Stremmel, A. J., & Hill, L. T. (2002). An invitation to join in a growing community for learning and change. In V. Fu, A. Stremmel, & L. Hill (Eds.), *Teaching and learning: Collaborative exploration of the Reggio Emilia approach* (pp. 5–11). Upper Saddle River, NJ: Merrill/Prentice Hall.

Gambetti, A. (2002). The evolution of the municipality of Reggio Emilia: An interview with Sandra Piccini. *Innovations in Early Education: The International Reggio Exchange, 9* (3), 1–3.

Gandini, L. (1984). Not just anywhere: Making child care centers into "particular" places. *Beginnings,* 17–20.

Gandini, L. (1998). Educational and caring spaces. In C. Edwards, L. Gandini, & G. Forman (Eds.), *The hundred languages of children: The Reggio Emilia approach—Advanced reflections* (2nd ed.; pp. 161–178). Greenwich, CT: Ablex.

Gandini, L., & Edwards, C. (Eds.). (2001). *Bambini: The Italian approach to infant/toddler care.* New York: Teachers College Press.

Gandini, L., & Goldhaber, J. (2001). Two reflections about documentation. In L. Gandini & C. Edwards (Eds.), *Bambini: The Italian approach to infant/toddler care* (pp. 124–145). New York: Teachers College Press.

Goldhaber, J., Smith, D., & Sortino, S. (1997). Observing, recording and understanding: The role of documentation in early childhood teacher education. In J. Hendrick (Ed.), *First steps in teaching the Reggio way.* Upper Saddle River, NJ: Merrill/Prentice Hall.

Jones, E., & Nimmo, J. (1994). *Emergent curriculum.* Washington, DC: NAEYC.

Hill, L. T. (2002). A journey to recast the Reggio Emilia approach for a middle school: A pedagogy of relationships and hope. In V. Fu, A. Stremmel, & L. Hill (Eds.), *Teaching and learning: A collaborative exploration of the Reggio Emilia Approach.* Upper Saddle River, NJ: Merrill/Prentice Hall.

Katz, L. (1998). What can we learn from Reggio Emilia? In C. Edwards, L. Gandini, & G. Forman (Eds.), *The hundred languages of children: The Reggio Emilia approach— Advanced reflections* (2nd ed.; pp. 27–45). Greenwich, CT: Ablex.

Katz, L., & Cesarone, B. (Eds.). (1994). *Reflections on the Reggio Emilia Approach.* ERIC/EECE, University of Illinois, Urbana and Edizioni Junior, Bergamo, Italy (Available from Reggio Children USA and ERIC/ECE.)

Katz, L., & Chard, S. (1989). *Engaging children's minds: The project approach.* Norwood, NJ: Ablex.

Kessler, S. (1991). Alternative perspectives on early childhood education. *Early Childhood Research Quarterly, 6,* 183–197.

Malaguzzi, L. (1993). For an education based on relationships. *Young Children, 49* (1), 9–12.

Malaguzzi, L. (1998). History, ideas, and basic philosophy: An interview with Lella Gandini. In C. Edwards, L. Gandini, & G. Forman (Eds.), *The hundred languages of children: The Reggio Emilia approach—Advanced reflections* (2nd ed.; pp. 49–97). Greenwich, CT: Ablex.

Mallory, B. (1992). Is it always appropriate to be developmental? Convergent models for early intervention practice. *Topics in Early Childhood Special Education, 11* (4), 1–12.

Mallory, B., & New, R. (1994). *Diversity and developmentally appropriate practices: Challenges for early childhood education.* New York: Teachers College Press.

Mantovani, S. (2001). Infant–toddler centers in Italy today: Tradition and innovation. In L. Gandini & C. P. Edwards (Eds.), *Bambini: The Italian approach to infant/toddler care* (pp. 23–37). New York: Teachers College Press.

Mantovani, S., & Musatti, T. (1996). New educational provisions for young children in Italy. *European Journal of Educational Psychology, XI* (2), 119–128.

Moss, P. (2001). The otherness of Reggio. In L. Abbott & C. Nutbrown (Eds.), *Experiencing Reggio Emilia: Implications for pre-school provision.* Buckingham, UK: Open University Press.

New, R. (1990). Excellent early education: A city in Italy has it! *Young Children, 45* (6), 4–6.

New, R. (1993a). Cultural variations on developmentally appropriate practice: Challenges to theory and practice. In C. Edwards, L. Gandini, & G. Forman (Eds.), *The hundred languages of children: The Reggio Emilia approach to early childhood education* (pp. 215–231). Norwood, NJ: Ablex.

New, R. (1993b). Italy. In M. Cochran (Ed.), *International handbook on child care policies and programs* (pp. 291–311). Westport, CT: Greenwood Press.

New, R. (1994). Reggio Emilia: Its vision and its challenges for educators in the United States. In L. G. Katz & B. Cesarone (Eds.), *Reflections on the Reggio Emilia approach.* Urbana, IL: ERIC/EECE Monograph Series, No. 6.

New, R. (1998). Theory and praxis in Reggio Emilia: They know what they are doing, and why. In C. Edwards, L. Gandini, & G. Forman (Eds.), *The hundred languages of children: The Reggio Emilia approach—Advanced reflections* (2nd ed.; pp. 261–284). Greenwich, CT: Ablex.

New, R. (1999). What should children learn? *Early Childhood Research & Practice, 1* (2), 1–19.

New, R. (2000). Reggio Emilia: An approach or an attitude? In J. Roopnarine & J. Johnson (Eds.), *Approaches to early childhood education* (rev. 3rd ed.). Columbus, OH: Merrill.

New, R. (2001). Reggio Emilia: Catalyst for change and conversation. *ERIC Digests.*

New, R. (2002). *The impact of the Reggio Emilia model on early childhood education in the U.S.*

Unpublished paper, commissioned by the Board of International Comparative Studies in Education's Committee on a Framework and Long-term Research Agenda for International Comparative Education Studies. Washington, DC: National Research Council.

New, R. (2003). Reggio Emilia: New ways to think about schooling. *Educational Leadership, 60* (7), 30–37.

New, R., & Mallory, B. (in press). Children as catalysts for adult relations: New perspectives from Italian early childhood education. In O. Saracho & B. Spodek (Eds.), *Contemporary perspective on families and communities and schools in early childhood education*. Greenwich, CT: Information Age Publisher.

New, R., Mallory, B., & Mantovani, S. (2000). Cultural images of children, parents, and teachers: Italian interpretations of home-school relations. *Early Education and Development, 11* (5), 597–616.

Newsweek. (1991, December 2). The 10 best schools in the world and what we can learn from them. *Newsweek,* pp. 50–59.

OECD (Organization for Economic Cooperation and Development). (2001). *Starting strong, early childhood education and care.* Paris: Organization for Economic Cooperation and Development. Available at: www.oecd.org.

Oken-Wright, P. (2001). Documentation: Both mirror and light. *Innovations in Early Education: The International Reggio Exchange, 10* (2), 1–4.

Oken-Wright, P., & Gravett, M. (2002). Big Ideas and the Essence of Intent. In V. Fu, A. Stremmel, & L. Hill (Eds.), *Teaching and learning, collaborative exploration of the Reggio Emilia approach* (pp. 197–220). Upper Saddle River, NJ: Merrill/Prentice Hall.

Project Zero. (2003). *Making teaching visible: Documenting group learning as professional development.* Cambridge, MA: Project Zero.

Project Zero & Reggio Children. (2001). *Making learning visible: Children as individual and group learners.* Reggio Emilia, Italy: Reggio Children.

Putnam, R. (1993). *Making democracy work: Civic traditions in modern Italy.* Princeton, NJ: Princeton University Press.

Rinaldi, C. (1993). The emergent curriculum and social constructivism. In C. Edwards, L. Gandini, & G. Forman (Eds.), *The hundred languages of children: The Reggio Emilia approach* (pp. 101–111). Norwood, NJ: Ablex.

Rinaldi, C. (1998). Projected curriculum constructed through documentation—*Progettazione:* An interview with Lella Gandini. In C. Edwards, L. Gandini, & G. Forman (Eds.), *The hundred languages of children: The Reggio Emilia approach—Advanced reflections* (2nd ed.; pp. 113–125). Greenwich, CT: Ablex.

Rinaldi, C. (2003). The teacher as researcher. *Innovations in Early Education: The International Reggio Exchange, 10* (2), 1–4.

Rogoff, B. (1990). *Apprenticeship in thinking: Cognitive development in social context.* New York: Oxford University Press.

Spaggiari, S. (1991). *Considerazioni critiche ed esperienze di gestione sociale.* [*Critical considerations and experiences of social management*]. In A. Bondidi & S. Mantovani (Eds.), *Manuale critico dell'asilo nido* [*Critical manual of the day care*] (pp. 111–134). Milan, Italy-Franco Angeli.

Spaggiari, S. (1998). The community-teacher partnership in the governance of the schools: An interview with Lella Gandini. In C. Edwards, L. Gandini, & G. Forman (Eds.), *The hundred languages of children: The Reggio Emilia approach—Advanced reflections* (2nd. ed.; pp. 99–112). Greenwich, CT: Ablex.

Stremmel, A. J., Hill, L. T., & Fu, V. R. (in press). An inside perspective of paradigm shifts in child development laboratory programs: Bridging theory and professional preparation. In S. Reifel (Series ed.), *Advances in Early Education and Day Care, Vol. 13.*

Super, C. & Harkness, S. (1986). The developmental niche. A conceptualization at the interface of child and culture. *International Journal of Behavioral Development* (9), 545–569.

Turner, T., & Krechevsky, M. (2003). Who are the teachers? Who are the learners? *Educational Leadership, 60* (7), 40–43.

Chapter 15

The Waldorf Approach to Early Childhood Education

Christy L. Williams ∽ Fairbrook First Steps Christian Preschool,
Pennsylvania Furnace, Pennsylvania
James E. Johnson ∽ The Pennsylvania State University

Nowadays increasing numbers of teachers and parents are becoming aware of Waldorf education. Like Montessori and Reggio, Waldorf has its roots in Europe and has been spreading world wide. Many are drawn to this approach because they see it as an alternative to traditional education and as an inspiration for improving education (Edwards, 2002). The Waldorf model of education is relevant to early childhood education (ECE) because it seeks to promote a healthy, unhurried, developmentally appropriate learning environment for young children. Waldorf early childhood education has been applied in a variety of service delivery settings including home- and center-based child care, parent and child groups, parent support programs, and kindergarten and mixed-age programs for children from 3 to 7 years of age (Oldfield, 2001). Lesser known in the United States, this approach founded by Rudolf Steiner was first implemented in Germany.

ᔈ RUDOLF STEINER AND ANTHROPOSOPHY

Rudolf Steiner was born in Austria in 1861, the son of a minor railway official. He spent his childhood in the peasant villages of Austria, a modest beginning for one who would eventually earn great respect for his work. As a young man, Steiner studied mathematics, physics, and chemistry to obtain his first degree from a university in Vienna; he then went on to earn a doctorate in philosophy from the University of Rostock. Trying his hand at new ventures, including tutoring and speaking engagements, he continued to nurture his thirst for spiritual connections to modern ways of thinking.

After World War I, he began to develop and promote the idea of a threefold social order, which was embraced by many as a welcomed renaissance. According to this conception, a healthy society requires the interdependent functioning of the *economic* sphere relating to the production, distribution, and consumption of goods and services; the *political* sphere, which concerns human social relationships; and the *spiritual* sphere or those ideations and activities emanating from deep within the individual human being. The guiding values for these three spheres were *fraternity* in economic or business matters, *equality* in things of a political nature, and *liberty* in the spiritual realm. Separately each is important; together they must negotiate among themselves to produce the unity of society (Childs, 1991a).

Unfortunately, at that time in Germany not enough support existed to overturn the traditional modes of thought, and Steiner's movement collapsed. Steiner's forward-thinking ways were not stifled, however, and his ideas manifested themselves in a number of other arenas. Steiner authored over 50 books and presented well over 6,000 lectures as a renowned scientist, artist, philosopher, architect, and educator before his death in 1925. Arguably his biggest legacy is the model of education that he designed based on his philosophical view of life and his theories about child development (Richards, 1980; Steiner, 1982).

Any overview of Steiner's philosophical beliefs would have to begin with *anthroposophy* (from the Greek: *anthropo* = man + *Sophia* = wisdom). Most simply stated, anthroposophy is the exploration of humanity in combination with the spiritual. The goal of anthroposophy is to bring about truths or new knowledge, not welded to any particular tenets or dogma that would make it an orthodoxy. Central is the quest to hear the truth about spiritual things (Wilkinson, 1996).

Anthroposophy is a spiritual-science movement with its roots in Christianity. Begun by Steiner, it has grown to be widely recognized and has followers all over the world. Two important components of anthroposophy are *oneness with the world* and *search for self*. Oneness with the world encompasses the idea that everything is interconnected, from the cycles of the moon, planets and earth, to the cycles of the seasons, to the cycles of human life and death. Each choice that we make will impact others in ways that we may not foresee.

An example that comes to mind is the current situation with our rainforests. As we continue to destroy the trees that make up the rainforests, not only are we destroying the plant and animal life there, but our actions are having many other far-reaching consequences. Because trees serve to "clean" our air by using CO_2 and producing oxygen, we are seeing an abundance of air pollution that was previously at least partially filtered by the vast acreage of forest. We are also seeing the effects of global warming, caused in part by abundant amounts of carbon dioxide in the atmosphere. Destruction of rare species of plants and animals in short periods of time also seriously disrupts the food chain, affecting other species that depend upon those that are disappearing. These effects, not even considered when the choice was made to harvest the rainforests, demonstrate the interconnectedness of every facet of our world. Anthroposophy sees the value in being aware of those connections, suggesting that life can be much more fulfilling and meaningful when we recognize and act upon them.

A second important component of anthroposophy is the search for self. Steiner stressed the importance for each individual to develop his or her own faculties in a variety of areas, in order to obtain a "wholeness." Through the study and exploration of intellectual subjects, artistic endeavors, craft and skilled labor, and spiritual meditation, a person can strengthen one's spirit and sense of self. "The human being cannot escape—indeed, should not seek to escape—worldly experiences, but he must be in a position to discriminate and not be dominated by them" (Wilkinson, 1996, p. 53). Steiner felt that through the philosophy of anthroposophy, the value of preparing the body, soul, and spirit for a life of continued learning and growth could be realized.

Steiner's Theory of Child Development

Consistent with his anthroposophical beliefs, Steiner created his own theory of child development. He proposed 7-year cycles that incorporate both physical and spiritual development. In the first 7 years of life Steiner felt that children's development is focused on their physical body. They imitate the adults around them to learn about their world. They practice "real" work through their play and through craft projects.

Simultaneously, spiritual development is occurring as well—Steiner's concept of "Will," which is also nurtured through imitative play. Important in this time period is the exploration of fantasy and imagination. At this stage, Steiner felt that formal academic instruction is inappropriate.

The next 7-year cycle encompasses the ages of 7 to 14 and is marked by the growth of the child's permanent teeth. In this stage of development the child is becoming more aware of the surrounding world and is thus ready to begin academic instruction. The spiritual concept of "Feeling" is being realized at this time, and the child is intrigued by imagery and pictorial stimulation that evoke emotions. Personal relationships are important at this stage as well.

The third 7-year cycle ranges from ages 14 to 21 and begins with the onset of puberty. Here young people are ready to combine their intellect with more abstract thoughts and applications, hence the spiritual development of "Thinking." A sense of independence takes root in this stage and propels the student to seek individually relevant explorations and connections. Steiner outlined 7-year cycles and their corresponding characteristics throughout the life span until the age of 85 years (Wilkinson, 1996).

Closely connected to his theories of development are Steiner's beliefs about education. He felt that schooling should stress the child's all-around development of body, soul, and spirit. The focus should be on educating the "whole" child because developing a child's faculties is more important than teaching subjects. This can be interpreted to mean that it is more important to teach children to learn and to think for themselves than to teach children facts and book knowledge. Steiner also believed that specific types of learning were appropriate primarily at certain ages and stages. These basic tenets served as his guidelines later on when Steiner was given the chance to open a school in Germany to put his ideas into practice.

History and Context of Waldorf Education

An opportunity presented itself to Steiner shortly after the First World War ended. Steiner was lecturing in war-torn Stuttgart, Germany, about his ideas for a new social order, a new sense of ethics, and a less damaging way of resolving conflict. After Steiner gave a lecture at the Waldorf-Astoria Cigarette Factory, the owner, Emil Molt, was so impressed by what he had heard that he asked Steiner to open a school at the factory for the workers' children. Steiner agreed to the challenge, with a few conditions. They were as follows:

1. The school must be run by the teachers, not administrators.
2. There would be a highly ambitious curriculum.
3. The importance was to be placed on imagination, a sense of truth, and a feeling of responsibility (to reflect his threefold social order).
4. Steiner would hand-pick the teachers and train them through lectures and meditations.

Emil Molt accepted these conditions, provided the site and necessary funds, and the first Waldorf school opened in 1919, named after the cigarette factory in Stuttgart. The enrollment more than doubled in the first few months after the school was open. Within 20 years, six more Waldorf schools had opened in Germany, seven others around the world. When the Nazi regime dominated Germany in 1939, the government closed down all of the Waldorf schools in the country, claiming that the schools "taught children to think for themselves." As soon as the Nazi regime collapsed, the schools opened again with a renewed vigor and continued to spread.

The Waldorf schools reflect German culture in the sense that they are very child centered and that they embrace Steiner's ideal of a threefold organization of society (the political, the spiritual, and the economical). South Germany, in particular, held special interest in Steiner's ideas of liberty, equality, and fraternity. When the over-all philosophical movement collapsed, out of it came Steiner education, a perfect remedy to the stale, traditional modes of thought that were dominating war-torn Germany. His fresh ideas not only appealed to Germans, but also to teachers and parents around the world. Currently more than 800 Waldorf schools exist in more than 40 countries, with more than 150 of those schools in North America. Sharing the same basic tenets but leaving room for innovations, Waldorf schools are independent, self-governing entities without separate administration and set curriculum; most follow the original ideas and theories defined by Steiner in his lectures. Some Waldorf schools only provide kindergarten education, while others provide schooling from kindergarten through the twelfth or thirteenth grade.

Waldorf Kindergarten   The kindergarten in Waldorf schools is very different from the other levels of schooling, as well as from most "typical" kindergartens with which we are familiar. A Waldorf kindergarten serves children between the ages of 3 to 6 years, consistent with the first 7-year cycle in Steiner's theory of development. The curriculum consists of imaginative play, fairytales, folklore and fables, imitation, art activities, "real" work such as knitting and baking bread, musical instruments, dance, drama, and awareness of nature, cycles, and seasons. This curriculum is based upon Steiner's ideas about the child at this stage. Since Steiner feels that young children are working to develop their physical body and their will, the activities are not academic in nature, but hands-on. Many opportunities exist for creativity and make-believe, traits that Steiner believed enhanced the development of the will. The toys at school are simple and open ended

to encourage imaginative uses. Many objects found in the classroom are natural materials, such as gourds, pinecones, branches, and pebbles. The purpose of these materials is to foster connections with nature and the concept of "oneness with the world."

Going into this kind of classroom environment has been compared to "stepping back into the nineteenth century," in the sense that the toys are simple and natural, the teachers are often busy mending cloths or baking bread, and the children are actively engaged in imaginative play or imitative work. The Waldorf kindergarten is designed to be an extension of the home. There is no formal academic instruction, no educational toys, and even books are rarely found in the classroom; this is based directly on Steiner's theory that academic instruction at this first developmental stage is inappropriate. A rich and stimulating environment is required with teachers providing language and literacy experiences through stories, poems, and songs. Mathematical experiences are naturally occurring through cooking and imaginative play. Likewise art experiences, music experiences, drama experiences, and science experiences have a place, but not in the overt manner so prevalent in the typical public school setting.

In the Waldorf kindergarten, children are expected to be children first and foremost. The stage of development they are in is well understood and appreciated by the teacher. Waldorf in this way contrasts with the reality of today in which children are often rushed through their childhoods in an attempt to help them become the best and the brightest. Unfortunately many children thereby miss the opportunity to simply be, to have the childhoods to which they are entitled.

Waldorf education respects the stages that a child goes through and feels that there is a right time for everything. Take the Waldorf approach to reading, for example. It is not unusual for a Waldorf student to begin to read in grade three or four, much later than the "typical" public school student. Waldorf preparation will allow the child as a whole person to be much better prepared for the reading experience when he or she reaches that point, even if it takes a bit longer. The essential matter is not how soon reading can occur. Short-term results are not that important. What is important is to build a solid developmental foundation that will contribute in the long term to a happier, healthier, and more well-rounded and competent child.

Waldorf Grade School At 7 years of age the child enters the next stage of development and schooling, corresponding to grades two through eight. During this period the child remains with the same teacher and class of students for the entire cycle. This serves to sustain important relationships (a key part of the second 7-year cycle) and to create more consistency in the child's schooling. This also is a way to keep the teacher from becoming stagnant, as the teacher will have to grow with the students over the 7-year period.

According to Steiner's theories, children at this second stage are now ready to learn academic subjects. They have a strong foundation from proper kindergarten experiences and can build upon it. Their awareness of the outer world is steadily growing. They are also developing their spiritual sense of "Feeling," so subjects, images, and pictures that evoke emotion are very effective learning tools. The main academic areas covered at this point are typically reading, writing, language skills, math, geography, history, and the sciences. It is the teacher's challenge to present these materials in such a way that the students can explore and master the content to the fullest extent possible.

A typical daily schedule in a Waldorf grade one through eight class would proceed as follows. Each morning, the teacher greets students individually as they arrive, assessing their mood and state of being in an attempt to be sensitive to their needs. Then the class gathers to recite the morning verse. This is usually an inspirational passage that the class "adopts" for the entire year. Next, the main lesson begins and its study lasts for a 2-hour time block. This block is used to approach the subject in a number of ways; not simply a lecture, but various related activities. The same subject is usually explored during this time for 3–4 weeks, and then a new subject is chosen for study. Two more lessons follow, of approximately 45 minutes each, with lunch perhaps in between. Then the afternoon is spent on less intellectual topics, such as art, music, and practical activities, which would include craft and skill work. Time periods and activities would be adjusted according to the developmental level of the class.

Waldorf Teacher Training Because the Waldorf philosophy is well organized and contains so many interlocking components, Waldorf teachers need to be trained in the philosophy and theories behind their craft, as well as in proper ways to incorporate these ideals into the classroom. Currently, there are over 50 full-time training schools worldwide, at least 8 of which are in the United States. The Rudolf Steiner College in California is one of these. The college offers a wide variety of programs and courses that train teachers, teacher educators, followers of the Anthroposophy movement, and others who are interested in Steiner and his applications. Programs are available full time or part time, during the summers, and through weekend seminars.

Diversity Waldorf education originated in Germany and has been adapted to other cultures worldwide. In America, adaptations have taken several forms. In public schools, in order to comply with separation of church and state regulations, Waldorf has been stripped of all religious and spiritual exploration. Even with such profound changes, Waldorf programs have been very successful, especially in inner-city public schools by changing the heavily Eurocentric readings and history to include American literature, history, and diversity perspectives. Moreover, multicultural perspectives and interests have been added as well. Private schools in America have been better able keep the spiritual side intact while also adding American and multicultural perspectives. Overall, and especially in private schools, the basic tenets of Steiner's original educational philosophy have remained at the heart of Waldorf education in America.

Waldorf education has been successfully adapted to numerous other cultures as well, such as in countries in Europe, Africa, the Middle East, Japan, and Australia. Waldorf schools in these cultures all profess the same original ideas, concepts, and philosophy of the very first Waldorf school in Germany. The curriculum is similar in subject matter and materials, although modified to incorporate the literature and culture of each particular country. Waldorf education is mostly found in countries that accept Christianity, given Anthroposophy's connection to this religion, even though Waldorf does not require the students to be of any particular faith. Each school is different because curriculum and administration is not fixed, leaving room for innovations. Waldorf curriculum is easily modified to accommodate multicultural points of view without compromising the basic philosophy.

Many embrace the ideals of Waldorf education because of its simplicity. In this time of technology, busy schedules, competition, and fast food, there is a growing sense of disconnectedness, a feeling that something is missing. Waldorf education strives to eliminate the rush, allowing us to focus on what is really important, to remember where we came from and what life is all about. Waldorf helps children to learn how nature supports us and how we must support nature, to be aware of its rhythms and cycles, and to become one with the world. Waldorf education is about learning who we are as individuals, learning what we can do and what we know, "finding ourselves," so to speak, and recognizing the spirit within us. It is about taking time to "smell the roses and to appreciate where they came from," an ideal that transcends cultural boundaries.

✍ PROGRAM CHARACTERISTICS

Creating a Caring Community of Learners

The Waldorf approach to early childhood education incorporates certain community elements into its design. The importance of the physical environment, age groupings, planned activities, schedules, and social relationships are all discussed in great detail by Rudolf Steiner. Each element is an integral part of the Waldorf kindergarten.

Children's Sensitivity to the Environment
Steiner begins with the environment, which includes the layout and design of the classroom as well as the outdoor area used by the children. As it will set the stage for future learning, the environment is an important place from which to begin. The aesthetics of the room play a key role in the general "feel" of the learning space and, as such, are tailored to the developmental needs and interests of the children who are served. The Waldorf early childhood environment nourishes the child's senses with beauty and order (Trostli, 1998).

Steiner feels that young children are extremely sensitive to their environment, absorbing information through all five senses and experiencing it throughout their entire body. For this reason, Steiner has specifically addressed issues such as the paint color on the walls, classroom materials, and furniture. He suggests that the walls of the early childhood classroom be "plain light colors without wallpaper designs" (Grunelius 1991). Colors play a very important role—loud, bright colors can be overly stimulating, grays and browns can be dreary, plain light colors will promote a light airy feeling, reminiscent of cherry blossoms or spring leaves. This aesthetic beauty

Wooden stands draped with cotton or silk cloth invite child-centered imaginative play.

stimulates the child's imagination and is at the same time also calming. The simplistic charm of the classroom is achieved by incorporating natural materials, such as solid wood furniture polished with beeswax, curtains made of natural fibers and colored with plant dyes, and toys handcrafted from natural materials.

The Waldorf early childhood classroom is seen as an extension of the home, in both design and function. The prevailing atmosphere is that of the traditional home, where daily chores provided the rhythm of family and community life. In these hurried times, when the pace of life dictates processed foods, synthetic products, entertainment in a box, and gadgets and machines that perform much of the chores that once provided satisfaction, Waldorf provides a sanctuary for children and adults alike.

The Importance of Imitation and Play

Steiner emphasizes two valuable ways in which young children develop a sense of community. One is imitation, the other is play. Young children are innately curious about the work of adults and instinctively imitate what they see to deepen their own understanding. Waldorf

teachers find it very important to give children something valuable to imitate. Therefore, they engage in the work of the home/classroom, such as mending classroom materials, preparing food for snack, polishing tables, washing floors, and caring for the plants that adorn the windowsills. Each of these tasks is rooted in meaningful, day-to-day necessity. The children are never forced to do this work alongside the teacher, but are always welcomed when they choose to imitate the teacher's actions. Through this self-initiated imitation, children learn not only to do their part for the classroom community, but they also learn to rely on others.

Play is another crucial method through which children develop a sense of community. Play provides "safe" opportunities to practice social interactions. Children can try out different roles, work through conflicts, and attempt various methods of communication, all under the pretense of play. In terms of social development, play is an opportunity for children to practice their social skills and to learn how to function within a group. Lengthy periods of time designated for true imaginative play in the Waldorf classroom allow children to *experience* community in a nonthreatening manner, while developing their emotional maturity along the way.

Benefits of Mixed-Age Grouping Another factor that contributes to Waldorf's caring community of learners is the mixed-age grouping of children. Children in a Waldorf kindergarten range in age from 3 to 6 years, meaning that they have the continuity of building a relationship with one another and with the teacher for up to 3 years. This design also promotes a family atmosphere in the sense that the class replicates siblings with a stratification of ages, much more natural than a class of children all the same age. This diversity in ages offers the younger children role models, with older children to look up to and learn from them. The youngest children's learning is scaffolded by the nurturing assistance that they receive from the older children. The older children benefit from this design as well. They gain an attitude of caring and responsibility and improve social cognitive skills. There is such beauty in watching a child begin as the youngest, attempting to imitate the actions of the older children, and progress over 3 years to become one of the oldest, now looking out for and nurturing the younger children.

Establishing Rhythm and Routine The rhythm and routine that is an integral part of the Waldorf kindergarten also serves to foster a sense of community. Teachers take it upon themselves to establish routines that are repeated daily, weekly, seasonally, and yearly. There is a rhythm to each day that involves a balance of time spent "breathing in" and "breathing out." These times offer children experience with both self-expression and communal moments. There is a rhythm to each week, with Monday designated as "bread-baking day" and Tuesday as "vegetable soup day" and each other day of the week with its own identity that the children come to recognize and depend upon. It is this predictability that lifts

children's anxieties and builds their trust in their social worlds, trust in the teachers. Children feel safe and secure in the community of their classroom—they know they can trust in what they will find there.

Teaching to Enhance Development and Learning

Underlying the very premise of Waldorf education is a profound respect for childhood. Sally Jenkinson, a former Waldorf kindergarten teacher, expresses Steiner's beliefs beautifully: "what remains constant (in Waldorf education) is a deeply held belief that childhood matters; that the early years are not a phase of life to be rushed through, but constitute a stage of tremendous importance needing to be experienced fully in its own right" (Oldfield, 2001, p. xvii). There are three feelings regarding early childhood education that Waldorf teachers espouse. They are *reverence, enthusiasm,* and *protection.* These three words demonstrate how Waldorf teachers respect and value the children that they work with daily.

Reverence, Enthusiasm, and Protection Reverence can be described as the attitude of a teacher toward a child. Steiner speaks of the first seven years of a child's life as critical. The child is very impressionable, absorbing stimuli from the environment through all senses and experiencing it with the whole body, making it vital for the teacher to provide beneficial stimuli. When a teacher approaches a child with reverence, caution should be taken to speak clearly so as not to confuse the child, to be worthy of imitation, and to allow the child to proceed at one's own pace, recognizing that it is the quality of development, not the speed, that is important.

Recognizing that the art of teaching presents many challenges, Steiner urges that those persons called to teach must accept their role with enthusiasm. Not every person's nature includes being a teacher, but those who choose this career should be truly dedicated and enthusiastic about the responsibility that they are undertaking. This will translate to the child, who senses a teacher's enthusiasm and cannot help but to get caught up in it. It is that true spirit of childhood, the sense of wonder, the inquisitive nature, the naivety that affords a child the ability to explore the world with such excitement and awe.

The third duty of the teacher is to protect all children in their care, physically, emotionally, socially, and psychologically. The Waldorf early childhood classroom is a sanctuary from all that works against the healthy development of young children. The teacher provides a stress-free environment with a slow, calming pace that allows children to take the time to build the foundation that will support their future learning. Children do not feel the pressure of standards, testing, or the necessity to read but instead enjoy rich literacy experiences that call on their imaginations to take them to fairytale lands of elves and gnomes. They are protected from the fast-paced, overstimulating bombardment of images from television and computer games. Instead, they dig in the earth under a tree fragrant with apple blossoms and discover the purpose in a worm's slow deliberate movement. In addition, the food that children in a Waldorf kindergarten eat is free from processing, free from pesticides and insecticides, and free from genetic alteration. It is natural and pure, promoting a healthy physical constitution.

Some criticize Waldorf for being overprotective, sheltered even. Eugene Schwartz (1995, p. 8) responds to this perception:

> To a degree, this is true: during the school day, Waldorf kindergartners are protected from the media, electronic devices, synthetic noises and processed foods. On the other hand, unlike most urban and suburban preschoolers, Waldorf kindergartners are exposed to a great deal as well: the realities of food preparation, the wind, the rain, warmth and cold, brambles and briars (on their daily walks); in some

settings, they encounter sheep and goats, chickens and ponies, birds and fish, in all their raw reality, uncaged and unlabelled. (Encountering animals who are unaccompanied by explanatory labels or animated software may not be "educational," but such meetings are memorable and very real.) So which child is the "sheltered" one, and which is the child really meeting *life*?

Respecting and Valuing Children   Inherent in respecting and valuing children is knowing each individual child. Waldorf teachers see each child as a riddle to be solved, a challenge to be met, and teachers strive to understand as much as possible about each individual child (Childs, 1991b). Teacher training in Waldorf education focuses on the lectures and writings of Rudolf Steiner; a solid understanding of his theory of child development is required to guide ECE practice. For example, Steiner goes into much detail to explain the four temperaments: melancholic, sanguine, phlegmatic, and choleric. He addresses characteristics of each, how they work together and against one another, the insights that they can offer into a child's nature, and how a teacher can work with a child's temperament to achieve a balance (Childs, 1991b). Based on a thorough understanding of Steiner's theory of child development, a teacher can better recognize the needs of individual children.

Another component of Waldorf kindergarten that supports knowing and understanding each child is the multiage grouping where the teacher first meets a child at 3 years of age and then proceeds to be an important part of that child's growth and development until the child turns 6 years old and is ready to enter the next level of Waldorf schooling. What valuable understanding of a child can be ascertained over a 3-year period, especially during such formative years!

Providing an Engaging and Responsive Environment   Teaching to enhance development and learning requires that teachers create an engaging and responsive environment. In a Waldorf classroom this takes many forms. The aesthetic beauty and a welcoming feeling of warmth discussed earlier is one important component. Another is the toys and materials that teachers make available to children. Waldorf kindergartens are full of materials that invite young hands and minds to touch, manipulate, create, and imagine. Baskets of natural items, such as pinecones, smooth pebbles, sticks, seashells, and moss are arranged in areas where children will incorporate them into their play. Wooden stands will be pulled out and draped with play cloths made of natural fibers, such as cotton or silk. These may be arranged in a variety of formations by the children, creating houses, stores, spaceships, or stages. Toys are handcrafted from wood in various forms that inspire creativity, unlike commercial toys marketed for young children today that have but one purpose and are often so realistic that they leave nothing for the child to add to the experience. Such commercial toys will not be found in a Waldorf classroom. Instead, you find children having a particular wooden toy for a phone one day, and then upon desire or necessity, it will be transformed into an airplane the next. This perspective on toys affords children the luxury of open-ended thinking. They learn that the possibilities are endless, rather than learn that there is one correct way to do something.

Children's Connection with Sensory Experiences   Another aspect to the environment of the classroom concerns Steiner's belief that young children are "wholly sense organ," meaning that young children are inextricably connected with their sensory experiences. Children are "united with sensation, and therefore deeply affected by what it conveys, and her psychological development is influenced by the immediate surroundings" (Oldfield, 2001, pp. 101–102). The natural materials in a Waldorf classroom, the lightly colored walls, the soft play cloths, the rich watercolor paints, the smell of the bread baking, and the rhythm of hands clapping in ring-time all provide sensory stimulation without creating sensory overload. Due to children's vulnerability to the environment and all that takes place within it, Waldorf educators take great responsibility in providing worthy sensory experiences.

Also important to consider is the quantity of sensory experiences that children encounter daily. Waldorf again seeks to protect its children from the bombardment of images, smells, sounds, tastes, and touches afforded by our fast-paced, thrill-seeking society. Infants who are subjected to loud parties with lots of people, conversation, and music usually fall asleep right in the middle of all the chaos. Do you imagine that this setting is calming to a child, inviting peaceful sleep? Well, it is not. The infant suffers from sensory overload and its natural defense mechanism is to shut down. The baby falls asleep to block out the stimulus. The same thing can happen to preschoolers. They can become overstimulated by factors in their environment and their body reacts by shutting down. This may not mean that they fall asleep like the infant, they may instead withdraw, manifesting as a "zombie-like" trance as the child stares at the stimulus or off into space (Healy, 1999). The child also may react by losing self-control and acting out in socially unacceptable ways. Waldorf education with its calming natural environment is an anecdote to the excitability that children so easily internalize.

Collaborating with Peers   Collaborating with peers is another essential part of healthy development and learning that Waldorf teachers foster in the kindergarten. Teachers provide many opportunities for children to work and play together. When children choose to imitate a teacher's work, perhaps kneading dough for the morning bread baking, they often join together with peers in this united purpose. From the youngest ages children are working

Waldorf green spaces and gardens nurture serenity, free thinkers, and the creative impulse.

side by side kneading their own piece of dough while enjoying the comfort of a common activity. Older children learn the give and take of working together, perhaps taking turns or assigning "jobs." These events and opportunities widen and deepen children's social and emotional experiences, thereby enriching their development.

Another scenario evolves out of free play. Consider two children playing together in a "hospital" that they have built. A third child asks to join in. The first two children must reconstruct their play in order to incorporate this third child. Not only are they learning valuable social skills, but they are also practicing flexibility and creativity. In a Waldorf classroom, furthermore, frequently children are seen working together polishing the tables with beeswax, working side by side as they sculpt their clay, joining together as one in ring-time to recite verses, or working in pairs to plant the vegetable garden. The rhythms of the day seem to naturally encourage children to interact in a variety of ways with their peers.

Children Learn Through Doing Waldorf teachers do not employ direct instruction as a teaching method in the kindergarten classroom, as they find it counterproductive to require this form of child participation. Their belief is supported by current brain research:

> Before brain regions are myelinated [and nerves have the outer coating needed to transmit impulses], they do not operate efficiently. For this reason, trying to make children master academic skills for which they do not have the requisite maturation may result in mixed-up patterns of learning. I would contend that much of today's academic failure results from academic expectations for which student's brains were not prepared – but which were bulldozed into them anyway. (Healy, 1990, p. 67)

Rather, Waldorf teachers encourage the children in self-discovery. When children choose to engage in imitation or play, they will do it wholeheartedly and gain much more than if they had been coerced. Steiner promotes the idea that children learn from doing, and whether they do it correctly or incorrectly, they are still receiving valuable information. The teacher's role, then, is to ensure that there are plenty of opportunities throughout the day for children to *do*.

Natural environments and materials are valued highly in Waldorf programs.

Responsibility and Self-Regulation   One of the foremost goals of the Waldorf early childhood curriculum is to help children develop a sense of responsibility and self-regulation. Steiner gives much attention to this topic in his lectures and writings. Again, this is one reason why children are not forced to participate in any activity, but are given the freedom to choose their own activities. Although they may not be able to articulate it, young children are astute when it comes to determining what they need. The young 3s may simply watch an activity first, absorbing the action of the other children. When they are ready, they will join in. It may only be a few minutes, or it may be months, but contrary to popular belief, these young children will choose the right timing for their own development, given the opportunity and their level of understanding. By having choices to make young children can begin to exercise their own self-control.

A concern connected to this idea is the concept of "learned helplessness," which children often exhibit in classes where teacher-directed instruction prevails. When teachers direct most activity, reducing the time for imaginative, creative, and self-directed play, children learn to depend on the teacher's directions. Lynne Oldfield asks two very important questions relating to this issue: "Is modern educational culture in danger of inculcating a habit of passive dependency, whereby the child waits for direction before becoming actively engaged in his own learning? Or are children being encouraged habitually to seek adult approval in order to substantiate their own efforts?" (2001, p. 56). This is quite the opposite of Waldorf's intentions; Steiner teachers strive to encourage children's independence.

An important part of this approach is recognizing that this development of responsibility and self-regulation is a process. Over the 3 years children are involved in the Waldorf kindergarten their skills gradually begin to emerge and blossom. In order for this to happen, they need sufficient time, space, and opportunity to practice making choices and exerting independence and interdependence under careful adult supervision and guidance. Because young children have limited self-control teachers set goals that are reasonable for their level of development and allow for approximation of meeting these goals.

Moreover, with imitation as a valuable teaching tool, Waldorf teachers can gradually guide their young children through this transformation. A sense of self-regulation, as well as group regulation, "involves the development of self control of movement, *i.e.* also knowing when *not* to move—for example, holding back inappropriate behavior" (Oldfield, 2001, p. 56). Lynne Oldfield also offers a beautiful vignette to illustrate this concept:

> One morning at snack-time, a mixed age group (3–6 years) was gathered around a table. On one side was seated a group of three and four year olds. One boy accidentally fell off his chair and then began to hit his chair, saying "Silly, silly, chair!". Immediately, all the other three and four year olds threw themselves on the floor and began banging their chairs, with a great deal of laughter. Across the table, seated next to the teacher (their favorite spot since they had turned six) were two girls. One said "I want to fall off my chair, but I won't"; and her friend replied, "So do I. But I won't either!" (2001, p. 57)

Constructing Appropriate Curriculum

The Waldorf early childhood curriculum is designed to educate the whole child: "the head, the heart and the hands" (Easton, 1997). It speaks to the development of the social, emotional, spiritual, moral, physical, and intellectual aspects of each individual child. It nurtures these important elements of the human being through a curriculum that seems very simple on the surface, yet in reality is amazingly complex.

Nurtures the Whole Child—"Head, Heart and Hands" The curriculum can be described by just a few activities, but the depth that they reach requires lengthy discourse. A typical kindergarten day is marked by the rhythm of familiar activities, alternating between "breathing out" (a time of self-expression) and "breathing in" (a time of quieter, teacher-led reflection).

The morning begins with a full hour of uninterrupted time in which children are free to choose their activities. They can be found caught up in artistic endeavors, imitating the teacher as they prepare the snack, or swept away in a playful adventure that is only bounded by their own imaginations. This time allows for all manner of developmental growth, from practicing social skills in a "restaurant" to learning the fundamentals of engineering by making a suspension bridge with the blocks. Yet the freedom of play alleviates any pressure for performance and gives wings to children's sense of self-direction. And, singing a familiar song or verse the teacher gently signals the transition from this activity to the next, which is ring-time.

Transition periods themselves are important parts of the curriculum. As the teacher carefully and deliberately places the art supplies back in their rightful spots, and washes the bowls and spoons used to prepare the snack, for instance, the children can absorb the teacher's sense of reverence and imitate the teacher's purposefulness. With the room returned to order, all gather together in a circle or ring.

Ring-time is one part of the daily schedule when the children participate as a large group with the teacher directing their activity. They often begin with a morning verse, repeated daily to allow even the youngest children to pick up the language and rhythm with which it is recited. Ring-time may involve movement, songs, poems, or finger plays, and is a dynamic, yet predictable time of the morning when the children direct their learning inward as they enjoy the sense of community that comes from participating in a group.

Next the teacher leads the group outside, where the children are free to explore the natural world. They revel in the changing seasons, comfortable with the pleasures each one affords. Out of doors their senses are stimulated. The colors of the changing fall leaves, the smell of fresh-cut grass, the feel of the mud between their toes and the taste of sweet snowflakes on

Children knit stockings to hold flutes they play in school orchestra and music class.

their tongues. Again they will play and imitate, as they busy themselves.

When children return to the classroom, they will wash themselves and settle at the small tables and chairs for a snack. The teacher will light a candle and they will join together in a poem of gratitude. The snack that they helped to prepare will be served and they will enjoy each other's company as they nourish their bodies. They transition easily from snack to the circle again for the culmination of their morning together. It is at this time that they engage their fullest mental capacities as they visualize the story that the teacher presents to them. The teacher does not read from a book, but tells the story, being careful to include a rich vocabulary of imagery, assisting the young children in painting pictures in their minds. At the end of the story, the children will gather their things and leave the kindergarten with fairytale creatures dancing in their minds. A seemingly simple curriculum, it incorporates so much content.

Enhances Holistic Development Waldorf strives to develop the whole child—not just intellectual capacities, but a balance among all faculties. *Social development* is stimulated and

practiced through imaginative play. Conflicts arise and children must work through them and find a solution. The give and take of social discourse is learned also during snack time, as the children converse with one another. *Emotional development* is supported in the close personal relationship that each child develops with the teacher and through friendships that the child builds with peers. The child learns to gain greater control of emotions with development as it occurs in an environment that is safe, secure, and free of stress. The child plays out situations and role plays various emotions, internalizing appropriate actions to accompany feelings. It is also through the arts that the child cultivates knowledge of feelings. The entire Waldorf early childhood curriculum is infused with an artistic element. From the design and decoration of the classroom to the art experiences offered, the child learns to feel the colors and shapes. The child learns that art is a form of expressing what is inside.

Spiritual development is fostered through imitation of the teacher's reverence for childhood, nature, the materials in the classroom, and the food eaten for snack. It is also learned through the sense of gratitude that permeates each aspect of the day. "Indeed, fortunate is the child who can thus imitate the very gestures and language of gratitude, thereby learning from early years to turn his attention to the source of the many and varied gifts of life, instead of concentrating on his own wants" (Pusch, 1993, p. 28). Steiner writes often of the spiritual nature of children and the responsibility that adults have to respect and nurture this element of the child's development. Spiritual development manifests itself as social responsibility and concern for the world; the foundation for both of these concepts is laid in the community of the Waldorf kindergarten classroom.

The importance of self-regulation has been discussed previously; children need to learn how to control their behavior and to make good decisions. Waldorf education is designed to lay these foundations for *moral development*. "If the goal is responsibility, inner discipline, the willingness to do one's share, and eventually the ability to give oneself direction and purpose in life, the soil for this blossoming will have to be prepared early in life" (Pusch, 1993, p. 27).

Physical development is nurtured through movement. Waldorf teachers recognize that young children learn through movement. They learn about spatial relationships, as well as internalizing the essence of whatever they touch and move. Children are on the go and Waldorf teachers support this high level of activity throughout the morning. Significant amounts of time spent outdoors encourage large muscle movement and development, while the many artistic projects encourage fine motor skills.

Intellectual development comes not from direct instruction, but through self-regulated discovery and imitation. Young children should be building a love of learning that will inspire them to continue to seek knowledge throughout their lives. Best accomplished by respecting a child's own pace, teachers provide an enriching, stimulating environment that offers many opportunities for children to build a strong foundation, in anticipation of subsequent stages of development and education.

Incorporates a Wide Variety of Disciplines

Through the Waldorf curriculum of play, imitation, art, and stories children also gain experience in a wide variety of disciplines. Many schools today are struggling to develop integrated curricula. Often teachers identify with their disciplines. Waldorf teachers, on the other hand, have always taught math, science, literature, the arts, and so forth as part of an organized whole. The foundations for literacy and numeracy, for instance, are laid through everyday experiences such as puppet shows and setting the table for snack. Science-related concepts are an inherent part of many activities, including cooking with the tasks of chopping, measuring, pouring, and weighing. Problem-solving skills and divergent thinking are instilled through the use of simple open-framework toys that leave much to the imagination.

Maintains Intellectual Integrity

A key component to the curriculum is intellectual integrity, which Steiner feels is very important. Because young children imitate the actions of those around them, the teacher must provide actions that are worthy of imitation. The teacher models everyday tasks necessary for the care of the school/home, including mending and cleaning, cooking and washing. These are all valuable, purposeful tasks worthy of imitation. With the decline of family farms and the trends of city living, fewer children have quality model behaviors to imitate. They need real-life experiences, activities that give a sense of satisfaction for a job well done.

Embraces Diversity

Waldorf education can be viewed as a model multicultural program since it easily adapts to the cultures and heritage of the children and community that it serves.

Persons not familiar with Waldorf often have a difficult time understanding this, especially when they confuse Waldorf education with its Christian roots. In fact, the worldview or philosophy of Anthroposophy that guides Waldorf education is not a religion at all. Anthroposophy promotes the idea that all human beings have a spiritual core and maintains harmony with many world religions and philosophies, while eschewing the tenets of a religion. In Waldorf education Anthroposophy per se is not taught but its influence can be seen in the curriculum and festivals. Many of the festivals are based around religious holidays, but not just Christian ones. Waldorf teachers are careful to delve "into diverse world cultures with as much reverence and depth as possible" (Ward, 2001, p. 3). The purpose of Waldorf education is to provide children with an "education toward freedom," which is why the goal is to help children develop strong independent judgment. Rudolf Steiner believed that the best way to accomplish this is to expose children to a wide variety of world religions and the values and traditions that they espouse. So the answer to the question "Is Waldorf Education Christian?" is "NO." This answer is based on the understanding that although stories from both the Old and New Testaments are introduced to children, and some plays and festivals are centered around biblical events, such experiences form only one set of influences in their studies of world cultures and religious traditions.

A more relevant and revealing approach is to ask: What image of the human being does the Waldorf schools seek to bring to the children as a model and inspiration? Here the answer is unequivocal. It is an image of the human being as loving, compassionate, reverent, respectful, engaged, tolerant, peaceful, joyful, patient, good, upright, wise, balanced, in harmony with the cosmos, nature and humanity. No religion or code of ethics can arrogate these fundamental and universal values as its unique possession. (Ward, 2001, p. 3)

There are numerous Waldorf schools in countries all over the world. Each one is unique in its culture, language, and materials, but each one upholds Rudolf Steiner's ideals. Tina Bruinsma, a teacher from Amsterdam supporting the Sloka, India, initiative, writes:

The Waldorf curriculum brings meaning to education. In an Indian context it can de-Anglicize the curriculum and promote the dignity of labour. Teachers and children come to the school with thirteen different mother tongues and seven different religions, and yet this form of education can embrace this diversity. In a country where education has come to mean merely performance, memory and competition bordering on rivalry, a Waldorf school brings with it the deeper meaning behind education. (Oldfield, 2001, p. 28)

Ann Sharfmann, teacher trainer, Centre for Creative Education, Cape Town, South Africa, writes:

Our work is to prove that Waldorf education can happen in less affluent circumstances, such as the South African township environment. And it does, and it works! Definitely not at all like the European Waldorf kindergarten model, and definitely not yet at all as we want it to be. But we are making a difference in our own small way and we are being noticed. For us, however, it is the growth and awakening that we see in the children. We have managed to deliver about 30 play kits to date—a cupboard containing blocks, puppets, felt animals, dolls, cloths, cones, shells, fabrics, etc. In many centers the children just sit and look at the toys as they are unpacked. They look and look but do not move. They cannot imagine that such beautiful things are meant for them. When invited to play, they are very hesitant at first, but soon gain in confidence and begin joyfully to play with everything. As you can imagine, even if nothing else changes, being able to play allows these little ones some real childhood activity and they begin to unfold as children. In some classes, where the children have a daily ring time, stories, puppets and the opportunity to draw, model, paint, the difference is astonishing. (Oldfield, 2001, p. 21)

The Waldorf curriculum, by its very nature, embraces diversity and creates a caring community.

☙ ASSESSING CHILDREN'S LEARNING

The purpose of the Waldorf ECE curriculum is not to teach basic academics and test-taking skills, nor help prepare students to meet government-declared "standards" for various ages/stages or grade levels. In fact, standardized testing is not a part of Waldorf education at any grade level. It is interesting to note, however, that many Waldorf graduates do pursue a college education and have performed well enough on the Scholarly Aptitude Test (SAT) to gain acceptance at such highly esteemed universities as Harvard and Yale (Oppenheimer, 1999).

Assessment is necessary even in the kindergarten to ensure that students are meeting the objectives of the curriculum. Waldorf teachers are very aware of the developmental progress of each of their individual students. So why and how do they do this without conventional methods of assessment?

"Why?" is simple. The purpose of Waldorf education is to foster in children a sense of individuality, self-esteem, and wholeness. Each day includes rich opportunities to develop all aspects of growth and learning—social, emotional, spiritual, psychological, physical, and cognitive. Children learn through art and music and movement and exploration and experience; through rhythm and routine and gratitude and beauty. Children learn to respect one another and to find their strength in community, not competition. Traditional methods of assessment pit one child against another, and create stress and feelings of self-doubt. Steiner writes that each child is filled with potential, it is simply a matter of giving every child a nurturing environment and

the freedom to unfold at one's own pace. This is what is meant by respecting childhood. Waldorf teachers exhibit the patience of gardeners, taking a long view of education. They believe that when the seeds of learning are sown in fertile soil and tender shoots emerge, there will be a rich harvest when all bears fruit at the end of a long growing season (Petrash, 2002).

So many early childhood programs do not appreciate this process and rush children into learning for which they are not ready. Steiner education warns against this:

> Even though it is necessary in modern civilization for people to be completely awake or "heads up" later in life, it is just as necessary to allow children to live in their gently dreamy experiences as long as possible so that they grow slowly into adult life. They need to remain in their imaginations, in their pictoral capacities without intellectualism, for as long as possible. The assumption is that if you allow the child to be strengthened without intellectualism, children will later grow into the necessary intellectualism in the proper way. If you do not you may ruin the person's soul for the remainder of life. (Trostli, 1998)

Waldorf education is based on the understanding that it is important for a child to develop a strong foundation and a love of learning as a prerequisite to developing necessary academic skills, which will come later when a child is ready.

In light of this perspective, assessment of young children is approached very differently by Waldorf teachers. Rather than pressure students to meet predetermined standards of learning, teachers use Steiner's theory of child development as a guideline and adjust curriculum and instruction to the pace of each individual child. They focus on the whole child, individual areas of strength and weakness, with the purpose of helping the child to develop into a well-balanced human being with a love of learning that will act as a motivator and guide throughout life. Waldorf kindergarten teachers gather information about each student's development and learning, but discreetly so as not to pressure the child. Teachers begin with perhaps their most valuable resource—parents. Parents are employed to give insight into the child's home life and experiences; often the teacher will even visit the child at home before the first day of kindergarten.

Classroom observation is perhaps the most frequently used tool to keep track of children's growth. ECE teachers are especially concerned with all areas of development and can learn much by simply observing a child during imaginative play. Insights into social development are apparent through interactions with other children. Play offers information about cognitive development and socioemotional well-being. In fact, it could be argued that true imaginative play is a window into the child's developmental state and well-being.

Throughout the kindergarten day there are many other behaviors to be observed as well. Ring time offers a chance to watch as children join in movement activities, songs and poems, and fanciful fairytales that call on the children's inner imaginations. Teachers are just as interested in learning about the external features of the children's development as the internal. They must carefully watch for children's reactions and mannerisms and moods to gain this valuable information.

Once gathered from many sources and many situations, teachers utilize this information not to grade or scale the students, but simply to develop a deeper understanding of the child so as to best facilitate development and learning in the classroom.

Establishing Relationships with Families

Waldorf education is so integrally entwined with the family that the two cannot be separated. Waldorf educators place great value on the role that parents play in their children's lives. Parental involvement and support has primary influence on children's success, and when combined with a school's influence that promotes

this dynamic, there is tremendous potential. Teachers need the support of the parents; the parents need the support of the teachers. Education is seen as a partnership, with both parties working together to further the natural and holistic development of the child.

Developing a sense of community is an important goal of Waldorf education. For this reason many Waldorf schools offer informational sessions for prospective parents. Parents are encouraged to learn how Waldorf schools approach education. They learn some fundamentals and receive applications, and then are invited to ask questions. This is often the beginning of a relationship of mutual respect between teachers and parents.

Given the deep reverence that Waldorf holds for the parental role, teachers naturally make every effort to further their connection with parents, to work together with them to develop goals for each individual child's learning, to share a sense of responsibility for the child's growth and development, and to strive for consistency between the home and school environments. This can only truly be accomplished through the continual communication between parent and teacher that is fostered by the welcoming nature of the Waldorf kindergarten. Frequent seasonal celebrations, parent education opportunities, and other events allow ample opportunity for parents and teachers to build their relationships and to share ideas and information within the community of the Waldorf school (Oldfield, 2001).

Waldorf education holds high standards for parents, the reason being that much of a young child's learning occurs in the context of the home environment. With only part of the child's the day spent in the kindergarten, parents are responsible to see that the important aspects of development are encouraged at home. Taking care to acknowledge parents' goals and choices for their children, Waldorf teachers also find themselves educating parents about Waldorf's goals for their students. An example that lends itself well to this topic is the issue of television. In the first stage of child development, from birth to 7 years of age, children learn best by doing and so need ample time to move—running, jumping, digging, climbing, and exploring. Critical also is protection from potentially harmful environmental influences. For these reasons, Waldorf educators encourage parents to limit their children's time spent in front of the television in favor of more appropriate activities that promote healthy development. Teachers also find that observing the parents and child at home is helpful and this usually can be arranged.

Rudolf Steiner continually reinforced the importance of providing a wholesome environment that offers young children valuable sources of learning. Again, children absorb all aspects of their surroundings, and in the years before children attend the Waldorf kindergarten, that environment is primarily provided by the family in the home. Therefore, Waldorf teachers, as a matter of policy, make home visits before the first day of school to gain a sense of the environment that had been provided for the child as an infant, toddler, and preschooler and to learn what sources of imitation were made available to the child, which in turn gives insight into the child's development. Being aware of the child's home life is considered just as important to teaching as being aware about what is done in the classroom (Trostli, 1998).

The community that develops around the parents, children, and teachers is what brings life to the school. Each school is vibrant and dynamic, constantly responding to the needs and interests of its members. In each locale, in each country where Waldorf is established, the school is a reflection of the culture that gave it breath. Holding to the same principles that Steiner espoused, each school is able to give attention to the individuals served. Families connect with one another, provide support, offer their services, and come together with other parents and teachers for the common purpose of giving their children the gift of an education that respects their childhood.

DISCUSSION

Waldorf and Other Approaches

The Waldorf approach to early education seems to possess certain distinct appeals and arguably compares very favorably with other well-known models. Certainly Waldorf has a great deal in common with developmentally appropriate practices (DAP) as set forth by the National Association for the Education of Young Children (NAEYC) (Bredekamp & Copple, 1997). In Table 15–1 we compare in summary manner the DAP guidelines with Waldorf early childhood education. Waldorf's approach contains features that qualify it as falling under the DAP orientation to the education of young children in all five categories: (1) Creating a caring community of learners; (2) Teaching to enhance development and learning; (3) Constructing appropriate curriculum; (4) Assessing children's learning and development; and (5) Establishing reciprocal relationships with families.

Although in general there is good correspondence between DAP and Waldorf under the five categories of program characteristics discussed in this chapter, DAP guidelines would appear to recommend a more differentiated approach to assessment than what is offered in Waldorf's nontraditional approach to assessment. An even more glaring discrepancy is under the dimension of constructing appropriate curriculum where DAP recommends or at least acknowledges the use of technology and urges its integration into a program. Indeed, mainstream ECE today recognizes the need to prepare future techno-citizens of the twenty-first century and has computers in programs for young children. Waldorf bucks this trend. Computers, to be sure, are part of Waldorf education, but only with children and adolescents well past the early childhood years.

TABLE 15–1
Comparison of DAP Guidelines and Waldorf Education

DAP Guidelines	Waldorf Education
1. Creating a Caring Community of Learners • The setting functions as a community of learners • Consistent, positive relationships with adults and children further healthy development • Social relationships are an important context for learning • A safe and stress-free environment promotes community • Children thrive on organization and routine	**Waldorf Aspects of Community** • Children's sensitivity to the environment • The importance of imitation and play • Benefits of mixed-age grouping • Establishing rhythm and routine
2. Teaching to Enhance Development and Learning • Teachers respect and value children • Teachers make it a priority to know each child well • Teachers create an intellectually engaging, responsive environment • Teachers foster collaboration with peers • Teachers use a wide variety of teaching strategies • Teachers facilitate the development of responsibility and self-regulation	**Teaching to Enhance Development and Learning in Waldorf** • Reverence, enthusiasm, and protection • Respecting and valuing children • Providing an engaging and responsive environment • Children's connection with sensory experiences • Collaborating with peers • Children learn through doing • Responsibility and self-regulation

3. Constructing Appropriate Curriculum
• Curriculum provides for all areas of development
• Curriculum includes a broad range of content across disciplines
• Curriculum builds upon what children already know and are able to do
• Curriculum integrates across subjects briefly
• Curriculum promotes the development of knowledge, understanding, processes, and skills
• Curriculum content has intellectual integrity
• Curriculum provides opportunities to support children's home culture and language
• The curriculum goals are realistic and attainable
• Technology is physically and philosophically integrated, when utilized
	Constructing Appropriate Curriculum in Waldorf
	• Nurtures the whole child—head, heart, hands
	  1. social
	  2. emotional
	  3. spiritual
	  4. moral
	  5. physical
	  6. intellectual
	• Incorporates a wide variety of disciplines
	• Maintains intellectual integrity
	• Embraces diversity

(Continues)

TABLE 15–1
Continued

DAP Guidelines	Waldorf Education
4. Assessing Children's Learning and Development • Assessment is ongoing, strategic, and purposeful • The content of assessments reflects progress toward important learning goals • Methods of assessment are appropriate to the age and experiences of young children • Assessment is tailored to a specific purpose • Decisions are never made based on a single assessment device • Developmental assessments are used to identify needs and plan accordingly • Assessment recognizes individual variation and allows for differences	**Assessing Children's Learning and Development in Waldorf** • Nontraditional approach to assessment • Freedom to unfold at their own pace • Assessing each child as an individual • Observation offers insights into child's development
5. Establishing Reciprocal Relationships with Families • Reciprocal relationships require mutual respect • It is important to establish and maintain regular, frequent, two-way communication • Parents are welcome in the program and participate in decisions about their child • Teachers acknowledge parents' choices and goals for their children • Teachers and parents share knowledge of the child • The program involves families in assessing and planning for individual children • The program links families with a range of services • Developmental information about a child is shared among all with educational responsibility for that child	**Establishing Reciprocal Relationships with Families in Waldorf** • Parents are welcomed into the schools from the beginning • Communication is a key element • The parents' role in their child's development is seen as critical • Waldorf promotes a community of families

Nevertheless, Waldorf early childhood education has many redeeming virtues. The case can be made that Waldorf contributes to cognitive and social competence, and even school readiness. Of course, school readiness would not be a priority in Waldorf ECE given its devotion to the integrity of childhood, and the fact that chil-

dren tend to stay in Waldorf throughout their school careers. Especially commendable, it would appear, moreover, is Waldorf's use of projects similar to Reggio and The Project Approach (see chapters 14 and 13, respectively, in this volume). Children in Waldorf ECE have a full hour of indoor and outdoor freedom to engage in fruitful learning encounters that usually take the form of long-term investigative activity. Moreover, like the Spectrum Approach (see chapter 11 in this volume), there are a multitude of diverse activities available in the curriculum that stimulate various budding talent areas in young children, consistent with the notion of multiple intelligences. These program features can serve to enrich intellectual and social-emotional development in children by providing an engaging learning environment that fosters positive dispositions and work habits.

Is Moral Education Neglected in ECE?

Waldorf defines moral development as acquiring a sense of responsibility, gratitude, and self-regulation, beginning at the early childhood level. These important aspects of character are learned not by direct instruction, but are incorporated into the curriculum in such a way that the children encounter situations that strengthen these characteristics daily. Do these have their roots in anthroposophy? We think Steiner would answer yes, but believe that these character traits could be considered universally valued virtues. Is there a culture that would not desire its children to grow up to be responsible, grateful, and able to regulate their own behavior?

Perhaps mainstream ECE does not seem to directly address moral development because it is seen as connected to the religious or spiritual, or maybe it is because morals have traditionally been instilled by the family. Controversy surrounds the debate over which aspects of development are the responsibility of the parents and which are the responsibility of the school. It has been argued that if the parents are not fulfilling their duties, then perhaps the school should attempt to fill this void. Others feel that the schools cannot possibly address something so dependent on personal values as moral development.

The Culture of Morality by Elliot Turiel (2002) examined various ideas, theories, and opinions concerning morality and expressed the view that the concept of "morality" is multifaceted and entails character, culture, judgment, social relationships, tradition, and emotion. Turiel contends that there are three imperatives to children's moral development: (1) emotional reactions, including sympathy and empathy; (2) relationships with adults to develop a sense of obligation and respect; and (3) relationships with other children. Given this interpretation of moral development, perhaps mainstream ECE has addressed these issues without labeling them as such. Indeed, ECE would be doing young children a great disservice by neglecting to address this critical aspect of a child's development.

How Does Waldorf Approach Special Education?

With respect to the area of special education you may be curious about the way in which Waldorf education approaches this sensitive, but increasingly important topic. Intriguingly, Rudolf Steiner calls it by a different name altogether—*curative education.* The very name suggests a novel way of thinking about the education of children with special needs. The attitude toward these children is one of respect with the recognition that each person, whatever the disability, has something to contribute to society.

> In curative education, an essential view is that a child's spiritual integrity remains intact regardless of the nature and severity of a disability that may be physical, sensory, mental, emotional or social, or a combination of any of these. The special child is viewed as in need of special soul care and the children are helped to cope with and overcome their disabilities in a carefully designed therapeutic setting in which their diverse and unique developmental, educational, and therapeutic needs can be met. (Juul & Maier, 1992, p. 212)

Teachers work with these children "in need of special care" in residential schools or villages designed to create a humanistic and holistic environment. These communities cater to the needs of their members, in an attempt to reach the whole child: head, heart, and hands. Teachers teach children in an integrated setting, working to achieve a balance within each child that will enable him or her to develop his or her abilities and work to overcome his or her disabilities. The curriculum is similar to that of a traditional Waldorf school, but also includes therapeutic art activities, adaptive physical procedures, vocational training, and occupational experiences (Juul & Maier, 1992).

Waldorf ECE has been popular in the United States for affluent families with children with disabilities, as well as for children born into deprived circumstances worldwide. Waldorf ECE is nondenominational, holistic, and based on a deep respect for children as people and on a profound understanding of human development and worth. There would appear to be something *intrinsically therapeutic* about Waldorf ECE, with its "homelike" physical features (curtains, carpets, subdued lights and colors, simple and natural furniture, etc.), with its emphasis on creative play and artistic expression, and with its delicate order and reassuring rhythmical nature. Accordingly, Waldorf seems ideally suited for children experiencing anxiety and stress-related symptoms, such as refugee children living in camps, children growing up in slums and poverty, or children in conflict situations where violence or war are present. Waldorf ECE is reaching out to just these children (Oldfield, 2001).

Criticisms of Waldorf Education

The strengths and benefits of Waldorf education have been highlighted so far, but all models of education have critics. What is being criticized about Waldorf? Certainly one can criticize Waldorf ECE for its neglect of technology. Others may see limitations in the way Waldorf views early literacy learning goals and its laid-back approach to reading, or its nonchalant stance concerning assessment. These are valid concerns already alluded to. However, other valid or not so valid objections to Waldorf have also been advanced.

An organization called PLANS (People for Legal and Non-Sectarian Schools) has created a Web site (www.waldorfcritics.org) that offers critics and "survivors" (of Waldorf schools) a forum to voice their opposition to Waldorf education. From the information available on this site, it is apparent that this group has very strong opinions about the Waldorf approach and that members are very outspoken in their concerns. There seem to be three major criticisms of Waldorf education that continually surfaced on the PLANS Web site: (1) Waldorf schools are religious schools, (2) Waldorf curriculum is based on Steiner's anthroposophical theories, and (3) Waldorf schools do not inform parents of their philosophy or ties to anthroposophy.

The first complaint relates to the recent movement of Waldorf schools into the public school sector. "Waldorf-inspired" public and charter schools in the United States, critics feel, are a violation of the separation of church and state laws. PLANS members argue that the religion of anthroposophy and Rudolf Steiner's spiritual beliefs are inseparable from Waldorf education and that any re-creation of Waldorf methodology in the public sector retains its anthroposophic roots and therefore is not acceptable. An example noted that changes being made to festivals celebrated in public Waldorf-inspired schools in an attempt to remove the religious nature are only acting on the surface, leading them to believe that the same "spiritually based" rituals are being performed under different names.

A second issue is the influence of anthroposophy on the curriculum as children are introduced to theories of history and science. Anthroposophy promotes some nontraditional ideas about the functions of the body's organs, reincarnation, karma, and historical events, to name a few. PLANS claims that this is "pseudoscience" in the Waldorf education, "crazy" anthroposophical ideas infiltrating the classroom.

Proponents of Waldorf, however, hold the position that teachers study anthroposophy but do not teach it in the classroom.

A third concern is that some parents are generally unaware of the philosophical beliefs surrounding Waldorf education, even intentionally kept in the dark by teachers who were unwilling to offer clear answers to their questions. The PLANS Web site also contends that:

> A huge amount of literature about Waldorf education has been produced within the closed system of Anthroposophy. Much of the available information fails to describe the spiritual mission of the Waldorf school system honestly. We have found that even experienced parents of Waldorf students usually know little about the anthroposophical principles that determine the teaching methods and the anthroposophical doctrine that permeates the curriculum. (www.waldorfcritics.org/active/concerns.html)

As a rejoinder, parents who choose not to send their child to a public school have the responsibility of educating themselves about the philosophy of the school that they decide upon for their child. Being informed about what a chosen school believes and how and what it teaches is the parents' responsibility. Parents can research on the Web and find a great deal of information, observe in the classrooms, and talk with numerous teachers before the child is enrolled, limiting the chance of surprises later on.

Can Waldorf Education Be Replicated in Public Schools?

This question is an important one to address with the popularity of this movement currently on the rise. With increasing attention on Waldorf education in the United States, there have been many new initiatives for Waldorf-inspired elementary school programs. Bruce Uhrmacher, an education professor at the University of Denver, has written a very informative article on the topic of borrowing ideas from alternative education. He offers two important factors to consider when making a decision about using an idea from another model or approach to education: recognizing where ideas come from and reflecting on where ideas go (Uhrmacher 1993, 1997).

First, the teacher must consider the context or framework from which to borrow and how that idea fits within that context. An example from Waldorf early childhood education might be the idea of providing a full hour of imaginative playtime at the beginning of the day. A teacher wishing to borrow this strategy and implement it in the classroom must understand the philosophy behind its use in the Waldorf approach. The teacher must understand that Waldorf values childhood and sees imaginative play as one of the most important expressions of childhood. True play to Waldorf teachers means giving children the freedom to be self-directed, allowing their inner thoughts and ideas to manifest in truly creative ways. A teacher who does not recognize this may apply this concept in an inappropriate manner, perhaps by interrupting the children's play in an attempt to encourage teacher-directed learning, such as asking children to explain what they are doing or to describe the colors they are using when building with the blocks. In the eyes of a Waldorf teacher, this draws the children out of their play experiences and undermines the importance of what they are doing.

According to Uhrmacher (1997), it is also important for a teacher who is considering borrowing an idea to anticipate how the application of this new idea will affect the current curriculum. With any change to an established routine there will certainly be disruptions to the current felt downstream. The teacher must carefully reflect upon how this new idea will fit with personal philosophy, and even the administration under which the program functions. Will the teacher have to make compensations elsewhere to balance this new addition? These are all important considerations and must be thoroughly addressed ahead of time. There is much debate over this topic of taking ideas from a particular approach to education and transplanting them in other programs. Some people feel that, when done properly, borrowing can be helpful and beneficial. Others feel that borrowing will always remove ideas from their intended context, causing inappropriate application.

In terms of Waldorf education, even Waldorf teachers are divided on this issue. Many feel that a Waldorf education has much to offer. If their particular methods of teaching are working for children, then why not encourage the widespread use of those methods, even if it means taking them outside of the Waldorf schools? Many other Waldorf educators, on the other hand, feel that these ideas will lose their meaning and, therefore, their inherent value when taken out of the context of the Waldorf schools. Teaching ideas based on Steiner's principles of child development are closely tied to the beliefs of anthroposophy. Teachers fear that without this contextual framework the ideas will not hold the same purpose or benefit to students. The strong spiritual aspect of Waldorf makes the transition to public schools nearly impossible because of the separation of church and state. Is Steinerian education without the spiritual aspect? Waldorf educators take varying stances on this hotly debated issue.

Nevertheless many success stories exist of Waldorf-inspired public school programs in the United States. One is the Urban Waldorf School of Milwaukee, opened in 1991 as the first public school to attempt to adapt Waldorf pedagogy as an effective model. Three years after it began, the program was evaluated by seven non-Waldorf affiliated educational researchers (Easton, 1997). The researchers found the school to be successful in providing a safe, warm educational environment for the inner-city children that were attending. Standardized test scores had risen dramatically and there was relatively little evidence of aggression, considering the violent neighborhood, or other negative social behaviors. Teachers working with the children were able to develop with them meaningful relationships, were able to consistently negotiate misbehavior, and were also able to help the students develop character and cognitive learning in preparation for good citizenship (Easton, 1997). Although this evidence suggests that this school was successful in meeting the needs of its students, questions still remain . . . how well did it apply the Waldorf pedagogy? Was it the Waldorf influence that was responsible for the students' success or were there other factors? Perhaps a Hawthorn effect was operating.

CONCLUSION

Despite its humble beginnings in war-torn Germany, Waldorf has remained timeless in its philosophy and is every bit as dynamic and progressive today as it was in 1919. Waldorf early childhood education and best practices in ECE as epitomized in the DAP guidelines (Bredekamp & Copple, 1997) are closely aligned. Both are seeking an appropriate approach to early childhood education based upon an understanding of child development. Both value the child as an individual and respect the importance of childhood.

Furthermore, we feel that in many ways Waldorf may have even exceeded the standards set forth by NAEYC, taking basic concepts to new heights through both application and attitude. For instance, while NAEYC addresses the whole child as physical, social, emotional, linguistic, aesthetic, and cognitive, Waldorf takes this wholeness to a deeper level by also considering a child's spiritual and moral development.

Currently, there are more Waldorf kindergartens than Waldorf grade schools in the United States, even though the published information tends to focus on grades 1–12. While having more information on the education of younger children from the Waldorfian perspective would be helpful, research data from third parties are even more important for a comprehensive and fair analysis of the philosophy and developmental and educational ideas of Waldorf

to our field of early childhood care and education. Much remains to be learned about Waldorf pedagogy in the early years. It seems an especially promising approach to educating young children, particularly in these troubled times, and the accelerated pace of our lives.

REFERENCES

Bredekamp, S., & C. Copple. (1997). *Developmentally appropriate practice in early childhood programs* (rev. ed.). Washington, DC: National Association for the Education of Young Children.

Childs, G. (1991a). *Truth, beauty and goodness: Steiner-Waldorf education as a demand of our time.* London: Temple Lodge Publishing.

Childs, G. (1991b). *Steiner education in theory and practice.* Edinburgh, Scotland: Floris Books.

Easton, F. (1997). Educating the whole child, "Head, Heart and Hands": Learning from the Waldorf experience. *Theory into Practice, 36* (2), 87–94.

Edwards, C. (2002). Three approaches from Europe: Waldorf, Montessori, and Reggio Emilia. *Early Childhood Research & Practice, 4* (1). Available online: http://ecrp.uiuc.edu/v4n1/edwards.html [2003, May 23].

Grunelius, E. M. (1991). *Early childhood education and the Waldorf school plan.* Fair Oaks, CA: Steiner College Publications.

Healy, J. (1990). *Endangered minds: Why our children don't think.* New York: Simon & Schuster.

Healy, J. (1999). *Endangered minds: Why our children can't think and what we can do about it.* New York: Touchstone Books.

Juul, K. D., & Maier, M. (1992). Teacher training in curative education. *Teacher Education and Special Education, 15* (2), 211–218.

Oldfield, L. (2001). *Free to learn: Introducing Steiner Waldorf early childhood education.* Gloucestershire, UK: Hawthorn Press.

Oppenheimer, T. (1999). Schooling the imagination. *The Atlantic Monthly, 284* (3), 71–83.

Petrash, J. (2002). *Understanding Waldorf education: Teaching from the inside out.* Beltsville, MD: Gryphon House.

Pusch, R. (Ed.). (1993). *Waldorf schools, Vol. I: Kindergarten and early grades.* Spring Valley, NY: Mercury Press.

Richards, M. C. (1980). *Toward wholeness: Rudolf Steiner education in America.* Middletown, CT: Wesleyan University Press.

Schwartz, E. (1995). Playing and thinking. Available online at: http://www.bobnancy.com/waldorf/es_play.doc [2003, June 10].

Steiner, R. (1982). *The roots of education.* London: Steiner Press.

Trostli, R. (1998). *Rhythms of learning: Selected lectures by Rudolf Steiner.* New York: Anthroposophic Press.

Turiel, E. (2002). *The culture of morality: Social development, context and conflict.* Cambridge, UK: Cambridge University Press.

Uhrmacher, B. P. (1993). Coming to know the world through Waldorf education. *Journal of Curriculum and Supervision, 9* (1), 87–104.

Uhrmacher, B. P. (1997). Evaluating change: Strategies for borrowing from alternative education. *Theory into Practice, 36* (2), 71–78.

Ward, W. (2001). Is Waldorf education Christian? *Renewal, 10* (1). Available online at: http://awsna.org/renchristrian.html [2003, February 18].

Wilkinson, R. (1996). *The spiritual basis of Steiner education.* London: Steiner Press.

WEB SITES

Alliance for Childhood
   www.allianceforchildhood.net

Anthroposophical Society in America
   www.anthroposophy.org

Anthroposophical Society World Headquarters
   www.goetheanum.ch

Association of Waldorf Schools in North America
   www.awsna.org
   www.waldorflibrary.org
   www.bobnancy.com

European Council for Steiner Education
   www.steinerwaldorfeurope.org

Rudolf Steiner Archive
   www.elib.com/Steiner

Rudolf Steiner College
   www.steinercollege.org

Waldorf World—Waldorf Education on the Web
   www.waldorfworld.net

Waldorf Materials Shopping Sites
   www.naturalplay.com
   www.waldorfshop.net

Waldorf Critics
   www.waldrofcritics.org/active/concerns.html

INTERNATIONAL WALDORF SCHOOLS ON THE INTERNET

Steiner School in Italy (language: Italian)
   www.rudolfsteiner.it

Steiner School in Australia (language: English)
   www.mrss.com.au

Swedish Waldorf Schools (language: Swedish)
   www.waldorf.se

Steiner Waldorf Schools in the UK and Ireland
(language: English)
   www.steinerwaldorf.org.uk

Federation of Waldorf Schools in Southern Africa
(language: English)
   www.waldorf.org.za

Nairobi Waldorf Schools in Kenya (language:
English)
   www.nairobiwaldorfschool.org

BOOKS RELATED TO WALDORF EDUCATION

Berger, T. (1992). *The harvest craft book*. Edinburgh: Floris Books.
Berger, T., & Berger, P. (1999). *Gnome craft book*. Edinburgh: Floris Books.
Jenkinson, S. (2001). *Genius of play*. Gloucestershire, UK: Hawthorn Press.
Leeuwen, M. V., & Moeskops, J. (1990). *Nature corner*. Edinburgh: Floris Books.

Masters, B. (1984). *Waldorf songbook*. Edinburgh: Floris Books.
Nobel, A. (1996). *Educating through art: The Steiner school approach*. Edinburgh: Floris Books.

Chapter 16

Montessori Education Today

Martha Torrence ❧ The New School, Cincinnati
John Chattin-McNichols ❧ Seattle University

Maria Montessori (1870–1952) was an extraordinary person by any standard who overcame great difficulties to become one of Italy's first female physicians. Her gift of observation was sharpened by her studies in anthropology, resulting in her first book, *Pedagogical Anthropology* (Montessori, 1913). She also worked with what were then called "defective children" at the state Orthophrenic School in Rome. In her work with this very diverse population, she drew from the work of Jean Itard and Edouard Seguin, French physicians and educators of developmentally disabled children (Loeffler, 1992). In 1907, she was asked to create a program to care for the children of families in a housing project in Rome serving a lower income population of 4- to 7-year-olds; this was the first Casa dei Bambini, or Children's House.

In the United States, there was a great deal of interest in her methods from 1910 to 1920 (Montessori's program was demonstrated with a model classroom in San Francisco at the 1916 World's Fair), but then Montessori education was all but forgotten in the United States until the late 1950s. However, during these three decades, Montessori schools increased in Europe and India.

What caused this initial failure in the United States? Elkind (1998) suggests that one reason for the poor reception may have been that modern parents at that time in America viewed childhood as a time of innocence when children are best cared for by their mothers. Four other reasons that contributed to the rapid downfall seem to have been (1) poor or uncomprehending reception by the educational leadership; (2) adaptation of Montessori's methods in a variety of ways with which she disagreed; (3) a focus on academics by demanding middle-class parents; and (4) a flood of "trainers" and authors eager to capitalize on Montessori. J. McVicker Hunt, in his introduction to a new edition of *The Montessori Method* (Hunt, 1964), claimed that on five central issues, educators and psychologists of the day disagreed with Montessori (see Table 16–1).

Table 16–1 shows the major differences between Montessori's ideas and the dominant theories in education and psychology in this country in the early part of this century. In terms of the effects of environment (vs. heredity), the mutability of intellect, motivation, the role of the senses in learning and development, and the focus on observable, testable behavior, Montessori was completely out of step. So much so that Kilpatrick's 1914 book-length criticism, *The Montessori System Examined*, was taken by most professionals as the last word—in fact the only word needed. If Columbia's "million-dollar professor" and colleague of John Dewey, William Heard Kilpatrick saw nothing new or of interest in Montessori, that settled it for most educational leaders in this country.

The million-dollar question today may be, why haven't many contemporary educational leaders noticed that theories in these same areas

TABLE 16–1
Montessori versus 1910–1920 Contemporaries

Montessori's Position	1910–1920 Contemporaries' Position
Importance of experience for 3- and 4-year-olds	
Absorbent minds: Montessori's concept of a period of development when certain kinds of things (e.g., language) are absorbed without external motivation.	Fixed intelligence
Specialized group settings could provide appropriate stimulation.	Only families (not outside agencies) should be involved in the education or care of young children.
Importance of predetermined development and usefulness of early teaching	
Appropriate learning environments can allow for growth and change.	Development is predetermined. Early studies of the "fade out" of practice (with traditional elementary school methods) showed uselessness of education before about age 8.
Motivation	
Internal motivation; children are intrinsically motivated to practice, especially at the edge of competence.	All behavior needs to be motivated externally, usually by primary drives such as food, painful stimuli, etc.
What should be the focus for education?	
Emphasis on the senses and the experience of the child. Little emphasis on testing.	Emphasis on behavioral responses.
Role of the teacher	
Facilitator, guide, teaching through the environment, short individual or small-group lessons; large part of day in free-choice time.	Traditional teacher role: direct, whole-group instruction. Froebel's "gifts."

Source: "Introduction" by J. McVicker Hunt in *The Montessori Method* by M. Montessori, 1964, New York: Schocken.

have changed and are now much more in line with what Montessori had proposed? Her language remains the same; it is admittedly dated and may therefore be interpreted as representing out-of-date thinking. But most of the mismatches between Montessori and current theories have been resolved through advances in our understanding of child development and learning. "With the broad acceptance and continued interest in developmentally appropriate practice, many educators are recognizing that what are nowadays spoken of as 'education reforms' have actually been part of Montessori practice for decades" (Lindauer, 1993, p. 252). Shute (2002) agrees that many of Montessori's once-radical theories, such as the importance of children learning through hands-on activity, the preschool

years being a time of critical brain development, and parents being included as essential partners in their children's education, are currently accepted as standard thinking in the field of early childhood education.

The contemporary American Montessori movement began in the late 1950s as a set of private schools serving an almost entirely middle-class population. Many of these early schools were founded by parents. In 1959 the American Montessori Society (AMS) was established. Its founder, Nancy McCormick Rambusch, asserted that not only adoption but also adaptation of Montessori's method was necessary, in order that it be both translated and "naturalized" into the diverse American cultural setting (Rambusch, cited in Loeffler, 1992).

A teacher shortage, predicated by the mush-rooming number of schools, resulted in the opening of private Montessori teacher training centers, typically freestanding—not associated with a college or university. The word *Montessori* has been used in the public domain in the United States, and so both schools and teacher education programs proliferated and were licensed without name-brand regulation or restriction. Some schools (then and now) used the name *Montessori* referring to programs that have little relation to the schools she described. The AMS, the Association Montessori Internationale (AMI), and a number of other organizations have established criteria as to what constitutes a quality Montessori school. But membership in these organizations is voluntary, and organizational criteria do not apply to state licensing standards.

Beginning in the late 1960s, parents in several school districts began to advocate for the public schools to offer the Montessori model for their children, many of whom had graduated from private Montessori preschools. This push was given a strong boost by the availability of federal funds for magnet programs. Today, more than 350 schools in 150 districts nationwide (Kahn, 1990; Schapiro & Hellen, 2003) offer some form of public Montessori program. These programs serve children from age 3 through high school. The combined total of public and private Montessori schools in the United States is just under 4,000 (Schapiro & Hellen, 2003).

KEY TENETS AND BACKGROUND INFORMATION

Since there are no restrictions on the use of the word *Montessori,* many people rely on a school's affiliation with a major Montessori organization to determine whether or not a program is in fact Montessori. Two of these organizations are the AMI and AMS. But many private Montessori schools and the majority of public Montessori school programs have chosen not to affiliate with any organization, usually citing financial considerations. What are some of the characteristics of a Montessori classroom, then, that differentiate it from a traditional early childhood classroom? What might a visitor to a contemporary Montessori classroom expect to see?

The first thing that an observer might notice is the mixed-age grouping: typically, 3-, 4-, and 5-year-olds are together, as are 6-, 7-, and 8-year-olds, and so on. Another difference is the arrangement of the room, with low, open shelves holding many carefully arranged materials from which the children can choose. Tables and desks are grouped to facilitate individual or small-group work, rather than an arrangement in which furniture is oriented in one direction to facilitate whole-group instruction. Open floor space allows for work on the floor. The amount of shelving needed to hold the required Montessori materials is more than is generally seen in other educational models, with all walls of the classroom typically containing some shelving, and shelving extending into the classroom at several points to create bays, or focus areas. The Montessori manipulative materials are designed for use by individual students or small groups, rather than as teacher presentation aides. For example, small globes are provided for children to handle and explore, rather than one big globe provided at the front of the room for teacher-centered instruction.

The single most important criteria for judging a program to be a good implementation of Montessori is the activity of the students. For major portions of their school day—from 3 to 4 hours per day, for children attending full-day programs—students should be engaged in individual and small-group work of their own choosing. These choices are, of course, guided and supervised by the teacher. (See the section entitled, "The Role of the Teacher," later in this chapter.) Classrooms that spend more than 1 hour a day in whole-group instruction have moved away from the Montessori model (see Baines & Snortum, 1973; Feltin, 1987).

Children working together using Montessori materials inventively.

Another important aspect of Montessori classrooms is an attitude of cooperation rather than competition in completing work. For example, in an elementary classroom, the answers to math problems and science or geography questions are freely available to the students. Students complete work independently and then check responses with the "control" material. Children in Montessori classrooms commonly ask other children for help, not perceiving the teacher as the sole source of information in the room.

This availability of a correct answer accompanies a reduced emphasis on conventional forms of testing. Although public and private Montessori schools comply with school district or state-level requirements for mandated achievement tests, these are seen by many Montessorians as being somewhat irrelevant to much of the learning that goes on. The new emphasis on authentic assessment methods, which include portfolios and performance-based assessment, is welcomed by many Montessori educators. In fact assessment in a Montessori classroom is typically based on extensive teacher observation. During individual and small-group presentations, students are asked to practice the relevant activities, giving the teacher an immediate assessment of the success of that lesson. Ongoing systematic teacher observation of children's work adds to the teacher's cumulative knowledge of child progress. Intervention to support a child who needs more individual instruction with a given skill or concept is always an option as a result of such observation.

Finally, there is strong emphasis on the development of individual responsibility. For example, children return materials to their place after use, the classroom is cleaned and maintained at least in part by the children, and they participate in the development of classroom rules.

The following vignette, taken from an observation of a Montessori environment for 3- to

6-year-olds, offers a glimpse of what a visitor might see on a "typical" day.

———————— ✂ ————————

9:05 A.M.: Several children are already engaged in individual activities (one is beating soapsuds with an eggbeater, another is placing pegged wooden pieces into a puzzle map of North America, a third is polishing a piece of silver). The teacher stands near the door, quietly greeting new arrivals. As each child enters the room, the teacher gets on his or her eye level and shakes his or her hand, welcoming each by name. Brief conversations with individual children ensue; for example, one child describes in detail the skunk that was in her family's garage the previous evening. The teacher listens and responds, asking detail-provoking questions.

The assistant teacher moves through the room, helping children to initiate individual activities, making suggestions to the hesitant or undecided. Two girls stand near the guinea pig's cage, observing as he nibbles at a fresh carrot. The girls chat about the guinea pig; one then gets a lap board, art paper, and colored pencils and begins to sketch this classroom pet. When finished she labels her picture "ginee pig" and places it in her cubbie.

By 9:15 all of the children have arrived, a total of 24. A fairly even mix of 3- 4- and 5-year-olds comprises the group. The children move about the room, some engaging in individual pursuits, others uniting in interest groups of twos and threes. One 3-year-old boy has chosen a stack of five sandpaper letters to trace; he asks the teacher to watch as he traces each and pronounces the letter's sound. He spontaeoulsy repeats this activity five times with each letter!

A 4-year-old girl paints on large paper at the easel. She uses the paint brush to apply paint, then tracks with a roller over the original paint, spreading it and adding texture. A 3-year-old chooses a basket of wooden zoo animals from the language shelf. She says, "This is animal matching," and proceeds to match each animal to its pair. She then names the animals. She accurately names the elephant and rhinocerous, calls the wolf

a fox but later renames it "wolf" when she gets to the actual fox, which she calls an "ant killer."

Two 5-year-olds collaboratively set up the "bank," a large collection of thousand cubes, hundred squares, ten bars, and unit beads, on a mat. Later they will use these quantities to build large numbers in the thousands, which they will match with corresponding numeral cards. One child will be the "banker," the other the "customer."

Two children decide to eat snack together. They don aprons, which are stored on each of two chairs at the small snack table. Each washes her hands at the nearby child-sized sink, then proceeds to serve herself a muffin from a basket on the serving table (a sign says "1" indicating the number each child may have). Each pours her own juice into a small glass, carries it to the table and sits down. The two chat as they eat. When finished each child places her napkin in the trash and her glass in the dish basin, then sponges her placemat.

A range of such activities ensues until, at 11 A.M. the teacher gathers the children for circle using a rhythmic call and response. With the support of the assistant, children put their respective activities back on the shelves. A few are in the midst of lengthy activities that cannot be completed prior to the group gathering. These children get their name cards from a collective basket; each places his or her name card on the work, marking his or her spot to return to it later.

The teacher shows and names the contents of a "c" object basket that a child has brought from home. She then leads the children in a group "I Spy" game, giving descriptive clues about each object as the children take turns guessing. The children are dismissed one at a time to line up at the door in preparation for playground time.

———————— ✂ ————————

MONTESSORI'S VIEW OF HUMAN DEVELOPMENT

Montessori viewed education as a vehicle for "giving help to the child's life . . . helping the mind in its process of development" (Montessori,

1967a/1949, p. 28). Her oft-cited phrase "follow the child" is meant to infer that by following the child's development, the educator can make the most helpful match between instructional methods, curriculum, and child. A discussion of Montessori's educational philosophy, then, must begin with her view of human development.

In Montessori's view, development does not progress in one continuous inclined plane, the implication of that model being that the child is simply a small adult, and that development proceeds in a linear or constant fashion from birth to maturity. A further implication of the inclined plane model is that mental activity on the more elevated end of the scale—representing an older, more developed person—is inherently more valuable than that of a very young child. On the contrary, Montessori viewed the first period of life to be the most developmentally dynamic and of the highest importance.

Montessori's developmental paradigm depicts a series of four related triangles, which she termed, "the constructive rhythm of life" (see Table 16–2). Each triangle represents a six-year period (or plane) of development: birth to 6 years of age (infancy); 6 to 12 years of age (childhood); 12 to 18 years (adolescence); and 18 to 24 years (maturity). Two of the planes, the first and third, are described as particularly volatile and active with respect to physical and psychological changes, with the other two as relatively stable periods of strengthening and integration (Grazzini, 1996).

Each plane is distinct unto itself, having its own particular characteristics; at the same time, each prepares the child for the one that follows. Montessori describes the key characteristics or mental tendencies that distinguish each plane as "sensitive periods." "These periods . . . are transitory, and confined to the acquisition of a determined characteristic. Once the characteristic has evolved the corresponding sensibility disappears" (Montessori, 1966, p. 38). Montessori viewed the sensitive periods as the most oppor-

tune time in life for an individual to develop key characteristics or abilities.

According to Grazzini, Montessori viewed development as a series of "births," or periods of heightened sensitivity, each sensitivity giving rise to new interests and skills. Although these sensitivities heighten to a crescendo then fall away, the acquired abilities remain for the whole of the individual's life (Grazzini, 1996). For example, Montessori noted that beginning at birth, but peaking in the 2- to 4-year-old, a sensitive period for order is manifested. During this period, young children exhibit an almost ritualized interest in putting or finding things in their exact place in the environment. This sensitivity manifests itself in many ways, including children becoming upset when events occur out of their usual order or then delighting in hearing the same story told in the same way, many times over.

Montessori viewed this love of order as the outward manifestation of the child's inner need for a precise and predictable environment. The child's drive for external order generally diminishes by about age 5 to 6 years, according to Montessori. By this time, the needs of this sensitive period will have been met, given time and experience in an appropriate environment. The child will have formed an "inner conceptual framework," which will serve her in the next plane of development, as she moves toward more abstract thinking, reasoning, and complex problem solving.

This example demonstrates two essential qualities of the sensitive periods: They are by nature both transitory (or passing) and retained, in the form of lasting mental capacities. One primary goal of the educator, then, is to maintain awareness of the natural drive of these sensitive periods and to prepare an educational environment that responds accordingly.

The Absorbent Mind

Montessori noted, with great respect, the unique capacity of the very young child to assimilate, or to take in, one's surroundings. She observed that

TABLE 16–2
Planes of Development

Planes	Characteristics/Sensitive Periods

0–6 The child is constructing himself from experiences.
- Need for order in the environment
- Exploration of the environment through use of hands and tongue (leads to language development)
- Movement
- Fascination with minute and detailed objects
- Interest in the social aspects of life

6–12 The child has constructed tools to explore the world, now wants to move outside the classroom.
- Exploration of culture
- The imagination
- Morality
- Social relationships

12–18 Child reconstructs himself now as a social being, in relationship with adults, peers, and society. This important social task means less attention is available for academic work, especially work with no obvious connection to the real world.
- Humanistic explorers
- Interest in justice
- Need for work in the real world

18–24 The young adult, having done the needed social reconstruction, now is able to make full use of available educational resources.
- Self-motivation in learning, application of knowledge to real-world problems
- Moral and spiritual development noticeable, have influence on choices

Based on Grazzini, 1996.

from infancy, this capacity enables the child to absorb each experience in a powerful and direct way. Through the process of such absorption, the mind itself is formed. Thus, the child directly assimilates the physical and social environment in which he or she is immersed, simultaneously developing his or her innate mental powers. As Montessori phrased it, "Impressions do not merely enter his mind; they form it. They incarnate themselves in him. The child creates his own 'mental muscles,' using for this what he finds in the world about him. We have named this type of mentality, *The Absorbent Mind*" (Montessori, 1967a/1949, pp. 25–26; emphasis in original).

According to Montessori, this powerful mental construction occurs between birth and the age of 6 years and consists of two distinct phases: From birth until about 3 years of age, the child is in the phase of the unconscious absorbent mind, during which time, the child explores the environment through the senses and through movement, also absorbing the language of the surrounding culture. The child retains memories of these experiences, but they are not conscious; that is, they cannot be called upon at will for the child's use. Montessori asserted, "If we call our adult mentality conscious, then we must call the child (of under 3 years) unconscious, but the unconscious kind is not necessarily inferior. An unconscious mind can be most intelligent" (Montessori, 1967a/1949, p. 23).

As an example, Montessori cited the very young child's powerful absorption of the sounds, rhythms, and structures of language. An infant hears a multitude of environmental sounds but is naturally and unconsciously cued in to the sound of the human voice. Gradually, but without conscious effort by the child or direct teaching by the adult, the child absorbs the sounds and rhythms of his or her native language, as well as its vocabulary, semantics, and syntax. The child, at least during the early stages of this process, does not have a conscious memory but must construct such memory through experience, absorbing the patterns of human language powerfully and directly (Montessori, 1967a/1949).

At about the age of 3 years, according to Montessori, the child's capacity for such powerful absorption shifts to a more conscious, purposeful type. At this point, the child becomes a factual, as well as a sensory explorer, noting relationships between things and making comparisons. At this point, the child begins to classify and refine sensory experiences, bringing to consciousness many impressions that were previously absorbed. In so doing, "he constructs his mind step by step till it becomes possessed of memory, the power to understand, the ability to think" (Montessori, 1967a/1949, p. 27). This process evolves throughout the period of the "conscious absorbent mind," approximately between the ages of 3 and 6 years. It is worth noting that Montessori's period of the unconscious absorbent mind correlates closely with Piaget's sensorimotor period birth to 2 years; the period of the conscious absorbent mind correlates closely with Piaget's preoperational stage (ages 2–7 years).

Discipline: The Development of the Will

Children, in Montessori's view, actively construct not only their own understanding of the world but also their own sense of inner discipline, or ability to control and direct their focus and actions. Thus, "discipline" in a good Montessori classroom arises not from the teacher's superimposition of will over the children's, but from each child's gradual development of a sense of inner purpose, originating in focused activity.

As children newly enter the learning environment, they are unaccustomed to its materials, social expectations, and ground rules. They can be impulsive and seem to lack focus. But when they discover something that is of deep interest, they begin to act on it. According to Montessori, such purposeful engagement deepens the experience and deepens children's ability to concentrate and direct actions in other situations as well. Through such a series of actions on the environment, the children's will, or ability to direct their own actions, begins to develop. Although "the school must give the child's spirit space and opportunity for expansion" (Montessori, 1967a/1949, p. 264), this is not a laissez-faire or permissive method in which anything goes. If this were the case, chaos would reign, and only the teacher's direct imposition of control would restore harmony. Rather, behavioral limits are designed and implemented so that all may work in peace.

In other words, within Montessori classrooms, an atmosphere of freedom within limits is maintained—freedom to choose and use materials with purpose and care, to direct one's own learning, to interact with others, to move about the space freely. Limits are imposed to offer children guidelines for peer consortium and bounds of appropriate use of materials and to maintain a sense of social dignity and peace. Ground rules are often described as being in place to ensure respect for oneself, for others, and for the environment. The peace that can arise through such a balance between freedom and limits is not to be mistaken for inaction or immobility. Rather, "a form of active peace" (Montessori, 1967a/1949, p. 254) is said to prevail in a disciplined Montessori classroom.

Given the unique capacities of the young child's mind, and the tenet that education should be a "help to life," what type of educational environment, materials, and methods match the task?

⚘ PROGRAM CHARACTERISTICS

The Prepared Environment

The child, in Montessori's view, is a constant inquirer who "absorbs his environment, takes everything from it, and incarnates it in himself" (Montessori, 1967a/1949, p. 66). Not a passive recipient of experience, the child ideally interacts purposefully and freely with a specifically designed, learner-sensitive environment for optimal development to occur.

The Montessori-prepared learning environment is both physical and psychological. The physical environment is designed to be ordered, proportioned to the child's size, aesthetically pleasing, and visually harmonious. Although the environment is carefully prepared before the entry of the children, it is constantly refined and adjusted to keep pace with the ongoing needs and interests of a particular group. In other words, it is orderly but not rigid, prepared but not fixed. The teacher constantly re-prepares or fine-tunes the environment based on observations of the children's interests and needs.

The preparation and subsequent refinement of the environment are central tasks of the Montessori teacher. Though not the central figure in the class, the teacher in a Montessori classroom is far from passive: The teacher supports the child's engagement with the environment by initiating a psychological tone of calm and focused activity; by responding genuinely, warmly, and with dignity to each child and his or her needs; and by helping to make the "good match" between child and material. Much of the success of the prepared environment will depend "on the teacher's ability to participate with the children in a life of becoming" (Lillard, 1972, p. 61).

Lillard (1972) outlined six essential components of the Montessori learning environment: (1) freedom, (2) structure and order, (3) reality and nature, (4) beauty and an atmosphere that encourages a positive and spontaneous response to life, (5) Montessori learning materials, and (6) the development of community life. Another characteristic that distinguishes a Montessori learning environment is its provision of extended, uninterrupted blocks of time for child-centered activity. These blocks of time enable children to repeat activities as often as they wish, extend their concentration spans, and to socialize, rest, reflect, and engage in a wide range of possible work choices within each routine day.

Freedom

In Montessori's view, the natural thrust of the child is toward independence, independence of the "I can do it myself" variety. In addition, the child internally possesses the blueprint for his or her own development, which will unfold quite naturally given an appropriate environment and the freedom to act on the directive thrust of this inner guide.

Freedom is necessary so that the child can choose from among the materials and experiences offered those that are of most use and interest at any point. The adult in turn observes the child's interest and activity, gaining insight into the child's personality and development, and fine-tunes or modifies the environment to meet the child's needs. It is only in an atmosphere of freedom, according to Montessori, that true discipline can begin.

When a child undertakes a purposeful task that satisfies an inner developmental need, attention is fixed on this task in a manner that lengthens the focus, attunes the "will" toward a purpose or object, and thereby begins growth toward self-discipline. The quality of freedom in a Montessori classroom is dependent on this internal development of focus and self-discipline. According to Montessori, one cannot logically occur without the other.

Structure and Order

"The child, left at liberty to exercise his activities, ought to find in his surroundings something organized in direct relation to his internal organization which is developing itself by natural laws" (Montessori, 1965, p. 70). The external organization of the environment, in other words, should both mimic and promote the internal order unfolding within the child. Given the young child's acute sensitivity to order (see Table 16–2), it makes sense that the rhythms and routines of the classroom should be predictable, the learning materials should be organized in a logical fashion, and the delivery of lessons as guides to action should be exact and concise.

The word *rigid,* however, does not apply. Such appropriate structure manifests in many forms in a Montessori classroom, from a routine cycle of activities each day, to finding a material in an expected location; to the carefully designed symmetry of the learning materials, to the predictability of the basic ground rules or limits that govern the behavior of all.

Reality and Nature

Because of the absorbent quality of the young child's mind, Montessori felt that the material placed in a child's hands should be of authentic quality and should tangibly represent the real world. She shunned the practice of offering materials of inferior quality to the young child as well as that of presenting fantasy-based images.

Children are provided with real, workable, child-sized tools of everyday living in the Montessori environment. Objects such as child-proportioned brooms, dust pans, and glassware are commonplace. The Montessori didactic materials are generally made of sturdy hardwoods, glass, and (in this age) high-quality plastics. Quality and authentic materials are advocated in teacher education programs.

Montessori felt strongly that young children should be immersed in a world of reality, not fantasy. Her position was that the child's imagination develops from a sensory base and a foundation in real-world experiences, rather than from an immersion in adult-created fantasy (Montessori, 1965). Lillian Katz seemed to concur on this point, applying it to the modern era of media and mass marketing. "I believe the majority of our young children suffer from a surplus of adult-generated fantasy. We have reached a stage that I call the abuses of enchantment; it is another aspect of treating children like silly empty-headed pets that have to be amused and titillated" (Katz, quoted in Loeffler, 1992, p. 193).

Because the child is inherently drawn to the natural world—to its cycles, rhythms, and inherent order—Montessori felt that nature should be a part of the learning environment. Plants, animals, and small gardens cared for by the children are standard in many Montessori classrooms.

Beauty and Atmosphere

Montessori advocated not only that aesthetic qualities be built into learning materials but also that the environment itself convey a sense of overall harmony. The environment should be clean, attractive, and well cared for. It should be colorful to attract the child, yet uncluttered so as not to overstimulate. In addition to the aesthetic qualities of beauty, Montessori advocated an overall environment of peace, nurturance, and, in a sense, spiritual beauty in which to immerse the developing child. Anita Rui Olds, in an essay entitled "Places of Beauty" (quoted in Bergen, 1988, p. 185), echoed this sentiment: "Japanese architecture features an arch called a 'torre' to signal the transition from profane to sacred territory, from that which is spontaneous and ordinary to that which is spiritually and aesthetically integrated. I have often thought that every child space should be framed by such an arch, and that the space should be designed to fulfill its meaning. Passage beyond the torre would then surround each child with beauty, wholeness, and care."

Montessori Learning Materials

"The 'prepared environment' is designed to help the child achieve a sense of himself, self-mastery and mastery of his environment through the successful execution and repetition of apparently simple tasks which are nonetheless linked to the cultural expectations the child faces in the context of his development" (Rambusch, 1962, p. 71). These "apparently simple tasks" refer to the Montessori didactic materials, generally associated with the Montessori method. To some, the sheer presence of these materials distinguishes a learning environment as Montessori in practice. However, it is not the materials themselves but, rather, their design principles that make them necessary, but not sufficient, components of a Montessori setting.

These inherent design principles isolate a particular concept or difficulty and contain a built-in control of error (i.e., auto-educational). They involve movement or activity by the child. They begin as relatively simple activities but add complexity as the child gains experience and judgment. Moreover, Montessori materials are designed to prepare the child both directly and indirectly for other subsequent learning. They have visual appeal and are aesthetically pleasing.

The isolation of a single difficulty is intended to induce clarity in the child's learning experience and to focus attention on a key concept. For example, the tower of cubes (or pink tower) is a series of 10 cubes, graded in size at exact increments. Each cube is exactly identical except for the single variable of size. This draws the child's attention to that quality, allowing the exploration of the size relationships among the cubes without unnecessary distraction. In contrast, many contemporary commercially made materials are designed with the notion that "more is better." In the commercial version, such sized cubes might be adorned with a variety of colors, letters, numerals, or textures. In Montessori's view, the child may be entertained by using such multifaceted cubes but also may be unnecessarily distracted by the extraneous stimuli offered.

The notion of control of error is often misunderstood to mean that children should be ushered by the materials through drill toward a sort of methodical perfection. Montessori, a scientist, viewed error to be inherent and a constructive

component of all learning. Errors are considered essential tools for cognitive self-construction in that the perception of "errors" stimulates the child's careful observation and analysis of the learning experience at hand. Montessori designed controls of error (or design cues) into her materials to offer feedback that children can read and interpret, liberating children from dependency on adult approval or disapproval. Montessori has assessed that, "The control of error through the material makes a child use his reason, critical faculty, and his ever increasing capacity for drawing distinctions" (Montessori, 1967b/1948, p. 103).

The most frequently cited example of this design principle lies in the Montessori cylinder blocks, which are blocks of solid wood containing 10 knobbed cylinders of graduated dimension, each of which exactly corresponds to an equally sized socket. In general, children quite naturally match cylinder with socket; any "error" in the match becomes apparent due to a cylinder not fitting into a socket, wobbling through having been placed in a socket too large, or remaining socketless due to a prior mismatch. The child detects "errors" through the process of observation and experimentation and thereby engages in a cognitive dialogue with the material. As the child gains such experience and, therefore, judgment, the external and obvious control of error in subsequent materials is diminished. For example, the knobless cylinders (a more advanced material) duplicate this initial experience except that there are now no blocks and no sockets into which to place the cylinders. The child grades the series without the benefit of a preset form to follow, replacing the guiding construct of the material with independent judgment.

Appreciative of the neuromuscular connection between physical movement and cognitive development, Montessori intended that child activity or movement be a part of all of her didactic materials. Children in Montessori classrooms lift, carry, balance, stack, pour, sweep, assemble, and grade various objects as they actively engage and manipulate the learning environment.

Such motor activity serves to sustain the child's interest in the learning experience. Montessori claimed that, "The ability of a thing to attract the interest of a child does not depend so much upon the quality of the thing itself as upon the opportunity that it affords the child for action" (Montessori, 1967b/1948, p. 104). Integrating movement with perceptual learning helps embed the activity or concept into the child's "muscle memory" and affords the child the opportunity to develop control of movement. The child adapts physical movements to the demands of a given activity, developing coordination, balance, and overall motor refinement.

Montessori didactic materials generally progress from simple to complex, adding one degree of difficulty as the child progresses to the next experience. This enables a child to reach a sense of internal mastery of a skill, material, or concept, before moving on to something that has more steps or requires increased judgment. Since the curriculum is child driven rather than teacher driven, there is no one blueprint for progression through the didactic materials. Materials are presented to each child according to interest and the requisite preparatory skills—the goal being child success and independence, not completion of a preset curriculum or a preset timetable.

In addition to progressing from simple to complex, Montessori materials are generally designed as scaffolding or indirect preparation for other, subsequent learning. For example, by grading sets of size-related materials such as the pink tower or red rods children indirectly prepare themselves for comprehension of the base-10 number system, as all of these graded series contain 10 elements. By using a three-finger grasp to handle the knobbed cylinders, children indirectly prepare their fingers for handwriting. By pouring liquids from one larger container into three equally sized smaller containers children indirectly prepare themselves for fractions and division.

Overall, materials are evaluated in their composite, not in terms of one exclusive set of materials. The greatest hallmark of good Montessori classrooms is the teacher as scientific pedagogue; under the guidance of this type of teacher, the Montessori materials become a well-designed set of possibilities, not a complete instructional package.

The Development of Community Life

It would be a mistake to take the thrust toward independence and individual development in Montessori classrooms as an indicator that little socialization occurs. In fact, some might say that nothing could be further from the truth. "To the question 'what provision is made for socialization?' one could reply that the very condition of learning in this Montessori environment depends on socialization as an atmospheric element" (Rambusch, 1962, p. 79). Liberated from spending long periods of time in teacher-led large-group instruction, children routinely interact with each other, sharing work, watching another's activity, offering or seeking peer help with a material, or sharing snack and conversation. Productive sociability, not mere togetherness, should be a prominent feature of a good Montessori class (Rambusch, 1962).

Although many activities are designed with an individual learner in mind, many others such as language activities are specifically intended for two or more children. Teachers are subtle but key community builders spending time moving about the room, offering lessons to individuals and small groups, making conversation, and helping children to mutually resolve conflicts.

Grouping together children of three different age groups, spanning 3 years (which is common to most Montessori environments), supports the development of community life as well. Older children are actively encouraged to support younger learners and to serve as leaders and role models. Children are free to choose friends from a wide range of possibilities and to discover and explore qualities in others unlike themselves. Cooperation and respect for others are foundational concepts in a Montessori classroom community.

CURRICULUM AREAS

The Montessori learning environment for 3- to 6-year-olds is generally divided into four basic areas: practical life (everyday living); sensorial (materials focusing on one or more of the senses); language; and mathematics. In addition, music, art, movement, and drama are included in the curriculum (American Montessori Society, 1994).

Practical Life

The curricular area called *practical life* is generally seen as the sine qua non of the Montessori curriculum, because, through involvement with practical experiences in everyday living, the child begins to develop these skills and tendencies that will support focused learning in all other classroom endeavors. Through involvement with familiar, home-based experiences such as sweeping, sewing, and gardening, the child begins to focus attention on a single activity and learns to follow a sequence from beginning to end, learns to coordinate movements toward a particular goal, and learns to organize each step of a given task, thereby attaining independence through self-directed activity. Thus, while the direct or practical aim of an activity such as carrot cutting may be the peeling, cutting, and serving of a carrot, the underlying or indirect aims include the development of independence, order, concentration, hand–eye coordination, the development of community life (through serving the carrot to others), and realistic self-esteem (through accomplishment). Practical life activities invite the child's participation in the surrounding culture through offering child-sized versions of activities commonly done in the home—reinforcing for the child a fluent transition from home to classroom. Specific activities involve self-care (e.g., tooth brushing, dressing frames for practice with various types of fasteners, nose blowing, hair combing); care of the environment (flower arranging, shoe polishing, table scrubbing, gardening); life skills (sewing, food preparation); fine motor development (transferring activities, e.g., pouring and basting); and community living (setting a table, saying "excuse me" or "thank you," etc.).

Since few practical life activities are standardized, teachers create most materials for this curricular area. Great diversity exists from one classroom to the next as each teacher responds to the needs, interests, and cultural makeup of the class. For example, in a Hawaiian Montessori school, teacher adaptations are made to reflect Hawaiian culture and the surrounding natural environment: Stringing is done with flowers, seeds, or leaves; pouring and scooping are done with small shells and seeds—large shells are often used as pouring vessels; dressing frames are made with Hawaiian tapa-cloth designs; food activities include preparation of rice sushi, pounding poi, and drying fruits and seeds Chinese style (Bogart, 1992).

As children mature, practical life involves more complex cooking activities, first aid, bicycle repair, telephone manners, computer skills, and knowledge of simple machines (Chattin-McNichols, 1992).

Sensorial

From birth, children are immersed in a stimulus-rich environment and unconsciously use all of their senses to absorb sensory impressions, in the absorbent mind (Montessori, 1973). In the third year of life, according to Montessori, the child can begin to order and classify impressions through hands-on examination of specifically prepared materials. Sensorial materials were designed with this purpose in mind; they originate from Montessori's own designs and are adapted from the work of Jean Itard and Edouard Seguin (Montessori 1967b/1948).

The sensorial materials are a series of sequenced exercises, aesthetically pleasing and seemingly simple in design, which are offered so that the child can "catalog and classify" (Montessori, 1967b/1948) sensory impressions. These activities refine and sharpen the senses and create a sensory foundation for further intellectual development. "The training and sharpening of the senses, has the obvious advantage of enlarging the field of perception and of offering an ever more solid foundation for intellectual growth" (Montessori, 1967b/1948, p. 99).

Materials appealing to the visual, muscular-tactile, auditory, gustatory, and olfactory senses are presented, serially, each isolating one specific concept or sensory perception. Examples are the long rods (which isolate length), the color tablets (which isolate color), the touch tablets (which isolate rough and smooth textures), the sound cylinders (which isolate sound volume), and the smelling jars (which isolate particular scents).

Each series proceeds from simple to complex. For example, in using the first color box, the child matches only the primary colors: red, yellow, and blue. In the final work of this series, the child grades seven shades of each of nine colors, from darkest to lightest. As the child progresses through the series, increased judgment and refined perception gained from prior lessons serve as inner guides.

These exercises also advance from an immediate and concrete experience to the child's more abstract awareness of the relevant concept or quality. For example, when using the geometric cabinet, an early activity that introduces geometric figures, the child handles a blue knobbed wooden triangle and places it into a corresponding inset (like handling a piece of a simple knobbed puzzle). The name *triangle* is introduced by the teacher at some judicious point. Through subsequent activity, the child eventually recognizes a thin blue outline on a card as *triangle* and later locates other triangles in the environment ("I see a triangle on your shirt!"). By doing this, the child has internalized the image and identity of *triangle,* and knowledge has reached the conceptual stage. Later, the child will construct a definition of *triangle* as well as of the various types of triangles earlier explored in this hands-on way.

When using sensorial materials, the child is initially encouraged to follow a pattern of comparison or gradation modeled by the teacher but is later urged to experiment with other possibilities to discover variations (alternative arrangements of a material) and extensions (discovery of the relatedness of two different materials or the extension of the activity into the environment) (Torrence, 1993). Many of the sensorial materials are open-ended sets and can be used to generate a variety of child-initiated designs, thus allowing for exploration and creativity.

Language

> [Language] is not a material; it is a process. If we consider the Montessori legacy for "language as process," the language area . . . expands to include much more—the whole learning environment and, in fact, the whole world. The language curriculum becomes a context rather than a content, a smorgasbord rather than a carefully prescribed diet; and the key to the pantry is the child's own spoken language. (Turner, 1995, p. 26)

Language development in a Montessori classroom is fostered throughout the environment: the social environment of community and free exchange between children; the exact terminology offered by the teacher through specific lessons; the songs, rhymes, and conversation shared during whole-group gatherings; the selection of quality books found in the library corner; and the specific didactic materials developed to promote language and literacy development. The Montessori classroom provides a rich context for oral language development, which lays the groundwork for the child's eventual conquest of the mechanics of written language.

Montessori would concur with current whole language theorists that spoken and written language are corollaries as means of self-expression (Montessori, 1964). According to

Montessori, for the child to learn to write (which is seen as social activity), he or she must first acquire the mechanics of writing. This is accomplished in part through use of didactic material called the "metal insets," which are a variety of metal geometric templates that allow for a large number of different tracing and drawing activities, appropriate to a wide range of pencil skills (Chattin-McNichols, 1992). The child's hand is prepared for these activities in the previous handling of practical life and sensorial materials.

Development of the mechanics of writing is also accomplished through the child's handling of individual wooden letters, as well as tracing sandpaper letter forms, which have been glued to masonite plaques (the sandpaper letters) (Montessori, 1964). Through the activation and association of visual, muscular-tactile, kinesthetic, and auditory modalities (the teacher makes the letter's sound as the child handles the letter), the child, with practice, retains a mental image of each letter as well as its related sound. Eventually, the child, with a storehouse of symbols and their sounds embedded in memory, begins to investigate printed language through "writing" (sound-spelling) words and messages, at first using a large box of wooden letters (the movable alphabet) and later forming such words with a pencil or some other writing utensil.

Montessori's method of acquainting very young children with alphabetic symbols may appear to some to be "pushing" early reading. But her intentions, on the contrary, were to acquaint children with the tools of written language at a key period of sensitivity, so that later, the child's "explosion" into written language would be experienced as spontaneous, rather than as an uninspired product of so much abide-by-the-rules drudgery and rote practice.

Most contemporary Montessori teachers consider the metal insets, the sandpaper letters, and the movable alphabet as core language materials which are expanded upon by a great variety of teacher-generated materials, all designed to meet the needs and interests of specific children. Additional activities commonly found include nomenclature cards, rhyming objects and pictures, sequence story cards, go-togethers, boxes of objects grouped by phonetic commonality, picture–label matching sets, dictation games, command games (which use both pictures and words to offer instructions), and grammar games.

The Montessori language sequence assumes that writing (or encoding) generally precedes reading (or decoding), but that the two are highly interrelated. Many specific activities supporting the skills of beginning readers (labeling activities, sight word cards, as well as a wide array of phonetic and predictable texts) are included in most classrooms.

Mathematics

Mathematical thinking originates in many other seemingly unrelated activities that happen prior to experiences in the math area proper. Montessori felt that the order, precision, attention to detail, and sense of sequence fostered through use of the practical life and sensorial materials lay the foundation for what she termed the "mathematical mind." "Prerequisite activities prepare a child for the exactness and logical order required for mathematics" (Scott, 1995, p. 26).

The concept of one-to-one correspondence, for instance, is embedded in the use of dressing frames (one button for each hole), the knobbed cylinders (one cylinder for each socket), and all matching activities. The child explores and compares similarities and differences through all grading and sorting activities, explores spatial relations through making relational patterns with sensorial materials, and explores temporal relations through experiencing the predictable pattern of daily routines. The child is indirectly introduced to the base-10 system through grading sensorial series that contain 10 objects (tower of cubes, broad stair). Moreover, grading various series (e.g., long rods, knobbed cylinders) acquaints the child with the concepts of *greater than* and *less than*.

The math sequence proper begins as a logical extension of a familiar sensorial experience. The child who previously graded the 10 red rods according to length is now introduced to identical rods on which red and blue segments, denoting quantity, are included. The child orders these rods from shortest to longest, counting each segment. Later, following a visual and tactile introduction to numerical symbols (sandpaper numerals), the child returns to the rod activity, relating numerical symbol to quantity. In similar fashion, all of the Montessori mathematical materials progress gradually from the concrete and known to the abstract and unknown, targeting one difficulty at a time; math materials are the physical manifestations of abstract concepts, or "materialized abstractions" (Montessori 1967b/1948, p. 174).

Montessori math materials are grouped into four categories: (1) 0 to 10 numeration and quantification; (2) linear counting (systematic number-line counting of increasingly large numbers); (3) the decimal system (using the classic golden bead material to represent place value—unit beads, 10 bars, 100 squares, and 1,000 cubes); and (4) operations (addition, subtraction, etc.). As is generally the case with the use of Montessori materials, presentations of the math materials are brief and are always offered to a willing and interested child; materials are chosen by the child, not assigned by the teacher. The purpose for their availability and use is not to push early academics, artificial abstraction, or memorization of math facts. Rather, Montessori believed mathematics to be a natural and satisfying function of the human mind. Systematic discovery of the relationships between numbers lead children to become mathematical thinkers and problem solvers. "Abstraction is a creative process undertaken by the child to construct knowledge" (Chattin-McNichols, 1992, p. 97). As stated in the American Montessori Society's "Position State-

ment on Mathematics Education" (American Montessori Society, 1996), "mathematics arose as a way of solving problems associated with daily life—involving space, size, and quantity." Children are urged to think clearly and to use concepts learned in new and imaginative ways. The ability to understand and use concepts in problem solving is considered the purpose of all education, not just mathematics education.

Artistic Expression

"Concurrent with emphasis on the developing cognitive skills must go attention to the child's affective life, inner thoughts and feelings, and modes of self-expression" (American Montessori Society, 1996). It is to these ends that contemporary American Montessori programs emphasize child self-expression through the visual arts, music, dance, and drama (American Montessori Society, 1994).

Montessori was a pioneer in environmental aesthetics in education and saw the profound effect that aesthetic quality and overall balance in the environment can have on the young child's development. She favored an indirect environmental approach to aesthetic education during the early years, feeling it important to include beautiful and carefully selected works of art in the early childhood environment (Montessori, 1964). A wide, rich array of sensory experiences, both through classroom materials and from the natural world (Montessori, 1964, 1965), provide an ample palette for the child's later blossoming of creative expression.

Today's Montessori classrooms reflect this focus on aesthetics and rich sensory experience as well as an awareness of the importance of the visual arts in child self-expression and symbolic meaning making. A wide range of expressive art media, such as paints, clay, collage materials, various drawing and coloring media, and papier-mâché, are generally included in contemporary Montessori environments. American Montessori training courses offer core instruction in modes of child artistic expression (MACTE [Montessori Accreditation Council for Teacher Education], 1996) and many professional development workshops (AMS and North American Montessori Teachers Association [NAMTA]) are offered to deepen teachers' awareness and skill level in this important area of child development.

Music

Musical awareness and expression and training in the basic elements of music are inherent in Montessori programs (AMS, 1997). Exercises that prepare the ear for the distinction of sounds, such as the "silence game," the sound cylinders, and the Montessori bells (for distinction of pitch), are considered core curriculum in Montessori early childhood programs (Montessori, 1967b/1948). Rhythmic activities (movement on the line to various rhythms), listening to classical and other types of music, group singing, experimentation with simple musical instruments, and simple music notation (using movable wooden notes on a large staff) are music activities additionally described by Montessori and found in contemporary settings (Montessori 1967b/1948).

Montessori programs in elementary schools typically offer children the opportunity to study various instruments, as well as to read and write music and to engage in group musical experiences. For example, two schools, one located in Albuquerque, New Mexico, and one in Cincinnati, Ohio, boast elementary and high school steel drum bands, respectively (Leto, 1996).

The Cultural Subjects: Geography and Science

Embedded in Montessori's philosophical frame is a cosmic view of the systematic interrelatedness of all living and nonliving things (Montessori, 1973). This view is based on assumptions that the universe is an organizing force and that in order for the child to reach understanding of individual facts and phenomena, he or she must also gain an appreciation of the interdependent nature of all life forms and elements (Duffy & Duffy, 2002). This philosophical view underlies the Montessori approach to the life and physical sciences, as well as to what Montessori calls physical and cultural geography.

Montessori viewed the needs of humans as universal, and the study of the diverse cultures of the earth as an investigation of the ways in which humans interact with nature to meet such needs (Montessori, 1965). Cultural celebrations, unit studies of a particular culture, or the use of objects or vessels from a varied range of cultural contexts—all are ways in which the child may absorb an awareness and knowledge of different cultures within a Montessori classroom. The child is invited to choose freely from a range of areas and activities that are provided to grant many possibilities in an integrated curriculum.

For example, in the first author's classroom during a study of Japan, the children transferred objects with chopsticks and rolled sushi with rice and seaweed in the practical life area; young children matched lovely flowered fabric patterns and tasted green tea in the sensorial area; they learned Japanese expressions of routine daily communication (*hello, excuse me, thank you*) in the language area; they counted polished stones on an enameled tray in math; they assembled the puzzle map of Asia (locating Japan) in geography; they created a Japanese rock garden (raking sand and arranging rocks in pleasing patterns) in art; finally, they constructed a Japanese tea house, and two at a time, donned kimonos, entered, and served each other green tea (after observing a tea ceremony presented by a visitor) as a combination practical life or dramatic play activity.

In most Montessori classrooms, children are offered physical models of land forms (e.g., an island to surround with water, a lake to fill with water) and puzzle maps of the continents and other areas of the earth.

Scientific exploration, for preschoolers, involves "direct observation (which provides the basis for generating and testing informal hypotheses). The role of the senses in direct observation of nature provides the experimental base for later abstract thought" (American Montessori Society, 1996). For the young child, this means direct daily contact with the natural world; the opportunity to experience, label, and begin to categorize natural phenomenon; the opportunity to ask "what?" and "how?" questions; and routine interaction with an adult who is willing to serve as mentor to the child's inborn sense of wonder.

✍ THE ROLE OF THE TEACHER

Montessori's goal was nothing less than to recreate the world into a more peaceful, compassionate, and purposeful place by focusing on both the nature and development of the child. Within this scheme, the teacher's role is to regard the child respectfully, appreciate the unfolding of each child's development, and protect the child's natural impulse or drive to create her own personality (Cossentino & Whitcomb, 2003).

This being the goal Montessori realized that a new paradigm or model of the role of the teacher would have to be created (Montessori, 1964). The school and the teacher must permit freedom within a prepared environment if the goals of this new type of education are to be reached. According to Montessori, the child who is given such freedom in a carefully prepared environment will develop according to the child's own natural timetable and tendencies. Therefore, the teacher's job is not to artificially "teach in" what the child lacks but rather to be a careful observer of each child's development, providing learner-responsive materials as well as guidance in the form of instruction, consistent structure, and appropriate encouragement.

The role of teacher as observer differed most radically in Montessori's day (as it still does today) from the common notion of the teacher as the controlling, central force in the classroom. Misunderstood by some as a laissez-faire or passive stance, the observation of a trained Montessori teacher is, on the contrary, the studied observation of a scientist. "The book for the teacher, the book which inspires her own actions, and the only one in which she can read and study if she is to become an expert, is the constant observance of the children as they pass from their first disordered movements to those that are spontaneously regulated" (Montessori, 1967b/1948, p. 55). As the teacher first observes these "disordered movements" exhibited (even today) by children new to the environment and unfamiliar with the routines and materials therein, he or she sets in motion active imagination; the teacher begins to imagine a child "who is not yet there." The teacher trusts in the eventual appearance of a focused and calm child who will reveal himself or herself through the purposeful activity referred to as "work" (Montessori, 1963).

The teacher's primary roles beyond this central one of keen observer (or in today's vernacular, "kidwatcher") are to carefully prepare and maintain the learning environment, to deal with disorderly children through redirection and attention to their perceived difficulty, and to present lessons with didactic materials to those children who show interest. Teachers are also responsible for conducting large group meeting times and for maintaining careful records on each child. They are generally expected to maintain close contact with each child's family through periodic communication such as conferencing.

Montessori's method is often confused with a standard set of didactic materials, many of which were designed by her and bear her name. It is true that she developed and routinely trained teachers in the specific use of these materials and that Montessori teacher trainees today spend much time and effort consumed in mastering presentations of same. But Montessori apparently did not intend for these materials and their use to define her work. As stated in *The Montessori Method*, "This book of methods compiled by one person alone, must be followed by many others. It is my hope that, starting from the individual study of the child educated within our method, other educators will set forth the results of their experiments. These are the pedagogical books which await us in the future" (Montessori, 1964, p. 373). Accordingly, in Montessori's view, the new relationship between teacher and child, based on observation, was to be noted as the hallmark of her method, much more so than a particular set of didactic materials.

Nevertheless, the classic Montessori didactic materials, along with teacher-generated materials, do play a vital role in the child's activity in a Montessori classroom. The teacher plays an active role in establishing the initial connection between child and materials and, as such, invites the child to investigate materials and provides specific lessons on their use (Montessori, 1967b/1948). These lessons should be brief, simple, and exact. They are offered to clearly demonstrate the purpose of an activity—blueprints for subsequent investigation by the child but not standards of perfection to be exactly emulated.

Paradoxically, although the teacher is expected to have worked each lesson to mastery, this same standard is not to be imposed on the child. The offering of each lesson is intended "to stir up life, but leave it free to develop" (Montessori, 1967b/1948, p. 111).

Upon the child's purposeful involvement, the teacher should take a back seat to the child's active interaction with the material. The primary learning is seen to reside in the child's doing, not the adult's teaching. "It is the child who uses the objects; it is the child who is active, and not the teacher" (Montessori, 1967b/1948, p. 149). The trained Montessori teacher must, in fact, specialize in observing the delicate balance between intervention and nonintervention in a child's activity. The control of error, designed into the material, is intended to assist the child in suc-

cessfully investigating the material. But how does this work in practice? One survey ($N = 422$) examined teachers' reported intervention in cases when children were making errors in seriating and classifying tasks. Teachers from four countries with a wide range of experience and from seven different Montessori teacher education backgrounds were quite consistent in reporting that they would be unlikely to intervene in these situations; however, their responses were much less consistent when asked about intervening in math and language errors or in fantasy play (Chattin-McNichols, 1991).

The teacher's role is to intervene and actively redirect whenever children exhibit roughness, rudeness, or disruptive behavior, but to sensitively observe and remove herself from interference with the child's spontaneous interest and involvement whenever the child's behavior corresponds with the intended purposes of the material (Montessori, 1967b/1948). The teacher observes, records, and thereby comes to know the needs and interests of the children, preparing and maintaining an attractive, ordered learning environment that contains both traditional Montessori learning materials and those originally developed. The teacher seeks the good match between children and materials through observation, serving as a potent but subtle catalyst for child activity. The teacher offers polished, streamlined, and concise lessons, demonstrating a clear set of impressions as to the purpose and direction of a given material. The teacher redirects in cases of inappropriate or abusive acts and maintains a watcher's stance when the child is engaged in purposeful, focused activity.

✍ RESEARCH ON MONTESSORI

The research base on Montessori education is small, especially considering the approximately 5,000 schools in the United States alone (Schapiro & Hellen, 2003). Although well over 100 studies have been published, the numerous problems that beset the research literature make it impossible to draw other than very tentative conclusions (Boehnlein, 1988; Chattin-McNichols, 1981, 1992). Methodological problems include the difficulty of separating the effects of parents who have chosen Montessori from the effects of the model itself. Another common weakness is the use of a single or small number of teachers in a classroom or school that is assumed (rather than demonstrated) to be representative of best Montessori practices. The short-term nature of most studies also is incompatible with the Montessori idea of a 3-year time in a single classroom with the same teacher. A further difficulty lies in the lack of specification of the Montessori model in some study samples. Evaluations of programs that may do only a partial implementation of a Montessori program do not advance our knowledge significantly.

Nevertheless, research examining Montessori classrooms suggests the following:

- Students spend relatively little time in whole-group instruction. Rather, they move about the classroom, choose activities, work individually or in small groups, and talk with each other. This behavior set has been described as characteristic of independence (Feltin, 1987; Miller & Dyer, 1975; Wirtz, 1976).
- Work with manipulatives is more frequent than in other preschool programs (Feltin, 1987; Schmid & Black, 1977; Stodolsky & Karlson, 1972).
- Children spend significant amounts of time conversing, and a relatively high portion of this is either related to school work or actual peer teaching. Lack of similarity in observation instruments obscures the extent to which this is true at different age levels (Baines & Snortum, 1973; Feltin, 1987; Wirtz, 1976).
- Montessori children do engage in fantasy and role-playing activities, although the typical program lacks a designated role-

play/dress-up area (Black, 1977; Chattin-McNichols, 1991; Feltin, 1987; Miller & Dyer, 1975; Reuter & Yunik, 1973; Schmid & Black, 1977; Stodolsky & Karlson, 1972; Torrence, 1992; Wirtz, 1976). Bear in mind that some of these findings are stronger than others, in terms of sample size, recency of data collection, and so on.

Researchers examining outcome effects or the impact of Montessori schooling have tentatively suggested the following:

- Early studies generally showed some initial gains from Montessori preschool experience with great difficulty establishing long-term gains. In perhaps the best controlled study, Montessori children showed the highest IQs compared to other programs and controls (Miller & Bizzell, 1983, 1985; see also Dawson, 1988; Dreyer & Rigler, 1969; Duax, 1989; Karnes, Shwedel, & Williams, 1983; Miller & Dyer, 1975; Takacs & Clifford, 1988).
- With respect to academic achievement outcomes, Montessori preschools are seen as strong as any program studied. Duax (1989) examined the performance of children in a Milwaukee public Montessori program and found that only one student did not score at or above the national mean. Parent selection bias may well be a factor. Still, Duax's teacher survey data showed that Montessori graduates in middle school had higher scores on the following five items:

1. Uses basic skills necessary to survive in middle school.
2. Is responsible and can be counted on.
3. Shows enthusiasm for class topics.
4. Is individualistic and not afraid to be different.
5. Exhibits multicultural awareness.

As far as more recent studies of achievement test results and other typical measures of learning, there are only a few to report. Duax (1995) examined a private Montessori elementary school in a diverse suburb and found high levels of achievement. Glenn (1993, 1996, 1999) employed a minilongitudinal approach in accessing achievement in a private Montessori school. At 10 years, his admittedly small sample scored above the average on achievement test scores as compared to the general population. Results of perhaps greater interest came from Glenn's online survey administered to these same students during their high school and college years. Forty-five students completed the online survey, which focused on psychological, social, and vocational issues. The study postulated two hypotheses: (1) the number of Montessori Education Years (MEY) would positively relate to qualities emphasized in Montessori education; and (2) participants with any Montessori education would be at least as successful as the general population. Although tempered by drop out sample bias, findings provided considerable support for the first hypothesis on lifelong learning and self-development. The personal value of lifelong learning was identified as most prevalent among students with 10–15 MEY. The striving for self-development was manifested by a strong desire for self-understanding, general personality development, self-direction and discipline, and a strong positive attitude toward social-interactive activities.

Positive results have been found for mathematics achievement (see Baker, 1988; Bausch & Hsu, 1988; Dawson, 1988; Fero, 1997; Glenn, 1989; Miller & Bizzell, 1985; Reed, 2000; Takacs & Clifford, 1988). In one longitudinal study, mathematics achievement for boys enrolled in Montessori was statistically significantly different from children enrolled in other preschool programs and control groups at that grade level (Miller & Bizzell, 1983, 1985; Miller & Dyer, 1975). In another study, the achievement test data from public Montessori school students in the Houston schools were examined by ethnicity to discern how Montessori served children from different ethnic backgrounds. All grade and ethnicity groups scored at least one half of a grade equivalent above their actual grade. Some fifth graders had a grade equivalent of mid-tenth grade in the area of math (Dawson, 1988). Reed (2000) who studied Montessori first through third graders' procedural and conceptual abilities on place value tasks, found that these students did well in the following areas: identifying the value of digits in a number, using standard addition algorithms for multidigit numbers, solving two-digit addition and missing addend questions with and without materials, and solving word problems involving three-and-four-digit numbers.

In addition to the above-cited studies, Cisneros (1994), Curtis (1993), Fero (1997), and Manner (1999) examined achievement test scores of students from Montessori and traditional programs. Fero's and Manner's studies are typical, showing no statistically significant differences between the Montessori students and comparison groups. In Manner's study, mathematics scores for groups of Montessori and traditional students were not observed to be significantly different, although following the initial observation, the Montessori group continued to produce higher mean scores than did the traditional students. Reading scores for the groups demonstrated marginally significant differences by one analytical method, and significant differences when analyzed with a second method. In the second and third years of the study, Montessori students produced means that consistently outperformed the traditional group.

DeVries and Goncu (1988) have suggested that Montessori children are less inclined to solve interpersonal problems without conflict than are children in constructivistic programs. They compared 40 four-year-old children from constructivist and Montessori preschool programs on sociomoral development. The children's social behaviors were evaluated to examine three specific hypotheses: (1) Children from Montessori and constructivist programs would perform equally well on cognitive measures. (2) Children from constructivist programs would use higher levels of interpersonal negotiation strategies. (3) Children from Montessori and constructivist programs would engage equally often in conflict, but children from constructivist programs would resolve conflicts more cooperatively. The evaluation task consisted of a board game played in a room within the children's school, without adult regulation. The assumption was that the children would be motivated to cooperate (to have fun) and would be likely to have interpersonal conflicts (out of a desire to win). The children's verbal and nonverbal interactions were videotaped and transcribed for coding and analysis. The instrument divided social-cognitive interactions into four levels: Level 0 strategies demonstrate "raw will" without reflection of self or another's perspective. Level 1 strategies reflect the actor's wishes or needs without reference to the needs or wishes of others. Level 2 strategies demonstrate an awareness of others' needs and opinions. Level 3 strategies are thought to demonstrate an awareness of the complexity and multiple meanings inherent in group processes. According to DeVries and Goncu (1988), these levels are developmental in nature, describing a normal hierarchical sequence in progressive understanding.

Results of the analysis of game play indicated that the children from the two programs did not differ from one another in general understanding of the game and ability to count. However, children from the constructivist program did significantly better on moving markers in the correct direction toward the goal, completing the game, and proposing new rules for the game. Likewise, children from the constructivist program took turns more effectively than did Montessori children.

Results of the analysis of interactions of the pairs of children showed that Montessori pairs had a significantly higher proportion of level-1 behaviors than did constructivist pairs and that constructivist pairs had a significantly higher proportion of level-2 behaviors than did Montessori pairs. Children from the constructivist program were generally more advanced in their use of interpersonal negotiation strategies than were children from the Montessori program. Interpersonal negotiation strategies were at a significantly higher level for constructivist pairs than for Montessori pairs.

DeVries and Goncu (1988) interpreted the findings of this study to suggest that sociomoral development in young children may be affected positively by preschool experience such as that provided by constructivist education with its emphasis on child autonomy and rich interpersonal experience. The authors contrast this with experience in the Montessori classroom, which they see as quiet, orderly, and controlled by teacher authority with little social interaction. In particular, they stress that the teacher's reactions to and encouragement of children's autonomy in contexts of interpersonal conflict are critical to the children's sociomoral development. Remember though that research suggests that social interaction is taking place in Montessori classrooms (Miller & Dyer, 1975). Moreover, interpreting evaluative research on a single Montessori school, as if it is representative of all American Montessori schools, would be grossly inaccurate.

An inconsistent pattern of results is found in the difficult-to-measure area of creativity. Dreyer and Rigler (1969) compared 14 matched pairs of 5-year-old Montessori and traditional nursery school children using the Torrance Picture Construction Test, a nonverbal task of the Minnesota Test of Creative Thinking. They found that the traditional nursery school children performed significantly better than the Montessori children did on this measure. Brophy and Choquette (1973) conducted a study to test the hypothesis that teacher instruction in the correct use of classroom equipment inhibits children's ability to generate other uses for that same equipment. Subjects were 31 matched pairs of 4- and 5-year-olds from two Montessori and two traditional nursery schools. Measures of creativity were four adaptations of the Unusual Uses Test from Torrance's Minnesota Tests of Creative Thinking and Writing. Children, given a variety of objects, were asked to tell as many different uses of these items as they could. The analysis of responses revealed no signs of reduced ability on the part of Montessori children to produce verbal responses regarding divergent uses for objects. Updated research is certainly needed in this area.

In summary, some support exists for the benefits of a Montessori education during the early years. However, better designed research projects are needed to answer the questions of the Montessori method's strengths and weaknesses in greater detail. Specifically, research should examine some of the unique aspects of Montessori education. For example, the geography and geometry curricula are significantly accelerated in many early elementary Montessori classrooms. Do students really learn more in these content areas? Are Montessori children less competitive and more cooperative? Are they more accepting of racial, cultural, and national differences? Are they more self-motivated to continue their own learning and better able to initiate their own learning projects?

✒ DISCUSSION

Misconceptions About Montessori Education

Misconception: Montessori is just for special learners. Several reasons can be offered why people may have this misconception. First, Montessori began her work with children in the State Orthophrenic School in Rome, before opening the first Casa dei Bambini. Another reason people might think Montessori schools are for children with special needs (especially learners who have learning disabilities or who are gifted) is because some Montessori methods are similar to those used with learners with special educational needs. For example, the use of concrete materials and the availability of materials in many sense modalities—sight, hearing, touch, even smell and taste—are considered very appropriate educational techniques for students with learning disabilities. Also, Montessori schools in some areas have acquired a grapevine reputation of schools well-suited to deal with children who are gifted or who have learning disabilities.

Misconception: Montessori schools are religious. This is another misconception that has had a great deal of staying power because of the half-truths it contains. Montessori herself was raised as a Catholic; and both she and her followers, such as E. M. Standing, have written and spoken about the religious education of children [see Montessori's *The Mass Explained to Children* (1933) and Standing's *The Child in the Church* (1964)]. This confusion may also be traced to the fact that many of the early Montessori schools in the second wave of American Montessori movement that began in the late 1950s were Catholic. Despite these early links between Montessori and Catholicism, the majority of Montessori schools are not aligned with any religious group. The public Montessori programs cannot be; and, even if this were not so, few private school administrators would want to limit their market by choosing a particular religious orientation for their school.

Misconception: Montessori is only for the rich (or poor). Interestingly, both criticisms have been made. Montessori's first Casa dei Bambini was designed for the children of low-income workers in the San Lorenzo district of Rome. But the second American Montessori movement that began in the late 1950s was primarily a private preschool movement dependent on tuition and supported primarily by middle- or upper-income families. This economic fact is not a limitation at the model level. Private and public Montessori schools today serve children from a wide range of economic and cultural backgrounds.

Misconception: Too structured (or too free). Rigidity and structure are relative terms. If Montessori programs are seen as too rigid or overstructured, this must be in contrast to other programs or perhaps to the home environment. The bulk of this criticism seems to be based on any one of three aspects of Montessori practice. First, many people react negatively to the structure inherent in the formal instructional presentation of Montessori materials. For instance, a common reaction by teachers in training is: "Why must I memorize 17 steps to teach a child how to scrub a table?" The layout of the materials is structured a great deal, and the standards for teaching performance are very exacting. One response to this criticism, however, is to point out that perhaps the child does not perceive the same level of structure in a layout or a presentation. The child's perception may simply be one of being shown a clear, step-by-step way to do something. The reason for the extra effort in structuring the presentation so carefully is to increase the chances of success for the child.

Restricting choices to particular materials in the classroom and structuring the way a child uses the material are two other areas of concern. The words *Montessori teacher* seem to conjure up for some a picture of a teacher waiting to swoop down on a child using a material incorrectly, either correcting the child sternly or whisking the material away. This stereotype is perhaps common among people who are confusing the elaborate details required in the teacher's presentation with the expectations that a teacher has for child performance. Others, unfortunately, may have seen some very poor Montessori programs. On the model level, Montessori's position about interfering with the child is very clear. No justi-

fication exists for intervening when a child is concentrating with a material. Child concentration is in fact a main goal of the whole Montessori method, entailing the child, the teacher, the environment, and the materials. Even necessary interruptions such as snack time can be minimized through self-service eating arrangements in the well-run Montessori classroom.

The teacher certainly intervenes if children are in danger of hurting themselves or other children or damaging the materials or the classroom. Decision making is more difficult when the child is using the materials in a nondestructive way but in a way unrelated to their intended didactic purpose. For example, the broad stair materials are designed to give the child experience with length, width, and height. Many free-form building activities with these materials would support this growth. However, using the stair as a sword would not be viewed as supportive and would not be permitted, even if the child is not endangering or disturbing others. Space fortresses built with the broad stairs would result in a borderline decision. To make a decision in a case like this would require additional information including the child's level of concentration, mastery of dimension knowledge given by the materials, self-esteem, and interests in other areas, and whether alternative building materials are available.

Whenever called for, teacher intervention is given in the form of a suggestion, redirecting activity to a different use of the material or toward another material. Even when teachers seem too quick to intervene and redirect, it is appropriate to keep in mind that the richness of the Montessori environment makes it likely that the child will be able to find another activity meeting the child's needs and interests.

Structure can be defined as control over or limitation of the child's choices. Many teachers in Montessori classrooms feel that a child must have a short teacher-led lesson with a material before working with it alone; sometimes teachers are content if the child has observed a lesson given to another child or group of children. Montessori teachers generally work very hard to make sure that each child has many activities from which to choose, introducing new materials and granting their independent use as quickly as is appropriate. Also, especially at the beginning of a new school year, materials are provided that need no introduction, such as Lego blocks and simple puzzles.

Whether Montessori children can do whatever they want is a question readily answered by observing any good Montessori classroom. Certainly, the children have a great deal of freedom. But choices have limits, set both by the teacher and the environment. Children learn in the atmosphere of the Montessori classroom at least as well as children in other programs.

Are the children allowed to play? Montessori was opposed to several very specific kinds of fantasy for children under 6 years of age, particularly teacher-directed fantasy in the Froebellian tradition (Montessori, 1965). Viewing pretense as "something of little importance," Montessori (1966) favored real-world activity, which she felt would offer children a sensory base for the development of their imaginations. Although dramatic play has not been a major focus in Montessori classrooms or in Montessori teacher education programs, with the increase in the number of Montessori child-care programs (as opposed to half-day preschool classrooms), teachers have increasingly raised the question of how to provide for this legitimate need within Montessori settings.

Scant research exists on teacher allowance or encouragement of dramatic play in contemporary Montessori classrooms. One questionnaire study ($N = 144$; Torrence, 1992) asked experienced Montessori teachers to identify classroom areas where unsanctioned play occurred, typical teacher reactions, and a list of play materials included in these environments. Results indicated that standard play materials

(puppets, dolls, dress-up clothes) were seldom included in Montessori classroom environments. Blocks and Legos were the play props most frequently found (70% of respondents). Almost all respondents indicated that they observed pretend play to occur at some point during the designated "work" time. Teachers divided their responses to specific situations: Many indicated that they would be unlikely to intervene with a child who was pretending with a didactic material, depending on the individual nature of the situation. Some respondents reported ambiguity in their feelings about dramatic play, recognizing its importance in child development yet feeling uncertain as to how to best provide for this need in a Montessori setting (Torrence, 1992).

In summary, because current theory and research support the importance of dramatic play in the child's overall development, present-day Montessorians are constantly reinvestigating this issue and are continuing to find new ways to incorporate dramatic play activity into early childhood settings.

Misconception: Too much (not enough) academics. The purposeful, ordered activity of a good Montessori classroom answers most people's concern that Montessori children can "do whatever they want." The criticism that Montessori schools push children too far, too fast, is unfortunately true for some Montessori schools, although it is the furthest thing possible from the Montessori model. Both Montessori's writings and the teacher education program that the Montessori model is based on stress the individual needs and capabilities of each child. Montessori's dictum "Follow the child" speaks for itself. But in almost every city, you may find what has been called "clipboard Montessori," in which a Montessori teacher may descend on a child to suggest that he or she now choose some math, reading, or "challenging work." The fact is that many Montessori schools serve middle- and upper-class families.

Increasingly, these families see preschools as a necessary first step in a child's education or even as a prerequisite to acceptance at the "best" private elementary schools. In far too many cases, administrators and teachers have given in to parent pressure to produce graduates of Montessori classrooms who are at a high level of competence in reading and math skills. Many children will develop these skills as a result of their own choices in the classroom. And the Montessori materials are quite successful at allowing children to learn even if the teacher and not the child has chosen an activity. But this force-feeding of children to bring them up to a certain standard by a certain age is clearly in contrast to Montessori's most central ideas.

Misconception: Montessori is out of date. The idea that a program as old as Montessori should have changed is based on the knowledge that we have learned a great deal in the fields of child development and early childhood education since the beginnings of the Montessori method. The most significant response to this question is that certain parts of the Montessori curriculum are designed to change with the perceived needs of a given group of children. For example, the practical life area should reflect the real world, in particular the culture or cultures of the children in the classroom. Practical life in Japan includes silk scarf tying, which may not be on the shelf in Cleveland.

As has been mentioned, almost all of the materials and activities on the shelves in the language area, both in programs for 3- to 6-year-olds and in elementary classrooms, have been developed by Montessori educators, rather than by Montessori herself. The core materials are still there: the metal insets, sandpaper letters, and the movable alphabet. But most of the other materials found in this area, especially materials made for English-speaking children and teachers, had to be subsequently created— and this area continues to grow and develop. The best Montessori schools and teacher education programs are true to Montessori's empirical traditions; they constantly make small changes and adjustments and carefully observe the children's reactions.

The elementary Montessori materials were developed by a number of people. Montessori herself, of course, created materials and activities but so did Maria Montessori and elementary teacher trainers, especially at the International Center for Montessori Studies in Bergamo, Italy. This curriculum continues to grow and change. For example, the science curriculum is constantly being revised, with new findings in physics and earth science, and with taxonomy changes in the life sciences. More infrequently, changes are made for pedagogic reasons (see Lanaro's 1984 article on classification development in the magazine *The Constructive Triangle* for examples of ways in which a better understanding of the child's development can affect the materials used).

Still, a great deal of what Montessori describes in her books can be seen in contemporary classrooms. Why has this not changed or been brought up to date? The answer is that it is still as up to date as it was when Montessori developed it. The sensorial curriculum still attracts children and still provides them with a rich and challenging (graded difficulty) environment in which to practice matching, seriating, and classifying activities. Montessori's ideas of the environment and of teacher behaviors and expectations still result in happy, self-motivated, and independent children. In many respects, some may even argue that early childhood education has taken decades to catch up to Montessori.

PUBLIC MONTESSORI PROGRAMS

Approximately 150 public school districts operate some kind of Montessori program. Ranging in size from a single classroom or a few classrooms run as a "school within a school", to districts like Cincinnati which has five complete schools (including a high school) using Montessori methods (Kahn, 1990).

A 1981 survey (Chattin-McNichols) collected data via questionnaire from 25 of the approximately 50 school districts known to have Montessori programs at that time. The only other known study is fortunately more recent (Michelessen & Cummings, 1991). The Michelessen and Cummings study received responses during the 1990–1991 school year from 63 school districts or schools.

The 1981 survey (Chattin-McNichols, 1981) asked questions about the origins of the public school Montessori programs, their costs, training of teachers, and other demographics. These data were limited by the 50% return rate (selection bias) and by the lack of control over who completed the survey (their positions varied, including principals, Montessori specialists, teachers, and support personnel). The newer survey (Michelessen & Cummings, 1991), while more current and comprising more respondents, suffers from the same limitations.

The 25 districts surveyed in the 1981 study served 5,035 children (Chattin-McNichols, 1981). In 1991, the number of students at the 63 schools studied averaged 233, with a total of over 14,000 students (Michelessen & Cummings, 1991).

Few public school Montessori programs serve children under age 5 years. While this climbed to 42% in 1991, only a minority of the public Montessori programs provide the full 3-year age span of 3-, 4-, and 5-year-olds (Chattin-McNichols, 1981; Michelessen & Cummings, 1991). Many others provide either a different age mix, such as 5-, 6-, and 7-year-olds, or only elementary Montessori. This points to one of the major issues in public Montessori: The extent to which the public programs are implementing a full Montessori model. Clearly, districts vary in the degree to which they fully implement the Montessori model.

In the 1981 sample, approximately one-third of the "Montessori" programs used single-age grouping, one third reported 3-year spans, and the rest used 2-year spans or did not answer the question. Initial impetus for the Montessori programs in the 1991 survey came from parents (26 cases), teachers (13 cases), administrators (39 cases), and in 17 cases, other sources. Some schools reported more than one source of impetus for the Montessori program (Chattin-McNichols, 1981; Michelessen & Cummings, 1991).

Perhaps the biggest problem in starting and maintaining a high-quality public program is the scarcity of good Montessori elementary teachers. To teach in a public program, the teacher must have both state teaching certification and Montessori elementary teacher training. Practically, this means that either a state certified teacher must become so enamored of Montessori to take either a year or at least a summer to study Montessori, or that a Montessori elementary teacher takes a year off to enroll in a program to become a state certified teacher. In either case, the teacher is paying tuition twice and is certainly having to sit through at least some of the same content twice. Even with the higher public school salaries and benefit packages (compared to private schools), public programs often have a hard time filling positions. This usually results in teachers working in Montessori programs without the combination of full elementary Montessori certification or state credentials.

Montessori programs usually are successful magnets in both attracting and retaining students and in educating them well, as shown by the achievement test data (Dawson, 1988; Duax, 1989; Takacs & Clifford, 1988; Villegas & Biwer, 1987). Duax (1995) looked at attrition patterns at a nonselective Montessori magnet school in Milwaukee and found that children were retained at a rate approximately twice that of the district average, and that there was no significant difference in retention of African American versus Anglo-American students.

Montessori programs are a continuous and steady presence in public schools today.

Up-to-date information on public Montessori schools is available. Descriptions of current public Montessori programs are available from a new resource group called The Montessori Public Schools Consortium, representing AMI, AMS, and NAMTA. This consortium can be reached at the NAMTA address given later. There is also a newsletter called *Public School Montessorian,* circulated free to all public programs, which provides a forum for discussion of the issues that impact public Montessori programs. The newsletter is published by Jola Publications, Box 8354, Minneapolis, MN 55408.

In general, public school Montessori continues to grow. The decline in federal support for magnet programs (especially start-up money) seems to have reduced only slightly the launching of Montessori public school programs. Those public programs started through persistent parent advocacy seem to be continuing, perhaps in part because of Montessori's continued success in the private sector. The charter school movement has led to additional publicly funded Montessori programs in seven states (Schapiro & Hellen, 2003).

Current difficulties continue to be the training of public Montessori school teachers and the tendency for the last years in the Montessori school (typically fourth and fifth grades) to become much more traditional, as concerns increase about the transfer to non-Montessori school settings. Also, the increased push for standardized achievement testing has emerged as an issue on which traditional education and Montessori education have sharply differing views.

✸ CONCLUSION

The Montessori approach to education has both historic and contemporary significance. Rooted in the early twentieth-century work of one person, it is tempting for critics to view this as a personality-based movement that is rigidly fixed in time. In truth, some of Montessori's most

Developmentally appropriate ways to teach academic content with specialized tools of learning—a major Montessorian contribution to early childhood education today.

ardent proponents, in an effort to replicate her method, do little to correct this impression, and many of her writings do appear dated, at least in style.

Yet Dr. Montessori's central vision as well as many key practices were well ahead of their time and remain as viable and relevant today as they were 80 years ago. Practices and constructs such as multiage groupings, peer tutoring, individualized and child-centered learning, holistic education, the prepared and learner-responsive environment, the teacher as observer and guide, the use of hands-on manipulatives as tools for learning, respect for each individual's inherent potential—all are central to the Montessori philosophy. Much more so than a particular set of didactic materials, these aspects are integral to good Montessori practice and make the Montessori approach a viable option with potent possibilities for contemporary educators. The Montessori approach seen in a high-quality fully implemented program accords with developmentally appropriate practices as espoused by the National Association for the Education of Young Children (Humphryes, 1998).

Furthermore, currently, the core Montessori curriculum continues to be developed and expanded by innovative teachers applying Montessori principles to new situations and to meet the interests and needs of diverse individual learners. Over the past two decades, Montessori programs have been incorporated into many public school systems as an experimental model, expanding the availability of this largely private school movement to a wider base of socioeconomic, racial, and cultural groupings.

Research has only begun to keep up with the results of the Montessori public school venture, as well as the long-term results of Montessori education in general. Hopefully, a range of longitudinal, experimental, and naturalistic studies can be undertaken to further document current practice and to seek answers to far-reaching questions regarding the nature and effects of the Montessori school experience.

REFERENCES

American Montessori Society. (1994). *Montessori education*. New York: Author.

American Montessori Society. (1996). *American Montessori Society position papers*. New York: Author. Available at http://www.amshg.org.

American Montessori Society. (1997). *American Montessori Society Position Papers*. New York: Author. Available at http://www.amshq.org.

Baines, M., & Snortum, J. (1973). A time-sampling analysis of Montessori versus traditional classroom interaction. *Journal of Educational Research, 66,* 313–316.

Baker, K. (1988). *The interpretation of subtraction held by children in the Association Montessori Internationale curriculum*. Unpublished master's thesis, University of Maryland.

Bausch, J., & Hsu, H. (1988). Montessori: Right or wrong about number concepts? *Arithmetic Teacher, 35* (6), 8–11.

Bergen, D. (Ed.). (1988). *Play as a medium for learning and development*. Portsmouth, NH: Heinemann.

Black, S. (1977). *A comparison of cognitive and social development in British infant and Montessori preschools*. Unpublished doctoral dissertation, Temple University.

Boehnlein, M. (1988). Montessori research: Analysis in retrospect. *Special Edition of the North American Montessori Teachers' Association Journal, 13* (3).

Bogart, L. (1992). Transmitting the tools of a culture. *Montessori Life, 4* (3), 27–28.

Brophy, J., & Choquette, J. (1973, March). *Divergent production in Montessori children*. Paper presented at the biennial meeting of the Society for Research in Child Development, Philadelphia.

Chattin-McNichols, J. (1981). The effects of Montessori school experience. *Young Children, 36,* 49–66.

Chattin-McNichols, J. (1991). *Montessori teachers' intervention: Preliminary findings from an international study*. Urbana-Champaign, IL. (ERIC Document Reproduction Service No. ED 341 499).

Chattin-McNichols, J. (1992). *The Montessori controversy*. Albany, NY: Delmar.

Cisneros, M. (1994). *Multiple measures of the effectiveness of public school Montessori education in the third grade*. Unpublished doctoral dissertation. University of North Texas.

Cossentino, J., & Whitcomb, J. (2003 April). *Culture, coherence, and craft-oriented teacher education & the case of Montessori teacher training*. Paper presented at the Annual

Meeting of American Educational Research Association, Chicago, IL.

Curtis, O. A. (1993). *A comparative analysis of elementary students' achievement in Montessori and SIGHTS programs in an urban school.* Unpublished doctoral dissertation, Texas Southern University.

Dawson, M. A. (1988). *Comparative analysis of the standardized test scores of students enrolled in HISD Montessori magnet and traditional elementary classrooms.* Unpublished master's thesis, Texas Southern University.

DeVries, R., & Goncu, A. (1988). Interpersonal relations in four-year-old dyads from constructivist and Montessori programs. *Journal of Applied Developmental Psychology, 8,* 481–501.

Dreyer, A. S., & Rigler, D. (1969). Cognitive performance in Montessori and nursery school children. *Journal of Educational Research, 67,* 411–416.

Duax, T. (1989). Preliminary report on the educational effectiveness of a Montessori school in the public sector. *North American Montessori Teachers' Association Quarterly, 14,* 2.

Duax, T. (1995). Report on academic achievement in a private Montessori school. *NAMTA Journal, 20* (2).

Duffy, M., & Duffy, D. (2002). *Children of the universe* Hollidaysburg, PA: Parent Child Press.

Elkind, D. (1998). *Reinventing childhood: Raising and educating children in a changing world.* Rosemont, NJ: Modern Learning.

Feltin, P. (1987). *Independent learning in four Montessori elementary classrooms.* Unpublished doctoral dissertation, Seattle University.

Fero, J. R. (1997). *A comparison of academic achievement of students taught by the Montessori method and by traditional methods of instruction in the elementary grades.* Unpublished doctoral dissertation, Montana State University, Bozeman.

Glenn, C. (1989). A comparison of lower and upper elementary Montessori students with a public school sample. *North American Montessori Teachers' Association Quarterly, 14,* 263–268.

Glenn, C. (1993). *The longitudinal assessment study: Cycle 3* (Seven Year) Follow Up. (ERIC Document Reproduction Service, No. ED 370679).

Glenn, C. (1996). *The longitudinal assessment study: Cycle Four (Ten Year) Follow Up.* (ERIC Document Reproduction Service, No. ED 403013).

Glenn, C. (1999). The longitudinal assessment study: Thirteen Year Follow Up. (ERIC Document Reproduction Service, No. ED 431543).

Grazzini, C. (1996). The four planes of development. *The NAMTA Journal, 21* (2), 208–241.

Humphryes, J. (1998). The developmental appropriateness of high-quality Montessori programs. *Young Children, 53* (4), 4–16.

Hunt, J. McV. (1964). Introduction. In M. Montessori (Ed.), *The Montessori method* (pp. xi–xxxix). New York: Schocken.

Kahn, D. (Ed.). (1990). *Implementing Montessori education in the public sector.* Cleveland, OH: North American Montessori Teachers' Association.

Karnes, M., Shwedel, A., & Williams, M. (1983). A comparison of five approaches for educating young children from low-income homes. In *The Consortium for Longitudinal Studies* (Ed.), *As the twig is bent: Lasting effects of preschool programs.* (pp. 133–169). Hillsdale, NJ: Erlbaum.

Katz, L. (1992). Questions about Montessori education today. In M. H. Loeffler (Ed.), *Montessori in contemporary American culture* (pp. 183–194). Portsmouth, NH: Heinemann.

Kilpatrick, W. H. (1914). *The Montessori system examined.* Boston: Houghton Mifflin.

Lanaro, P. (1984). Classification development in the Montessori classroom. *The Constructive Triangle, 11,* 1, 4–11.

Leto, F. (1996). Let the music flow: A conversation with Frank Leto. *Montessori Life, 8* (5), 22–26.

Lillard, P. (1972). *Montessori. A modern approach.* New York: Schocken.

Lindauer, S. K. (1993). Montessori education for young children. In J. L. Roopnarine & J. Johnson (Eds.), *Approaches to early childhood education,* 2nd ed. (pp. 243–259). Upper Saddle River, NJ: Merrill/Prentice Hall.

Loeffler, M. H. (1992). Montessori and constructivism. In M. H. Loeffler (Ed.), *Montessori in contemporary American culture* (pp. 101–113). Portsmouth, NH: Heinemann.

MACTE. (1996). *Montessori accreditation council for teacher education standards for teacher education programs.* Pasadena, CA: Author.

Manner, J. A. (1999). *A comparison of academic achievement of Montessori and non-Montessori students in a public school setting.* Unpublished doctoral dissertation, Florida International University.

Michelessen, P., & Cummings, L. (1991). *Survey results: Public Montessori school survey.* Rockford, IL: Rockford Montessori School Parents Group.

Miller, L., & Bizzell, R. (1983). Long-term effects of four preschool programs: Sixth, seventh, and eighth grades. *Child Development, 54* (3), 727–741.

Miller, L., & Bizzell, R. (1985). Long-term effects of four preschool programs: Ninth- and tenth-grade results. *Child Development, 55* (4), 1570–1587.

Miller, L., & Dyer, L. (1975). Four preschool programs: Their dimensions and effects. *Monographs of the Society for Research in Child Development, 40* (Serial No. 162).

Montessori, M. (1913). *Pedagogical anthropology.* New York: Stokes.

Montessori, M. (1933). *The mass explained to children.* London: Sheed & Ward.

Montessori, M. (1963). *Education for a new world.* Madras, India: Vasanta Press.

Montessori, M. (1964). *The Montessori method.* New York: Schocken.

Montessori, M. (1965). *Spontaneous activity in education.* New York: Schocken.

Montessori, M. (1966). *The secret of childhood.* Notre Dame, IN: Fides.

Montessori, M. (1967a). *The absorbent mind.* New York: Dell. (Original work published 1949).

Montessori, M. (1967b). *The discovery of the child.* Notre Dame, IN: Fides. (Original work published 1948).

Montessori, M. (1973). *From childhood to adolescence.* New York: Schocken.

Rambusch, N. M. (1962). *Learning how to learn.* Baltimore: Helicon.

Reed, M. (2000). *A comparison of the place value understanding of Montessori and non-Montessori elementary school students.* Unpublished doctoral dissertation, Ohio State University.

Reuter, J., & Yunik, G. (1973). Social interaction in nursery schools. *Developmental Psychology, 9,* 319–325.

Schapiro, D., & Hellen, B. (2003). *Montessori community resource.* Minneapolis, MN: Jola.

Schmid, J., & Black, K. (1977). An observational study of the choice and use of toys by Montessori and non-Montessori preschoolers. In S. Makhick & J. Henne (Eds.), *Evaluations of educational outcomes: Proceedings of the national conference on the evaluation of Montessori and open classrooms* (pp. 79–92). New York: American Montessori Society.

Scott, J. (1995). The development of the mathematical mind. *Montessori Life, 7* (2), 25.

Shute, N. (2002, September). Madam Montessori. *Smithsonian,* 70–74.

Standing, E. M. (1964). *The child in the church.* Notre Dame, IN: Fides.

Stodolsky, S., & Karlson, A. (1972). Differential outcomes of a Montessori curriculum. *Elementary School Journal, 72,* 419–433.

Takacs, C., & Clifford, A. (1988). Performance of Montessori graduates in public school classrooms. *North American Montessori Teachers' Association Quarterly, 14* (1), 2–9.

Torrence, M. (1992). Montessori and play: Theory vs. practice. *Montessori Life, 7* (3), 35–38.

Torrence, M. (1993). From percept to concept: The sensorial path to knowledge. *Montessori Life, 5* (3), 28–30.

Turner, J. (1995). How do you teach reading? *Montessori Life, 7* (3), 25–34.

Villegas, A., & Biwer, P. (1987). Parent involvement in a Montessori program: The Denver public school experience. *North American Montessori Teachers' Association Quarterly, 13* (1), 13–24.

Wirtz, P. (1976). *Social behavior related to material settings in the Montessori preschool environment.* Unpublished doctoral dissertation, George Peabody College for Teachers.

MONTESSORI WEB RESOURCES

Who Was Maria Montessori

www.montessori-namta.org/NAMTA/geninfo/
   mnbio.html

This site gives an introduction to Maria Montessori, a bit of history, and an introduction to her ideas.

All about Montessori Schools

www.montessori.org/search/searchuschool.html

This URL will let you search a database of Montessori schools by location, name, or other keywords.

Technology and Research in Montessori Classrooms

http://tac-staff.seattleu.edu/jcm/montmain.html

This site (maintained by one of the authors of this chapter) has some general information but is focused on the use of technology in Montessori classrooms and on research, especially teacher research. It includes an annotated bibliography of Montessori books.

All about the American Montessori Society

www.amshq.org

This is the American Montessori Society's site, including a database of schools, position papers, upcoming conferences, teacher education program listings, award winners for the best research thesis and dissertation on Montessori, and more.

All You Need to Know about NAMTA or NAMTO

www.montessori-namta.org

This is the site for the North American Montessori Teachers Organization, with information on its activities, including upcoming conferences.

What You Need to Know about the Toronto Montessori School

www.toronto-montessori.on.ca

The Toronto Montessori School's site has a long list of other resources on Montessori.

MAJOR U.S. MONTESSORI ORGANIZATIONS

American Montessori Society (AMS)
281 Park Ave. South, 6th Floor
New York, NY 10011
212-358-1250

Association Montessori Internationale
(AMI/USA)
410 Alexander St.
Rochester, NY 14607–1028
716-461-5920

Montessori Accreditation Council for Teacher
Education (MACTE)
17583 Oak Street
Fountain Valley, CA 92708
888-446-2283

North American Montessori Teachers Association
(NAMTA)
11424 Bellflower Rd. NE
Cleveland, OH 44106
216-421-1905

Chapter 17

The Pyramid Method

Jef J. van Kuyk ∽ Citogroep, Arnhem, The Netherlands

yramid is an educational method for all children between the ages of 2½ and 6 years. The method has a number of special features for children who need extra support. These include extra language stimulation, extra play and learning activities, and tutoring (Kuyk, 2001).

Education in the Pyramid Method means that we start close to the vulnerable child who cannot yet manage daily tasks without our help and support. At the same time we stimulate children to distance themselves from us so they can learn to manage on their own.

One of the most interesting discoveries in recent times has been that we now know that we do not have to wait until the brain is ready for development to occur. Research has shown that the first years are very important for the development of the child's brain and that its potential needs to be supported by the child's environment and experiences (Shonkoff & Philips, 2000). Through these experiences linkages are created between brain cells. Children need these linkages in order to learn at a higher level. For this reason alone we should offer children a wide variety of enriching experiences. We do not need to wait. We should, in fact, stimulate children from an early age.

Research that goes beyond the theories of Piaget (1970) and Vygotsky (1962) also shows that when children are well supported by adults—that is to say receive the sort of support that allows them to progress but also to retain their own initiative—they will begin to function at higher levels than would otherwise be the case (Fischer & Bidell, 1998). If we let children play alone, they will continue at the same level for a long time, but they will learn at a higher level if supported. The teacher can give this support by playing with the children, providing support in initiative learning, giving directions, and showing them things in such a way that they can discover for themselves where they should go. Children like it when we play and learn with them; they are interested in being given instructions that help them make progress. They not only learn but they also persevere longer in looking for solutions; in fact, they are more motivated to keep on trying to find solutions. And—for learning—this is an important attitude (Bowman, Donovan, & Burns, 2000).

BASIC CONCEPTS

The Pyramid Method is built upon a number of basic concepts. One should see the method as a closely woven construction, a Pyramid. It has a broad base and as such can offer security to many children. There are four basic concepts that are the cornerstones of the Pyramid (see Figure 17–1).

Nearness

In educating children, it is important that the attachment between the child and the educator

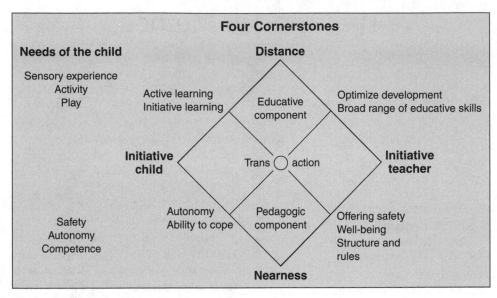

FIGURE 17–1 Pedagogic and Educative Components

is a solid one (Ainsworth, Bowlby, 1969; Blehar, & Waters, 1978; Erikson, Sroufe, & Egeland, 1985). It is important that the child has the feeling that the educator is close by. This makes the child feel safe, secure, and free enough to go on and explore the world. The educator gives the child this freedom but, at the same time, creates a clear structure and establishes rules. These rules are not to restrict the child, but to indicate where there is room for playing and learning. Structure and rules also give the child a sense of safety. In a safe environment children take the initiative and go and explore the world. The task of the educator is to pick up signals from the child and to find the answers that will allow the child to be himself or herself. The educator gives emotional support when needed and respects the autonomy of the child. Children may, for example, show signs that they are not yet ready to take part in group activities. Such signals should be respected. If children are playing intensively, the educator should remain in the background. If they reach an impasse, then he or she can offer more intensive guidance. We refer to this as a *sensitive response attitude.*

Distance

The distancing concept is based on distancing theory (Cocking & Renninger, 1993; Sigel, 1993). Distancing can serve as instructions within Vygotsky's zone of proximal development (Vygotsky, 1962). Under the condition of nearness the teacher takes distance from the here and now. He or she must begin close to the child in here-and-now situations, things that can be directly observed with the senses or by using concrete material. At the same time, the teacher must help the child establish more and more distance from these things. The teacher asks here-and-now questions but then also asks questions and talks about things that are not in the here and now. In this way children learn that the world existed before they were born and that their mothers and fathers were also small children once. They also learn to think about places that they have never seen before or things that have happened long ago or that have not yet happened. For example, we are going on holiday. What will the place we are going to look like? What did you do yesterday? What are you going to do tomorrow or next week?

In this way children learn to create representations that can be recalled later on. Research has shown that children with parents who do all sorts of things with them outside the here and now develop very strongly. Parents who stay in the here and now have children who are less developed or who may even display signs of underdeveloped skills (Sigel, 1993). The basic principle is: Begin close by with very concrete situations and materials and then start making those things that are not in the here and now present by using fantasy, representations, and questions.

The Child's Initiative

The question raised here is: To what extent can children optimize their development on their own? According to the theory of Piaget (1970), children have enough cognitive power to direct their own development. This is done through confrontation with objects from their physical and social environment. The child's initiative is the beginning and end of the educational process. The human being is oriented toward self-regulation (Fischer & Bidell, 1998). As soon as a child is born, we see that he or she wants to discover the world. At a very early age, children begin to grasp objects. They listen to sounds and follow movements. They pay attention to things that interest them and lose interest when things are known. They learn to make choices by themselves. The first objective of the Pyramid Method is to support and optimize the child's capacity to take the initiative. It is also the ultimate objective, because later the child must be able to manage everyday life. For this, a child's own initiative is essential.

The Teacher's Initiative

The question asked in the teacher's initiative context is: What teacher initiative secures optimum development? The initiative of the teacher is essential in the education process (Fischer & Bidell, 1998; Geert, 1998). The role of the teacher is to scaffold children in their development. It is an image that suggests aiding someone to work in areas that cannot be reached without support (Bowman, Donovan, & Burns, 2001). During play the teacher can support the child by stimulating him or her to take the initiative. However, the teacher also takes initiatives that encourage optimal development. He or she does this during group activities or when children are carrying out tasks on their own. The teacher has a broad spectrum of educative skills. The teacher creates possibilities, offers support, motivates, sets a good example, gives instructions, and guides children in learning to think about and solve problems.

THE RELATIONSHIP BETWEEN THE BASIC CONCEPTS

In the Pyramid Method, we identify four basic concepts, and emphasize the strong interrelationship among them. If the child takes strong initiatives, the educator can stay in the background. If the child shows little initiative, the teacher must provide some support. Nearness and distance are strongly related to each other. Through nearness it is possible to take distance: If children feel safe they can start to explore, they can take distance from the here and now.

All four concepts come together in the pedagogic and educative components. The pedagogic component relates to the way in which the teacher treats the children and deals with them, offering safety and well-being, having respect for the autonomy of the child, and offering structure, rules, and optimal conditions such as quietness and the avoidance of stress. The teacher takes into consideration the pedagogic needs of the child: the need for safety, the need to be oneself (autonomy), as well as the need to get a grip on things (competency). The educative component relates to the way the teacher stimulates and optimizes the child's development. The teacher has a broad range of educative skills to stimulate the child's development. The most important skills are supporting and enriching play, providing support for initiative learning to let the children keep the initiative with a maximum result, providing examples to learn concepts, and giving instructions and scaffolding. Expert scaffolding is the highest skill. Here the teacher uses his or her experience and knowledge to ask open and distant questions in order to teach high-level representations (anticipation, evaluation, conclusion, reflection) (Fischer & Bidell, 1998; Sigel, 1993). The teacher must take into account the educational needs of the young child including the need for sensory experience, the desire to do things in an active way, and the need to play.

🐌 OPTIMIZING

We have shown that the way we work in the school situation is much the same as in the home situation, but the environment is much more complex. Let us reflect on how we do this. Research has shown that children can function at many different levels of thought and action (see Figure 17–2). It is not true that

they always function at the same level. The level they will function at will depend on the circumstances (Fischer & Bidell, 1998). If the pedagogic environment is good, the child will act in a normal way. If circumstances are less favorable, if there is unrest or stress, then the child will function at a minimal level. If for instance children are disturbed by lack of structure and rules they will not be able to function at a normal level.

If the pedagogic component is not in order, a child cannot develop well. In educational terms, however, it is a fact that we can stimulate children to rise above their normal level. From research it appears that good educational support can lead to children reaching an optimal level of development (Fischer & Bidell, 1998; Sigel, 1993). This can be done, for example, by supporting children in their play and by stimulating initiative learning. During individual activity the teacher can enrich the child's play by introducing a new role or material or he or she can support the writing of a word the child has chosen. In group activities he or she can provide clear examples, describe the main features of a situation, or guide the process of growth in a plant. To help children learn in an active way

FIGURE 17–2 Levels of Action and Thought and Social Support

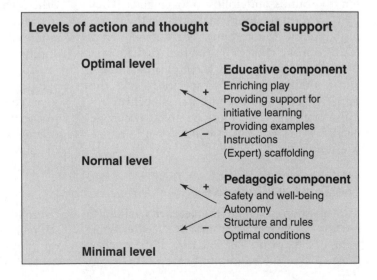

scaffolding is provided giving support that can bring the child to a higher level. Support is given only to the extent that it does not impinge on the capacity of the child to take the initiative: Vygotsky's proximal zone. Expert scaffolding provided by a teacher with considerable knowledge and experience is the best. For this reason, we attach special importance to stimulating the development of all the children in the Pyramid Method. By stimulating children at an early age we lay the basis for success at school and encourage them to deal with everyday tasks by themselves.

As far as the education of young children is concerned, we should ensure the pedagogic component is such that children can function in a normal way. The educative component will then ensure that children reach their optimal level. This requires considerable professionalism because we are not just concerned with optimizing the development of one child but the whole group. This demands a broad repertoire of educational skills.

INITIATIVE LEARNING AND LEARNING TOGETHER

Piaget (1970) was an advocate of the principle that children should learn and discover things for themselves. Vygotsky (1962) championed the fact that children should learn in the company of an adult. In the Pyramid Method, we make use of the advantages of both these approaches by giving children the chance to play and learn by themselves and with teachers (Geert, 1998). Does this mean that the teacher should continually strive for an optimal level of development with each child? Even though this might be desirable, it is not possible. We cannot continually operate at top capacity and neither can a child. It is necessary to alternate between concentration and relaxation (Fischer & Rose, 1998). The teacher has to provide for a large group of children—between 12 and 15 in the case of young children and sometimes between 20 and 25 in the case of the older ones. It is impossible to give all children individual attention at all times. It is important that the teacher finds a balance between what children themselves can learn and things that must be learnt with the teacher. The teacher offers the pedagogic and educational support that the child requires for active learning given his or her level of development and independence.

THREE LEVELS OF INTERVENTION

We differentiate three levels of intervention in order to ensure that the support children need when they decide to take the initiative, and what children must learn as individuals or in a group supported by the teacher's initiative, are in good balance and attuned to each other. (See Figure 17–3.)

Low Level

The children play and learn independently without intervention from their teacher. The teacher gives little or no support. If support is necessary, the teacher will adjust it to the developmental level of the child and the degree of independence displayed.

Middle Level

The children play and learn together with the teacher. A middle level of support is given either in large or small groups. During the projects the teacher initially gives more than the average amount of support to help get the process started. Then, slowly, the teacher tries to hand over activities to the children bit by bit. The amount of help offered depends on the level of development and the degree of independence the children display.

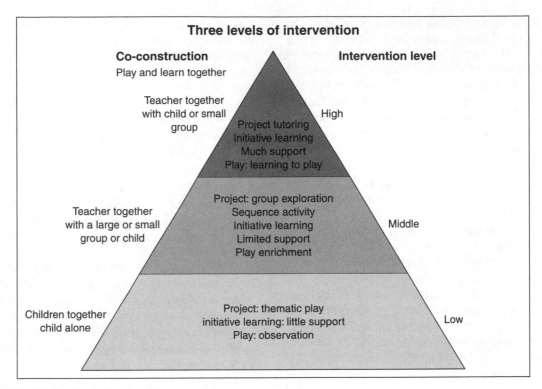

FIGURE 17–3 Three Levels of Intervention

High Level

The teacher or tutor (individual support by a special teacher) plays or teaches individual children or smaller groups requiring extra help. The teacher or tutor, therefore, gives considerable support. In general the developmental level of the children will be low and their degree of independence limited. The intensity of help is in proportion to what is needed to bring children to a higher level of development and to make them more independent.

✑ FOUR PROGRAMS

In the Pyramid Method we have four programs to work out the pedagogic and educative components from the initiative of the child or the initiative of the teacher to optimize the development of the children. Two programs are

initiated by the child: play and initiative learning. *Initiative learning* is a new term we use to make clear that children want to learn and are ready to take the initiative in doing so. Two other programs are initiated by the teacher: project themes, in which the teacher explores the outside world with the children, and sequential activities in which a hierarchy of activities is offered for the children to learn (see Figure 17–4).

Initiative child	Initiative teacher
Play	Project themes
Initiative learning	Sequenced activities

FIGURE 17–4 Various Initiatives Expressed

Two Programs that Proceed from the Child's Initiative

In the Pyramid Method we focus strongly on the fact that children should regulate themselves. Children are stimulated to take the initiative and to make choices for themselves in both play and learning activities. When children are able to choose their own learning activities we call this initiative learning. Providing a rich and stimulating play and learning environment facilitates this.

Two Programs that Proceed From the Teacher's Initiative

We know that children cannot learn everything by themselves. In fact, they learn a great deal from other children and especially from their teachers. The teacher's initiative is important in teaching children new things. This can be done on an individual basis through tutoring (Slavin, Madden, & Karweit, 1994), for example, when a teacher gives guidance to individual children who need extra support or more learning time. However, this is expensive. It can be done better and more efficiently by tackling subjects and exploring them in groups with the help of projects and sequential programs. In the projects and sequenced activities the teacher takes the initiative. He or she sets an example, instructs the children, and supports them in active learning. He or she motivates the children and teaches them what they should know and be able to do.

✍ PROCESSES

In the introduction, we indicated how we work with children and how we try to optimize their development. This is the basis of the method. The question is, of course, what is the focus of our efforts to optimize development? What development is being fostered? In terms of these processes we have been inspired by the theory of emotional intelligence of Salovay and Mayer (1990) and by Gardner's (1993) multiple intelligence theory. We describe the processes of the Pyramid Method (Kuyk, 2003). We indicate which development areas are involved in these processes. In the Pyramid Method, we deal with these in a balanced way.

✍ THREE INTELLIGENCES

In the Pyramid Method we proceed from three intelligences (see Figure 17–5). In daily life we often speak of the gift of the head: cognitive intelligence; the gift of the heart: emotional intelligence; and the gift of the hand: physical intelligence. Children have these gifts or intelligences in varying degrees. We have differentiated them in this way because we want to offer each child a balanced development path that involves all three and not because we focus the learning process on those intelligences where the most capacity exists. Because the intelligences are abstract and general we have concretized them in development areas that are recognizable worldwide to all those involved in teaching young children. We also identify three levels of action and thinking, reflecting an increasingly individual but also more flexible and conscious use of what is being learnt.

Cognitive Intelligence

Cognitive intelligence is the capacity to control language and thought and to work with them. Here we see the development of perception, language, thought, and orientation in space and time. All perceptions, language, and thought take place in space and time. Children learn to get a grip on the everyday world by developing these areas. They learn to distance themselves from the here and now. Language has a double function. Language is the means whereby children can communicate and learn from the teacher. Language is also an important educational objective.

Emotional Intelligence

By emotional intelligence we mean the capacity to sense one's own emotions and the emotions of others and to conduct oneself in a social way.

FIGURE 17–5 Intelligences and Development Areas in the Pyramid Method

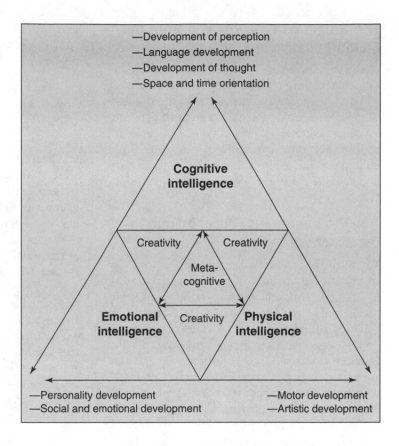

This intelligence area includes personal development and socioemotional development. The children learn to develop confidence, learn to persevere, learn to get themselves under control, and learn to play and learn either alone or with other children with motivation and curiosity. In addition, they learn to recognize their own feelings and those of others and to show respect for these in the way they behave and conduct themselves (moral development).

Physical Intelligence

Physical intelligence is the capacity to initiate movement, to control it, and to express oneself creatively. Here we make a distinction between motor development and artistic (music and art) development. Within these areas children learn to move, to act, and to control their bodies and learn their boundaries. They learn to be creative in relation to their own body, they learn how to develop their body's language, and they learn to work with materials, tools, and instruments in the process of artistic development. They learn with their bodies and with the help of appropriate materials and instruments to create new things and to express themselves in art and music. Most of the time this is a total experience.

LEVELS OF ACTION AND THINKING

We also identify three levels of action and thinking, reflecting an increasingly individual but also more flexible and conscious use of what is being learned.

Basic Level

The basic level involves basic knowledge and skills. This is what the child copies and learns from others through imitation and examples. This is the level children learn in the first steps of the projects and in sequential activities.

Creative Level

The second level hinges on creativity. By creativity we mean the capacity to create or think of something that is new and worthwhile. It is this creativity that differentiates human beings from animals. An animal can only survive by following fixed patterns. The human being can add new things and introduce change into existing situations. They play with what they have learned and begin to follow new paths. In play and initiative learning and in the project steps in which active learning is indicated, children learn to use knowledge and skills in a creative way.

Metacognitive Level

At the highest level of knowledge and skills, we speak of metacognition. This level is attained when children are aware of their knowledge and skills and consciously change their own behavior. Under the direction of cognitive intelligence, children can become conscious of their physical, emotional, and cognitive actions and work with them in a flexible and creative way. In reflections on play and initiative learning (what is important, can you find the solution?) and in the active learning in projects, the child is stimulated to learn and think on a metacognitive level.

✏ ELABORATION OF THE FOUR PROGRAMS

As we noted already, the four programs include two that stem from the child's initiation (play and initiative learning) and two are the result of teacher initiatives (projects and sequential programs).

Play

Play is an activity that is initiated by the child himself or herself. Children can play freely and, in a rich play environment, make choices for themselves. This is also possible in the projects discussed in *The Pyramid Play Book*. These projects also include a play program.

There are several possible ways to encourage children and optimize children's play. In the Pyramid Method there are three levels:

Creating Rich Play Situations We identify five different sorts of play and each one of these puts different demands on the play environment. In the Pyramid Method we distinguish between five sorts of play: material play, motor play, make-believe play, imagination play, and rule play. *The Pyramid Play Book* describes all these different types of play in greater detail.

In addition to creating play situations in the material environment, it is also important to stimulate children toward rich play. If there is not enough rich play then we evidence the second level.

Play Enrichment In the past, teachers often thought they should not disturb children when they are playing. This is still the case when children are playing richly and deeply. In Pyramid, we proceed from the idea that adults can and should play an active role in enriching play. Children like to play with adults, but what is more important and what scientific research has confirmed is that children will act and think at a higher level if an adult guides them in their play. The process of enrichment can take two forms:

- *Joining in the Play* By playing together with the child or a group of children, the teacher shows that he or she values and enjoys the play the child is engaging in. The child feels valued and from this position the teacher can work to enrich play. Once he or she is involved as a participant in the child's play or the group's play, he or she can do many

Pyramid teachers expect learning in specific sequences in
large or small groups.

things. The teacher can even give orders if
this fits into his or her role or he or she can
play the role of the mean teacher,
something he or she may have wanted to
do for a long time!

- *Enriching Play* Each day the children play
  at drinking tea in the Home Corner.
  Every day the teacher comes to visit them
  and drinks tea with them. After this ritual
  has been completed the children do the
  washing up. The teacher can observe their
  play and assess the degree of involvement.
  Do the children take the initiative? Do
  they make their own rules? Is the play
  still exciting enough? Are the roles
  becoming too stereotyped? Is fantasy
  being used? The things that show that
  the play is not rich enough can often be a
  source of inspiration for enriching play. In
  this way the teacher can introduce a new
  role into play: What do I hear? Is that a
  bell? Who can that be? Who is coming to
  visit us? Tea can suddenly become a magic
  potion. If you drink it strange things will
  start to happen.

Learning to Play Sometimes it happens that
there are children in a group who do not play.
They may feel ill, or be worried or afraid. Some
children do not have a good command of
language and feel themselves left out. There are
also children who are not used to play. Their
play has never been appreciated or their play has
been forbidden or rejected. How can we get
them to play? In the Pyramid Method we teach
children to play. We do this in three stages:
showing how it goes, playing and encouraging
the children to play by themselves, and finally
letting them play independently.

- *The Teacher Plays First.* The teacher
  chooses a play or a theme that interests
  the child. Often this is make-believe play.
  He or she begins to play without seeking
  the child's attention. The bear is sick. The
  bear is a substitute for the child. "Shall I
  get the bear out of bed? Oh he is sick. I
  shall get the thermometer. He has a fever.
  I'll put him back to bed quickly." The
  teacher talks to the bear and at the same
  time talks about everything he or she does

so the child can see and hear everything that is going on.

- *The Teacher Plays a Double Role*. The aim is to involve the child in the play as it is being played. In the beginning this will be chiefly imitation. "Take the bear out of bed. He is warm. Has he got a fever?" The teacher encourages the child to play as well but continues to play the role of mother.
- *The Teacher Gradually Withdraws*. The child slowly learns to play without the intervention of the teacher. It can be useful to get the child to play with a peer who is more receptive to the play and who can show how the play can be taken over from the teacher.

Initiative Learning

Children do not want to only play. They also want to find out how things work and they are motivated to understand the world around them. They set themselves goals. We see this very clearly in the area of beginning literacy, beginning numeracy, and exploration of the world. In the Pyramid Method it is exactly this motivation and curiosity to act out the adult world and to come to know and master it that we try to stimulate. Here we must give the child's initiative a chance and make sure the teacher adjusts his or her approach accordingly. Linked to this is the development of perception and thought. In the Pyramid Method development materials are used to encourage initiative learning. They have specific objectives and have been designed to be as attractive as possible so that they work. Children learn specific things using these materials such as concepts like long and short as well as particular ways of thinking (meaning) such as seriation, for example.

Inspiring Initiative Learning   In general the inspiration for initiative learning will come from the child himself or herself, but we can also inspire children to learn on their own. The best way to do this is to give children a good example. In the beginning, the emphasis is placed on developing interest not skill. The teacher can achieve this by letting children see many examples of reading, writing, and math. The teacher makes notes on the board, writes notes using text and numbers, he or she studies the water to see how the tadpoles are getting on in the spring, and then checks to see if the seeds are germinating.

Talking to children about what they are doing is a second source of inspiration. We can talk about the value of writing and math and of their usefulness later. The teacher gives the children meaningful examples of where communication is necessary (shopping). They look for ways to formulate what they want. In the shop you need a shopping list and you must pay for what you buy. With young children, it is necessary to make links with their experiences: Begin close and slowly take more distance.

Offering Support with Initiative Learning
It is clear that knowledge and skills are needed to be able to support young children. The most important condition is that the children themselves retain the initiative and a feeling of competency. That is to say, they feel they have achieved the best possible result. It is, therefore, necessary to offer strategic help but only as much as children need to complete their chosen task. Earlier we referred to this strategic help as scaffolding. Before the teacher provides support and determines a strategy, he or she observes the level of development, the degree of independence, and the amount of motivation the child has.

- *Little Support*. Children who have a high level of development and a large measure of independence do not need much support. If they need support it will be support at a high level. The teacher poses open questions, asks about the child's plans, and encourages him or her to solve problems alone. The teacher also asks

Children need to feel they are in control of what is being done. Pyramid Method materials are used to encourage this imitative learning.

questions that prompt evaluation. For example, "Please, Miss. I want to write dinosaur." "Where can you find that word? What have you done about writing it down? Look for that book and see if you can find that word in it."

- *Limited Support*. Children with a middle development level and a moderate level of independence only need a limited amount of support. The teacher carefully observes whether children require substantive help or if they need help with the way they work. For example, "Miss, I have made a drawing and I want to write a six by these circles." "Where can you find a six in this class? Can you point to the six? Can you write a six

yourself? Try it out and see what you can do; I'll help you if you can't manage."

- *Much Support*. If children have a low level of development, the teacher must help them carry out activities at their own level. If children have very little independence, then they will need a lot of help. This will mainly be substantive help, although sometimes the teacher will also have to help children with the way they work. It is difficult to let children retain the initiative and not take over everything oneself. However, although many examples may be necessary, they must retain the feeling that they are still in control of what is being done. For example: "Miss, I want to write my name." The child is still unable to write letters. "I will write it first and then we can write the first letter of your name together." Together the teacher and the child write the first letter of the child's name. A big achievement!

Projects

A project is a well-balanced body of activities. These activities are closely linked to each other and built up around a particular theme that fits the experience and interests of young children. Each year there are 12 projects. A network of concepts forms the basis of each project. In the Pyramid Method the teacher brings the outside world inside the classroom where he or she explores a particular theme together with the children.

A project is a complex body of three programs set out in a project book of some 80 to 100 pages. Each project begins with a play program. On the basis of project themes children can make play choices for themselves and carry out initiative learning activities within the context of a rich play and learning environment. This play program can be compared to the free play described before, but there is one difference. The teacher introduces new elements into the play and learning environment during each project in order to give the children a new stimulus to play with and learn.

At the core of each project is the group program, during which children explore a particular theme on the initiative of the teacher. In addition, the project offers a number of sequenced activities that can be carried out in the circle. After the group program activities have been completed, the skills learned can be implemented during individual and group work (cooperative learning). Two measures can be taken to accommodate the differences among the children in the group program: one involves the group teacher and the other the tutor.

The activities in the group program are presented in a differentiated way: activities are made easier or the level of difficulty is increased. There is a separate manual to help teachers deal with the differences present in heterogeneous groups. The most important and effective measure is tutoring. In the tutor program—which is directly tied to the group program—children who have been identified as in need of tutoring are given extra time with a tutor before each step in the group program is undertaken.

In addition to these programs, there is a parent program component in the projects, parallel to the daily program.

Projects have a double function in the Pyramid Method. In the first place, during group exploration, children learn about important things in the world as they experience them. They learn to recognize an integrated body of concepts that—in a particular context—belong together. In the second place, the projects provide the children with examples of how they can learn a variety of things on their own using their own initiative. The projects, therefore, provide examples of initiative play and learning.

Learning to Take Distance   One of the basic concepts in the Pyramid Method is achieving distance. From research (Sigel, 1993) we have seen that children whose parents or teachers go beyond the here (other places, close by and far off) and now (what has happened earlier and what will happen) appear to develop well. Here is an example. Imagine a picture of an elephant against a green background. When the picture is shown to the children we ask a few "nearby" questions (the answers can be found on the picture) and a few "distance" questions (the answer must be thought up, fantasized, or found by using earlier knowledge) (see Figure 17–6). Should we only ask "distance" questions? "Nearby" questions are also important. They are closer to the children, they give them something to hold on to, and they provide them with a feeling of safety. They give children a stable

"Nearby questions"	"Distance questions"
What color is the elephant?	Where is the elephant going?
Where is his trunk?	What does an elephant eat?
How many ears does the elephant have?	Why is his trunk so long?
Where is the elephant standing?	Where does an elephant live?

FIGURE 17–6 Question Types and Illustrations

basic knowledge. But we must not be satisfied simply with asking "nearby" questions. In fact, we should ensure we ask many of both kinds of questions.

Learning to take distance occurs in two ways: in the short term and in the long term.

Short term A number of steps are taken in the group exploration component of each project. We begin close to the world as the child experiences it and bit by bit we take distance from it. The child must learn to make representations. These are mental images that enable the child to think and they begin to develop from the age of 2 years. At first these represen-

tations are very concrete but slowly they become more abstract: first simple representations and later more complex ones. The period between 2 and 6 years is a particularly sensitive one, during which children begin to make representations on their own. This process takes place in four stages.

1. **Orientation** This first step is not a learning step but is intended to help children orient to the context of the theme. This takes place mainly by linking onto children's experience and what they already know about the theme. This gives them a sense of safety and a feeling that they can trust the coming activity. It puts children in a good mood.

2. **Demonstration** This first learning step begins close to the world as the children experience it. The teacher presents clear examples. In this first step, a great deal of work is done with the senses and, in this way, children gain multifaceted experiences. The teacher points out the most important aspects to the children. Concepts are discussed and named. The teacher shows, (display), and tells the children at the same time what he or she is doing. The teacher makes use of concrete

---

Playing with Water

Objective: The children review concepts from the playground project by playing with water.

Put an empty water table and one or more tubs in the circle or in the playground. Perform the activity with the entire group. You can do this by setting assignments in turns or by having small groups of children experiment with the materials when playing (indoors or outdoors). Have the children help you fill buckets with water from the tap and empty them into the water table and tubs. You can say:

We are going to play with water.
Where can we get water? (tap)
Do you hear the water running into the bucket?
Have a feel, is the water warm or cold?
Just add a little bit of warm water.
Does the water feel nice now?

Feeling

Objective: The children explore the water by feeling it.

Have the children first feel some drops of water on their hand and on their face. Use a drip or a plant spray to do this. You can say things like:

Do you feel the wet water drops?
Do they cling to your arm?

You can have the children experience the differences between wet and dry by having them wet some objects, for instance, a sponge, a piece of toiletpaper or paper towel.
Have the children then experience the difference in temperature by having them put their hands in cold and warm water alternately. Use buckets of cold and warm water for the purpose. Ask questions like:

Is this water cold or warm?
What gives the nicest feel?

---

situations and concrete materials and on the bases of this children build up a great deal of sensory experience. The teacher provides clear examples to help children understand. The teacher also uses pictures to illustrate his or her points. Children learn concrete representation in this way.

3. **Broadening** Broadening refers here to the broadening of concepts. Relevant characteristics are sought in various examples. Comparisons are made: What are the similarities and what are the differences? Now more difficult examples are introduced. Language plays an important role in comparison. The teacher also draws heavily on the children's own experience in the comparisons. He or she helps the children acquire more and more distance. He or she begins to ask distance questions. He or she reminds them about things that have happened earlier, refers to things that are not actually present or that have not yet happened.

What is the water for?

Objective: The children explore other examples of water and the function for which it is used.

In and outside the classroom the children go looking for places where they can find water. Put down some additional water-filled objects in places where the children can easily see them, like a water-filled watering can, plant spray, a glass vase with flowers, a glass bucket with water, and perhaps a fish bowl or fish tank. In and outside the classroom the children might also discover the water table or water in the paint pots, the sink, the washbasins, the toilets, the kitchen, and possibly rain on the windows. Have the children discuss the function for which the water is used. You can ask questions like:

Where do you see water here?
What is this water used for?
Is there anything else with water in it that you use for watering plants?

4. Deepening This last step aims to encourage the child to use what he or she has learned by demonstration and broadening in new, sometimes more difficult situations. Some of these situations will be familiar but some are new. Children must learn to solve problems by themselves. The business of thinking things out now takes an important place alongside sensory experience and language. By going into more depth children learn to be flexible in using what they have learned and experienced. They learn to switch between different senses and between different types of representations. "Distance" questions become the main type of question asked. The teacher allows the children to anticipate new situations. He or she encourages them to reflect on what they have learned and to draw conclusions from what they have experienced (metacognition). In this way, representations become more complex and abstract. These representations are necessary for future learning. In order to go more deeply into a subject a certain amount of knowledge is necessary in order to ask the most appropriate "distance" questions and to provide the most suitable answer.

In taking the initiative the teacher is supported by a wide range of educational tools designed to motivate children each step of the way. During the first step the teacher assumes that the group does not have much information about the subject. He or she gives examples and instructions. During subsequent steps the teacher motivates the child to use what he or she has learned by providing (expert) scaffolding. This will enable the children to make use of their deeper knowledge and reflection in other learning activities.

Long term   For children between the ages of 2½ and 6½ years—the period of representation (Fischer & Bidell, 1998)—a three year plan is implemented. Each year Pyramid begins with a welcome program followed by 12 projects that are carried out every two or three weeks. The youngest group (2½ to 4 years), the middle (4–5 years), and the oldest group (5–6½ years) explore the same theme. Each year the teacher and children explore at a

---

Soluble or not?

Objective: The children use their senses to find out that some substances can be dissolved in water.

Show the children a glass of sugar water and ask them who wants to take a sip. Wait for the reactions before telling the children that they have been tricked. Tell them that it is sugar water and that the sugar you have added to the water is no longer visible (it has dissolved).

Put some glasses with clear water and some trays with substances that can and cannot be dissolved in water, like sugar, sand, salt, flour, on a table in the circle. The children can add a different substance to each glass of water and determine whether or not this particular substance dissolves in water. Ask questions like:

What is happening? How can you know that the sugar dissolved?
Which substance has dissolved and which hasn't?
What can you tell from the water?

The Pyramid Method includes an emphasis on emotional learning; the capacity to sense one's own emotions and the emotions of others and to conduct oneself in a social way.

higher level. For example, the project "House" is the third thematic project of the year. In the youngest group the project is referred to as "I live here." It is a theme that comes close to the world as the young child experiences it and is closely associated with the child's need for security. In this project the child's own home is discussed in a general way (What does it look like?). Children are stimulated to understand their home and the concepts related to it. The project theme for the middle group is entitled "Rooms in a house." The house is looked at from the inside in terms of the location and function of its various rooms. The children learn and relearn to think about their home at a higher level and in a more differentiated way. They learn to look at the different rooms separately and to compare them with each other. In the oldest group the theme "Moving" is introduced. Here the child learns to take even more distance from its own home. It has to imagine not only its own familiar house but also another, new house and the consequences of moving there in the emotional

sense (saying goodbye, the fear of the unknown) and in the cognitive sense (What is different, what is the same?) What problems will the child have to solve when he or she leaves one house and goes to another one, for example? The children learn and relearn to make representations at an increasingly higher level and with greater complexity and abstraction.

Sequential Programs

In a sequential program there are activities that the children learn in a particular order that range from easy to difficult (see Figure 17–7).

The teacher teaches the children specific skills—sequenced activities. This takes place in the context of either a large or a small group but requires a great deal of concentration. The teacher also takes the initiative to give children tasks from the Project and Sequential Programs.

Sequenced Activities   The sequenced activities in the projects are designed for children

FIGURE 17–7   Short- and Long-Term Cycles in the Pyramid Project (see also Fischer & Bidell, 1998)

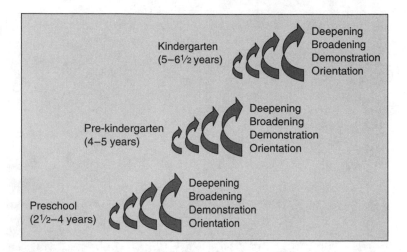

Kindergarten (5–6½ years)

Deepening
Broadening
Demonstration
Orientation

Pre-kindergarten (4–5 years)

Deepening
Broadening
Demonstration
Orientation

Preschool (2½–4 years)

Deepening
Broadening
Demonstration
Orientation

between the ages of 4 and 6 years. The activities are related to:

1. Fine motor development, drawing and writing skills;
2. Language development and preparation for reading and writing;
3. Thinking and numeracy development;
4. Orientating in time and space and discovering the world. These activities are derived from sequential programs. In the projects they are organized according to degree of difficulty and are placed in the context of the project theme. Sequenced activities are mainly carried out in the sequential circle. In this circle, which usually does not take long, sequenced activities are learned, practiced, and repeated.

The Sequential Programs   Sequential programs have been developed (or are being developed) for each development area. The programs include activities of increasing levels of difficulty and these are not tied to specific themes. They can, in fact, be used in all contexts and themes. They can also be used independently of context. The hierarchical structure provides a reference

point for those project activities in which all development areas are connected. As we have indicated, sequenced activities are also built into the projects. These activities follow the order given in the year-long program. This makes it possible to include sequenced activities in the projects with different degrees of difficulty. Sequenced activities are rooted in the sequential programs. In the projects designed for youngest children (ages 2 ½ to 4 years of age), no separate sequenced activities are included. The sequential activities of all development areas are built in the project books. Sequential programs without project themes are in development.

Two general sequential programs have been developed to support play and initiative learning: *The Pyramid Play Book* and the *Pyramid Learning Book* (see Figure 17–8). In addition, the year begins with a welcome program that focuses on welcoming all the children personally and teaching them how to use rules and rituals in an independent way while they learn to work on their own and look after themselves. The teacher helps them to take leave and to start play if they have problems saying goodbye. Younger children learn how to go into the circle, how to go to the toilet alone, how to tidy up materials, how to choose activities and play, and how to use the day-rhythm

Development Area	Sequential Program
All development areas	Pyramid Play Book
Beginning literacy, numeracy, exploring the world	Pyramid Learning Book
Personality development	Welcome Program
Social-emotional development	Sequential Program Social-Emotional Development
Motor development	Sequential Program Physical Education
	Sequential Program Dance
	Sequential Program Drawing and Writing Motor Skills
Artistic development	Sequential Program Art Development
	Sequential Program Musical Development
Language development and literacy	Observation and Sequential Program, Pleasure with Language
Development of perception, thought and numeracy	Observation and Sequential Program, Ordering
Spatial orientation	Observation and Help Program Spatial Orientation
Orientation in time	Sequential Program Orientation in Time

FIGURE 17–8   Sequential Programs

board. Older children also learn how to work independently for a longer time, how to use the play-work board, and how to choose their project activities. Independent work is also important. Here the teacher gives extra help without disturbing the child. The cognitive sequential programs—the development of language, reading and writing (pleasure in language), perception, thought and numeracy (ordering), and orientating in space and time (orientation in space)—all have an observation program.

The Parent Program   The Parent Program provides strong support for the earlier-mentioned programs and runs parallel with the yearly projects. Parent involvement is important as has been made clear in the meta-study conducted by Royce and colleagues (1983). The educational task is shared by school and parents (Gestwicki, 1987). Parent activities are important: They are the manifestations of the cooperation between education at home and at school. Parents can help to extend the child's learning time and this can have an important

effect on development. Thus, effective educational aspects support each other to create optimum development.

Parents can be involved in the following ways:

- The teacher makes an annual parent plan, outlining the various interrelated parent activities.
- Every morning there is "open-house play"—parents are free to play with their children in the classroom. This low-threshold activity links the education at home with the education in the playgroup or in kindergarten.
- At the beginning of each year there is a parent week. During this week parents work with their own child in the group after the teacher has demonstrated an activity, for instance, interactive reading aloud or explaining an assignment. These activities may be continued in the home environment.
- In the welcoming program at the beginning of the year and in all projects, parents take

home play and learning activities to extend the learning time of their children at home. These activities enhance the project activities in the group or classroom. If necessary instruction is given in the parents' own language. Parents are also encouraged to provide their children with theme-related materials, including materials that are part of their specific culture, to take to school with them.

The involvement of parents in the project activities creates a special "binding agent" and children benefit frequently and permanently from activities that can be carried out in the home environment. Open-house play and the discovery table that accompanies each project theme introduce parents to the project theme in a very visible way.

Evaluation

In the Pyramid Method we work toward optimizing the child's development. It seems obvious, therefore, that we should follow the development of each child over the whole Pyramid period and where possible improve the education process. In doing so we take note of the children's behavior (can the child work independently?) and the results achieved (for example, vocabulary size). We study both the individual child and the whole group. We refer to this as child assessment. We also approach the evaluation process from the perspective of the teacher. How does the teacher interact with the children (is he or she available for each child?) and is the teacher capable of organizing the process in such a way that the children are able to achieve good results? We refer to this as *teacher evaluation*. Finally, we ask ourselves whether the Pyramid Method is a good method and worth using in practice. Is it as good or better than other methods when compared with control or reference groups? We refer to this as *program evaluation*. Assessment is integrated into the entire Pyramid Method as it affects children

between the ages of 3 and 6 years of age. We describe the evaluation procedures we use to perform these different evaluations.

Child Assessment   Child assessment is the most important of the three evaluation processes and helps us support the child's learning process. We do this in a balanced way. In the Pyramid Method children develop through play and they learn both from taking initiatives themselves and through the initiatives taken by their teachers. A balanced assessment is sought to reveal how development takes place in each development area and how well the objectives or teacher aims are achieved. Development steps that we have described for each development area provide a good reference point in evaluating play and initiative learning. The objectives described in the program aims are used to evaluate the learning process initiated by the teacher. We have selected the evaluation procedures that suit these two processes best.

Authentic and Individual   In order to come as close as possible to what the child does, we use reliable procedures that focus on the individual child. These are procedures that fit into the child's natural play and learning environment. We examine the child's actual behavior: How does the child behave and what are the child's achievements? In this way we are able to come close to the uniqueness of the individual child, the child's creativity and "own learning power," as Piaget (1970) has formulated.

Systematic and Communal   To ascertain the extent to which the children have realized the objectives set for them, we use systematic, standardized procedures that relate to all children to the same degree. We look at their behavior and achievements in order to see the extent to which they use their own initiative and how much they rely on the initiative of their teacher (see Figure 17–9).

FIGURE 17–9   Portfolio: Child's Drawing

Instruments In order to carry out the various evaluations, we make use of several different instruments. There is no single instrument suitable for all goals. Each instrument has its advantages and disadvantages (see Figure 17–10). We also look at the quality of the instruments: the importance of the decisions reached and the period to which they apply or the consequences they have, for example, the more exacting our demands will be. The quality criteria are reliability (each teacher comes to the same result), validity (to measure what should be measured), and practicality (easy collection of information in a short time). More than 2,000 teachers have tested their practicality and the *Cito Group* (International Institute for Educational Assessment in the Netherlands) has studied their reliability and validity using Item Response Theory (Eggen & Sanders, 1993). We make use of observation scales and tests that require decisions taken over a longer period of time. These instruments are used to support both pedagogic and educative decision making. There are three sorts of evaluation using different types of procedures:

- Daily evaluation
- Half-yearly evaluation
- Diagnostic evaluation

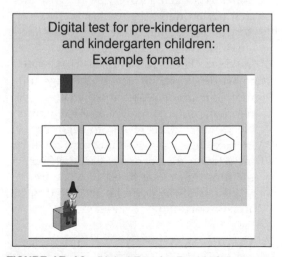

FIGURE 17–10 Digital Test for Pre-kindergarten and Kindergarten Children

These are tailored to specific functions and involve as few disadvantages (subjectivity in observation by making observation scales; computer-assisted testing to prevent subjectivity in data collection).

Daily evaluation   Daily assessment takes place in the everyday, natural environment of the group. In the Pyramid Method both the child's behavior and the results he or she has achieved are assessed.

1. **Observation** As he or she works, the teacher uses his or her pedagogic and educational knowledge to observe the child. As far as the pedagogic component is concerned the accent lies on safety, autonomy, emotional support, structure, and rules. In the educative component the activities that the child undertakes on his or her own initiative, such as playing and learning, are emphasized. The teacher also observes the child during group exploration sessions, sequential circle, and as he or she carries out tasks.

2. **Registration and portfolio** The teacher keeps a register of what the children have done. To obtain an overview of what the children produce, the teacher keeps a portfolio and collects the things that the child has made on his or her own initiative. These can be things that relate to art development such as drawings and three-dimensional objects—digital, photographs are useful here. Also, written pieces or products related to beginning literacy, numeracy, and discovery could be included in the portfolio. Each half-year the most important pieces of work are taken out of the portfolio and saved in the archive portfolio.

Six-Month evaluation   Twice a year the teacher distances himself or herself from everyday duties and goes through an observation list and some tests with the children. This assessment focuses on the child's behavior and what the child has learnt from the initiatives taken by the teacher, such as projects and sequenced activities. The objective of this evaluation is to find out whether the child has learned enough and whether the program that the child has followed during the last six months should be adjusted. Also, the teacher tries to see whether there are children who should receive tutoring in the coming six months. Assessment takes place over a longer period of time and has important consequences as far as tutoring is concerned.

In assessing physical and emotional intelligence, we make use of observation scales and for cognitive intelligence we use tests. In this way the development of the child can be followed every half-year. Using set norms we can compare the behavior and skills of every child with those he or she had a half-year earlier and with the norm for the group.

1. **Observation scales** In order to be able to observe the motor skills, the social and emotional development, and the play–work behavior of the child, the teacher uses two observation scales: the preschool scale (see Figure 17–11) and the pre-kindergarten–kindergarten scale.

2. **Tests** Three tests for cognitive intelligence are:
   a. language development and the development of reading;
   b. the development of thought and numeracy;
   c. orientation in space and time.
   The tests allow us to follow the development of each individual child and the whole group in the same way and allow us to identify which children require tutoring according to set procedures.

3. **Adaptive tests** After an extensive investigation to see if children can take a computer test (they like it, understand it, they do it quickly, and the results are

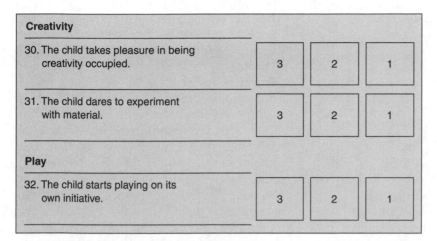

FIGURE 17–11 Example from Preschool Scale

stable), we developed computer tests for young children. Children like working with the computer; they can concentrate on the tasks. The tests are also adaptive. This means that the children only make those assignments that are appropriate to their skill level. They are not given tasks that are either too difficult or too easy for them. In addition the computer ensures that the procedure is objective and the same for each child. The test is no longer influenced by differences in interpretation on the part of the teachers. Extensive research has shown that young children can work easily with a computer mouse, sometimes after practicing with a mouse module and that, with the help of a funny figure that keeps motivating and supporting them in a playful way (a virtual coach, named Primo), they can easily complete the test themselves. Schools with a powerful computer can let the children work with it. Registration and making of graphs and tables can be automatically generated when the computer program developed by the *Cito Group* is used. According to the Netherlands Institute for Psychology (NIP), these tests conform to

a high standard. With the help of the scale described later, the teacher can follow the development of each child.

Diagnostic evaluation   Although, in general, the procedures mentioned earlier appear to be satisfactory and allow us to follow the child's development and make decisions, there are also diagnostic instruments available for exceptional cases and difficult problems. These are useful when a teacher is not certain how to proceed with a particular child.

1. **Diagnostic interview** A diagnostic interview is used to build up a picture of the child's behavior.
2. **Observation programs** The teacher can use three observation programs in order to establish how far the child has come in the cognitive domain:
   a. language development (Language Pleasure)
   b. development of thinking (Ordering)
   c. orientation in space (Orientation in Space)

The observation programs are not norm- but criterion-oriented: What has the child mastered and what has it not mastered yet? On the basis of this diagnosis the teacher draws up a plan of action.

Teacher Evaluation The teacher evaluation focuses on the way the teacher deals with each child (pedagogic component) and the extent to which it optimizes the development of each child (educative component). Teachers working with the Pyramid Method receive a professional training from a diploma-holding Pyramid trainer. The training takes 18 days and is spread over a period of 2 years.

During the training During the training the teacher is coached on the "work floor." In order to carry out the training in an effective way, the trainer makes use of the Pyramid Implementation Assessment (PIA). This instrument covers all the relevant objectives of the Pyramid Method presented in an easily recognizable way. Trainer and trainee can decide together how to work to optimize the skills that the trainer must observe.

After the training After the training has been completed it is necessary to keep these skills up to date. Pyramid has developed a Web-based competence "mirror"—known as Pyramid Competence Mirror (PCM)—for this purpose. This instrument in based on the PIA. All trained teachers can check the status of their skills on the basis of seven competencies. Teachers are confronted with a number of questions that address both the desired behavior as well as the actual behavior displayed by the children. Following, we give an example of one of the questions and the overview that the teacher gets on the Web once he or she has filled in the list. On the basis of this the teacher can improve his or her skills or ask for help from the supervisor.

Program Evaluation

Internal evaluation Within the school, internal evaluation is an acceptable procedure (see Figure 17–12). Schools can evaluate their own teaching with the help of the Pyramid instruments (curriculum independent) developed

FIGURE 17–12 Web Site Mastery of Competencies

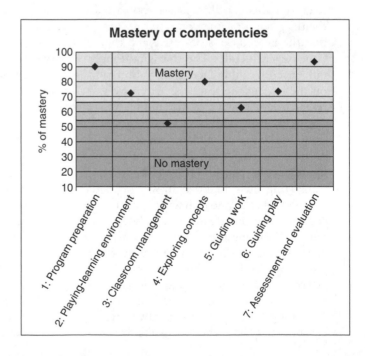

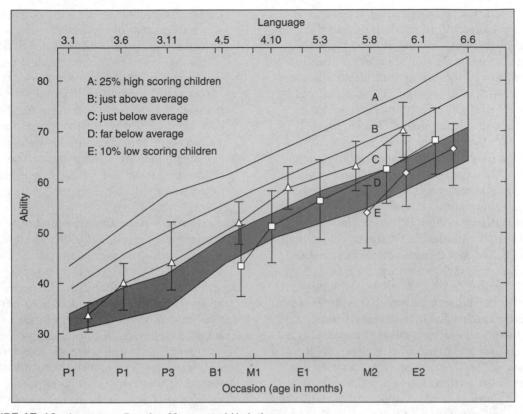

FIGURE 17–13 Language Results, Means, and Variations

by the Cito Group. At a higher level of aggregation the standardized tests can be used to establish school results, results from groups of schools, a municipality or a random, national sample of schools. In this manner a child's development can be followed over a period of 3 years. Using the computer program from the Cito Group, available data can be aggregated at a higher level. It is easy for each school and municipal to use the computer to discover the effectiveness of the Pyramid Method for themselves. Figure 17–13 demonstrates a scale used to establish the results of an internal evaluation. From the scale we can read not only average results but also the distribution of results set against a national reference group whose norms have been already established.

From the scale it appears that when compared to a national reference group, children who started with the Pyramid Method when they were 3 years old achieve better results. Children who start later—when they are 4 or 5—also achieve good results but to a more limited extent. It is also clear that children who follow the whole program from the beginning to the end have the best results. The conclusion here is: Begin early at age 3 years and use the Pyramid Method all the time.

External evaluation

1. **National experiment** In order to be able to present acceptable research findings it is better to have an external evaluation

carried out by independent researchers. The University of Amsterdam and the University of Groningen have made a study of the Pyramid Method at the request of the Ministry of Heath and the Ministry of Education. They carried out their study in preschools (3–4 years), pre-kindergarten groups (4–5 years), and kindergartens (5–6 years) with a relatively high proportion of children from disadvantaged backgrounds, particularly migrant children. They studied the level of implementation (Groningen) and effectiveness (Amsterdam) of the Pyramid Method and an American method adapted to the situation in the Netherlands—the High Scope (Kaleidoscope) Method (Homann & Weikart, 1995). Children who needed extra support were given an extra teacher for four sessions a week (Kaleidoscoop) or a tutor (Pyramid). The research was carried out between 1996 and 1999. The results were compared to those of a control group.

From the data it appears that the level of implementation of both approaches was high and that the level of involvement of the children in educational activities was very high. However, the researcher did have a number of critical comments. In the Pyramid Method, it was concluded, language development—given the focus on children from disadvantaged backgrounds—was not emphasized enough in the programs available and the steps taken to increase the breadth and depth of group exploration were insufficient and not clear.

The effectiveness of the Pyramid Method—just like the effectiveness of the Kaleidoscoop Method—was weak to strong positive effects. In terms of the Cohen effect (.20 = weak, .50 = moderate, .80 = strong), it appeared that language development and the development of

reading, when compared to the control group, was weak to moderate. Kaleidoscoop had a somewhat better effect. In the areas of thought and numeracy development, the results were moderate to strong and the results of Pyramid were stronger than those of Kaleidoscope. The conclusion here was that the Pyramid and Kaleidoscope programs should begin early and keep going for a longer time. The results were promising and an improvement in the program could only lead to more positive results.

2. **Amsterdam Experiment: preschool–kindergarten** Between 1998 and 2000, after the national experiment, the University of Groningen carried out a similar study in Amsterdam. The necessary improvements had been introduced into the Pyramid Method. Namely, a new language approach had been incorporated into the projects with a specific structure for vocabulary development. Also, the steps toward broadening and deepening of group exploration in the project books had been made more explicit. This study involved a population of preschool (3–4 years), pre-kindergarten (4–5 years), and kindergarten children (5–6 years) and contained a high proportion of children from deprived situations, particularly migrant children. Children who needed extra support were given an extra teacher or tutor (see Figure 17–14). From the study it appeared that the Pyramid Method proved to have a stronger effect in the area of language than when results were compared to those of a control group. The effect of Kaleidoscoop was weak to moderate in Cohen's terms. As far as the development of thinking was concerned, the effect of Pyramid was nearly as strong and that of Kaleidoscoop weak to moderate. From observations it appeared that neither the extra teachers (Kaleidoscoop) nor the

Preschool Experiment Amsterdam, University Groningen			
Cohen effect: .20 = weak; .50 = moderate; .80 = strong			
Pyramid		Kaleidoscoop (Highscope)	
From preschool		From preschool	
Language		Language	
Language test 3–6 years	1.08	Language test 3–6 years	.38
Thinking		Thinking	
Ordering 3–6 years	.72	Ordering 3–6 years	.35

FIGURE 17–14   Preschool–Kindergarten Experiment, Amsterdam

extra tutors (Pyramid) had been able to function effectively. The tutor had to fill in for the group's teachers when they were sick or absent for other reasons. Nevertheless, Pyramid had an effect that the researchers categorized as strong. Pyramid appeared to be a robust method that could be effectively used in less-favorable circumstances.

In all three studies Pyramid was shown to have a positive effect. We see the same effects at the local level. The Pyramid Method appears to be an efficient one that helps teachers provide successful preschool and kindergarten education. The method is, therefore, promising for other preschools and kindergartens and would even be more effective if conditions, such as the effective application of tutoring, are optimal.

REFERENCES

Ainsworth, M. D., Blehar, M. C., & Waters, E. (1978). *Patterns of attachment: A psychological study of the strange situation.* Hillsdale, NJ: Erlbaum.

Bowlby, J. (1969). *Attachment and loss.* Vol. 1. London: Horgarth.

Bowman, B. T., Donovan, M. S., & Burns, M. S. (2000). *Eager to learn. Educating our preschoolers.* Washington, DC: National Academy Press.

Cocking, R. R., & Renninger, K. A. (Eds.). (1993). *The development and meaning of psychological distance.* Hillsdale, NJ: Erlbaum

Eggen, T. J. H. M., & Sanders, P. F. (ed.). (1993). *Psychometrie in de praktijk Psychometrics in practice.* Arnhem, The Netherlands: Citogroep.

Erickson, M. F., Sroufe, L. A., & Egeland, B. (1985). The relationship between quality of attachment and behavior problems in preschool in a high-risk sample. In I. Bretherton & E. Waters (Eds.), *Growing points of attachment theory and research.* Monographs of the Society for Research in Child Development, 50 (pp. 147–166).

Fischer, K. W., & Bidell, T. R. (1998). Dynamic development of psychological structures in action and thought. In W. Damon & R. M. Lerner (Eds.), *Handbook of child psychology* (pp. 467–561) . New York: John Wiley and Sons.

Fischer, K. W., & Rose, S. P. (1998). Growth cycles of brain and mind. In *Educational Leadership* (November 1), 56–60.

Gardner, H. (1993). *Multiple intelligences: The theory in practice*. New York: Basic Books.

Geert, P. Van. (1998). A dynamic systems model of basic developmental mechanisms: Piaget, Vygotsky, and beyond. *Psychological Review, 105* (4), 634–677.

Gestwicki, C. (1987). *Home, school and community relations: A guide to working with parents*. Albany, NY: Delmar.

Groot. K. T. (2002). *Piramide Spelboek, Pyramid Play Book*. Arnhem, The Netherlands: Citogroep.

Homann, M., & Weikart, D. P. (1995). *Educating young children*. Ypsilanti, MI: High/Scope Educational Research Foundation.

Kuyk, J. J. van. (2001). Piramide, educatieve methode voor 3–6 jarige kinderen. [Pyramid, educational method for 3 to 6 year old children.] *Theorie en onderzoek.* [*Theory and research.*] Arnhem, The Netherlands: Citogroep.

Kuyk, J. J. van. (2003). *Pyramid. The method for young children*. (English version). Arnhem, The Netherlands: Citogroep.

Piaget, J. (1970). *Genetic epistemology*. New York: Columbia University Press.

Royce, J., Darlington, R., & Murray, H. (1983). Pooled analysis-findings across studies. In Consortium for Longitudinal Studies *As the twig is bent Lasting effects of preschool programs*. Hillsdale, NJ: Erlbaum.

Salovay, P., & Mayer, J. D. (1990). Emotional intelligence. *Imagination, cognition, and personality, 9*, 185–211.

Shonkoff, J. P. & Philips, D. A. (Eds.). (2000). *From neurons to neighborhoods. The science of early childhood development*. Washington, DC: National Academy Press.

Sigel, I. E. (1993). The centrality of a distancing model for the development of representational competence. In R. R. Cocking & K. A. Renninger (Eds.), *The development and meaning of psychological distance* (pp. 141–158). Hillsdale, NJ: Erlbaum.

Slavin, R. E., Madden, N. A. & Karweit, N. L. (1994). Success for all: A comprehensive approach to prevention and early intervention. In R. E. Slavin, N. L. Karweit, & B. A. Wasik (Eds.), *Preventing early school failure: Research, policy and practice*. Boston, MA: Allyn & Bacon.

Vygotsky, L. (1962). *Thought and language*. Cambridge, MA: MIT Press.

Epilogue

Making Progress? Conceptualizing and Reconceptualizing Approaches to ECE and Child Care in the Twenty-First Century

Marianne Bloch ᔧ University of Wisconsin–Madison

ᔧ CONCEPTUALIZING HISTORY, POLITICS, AND ECONOMICS OF EARLY EDUCATION FOR THE TWENTY-FIRST CENTURY

As we move into the twenty-first century, the field of early childhood education has a long history from which it can, and, to a great extent, must draw. The historical chapter by Patricia Nourot in this volume discusses many of the ways in which this field is not at all "new," and many of the ways policies, pedagogical practices, and debates of today are foreshadowed by the explicit and implicit policies, pedagogical choices, and debates of long ago. Yet at the same time, stories of the history of early childhood education (ECE) can be told in many ways (e.g., Beatty, 1995; Bloch, 1987, 1992; Cannella, 1997; Lascarides & Hinitz, 2000; Michel, 1999). Similarly, interpretations of early childhood practice, policy, theory, research, and their relations can be highlighted and interpreted in a variety of ways. As an epilogue to this book, and at the beginning of a new century, we need to look backward and forward to see the general themes presented in the various chapters, and by their writers.

We also need to look at the broader field of early education and child care at this point in time, and in the particular national-cultural contexts in which the majority of programs and approaches have originated, as well as those in which they have been implemented. Finally, we need to open up to new possibilities for the future for our own and "other people's" children (see Delpit, 1995), to recognize the interconnectedness of the world, and the necessity for socially, economically, and educationally just *ways* to enhance and provide opportunities for all children and their families. The need to understand the collective rather than the individual and private nature of our actions as also imperative, as we move toward opening up possibilities for the future, rather than closing opportunities down for many.

Different Histories of Early Education and Child Care

Many of the "approaches" described in this volume are products of historical ideas from centuries ago, as well as specific programmatic developments from the 1960s. Head Start and Follow Through Planned Variation were contextualized by the specific historic and cultural contexts in the United States where Head Start was initiated as a reform to equalize economic and educational opportunity for low-income children from diverse backgrounds. While some of the approaches represented in the volume, such as the Developmental-Interaction approach at the Bank Street College of Education program, the Project Approach, the Montessori Method, and the Waldorf School, are historically grounded in the ideas of the late nineteenth- and early twentieth-century Western Europe, Great Britain, and the United States (e.g., in the theories of John Dewey, Maria Montessori, Patty Smith Hill, Edward Thorndike, Caroline Pratt, Lucy Sprague Mitchell, Susan Isaacs, Erik Erikson, and Rudolf Steiner), other approaches represented in the book (e.g., Project Spectrum, the Pyramid Approach) are relatively new in design, experimentation, and implementation. They represent theoretical and empirical ideas of the late twentieth century (e.g., Howard Gardner's multiple intelligence theory; Feldman's emphasis on domain-specific forms of cognitive and intellectual activity and skills; information-processing theories; Derman-Sparks and Ramsey's work on multicultural, antibias and different cultural/social theories in education) as these are now applied to early education and child-care programs and policy. Still others in the book became prominent when psychological theories, developed in the early twentieth century by Jean Piaget and Lev Vygotsky, became well-known and prominent only in the second part of the twentieth century. Although 40 years old, David Weikart's High/Scope program, as well as the Reggio Emilia program that has developed in Italy, is representative of this last group; these programs drew from the ideas of Jean Piaget and Lev Vygotsky only in the postwar, civil rights era of the 1960s. In their respective and unique ways, they illustrate different ways in which early childhood and children's

thinking could be envisioned and represent a midcentury shift toward cognitive development and learning that remains part of the heated debates related to the "whole child," a balanced curriculum, need for attention toward academics in early education, and/or how to define the integration of different types of learning and development with pedagogy, instructional choices, and assessments of the effectiveness of different approaches.

All of the different ideas in the volume represent approaches that have, in general, borne the test of time—the variations, contrasting ideas, and similarities in approaches have remained important in the field of early education for a very long time. So, interestingly, have the variety of approaches represented in this volume. This is surprising in some ways, given recent efforts by the National Association for the Education of Young Children (NAEYC) and other organizations to consolidate "best practice" into a single set of recommendations representing "developmentally appropriate practices" or DAP (see, for example, Bredekamp & Copple, 1997). In addition, recent attempts to find and set universal standards for educational processes, outcomes, and teacher as well as child competencies in early and later schooling also are attempts to homogenize a field of practice in early and later education that, at least at the early childhood/child-care level, is difficult to achieve, and, potentially, undesirable to achieve. The recent "No Child Left Behind" policy and the related *Good Start/ Grow Smart* (2002) legislation that has been applied for the first time in all U.S.-based Head Start programs in 2003 are two examples of this reemerging trend to establish standards in what constitutes the best practices for "all" children.

Despite recent attempts at homogeneity, however, as suggested in the chapters in this volume, there are still many different approaches to early education and child care in the United States, as well as internationally. The majority described in this volume are grounded in psychological experimentation and theoretical ideas that developed over the nineteenth and twentieth centuries. However, despite long historical "roots," quite a few were primarily implemented across the United States (and now elsewhere) as early education programs when Head Start and then the Follow Through Planned Variation intensive experimentation in the mid-1960s to early 1970s began (Zigler & Muenchow, 1992; Zigler & Valentine, 1979). At the time of the Head Start, a comprehensive set of program characteristics were described but with multiple variations. In the Planned Variation study in the national Project Follow Through, 22 "differentiated" ideas for model programs were explored (Goodwin & Driscoll, 1980, p. 432). Other volumes by Evans (1975) described six distinct approaches with variations with each, while earlier volumes related to preschool "models" provided an array of varying approaches to early education, most of which were historical variations, that remain in our variations of programs today (see, for example, Day & Parker, 1977; Peters, Neisworth, & Yawkey, 1985). It seems that we have a continuing use of these same, yet "different," approaches, while a few new ideas have been added, or have become quite popular worldwide once again (e.g., the Waldorf and Montessori approaches). Whether one composite "best practice" and "standard" curriculum for all can be gleaned from (is represented within) these varieties of ideas (such as DAP), and whether "one model" could or should be a *standard* fit for all children and families, particularly worldwide, are two questions in a central debate in educational policy and pedagogical practice today. When research has been used, over time, to examine the effects of different programs, against each other in controlled experiments, the results have been consistent that, despite varying pedagogical goals and methods, systematically planned and supervised programs, taught by well-trained teachers (who know what they are teaching and why), appear to have good

and similar long-term effects (National Research Council, 2002; Weikart and Schweinhart's chapter, this volume). This empirical result suggests that one standard model that fits everyone in the world is certainly not necessary, and, with great likelihood, is not desirable. However, this result does reinforce the notion that having well-supported programs and teachers with training and time to be critically reflective about their practice (and with time to interact with each other, families, and children) are both important elements of programs that are considered good.

From Cultural Deprivation and Educational Disadvantage and Deficiency to "at risk" for School Failure

At the time of Head Start, programs expanded and proliferated based upon a context of acceptance of ideas from psychological theories and research, and from political and cultural theories that were focused on low-income children and their families. In the 1960s, these political/cultural ideas framed children from low-income and non–Euro-American backgrounds and their families as culturally or educationally "deprived," "disadvantaged," "deficient," or "different" from the normal child and family and in need of educational/cultural intervention. Today, these words are related to the language of families/children "at risk" and the continuing perception that early childhood programs can prevent (save?) low-income and other peoples' children from failure (see Swadener & Lubeck, 1995). This is expressed in terms of statistics that try to illustrate the costs and benefits of early childhood education in terms of children's achievement throughout their different years of public schooling, their eventual improved ability to graduate from high school, and the reduced likelihood of children's assignment to special educational classes, rates of imprisonment, and the like. While the language of "at risk" and the emphasis on the costs and benefits to society of early childhood education in terms of reductions in, for example, the likelihood of prison time is a language that catches the ideas of legislators and calls attention to the importance of early childhood education and child-care programs for all children and their families, this same language often "frames" and constructs children and their families as different, dangerous, and abnormal (Burman, 1994; Cannella, 1997; Dahlberg, Moss, & Pence, 1999; Lubeck, 1994, 1996).

The message is clear that the language of policy and practice in early education and child care must constantly be critiqued and reexamined. In the twenty-first century, we need to open up to new ways of thinking about the richness and diversity of cultural, linguistic, gendered/sexual, religious, and differently abled children and their families rather than the *risk* "differences" pose to society. The chapters of this volume that focus on the value of mixed-age and multicultural classrooms and of the multiplicity of ways to incorporate and value knowledge and competencies from children with diverse backgrounds and home languages are excellent contributions to prompt further work in the field of early education and child care.

Again, can one standard fit all? While high expectations for *all* are important, culturally relevant pedagogy that values the multiplicity of identities and cultures of difference rather than punishes children (or families) for difference are critical aspects to include in today's and tomorrow's programs for younger and older children (for example, see Ladson-Billings, 1995, 2001; Garcia, 1995; Soto, 2002).

Similarly, a concept expressed in the Reggio Emilia approach, that all children should be seen as rich and with multiple competencies, might be a viewpoint that could permeate the field of practice to a greater degree than it has (see Dahlberg et al., 1999; Edwards, Gandini, & Forman, 1998).

Public Policy and Funding of ECE/Child Care and the Concept of "Educare" or Child-Care Systems

In the United States and elsewhere, the differential costs of half-day and full-day child-care and preschool programs for children and the low wages paid to their caregivers at all levels outside the public school system embody historical assumptions that have been described as maternalist, class- and ethnicity/race based (Bloch, Holmlund, Moqvist, & Popkewitz, 2003; Cannella, 1997, 2003; Michel, 1999; Polakow, 1993; Swadener & Jagielo, 1998). These patterns, built into a long history of early education and child care in many countries (see Bloch et al., 2003; Michel & Mahon, 2002), are part of the history of welfare policy in the United States, where since the nineteenth century, policies have resulted in a segregated system of largely privately funded child care, half-day nursery school or preschool, and public funding (by the 1980s) of 5-year-old kindergartens in public school settings. The cultural history of these differences is represented in a variety of ways (see Beatty, 1995; Bloch et al., 2003; Michel, 1999; Polakow, 1993, for several examples), but these assumptions must be fought against as we move into this next century.[1]

As the ideas of targeting poor families for "relief" and welfare, or for punitive practices (rather than providing for universal funding for child care), move from liberal and neo-liberal welfare state regimes (such as the United States, Great Britain, and Australia) to other countries

---

[1]I have recently told my undergraduate students, teachers in training, that public financing for early childhood education/child care and better wages for caregivers/teachers will not happen during my career—that this fight will be passed on to them. While this is a pessimistic view given the new initiatives for universal 4-year-old programs across the United States, cross-national analyses and current U.S. reform initiatives with Head Start still make me feel pessimistic (see *Good Start/Grow Smart*—President Bush's new reform initiative for Head Start presented at the State of the Union Address, 2002).

and continents, it is ever more important to interrogate and shift our collective and individual national policies and practices. As the United States is the only industrialized country in the West, according to recent cross-national reports, that fails to provide adequate funding for its child-care systems (defined as including full-day child care, half-day child care and preschool programs, and "pre-primary" programs for 5 or 6 year olds in public elementary schools), or for families and children who must pay for them (Kagan & Cohen, 1996; OECD, 2000), the questions addressed to U.S. policy makers must be made over and over again.

With current U.S. welfare reform policies also targeting poor families and their young children in new ways with work requirements outside the home without adequate child-care support for infants and toddlers or for older children, we must indeed ask how important early childhood education really is in our country. We must ask why different families' well-being is treated in different ways and why there is no universal policy related to adequate money and attention to universal "quality" in child care/early education choices. As we examine these debates and issues further, we can open new doors for dialogue and possibilities in policy and practice in our approaches to early education/child care, or "educare," which combines both ideas.

❧ THE LOGIC OF PRACTICE AND THE PRACTICE OF LOGIC

While each program described in the volume has a particular disciplinary and cultural-historical "time" that frames the way the program or programs developed over the twentieth century, most are also firmly grounded in several common belief systems characteristic of nineteenth- and twentieth-century modern philosophies of education. These beliefs are related to (1) a logic of empirical positivism (see Bloch, 1992; Cannella, 1997; Popkewitz, 1984), (2) the conception

that scientific developments and experimentation will lead to progress, (3) the notion that individual, autonomy, rationality, and logic (often related to a focus on thinking, intellectual, academic, and cognitive development) can be separated from dependency, emotion/irrationality/lack of logic, and (4) a belief that the objective can and necessarily must be separated from subjective in researching effects on children and families. Each of these belief systems, characteristic of the nineteenth- and twentieth-century dominant ideologies of science, progress, and development must be recognized as we move into greater periods of uncertainty, unpredictabililty, and recognition of multiple ways to represent truth and the relations between power and knowledge, trends in our postindustrial, knowledge-based, and globalizing interdependent world. The analyses of curriculum must include what and whose knowledge is counted as valuable in the curriculum, how the child, childhood, family, community, and nation is understood, and upon what knowledge and reasoning systems pedagogical choices are based.

For example, in the majority of early education and child-care programs now in practice, it is normal to assume that the young child is "special" and that the stages of early childhood are, in general, to be treated as a different moment in time as the child develops along predictable lines from a dependent, immature child, lacking in reason, to the mature adult, who ideally will be rational, logical, and autonomous. This mature, developed adult, based upon a variety of Western philosophies—from Descartes to Rousseau to Locke to Dewey and others, whom the young child will ideally develop into—should also be of *good* moral character. The "good" child, as he or she develops, should also be capable of participating in economic and political activities as a good democratic citizen. These ideas characterize the majority of programs in early childhood education that draw on philosophies and pedagogical practices of Froebel, Dewey, Erikson, Piaget, and

Vygotsky. These ideas are also seen within the assumptions of childhood in most of the early education curriculum approaches that have been described in this volume and elsewhere.

While these ideas may seem distant from the detailed discussions of different programs of early childhood education, the historical assumptions that frame the notion of the good developing child (and the adult he or she will become) remain core "frames" within which we see the child and his or her parents and other well-educated, well-developed citizens in modern societies of the early twenty-first century. The chapters by Derman-Sparks and Ramsey, by New, and others in this volume, however, ask us to question the "logic" of these practices, as well as the practice of this logic within the philosophies of Western and Northern European and American enlightenment (see Baker, 2001; Cannella, 1997). The philosophical foundations of Jean-Jacques Rousseau ("the natural child" for whom child-centered pedagogy is most appropriate) or other philosophies, such as that proposed by John Locke (for whom the environment must define different individual ways in which the child can be led toward certain desirable behavior), are still key debates in education/early education; both point toward the reasoning child of good social-moral conduct as the ideal of education.

The philosophies of Johann Pestalozzi, Friedrich Froebel (the founder of the kindergarten in Germany, see Wollons, 2000), John Dewey, Caroline Pratt, Lucy Sprague Mitchell, G. S. Hall, Erik Erikson, Lev Vygotsky, and Jean Piaget, to name only a few, provide a common background of logic as well as practice that also provides a reasoning about childhood and adulthood that includes some, while excluding many types of conduct and identities from the idea of normal and good (development/learning/ growth/maturity/citizenship). A different way to approach the practice of logic, and one that would lead toward different logics of practices in pedagogy, would be to open up to more diverse notions of identity (women/men; girl/boy; European-American/African-American/Asian-American/Hispanic; heterosexual/homosexual; English speaking or not; mother/father; family/ nonfamily, to name some examples). By opening our reasoning about our own and others' identity and conduct to scrutiny, we can open up to new possibilities about childhood, families, different communities, and what the good child, teacher, or parent/family is and could be.

Cultural-Historical Specificity and U.S. Early Education

While many of the approaches described have been tried in a variety of other countries, the majority of the different early educational approaches or models in the volume were developed within the United States in the past half-century. Therefore, while they merge different values and practices from multiple centuries of philosophizing about childhood and the child, his and her family, and development and learning, the programs also embody particular characteristics of history in the United States. Nourot's chapter does an excellent job of bringing some of these historical frames to bear on the development of different programs by looking at varying conceptions of the parent, teacher, and for children in different eras and programs, at different historical moments. However, when reading this book, it is important to recall this particular cultural-national framing, as well as the specific histories that colored the development of the ideas and practices embedded within each set of curricular and pedagogical practices.

One critical example is the Bank Street program, which was linked to the progressive pedagogy of John Dewey and other social reformers' ideas of the early twentieth century; a particular brand of American democracy—a pragmatic and functional idea of the child's relationship with education and society—was formed. At the same time, the growth of psychology and a certain brand of American behaviorism tied to "habit formation" and skill development through carefully organized and structured learning and reinforcement sequences were developed. The particular way that scientific experimentation became the hallmark of progress also became embedded in the minds of teachers, teacher-trainers, and researchers who were to inform pedagogical practices throughout the twentieth century. These different pathways, and assumptions about how a good future citizen can be best educated, continue to frame some of the serious educational debates one can see in the program descriptions and different approaches to education within the volume, as well as the way "effects" of programs are studied and represented as evaluation data about best practices.

While the scientific study of differential program effects is important to the field of child care and early education, the history of objective evaluation research needs further historical and cultural critique, as well as a more interdisciplinary methodological and foundational base. What this means for the logic of practice, and the practice of logic, is that there are many ways to represent effective programs and pedagogical practices, that there are different ways to study "the child" and different families, and that there are many ways to tell the story of what a "quality" program is for different parents/families, teachers, and children (see, for example, Holloway, 2000; Holloway, Fuller, Rambaud, & Eggers-Pierola, 1997).

These differences in assumptions about the education of future citizens (focus on present learning and/or on the improvement of academic skills and learning for the future) merged with the political postwar turmoil of the 1950s and 1960s American civil rights movement to frame the desire to provide economic and educational opportunity to children who had been left behind, and to prepare all of America's children to have at least an equal start in schooling. This resulted in Project Head Start, and eventually in the Planned Variation Follow Through Project (Zigler & Muenchow, 1992; see Douglas

R. Powell's chapter, this volume). A brand of liberalism—equal opportunity for all, choices, and an emphasis on the right of families to participate "freely" in choosing programs for their children in the private sector of the American early education/child-care market—focused on the individual parent who could autonomously make choices and who had resources to examine different programs, and those who could pay for early education or child care. In addition, the American welfare policy of targeting families who are low income or perceived as at risk, combined with the political discourse of choice, led toward the provision of federally financed programs for those targeted children and their families who were perceived as needing help; other families were allowed to choose within the private market of early education and child care the kind of program they desired for their children and could afford. This historical portrayal of welfare state policies in liberal and neo-liberal welfare regimes is also part of the epilogue to this book as it provides another window into why so many different programs have evolved over time (a market of choices) and remain as "private" choices. It also provides a window into the continuation of a fragmented and differentiated "market" of choices for families and children that includes some who have resources, while excluding many others who do not (Cannella, 1997; Delpit, 1995; Polakow, 1992; Polakow, Halskov, & Jorgenson, 2001; Swadener & Lubeck, 1995).

Cultural, Linguistic, Age, Ability, and Gender Differences

The programs that developed in the 1960s as part of Head Start and the Planned Follow Through Variations were to ameliorate conditions of deficiency in low-income ethnically and linguistically different children and their families, or to intervene into these conditions and include children with "special" abilities and/or disabilities. Lasting 40 years at this point, each still embeds certain assumptions from their inception about the children to be educated, the outcomes and processes of their programs that should be examined to evaluate effectiveness, ways in which parents were and are to be seen and involved, and how different curricular goals and values should be focused on children who were considered, initially, as culturally deprived or at-risk for failure in school and in society (see Swadener & Lubeck, 1995). We can see this in the analysis of costs and benefits of different programs in terms of how many children are saved from going to prison or from becoming juvenile delinquents, for example. These assumptions, built into our framing of "benefits" of early childhood education, compared with costs to society, must constantly be interrogated. They are a product of historical understandings of what it means to be normal and good, how the good child and family are defined, and, by comparison, how the abnormal child and his or her family are constructed (see Cannella, 1997). Cultural, class, race, gender or sexuality, linguistic, ability, and age-related assumptions continue to characterize many of our programs presumed good for *all* children—in many nations. We need careful scrutiny of the assumptions about the universality of child development— and careful attention to national, cultural, language, and community variations required in pedagogical practices and in the evaluative assessments prescribed for children within new educational reforms (see again the new reforms in Head Start) and in policy (for example, see Garcia, 1995; Perry & Delpit, 1998; Soto, 2002).

National and International Dimensions of Approaches to ECE/Child Care

How we see the field of early education and child care in the twenty-first century—in the United States as well as globally—is also critical. We need to examine the relationships among the state, different societal expectations, different community expectations, and individuals in our

descriptions (and prescriptions?) of and for international, national, and local care and education for children and families. The very concept of "quality" of education (Dahlberg et al., 1999), so important when addressed toward children whose parents can afford costly "quality" care in the United States, is different when addressed toward children who are poor, and toward parents who are to work in the new welfare-to-work programs that have permeated the space of child care at the end of the twentieth century in the United States, in Great Britain, and in Australia. And these ideas have spread to many other countries around the world (see Edin & Lein, 1997; Newman, 2000; Polakow, 1993; Polakow et al., 2001).

The restructuring of the welfare state worldwide is complex and requires careful attention to a vast array of different ideas about child care and education as we move further into postindustrial and globalized systems. The reliance on past models for early education and child care, and the indifference to the care given to some, while constantly trying to improve the care given to others, is insufficient for a world that will be increasingly interdependent. In short, the well-being of children around the world has taken on increased importance. Societies that care for their own children and other nation's children, therefore, must be sensitive to international economic and political differences and the ability to provide social services to an ever-widening array of young children and families, while also being sensitive to culturally indigenous models of education and care that are often "trampled" or "colonized" by a notion of universal rights, justice, childhood experience, and scientifically universal pedagogical practices (see Bloch et al., 2003).

In the chapters presented in this volume, we can see greater attention to global issues related to childhood, to a spread of "quality" programs to many other countries in the past two decades, and yet there is some insensitivity toward local cultural customs in this diffusion of best practice and developmentally appropriate practices developed in the United States and Western Europe. However, there is an odd sense of déjà vu in the global spread of knowledge that constructs the child and childhood as universal and in the need of greater attention, care, and educational intervention from the prenatal stage to young adulthood. The Portage Project—now in many countries of the world—extends the ideas of intervention into families and community spaces. The demand for these programs and their perceived benefits appear to be great, particularly in poor countries of the world. However, as with all other programs, perceived benefits must always be qualified by collaborative efforts with communities, and with enormous respect for the indigenous knowledge systems and resources that can be used to develop local approaches to programs. Finally, with the greater economic resources with which to begin in the broader society, many of the issues addressed by some early education interventions would not be necessary. Locating the problem at the right level—not always with the individual, the family, or school, but in relation to broader inequalities—is crucial to the work of ECE or child care in this next century.

This volume's title, *Approaches to Early Childhood Education,* speaks to the political and economic, as well as social, conflicts we have in the United States and in many other countries about whether early education should also be child care for children of employed parents. Should early education be focused on academics, cognitive development, and/or care for children when away from home care? Should child care for young children exist outside the home; and/or, as Kim Whaley, in her chapter in this volume, so correctly points out, do we have that choice given the demographic changes in family life, employment of men and women, and need for early and later full-day child care in the United States as elsewhere? The historical conflicts between "mothers' interests and children's rights," so carefully discussed by Sonya Michel

in her book by that title (Michel, 1999), reflects the continuing gendered, class-based, and ethnic strains in the way policies in early educational programs are formed, not only in the United States, but also worldwide (see Michel & Mahon, 2002; Schram, 2000).

Often we speak about early educational programs as though they embody "education," with little attention to the care of children. The debates about the whole child in relation to academic priorities versus social-emotional priorities in the curriculum also embody a reluctance to admit that all programs of care are educational; all programs of care include language, cognitive, emotional, social, physical, and other forms of development and learning experiences. The values related to what to teach, and in whose interests different things are taught, however, is rarely discussed (see Kessler & Swadener, 1992; Kliebard, 1986/1995). Which children are being targeted for what types of programs or curricular emphases? What are the assumptions that lead us to develop and/or promote one type of "quality" program over another for particular groups of children? In what ways are we reducing bias, a call made clearly by Louise Derman-Sparks and Patricia Ramsey in their chapter, and in what ways are implicit biases reinforced? These are hard questions to ask, and hard questions to answer. But as we move further into the twenty-first century, they are questions we must pose. If we fail children in early education and child-care programs, and if we fail their families, if we extend the discourse of quality programming around the world without appropriate sensitivity to cultural, ethnic, language or national differences, we as researchers, educators, and policy makers or informers are failing.

In a variety of recent studies, it has been re-emphasized that young children are in different care-taking and educational settings (see Holloway et al., 1997), ranging from at-home care by parents to family child care to a great variety of half-day preschool and child-care programs. Speaking about early education as programs outside of home settings, at times as though we are speaking only of those programs that have "educational" components and "curricula," ignores most full-day child-care programs for infants and toddlers, for preschoolers, and for kindergartners (see, especially, Whaley, this volume). With more than two-thirds of the young children under age 6 years in the United States in one or another form of care outside the home during all or part of the day (and with nearly 80% of children in many other industrialized countries in care outside the home), it is clear that discussions of educational programs need to be inclusive of a variety of types of settings. These include care and education by relatives or other caregivers in home or home-like settings; large-group child-care and early education programs in settings as diverse as churches, elementary schools, private preschools, and child-care programs, and, increasingly, public state-funded programs. Discussions need to be inclusive of children with different abilities and different cultural, linguistic, gendered, and class-related backgrounds. Discussion of parents' roles in programs with their children continually needs to be prioritized. Despite work schedules outside the home, parents and other family members and friends are the most consistent adults in children's lives across their years in early education and child care, and in both public and private school settings.

The historical picture of early education and child care in the United States has been characterized by incredible diversity at its best, and characterized as extremely fragmented and as the starting point of a class-, race-, and gender-based segregated educational system for children and their families at its worst (Bloch, 1987; Cannella, 1997; Swadener & Jagielo, 1998). As we begin the twenty-first century, those of us who have participated in this field for the majority of our adult lives (I am one of these persons) look to ourselves and to the readers of this volume to continue to press for more equitable beginnings for young children,

for greater access to good early education and full-day child care for our children and our children's children, and for greater recognition and equitable wages and benefits for our teachers and caregivers of young children. As I look at data from around the world, inequalities strike me:

- Too few male teachers or caregivers; too few teachers of color
- Too few teachers who can speak the home language of children and their families
- Too many teachers who are paid too little to choose to teach young children
- Too little subsidization of early education and child care for parents, and the teachers who help to subsidize early education and child care by being forced to accept low salaries, or to leave the teaching field with young children
- Too many families who cannot afford child care or preschool, or cannot access a program in their neighborhood that is affordable and comfortable for them
- Too many children and their families who would like their children to attend a good preschool or child-care center but who cannot find them
- Too many children and families who are not served well by the education or child care they have because of inconsistent "quality," low teacher wages, or public or educational policies that reinforce universal standards of good practice that are not inclusive of cultural, language, or other aspects of children's and families' diversity

TOWARD AN UNCERTAIN FUTURE WITH OPEN-ENDED POSSIBILITIES

The ending of a book on current approaches should address achievements of the past as well as baby steps toward "progress" in the field for the future:

- First, we have new policies and practices on both the local and global stage that call for greater funding for early childhood and child-care programs in most countries of the world. This is an achievement, but one that has to be examined with caution and care—as programs that are neither culturally compatible nor relevant to different sites and cultural/linguistic patterns around the world are often being presented as a solution or an answer without appropriate cultural translation.
- In the United States, the latest reforms in Head Start with new calls for standards and assessments present opportunities as well as risks. There are many now calling for a decrease in funding of this federal program, even as most early childhood professionals and parents are calling for further state and federal subsidies for programs, and more supportive and universal family policy to help in the difficult combination of employment and family life.
- A restructuring of welfare state policies is occurring in relation to restructuring of governing patterns occurring globally; there are opportunities and limitations in this opening up of new possibilities. We need to investigate whom new policies benefit, and who fails to benefit from new opportunities.

- The spread of new ideas and practices can be beneficial to many, as can all of the choices offered to different families and children, as well as to teachers of young children. However, we must watch whose knowledge is included in curricular practices and pedagogical ideas, and who is defined once again as at risk and in need of fixing. Which children and families are targeted for intervention and involvement? Which families are good enough to avoid intervention?
- With a call for standards, common yard sticks for evaluation, and renewed emphasis on academic skills in preschools, Head Start programs, and child-care programs, will we benefit children and families? Does a common yardstick fit everyone? What "historical" traditions in the field of early education and child care must be advocated so as to be included in the notion of "best practice"? Are some of these traditions in danger or at risk?

The contribution of this volume is to renew our attention to the diversity of ideas in the field of early education and child care and to the continued importance of dialogue across ideas. The editors have brought together many voices to illustrate some of the continuing debates and questions in the field. This, again, is our collective challenge for the years to come.

REFERENCES

Baker, B. M. (2001). *In perpetual motion: Theories of power, educational theory, and the child.* New York: Lang.

Beatty, B. (1995). *Preschool education in America: The culture of young children from the colonial era to the present.* New Haven, CT: Yale University Press.

Bloch, M. N. (1987). Becoming scientific and professional: An historical perspective on the aims and effects of early education. In T. S. Popkewitz (Ed.), *The formation of the school subjects: The struggle for creating an American institution* (pp. 25–62). Philadelphia: Falmer Press.

Bloch, M. N. (1992). Critical perspectives on the historical relationship between child development and early education research. In S. Kessler & B. B. Swadener (Eds.), *Reconceptualizing the early childhood curriculum: Beginning the dialogue* (pp. 3–20). New York: Teachers College Press.

Bloch, M. N., Holmlund, K., Moqvist, I., & Popkewitz, T.S. (Eds.). (2003). *Governing* children, families, and education: Restructuring the welfare state. New York: Palgrave Macmillan Press.

Bredekamp, S., & Copple, C. (Eds.) (1997). *Developmentally appropriate practice in early childhood education* (Rev. ed.). Washington, DC: National Association for the Education of Young Children.

Burman, E. (1994). *Deconstructing developmental psychology*. New York and London: Routledge.

Cannella, G. S. (1997). *Deconstructing early childhood education: Social justice and revolution*. New York: Lang.

Cannella, G. S. (2003). Child welfare in the United States: The construction of gendered, oppositional discourse(s). In M. N. Bloch, K. Holmlund, I. Moqvist, & T. S. Popkewitz (Eds.), *Governing children, families, and education: Restructuring the welfare state*. New York: Palgrave Macmillan Press.

Dahlberg, G., Moss, P., & Pence, A. (1999). *Beyond quality in early education and care: Postmodern perspectives*. London: Routledge Press.

Day, M. C., & Parker, R. K. (1977). *The preschool in action* (2nd ed.). New York: Allyn & Bacon.

Delpit, L. (1995). *Other people's children: Cultural conflict in the classroom*. New York: New Press, distributed by W. W. Norton.

Edin, K., & Lein, L. (1997). *Making ends meet: How single mothers survive welfare and low-wage work*. New York: Russell Sage Foundation.

Edwards, C., Gandini, L., & Forman, G. (Eds.). (1998). *The hundred languages of children: The Reggio Emilia approach—Advanced reflections*. Greenwich, CT: Ablex.

Evans, E. (1975). *Contemporary influences in early childhood education* (2nd ed.). New York: Holt.

Garcia, E. (1995). *Meeting the challenge of linguistic and cultural diversity in early childhood education*. New York: Teachers College Press.

Good Start/Grow Smart. (2002). Available at: http://www.whitehouse.gov/infocus/early-childhood,toc.html. Washington, DC: Department of Health and Human Services.

Goodwin, W. L., & Driscoll, L. A. (1980). *Handbook for measurement and evaluation in early childhood education*. San Francisco: Jossey-Bass.

Holloway, S. (2000). *Contested childhood: Diversity and change in Japanese preschools*. New York: Routledge Press.

Holloway, S. D., Fuller, B., Rambaud, M. F., & Eggers-Pierola, C. (1997). *Through my own eyes: Single mothers and the cultures of poverty*. Cambridge, MA: Harvard University Press.

Kagan, S. L., & Cohen, N. E. (Eds.). (1996). *Reinventing early care and education: A vision for a quality system* (1st ed.). San Francisco: Jossey-Bass.

Kessler, S., & Swadener, B. B. (1992). Introduction: Reconceptualizing curriculum. In S. Kessler & B. B. Swadener (Eds.), *Reconceptualizing the early childhood curriculum: Beginning the dialogue* (pp. xiii–xxviii). New York: Teachers College Press: xiii–xxviii.

Kliebard, H. M. (1986/1995). *The struggle for the American curriculum, 1890–1958* (2nd ed.). New York: Routledge Press.

Ladson-Billings, G. (1995). *The dreinterrogate-Culturally relevant pedagogy for African-American children*. New York: Jossey-Bass.

Ladson-Billings, G. (2001). *Crossing over to Canaan*. New York: Jossey-Bass.

Lascarides, C., & Hinitz, B. F. (2000). *History of early childhood education*. New York and London: Falmer Press.

Lubeck, S. (1994). The politics of developmentally appropriate practice: Exploring issues of culture, class, and curriculum. In B. Mallory & R. New (Eds.), *Diversity and developmentally appropriate practice(s)* (pp. 17–43). New York: Teachers College Press.

Lubeck, S. (1996). Deconstructing "child development knowledge" and "teacher preparation." *Early Childhood Research Quarterly, X*(11), 147–167.

Michel, S. (1999). *Children's interests/mothers' rights: The shaping of America's child care policy*. New Haven, CT: Yale University Press.

Michel, S., & Mahon, R.(Eds.). (2002). *Child care policy at the crossroads: Gender and welfare state restructuring*. New York and London: Routledge Press.

National Research Council. (2002). *Eager to learn*. Washington, DC: National Academy of Sciences Press.

Newman, K. (2000). *No shame in my game: The working poor in the inner city*. New York: Vintage Books.

Organization for Economic Cooperation and Development (OECD). (July, 2000). Early childhood education and care policy in the United States of America. *OECD Country Note*. Paris: OECD.

Perry, T., & Delpit, L.(Eds.). (1998). *The real ebonics debate: Power, language, and the education of African-American children*. Boston, MA: Beacon Press.

Peters, D. L., Neisworth, J. T., & Yawkey, T. D. (1985). *Early childhood education: From theory to practice*. Monterey, CA: Brooks/Cole.

Polakow, V. S. (1992). *The erosion of childhood* (2nd ed.). Chicago: University of Chicago Press.

Polakow, V. (1993). *Lives on the edge: Single mothers and their children in the other America*. Chicago, IL: University of Chicago Press.

Polakow, V., Halskov, T., & Jorgenson, P. S. (2001). *Diminished rights: Danish lone mother families in international context*. Bristol, England: Polity Press.

Popkewitz, T. S. (1984). *Paradigm and ideology in educational research: The social functions of the intellectual*. Philadelphia: Falmer Press.

Schram, S. (2000). *After welfare: The culture of postindustrial social policy*. New York: New York University Press.

Soto, L. D. (2002). *Making a difference in the lives of bilingual/bicultural children*. New York: Teachers College Press.

Swadener, B. B., & Jagieolo, L. (1998). Politics at the margins: Feminist perspectives on early childhood policies and programs. In M. E. Hauser & J. A. Jipson (Eds.), *Intersections: Feminisms/early childhood education* (pp. 327–337). New York: Lang.

Swadener, B. B., & Lubeck, S. (Eds.). (1995). *Children and families at promise: Deconstructing the discourse of "at risk."* Albany: State University of New York Press.

Wollons, R. E. (2000). *Kindergartens and cultures: The global diffusion of an idea*. New Haven, CT: Yale University Press.

Zigler, E., & Muenchow, S. (1992). *Head Start: The inside story of America's most successful educational experiment*. New York: Basic Books.

Zigler, E., & Valentine, J. (1979). *Project Head Start: A legacy of the War on Poverty*. New York: Free Press.

Author Index

Subject Index